Springer Japan KK

Ifo Institute for Economic Research
Sakura Institute of Research

A Comparative Analysis of Japanese and German Economic Success

With 98 Figures and 66 Tables

Springer

Ifo Institute for Economic Research
Poschingerstrasse 5
81679 Munich
Germany

Sakura Institute of Research
5-3 Kudanminami 1-chome
Chiyoda-ku, Tokyo, 102 Japan

This publication is supported by the Japan Foundation.

ISBN 978-4-431-65867-2 ISBN 978-4-431-65865-8 (eBook)
DOI 10.1007/978-4-431-65865-8

Printed on acid-free paper

Originally published by Springer-Verlag Tokyo in 1997

Softcover reprint of the hardcover 1st edition 1997

Preface

In the half-century since the end of World War II, Germany and Japan have achieved miraculous economic development by virtue of their highly skilled work forces and their technological prowess. Both countries recorded high growth during the post-war reconstruction period and overcame numerous economic crises as they evolved into leading international economies. In the 1990s, however, the world has entered an era of super-competition resulting from factors that include the end of the Cold War and the narrowing of the gap between advanced economies and the emerging economies of Asia and elsewhere. Both Germany and Japan are now confronted by the need to adapt to a considerably altered environment. The most urgent tasks for Japan are the elimination of closed sectors in its economy through deregulation and other means, and the creation of systems that are open to the international economy and community. As a leading force of European integration, Germany also needs to create flexible systems that can accommodate change.

This comparative study of economic and industrial systems in Germany and Japan began in 1993 as a joint project by the Ifo Institute for Economic Research and the Sakura Institute of Research. The initial objective was to identify the factors behind the economic success of Germany and Japan. As the study progressed, it became increasingly clear that, in both cases, economic success was the result of efforts to match social and economic factors in each country with the contemporary environment. As will become apparent from a perusal of the research findings, Germany and Japan now need to move into a new phase of development by adapting to a new epoch in an environment of increasing political, economic, and social internationalisation.

A feature of this study is its emphasis on corroborative analysis that goes beyond the macro-economic level to encompass semi-macro-economic aspects at the industrial sector level. There have been numerous studies about the political, economic, and social developments in Germany and Japan, but we are confident that there have been no other international comparative studies with the breadth of this research, which also encompasses the industrial sector. The Ifo Institute for Economic Research and the Sakura Institute of Research, together with the individual researchers who participated in the study, are honoured to present the findings of this research to the international economic and business community. We hope that it will contribute to future development, not only in Germany and Japan but throughout the world.

Karl Heinrich Oppenländer, President
Ifo Institute for Economic Research

Takeyoshi Ohno, President
Sakura Institute of Research

March 1997

The List of Contributors

Ifo Institute for Economic Research

Supervisor	Helmut Laumer (formerly Member of the Ifo Board of Directors)
Editor	Rigmar Osterkamp (Head of Ifo Academy for Economic Policy)

Sakura Institute of Research (SIR)

Advisors	Kazuo Yoshida (Professor of Economics, University of Kyoto) Shunji Fukinbara (Senior Advisor, SIR)
Supervisor	Yukio Takayama (formerly Senior Managing Director, SIR: currently Senior Managing Director, Mitsui Finance Service, Co., Ltd.)
Editor	Kaoru Takahashi (formerly General Manager of Economic Research Dept. II, SIR: currently General Manager, Sakura Bank Machiya Branch)

Writers	Ifo	SIR
Chapter 1	Rolf H. Dumke	Motoko Hattori
Chapter 2	Rolf H. Dumke	Mitsuhiko Nakano
Chapter 3	Wolfgang Gerstenberger	Mitsuhiko Nakano
Chapter 4	Rigmar Osterkamp	Mitsuhiko Nakano
Chapter 5	Alexander Juchems	Mitsuhiko Nakano
Chapter 6	Kurt Vogler-Ludwig	Mitsuhiko Nakano
Chapter 7	Lothar Scholz	Mitsuhiko Nakano
Chapter 8	Alexander Juchems	Shigetaka Sato
Chapter 9	Joachim Jungfer	Shigetaka Sato
Chapter 10	Anneliese Herrmann	Shigetaka Sato
Chapter 11	Ralf Köddermann	Shigetaka Sato
Chapter 12	Kurt Vogler-Ludwig	Motoko Hattori
Chapter 13	Hanns Günther Hilpert, Joachim Jungfer, Uwe Täger	Shigetaka Sato
Chapter 14	Wolfgang Gerstenberger	Mamiko Hirowatari
Chapter 15	Anneliese Herrmann	Shigetaka Sato
Chapter 16	Rolf-Ulrich Sprenger	Taro Ohmura
Chapter 17	Eva Mang	Shingo Miyahara
Chapter 18	Stephan O. Hornig	Yukinobu Iida
Chapter 19	Hans-Günther Vieweg	Kazue Takayama
Chapter 20	Reinhard Hild	Fumihiko Tsuzuki
Chapter 21	Hans Schedl	Tadashi Nishi

Contents

Introduction: Background of Japanese and German Economies

The social and economic developments in Japan and Germany after World War II have already been examined in numerous publications. Most studies, however, concentrate on one of the two countries. An important feature of this work is the systematic comparison of post-war economic development in Germany and Japan. The long-term statistical time series available today make such an analysis possible. This is an inviting task for researchers and—we hope—a beneficial approach for the reader.

The study is based on the non-commonplace understanding that two quite different versions of a market-economy system can lead to similarly successful economic and social developments.

The two-fold task of this study is, firstly, to contribute to the international discussion in this area; hence it is addressed to specialists working in similar fields. Secondly, we also believe that the questions raised here are not only of interest for economists and social scientists. The experience in shaping economic and social developments in postwar Japan and Germany may also be instructive for politicians and economic policy-makers in countries where the economic and social order is currently undergoing transformation. We believe that looking at the Japanese and German experience could stimulate positive developments—and prevent some misguided decisions—not only in Eastern Europe, Central Asia and East Asia but also in many countries in Latin America and Africa.

The main objective of this study is to determine the success factors in Germany and Japan and to examine the causal relationship of these factors. Obviously, this goal did not prevent the authors from critically examining those developments which must be regarded as unsuccessful.

In analysing the factors that led to successful (or less successful) developments, we have placed emphasis on the economic, industrial and social policies that were practised in post-war Japan and Germany. Parts III and IV look directly at specific aspects of economic- and social-policy decisions. Also, in the chapter that examines developments in individual industries (V), it is shown that these were influenced by national economic policies.

With regard to the lessons that can be drawn from the Japanese and German experience, focusing on the alternatives that faced economic policy-makers is particularly important since these are the only factors that national policy can shape independently, that it can influence in the short term, and that often show rapid effects. In contrast, factors such as natural resources or the intrinsic work ethic only change, if at all, in the long term.

This study is a joint undertaking of two economic research institutes, with contributions by numerous specialists at both. The proposal for the study was made by the two institutes in 1992. In 1993 a detailed concept was developed and empirical groundwork was undertaken in many areas. In 1994, the actual formulation of the texts began, which was concluded in the late summer of 1995. In each topic area, the German and Japanese authors conferred with each other, and the final articles bear the fruit of this intense co-operation.

The consultation process caused several delays in the project (along with other external constraints). We believe, however, that the intense discussion between the two partner institutes has enhanced the quality of the study. We hope that this study will contribute to the discussion on long-term economic developments and shaping of reform processes by economic policy-makers.

Ifo Institute for Economic Research
Munich

Sakura Institute of Research
Tokyo

Part I
Background of Japanese and German Economies

1. Historical and Cultural Background

1.1. Japan's Historical and Cultural Background

Japan's post-war reconstruction began with the reforms implemented by the Occupation administration (General Headquarters, or GHQ). Yet, despite a series of thorough reforms, including demilitarisation and democratisation programmes, some components of the control systems of the wartime period remained in place, albeit in changed forms. Moreover, the material and spiritual legacies which had developed since the Meiji era (1868–1912) were still intact. In a broad sense, these were the conditions inherited by post-war Japan and served as its foundation for growth.

1.1.1. Geographical and natural conditions

The modern Japanese stem from an admixture of several races of prehistoric age, including Mongoloid, South Asian and Ainu types. Experts believe that the formation of the Japanese race as a single ethnic group with Japanese as its native language and life-style based primarily on rice farming was generally completed during the period of the Yayoi culture, which flourished in the third and second centuries BC. Since this time Japanese society has been dominated by the concept of itself as a homogeneous group of human beings with a common culture and a single language.

Geographically, Japan is an island nation separated from the Asian continent. The seas surrounding Japan formed an isolating barrier that prevented the ordinary people from travelling to and from the continent with ease. Since ancient times, the people of Japan have been influenced by foreign cultures through contacts with the regions that are present-day China, Korea and other countries. Japan has selectively accepted foreign culture and technology, and adapted it to its own conditions and culture, without being dominated by foreign culture.

Japan's small territory is divided into a number of flat areas by a mountainous topography. This landscape made the geographical movement of people difficult, and until the Edo period (1603–1868) political power was scattered among the regions. After Japan became reliant on imported raw materials to feed its industries from the Meiji period onwards, its long and heavily indented coastline became an advantage in terms of siting conditions for heavy and chemical industries.

Japan experiences rainy spells in early summer, with the exception of Hokkaido, and several typhoons in autumn. Its climate, which remains relatively mild throughout the year, is characterised by high humidity and the division of the year into four clearly defined seasons. The high temperatures and humidity of the Japanese summer are ideal for rice growing, and water resources are also abundant. Japan is thus blessed with an environment that enables it to maintain minimal living standards in terms of food supply and demand.

Japan has abundant marine resources, but the only key industrial resource, with which it is significantly endowed, is coal. Its reliance on other countries for industrial raw materials was a basic restrictive factor during the industrialisation process. However, Japan was able to restructure its industrial mix and achieve high economic growth by taking full advantage of processing trade, whereby it imported raw materials and exported industrial products.

Even where geographical and natural conditions are favourable for economic growth, they may fail to play a significant role in the economic development process or even have an adverse effect on growth. Conversely, the need to overcome adverse conditions can help to accelerate economic development. It is not always appropriate, therefore, to emphasise the geographical and natural conditions as prerequisites for economic development. As for Japan, it has achieved economic development by adapting itself to its environment.

1.1.2. Japan's emergence as a modern state

1.1.2.1. Formation of modern political and social organisations

The Meiji Restoration of 1868, which was led by young low- and middle-ranked samurai in the Satsuma and Choshu Clans, marked the collapse of the shogunate government and a return to direct rule by the emperor. This change was a revolution that affected not only Japan's political structure but also its economic and social systems. The aim was to build a modern industrial state capable of dealing with the Western powers on an equal footing and with equal strength. The factors that triggered the transformation were rising nationalism and alarm at the possibility of colonisation as the logical consequence of the historical events that had forced Japan to open the country in response to external pressure. Japan recognised its own backwardness, and instead of confronting the advanced Western countries or trying to isolate itself in the world, it actively sought to introduce the advanced culture and technology of the West.

At the political level, the aim of the transition from the Tokugawa shogunate to direct imperial rule was to bring about a return to an earlier order and establish a centralised system of rule. In order to restore its sovereignty over tariffs and judicial matters, which was not recognised under unequal treaties concluded with Western powers, Japan introduced a constitution-based legal system patterned on modern Western models. It also began to develop a modern army through the introduction of universal conscription system. Changes to social systems included the abolition of the feudal caste system, which had divided society into four ranks: samurai, farmers, artisans and merchants. The creation of a society in which all people are equal fostered the spirit of independence, self-respect and self-help. The resulting increase in social mobility also facilitated the redistribution of human resources, which was essential to economic development.

1.1.2.2. Establishment of a modern economic system

Recognising that economic development was vital to the maintenance of national independence, Japan began to create a modern economic system through the modification of old systems to provide institutional support for free economic activities. A number of changes were made to key systems during this period. First, in 1873 the land ownership system was reformed, and the old land taxation system, which was based on payment in kind, was replaced with a system based on payments in money equivalent to 3% of land value. Second, a banking system was created with the 1872 promulgation of the National Bank Ordinance to promote the establishment of banks capable of issuing bank notes backed by convertibility with government currency. The aim of this move was to create a framework for the raising and supply of industrial capital. Third, the enactment of the Commercial Code in 1893 established the joint-stock company system. A succession of companies was established in the modern industries that were being transplanted from the West, including railways, spinning and banking, all of which required vast amounts of capital.

1.1.2.3. Economic development through industrialisation

(a) The economic base of the Edo period (1603–1868)

In the Meiji era (1868–1912) and beyond, economic development was achieved through industrialisation. Yet industrialisation was possible thanks to the existence of the agriculture-oriented economic base that had been formed during the Edo period. By the middle of the nineteenth century, the development of new rice fields, the introduction of fertilisers and the improvement of agricultural equipment had led to increased agricultural production, and agricultural products were being traded as commodities. There were also widespread industrial activities, albeit in the form of cottage industries, including cotton spinning, silk yarn production and sake brewing. The level of economic activities in the closing years of the Edo period was higher than is generally assumed.

(b) Human resources

Japan's population at the time of the Meiji Restoration was thirty-four million, including a working population of twenty-one million. Japan thus had a vast labour force, and its human resources were quantitatively excessive in relation to the level of economic activities at that time. However, the high quality of those human resources made them extremely adaptable to new economic and social systems. The spread of "temple schools" (privately operated elementary schools) during the Edo period contributed to the quality of Japanese labour. There were over ten thousand of these temple schools by the end of the Edo period, and by the time of the Meiji Restoration they were providing education for 43% of males and 10% of females. Japan was thus maintaining a very high standard of education in quantitative as well as qualitative terms. Education during the feudal period contributed to economic development after the Meiji Restoration, not only by imparting the basic skills of reading, writing and arithmetic but also by supplying society with a labour force that was ready to accept vocational training. Although the feudal system of the Edo period was based on strict rules of social status and order, it was accepted that people could develop their abilities and knowledge by increasing their virtue through education. Even the common people were extremely eager to have their children educated.

It was against this historical backdrop that the Meiji government introduced its educational system in 1872. The government gave priority not to education for the elite, but rather to the provision of elementary education for all people. Initially, elementary schools charged fees, and in 1874 only 35% of children attended elementary school. However, by 1909 the ratio had risen to 98%. The Meiji government introduced a merits-based educational system, under the innovative concept of integrating the clan schools, which were established for the children of the dominant samurai class, with the temple schools, where the children of peasants and townspeople learned. Regardless of family background or status, a person who learned hard and graduated with excellent marks could look forward to a bright future. Together with the abolition of the caste system, this change helped to stimulate motivations towards advancement among individual Japanese. The rapid extension of education to the masses thus appears to have contributed to the growth of the Japanese economy.

(c) Capital

In the samurai class, there were many outstanding individuals with a strong sense of patriotism and self-sacrifice. In the new environment these people exhibited a powerful entrepreneurial spirit and worked with dedication to develop modern industries. During the Edo period, the merchant class was accorded the lowest social status; however, the merchants had economic power. They played, therefore, a key role in the expansion of business and the development of the commercial economy in the Meiji era.

Immediately after the Meiji Restoration, the Meiji government sought to promote industrialisation by establishing model government-owned coal and copper mines, shipyards and factories in such areas as cement, paper, spinning and brewing. When these operations were sold to private enterprises in the 1880s, they were purchased by privileged merchants with strong government connections. This would eventually lead to the formation of the *zaibatsu* (industrial conglomerates).

(d) Technology

The Meiji government encouraged the introduction of advanced Western technology, which was vital to the development of industry. It was possible to achieve development in the agricultural sector through the nation-wide dissemination of farming technology accumulated in different regions during the Edo period. However, the introduction of large-scale Western farming methods or other models as part of efforts to boost production and foster industry frequently ended in failure. In the textile industry, technology introduced from the West was used not to replace Japanese technology but to improve it. This enhanced the industry's international competitiveness and led to the expansion of exports.

It is often said that the technical abilities of the Japanese were limited to manual dexterity and imitation. When a country endeavours to catch up with more advanced nations, however, the introduction of superior foreign technology is a logical strategy. Furthermore, the introduction of technology is merely a prerequisite for the development of technology, and the ability to assimilate technology perfectly as an imitator in itself is a valuable quality. The continued development of improved technology based on technology imported from other countries provided the driving force for Japan's industrialisation.

(e) Social capital

The Meiji government placed particular importance on the construction of a railway network. This emphasis was prompted in part by political and military considerations, since the construction of railways was seen as a means of establishing a centralised system of rule. The main reason, however, was the government's recognition that the creation of a physical distribution system, capable of carrying large quantities of goods, was essential to economic development. Railway construction was in principle led by private railway companies and did not rely on foreign investment. Japan also developed telegraph services and a postal system, which were introduced in 1870 and 1871 respectively. Many private companies also participated in the electric power industry. This stimulated competition, and the resulting availability of cheap power contributed to the growth of heavy and chemical industries. A virtuous circle was formed, in which the development of social capital stimulated the dynamic growth of production, distribution and consumer markets, which in turn generated increased demand for social capital.

(f) Changes in Japan's industrial structure in the period up to World War II

During the period from the Meiji Restoration to the mid-1880s, Japan reformed its social and economic institutions and built economic and social infrastructure. This was also a period of transition to economic development through industrialisation. The industrial structure was still dominated by agriculture, and the food and textile industries were limited to a subsidiary role in relation to agriculture.

Japan began to industrialise in earnest from around 1886 onwards. The combination of a vast labour force with limited capital goods resulted in the development of labour-intensive industries. Traditional industries, such as tea, coal and silk, expanded their exports. Other industries, such as cotton yarn and cotton textiles, also joined this export growth trend. Japan imported machinery from advanced countries and industrial raw materials, such as raw cotton, from developing countries.

Japan participated in World War I (1914–18) but remained outside the main theatres of war. As a result, its exports increased dramatically, leading to the growth of heavy industries, especially shipbuilding and steel, and chemical industries such as dyes, chemicals and fertilisers. After World War I, the development of heavy and chemical industries continued under government control. Small- and medium-sized enterprises contributed to this development through their role as subcontractors. In the period between the two world wars, industrialisation occurred in an environment characterised by the formation of closed economic blocs and the growth of military demand.

Meiji Japan went through its industrial revolution thirty to one hundred years after the Western countries. Yet in the eight decades before the start of World War II, it maintained an average real economic growth rate of 4.5% per annum, which was the world's highest in that period. In the early years of the Meiji era, government intervention played a major role in the establishment of modern economic and social infrastructure and modern institutions. Thereafter, economic development was led by free economic activity in the private sector.

1.1.3. National character and attitudes

1.1.3.1. Attitudes to religion and ethics

Most modern Japanese take little interest in religion in the context of their daily lives. However, there are many religious customs surrounding turning-points in life, such as ceremonies for births, weddings and funerals. Shinto customs, for example, are observed in new year shrine visits, shrine festivals at the harvest time, and ground-breaking ceremonies for new houses. Weddings are celebrated in accordance with Shinto custom, while funerals are Buddhist in many cases. According to the 1993 Yearbook of Religion published by the Agency for Cultural

Affairs, the total number of believers in all religious organisations in Japan is 220 million, which almost doubles Japan's total population. Shinto groups account for 118 million (53.8%) of this total, Buddhist groups for 89 million (40.4%), miscellaneous religious groups for 11 million (5.1%) and Christian groups for 0.7%. These figures reflect the Japanese tendency to belong to several religions, as well as an ambivalent attitude towards religion.

(a) The birth of Shinto

The everyday beliefs of the Japanese people have been based primarily on Shintoism, which evolved together with the formation of an agrarian society in Japan. Shintoism originated as an animistic religion. The Japanese believed that many spirits inhabited the natural world, and they came to worship local gods. They worshipped nature itself and did not look for any transcendent or absolute authority over this world. The basic teachings of Shintoism emphasise sincerity and purity of heart. The emphasis placed on benefits in this world in the Japanese view of life is said to be attributed to this Shinto influence.

(b) The arrival of Buddhism

Another religion that has had a major influence on the Japanese people is Buddhism, which arrived in Japan in the sixth century. By accepting Buddhism as a religion that explained the uncertainty and impermanence of human activity, the Japanese sought to resolve unfulfilled human desires. Awareness of sin weakened after the emergence of the Japanese-style belief that all people, however sinful, had an equal opportunity to be saved, if they recognised their sins and prayed to Buddha. Buddhism gradually spread to the common people between the tenth and fifteenth centuries, but belief in local gods was never totally eliminated. Japanese religious life became characterised by co-existence between Shintoism, which was used when praying to the gods concerning matters of this life, and Buddhism, which was used when praying to Buddha concerning matters after death.

(c) The influence of Confucianism

In contrast with Shintoism and Buddhism, Confucianism has few religious ceremonies and no priests. It has had a considerable influence, however, on Japanese thought patterns. Confucianism, which is based on the teachings of Confucius, reached Japan between the sixth and ninth centuries. However, it was after the establishment of the Tokugawa shogunate in the seventeenth century that it became linked with politics and rose to prominence. The moral values of Confucianism include the five principles: loyalty to one's ruler, filial piety to one's parents, wisdom, philanthropy and love. Confucianism also places particular significance on human relations and human sincerity, and reliance on education and diligence. Such a sense of moral principles were incorporated into the Imperial

Prescript on Education, which was promulgated in 1890, and into moral education curricula during the pre-war and wartime periods. Although these policies disappeared after the end of the war, Confucian values and ethics are still deeply ingrained, and are reflected in the Japanese reliance on natural science, progress and growth, on democratic ideals and values, and on diligence and frugality.

(d) Haji no bunka

It is clear that the norms of day-to-day behaviour in Japanese society have been determined less by religion than by the natural rules of village life, and by the dominance of *haji no bunka* ("shame culture," i.e., introversive dispositions, such as timidness, shyness and reservedness, in contrast to a Western "guilt culture"). However, Japan's economic development in the post-war era has led to the breakdown of communities based on farming villages and to the collapse of a way of life based on harmony between Shintoism and Buddhism. The price paid for economic development has been the erosion of traditional ethics.

1.1.3.2. Attitudes to work and life

Diligence is often emphasised as part of the Japanese value system. As discussed above, this quality is attributable in part to the influence of Confucianism. However, it also appears to have evolved naturally during Japan's long history, owing to the dependence of the Japanese people on rice farming, which is influenced not only by natural conditions but also by human labour. The Japanese propensity for frugal living similarly appears to have evolved under the influence of the internal rules of farming communities, which necessitated a conservative approach to life.

When people were released from the fetters of the feudal caste system after the Meiji Restoration, this emphasis on industry and frugality was replaced by dedication to advancement and success. The embodiment of this concept was Ninomiya Sontoku, whose example has been deeply imprinted on the national consciousness through school education. The Japanese thus have a great respect for work, and both believe and put into practice the view that work should be placed above all else as the purpose of life.

Whilst contemporary Japanese have not lost this diligence, the improvement of living standards and the diversification of values are reflected in a shift in the pattern of diligence, away from self-sacrificing hard work towards an emphasis on the quality of personal life. This is reflected in the tendency to seek comfort and spiritual enrichment in one's life as an individual. In addition, the generation of Japanese born since Japan's achievement of material wealth and high economic growth are increasingly abandoning the traditional spirit of simplicity and frugality.

1.1.3.3. Communication styles and behaviour patterns

The dominant styles of communication in Japanese society are *ishin-denshin* (communion of mind with mind or tacit understanding), whereby people somehow perceive the feelings and thoughts of others, and *nemawashi* (digging around the roots before transplanting, that is, making preliminary negotiations behind the scenes, or through informal channels, to obtain a predetermined agreement), which is the sharing of opinions through informal channels. The Japanese are generally not skilled in decision-making based on the democratic process, which involves expressing one's views clearly in public and reaching a conclusion after accepting or disputing the views of others. Although Japan has adopted the principle of majority rule, the people of Japan have traditionally preferred to achieve unanimity. This reflects the formation of a homogeneous society with a strong tendency towards conformity, and the relative ease with which information can be disseminated thanks to a common language. It can also be attributed to the fact that there was little need to express one's philosophy and views clearly in Japanese society.

This vague communication style is closely linked to a tendency to identify with groups and give priority to the values of the group rather than the individual. Until the end of the Edo period, people lived in static groups defined by the caste system. The peasants had their farming communities, and the samurai had their clans. Since the Meiji Restoration, this group orientation has become a source of economic dynamism through its realignment towards an emphasis on goal- and competition-oriented groups.

In order to maintain harmony, however, in a system based on competition-oriented groups, the people of Japan avoided facing problems, such as the inconsistencies and distortions resulting from the pursuit of a single goal, by skilfully separating *tatemae* (stances or principles) and *hon-ne* (true feelings or real intentions). In Japanese society this behaviour has been responsible for a tendency to postpone the achievement of real solutions to problems and for the formation of systems of collective responsibility in which no one is really responsible. Such thought and behaviour patterns based on self-suppression prevent people from exercising their ability to achieve self-reform in response to today's massive environmental changes. They have also led to a loss of balance amongst diversified values.

1.2. Germany's Historical and Cultural Background

Elements of West German history, culture and geography undoubtedly provide important ultimate and proximate sources of economic growth. Both historical shocks and the evolution of institutions over time have influenced the economic organisation of society and may have set up a time-dependent, unique path of development for this country, both in comparison with other countries and with the German Democratic Republic.

German cultural traits have also influenced economic growth, insofar as they affect savings propensity, investment and the intensity and quality of work, if not the extent of work. It should not be surprising that the Germans show elements of the individualistic Protestant ethic, which Max Weber argued was the base for the modernisation and economic success of northwestern Europe since early modern times. Nevertheless, it should be clear that the task of identifying specific German virtues is beset with the same large methodological problems which confront the literature on the cultural reasons for slow growth in England in the last hundred years ("the decline of the industrial spirit"): most of the arguments are anecdotal.

In contrast, the geographical dimensions—the availability of mineral resources, especially hard coal, and good farming land in temperate zones, the navigable rivers Rhine, Main and Weser, and a large internal market—have had a clearly positive economic impact.

1.2.1. Identifying German institutional and cultural virtues

1.2.1.1. Patterns of development and investment in human capital

A significant contribution to identifying paths towards economic modernity was made by Hollis Chenery and Moises Syrquin (1975) in their study of patterns of development, i.e., of the dynamics of population growth, of investment behaviour by the private sector and the state, of income inequality, of sectoral resource allocation and structural change, all contingent upon the rise of per-capita incomes. On the basis of cross-sectional data, the authors identified a "normal" path towards higher per-capita incomes which is shared by all larger countries in the twentieth century.

Nicholas Crafts (1985) has applied this approach to Great Britain and other European countries in the nineteenth century in order to assess whether Britain, the first industrial nation, was different from its industrial followers. It was; its agriculture was vastly more productive and the scale of urbanisation was far larger than in other countries at a similar level of development. Crafts' major finding is that the laws of nineteenth century development are identical to those of the twentieth century, with the exception of population growth, which has been strongly influenced by disease prevention technology in this century.

Of special interest for the topic of this chapter is Crafts' finding that Germany fits the European norms of the nineteenth century in all dimensions, except for its superior investment in education. The early institution of universal elementary public school education in Prussia and Germany was an exceptional cultural achievement. Undoubtedly, this basic education combined with another German institution, the training of craft skills, resulted in a well-trained and well-educated labour force.

This has been correctly seen as a linchpin of German economic growth in the nineteenth century, while Germany was catching up with Britain and in the twentieth century while surpassing British productivity, as numerous studies by the National Institute of Economic and Social Research in London have shown for the period after World War II (O'Mahoney, 1994). In a further study by Crafts and Thomas (1986), Germany's comparative advantage in international trade in the late nineteenth and early twentieth centuries was seen to be based in goods requiring skilled labour.

Germany not only stood out in the nineteenth century because of its universal primary schools, but also because of the establishment of a new research and teaching institution embodying Wilhelm von Humboldt's idea of a university as an autonomous body for research and teaching, co-opting its new members on a basis of substantial research reputation. Following the founding of the Humboldt University of Berlin in 1810, German universities became vastly superior research institutions in comparison with those in other countries. By the end of the century German universities were the model copied everywhere in the world, so for example, in the United States as well as in Japan.

The establishment of technical universities in the nineteenth century and the training of industrial entrepreneurs in those institutions was also a German hallmark, improving the technical know-how of industrialists and leading to an appreciation of basic and applied research—as well as research laboratories—in German industries. This helps one to understand the dramatic development of the German chemical industry to world leadership already by the turn of the century.

In summary, one can see that the existence of exceptional coal deposits in Germany combined with superior educational, training and technical research institutions put Germany on a development path over the last century, a competence in heavy industrial products, in iron and steel, and chemicals with established export capabilities.

West Germany was to inherit a large percentage of German heavy industry and chemical industries after the division of the country into different military zones after 1945. Thus, a combination of specific resources, institutions and good fortune were key elements in West Germany's path of development in these industries.

1.2.1.2. "Relative backwardness" and the role of universal banks

According to Gerschenkron's analysis (1962) of industrialisation of the industrial followers in nineteenth-century Europe, the more backward a country was compared to Great Britain, the more specific institutions and development paths were established. In particular, Germany, as well as Belgium, France and the rest of the western Continent, were seen to develop and employ new financial institutions, the universal banks, in an effort to channel scarce savings towards industrially productive, large-scale investment projects, such as railway development.

The close connection between banks and industry characteristic of the universal banking practice, with banks acting as investment bankers, placing and holding the shares of new firms in new industries and supporting the firms' regular need for business credits, has been seen by financial historians—especially Richard Tilly and William Kennedy—as a great benefit to Germany before World War I. The universal banks are also thought by many Anglo-Saxon economists to benefit the German economy today.

The close relationship between banks and industrial firms is thought to be beneficial, because it a) diminishes information asymmetries between borrowers and lenders and, therefore, leads to a more efficient allocation of investable funds than in Anglo-Saxon countries, and b) diminishes agency problems because the placing of bank directors on the boards of client firms reinforces the interests of the owners versus those of the managers. By increasing the efficiency of investment and raising returns to investments, the universal banks are said to have a direct impact on economic growth and indirectly by encouraging more savings and investments.

Moses Abramovitz (1986) has argued that the institutions discussed above—those supporting investment in human capital, technological competence and the financial institutions—are the "social capabilities for growth," necessary to support the process of technological catch-up growth, which characterises the twentieth century. The new growth theory has also begun to emphasise the importance of human capital formation and of efficient financial intermediation for growth in the long-run.

1.2.2. Learning from history

1.2.2.1. The hyperinflation and Germany's *inflationsangst*

Because societies learn from historical experience, history is important today. German society was gravely affected by the hyperinflation after World War I. The distribution of wage income was levelled; income and wealth inequality levels, which had taken over fifty years of prior industrialisation to be established, were eliminated in a few years; liquid assets were destroyed and a class of *rentiers* was eliminated, as C. L. Holtfrerich has pointed out (1980).

This experience has been etched into the German collective memory and has shaped the German approach to monetary policy for the rest of this century. Thus guaranteeing the stability of the German currency was the most important macro-policy in Germany in the post-war era. The independent Bundesbank has fought for this goal, at times at the expense of the loss of a significant amount of employment, as after the oil price shocks of the 1970s. The rate of inflation in Germany in forty years of the post-war era (1950–1990) was the lowest in Europe.

One can argue, as the recent World Bank report on the economic miracles in Southeast Asia does, that a stable macro-economic environment with low inflation rates is a policy suitable for high growth. In the 1950s *"Wirtschaftswunder"* years in Germany, this view prevailed.

1.2.2.2. The 1920s vs. 1950s and 1960s vs. 1990s: learning and unlearning lessons of corporative compromise

Several recent studies have compared the two post-war periods in the twentieth-century Germany in order to assess why there was strong productivity growth and a *Wirtschaftswunder* (economic miracle) after 1945, but not after 1918 (Carlin, 1993; Paqué, 1994; Maier, 1987; Olson, 1982).

In Olson's view the relatively high post–World War II growth must have been occasioned by the greater destruction of German society caused by World War II. According to Olson, growth in stable, and especially democratic, societies is fated to slow down, as in Britain, because of the rise of an ever more dense network of interest groups which redistribute income and throttle productive activities through political influence over taxes, tariffs and regulations of industry.

This view that German interest groups were largely destroyed after World War II and that, therefore, the brakes to growth were removed in Germany was challenged by Paqué. Paqué showed that the old networks of business interest groups quickly re-established themselves after World War II.

What was new after World War II, Paqué and Carlin argued, was the relative quiescence of unions. Union wage demands remained substantially behind productivity increases for most of the first post-war era lasting until the end of the 1960s. This is in contrast to the Weimar economy, which, as Knut Borchardt (1982) has argued, was stymied by a profit squeeze due to compulsory arbitration procedures which resulted in wage increases surpassing productivity rises.

Charles Maier explained the post–World War II "politics of productivity" in Germany and other European countries by arguing that, in contrast to the failed class compromises everywhere in Europe after World War I, this was the outcome of a stable corporatist class compromise between business and labour. The compromise after World War II gave entrepreneurs the markets in which to produce and sell, and gave workers employment opportunities arising out of high investments as well as a social safety net provided by the government to insure against market risks.

In this corporatist arrangement, governments should be also seen as playing an important role in reducing the problem of the time inconsistency of plans. Unions would only lower wage demands, if employers used increased profits for investments, but unions could not bind employers to do that. Employers would only increase investment if they were sure that governments would maintain aggregate demand, possibly by maintaining the purchasing power of the population by improved social security legislation.

The solution—low wage demands, high investment and social welfare programmes of the state—which characterised the social market economy in

Germany after 1948 resulted in high growth and strong *ex post facto* wage increases.

In Germany this arrangement broke down in the late 1960s with rising labour shortages and rising union demands to change the distribution of income, as in the 1920s. The great depression and high unemployment ushered in by the Bundesbank's restrictive monetary policy after 1979 and in the early 1980s brought a return to more modest union demands in the late 1980s.

With the re-unification of Germany, a peculiar class compromise seems to have taken place between unions and employers in West Germany at the expense of the rest of the society. Both interest groups were afraid of the threat of competition from a low-wage economy in eastern Germany. Both groups decided upon a fast path towards high western wages for the eastern German economy. This was a path which resulted in pay increases rising dramatically over productivity increases and in a massive job destruction in eastern industry (Sinn, 1995). This path was only possible by relying upon massive transfer payments from the eventual taxpayers of West Germany. It remains to be seen, if this wage policy will be conducive to *Wirtschaftswunder* in eastern Germany.

1.2.3. Assuring a market economy by integration with the West

Undoubtedly, the major event of twentieth-century German history was the shock of defeat after World War II and the uncertainties ensuing from unconditional surrender, which put the welfare of the German nationals into foreign and possibly hostile hands. The situation of the post-war German economy is described in detail in the following chapter. Here, it should suffice to point out that, although there were de-industrialisation plans ("Level of Industries Plan") initially favoured by the United States and the Western Allies, economic sense led them to be scrapped by 1947.

Replacing the Level of Industry Plan was a Western Allied understanding that after the disintegration of the German economy into different military zones, West Germany could only survive by integrating its heavy industry into Western Europe. While East Germany was being integrated into a Soviet-style socialist planned economy which eradicated entrepreneurship and the market economy, West Germany was fortunate. It was the policy of the United States to ensure the Western integration of the West German economy and to support its market orientation, the "Americanisation" of the West German economy. Recent studies of the Marshall Plan (Eichengreen, Uzan, 1992; De Long, Eichengreen, 1993) argue that it served to reinforce a market economy focus in Western Europe, especially in the West Germany.

2. Immediate Post-war Situation

2.1. Japan's Immediate Post-war Situation

Almost fifteen years of continuous war, which started with the Manchurian Incident in 1931, followed by the war between China and Japan and the Pacific War (World War II), ended with Japan's unconditional surrender to the Allied Forces and its acceptance of the Potsdam Declaration in August 1945, and resulted in the collapse of the Japanese Empire. Japan entered the post-war era with its economy totally crippled by the war. After a period of extreme confusion, Japan began to rise again from the ashes of war and subsequently achieved a miraculous reconstruction and development. In order to examine Japan's post-war economic development, it is first necessary to ascertain the extent of human and material losses that Japan suffered in World War II and to evaluate the economic and social conditions that existed in the immediate post-war period.

2.1.1. Changes during the war and post-war era

Japan's real GNP statistics for the period from 1930 onwards (1934–36 prices) show rapid growth during the period of the Manchurian Incident and the war between China and Japan. This growth peaked in 1939, and the economy remained flat in subsequent years. From 1943 onwards the Japanese economy began to register negative growth in real terms (Fig. 2.1-1). In terms of individual demand items, the period between the start of the war between China and Japan and the end of World War II was characterised by ballooning government current account expenditure and fixed capital formation, as well as by shrinking private-sector expenditure (Fig. 2.1-2).

In the absence of figures for 1945, it is not possible to gauge Japan's GNP level immediately after the end of World War II. However, GNP amounted to ¥10.9 billion in 1946, a decline of ¥9.2 billion (46%) compared with the 1944 figure, and a ¥11.2 billion (51%) drop from the pre-war peak of ¥22.1 billion. (There was little decline in consumer spending during this period, but government current-account expenditure fell to less than one-seventh of its previous level, while total fixed-capital formation slumped by more than one-half.)

If the Japanese economy had continued to grow from the 1936 level at the pre-1936 average growth rate of 3% (in other words, if World War II had not happened), Japan's 1946 GNP would have reached ¥23 billion, which is ¥12.1 billion (53%) higher than the actual figure for that year.

After growing rapidly for a period during the war, the Japanese economy went into sharp decline as the war drew to a close. This contraction was caused not only by direct damage to production facilities as a result of air raids but also by the

Fig. 2.1-1 Trend of GNP growth around the war time

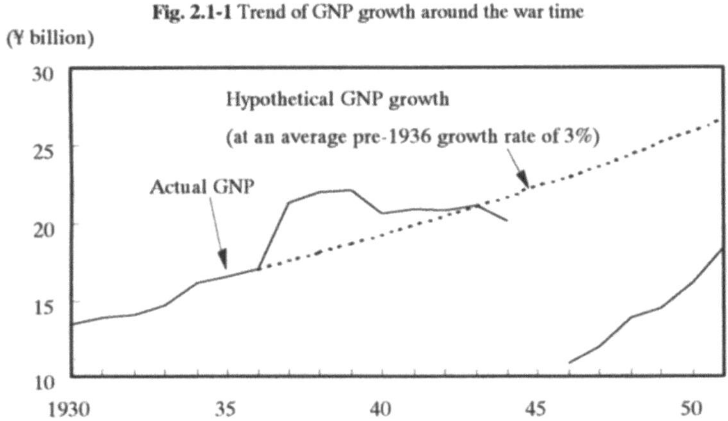

Source: Ohkawa, Long-Term Economic Statistics; National Income

Fig. 2.1-2 Components of expenditure on GNP

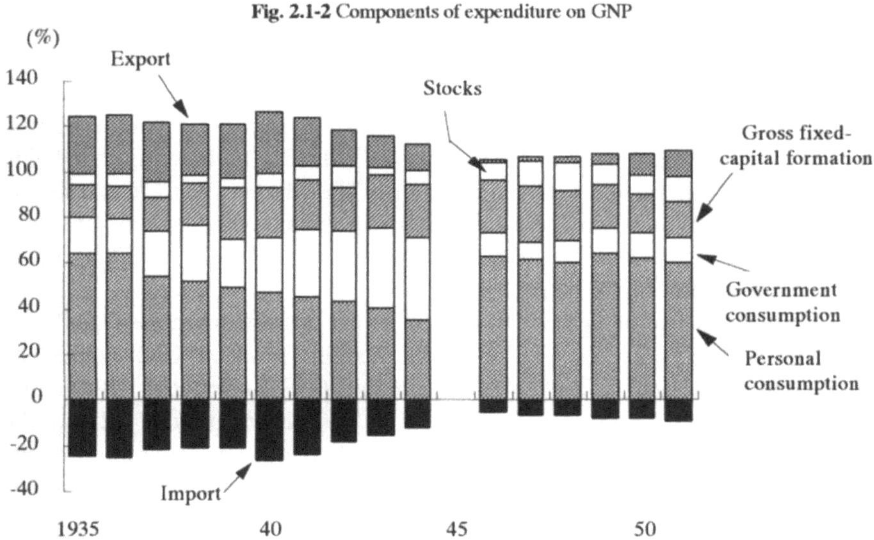

Source: Ohkawa, Long-Term Economic Statistics; National Income

Table 2.1-1 Destruction of national wealth
(¥ million, %)

	Value	Ratio
Total	64,278	25.4
Buildings	22,320	24.6
Industrial machinery and equipment	7,994	34.3
Ships	7,359	80.6
Movable property	17,493	21.6

Note: loss of purely military assets excluded.
Source: EPA, The post-war history of the Japanese economy, vol. 1

gradual exhaustion of economic activities due to human losses and difficulties in obtaining supplies of raw materials and fuel. It was only in 1951 that real GNP recovered to the level attained in 1936, prior to the Marco Polo Bridge Incident.

2.1.2. Damages caused by the war

2.1.2.1. Destruction of national wealth

During World War II Japan suffered from repeated air raids directly on its mainland, including two nuclear bomb attacks. The result was massive damages, especially to major cities. According to figures compiled by the then Economic Stabilisation Board, the damage to Japan's domestic national wealth[1] amounted to ¥64,278 million at war-end prices, and the loss ratio was 25.4% (Table 2.1-1). If losses of purely military assets, such as aircraft, are included, the cost of damage rises to ¥134.3 billion and the loss ratio to 41.5%. Damage to buildings, the biggest single loss category, amounted to ¥22.3 billion (24.6% loss ratio), followed by damage to movables (goods and chattels) reaching ¥17.5 billion (21.6% loss ratio), industrial machinery and equipment (¥8 billion, 34.3% loss ratio) and ships (¥7.4 billion, 80.6% loss ratio). National living standards were affected by massive losses in housing. War damage and compulsory demolition claimed 2.7 million housing units, or approximately 20% of total housing stocks. These losses, coupled with increased demand owing to the subsequent repatriation of Japanese from overseas, created a housing crisis in post-war Japan.

1 All material assets, including buildings, ports, canals, industrial machinery and equipment, production goods, railways, shipping, vehicles, electric power, gas and water facilities, telephone and other communication facilities, household goods and furniture.

2.1.2.2. Damage to industrial production capacity

The level of damage to industrial production capacity varied from industry to industry. For example, there was no damage to hydroelectric facilities, while 30% of thermal power generation capacity and 60% of oil-refining capacity were destroyed (Table 2.1-2). There was little damage to the iron and steel industry, yet in the machinery sector the vehicle and delivery equipment industry suffered loss ratios as high as 20–30%. In the chemical sector, the production capacity for ammonium sulphate and rubber was reduced by 40–50%. The fact that damage was heavy in industries close to the finished-product sector and light in key industries appears to have been behind the strong emphasis placed on heavy and chemical industries, such as iron and steel, and shipbuilding, in Japan's post-war industrial reconstruction policy (Arisawa, 1994). However, the level of national wealth does not provide a full picture of the extent or impact of the losses. For example, virtually all resources were allotted to military use during the war years, while production facilities belonging to the textile industry and other industries were converted to military production, resulting in a serious imbalance in the

Table 2.1-2 Damages to industrial production capacity
(%)

	Ratio		Ratio
Power generating		Chemical	
Thermal power	30.2	Ammonium sulfate	54.1
Hydroelectricity	0.0	Caustic soda	35.7
Gas	31.5	Cement	27.0
Synthetic petroleum	44.6	Rubber	42.7
Non-ferrous metals		Machinery	
Electrolytic copper	22.1	Machine tools	25.0
Aluminium	23.9	Automobiles	20.8
Alumina	12.6	Rolling stock	24.6

Source: EPA, The post-war history of the Japanese economy, vol. 1

Table 2.1-3 Human losses
(thousands)

	Number
Total	2,645
Dead and missing civilians	690
Dead and missing military	1,860
Disabled military	95

Source: EPA, The post-war history of the Japanese economy, vol. 1

distribution of industry. It is necessary, therefore, to take account of these factors when evaluating economic activities in the immediate post-war period.

2.1.2.3. Human losses

Total human losses, including civilians and military personnel killed or missing, reached 2.6 million (Table 2.1-3). This figure is equivalent to approximately 3.5% of Japan's population at the start of World War II (71.9 million). US bombing raids focused primarily on major cities, and it is estimated that around 28% of people living in these cities were affected. If we assume that Japan's working population in this period was 37 million, which is the total of one-half of the general populace together with military personnel and employees, then the war claimed 7.0% of that working population.

2.1.2.4. Impact of war losses

As has been described, the war inflicted massive losses on the material and human assets of the Japanese economy. Japan's economic level, which had already been lower than that of the West, lost even more ground (Japan's GNP and per-capita GNP in 1940 were equivalent to one-fifth and one-tenth respectively of those of the United States). As a result, most Japanese people, especially those in low-income groups, started the post-war era with living standards that were characterised by a struggle to find enough to eat. Food crises, housing crises and serious inflation forced large numbers of people to rely on black market goods.

2.1.2.5. US aid to Japan

The stabilisation of national living standards was an urgent priority for the government of this period. The government itself, however, lacked the ability to rule while Japan remained under the US military occupation. The *de facto* government was the General Headquarters (GHQ) of the occupying forces. GHQ sought to alleviate shortages in post-war Japan by using its military budget to provide assistance under the Government Appropriation for Relief in Occupied Areas (GARIOA) system. The main items supplied under this system were foodstuffs, fertilisers, petroleum and pharmaceuticals. GHQ also provided reconstruction funds under the Economic Rehabilitation Account in Occupied Areas (EROA) system. These funds were used mainly to purchase raw cotton, minerals, raw materials and machinery. The total amount of aid provided between 1945 and 1951 was approximately $1.9 billion. During the period of post-war confusion, Japan was unable to import essential goods with its foreign currency reserves exhausted. Aid from the United States enabled it to import urgently needed supplies. Without those aids, post-war Japan would have faced extremely severe economic problems that would inevitably have delayed its economic reconstruction.

2.1.3. Post-war changes in Japanese national attitudes

2.1.3.1. US occupation policy towards Japan

The biggest influence on Japanese national consciousness or their way of thinking in the post-war period was exerted by the policies of the US government and GHQ. In September 1945 the US government announced its initial policy towards post-surrender Japan, with its primary emphasis on democratisation. General Douglas MacArthur, who headed GHQ and was responsible for the actual implementation of occupation policies, issued in October 1945 a directive called "five major reforms relating to human rights".[2] In January 1946 the emperor renounced his divine status by declaring himself to be a human being. Under the new Constitution promulgated in November 1946, sovereignty was transferred from the emperor to the people, and Japan renounced militarism and made peace its national goal. At the same time, a number of laws, including the Fundamentals of Education Act and the Labour Standards Act, were enacted, creating a new legal framework. These changes implied that the then existing values were no longer valid, and it became necessary to formulate a new value system. However, national consciousness remained unstable due to the combination of a sense of defeat and anger resulting from Japan's first experience of losing a war, a sense of relief that the war had finally ended, and a feeling of social liberation resulting from the democratisation measures introduced by GHQ.

Meanwhile, from an economic perspective, most Japanese faced lives of considerable hardship. According to a survey conducted in July 1946, expenditure on foodstuff accounted for 73% of total household expenditure in Tokyo, indicating that people were devoting much of their effort in this period to the task of finding food (Ishikawa, 1981). At the same time, the people of Japan were learning about American life-styles and attitudes through the occupation forces. Affluent American life-styles seen in the media became the focus of envy as well as goals for the future.

2.1.3.2. Changing mental attitudes towards the economy

The agricultural land reforms implemented between 1946 and 1949 played a major role in the changing mental attitudes of the Japanese people towards the economy. In pre-war Japan, the patriarchal system and the feudalistic lord and vassal system were deeply rooted, especially in rural communities. The land reforms effectively accelerated the breakdown of these old systems, since tenant farmers became economically independent land-owning farmers. However, a series

---

[2] The five areas targeted by these reforms were the emancipation of women; the right of workers to organise; the introduction of liberal ideals in education; the abolition of the absolutist political system; and the democratisation of the economy. A law enfranchising women (women's suffrage) was established in 1945.

of ensuing government measures to protect agriculture ended up in delaying the centralisation of farming and the improvement of competitiveness in the agricultural sector owing to the continuing existence of independent farmers working small areas of land during the following years of economic development.

GHQ also moved to break up the huge industrial conglomerates known as *zaibatsu* and to remove people who had co-operated in the war effort from public office. These measures helped to reform mental attitudes as the economic circles shifted from pre-war systems to new systems. GHQ's purge of public officials, meanwhile, accelerated the introduction of new blood into the government ministries responsible for guiding industry. At the corporate level, young entrepreneurs sought to manage their companies in ways not bound by the old norms, thereby paving the way for Japan's future economic development.

2.1.3.3. Changing social attitudes

One major change on the social front was the rapid growth of the labour movement. This occurred partly because GHQ encouraged the formation of labour unions as part of the democratisation process. The expansion of unions was also a reaction to the suppression of unionism during the war. One consequence was an increase in the frequency of labour disputes. There was also an accelerating shift towards labour militancy, typical examples of which were food protests on May Day in 1946 and the general strike of 1 February 1947 which was halted by a GHQ directive.

The social confusion of the times was also manifested in a series of incidents that spread disquiet amongst the people of Japan. These included the Teikoku Bank Murders[3] in 1948 and three major incidents in 1949 (the Shimoyama Incident, the Matsukawa Incident and the Mitaka Incident), which resulted from mass layoffs of workers employed by the national railway system. In many cases, the authorities were never able to discover either the perpetrators of these crimes or their motives.

Japan's post-war social environment was thus characterised by widespread confusion resulting from the loss of traditional mental and spiritual props, and the removal of restraints imposed by pre-war systems. This situation persisted until Japan's future course started to take shape in the late forties through the economic upswing triggered by the outbreak of the Korean War in 1950 and by the signing of the San Francisco Peace Treaty and the Japan–US Security Treaty in 1951. However, there is still room for debate about whether the various policies implemented during this period really caused fundamental change in the Japanese people's sense of values existing since pre-war times. The Confucian patriarchal system and the spirit of diligence and frugality are still inherited in Japanese mental attitudes. These qualities appear to have led to the formation of the hard-working labour force that sustained the rapid growth of Japan's post-war economy. It took

---

3 The Teikoku Bank Murders resulted in the deaths of fourteen bank employees at its Shiinamachi branch of the Teikoku Bank.

considerable time for Japanese social attitudes to change at a more fundamental level.

2.1.4. Systems remaining after the war

The immediate post-war period was the starting point for developments that determined the future course of the Japanese economy. Although there was massive damage to the infrastructure, including production facilities, housing and railways, it is also apparent that some industrial structures and systems formed during the war years remained in existence during the subsequent reconstruction and development of the Japanese economy (Noguchi, 1995).

The first of these elements was the administrative organisation of the government. The pre-war bureaucracy was further strengthened under the "new economic system" of 1941, which concentrated power in the hands of the central agencies, especially the Ministry of Home Affairs (*Naimusho*). After the war, the functions of the Ministry of Home Affairs were transferred to ministries and agencies, such as the Ministry of Health and Welfare, the National Police Agency and the post-war Ministry of Home Affairs (*Jichisho*). Despite this, there was no significant change in the concentration of authority in the hands of central government agencies related to economy. This tendency increased as a consequence of a change in US policy to treat Japan as an ally after the outbreak of the Korean War. Another factor that helped to concentrate more power in the hands of the bureaucracy was the destruction of the power structure before and during the war supported by the military and *zaibatsu*, and this change further expanded the role of government in Japan's post-war economic growth.

The second element to survive from pre-war days was the tax system. Japan's post-war tax system initially gave priority to fair taxation in line with the Shoup recommendations, which emphasised direct taxation. Fairness of taxation was lost under subsequent taxation reforms, giving priority to the accumulation of capital. However, the core emphasis on direct taxation has remained to the present day (although a consumption tax was introduced in 1989). The system of withholding tax on salary and wages, which is the main method of tax collection, was introduced under the 1940 tax reforms (JFCPTA, 1987). These reforms were accompanied by the separation of corporate tax from income tax under an independent corporation tax law.

The third pre-war element to be maintained in the post-war era was the industrial structure. Japanese industry had been increasingly dominated by heavy and chemical industries since 1930. The industrial base in these sectors was further strengthened during the war years with the development of industries to meet military demands. In 1940 heavy and chemical industries accounted for 58.8% of manufacturing production. This is even higher than the figure of 55.1% recorded during the high-growth era in 1960 (Nakamura, 1978). The wartime industrial structure was basically maintained under Japan's post-war economy. By rebuilding its industrial facilities, training technical personnel and acquiring up-to-date technology from advanced countries, Japan once again began to move towards industrialisation in the heavy and chemical sectors.

The fourth element retained from pre-war days was the financial structure. During the war the government established the designated bank system and others in the name of national policy. This led to a transition from a system in which the business sector relied primarily on direct finance to one dominated by indirect finance supplied mainly through banks. The formation of the *zaibatsu* (or big business concerns) was a phenomenon associated with the concentration of capital, which had begun in the nineteenth century. Thus it is not entirely accurate to attribute their emergence to the war. The war, however, did cause the *zaibatsu* to form stronger bonds around their banks, resulting in the establishment of a system under which major banks dominated the supply of funds to the business sector. This appears to have become a remote cause for the formation of corporate groups centering on banks as a response to the fund shortage of the post-war era.

2.1.5. Impact of conditions in the post-war period and its evaluation

Japan's situation in the period immediately after World War II affected its subsequent economic development in a number of ways.

First, the people of Japan responded to rapid economic and social change by developing a commitment to self-help. Despite the desolation of post-war Japan, economic and social democratisation appears to have convinced individual citizens that their efforts would produce results. The introduction of Western-style democracy by GHQ was extremely significant in this context. Yet in some respects Japan failed to present its ideals as a peaceful nation effectively to the international community. It was for this reason that other nations began to criticise Japan for giving first priority to its economy, or for being "inscrutable".

Second, most of Japan's physical production facilities were eliminated by the war. While this loss of industrial stocks was a handicap, it also enabled the Japanese economy to make a completely new start. In fact it was the concentration of limited industrial resources and the introduction of new technology that triggered the rapid economic growth of later years.

Third, Japan maintained the centralised economic system that had formed during the war years, including its bureaucratic organisations, the tax system and its financial structure. However, this does not mean that all legacies inherited from the war years continued to function in the same way as they had during the war. Although systems may have been similar in form to their wartime counterparts, we must recognise that their functions were modified whenever necessary to keep pace with the post-war development of the Japanese economy. On the other hand, it cannot be ignored that some aspects of these systems had a negative impact on the situation in the immediate post-war period and on Japan's subsequent development. Many of the laws, organisations and structures created after the war were based on the abnormal conditions that existed immediately after Japan's defeat in World War II. Failure to modify these elements in response to subsequent environmental change clearly reduced overall economic efficiency and prevented companies and other organisations from becoming fully self-sufficient.

The situation in the immediate post-war period thus defined Japan's subsequent direction. The people of Japan consciously worked to overcome and improve the harsh conditions that faced Japan immediately after World War II. The task confronting Japan today, fifty years after the end of World War II, is to go back to the starting point and review the situation that existed in the immediate post-war period so that Japan can create a new framework for the definition of its future course.

2.2. Germany's Immediate Post-war Situation

The situation of the West German economy after mid-1945 was incomparably more complicated and desperate than the post-war phase in any other major European country and in comparison with the German past since Napoleonic times. Not only was there vast destruction of German cities by Allied wartime bombing, with a corresponding breakdown of transportation and energy networks and of industrial production, the economy was paralysed for almost two years by Allied policy uncertainty. As well, the disagreements among the Allied powers about the potential role of Germany in the post-war international order and disagreements among the leaders of the Allied military occupation zones of Germany about economic policy led to a *de facto* disintegration of the highly integrated German economy into separate autonomous zones.

West German post-war recovery and reconstruction was complicated by the fact that a West German state and economy was actually not being reconstructed, but was being built out of the remains of a discredited, defeated and dismembered German Empire. Because there was no predecessor to the Federal Republic of Germany, there are statistical problems in determining how quickly or how well the recovery process proceeded; data for a hypothetical West German economy before 1945 have to be made up. The German Federal Statistics Office, as well as the authors of other German statistical studies, have had to create a historical artifact, a West German economy since 1924 which is based on the regional desegregation of the two pre-war German national industrial censuses of 1925 and 1938. Non-German analysts (e.g., Maddison, 1984; Sommariva, Tullio, 1987) have dared to project a fictitious West Germany far back into the nineteenth century in order to present "historical" data with which to compare the post–World War II West German economy. Although we will continue with this practice here, it is necessary to add this note of caution.

2.2.1. Post-war output levels compared

The extent of the breakdown of the German economy in the post-war period is indicated by information on industrial production. Figure 2.2-1 compares indexes of industrial output for Germany, Europe and the world after World War I and World War II in comparison with the pre-war years 1913 and 1938 (Mendershausen, 1955). It is evident that the decline of the index of industrial production in West Germany, from 100 in 1938 to 28 in 1946, is not only more than twice the decline of the German index from 1913 to 1921; the decline in West Germany exceeds by far the declines in the rest of Europe, where the index is around 90 in the year 1947. More precise data on industrial production in European countries has since been forwarded (Abelshauser, 1975; Wolf, 1993; Paqué, 1994), but the general trends found by Mendershausen do not change. Interestingly, the decline in East German manufacturing output seemed less than in the West Germany. Compared with 1936 (100), the index of manufacturing output in East Germany dropped to 46 in 1946 and 52 in 1947; it reaches 87 in 1950 (Ritschl, 1994).

The index of GDP, in contrast to industrial output, declines substantially less between 1938 and 1946 (it decreases from 100 to 49) because non-industrial sectors, especially agriculture, were not so heavily hit as industry. According to an Ifo study (Ifo, 1953), the index of agrarian output (1935/39 = 100) declined to 67 in 1946 and 58 in 1947. The GDP drop from 100 to 49 also occurs in GDP per capita, according to Paqué (1994). Fig. 2.2-2 indicates that the index of per-capita GDP rose during World War II to 120 in mid-1944. Consequently, there was an almost 60% decline in the following two years, no doubt one of the biggest short-term decline in western Germany in a period of over a hundred years.

What does this mean for comparative consumption levels? The index of per-capita consumption in West Germany declined from 100 in 1936 to 52 in 1947 (and 58 in 1948) (Ritschl, 1994). This is the same order of magnitude as the per-capita GDP decrease discussed above.[4] It should be clear that the decline in output is not the only reason for declining living standards. Western Germany's population grew dramatically after 1945 due to the inflow of refugees from the Soviet occupation zone and displaced persons from Germany's lost eastern provinces and Czechoslovakia. Between 1939 and 1946 the population in western Germany (in the British and American zones) rose from 34 million to 38.9 million, an increase of 4.8 million. During that time 6.7 million or 17.5% of the population of the year 1946 were migrants, refugees and expellees (or victims of "ethnic cleansing", in present parlance).

[4] In East Germany, in contrast, per-capita consumption declined yet more, to 36 in 1947. East Germany's relative position was to deteriorate in the late 1940s.

Fig. 2.2-1 Indexes of industrial production: Germany, Europe, and the world

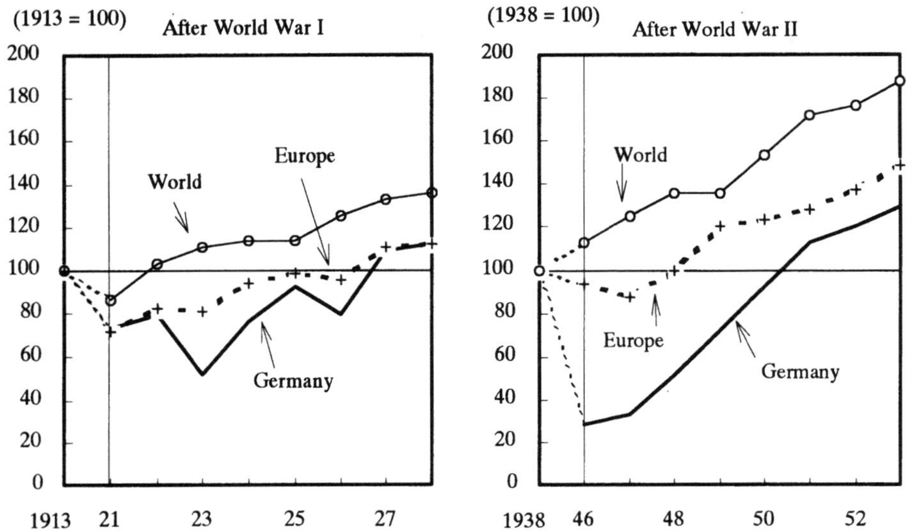

Source: Menderhausen, 1955

Fig. 2.2-2 GDP per capita, Germany 1913-38 and 1938-63

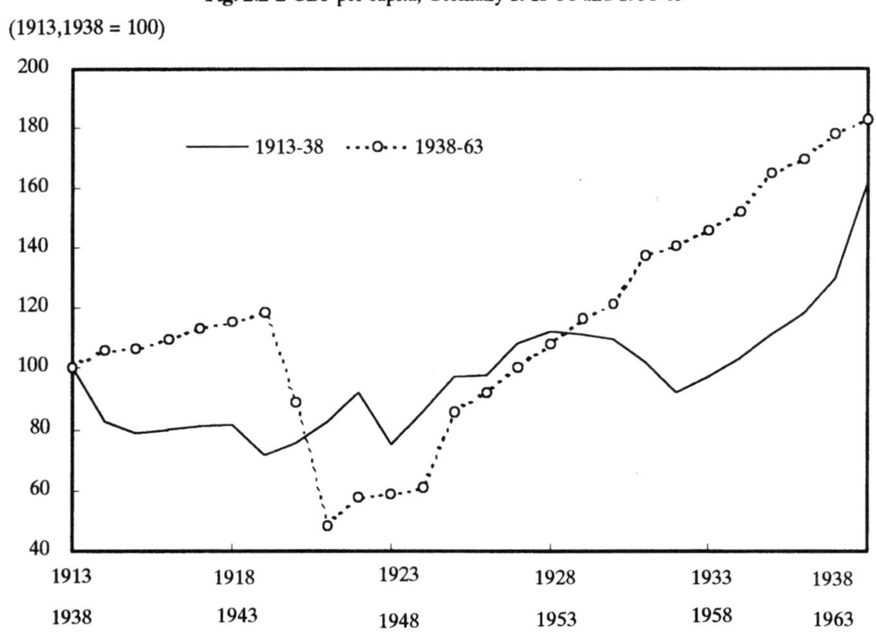

Source: Calculations by Paqué (1994) based on estimates of GDP at constant prices and of population by Maddison (1991), For details of definition, see Maddison (1991).

2.2.2. Defining the recovery stage

Besides providing information on the massive breakdown, Figs. 2.2-1 and 2.2-2 also show that West German industry (and GDP per capita) recovered very rapidly after 1947 and that the 1938 levels of output were again attained in early 1950 (1952, for GDP per capita). Re-attaining pre-war levels is one usual definition of recovery, the initial very fast growth stage of the reconstruction phase in German economic history.

Another definition by the Ifo Institute (1953) looks at the industrial structure of the West German economy in 1952—as measured by industrial goods sales shares in 1936 prices by different industries—and compares it with the structure of the western German economy in 1936. In 1952 the West German economy evidences a larger weight of the investment goods sector, a reflection of the comparative advantage of West Germany in international trade. Nevertheless, the iron and steel industry lost almost half of its 1936 importance. The Ifo report suggests this is due to the loss of customers in East Germany. The weight of the chemical industry also increased because of rapid technical change and product innovation. On the whole, the Ifo report suggests that recovery (*Wiederaufbau*) was largely complete by 1952 and that West Germany had an industrial structure appropriate for peace time and one which could provide sufficient exports to finance agrarian and raw materials imports. This definition of recovery, therefore, focuses on eliminating balance of payments constraints by restructuring an economy which was bloated by wartime production and distorted by the post-war disintegration of the German economy.

2.2.3. Comparing the recoveries after World War I and World War II

A comparison of the recoveries after both World Wars in Germany and Europe has profound implications about the nature of the ultimate causes of faster growth after 1945. Such a comparison is an analytical tool which serves to highlight the influence of different policy regimes on the economy.

Figs. 2.2-1 and 2.2-2 help to make the point that the recovery stage itself is made up of separate identifiable stages, the pre-reform and post-reform years. An important reason for the relatively slow and lengthy recovery after World War I, where pre-war levels of industrial output were only reached fourteen years later (in 1927), was due to the negative effects of hyperinflation in contrast to the repressed inflation and the price controls after World War II (Mendershausen, 1955). Hyperinflation is worse than repressed inflation: that is the interesting message. When the paths of output after the currency reforms in 1923 and 1948 are compared, similar fast rates of growth are to be found in the period 1923–28 and 1948 onwards. In other words, the state of the economy during the time before the currency reforms turns out to have important consequences in the interpretation of what went wrong after World War I.

The fact that post–World War I reconstruction was incomplete apparently had less to do with the quality of the economic reforms and currency stabilisations than with the length of time during which economic growth could take place before, and after, the reforms. The slow-down of the economy after 1927/1928 can be usefully contrasted with the continued fast growth after 1950. These differences can be explained by the different evolution of demand: the slide into a world of depression in the 1930s versus the Korean War boom of the early 1950s, a fortuitous demand boom. Consequently, Wolf (1993) is correct when he states that an important element of the success of the post–World War II West German economy is fortuna. Others have commented that "it was only through a number of fortuitous circumstances that an Ordoliberal (i.e., market economy) programme could finally be implemented" in West Germany and a socialist political alternative with significant state intervention and planning be avoided (Giersch, Paqué, Schmieding, 1992).

The recoveries of the post–World War I and post–World War II epochs of Britain, France and Germany have also been compared and contrasted in the aggregate by Bradford De Long and Barry Eichengreen (1993). Like Paqué in our Fig. 2.2-2, they superimpose the movements of indexes of GDP per-capita levels over time, starting with the pre-war levels (1913 and 1938 = 100). For all three European countries in the aggregate, it is even more evident than in the German case that the post–World War II recovery is very much more dynamic than the stalled recovery after 1919. The authors use this information to hypothesise that a better international policy environment, the Marshall Plan which was common to all three countries, encouraged this dynamism. "The availability of Marshall Plan aid to nations that had accomplished stabilisation provided a very strong incentive to compromise ... distributional conflicts early and gave European countries a pool of resources that could be used to cushion the wealth losses sustained in restructuring" their economies from wartime to peacetime output. Because such help was not available after World War I, Europe's recovery of output was repeatedly interrupted by distributional struggles, which produced instability in government finance, politics and labour relations.

2.2.4. Proximate causes of the fast recovery after 1945

In the traditional neo-classical growth framework, output growth is a function of the growth of inputs, especially labour and capital, and of the efficiency of inputs, i.e., technical change. The relevant magnitude to analyse is potential output growth, assuming the full employment of factors and an orderly, efficient functioning of markets. However, war can have a negative impact on growth by both destroying factors of production, thus diminishing potential output, and by disorganising the efficient functioning of the economy, diminishing actual output below potential output. The first effect is a negative growth effect wherein the production possibility curve is shifted inward towards the origin; the second effect is to push the economy temporarily below the existing production possibility curve. By affecting the relative abundance of the factors of production, the capital-labour ratio and the capital-output ratio, war destruction of capital stock can also usher in a rapid post-war transition growth during which the marginal efficiency of capital is unusually high.

To what degree are the severe war damages incurred to the West German economy during World War II responsible for the initial massive breakdown of output levels and the subsequent high growth rates? Surprisingly, the massive destruction of the housing stock in cities, which influenced contemporary opinion on the extent of capital damage to the West German economy, was not equalled by the destruction of the industrial capital stock. According to the Ifo report (1953), the war destroyed about one-fifth of the total housing stock in West Germany. As many as 2,300,000 flats were destroyed or so badly damaged that they were unusable. This figure is the equivalent of the complete housing stock of the eleven largest West German towns which housed 9.7 million persons before the war. Fourteen large cities lost more than half of their housing accommodations.

In contrast, West German industrial capital stock in 1946 exceeded the capital stock in 1938. This was a reflection of ineffective strategic bombing of industrial locations and an investment boom just before the war, since net investment during the war exceeded wartime destruction and post-war dismantling. Led by John Kenneth Galbraith, a team of Anglo-Saxon experts came to the conclusion in the remarkable United States Strategic Bombing Survey of October 31, 1945 that the decline of industrial output in Germany since the middle of 1944 was not occasioned by the destruction of industrial capital but was due to the laming of the transport system by air attacks (Abelshauser, 1975). Table 2.2-1 provides the relevant figures on the evolution of industrial capital stock in West Germany. Because of the abundant capital in the immediate post-war era, little industrial investment took place between 1945 and 1948. Consequently, capital stock declined over this period, largely due to depreciation. Still, in 1948 capital stock in the British and American zones exceeded levels in 1936 by 11%, according to Abelshauser (1975), who concluded that a capital shortage was not a limitational factor in the German economy in 1945 or in 1948. Nevertheless, a number of key sectors—steel rolling mills and ball bearing plants—did suffer

Table 2.2-1 Industrial capital stock
(billion Reichsmarks, 1950 prices)

Capital stock in 1938	49.3
Plus net investment	25.2
Minus bombing damage	13.8
Minus dismantling	2.8
Capital stock in 1947	57.9

Source: Krengel, 1963.

extensive damage, which created short-term bottlenecks during the post-war period.

Whilst the shock to industrial capital was relatively negligible, the same cannot be said for the capital-labour ratio, because West Germany received millions of refugees and expellees from the East in prime working age. Abelshauser calculates that the capital-labour ratio in the West German economy declined from 100 in the year 1936 to 42 in the first half of 1948 and 56 in the second half. This is a major but indirect war effect which could lead to the kind of fast transition growth discussed above.

However, one should not expect an immediate start of such growth because of the extreme regional mismatch of the labour force (Abelshauser, 1975). The new migrants found housing in agrarian regions, such as Schleswig-Holstein, far from the industrial capital stock. This is one reason for the relatively low-capacity utilisation rates of industrial capital in the early post-war era. The capacity utilisation rates for West German industry in 1936 (84.2%) by far exceeded the rates in the first half of 1948 (35.9%) and in the second half of 1948 (50.9%).

Consequently, one should view housing investment and the substantial programme of public housing of the early 1950s as having had important efficiency effects. Not only would one expect that housing investment in this environment would shift the Beverage curve in Germany inward, improving the efficiency of labour markets. Housing investment should also be seen as complementary to industrial investment, substantially raising the productivity of the industrial capital stock. These arguments have not been sufficiently studied in Germany and await future research.

The only research which takes account of the productivity argument, if only indirectly, is the study by Sommariva and Tullio (1987), which employs total (i.e., industrial and housing) capital stock in a macro-production function. Not surprisingly, in this case there is a substantial shock to West German capital and to the capital-labour ratio. The authors argue: "It appears that the destruction of the wars has given rise to long phases of higher-than-average growth rates in the post-war periods, bringing the stock of capital and NNP per capita after some time back to the level which would have prevailed in the absence of wars ... The destruction of capital due to the war led to a drop in the capital-labour ratio and to a sharp rise in the marginal product of capital. These factors constituted the main driving force behind the high rate of capital accumulation" in the 1950s and 1960s.

Abelshauser (1975) calculated a rise of 17.7% of the labour market potential—defined as the sum of all males aged 16 to 64 and females aged 14 to 49—in the British and American zones between 1936 and 1948. The restructuring of the war economy to peacetime purposes meant both the substitution of the relatively unskilled foreign and prisoner-of-war labourers—which amounted to almost one-third of the industrial labour force in July 1944, at the high point of wartime output—and the employment of the relatively skilled demobilised soldiers.[5] Abelshauser summarises the development of the West German labour force as being on the whole favourable to growth: labour force potential had increased and compensated for the older age, higher female labour force proportions and lower labour force participation ratios. There was no decline in the factor of labour.

Because both labour and capital inputs were higher in the post-war years, potential output did not decline. The reason for the drastic output decline in the post-war era was, rather, the unemployed and under-employed factors of production in a chaotic, badly functioning economy. Consequently, it was possible for output to rise quickly, for actual output to approach potential, once a functioning economic order was established in which efficient markets could allocate resources properly. The years 1945 to 1948 have thus rightly been called "the establishment of a liberal order" (Giersch, Paqué,Schmieding, 1992).

2.2.5. Ultimate causes of growth in the recovery phase

2.2.5.1. Before currency reform

"Ultimate causes" of growth include significant historical events, the nature of the basic social order, the degree of socio-political conflict, as well as macro-economic policies for growth and stability, in contrast to the previously discussed "proximate causes" of growth which are stressed by growth accountants (Maddison, 1984).

Amongst the significant historical events which affected West Germany after May 1945 is the initial attempt by the Allies to de-industrialise and to permanently demilitarise Germany, a goal which found expression in the Level of Industries Plan of March 1946. To de-industrialise Germany meant a change in the basic social order of this highly industrialised and efficient economy. According to this plan, industrial output was generally to be restricted to 55% of the level of 1936. The corollary of this policy of industrial disarmament was the virtual restriction of foreign trade and the dismantling of capital goods to be used as reparations in kind. As Giersch, Paqué and Schmieding note (1992), this policy was clearly likely to delay and impede West Germany's economic recovery. In July 1947, after a two-year experience of miserable levels of consumption and massive and expensive

---

5 In the year 1944 there were 9.1 million soldiers in the *Wehrmacht*. In March 1947, 2.4 million were still located in prisoner-of-war camps. These figures are aggregate German figures which are difficult to disaggregate regionally. Further aggregate figures are to be found in Harald Winkel. According to Winkel (1982, 101), German wartime casualties summed to more than 8 million persons. Of the 17.6 million Germans living east of the Oder/Neiße in 1939 (9.6 million) and outside the borders of the Reich in other countries in the year 1937 (8 million), over 14 million were able to flee to Germany by 1950. A major social problem was caused by the wounded, widows and orphans (4.3 million in 1952). The extent of the foreign labour force active in German industry during the war is estimated to have been 10 million persons.

food shipments to West Germany by Britain and the United States, the Level of Industries Plan was revised to allow the American and British zones to retain a level of output approximate to the level of 1936.

Yet actual industrial output between 1945 and early 1948 stayed at about one-third of the level of 1938; this was below the initial Level of Industry Plan (Giersch, Paqué, Schmieding, 1992). The disorganisation of the West German economy by the Allied decisions to continue wartime rationing, the Nazi price and wage controls of 1936, the relative prices of that year for most commodities and an almost worthless currency was, apparently, a more substantial handicap.

Ch. Buchheim (1991) has pointed out that, given this constellation and the private ownership of means of production, firms' objectives are not to produce the goods which society needs but to follow a course of survival by hoarding raw materials and semi-finished products, repairing damaged capital and binding skilled labour until the time of the inevitable currency reform. Hoarding, production boycott, and barter are the phenomena which characterise economies with such a fundamental inconsistency: bad money and private ownership.

2.2.5.2. German currency reform and Ludwig Erhard's price reforms

There are two ways of eliminating this inconsistency, and both were chosen in Germany. In the Soviet zone, private property was eliminated and central planning established in 1947, thus breaking the production boycott and the hoarding of inputs before the Bizone's answer, the currency reform of 20 June 1945 and Ludwig Erhard's price reforms.

The currency reform was in fact directed by the three western military governments of Germany and involved three main steps: a dramatic contraction of the money supply by the introduction of the Deutsche Mark in replacement of the Reichsmark, the consolidation and restructuring of private and public debt, and establishing institutional safeguards against future inflation by creating an independent central bank, the Bank Deutscher Länder, and the forbidding of budget deficits by order of the Allied military governments.

The different economic orders or systems in action in the different occupation zones in Germany provide an interesting laboratory for testing the effect of different combinations of currency and price reforms and planning. In the Soviet zone, the establishment of central planning in 1947 raised output levels substantially before they rose in West Germany. However, the almost simultaneous currency reform in 1948 in the East did not accelerate output. In a planning environment a currency reform can restore the function of the store of value to money, but realistic relative prices will not be established, nor will they have an impact on the allocation of factors and goods.

In the French zone, where the currency reform was initiated at the same time as in the Bizone, price reforms were delayed until 1949. Thus, output growth was not as spectacular as in the British and American zones following both the currency and price reforms of 1948. In the Bizone it was Ludwig Erhard's policy to lift price controls off the great majority of industrial goods and some foodstuffs. The combination of reforms in the Bizone resulted in a surge of production. In the second half of 1948, industrial output grew at an annual rate of 137%! The sudden appearance of goods in shops with the advent of the currency reform reflected the end of hoarding and the impact of a scarce and stable currency. The continued production and sale of manufactured goods was induced by more appropriate prices for goods and factors of production. For example, the increase in the number of hours worked was a main cause for higher production; the incentive structure had changed from spending time in searching and bartering for food and other necessities to working in factories (Giersch, Paqué, Schmieding, 1992).

Thus, the Bizone, the German occupation zone, which had established both stable money and functioning markets at the earliest date, was the most dynamic of German zones in the late 1940s. Both of these concerns, the interest in price stability and well-functioning markets, characterised a group of influential German economists called the Ordoliberals, who stressed the vitality and cohesion of societies with well-functioning markets, a strong anti-Keynesian position, just at the time when Keynes' ideas began to rule economic policy in the rest of Western Europe.

Part II
Economic Development after World War II

3. Phases of Economic Development

3.1. Japan's Phases of Economic Development

3.1.1. History of Japan's post-war economic growth

3.1.1.1. Trends in post-war economic growth

In general, the stages of a nation's economic development can be defined and examined in terms of different rates of growth or in terms of changes in the key factors of economic influence. Interestingly, in the case of post-war Japan, either approach tends to result in closely overlapping divisions. Consequently, the stages of development are tentatively defined here as set out below, and Japan's pattern of economic growth will be reviewed with attention to the qualitative and quantitative dimensions of each transition. In addition, the stages of development will be verified on the basis of changes in the government's economic plans.

(1) Post-war reconstruction phase (1945–54)
(2) High-growth phase (1955–72)
(3) Oil-shock phase (1973–84)
(4) High-yen and bubble economy phase (1985–).

Gauged in terms of the rate of real GDP growth, trends in the Japanese economy roughly diverge around the point of the first oil shock (Fig. 3.1-1). Up until then, real annual growth averaged over 9%. In fact, the real annual pace averaged a dramatic 11.2% from the days of the Tokyo Olympics (1964) and on through the late 1960s. However, following the first oil shock, the real growth rate fell substantially at around 4–5% annually until the Heisei Recession of the early 1990s. Roughly speaking, then, Japan's growth rate can be portrayed as having veered sharply downward around the time of the first oil shock.

3.1.1.2. Change in economic demand

If examined on the basis of demand sources, the following features are highlighted (Fig. 3.1-2). First, growth in fixed-capital formation (plant, equipment and housing) was extremely fast paced. From 1950 to 1970 its growth rate averaged above 10% and it functioned as the key engine of overall economic

Fig. 3.1-1 Trend of GDP growth

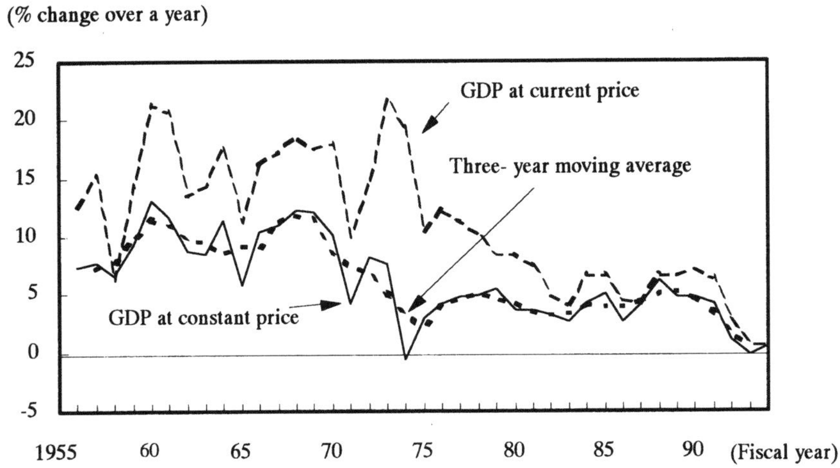

Source: EPA, Annual Report on National Accounts

Fig. 3.1-2 Change of economic demand

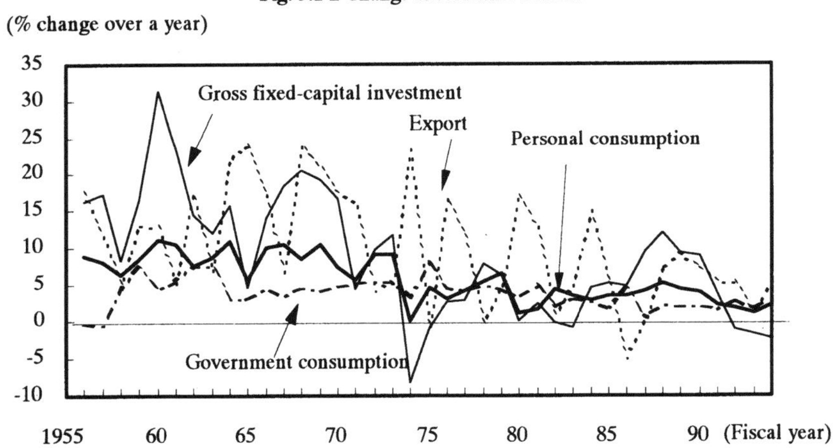

Source: EPA, Annual Report on National Accounts

growth. To be sure, during the Jinmu and Iwato expansions of 1955–61 and the Izanagi expansion of 1965–70,[1] total fixed-capital formation expanded at a pace of 17.6%. In particular, capital spending in the private corporate sector increased by a margin of around 20% each year during these two periods. But following the first

[1] In Japan it is sometimes customary to name an economic expansion after an emperor, an important individual or a special event in Japanese mythology.

oil shock, growth in fixed-capital formation tumbled to an average of only 3–4% in annual terms, except for the bubble economy years of the late 1980s.

Second, the growth in imports and exports (more precisely, of goods and services combined) registered a double-digit rate of increase up to 1970. This reflected a typical pattern of Japanese trade: namely, that of importing basic materials and exporting manufactured finished goods. From 1970 on, however, the exports continued to expand at a steep pace, while conversely imports tended to decline gradually. In return, Japan ran up a growing trade surplus. (As an exception to the overall trend, the flow of imports increased sharply under the influence of the speculation-driven economic bubble that took shape in the late 1980s.) As a result, overseas demand, as measured by net export of goods and services, replaced fixed-capital investment as a locomotive to lead the economy.

Third, household consumption expenditure rose at a strong pace of around 10% from 1955 to 1970, then fell back to a steady and sustained pace of 4% thereafter, until the onset of the Heisei Recession. Taking into account per-capita figures in order to exclude a factor of population increase, household consumption expenditure continued to grow by more than 7% up to 1970, and from 1970 onwards until the Heisei Recession, it remained stable at 3% or so on an annual average. Private consumption, thus, played a role in supporting the economic growth during this period.

In summary, from the latter half of the 1950s to the early 1970s, Japanese economic growth was powered chiefly by expanding levels of capital investment. Thereafter, growth was led by exports, which had become more competitive in the international market as a result of the earlier capital investment drive. In the meantime, though, the nation's steadily growing consumer sector formed the core of domestic demand to support its growth.

3.1.1.3. Scale of economy

In fiscal 1946, Japanese nominal GNP recorded $1.36 billion (¥448.7 billion at ¥360/dollar). By contrast, the US nominal GDP amounted to $211.9 billion in the same year, 156 times as large as Japan's. In 1967 Japan surpassed the leading European economies of former West Germany, France and Britain to assume its position as the world's second-largest economy after the US (ranking hereafter excludes the former Soviet Union and the countries of the Eastern bloc). In GDP terms, however, it still measured only one-seventh the scale of the US. Although two major oil shocks effectively blunted its growth rate in later years, Japan still managed to outpace the other leading industrial economies. In 1993 the most recent year for which comparative figures are available, Japanese GDP reached $4,198.0 billion, which is equivalent to about two-thirds of the US's that year ($6,245.4 billion).

In per-capita GDP terms, Japan reached the $2,000 mark in 1971 at $2,205, surpassing Italy (at $2,180). Nonetheless, that figure was equivalent to only about 40% of the corresponding US level, ranking Japan no higher than eighteenth among the twenty-four nations comprising the OECD. Over the 1970s, however, Japan increased its growth pace relative to the other leading industrial nations with its scale of per-capita GDP and its ranking steadily climbing among the OECD states. In 1984 its per-capita GDP had broken the $10,000 mark, placing Japan alongside the leading West European countries in terms of sheer scale. The latest figure for 1992 was $29,525, second only to Switzerland, among the OECD economies, and 1.3 times as large as that of the US ($23,215).

Of course, given the wide fluctuations in foreign exchange rates through the 1980s and thus far in the 1990s, it is difficult to gauge precisely the GDP-based economic scale using pure currency translations. Thus, as one useful alternative, some post-1970 GDP comparisons based on OECD-determined purchasing power parity (PPP) are presented here. In 1970 Japanese GDP registered $293.5 billion in scale, then already the second-largest of any country in the world, but still just less than 30% of the corresponding US figure ($1,011.6 billion). The relative scale of Japan's economy kept the same level up to the mid-1980s. Thereafter and into the 1990s, its relative scale gradually enlarged. In 1992 Japanese GDP totalled $2,481.4 billion, 42% of the US GDP ($5,920.2 billion).

Based on calculations using purchasing power parity, Japanese per-capita GDP equalled 57% of the US scale in 1970, and about 80% of the scale of Germany and France, having shown thereafter little change until around 1980. Measured in terms of purchasing power parity, the relative scale of Japanese per-capita GDP began a gradual expansion in the 1980s; in 1990 it closely paralleled the French figure, and by 1992 climbed to about 85% of the corresponding figure for the US, effectively ranking Japan fourth-largest after the US, Switzerland and Germany. Comparisons in terms of purchasing power parity accordingly suggest that the exchange-rate-based comparison actually exaggerates the scale of Japanese GDP and GDP per capita by about 1.5 to 1.6 times. While Japan has demonstrated a rapid rate of economic growth, Japanese relative economic volume in terms of purchasing power parity does not support the claim that its economy has expanded as much as its record of fast growth nominally suggests.

3.1.2. Industrial sector transitions in the Japanese economy

3.1.2.1. Value-added analysis

Retracing the pattern of transition in industrial structure is an effective means of clearly identifying qualitative changes in Japan's post-war economic development.

Of the three general industrial categories, Japan's primary industry accounted for about 30% of the total of real value added immediately following the end of World War II, but declined steadily thereafter (Fig. 3.1-3). In particular, value added of the primary industry, that is, farm, forestry and fishery industries, increased no more than 3.8% over the entire thirty-seven-year span from 1955 to

1992. The value added furnished by mining industries expanded strongly up to around 1970, but since then has demonstrated slow growth. Construction's contribution followed much the same pattern, growing at a brisk 10% or so up to 1970, but slowing down in later years (excluding the bubble economy period).

The secondary industry accounted for just under 20% of total value added at the end of the war. However, as manufacturing output recovered, that share later expanded at a double-digit rate, eventually outpacing the primary-industry share to become the largest in GNP. Since the early 1970s it has averaged a much slower rate of growth, around 5%. The metal and transport machinery industries continued to account for a rising share of total manufacturing output during the high-growth period, reflecting a relative decline in the textile industry and a rapid growth in the iron and steel and shipbuilding industries. Through the 1970s, however, the share of the metal industry continued to rise, but its growth rate slackened off sharply. Various trends in the machinery trades have highlighted a steady shift in the focus of growth. Whereas slowing growth characterised the general machinery field, electrical machinery sustained its fast pace. Furthermore, automobiles replaced shipbuilding as the most important sector of the transportation equipment field. Owing largely to these developments, a line-up of core industries contributing to economic growth showed a gradual change.

By comparison, the share of value added attributable to the tertiary industry remained relatively unchanged up to around 1970, at which point it began growing gradually, since its growth rate outpaced that of the secondary industry. In terms of growth rates alone, though, the value added produced by the tertiary industry actually expanded at a double-digit pace until 1970, but then it receded from the early 1970s onwards. Thus, the tertiary industry also witnessed a shift towards slower growth.

Fig. 3.1-3 Share of value added by industry

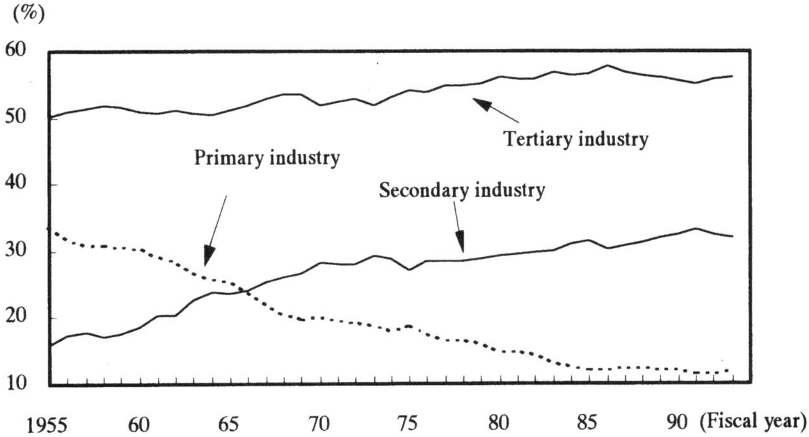

Source: EPA, Annual Report on National Accounts

3.1.2.2. Change in employment

Shifts in the share of the total work force paint a rather different picture from that suggested by trends in value added. Since 1970 the primary and secondary industries have together accounted for a steadily and gradually declining share of the total, whereas the share in the tertiary industry has followed a consistent growth track, having absorbed a steadily growing share of the labour force. Since the early 1980s, though, the share of the work force employed in the secondary industry alone has stabilised. By sub-industry, the share of the textile industry in the total employment fell sharply, while the machinery industry demonstrated a growing share. Since the beginning of the 1980s, employment has expanded particularly rapidly in the electrical machinery field, effectively contributing to a sharp up-trend and reflecting a structural change within the machinery industry.

3.1.2.3. Capital spending

As to the share of capital investment during the initial period of rapid growth in the late 1950s, the primary industry accounted for 20% of the total, compared with shares of about 40% each for both the secondary and tertiary industries. In the ensuing era and high-growth era, the share of the secondary industry widened, peaking at 53.0% in 1961. By sub-industry, the metal and machinery industries expanded their capital spending at an annual rate of around 30% between 1965 and 1970. The share of total capital spending attributable to the electrical machinery and transportation equipment fields has risen since the beginning of the 1980s.

One feature of the growth pattern through the late 1970s is the extremely volatile cycle of steep ups and downs. In the early 1980s the growth pace in capital spending slackened off, and the margin of fluctuation narrowed. During the bubble economy later that decade, it shot up again and then abruptly contracted. In contrast to the secondary industry, the share attributable to the tertiary industry began to grow and has continued to run above the 50% level since the late 1980s, reflecting the shift to low growth economy and the change of industrial structure.

3.1.2.4. Export growth

As for export growth, the general trend from the rapid-growth years to the era of stable growth was one of gradual decline, especially from the mid-1960s to the mid-1970s, Although metals, textiles and other industrial-use materials accounted for a significant portion of the total share in exports, capital goods and consumer durable goods recorded a higher increase in terms of growth rate. Reflecting the late-1970s shift to new growth industries, exports of capital goods, led by machinery, eventually accounted for the largest share and demonstrated the fastest growth as well. By comparison, although exports of consumer electrical appliances and other consumer durable goods registered an annual growth of above 20% up to the late 1970s, their pace has fallen since 1980. This, however, appears to reflect the fact that such industries set about relocating their manufacturing bases offshore earlier in the 1980s than machinery and capital goods industries did.

In summary, the primary industry was the driving force of the economy during the post-war reconstruction years. Later, during the period of fast-paced growth, the secondary industry took over this role. The emphasis has changed from foods and textiles in the reconstruction years, to iron and steel and shipbuilding in the high-growth years and then to general machinery, automobiles and electrical machinery in the stable-growth years. This, in turn, highlights a shift from light to heavy industry and then to advanced processing and assembly trades engaged in the production of higher value added. Although in output terms the manufacturing industry continued to play a leading role in the economy following the second oil shock, the tertiary industry has attracted a growing share of the nation's total labour supply and has become a leading factor in the economy's stable growth.

3.1.3. Defining eras in terms of changes in economic planning

On the basis of the preceding analysis, it is possible to identify a number of characteristics, including changes in economic policy, that define certain eras in the half-century since the end of World War II.

3.1.3.1. Post-war reconstruction (1945–1954)

This was a period in which Japan was searching for paths to rise from the desolation of the immediate post-war period and achieve economic self-sufficiency. Of the five economic plans that were formulated between 1948 and 1953, four were targeted towards economic self-sufficiency.[2] This period can be divided into two phases. During the first phase, Japan overcame the production slump and inflation of the immediate post-war years through the priority production system and the establishment of the Reconstruction Finance Bank, and through changes in supply-side conditions in the form of a shift in US occupation policies towards Japan. In the second phase, special demand generated by the Korean War created a pattern of economic growth led by capital investment, thereby laying the foundations for Japan's subsequent economic development. The outbreak of the Korean War in June 1950 generated massive special demand, including the need to supply US forces engaged in the war. This factor, together with rapid export growth, brought a sharp increase in Japan's foreign currency reserves and stimulated domestic consumption and investment. The structure that enabled the Japanese economy to achieve self-sustaining development appears to have been basically completed during this period.

---

2 During this period, economic plans were formulated and implemented by revising and continuing previous plans. Changing economic circumstances and changes in government resulted in the formulation and implementation of new plans prior to the completion of the previous ones.

3.1.3.2. High growth (1955–1972)

The high-growth era began with an economic upswing that became known as the Jimmu Boom and ended after the Izanagi Boom. During the period of approximately seventeen years, the economy went through four major expansionary phases: the Jimmu Boom, the Iwato Boom, the Olympic Boom and the Izanagi Boom. The high-growth era was characterised by Japan's efforts to catch up with the leading industrialised nations by improving living standards. This was reflected in the pursuit of quantitative expansion under policies that gave priority to growth. The "National Income Doubling Plan", formulated by the Ikeda cabinet in 1960, targeted full employment and the improvement of living standards, and can be described as the symbol of Japan's preoccupation in growth. Virtually all capital and labour were channelled into the achievement of economic growth, creating a pattern of growth driven by the dual forces of capital investment and exports. However, pollution and other distortions caused by high growth came to the fore towards the end of this period, raising doubts about the qualitative state of the economy. The result was a gradual shift in economic planning targets, from a primary emphasis on growth to the achievement of balance between quantity and quality.

3.1.3.3. Oil shocks and a low yen (1973–1984)

The oil shock period was a transitional phase in which the Japanese economy underwent a structural change from high growth to stable growth. Sudden changes in supply conditions owing to soaring crude oil prices made structural change inevitable. Even during the closing years of the high-growth era, Japan was already under pressure domestically and internationally to develop a more balanced economic growth structure. The oil shocks provided the impetus for this change. The "Basic Economic and Social Plan," formulated by the Tanaka cabinet in 1973, focused on the creation of a welfare society and the improvement of national welfare, and on the development of an internationally harmonious socio-economic structure. This adjustment of Japan's growth path was also accompanied by change in its industrial structure. The focus shifted from heavy material industries to higher-value-added processing and assembly industries. Tertiary industries, such as business services and communication services, also began to grow. The oil shock and low-yen period can thus be characterised as a search for ways to achieve qualitative improvement in the high economic level attained during the high-growth period.

3.1.3.4. High-yen period (1985–)

A feature of economic planning in the high-yen period is the emphasis on continuing qualitative improvement of Japan's economic structure. Another key issue is the correction of external imbalances caused by overwhelming export competitiveness as manifested in the trade surplus. For this reason, the focus of economic planning has shifted to the achievement of a better "quality of life" or a life-style that will enable people to enjoy Japan's wealth. This was made possible by moving from an export-led economic structure to one led by domestic demand. One of the goals pursued in this context is the improvement of economic vitality through deregulation. Japan's traditional economic structure has become the focus of concern, particularly with regard to the gap between domestic and foreign prices is preventing Japanese consumers from enjoying the benefits of a high yen. However, the conversion of Japan's economic structure has not been an easy task, and the problem of external imbalances remains unresolved. Distortions in the Japanese economy were amplified during the bubble economy of the late 1980s by such phenomena as soaring land prices. This was not the outcome envisaged when Japan began to work towards the achievement of a "rich national life-style". Japan's growth performance in the low-growth era has been healthy. From the viewpoint of its industrial structure, however, the economic characteristics that took root during the oil shock period have been reinforced. For the Japanese economy as a whole, this period has brought little progress in the direction set down in economic planning.

The bubble economy created a massive production capacity surplus and triggered stock inflation. As a consequence, the Japanese economy has been affected since the bursting of the bubble by severe stock adjustments and a deflationary trend in the prices of real estate and other stocks. This situation has necessitated a major rethinking of Japan's traditional economic structure, which was based on the assumption that growth would continue indefinitely. In particular, drastic changes are needed in the employment system, which is based on the concept of lifetime employment. Economic plans are still targeting the qualitative improvement of living standards, but the achievement of goals in this area will not be easy. Japan has also worked to alleviate external imbalances, but progress has been disappointing, and the industrial sector is concerned that the rapid appreciation of the yen will lead to a "hollowing-out" effect. This situation reflects Japan's failure to implement adequate structural economic reforms after the oil shocks. Even in the areas in which there was progress towards reform, there now emerges a vicious circle in which reform strengthens international competitiveness, thereby causing the yen to rise even further.

3.2. Germany's Phases of Economic Development

3.2.1. Delimitation of phases

The post-war economic history of West Germany shows clear changes in the economic development measured by patterns of growth, employment, rate of inflation and structural change during the last fifty years. The different phases are, however, not sharply delimited from each other. The transitions were gradual, as a rule, and took a number of years, as several events at different points in time had to combine to bring about a new pattern of economic development.

Because of the gradualism in the development, every delimitation of phases by individual years remains arbitrary. The starting years of the following phases, which are defined for convenience's sake, only mark the end of a period of transition lasting several years. The following periods are differentiated:

(1) Post-war reconstruction and recovery or the *Wirtschaftswunder* (1945–59)
(2) Full employment and the golden 1960s (1960–73)
(3) External shocks and adjustment problems (1974–present) with the subdivisions
    (a) Oil shock phase (1974–1986) and the
    (b) Phase of internationalisation (1987–present)

The post-war reconstruction and recovery period can also be divided into the phase of the establishment of a liberal order (1945–48) and the phase of spontaneous growth (1949–59) (Giersch, Paqué, Schmieding, 1993).

3.2.2. Characteristics of the different phases

3.2.2.1. Post-war reconstruction and recovery (1945–1959)

The post-war recovery was a phase of extremely fast economic growth and strongly increasing demand for labour. Despite the vigorous demand, inflation rates normalised after the price peak in the early 1950s induced by the Korean War. The growth phase started with the big bang of the currency reform and the removal of price controls in 1948. Because the upswing of German industry was very strong by the standards of other industrialised countries, it was named the *Wirtschaftswunder*, or economic miracle.

It is difficult to decide whether the economic miracle was mainly caused by the freeing of market forces (Giersch, Paqué, Schmieding, 1993) or was due to a catching-up process which closed the large gap between realised and potential output after the war shocks (Dumke, 1990; Abelshauser, 1987). On the one hand, the poor development of the former GDR in a similar socio-cultural environment proves that the economic order made a difference. On the other hand, it cannot be denied that the position of a follower with under-utilised capacities helped Germany very much to recover quickly. The under-valued currency, in addition, facilitated the realisation of export-led growth in the 1950s. Therefore, it was probably the combination of both factors that explains the extraordinary high growth in this era.

The end of the post-war phase is marked by the establishment of the institutions and the completion of the legislation that still characterise the economic order in Germany. It is important to note that only a core of industries (mainly manufacturing) was deregulated and liberalised in the 1950s. A significant degree of government intervention remained in agriculture, in the production of energy, in transport and communication services, in financial services, and in health and education services. The start of the European Economic Community in 1958 marks the beginning of a first phase of opening German industry to international trade and competition. Full employment was reached at the end of the 1950s. The diffusion of oil in the second half of the 1950s and the emerging nuclear power sounded the bell for the end of an era with coal as the main energy resource of the German economy.

3.2.2.2. Full employment and the golden 1960s (1960–1973)

Whereas the post-war period was an era of pronounced economic and social change, the 1960s were characterised by a relatively stable economic environment. As the 1960s brought about a pronounced increase in welfare and full employment, German society was able to harvest some of the fruits of the milestone decisions of the 1950s. The importance of stability in this era is underlined by the fact that the most important economic legislation of this era, the Law of Stability and Growth of 1967, was aimed at reducing the risks of business fluctuations. In the Keynesian spirit, the government's responsibility for full employment was formalised. The law is still in effect today.

The great stability of the economic framework did not mean a lack of structural change (Gerstenberger, 1984). The rising demand for labour of the expanding industries compensated for labour shedding in the declining industries. Foreign workers, mainly from Southern Europe, had to be introduced to balance demand and supply on the labour market.

With other nations also prospering in the 1960s, the phase of stability came to an end because of the resulting tensions in the world economy (Gerstenberger, 1984). The dynamic catching-up process in Germany, in other European countries and in Japan, and the expansive monetary and fiscal policy in the United States put the Bretton Woods system of stable exchange rates more and more under strain. It finally collapsed in 1971. The expansion of the world economy caused more and more raw materials and energy markets to turn into supplier markets. Thus, the first oil price shock of 1973 also had economic reasons. Last but not least, the long phase of full employment shifted the balance of power from employers' organisations to trade unions in Germany as well as in the other industrialised countries. Wage policy became more aggressive and was targeted at a change in the distribution of income (see also Giersch, Paqué, Schmieding, 1993). Rising labour costs and rising prices for raw materials and energy inputs stimulated inflation. Consequently, the end of the era saw rising inflation rates.

3.2.2.3. External shocks and adjustment problems (1974–)

The changes in the early 1970s sounded the bell for a phase of turbulence and disturbances of economic development. The two oil price hikes in 1973 and 1979 were only two of several supply-side shocks. The environmental problems associated with the production and consumption of goods and services had become a constraining factor for growth. This implied an even greater change in the economic framework than the phase of expensive energy starting with the first oil price hike. On top of the supply-side shocks, conflicts emerged between monetary policy and wage policy. These conflicts resulted in two deep recessions in the mid-1970s and in the early 1980s. Exaggerations on the currency markets after the liberalisation of exchange rates and the high German interest rates associated with the strict monetary policy of the Bundesbank led to a phase of an overvaluation of the D-Mark, which was ended by the dollar strength in the Reagan era.

The European Community's single market initiative marked the start of a new phase of internationalisation and opening of the German economy. Especially the protection of service industries from competitors from abroad has been reduced since the mid-1980s. German manufacturing industry, which was opened to international competition in the 1950s, was challenged by new competitors from East Asia already in the 1970s. The collapse of the former Soviet Union and the associated political and economic changes in Central and Eastern Europe resulted in an even greater impetus to internationalise the German economy. Suddenly a large force of qualified labour at low cost emerged in Germany's vicinity, awaiting integration in the international division of labour. The unification of Germany strained the financial capacity of the nation.

As in the other industrialised countries, the massing of external and internal shocks overtaxed the adjustment capacity of the German economic and social system. Growth friction and inflexibility in the labour market led to a rising trend in unemployment. Because of the high level of unemployment and the financial burden of unification, the financing of the well-developed German social security system became more and more difficult. Pressure for a fundamental reform of the system has increased sharply. Unemployment also rose because the labour supply increased considerably in Germany as a result of immigration. Taking into account this handicap, the adjustment efforts of the German economy to the challenges have been adequate and balanced. Despite unification, Germany is among the few European countries likely to meet the Maastricht Treaty criteria for monetary union.

Inevitably, the phase of shocks also called for a different economic policy. The Keynesian approach was abolished in favour of monetary and supply-side thinking. Deregulation, privatisation and flexibility have been the key words in economic policy since the 1980s.

3.2.3. Development of growth, employment, capital stock, and inflation

Growth of real GDP followed a downward trend over most of the post-war decades (Fig. 3.2-1). A stabilisation of growth at around 2.5% was detectable since the early 1980s. Inflation rates dropped to 2–3% after the price peaks in the early 1950s, measured by the deflator of private consumption. Taking into account the trend towards rising prices for services,[3] this increase in prices is close to the inevitable rate of inflation. The tensions emerging after two decades of strong growth led to a rise in inflation rates prior to the phase of internal and external shocks. The two oil price hikes brought peak values of increase in overall consumer prices. Inflation rates again reached the area of the inevitable price increases in the mid-1980s. This becomes more evident when analysing the development of the GDP deflator. This indicator shows that the price increase associated with the unification boom of the early 1990s was self-inflicted.

Similar to the growth trend, the trend in the growth of employment and of capital stock has been affected by business-cycle fluctuations. An elimination of the fluctuations shows a stagnation in employment from the mid-1960s to the mid-1980s (Fig. 3.2-2a). In the last ten years, growth has again become more labour-intensive, mainly because of an increase in part-time work and other forms of flexible employment. Also, due to an increase in the labour force, this expansion in labour demand was not strong enough to avoid a long-term increase in unemployment (Fig. 3.2-2b). The number of long-term unemployed increased considerably, despite different measures of labour market policy (including early pension schemes).

The downward trend in the growth of German capital stock lasted till the mid-1980s. This was true both for the capital stock of business and the capital stock of houses and public infrastructure. The latter serves as a proxy for the capital stock with no direct effects on the number and the quality of jobs. Between the 1950s and the early 1970s, business-oriented investment experienced a clear preference, indicated by the higher growth rates. In the phase of shocks, the growth of both categories of capital stock met at a lower level.

It remains to be seen whether the revival of business investment after 1985 will be permanent.

In the 1950s the growth of capital stock was accompanied by a significant increase in employment. With the achievement of full employment at the end of the decade, a process of capital deepening started. The increase in the capital stock per employee (capital intensity) was one of the main sources of the increase in

[3] This trend is due to difficulties in increasing productivity in certain services. Limits to improving the productivity in labour exist especially in the area of personal services, which requires interaction between producer and user to produce the services.

Fig. 3.2-1 Growth and inflation in West Germany: change from previous year

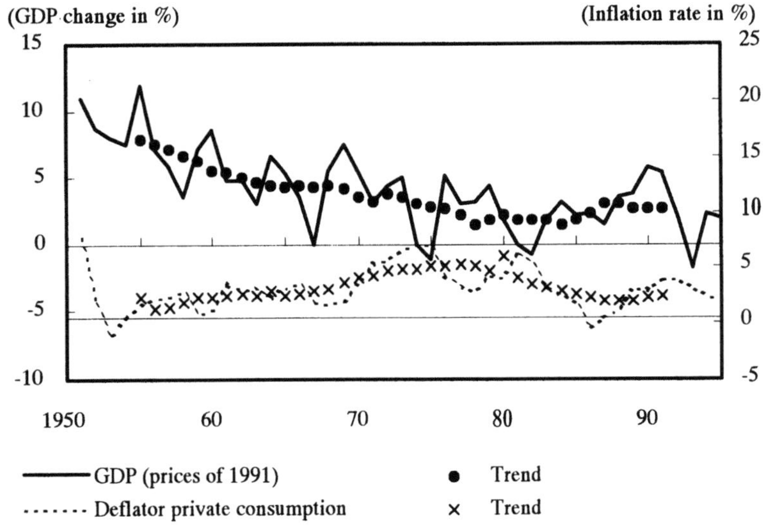

Source: Federal Statistical Office, Ifo calculations

Fig. 3.2-2a Employment and capital stock in West Germany: change from previous year

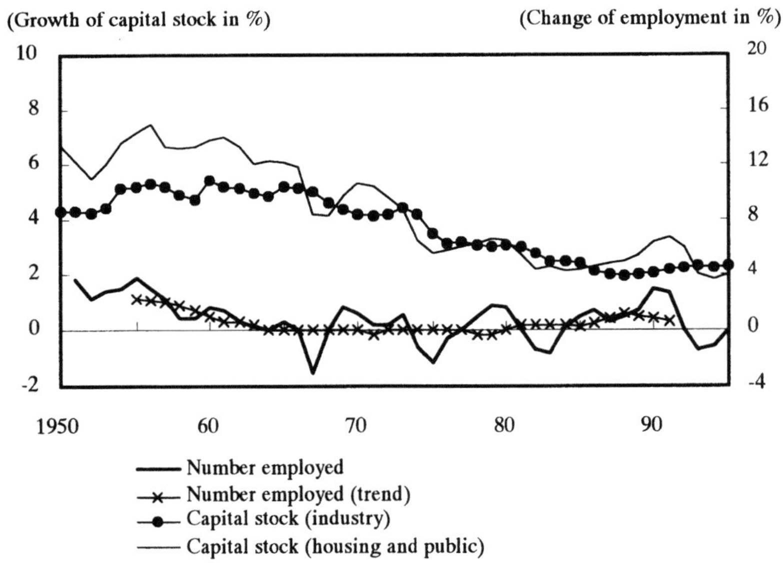

Source: Federal Statistical Office, Ifo calculations

Fig. 3.2-2b Labour force and employment in West Germany

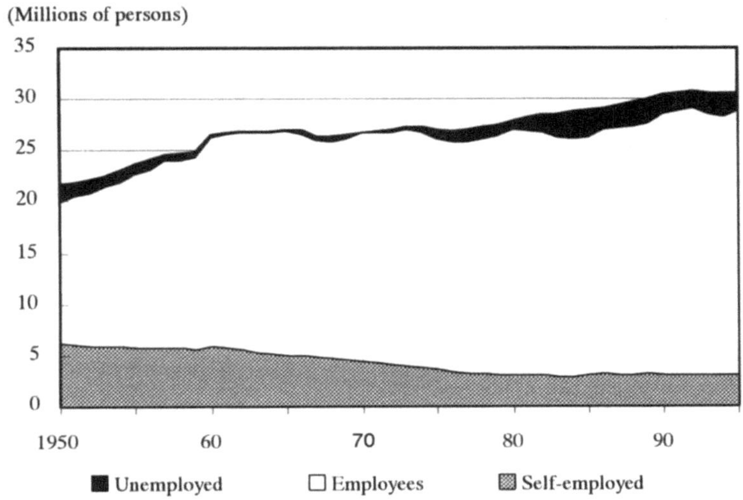

Source: Federal Statistical Office

Fig. 3.2-2c Index of labour and employment as sources of growth in West Germany

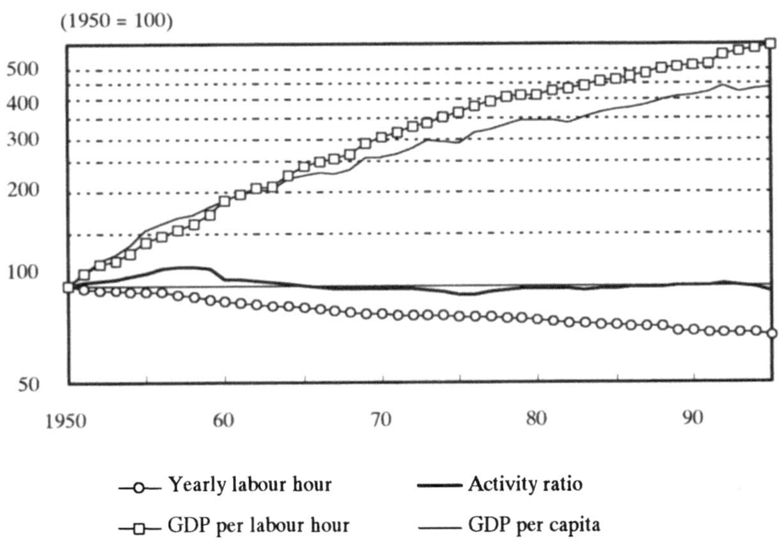

Source: Federal Statistical Office, Ifo calculations

labour productivity.[4]

The increase of labour productivity was the main source of the rise in real GDP per capita of the German population (Fig. 3.2-2c). It grew four-fold between 1950 and 1995. The development of GDP per capita can be divided into different components: the increase of labour productivity, the change in working time and the change in the activity rate. The latter is measured as the share of people gainfully employed in the total population. The increase in labour productivity was sufficient to allow a considerable reduction in working time and a reduction in the activity rate since the 1950s. Only since the mid-1980s has the activity rate been on the increase again.

3.2.4. Structural change

The growth process was intertwined with a pronounced change in the German economy. The importance in the creation of value added shifted first from the agricultural and extracting industries to manufacturing and then to services. The pattern and timing of the change in the production by industry were similar to that shown by the distribution of employment by industry (Fig. 3.2-3).

Employment in agriculture, forestry and fishing decreased since the early 1950s. In the early 1990s only 3% of German employees worked in agriculture compared to nearly one quarter in 1950. They produced 1% of total value added of the German economy compared to 10% in 1950. The social effects of this shrinking process were buffered by a rising amount of financial aid. Also in the 1990s, in the framework of European regulations of agricultural markets, consumers pay twofold for the adjustment of agricultural income to the level of industrial income and for farmers' old-age pensions. Firstly, they have to finance the subsidies with higher taxes. Secondly, they have to pay prices for agricultural products which are significantly above world-market levels.

The opening of German industry to international competition put a downward pressure on coal mining and on the production of textiles, clothing and leather. The advantages of oil as an energy sources were additional factors for the decline of coal. Whereas the shrinking of coal mining was buffered both by protection against foreign competition and subsidies, the textile clothing sector

---

4 Assuming a dependency of the rate of growth of labour productivity (GDP at constant prices per hour worked) (WPROD) on the rate of growth of capital intensity (WKI) and on the rate of GDP growth (WO) renders the following results:

$$\underset{}{WPRODt} = \underset{(0.0)}{0.01} + \underset{(11.0)}{0.47}\, WKIt + \underset{(20.0)}{0.68}\, WOt - \underset{(2.9)}{0.09}\, WOt\text{-}1 + e_t$$

D.W. = 1.47, R^2 = 0.931

T-values in parentheses below the parameter estimates, D.W. = Durbin-Watson Statistic, R^2 = coefficient of determination, e_t = error term, t = year (1952–95).

The rate of GDP growth serves to take into account scale effects and the effects of fluctuations in the rate of capacity utilisation on the growth of labour productivity.

only received some reduction of the adjustment pressure by the Multi Fibre Agreement between industrialised and developing countries.

During the 1950s and 1960s the decline in the sector mentioned was more than balanced by the rising demand for labour in other industries. Germany's strength as a location for engineering and know-how intensive industries led to a prospering of mechanical and electrical engineering, the production of means of transport and chemical and allied industries. The expansion of basic chemicals and mineral oil refining was favoured by the triumphal march of plastics as a material and the rapid motorisation of Germany. Employment in construction expanded only until the mid-1960s. The year 1965 marked the end of the post-war phase of recovery for this industry.

The demand for private and public services grew even stronger than the demand for manufactured products. Market services expanded despite a variety of regulations. The share of industry in value added and in employment peaked in the first half of the 1960s (Fig. 3.2-3). Since then, industry has been losing importance as an employer and generator of income within the German economy. Service industries which depend on the production of goods, such as wholesale and retail trade and transportation services, have also felt the changing climate in industry: Job creation in these industries has ceased since the mid-1960s. The importance of industry in Germany, however, has remained far greater than in other Western European countries. This reflects not only the less favourable conditions in Germany for touristic services; more important is the strong competitive position of Germany's manufacturing industry within Europe (Gerstenberger, 1990).

The phase of shocks also brought a modification in the pattern of sectoral change. Due to rising prices for oil and energy and due to environmental problems, chemical and allied industries lost their role as growth industries. Instead of creating jobs as in the 1950s and 1960s, the number of employees has stagnated in these industries since 1973. In addition, the electrical industry (especially electronics), optical and camera industry and shipbuilding came under strong competitive pressure from Japanese and other companies from East Asia and had to reduce capacities in Germany. As mechanical engineering and the car industry suffered from the strong D-Mark during the 1970s, these core industries also did not expand strongly in this period. The construction industry experienced a decline due to the dampening effects of high interest rates on the demand for housing and non-residential construction. The problems in the forward-linked industries resulted in a reduction of steel consumption and brought about a downward trend for the iron and steel industry. Thus, hardly any manufacturing industry remained to create jobs in the 1970s and most of the 1980s. In the second half of the 1980s and the early 1990s, an improvement in the investment climate in Europe came about which has strengthened the capital goods producing industries. This process was interrupted, however, by the last recession in 1992/93.

Both market services and non-market services expanded in the 1970s and the 1980s. The increase of employment in non-market services has become increasingly difficult to finance, however, due to the associated increase in the

Fig. 3.2-3 Employment by industry in West Germany

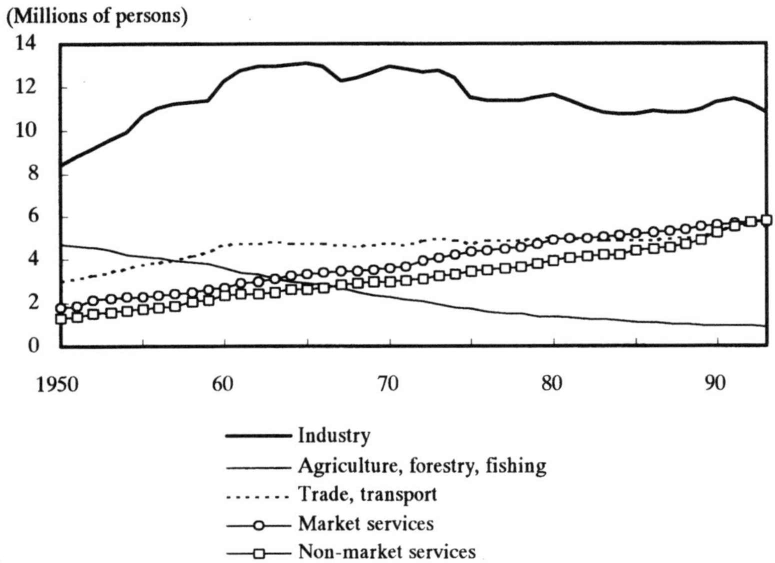

Source: Federal Statistical Office, Ifo calculations

burden of taxes and social contributions on the economy. The financial services and the business-oriented services grew strongest within the group of market services. Compared with the United States, the expansion of the service economy has been weaker in Germany. This weaker performance is to a large part due to the stronger regulations in Germany.

3.2.5. Economic policy stance in the different phases

The post-war reconstruction phase was the era that defined the German economic order. The new order of the social market economy was not established with the break up of large trusts in the phase 1945–47, the currency reform and the liberalisation of prices in 1948. The phase of liberalisation of the strongly regulated German "war economy" stretched out over several years. The interventions of government in the energy and steel sector were not abolished until 1952 (Ifo, 1953). The capital market became truly free only with the convertibility of the D-Mark in 1958. In this year also a law established the Deutsche Bundesbank as an independent institution for monetary policy. The cementing of the basis of liberal order for the German economy by the *Kartelgesetz* (law against restraint of trade) took place only in 1957. The pillars of the German social market economy, the old-age pension scheme and unemployment and health insurance were also established by legislation in the second half of the 1950s.

In the 1960s, these elements of the economic order were completed by defining the targets and instruments of macro-economic policy in the Law for Promoting Stability and Economic Growth (*Gesetz zur Förderung von Stabilität und Wachstum der Wirtschaft*, 1967) and by specifying the rules for government interventions in the process of structural change.[5] This doctrine for industrial policy established as a main target for government the facilitation of structural change and the intervention in declining industries in order to bring the speed of shedding labour and capital to a socially acceptable level. The phase of internal and external shocks put these guidelines for economic policy to a hard test.

Already the recession in 1974/75 revealed the limits of the law for stability and growth. After learning more and more about the constraints of government interventions in the process of economic growth and structural change, a new vision of the role of the state in business emerged and gained acceptance among decision-makers. The trend towards a more subsidiary role of government brought about several changes:

- In the field of macro-economic policy, the responsibility for full employment was shifted to trade unions and employers' organisations. The regulations concerning hiring and firing were eased and legal limits to flexible working time agreements were lifted.
- Monetary policy was concentrated more exclusively on the target of price stability than in the 1960s and early 1970s. Fiscal policy successfully cut back the growth of government expenditures and succeeded in reducing the tax burden somewhat during the 1980s.[6] Several reforms were aimed at reducing the growth in the expenditures of the mandatory social security system. These efforts were, however, not crowned by permanent success.
- Government started to retreat as a service provider. State-owned enterprises in energy supply, waste management, transportation and communication were partially or fully privatised. Municipal services in transportation and waste management were closed down to offer new chances for private service providers.
- Induced by the programme for the completion of the European single market, service markets in addition were deregulated and opened to international competition. The liberalisation affected primarily financial services, transportation and communication services, the pharmaceutical industry and the construction industry.

To date, the scaling down of the influence of government on the economy has not brought forward the improvements hoped for on the labour market. This is

5 Grundsätze der sektoralen Struktur- und der regionalen Wirtschaftspolitik der Bundesregierung, Bundestagsdrucksache V 2469 of 16.1.1968.

6 German unification brought a setback to these efforts. Today the high burden of taxes and social insurance contributions is again the factor that endangers Germany's position as a location for investment.

certainly partly due to the new shocks (collapse of the Soviet Union, unification) which have hit the economy. The new paradigm in economic policy was, however, only implemented in small steps and half-heartedly. This gradualism is another explaining factor for the poor results. Due to the lack of success and influenced by the "new growth theory", an even more active role of government in the growth process is being discussed today.

3.3. Comparative Summary of Economic Development Phases

It is possible to identify a number of interesting similarities and differences between Japan and Germany in terms of the phases of economic development based on the methods used to identify changes in economic growth rates, quantitative and qualitative change in growth factors, changes in economic policy and long-term growth processes.

3.3.1. Changes in economic growth rates

After World War II, the Japanese and German economies both went through vital post-war reconstruction phases and experienced periods of rising economic growth rates. The rising growth phase was called the "golden age" in Germany and the "high-growth period" in Japan, both of which were driven by plant and equipment investment as well as by exports. In both Japan and Germany, the miraculous development of the post-war era reached a major turning point with the first oil crisis.

However, signs of a shift in the economic growth rate were apparent in both Japan and Germany even before the oil crisis, and it is interesting to note that both countries were reaching a certain stage of maturity, following the high growth of the post-war era. In Germany, the balance of power between management and labour shifted in favour of the trade unions in the late sixties and early seventies with the result that rising labour costs began to restrict growth. In addition, manufacturing suffered from the breakdown of the Bretton Woods fixed exchange rate system and the resulting sharp revaluation of the D-Mark. In Japan industries producing basic materials subsumed under the descriptions "heavy, thick, long and big," were burdened with excessive supply capacity and faced the problem of insufficient demand.

On the surface, both Germany and Japan experienced a decline in their growth rates after the first oil crisis. However, it is essential to recognise fully that the two countries faced this situation under totally different economic systems. There was a structural difference in the sense that Germany's growth rate declined under the full market economic system that it had maintained throughout the post-war period, while Japan's government-led economic system had reached an impasse. As a natural result, the two countries adopted different policies as they strove to restore their growth rates. In Germany the government consistently played a supplementary role, but Japan adopted the policies of demand stimulation and structural adjustment under government leadership.

3.3.2. Changes in growth conditions

The phase of high growth after the war reflected partly a catching-up process in both countries. It was associated with a rapid transition of employment from agriculture to manufacturing and services and resulted in full employment. Thus a switch from extensive to intensive growth occurred in both countries. Efficiency gains constituted the dominant growth factor during the last four decades.

The decline in growth rates during the last two decades was not only brought about by frictions caused by the oil price shocks. Changing exchange rate regimes played an important role, too. From this perspective, the Plaza Accord of 1985 can be seen as the start of a new era in Japan. The German economy already had experienced a phase of over-valued currency in the seventies. For the development in the last ten years, the completion of the internal market of the European Community and the changes associated with the collapse of the Soviet Union (including German unification) were more important than the exchange rate adjustments.

3.3.3. Changes of economic policy

The last four decades also saw changes of paradigms of economic policy. Japan and Germany started the post-war period with different paradigms. Whereas German economic policy relied mainly on market forces during the fifties and early sixties, concentrating on securing price stability and competition in manufacturing and service sectors, Japan favoured an interventionist policy approach for the transition of the economy towards becoming a leading industrialised country. During the sixties, both countries adopted elements of Keynesian policy and tried to control total demand. Due to the problems of the Keynesian approach to fighting stagflation, the eighties saw a shift towards supply-side policy in both countries. Deregulation, flexibilisation and privatisation are the keywords of the last ten years. Market elements are enforced, especially in services, mainly to realise the growth potential of the transition towards the information society.

3.3.4. Conclusions

The comparison of Japan and Germany shows differences and similarities in the economic development since the fifties. A closer look reveals that the German model was less market-driven and the Japanese less government-driven than generally believed. The policy stance changed considerably during the post-war period. Since the mid-eighties, supply-oriented policies and monetary discipline have dominated in both countries. The growth phases were only partly determined by specific processes. Exogenous shocks like the oil price shocks and changes in the international framework affected growth conditions and led to lower growth in both countries since the mid-seventies. The nineties have brought difficult adjustment problems; the post-war success stories are fading.

4. Political and Social Systems

4.1. Japan's Political and Social Systems

While Japan's political, economic and social systems have evolved through separate historical processes, they have also functioned through reciprocal interaction. Japan's achievement of high economic growth was attributable not only to the successful functioning of its economic system but also to the role of the political and social systems in supporting the economic system. Yet, this does not mean that these systems have always been functioning appropriately in terms of their basic aims. In this chapter, the role played by Japan's post-war political and social systems in economic growth will be examined.

4.1.1. Political system

4.1.1.1. Parliamentary and cabinet system

Under Japan's post-war Constitution, sovereignty resides with the people, and the emperor is the symbol of the state. The Constitution also divides the powers of legislation, judicature and administration. (Under the pre-war Constitution, sovereignty resided with the emperor, whose authority encompassed all three powers of the state.) Law-making authority rests with the Diet, administrative power with the cabinet and judicial power with the courts, and each arm of the state is organised independently. The assembly responsible for the state at the national level is the National Diet, which is a bicameral structure consisting of the House of Representatives and the House of Councillors. Members of the House of Representatives have traditionally been elected under a medium-constituency system. However, the passage of an amendment in October 1994 resulted in the adoption of a proportional representation system in parallel with a single-member electorate system. The House of Councillors consists of members elected on a proportional basis from the national constituency, and those elected from regional electorates under a large constituency system. In general, the passage of legislation requires a majority in both houses, but the Constitution gives the House of Representatives precedence on such matters as the nomination of prime ministers, the adoption of budgets and the signing of treaties.

Japan has a parliamentary cabinet system, under which the cabinet must have the confidence of the Diet. Cabinet members are normally chosen from among

Diet members, but non-members can also be appointed to cabinet posts. Prolonged rule by the Liberal Democratic Party (LDP) after the formation of the conservative alliance in 1955 led to collusive relations between the political and administrative sectors of government. In other words, the increasing dependence of the political system on the bureaucracy, partly because of frequent changes of cabinets, resulted in the formation of a system under which requests were made to the bureaucracy through powerful Diet members. This system was not without merit, since it enabled requests to the bureaucracy to be handled with greater flexibility. However, it also resulted in numerous cases of corruption during the period of LDP rule and was thus responsible for a loss of confidence in the political system.

4.1.1.2. Administrative organisations

The head of the central government is the prime minister, who is nominated by the Diet. The government consists of the Prime Minister's Office and twelve ministries, together with the Cabinet Legislative Bureau, the National Personnel Authority and the National Security Council. The Prime Minister's Office consists of three commissions and nine agencies.

Local authorities form administrations under mayors elected by residents. The central government has far greater powers than local authorities, since the Ministry of Autonomy is given the power to distribute local allocation tax, and treasury subsidies from the central government account for a large proportion of the revenues of local authorities. Treasury subsidies accounted for 17.5% of revenues in local authorities' fiscal plans for the 1994 financial year. These subsidies give the central government considerable legal power over local authority's fiscal policy, which has been described as a "castle in the air" with treasury subsidies as its foundation (Ito, 1992). The power of the central government is further reinforced by its authority to make decisions over public investment in such areas as road construction, which accounts for a high proportion of economic activities in Japan. For this reason, it is now general practice among local authorities to seek treasury subsidies by making representations to the central government through locally elected National Diet members. The power structure that has formed between the bureaucracy and Diet members is reflected in the ability of leading Diet members to influence the administration.

4.1.1.3. Mechanism of political decision-making

Japan's political and economic systems are in essence based on democratic and market economy principles. Government intervention in private-sector activity takes such forms as the establishment of laws and regulations, the exercise of licensing and approval authority, and the provision of administrative guidance. In the economic sphere, the government formulates its own economic plans and works to implement them through the passage of new laws and the preparation of budgets. A total of seventeen economic plans were formulated between 1948 and

1992, each reflecting prevailing priorities. However, long-term rule by the Liberal Democratic Party resulted in a situation in which political decisions were made in the midst of a power struggle among various factions pursuing their own interests, and politicians and bureaucrats formed the collusive relations. Thus, the role of bureaucrats became more important than those of politicians in the formation and implementation of economic plans. In particular, budget decisions were made through a tug-of-war process between the LDP and the Ministry of Finance. The result was a firmly entrenched system of decision-making by bureaucrats. This environment also produced the uniquely Japanese system of "administrative guidance", which was not necessarily based on law and was often in the form of verbal advice from bureaucrats.

4.1.1.4. The defence system

Under its Constitution Japan renounced the right to wage war, except in self-defence, and thus does not maintain armed forces as a means of resolving disputes with other nations. For this reason, Japan has no conscription system. The Self-Defence Forces, which were officially established in 1954, were based on the Police Reserve Force of the early post-war period. Their mission is to protect the peace and independence of Japan's territory and to maintain security.

Under its security treaty with the United States, which was first signed in 1951, Japan is essentially dependent on the Japan–US security system for its external security. The scale of Japan's defence expenditure in terms of GDP ratio is one of the lowest amongst developed countries. The scale has been actually kept below 1% of GNP and is based on a principle that was first adopted by the Miki Cabinet in 1976. Low defence expenditure has been cited as one of the factors that enabled Japan to achieve economic development. From the perspective of overall resource allocation, it indeed appears that Japan's economic development has benefited from the fact that government funds were channelled into civilian areas rather than into non-productive military activities.

4.1.2. Social system

Since Japan's social system is examined in the section on education in the chapter on social policy, the following discussion focuses on the general social framework, economic organisations and labour unions. To understand contemporary Japanese society, it is also necessary to examine the issues of shrinking family sizes and the growth of the aged population. Space, however, does not permit the discussion of these issues in this chapter.

4.1.2.1. General social framework

The first characteristic of Japan's general social framework is the role played by the family system. Since World War II, the family system has evolved from the pre-war household system, which was based on extended families, into a system based primarily on nuclear families. This change is closely linked to the conversion of huge numbers of workers into employees during the high-growth era. However, there has been little change in parent-child relationships. In general, there is a strong tendency for parents to support their children until they become adults and establish their own independent households. For example, parents commonly pay most of their children's university tuition fees and even wedding expenses. There is also a strong expectation that children will reciprocate by caring for their parents in their old age. These attitudes have started to change in recent times. The relative status of husbands and wives in the family has been influenced by the expectation that women should care for the home. As a result, women have endured a lower social and economic status than men. (This tendency exists to a greater or lesser degree in all developed countries.) In recent years, however, women have responded to their rising status by increasingly demanding their rights.

A second characteristic of Japan's social framework is the importance placed on regional links and blood ties. Whilst this tendency has weakened in recent times, it is still firmly entrenched in provincial communities. The strength of community ties has a bearing on the high standards of law and order that characterise Japanese society. Factors contributing to Japan's excellent law and order record appear to include not only the prohibition of weapon ownership in principle but also the close links that bind local communities (and make it difficult for outsiders to penetrate) and the development of a law and order structure based on the *koban* system.[1] However, in recent years, there has been an increase in the incidence of heinous crime, and it is clear that the law and order situation has deteriorated compared with earlier times.

A third characteristic is the land system. Private land ownership was actively promoted, partly because of the post-war farmland reform and resulting creation of self-supporting farmers and partly because of housing policy in post-war Japan. Attitudes to land were also shaped by the "land myth" that land prices would never fall because of the limited supply of habitable land in Japan and increase of continuing demand for land in line with the economic development. These factors caused land prices to soar far above utilisation values. This private land ownership system made land a useful collateral for loans from financial institutions and thus contributed to economic expansion. However, the precedence given to private ownership frequently became a barrier to infrastructure development. The "land myth" was finally laid to rest with the collapse of the speculative bubble in the first half of 1990s. As a result, huge amounts of land became non-performing assets.

---

[1] Under the *koban* (police box) system, police officers are stationed in the smallest administrative districts to maintain law and order.

Since these bad assets were difficult to settle, deep scars were left on the balance sheets of financial institutions and ordinary companies, triggering an unprecedented crisis for the Japanese economy.

4.1.2.2. Economic organisations

The four major economic organisations in Japan are the Federation of Economic Organisations (Keidanren), the Japan Federation of Employers' Associations (Nikkeiren), the Japan Association of Corporate Executives (Doyukai) and the Japan Chamber of Commerce and Industry. There are also numerous industry-specific organisations. These economic organisations can be divided into those that evolved from the wartime "Control Associations", which were established in 1941 to 1942 to regulate individual industries, and organisations that were newly established in the post-war environment. In addition to their role as employer groups in opposition to labour organisations, economic organisations have also functioned as channels for presenting the views of industry to government administrators and for accepting administrative guidance. They have made an important contribution to the implementation of government industrial policy by absorbing the wishes of the relevant government agencies and co-ordinating industry efforts and by informing the government about the wishes of industry, such as protection measures and tax breaks. The Keidanren has played a particularly important role in protecting the interests of industry and management by seeking to act as a channel for business donations to ruling LDP party politicians,[2] thereby enabling it to work through politicians to reconcile industry wishes with those of government administrators. However, this relationship sometimes had a negative impact by allowing excessive administrative intervention in industry and by limiting free competition.

4.1.2.3. Labour unions

Most labour unions in Japan are enterprise unions. Enterprise unions are affiliated to Tansan (the Federation of Single-Industry Labour Unions). The smooth and harmonious labour relations are often cited as one of the factors that helped Japan to achieve economic development. However, this situation did not occur spontaneously from the outset. Although enterprise unions were certainly forming the mainstream "Patriotic Industrial Associations", which were by nature considered informal, gatherings between capital and labour started to be formed in various districts as of 1937 under the guidance of the Ministry of Home Affairs. When GHQ gave a directive to organise labour unions immediately after the war, the Patriotic Industrial Associations were almost automatically succeeded by enterprise unions. However, after a phase of fierce labour-management

---

2 In September 1993 the Keidanren announced that it would cease acting as a go-between for business donations to political parties.

confrontation during the immediate post-war period, today's labour relations evolved through the political changes that resulted from the establishment of the Japan–US security pact and through changes in Japan's economic circumstances during the high-growth era.

The superstructure of the industry unions was divided into left-wing and right-wing union movements. Typical of the left-wing movement was the Sanbetsu Kaigi (Congress of Industrial Organisations). Because of its growing leftist tendencies, Sanbetsu was severely weakened by the purging of communists. The right-wing union movement was embodied in Sohyo (the General Council of Trade Unions of Japan), which was established as a national centre in 1950. However, Sohyo subsequently shifted gradually to the left. As a lateral organisation of enterprise unions, Sohyo played a leading role in labour activities, including spring wage rounds, for many years. The right wing of the labour movement was inherited by Domei (the Japanese Confederation of Labour).

There was a qualitative change in the 1950s and early 1960s, when private sector unions shifted to labour-capital reconciliation and public sector unions of government workers and employees led the labour movement in criticising the established systems. Subsequent change both in the economic and political environment throughout the world brought dramatic change in labour-management relations, necessitating a restructuring of the Japanese labour management. Sohyo and Domei were disbanded in 1989, and new alliances were formed to become Rengo (Japan Trade Union Confederation), which aims to gain its own political power trough securing seats in the parliament.

4.1.3. Political and social change in post-war Japan

The political and social evolution of post-war Japan can be divided into four phases. The first phase lasted from the end of World War II until the achievement of stable LDP rule via the conservative alliance in 1955 (1945–60). The second phase was the period of stable LDP rule (1960–72). The third was the period of repeated instabilities in the LDP administration (1972–93), and the fourth is the period since the LDP's fall from power, albeit temporary (July 1993–present). Although there is some discrepancy between phases in the political situation and shifts in the economic situation, the periods generally match.

4.1.3.1. Before the achievement of stable LDP rule (1945–1960)

In the immediate post-war period, central government politics in Japan were dominated by pre-war pro-American conservatives. A resurgence of labour unions, which had been suppressed during the war, gave the Socialist Party a temporary hold on power, but basically leadership resided with the pro-American conservatives. Yet there were also serious differences of opinion within the pro-American conservative camp, and the political situation remained unstable. Some historians believe that the turning point was reached in 1955 with the formation of the Liberal Democratic Party as a conservative alliance and the unification of the Socialist Party as a critical power. In reality, however, the Yoshida faction from the old Democratic Liberal Party clashed with the Kishi faction from the old Japanese Democratic Party over the handling of the Japan–US security treaty. Political stability was not achieved until the signing of the mutual security treaty in 1960. The achievement of stability owed much to the settlement of the controversy over Japan's foreign policy stance, which had been a major issue in the post-war period, as well as to the establishment of a framework for the pursuit of economic growth under an American umbrella.

The confused political situation of the post-war period produced numerous labour disputes, such as the first Yomiuri struggle (October–December 1945). There were also moves to organise workers, and in August 1946 the right-wing Sodomei (an organisation which later split into Sohyo and Domei) and the left-wing Sanbetsu Kaigi both held inaugural rallies. The rise of the labour movement was manifested in plans for a general strike on 1 February 1947. GHQ issued a directive banning the strike, however, owing to fears of social confusion. GHQ also banned a power generation strike in August 1948. Moves such as these demonstrated that the labour movement was subject to certain limitations under the occupation administration. In June 1947 the national railway union and the teachers' union held a joint rally, signifying the start of moves to organise government workers and employees of public sector corporations. GHQ was alarmed by the emergence of leftist tendencies with the growth of the labour movement, and in June 1950 it initiated a purge of communists. In July of the same year, Sohyo was formed under GHQ guidance.

4.1.3.2. Achievement of stable LDP rule (1960–1972)

The confusion of the first fifteen years of the post-war period was followed by a period of political stability under conservative parties. During this period Prime Minister Ikeda held office for four years and four months, and Prime Minister Sato for seven years and eight months. The key political issues during this period were opposition to the war in Vietnam, student unrest and Okinawa's return to Japanese sovereignty. None of these issues actually caused the fall of a cabinet, however. The prolonged period of single-party domination by the LDP is attributed to three factors. First, there was a proliferation of opposition parties. Second, the policies of the Socialist Party, which was the largest opposition party, were too unrealistic for the party to gain the confidence of the people. And third, the LDP's political management was characterised by its conciliation in accepting some claims of opposition parties (Sato, 1994). Moreover, after the dissolution of the Sanbetsu Kaigi in 1958, enterprise unions became the dominant form of labour organisation. This contributed to the stability of LDP politics, since it led to a general weakening of the labour movement's readiness to engage in political confrontations.

The continued stability of LDP government was attributable in part to the success of policies that gave priority to economic growth and to a strong national desire for stability. In addition, the period was free of economic uncertainty, owing to the absence of economic crises on the scale of the oil shocks. The backlash against LDP rule occurred at the regional level rather than in the national political arena. In the early 1960s, progressive local authorities were formed through co-operation among the Socialist Party, the Komeito (Clean Government Party), the Communist Party and others. Reasons for this increase in activity at the regional level include the emergence of pollution and other problems caused by the distortions of high economic growth, which began to threaten the environment. Another factor was the emergence of the public sector unions as the mainstay of the labour movement rather than the enterprise unions.

4.1.3.3. Period of short-lived LDP cabinets (1972–1993)

With the exception of the Nakasone administration of the mid-1980s (November 1982 to November 1987), the establishment of the Tanaka cabinet in 1972 marked the start of a period in which the LDP cabinets tended to be short-lived. At times the LDP also lost its majority in the House of Representatives and was forced to form coalition governments with other conservative parties. This short-lived tendency was not unrelated to the prevalence of faction politics within the LDP. First priority was given to factional interests, chairs of ministers were allocated to factions by turns, and various alliances were formed to topple more powerful groupings. This transition occurred around the same time as the end of the high growth era after the first oil shock. Meanwhile, progressive local authorities began to fade from the scene in the late 1970s. This resulted from the fragmentation of the alliances that had led to the formation of progressive local authorities, as well as fiscal problems resulting from the expansion of welfare expenditure at a time when tax revenues were falling in the wake of the second oil shock. This had the effect of strengthening the authority of the central government.

This period was also characterised by widespread criticism of money politics, which had become entrenched under stable LDP rule in the 1960s. The mingling of politics and money was a constant issue, as evidenced by the Lockheed and Recruit scandals and accusations of wrongdoing by major construction contractors. These problems were a manifestation of a situation caused by the "iron triangle" pattern of decision-making by politicians, the bureaucracy and industry, which rejected policies that would threaten vested interests and encouraged political corruption.

Japan's rising international profile brought a gradual increase in criticism of the Japanese political decision-making process. In addition, the end of high economic growth ignited a strong public backlash against money politics which benefited only a few interest groups.

The Nakasone administration during the mid-1980s continued for an exceptionally long time. This was a result of tie-ups with other conservative parties, but also because the cabinet fostered the privatisation of the three public enterprises including the National Railway, and because the next generation of leaders had not yet emerged within the LDP. The longevity of the Nakasone administration can be regarded as a special case, resulting from a combination of circumstances, including Japan's emergence from the recession triggered by the second oil shock, the appreciation of the dollar and the weakening of the yen, which were reflected in strong performance by exporting industries. Another factor was the global swing towards neo-conservatism.

4.1.3.4. Period after formation of non-LDP administrations (July 1993–)

The resignation of the Miyazawa cabinet in July 1993 signalled the end of LDP rule. Money politics were exposed to strict criticism by the people with accusations of corruption directed at major construction contractors, especially in their dealings with the construction administration. This triggered a split within the LDP. The Shinseito (Renewal Party) withdrew from the LDP and formed a coalition government with former opposition parties, thereby creating a non-LDP administration. The former opposition parties, which had previously opposed the LDP, were prompted to join a coalition with part of the LDP by the disappearance to all intents and purposes of anti-LDP politics. It became quite hard to distinguish policies between the LDP and the former opposition parties. This resulted from a number of factors, including the formation of a policy tie-up (by LDP, Komeito and Democratic Socialist Party) at the central government level, the replacement of the progressive local government administrations of the 1980s with coalitions between the LDP and certain opposition parties, especially in the local political arena, and the Socialist Party's shift to a more realistic policy line, including acceptance of the Japan–US security pact and the Self-Defence Forces. In practice, the policies of the non-LDP coalition differed little from traditional LDP policies. The coalition collapsed after less than a year, and the LDP then formed a new coalition with its mortal enemy, the Socialist Party. This move demonstrated that there was little policy difference between the two parties participating in the administration.

On the economic front, the collapse of the speculative bubble of the late 1980s triggered the deepest recession of the post-war era. This highlighted problems in Japan's traditional economic systems. In addition, public dissatisfaction with the decision-making processes followed by the LDP during its long years in power came to a boil in an environment of economic stagnation. This dissatisfaction was manifested in the election of candidates with non-partisan support to the governor-ships of Tokyo and Osaka in the nation-wide regional government elections of April 1995.

The close interaction of post-war political, economic and social systems has contributed to Japan's economic success. However, this situation has also given rise to a wide array of problems and distortions. The priority from now on will be the linkage of political, economic and social systems into a new interactive structure that is in keeping with Japan's current status in the world.

4.2. Germany's Political and Social Systems

4.2.1. Preliminary remarks

This chapter addresses the question of what importance should be assigned to the political and social institutions in explaining economic and social developments in Germany after World War II. In answering this question recourse will be taken to the findings of the internationally young discipline, institutional economics. This specialised field analyses problems which in Germany have been examined for many years under the term "economic order" (*Wirtschaftsordnung*).

An economic order is understood as the totality of rules and institutions that determine and coordinate the economic activity of economic subjects or the actions of economic-policy decision-makers. A broad definition of institutions also includes rules and norms, so that economic order can be viewed as the totality of (relevant) institutions. Moreover, since the boundaries between economic and social institutions are not clearly drawn, we shall treat the social institutions in this chapter in a broad sense, thus including the economic aspects. We thus can either speak of socio-economic institutions or, with the same meaning, of an economic and social order.

This chapter will first examine the political system in Germany and then turn to several of the economic and social institutions that are typical for Germany's "social market economy". First, the question of the significance of the economic order in comparison to other explanatory factors for economic growth is raised. Next, the special question will be addressed of what importance can be assigned to a market-economy order in comparison to a centralised command economy in explaining long-term socio-economic development processes. Finally we will discuss the economic freedoms and goals of the economic order in Germany—the social market economy—as well as important characteristics of some of its institutions.

4.2.2. German political system and its potential significance for economic development

After World War II—under the direction of the occupying forces—a process of denazification and political-ideological renewal took place in Germany. In its occupation zone the Soviet Union helped the East German Communist Party (SED) gain a permanent political monopoly—a situation which lasted until German reunification.

In West Germany a parliamentary democracy was introduced. The election system, which contained elements of proportional and majority vote systems, usually led to coalition governments and several shifts in political power. The political system is federally organised. The German Constitution (*Grundgesetz*) expressly states that the definitive authority is not the federal government (*Bund*) but the states (*Länder*). Article 30 specifies: "The exercising of state authority and the fulfilling of the state's task is a matter for the Länder."

Moreover, the political system displays the characteristics of a party democracy. According to the Constitution, the political parties play a special role in the formation of political objectives among the electorate and in strengthening democracy. For this reason they need only raise part of their finances from membership fees and contributions as they are entitled to considerable funds from tax revenues.

In the public administration at the federal, state and local levels, politically neutral specialists are employed—apart from the top administrative posts. As a rule they have the status of civil servants (*Beamte*) which means that they are not allowed to go on strike and that they can be called on in special cases to provide additional, unpaid services. In return, the state as employer is obligated to provide for the welfare of its civil servants.

With the reunification of West and East Germany in 1990, the West German political system (and its economic order) was transferred to East Germany virtually unchanged.

The importance of the political system, especially democracy, for economic development is appraised differently in the academic literature. On the one hand, it is highly plausible that democratic rights strengthen the motivation and capability of the individual, which would have a positive effect on economic development in the long term. On the other hand, comparative international studies (e.g., Barro, 1994) show that growth can take place precisely under undemocratic conditions, and in many countries democracy emerges only after a positive economic development has occurred. This research may cast an interesting light on many past developments. However, with respect to economic policy and decision-making, they are largely worthless, since it would be fallacious to conclude that dictatorships are conducive to economic growth. It is at least just as likely that a poor country is easier to rule dictatorially than a rich country.

For individual cases such as Germany—in contrast to a comparison of many countries—it is hardly possible to offer convincing proof of the relationship between the political system and economic development. However, hardly anyone in Germany today would view this relationship as relevant. Democracy and political freedom are viewed as values in themselves and not with regard to how they may stimulate economic development.

4.2.3. Economic and social institutions and their importance for economic development

4.2.3.1. Economic order and the catching-up hypothesis

Germany's rapid economic development after World War II—and that of other Western European countries—has been interpreted by some economic historians (e.g., Abramovitz, 1986) as primarily a catching-up process which received its impetus above all from the difference in the initial position of the economic and technological leaders and that of those countries that lagged behind (or were thrown back by the war).

Recent empirical research (e.g., Dumke, 1990; Eichengreen, 1994; Klump, 1995) stresses that the catching-up phenomenon is at most a partial explanation of the post-war economic development. Of at least equal importance is the institutional constellation that was more or less consciously and purposefully designed by national economic policy.

In the case of Germany there are many indications that the creation of a functioning economic order, in comparison with the mere mechanism of the catching-up process, played a much more significant role in post-war economic development. This argument is also supported by the fact that, although the dynamic post-war development in Germany slowed down in the course of time, it still surpassed the position of many of the World War II victors.

4.2.3.2. Free market and command economy

Having looked at the relative importance of an economic order as an explanatory factor for economic and social development, our attention now turns to the effects that two completely different systems—the free market and the command economy—had on long-term developments. Examples here include the divided countries with different economic systems such as Germany (from 1945 to 1989), Korea and China. Another group of countries changed economic systems within a short period of time (e.g., Mexico in the 1980s and other Latin American countries, as well as quite a few African countries). (For a detailed presentation and analysis see Helmschrott, Osterkamp, Schönherr, 1992.)

The result of these comparisons is that the market economies experienced a significantly more favourable economic development, on average, than countries with a planned economy or *dirigiste* orientation, although the quality of the economic policy practised within the framework of the economic order that was chosen is also significant.

The example of the two former German states is a particularly clear confirmation of this conclusion. At the end of the 1980s, the crass difference in living standards and technological development in East and West Germany was primarily attributable to the different economic systems.

4.2.3.3. Arrangement of market-economy institutions in Germany: economic freedoms and economy-policy goals in the social market economy

(a) Economic freedoms of the social market economy

The basic philosophy of the social market economy is that the political freedoms which democracy provides the individual citizen (e.g. suffrage, freedom of expression, the right to demand accountability of the public administration, etc.) are incomplete or endangered without economic freedoms. These include the freedom to purchase goods, to invest, to sign and cancel purchase or labour contracts, the freedom of association (especially to form employee groups), freedom of trade and freedom to choose career and employment.

In real-world market economies all of these economic freedoms are subject to limitations. The characteristics of the German social market economy are seen in how these limitations are defined, and they tend to be more restrictive than in other market economies.

In the context of an individualistic and liberal philosophy, which ultimately underlies the concept of the social market economy, economic freedoms are not viewed instrumentally with a view to possible economic growth but are pursued because they are an important component of human freedom and are also necessary to ensure and maintain political freedom.

(b) Economic policy goals in the social market economy

At the heart of the economic policy goals of the social market economy are the goals of economic growth, price stability and full employment. These three goals are not pursued as ends in themselves but for their contribution to social justice. Economic growth improves the standard of living of all citizens and creates additional scope for redistribution to those who are poorer. Moreover, growth is generally linked with structural change and thus reduces the value of inherited wealth.

Two phases of hyperinflation in Germany have left the deep impression that the economically weaker members of society suffer additional losses during inflation. Even if the state wanted to help, it is even less in a position to do so in inflationary times. Thus, stable prices are viewed as particularly effective measures in connection with social justice.

Social justice must, of course, also be achieved or pursued with a wealth of other measures.

4.2.3.4. Arrangement of important sub-areas of the social market economy

The arrangement of institutions in important sub-areas of the economic order are analysed and described in detail in other chapters in this study. The following comments are thus in summary form and stress the features that are characteristic of the German social market economy.

(a) Competitive system

A fundamental component of the social market economy is the competitive system. The functions of competition are to prevent economic power (monopolies) from assuming political power; to create equal opportunity by enabling market access to all suppliers and purchasers; and to enhance the performance of suppliers for the benefit of consumers.

The proponents of the social market economy assume that competition does not come about on its own, but that economic entities try to prevent it wherever possible. The establishment and preservation of competition is thus a task that public officials must constantly fulfil. In Germany there are laws to this end and a special administrative agency, the Federal Cartel Office (Kartellamt).

The basic philosophy of the social market economy is not national but international. Accordingly, foreign suppliers should not be prevented from competing in the domestic market. A consequence of this position on competition is that economic policy should not aim at preventing the structural change that comes in the wake of national and international competition. Maintaining this stance during all phases of the business cycle is not an easy task. Nonetheless, structural change has basically been accepted in Germany—also that originating from foreign competition—and has at most been constrained or made socially palatable, but never prevented. The long-term growth and welfare effects brought on by structural change are thus ultimately attributable to the idea of competition. (A more detailed description of competition policy is found in Chapter 9.)

(b) Monetary system

Of particular importance in this connection is the constitutionally guaranteed independence of the German central bank (Bundesbank) from government interference. The Bundesbank has the task of ensuring monetary stability. At the same time it is obligated to support the policies of the federal government. This can lead to conflict, although in such cases the Bundesbank almost always decides in favour of monetary stability.

A number of comparative studies have concluded that a strong connection exists between the central bank's independence and monetary stability. Also in the case of Germany, there is no doubt that the high degree of monetary stability that has prevailed since the war is attributable to the autonomous actions of the

Bundesbank (along with the partnership between trade unions and employers). (More detailed discussions on the monetary system are found in Chapters 8.)

(c) Labour market system

The arrangement of working conditions, especially the determination of wages, is the domain of trade unions and employer organisations (the collective bargaining partners); it is not a matter of government agencies and, in general, not left to the individual employee. In arbitrating disputes between the collective bargaining partners, especially in cases of strikes, there is a strike procedure agreed to between the partners, and not legislated by the government. These strike procedures are so arranged that calling a strike is difficult (democratic agreement among strikers requiring high levels of consent) and calling one off easy.

Although, in general, only a minority of the employees of a bargaining district are union members, the wage agreements apply almost automatically to all employees of a company or bargaining district. The conditions negotiated for a bargaining district are transferred to companies outside this district, usually in the form of a "declaration of universal validity" issued by the Federal Minister of Economics.

Unions are organised according to industries and not according to trades, as in the UK. The public labour administration is responsible for job placement, the retraining and further education of the unemployed, and for paying unemployment compensation. The monopoly held by the state in job placement was lifted in 1995.

A specific aspect of the social market economy is a system called *Mitbestimmung*, or co-determination. In larger companies, the employees' elected representatives (often labour union functionaries) have the legal right to half of the seats in the supervisory boards. In this way the employees can participate in far-reaching company decisions—normally the domain of the company's shareholders.

Management and labour seeing themselves as partners, the organisation of the entire collective bargaining process by the partners themselves, and not least the particular way that strikes are handled in Germany, have significantly contributed to an overall favourable economic development with little inflation and few social hardships. (A detailed treatment of the labour market and wage policies is contained in Chapter 7.)

(d) Social system

Germany's social system is basically characterised by two features: the redistribution of income and wealth, and mandatory social insurance.

Even if government-protected competition provided equal opportunity, this would not mean that the resulting incomes and wealth would be acceptable in terms of amounts and distribution. In normal cases—not only in Germany—the wish for redistribution to establish greater equality prevails politically in the form of progressive income tax and in the taxation of inheritance and donations. The highest income tax bracket in Germany is currently more than 50%.

White- and blue-collar workers, insofar as their incomes remain under certain levels, are obligated to insure themselves against the risks of illness, unemployment, accidents at work, and invalidity as well as to save for retirement. These insurance plans are called social insurance. The insurance contributions are divided fifty-fifty between employee and employer.

Although the social system has made a major contribution in increasing the security of the individual in difficult situations, many now question whether the system is not too expensive and whether it does not have unfavourable effects, especially on the motivation to work. (For particulars on the social system, see Chapter 12.)

(e) Fiscal system

In keeping with the importance of the Länder vis-à-vis the federal government in the German political system, the system of taxation also has a federal structure.

In order to limit the power of the central state, the subsidiarity principle must be strictly applied. This principle stipulates that a higher level of government can only become active when citizens themselves or the next lower level of government are not able to perform the task at hand.

Budgets of public authorities may not accrue debts with the Bundesbank, but only with domestic (or foreign) commercial banks or private households. Moreover, the extent of new borrowing of a public authority is limited to the extent of investment in the same period. (Further discussion of the financial system is found in Chapters 5 and 8.)

4.2.4. Evaluation

The political, social and institutional arrangement in Germany has doubtlessly proved to be successful. Especially the social elements of the German social market economy have contributed to the stability of the system. Nevertheless, these elements also have the potential to reduce the system's efficiency. The declining trend in German economic growth can be attributed in part to the continuous strengthening of the social elements—to some extent at the expense of market and efficiency considerations.

If this trend continues, the performance of the social system will be endangered in the long term. This realisation, which is widespread in Germany today, was also not foreign to the founders of the social market economy: the truly social aspects of the social market economy are the market elements, e.g., the partial reduction in the value of inherited property by means of competition and structural change, especially in the long-term perspective (economic growth).

4.3. Comparative Summary of Political and Social Systems

4.3.1. Similarities and differences

Because of completely different historical developments that have occurred in Japan and Germany in their emergence as leading industrial countries, the political and social systems in both countries display great differences. There are, however, a number of common features that are of particular importance for the successful economic and social development of both countries.

Both countries have an established and functioning democratic constitution which gives the citizens in general—but also enterprises and employees, investors and consumers—a predictable legal system and thus a reliable framework for economic decisions.

The economic system in both countries is a market economy which has differing individual features but at its core displays the following three characteristics: autonomous decisions of economic subjects are possible and necessary; the market and not government officials decides the merit of these decisions; and the positive or negative results of these decisions are to be borne by those responsible for them.

4.3.2. Political systems

Japan and Germany both have parliamentary democratic systems and are governed by cabinets led by premiers elected from the National Diet or the Bundestag. Supreme executive authority rests with the prime minister or chancellor, who is generally the leader of the top political party. Japan has been ruled throughout most of the post-war era by conservative parties or the Liberal Democratic Party (LDP), and changes of government were synonymous with power shifts within the LDP. This political framework has had a harmful effect in the sense that it has led to a heavy bureaucratic involvement in policy formulation, and at times to unnecessarily close links between the legislative and administrative arms of government. In Germany, the Christian Democratic Union (CDU) and the Social Democratic Party (SPD) have taken turns at power or formed coalition governments. For this reason, there has been a lesser degree of collusion between politicians and bureaucrats in the area of economic policy.

Although the German and Japanese systems are similar in form, there are significant differences in the actual content of each system. The common feature of both systems, however, is the maintenance of political stability throughout the half-century of the post-war era. Germany has introduced the 5% rule to prevent the proliferation of minor parties under its small-electorate system. In Japan, the formation of factions within the LDP has allowed changes of government, albeit within the LDP, under Japan's medium-electorate system.

4.3.3. Administrative systems

Of great importance for the economic and social success of both countries is their efficient public administrations. Civil servants are not only well trained and well paid but are also closely supervised. Although cases of corruption cannot be prevented, they are contained and rigorously prosecuted in both countries.

The relationship between central and local governments in Japan and Germany differs considerably in terms of actual authority. The states enjoy a strong position under Germany's federal system, whilst in Japan there is a strong emphasis on centralised power. This reflects differences in the historical evolution of the two countries. In Germany there was a strong tendency towards territorial states, whilst Japan moved rapidly towards centralised power after the restoration of the imperial system in 1868.

4.3.4. Economic systems

The most important feature of the German economic system is the fact that it is a "social market economy". This system is identical to the ordinary free economic systems of the United States or the United Kingdom in the sense that it guarantees the economic freedoms of the individual. However, it imposes certain limitations from the standpoint of social equity. The German system is open to foreign participation. In fact, Germany has been very willing to encourage competition between domestic and foreign industries. The social economic system can be attributed to the priority that was placed on providing assurances to the people in the environment that existed after Germany's defeat in World War II.

Although Japanese society is characterised by fierce competition within specific limits, its overall economic system has shown a strong tendency towards government intervention that goes beyond legally specified regulations, typically through "administrative guidance." This approach is based on the view that the avoidance of economic concentration is a basic requirement for social development, a philosophy that was manifested in the efforts of GHQ to break up the *zaibatsu* (conglomerates). However, these restrictions have frequently become a barrier to new market participants. For example, the entry of foreign capital was restricted until a certain point in time in order to protect domestic industries. This is a major and extremely interesting difference from the approach taken by Germany, which opted for a more competitive economic system already shortly after World War II.

4.3.5. Social systems

One similarity between the Japanese and German social systems is the fact that business organisations and organisations representing workers, such as unions, have both worked to support the economic system. However, union formats differ:

Japan has enterprise unions while Germany has industry unions. But both countries have managed to develop generally stable and co-operative relationships between labour and management. In Germany, unions participate directly in management through management councils. This system, which is not found in any other advanced industrialised economy, appears to have contributed greatly to stable labour-management relations.

Japan's overall social system underwent dramatic changes in the post-war era, including the abolition of feudalistic systems and the reform of the educational system. Yet it is also possible to conclude that the enormous psychological shock of defeat in World War II left the Japanese people receptive to change, with the result that there was little resistance to the new social system. Germany's experience contrasted sharply with Japan's. It achieved a relatively smooth transition from Nazi military rule to democracy, partly because of its experience of republican government under the Weimar Constitution. The common factor in the Japanese and German social systems was that defeat in World War II caused both to become more democratic than the systems that existed during the war.

4.3.6. Conclusions

A comparison of political and social systems in Japan and Germany shows that the similarities and differences in these two nations are common with those that characterise most advanced economies. As stated in the Ifo Institute interpretation, political and social systems are created as ends in themselves and not necessarily as means of achieving economic development.

It is not clear how similarities and differences in political systems have affected economic development. In fact, it is possible to conclude that the pre-war political systems of Japan and Germany, which were always a threat to domestic and international peace due to their transformation by militarism or national socialism, created the conditions necessary for economic development and the maintenance of long-term stability under democratic systems in the post-war era. This is because the existence of political systems in which the views of the people were represented created a sense of security and enabled economic activities to be pursued efficiently.

The historical backgrounds of Japan and Germany are strongly reflected in their post-war social systems. The World War II Allies imposed few changes to Germany's systems, which meant that its traditional social system remained more or less intact. In Japan, the Allies implemented drastic social reforms, but the pace of change was gradual due to the fact that traditional Japanese thinking was preserved in the people. This suggests that the most important factor for a country is not the rapid introduction of reforms from outside, but rather the maintenance of stability based on that country's historical background. In other words, it appears that gradual social reform is a success factor in relation to economic growth.

5. Factors of Production: Capital

5.1. Japan's Factors of Production: Capital

5.1.1. Positioning of capital

Japan's capital has played a vital role in economic growth. During the period when the raising of capital from overseas was restricted, the effective utilisation of domestic savings was the key to economic growth. One of the factors that drove Japan's rapid economic growth was the linkage of abundant domestic savings with vigorous capital investment. However, a high level of savings does not necessarily translate into high economic growth. Since the transition to low economic growth and the start of financial liberalisation in the 1980s, the efficient utilisation of Japan's massive savings at home and overseas has become a vital issue for the Japanese economy. In this chapter we will examine the structure of Japanese capital and the mechanisms that linked capital to high economic growth. We will also evaluate the role played by capital in Japan's economic growth.

5.1.2. Sectoral evolution of savings—quantitative evaluation of capital

5.1.2.1. Savings-investment balance

Japan did not start the post-war period with ample domestic savings. It remained a net importer of overseas funds until the late 1960s because of the need to feed its voracious domestic demand, and the country as a whole faced a chronic shortage of funds. In terms of the savings-investment balance, it was not until the early 1970s that Japan began to register a consistent savings surplus at the national level.

Individuals have supplied most of Japan's domestic savings, and the personal sector has consistently registered a savings surplus equivalent to around 10% of GDP (Fig. 5.1-1). The corporate sector, on the other hand, has consistently relied on borrowings to offset a chronic savings deficit. The public sector has also remained chronically short of funds, except for a brief period in the late 1980s, when fiscal reconstruction and the so-called bubble economy produced a savings surplus. The combined shortage of funds in the corporate and public sectors remained at around 10% of GDP until the early 1980s, thereby matching the

Fig. 5.1-1 Trend of savings and investment balance

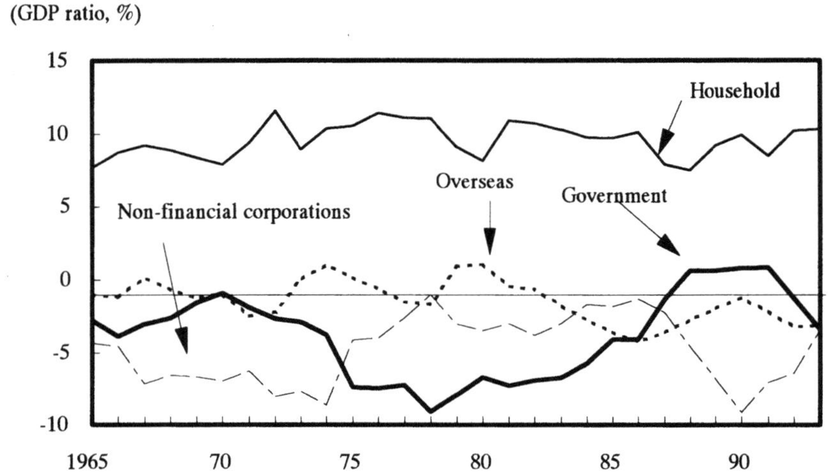

Source: BOJ, Economic Statistics Monthly

savings surplus in the personal sector.

5.1.2.2. Personal savings

Personal savings account for the bulk of Japan's domestic savings. Its ratio to disposable income (savings ratio) was around 12% during the early phase of the high-growth era. It rose gradually as the economy expanded, and between 1973 and 1978 it was above 20%. After the oil crises the personal savings ratio followed a gradual downtrend, in step with the downtrend in the economic growth rate, and by the late 1980s it had fallen to around 15%. However, this ratio is still high by international standards. Japan's high personal savings ratio has been attributed to a number of factors, including a pyramid-shaped demographic structure, government measures to encourage savings, the need to save for old age because of Japan's limited social security system, the need to support educational expenses of children, the high cost of housing relative to incomes, and the frugality of the Japanese character derived from Confucianism.

Savings deposits have traditionally accounted for the bulk of personal financial assets because of the limited range of savings methods available. Savings deposits accounted for around 60–70% of personal financial assets in the 1960s. The percentage subsequently declined gradually, reaching the middle of the 50% range by the start of the 1990s. The next most important category of savings after savings deposits is life insurance. Its share of personal financial assets has risen from around 10% in the 1960s to the low end of the 20% range in the 1990s. In addition, investment trusts have won an expanding slice of the savings pie since the liberalisation of the capital market in the 1980s. With the exception of the 1960s and the bubble period, personal investment in shares has remained below 10% of personal financial assets and has never been a major method of savings. The share of each type of financial product has varied in step with the change of the financial and capital markets.

5.1.3. Capital investment and capital stocks

5.1.3.1. Capital investment and savings

The increase in savings was manifested in an increase in gross fixed-capital formation, particularly in private-sector capital investment. Gross fixed-capital formation did not grow during the immediate post-war period from 1945 to 1955. However, it registered double-digit growth during the high-growth era and led to an increase in capital stocks. The increase in capital stocks induced other new investment, resulting in the so-called induced investment cycle.[1] The main resource fuelling the basic up-trend in capital investment in Japan was abundant household savings. A comparison of the GDP ratios of private-sector capital investment and household financial assets shows that they have followed similar trends in general (Fig. 5.1-2).

On the other hand, interest rates were kept lower than returns on investment

Fig. 5.1-2 Trend of fixed investment and household financial assets

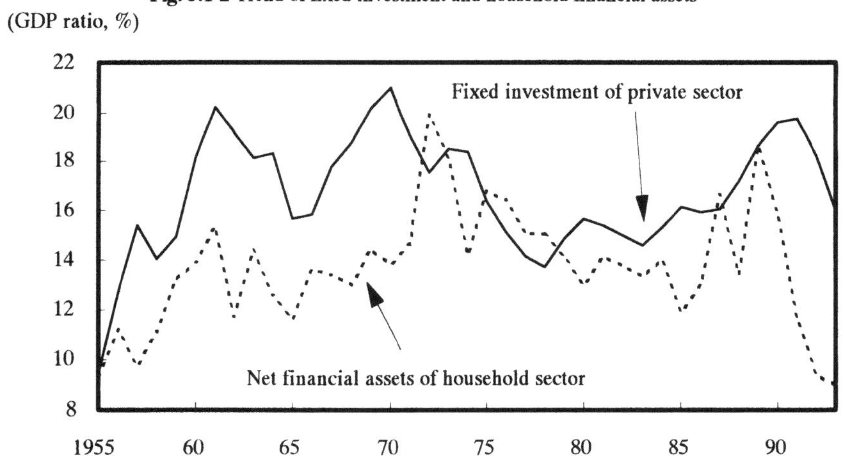

Source: EPA, Annual Report on National Accounts

[1] A general capital investment model assumes a certain level of demand, and an increase in capital stocks is regarded as a factor that limits new capital investment. During Japan's high-growth period, however, vigorous capital investment caused an increase in demand with the result that the increase in capital stocks stimulated rather than limited new capital investment.

through the Bank of Japan's policy of maintaining artificially low interest rates. This mechanism contributed significantly to the expansion of capital investment. At the same time, private companies could continue aggressive capital investment because domestic industries were protected by restrictions on foreign direct investment. (With the exception of four industries, foreign direct investment was totally liberalised in 1976.) Artificially low interest rates and restrictions on foreign direct investment thus enabled Japanese companies to secure large profits through the investment of capital. This accelerated the expansion of assets and the accumulation of shareholders' equity.

5.1.3.2. Change in capital investment trends

An industry-by-industry analysis of post-war trends in capital investment shows that the main change in the period up until the high-growth era was a sharp increase in the share of the manufacturing sector owing to the expansion of the market for consumer durable goods. After the oil shocks, the share of the manufacturing sector gradually declined, reaching about 35% in the 1980s. Within the manufacturing sector, the shares of the transportation equipment and electrical machinery industries increased rapidly from the 1970s onwards. In contrast with the manufacturing sector, the share of the non-manufacturing sector started to increase in the first half of the 1970s and reached about 50% by the end of 1980s. The pattern of capital investment in Japan has thus changed in step with shifts in the industrial structure.

An analysis of capital investment according to company size reveals that the share of small- and medium-sized companies increased from 10–15% in the early 1960s to over 25% in the first half of the 1970s and 30% in 1989, during the bubble economy period. This change reflected the fact that while major corporations in heavy industries were forced to review their mass-production systems after the oil shocks, small- and medium-sized companies in processing, assembly and service industries were able to adapt flexibly to market changes and were thus able to increase their capital investment. After the collapse of the bubble economy, however, small- and medium-sized companies were struck by rapidly declining demand and the accelerating appreciation of the yen, and by 1994 their share of capital investment had fallen to 23%. This phenomenon has highlighted the vulnerability of small- and medium-sized companies in Japan.

5.1.3.3. Trends in capital stocks and the capital-output ratio

Vigorous capital investment led to the steady accumulation of capital stocks in Japan. In theory, a cumulative increase in capital stocks leads to a decline in marginal productivity and a rise in the ratio of capital stocks to output. In practice, however, Japan's ratio of capital stocks to output either dropped or remained static until the end of the high-growth era in the 1970s (Fig. 5.1-3). This reflected efficient investment due to the matching of capital investment with strategic industrial policies that focused on heavy industries. From the first oil crisis in the 1970s onwards, the ratio of capital stocks to output followed a gradual upwards trend, reflecting the shift to a low-growth economy. The ratio has risen more rapidly since 1992 because of the collapse of the bubble economy. This rise in the ratio of capital to output is attributable to a shift in the industrial structure. The mass production and mass consumption approach was possible during the high-growth period, but mass production is not a suitable approach in a low-growth economy, and the centre of gravity of the production mix has thus shifted to non-manufacturing industries and high-value-added industries. The period since the 1980s has seen a gradual decline in the contribution of capital stocks to economic growth and a relative increase in the contribution of research and technology development.

5.1.4. Capital supply methods—qualitative evaluation of capital

The criteria for the qualitative evaluation of capital are continuity and stability. The issue of stability and continuity of capital can be seen by judging who undertakes the risk of capital input in the midst of the changing market and environment, and to which extent and for what duration. The analysis of capital supply channels thus provides an effective approach to the qualitative evaluation of capital.

Fig. 5.1-3 Trend of capital stocks to GDP

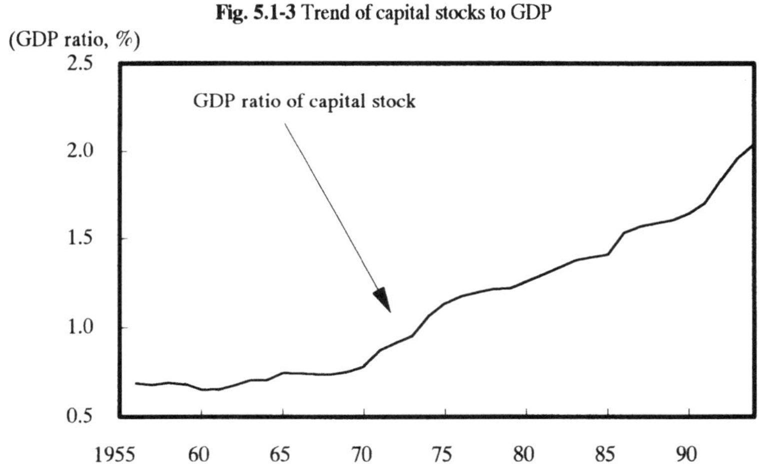

Note: GDP ratio of capital stock = capital stock/GDP

Source: EPA, Annual Report on National Accounts

5.1.4.1. Financial markets (intermediate finance)

In Japan, indirect finance was traditionally the principal method of supplying capital to the business sector, and borrowings from financial institutions have played an important role in companies' fund-raising activities. Until the late 1970s, funds on hand consistently covered about 50% of companies' net funding needs (Fig. 5.1-4). The remainder came from outside funds, mostly in the form of indirect finance. The contribution from indirect finance rose between the 1960s and the second oil crisis, reaching about 40–50%. Private-sector finance played a dominant role, accounting for around 40% of total funds raised. Government-affiliated financial institutions contributed less than 5%. Indirect finance could not function adequately in the confusion of the immediate post-war period. However, in the late 1940s economic growth triggered a rapid increase in lending, particularly for capital investment. During the high-growth period, private banks functioned as a channel for absorbing deposits, primarily from individuals, and for supplying those funds exclusively to industry in the form of loans. Around 30–40% of private-sector loans were used to fund capital investment. The main bank system played a particularly important role by supplying key industries with a reliable source of capital investment funds. After the oil crises, the role of indirect finance in corporate fund raising began to decline because of the curbing of private-sector capital investment and the development of the capital market. As a result, financial institutions began to focus on the expansion of their business with individuals, including housing investment and consumer loans.

Fig. 5.1-4 Share of corporate finance by type of funds

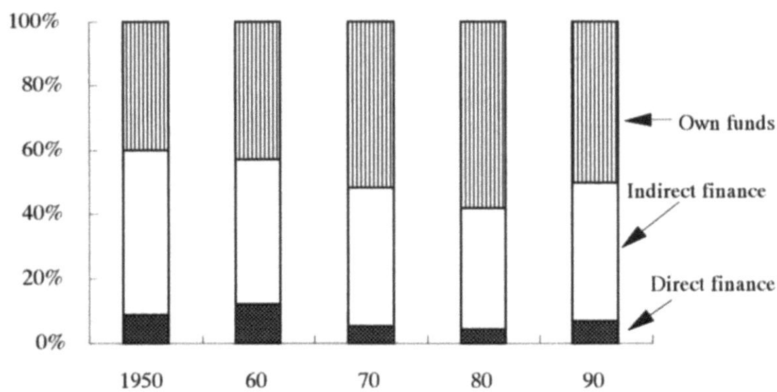

Note : 1. Own funds = Depreciation + Retained profits
Indirect finance = Private and public borrowing
Direct finance = Equity + Bond issues
2. Fiscal year for 1990

Source: BOJ, Economic Statistics Monthly

5.1.4.2. Stock market

With the exception of the immediate post-war era and the bubble economy period, the stock market has accounted for just 2–4% of total corporate fund raising. There were several reasons for the limited development of the stock market. First, the financial assets of individuals were dominated by deposits, with the result that the share of stock investment remained minimal. Second, market systems were still inadequate and market functions were virtually lost by factors such as the 1965 securities crash and the tightening of regulations. Third, cross-stockholding limited the volume of shares distributed through the market. The low level of fund raising through shares is reflected in the shareholders' equity ratios[2] of Japanese companies. During the first half of the high-growth period, shareholders' equity ratios averaged around 20% on an all-industry basis and about 25% in the manufacturing sector. Both averages subsequently declined to around 10% by the late 1970s. Shareholders' equity ratios began to rise gradually in the 1980s due to the curbing of capital investment and the expansion of share market activity. By 1992, the all-industry average had reached 20.0% and the manufacturing sector average 31.9%.

5.1.4.3. Bond market

Until the 1980s, the bond market was used merely to complement indirect finance provided primarily by banks. From the 1950s onwards, bonds accounted for less than 5% of total corporate fund raising. This share began to rise during the prolonged low-interest phase of the late 1980s, when activity in the stock and bond markets surged in the midst of a bubble economy. However, fund raising through the capital market began to decline once again after the collapse of the bubble. The sluggish development of the bond market in Japan was attributable to the lack of a distribution market, caused by government bonds being underwritten by private-sector financial institutions under the regulated interest rate system. It was also attributable to the existence of restrictions on the issuance limit of corporate bonds and to issuing costs that were high compared with overseas markets. In addition, there was a strong possibility that a bond distribution market would have destabilised the regulated interest rate system through the formation of market interest rates.

In the second half of the 1970s, however, market absorption became essential because of the expansion of deficit-covering bonds issues during the oil crisis period, and in 1977 the ban on selling government bonds in the market was lifted, except for bonds within a year after issue. The legalisation of government bond dealing by financial institutions in 1984 led to the formation of a secondary bond market. Thereafter the efficiency of bond market functions improved with the liberalisation of the capital market through measures that included the phased

---

[2] Shareholders' equity ratio = (capital + internal reserves) ÷ total assets.

introduction of the government bond auction system and the easing of bond-issuing conditions. The relatively high level of issuing costs, however, has remained a disadvantage that has prevented the formation of secondary markets for bonds other than government bonds.

5.1.5. Characteristics of capital

The evolution of Japanese capital in the various eras can be traced by comparing the demand generated by industry and the supply generated by savings.

5.1.5.1. Post-war reconstruction period (1945–1954)

On the supply side, there was a lack of savings and assets owing to losses suffered during the war. On the demand side, it was necessary to concentrate investment in key industries, such as coal and iron and steel, in line with the priority production system. This situation was reflected in the policy-based distribution of funds through fund allocations and other types of finance provided by the Reconstruction Finance Bank and the Bank of Japan.

5.1.5.2. High-growth period (1955–1972)

On the supply side, the growth of income resulting from high economic growth caused a rapid increase in personal and corporate savings. In industry, major corporations were leading an upwards trend in the demand for stable long-term funds, especially for capital investment, and there was a chronic shortage of funds. Private-sector financial institutions were the main suppliers of funds.

5.1.5.3. Oil crisis and low-yen period (1973–1984)

On the supply side, the personal savings ratio temporarily climbed above 20%, reflecting increased motivation to save for housing acquisition. The demand for funds in the business sector, however, contracted rapidly with receding capital investment demand resulting from the transition to low economic growth. In addition, companies, especially major corporations, began to reduce non-essential, non-urgent borrowing, whilst increasing the use of direct financing methods, such as bond and share issues, to raise funds. As a result, financial institutions began to focus on lending to small- and medium-sized businesses and individuals. Financial institutions also underwrote large volumes of deficit-covering bonds. In the 1980s, the liberalisation of capital transactions led to the aggressive introduction of foreign currency funds and to increased lending to overseas borrowers as a source of earning opportunities.

5.1.5.4. High-yen period (1985–1990)

Although low growth brought a decline in the savings ratio, there was still a large surplus of personal funds. As the economy expanded and the demand for capital investment funds grew, stock inflation in a low-interest environment led to increased demand for funds in the real-estate sector. Financial institutions focused on real-estate finance, and they also aggressively expanded their overseas lending.

5.1.6. Evaluating the role played by capital in economic growth

Capital contributed to economic growth in a number of ways. First, there was the efficient recycling of domestic savings, including personal savings, within Japan. The existence of abundant savings does not guarantee that those savings will be used adequately. In this sense, Japan appears to have benefited from the enclosure of domestic funds through the restriction on external investment and the concentration of such capital into indirect finance due to the premature state of the capital market. Channelling capital through financial institutions reduced the risk to lending or investing the funds and allowed them to be recycled smoothly. Under the regulated interest rate system, financial institutions were able to meet companies' funding needs without worrying about interest rate risk or liquidity risk. However, there were also negative consequences, including excessive financial administration and the decrease of management autonomy on the part of financial institutions.

Second, the policy of keeping interest rates artificially low enabled companies to accumulate earnings. This stimulated aggressive capital investment, which led to high economic growth. During the high-growth period, the supply of capital was far from adequate in relation to demand. However, companies were able to increase their internal reserves by raising funds at interest rates far lower than rates of return on capital invested. The prerequisites for the maintenance of artificially low interest rates were the predominance of indirect finance, a regulated interest rate system and the restriction of capital transactions. Whilst the low-interest policy stimulated high growth and increased national income, there were also implications for income distribution, since the policy meant that depositors did not receive fair interest. Some economists maintain that the low-interest policy thus delayed the accumulation of personal wealth (IMES, 1986).

Third, the system of separating financial institutions according to business formats helped to avoid excessive competition and facilitated the supply of capital in line with industrial policy. The separation of short-term and long-term finance clarified the roles of financial institutions and enabled them to carve out their respective niches. The existence of policy-oriented special financial institutions helped to reduce a lending risk that the private sector would have been unable to bear. This separation of business areas played a valuable role in the growth process. As is apparent from the trend towards financial liberalisation in the 1980s, however, structural changes and the internationalisation of the Japanese economy necessitated the restructuring of the financial system. Unfortunately financial institutions have not adapted adequately to these changes, partly because of the existence of practices that date back many years.

Any attempt to predict the future relationship between capital and economic growth must be based on a proper understanding of the changing nature of capital. The financial and capital markets have become more transparent through financial liberalisation. Moreover, the accumulation of financial assets is reflected in increased selectivity with regard to interest rates, and the income expectations of capital suppliers, including depositors and investors, are vastly higher than in the past. The range of savings methods available is no longer limited to domestic savings mechanisms, and in today's environment choices are invariably based on comparisons with opportunities available in other countries. To ensure that capital can make a continuing contribution to economic growth, it will be necessary to allocate capital not only to enlargement of equipment investment but also to new and innovative technology-oriented and growth industries. The priority from now on will, therefore, be to develop capital supply channels, in order to improve their efficiency, and to form systems that enable the suppliers of capital to reap adequate benefits.

5.2. Germany's Factors of Production: Capital

5.2.1. Methodology, general developments and definitions

The aim of this chapter is to measure the efficiency of investment financing. The main focus is on the capital spending of so-called producing enterprises (39% of total capital formation in 1991–93), but housing and public-sector investment are also considered (36% and 20% of total capital formation, respectively; see Table 5.2-1). Financial markets will be assessed in terms of allocative efficiency, i.e., the absence of distortions. An artificial encouragement for financing real investment without good reasons, i.e., through general interest-rate ceilings, is not seen as a contribution to efficiency and does not qualify as a success factor of German post-war economic development.

Transactions on financial markets take place for several reasons. They can serve the financing of net real investment—the increase of physical wealth after depreciation—which is the focus of this chapter. When this transaction takes place, funds are transferred from net-lenders to net-borrowers. Funds may also be transferred from one net-lender to another for reasons of shifting net wealth (i.e., to achieve the optimum portfolio allocation). There may also be shifts of debt between net-borrowers. Table 5.2-1 shows real capital formation (I), saving (II) and the net balance of investment and saving (III) by sector. Table 5.2-2 shows all gross financial flows. Netting out the gross financial flows for each sector yields the net financial position by sector (Table 5.2-1 (III)).

As is evident from Tables 5.2-1 and 5.2-2, there is a detachment of financial assets from real assets. The so-called "financial superstructure" has become bigger in the post-war period. In 1960 the relation between total domestic acquisition of financial assets and total domestic capital formation was about 1:1; since 1980 it has been around 3:1 (see Tables 5.2-1 and 5.2-2). In other words, fewer financial transactions go towards the financing of real investment today. This increases the transaction volume, i.e., "market-depth" of the financial markets. Deep markets guarantee high market transparency. Transaction costs, especially the information costs of financing, are brought down.

The exchange of financial assets/liabilities is accompanied by different transformation procedures. A financial transaction may require a transformation in space (lender and borrower may live in different places), in time, in volume and in risk. The transformations are accomplished either by markets or by financial institutions. It is evident from Table 5.2-2 that financial flows in Germany run to a significant extent through financial institutions: more than half of all financial assets are bought by financial institutions (thus, in 1993, the acquisition of assets by the financial sector was significantly more at DM 639 billion than that of the non-financial sector with DM 436 billion). This is one characteristic of the German financial system: the dominance of financial institutions, especially banks.

A precise definition of the notions "credit" and "capital" is necessary because they are employed differently. On the credit market, financial claims and liabilities are exchanged in unsecured form. Furthermore, credit is customised, terms and volume are specified after lengthy negotiations. In contrast, the exchange of financial assets/liabilities on the capital market is highly standardised; it takes place in secured form on highly organised markets. As defined here, the capital markets include the market for long-term financial funds (bond market), the stock market and the market for short-term maturities. The latter is often called "money market", especially in the Anglo-Saxon literature. In the German literature the notion of a money market is reserved for inter-bank transactions in central bank money as well as for transactions between the Bundesbank and the banking community. Non-banks do not transact in the money market.

5.2.2. Finance from internal sources

In the post-war era, the producing enterprises have mostly financed their capital formation from internal sources. On average, internal funds accounted for more than 65% of producing-enterprise finance (Table 5.2-3). Internal financing may be subdivided into self-financing (from profits and transfers), financing through asset shifting (mainly from depreciation) and financing from provisions for pensions. The share of retained profits, transfers and depreciation in gross capital formation (the Bundesbank's so-called internal financing quota, a definition that

Table 5.2-1 Overall capital formation

Position DM billion	1960	1965	1970	1976	1982	1986	1990	1991	1992	1993
I. Overall capital formation (net investment)										
Enterprises	50	68	89	81	69	99	178	209	241	193
Producing enterprises	32	40	55	37	12	47	108	128	126	64
Housing	17	26	32	40	53	47	66	75	104	120
Financial institutions	0	2	3	4	4	4	4	5	10	8
Government	9	18	28	33	34	33	40	42	62	61
Central, regional and local authorities	9	18	27	32	33	33	40	42	62	61
Social security funds	0	0	1	1	1	0	0	0	0	0
Net lending to the rest of the world	3	-7	3	8	10	79	81	16	-40	-41
Total capital formation	63	80	121	122	114	212	300	267	264	213
II. Overall saving										
Private households	16	34	54	87	117	127	178	190	228	222
Enterprises	29	30	37	40	15	76	127	116	51	33
Producing enterprises	20	18	21	17	-15	39	78	64	-6	-14
Housing	7	9	11	13	10	20	21	17	20	7
Financial institutions	1	2	5	10	20	17	27	34	38	40
Government	17	16	29	-5	-18	8	-6	-39	-16	-40
Central, regional and local authorities	14	12	22	-6	-27	-1	-27	-56	n.a.	n.a.
Social security funds	3	4	6	1	8	9	21	17	n.a.	n.a.
Total saving	63	80	121	122	114	212	299	267	264	213
III. Financial surplus or deficit (II-I)										
Private households	16	34	54	87	117	127	178	190	228	222
Enterprises	-21	-39	-55	-40	-54	-22	-50	-92	-190	-162
Producing enterprises	-12	-21	-34	-20	-27	-7	-29	-64	-133	-79
Housing	-9	-17	-20	-26	-43	-27	-44	-57	-84	-113
Financial institutions	0	1	2	6	16	13	23	29	27	30
Government	9	-3	1	-38	-52	-25	-46	-82	-78	-101
Central, regional and local authorities	6	-6	-5	-39	-60	-34	-67	-98	n.a.	n.a.
Social security funds	3	3	6	1	7	9	21	16	n.a.	n.a.
Total financial account of the German economy	3	-7	3	8	10	79	81	15	-40	-41
- Differences in sums due to rounding; since 1992, including the new Länder -										

Source: Deutsche Bundesbank, Sonderdrucke der Deutschen Bundesbank, No. 4; Summary of Financial Accounting of the German Bundesbank 1982-91; 1960-82; and Monthly Report of the Deutsche Bundesbank

Table 5.2-2 Acquisition of financial assets and incurrence of liabilities

Position DM billion	1960	1965	1970	1976	1982	1986	1990	1991	1992	1993
I. Acquisition of financial assets										
Private households	17	36	59	101	126	137	202	219	252	237
Non-financial[a)c)] enterprises	6	11	22	45	49	58	187	141	118	145
Producing enterprises	6	12	22	44	46	54	188	143	115	138
Housing	3	1	0	0	3	1	0	0	2	6
Government[a)]	11	6	10	8	16	17	48	26	28	53
Central, regional and local authorities	8	7	4	7	8	7	26	10	n.a.	n.a.
Social security funds	3	1	6	1	7	9	20	16	n.a.	n.a.
Non-financial sectors	35	53	91	154	192	213	438	386	399	436
Financial sectors	34	47	102	157	201	239	461	352	474	639
All domestic sectors (A)	69	100	193	311	393	452	899	739	873	1, 075
II. Incurrence of liabilities and issue of shares										
Private households	1	1	4	14	9	10	23	28	24	15
Non-financial[a)c)] enterprises	28	50	78	91	120	89	220	243	332	355
Producing enterprises	18	33	58	64	74	61	176	185	244	235
Housing	10	17	19	27	45	28	44	58	86	119
Government[a)]	3	8	8	46	69	42	94	108	106	155
Central, regional and local authorities	3	9	9	46	69	42	94	108	106	155
Social security funds	0	-1	-1	0	0	0	0	0	0	0
Non-financial sectors	32	60	91	153	198	146	338	377	463	526
Financial sectors	34	47	99	151	184	226	438	322	446	608
All domestic sectors (B)	66	107	190	304	383	372	776	700	909	1, 134
Net acquisition of financial assets (= (A)-(B))	3	-7	3	8	10	79	122	38	-36	-59
Statistical difference[b)] to total financial account	0	0	0	0	0	0	41	22	4	17

- Differences in sums through rounded figures; since 1992, including the new Länder -

a) After consolidation of intra-sectoral flows.

b) Difference between the total financial account from Table 5-2.1 and the net acquisition of financial assets because of non-divisible payments with foreign countries and (mainly) the new Länder.

c) The net incurrence of liabilities of the non-financial enterprise sector since 1990 does not coincide with its net financial deficit from Table 5-2.1 because of the non-divisible payments of enterprises with foreign countries and the new Länder. The difference corresponds to the difference in the last line of this table.

Source: Deutsche Bundesbank, Sonderdrucke der Deutschen Bundesbank, No. 4; Summary of Financial Accounting of the German Bundesbank 1982-94; 1960-82; Monthly Report of the Deutsche Bundesbank ignores pension provisions) is shown explicitly in the financial accounting framework of the Bundesbank: it increased from an average of 76% in the period 1950–64 to nearly 90% in the period 1985–93. By adding provisions for pensions, an even stronger bias towards internal financing becomes obvious. This bias can also be seen in the ever-increasing acquisition of financial assets by this sector. These assets serve as reserves for internal financing.

Internal financing has also been important in the housing sector, which is mainly financed by private household savings. Table 5.2-3 shows the importance of different sources of finance in the sectors discussed.

The components of internal financing differ in their importance: financing from provisions for pensions accounted for 1% to 3.5% of the yearly financing requirements of enterprises. It offered a cheap source of funds especially for larger producing enterprises because interest paid on them is low relative to the internal yield of enterprises. The German legal framework for depreciation, one of the most intensively used instruments of German economic policy, guarantees a favourable source of finance: accelerated depreciation which precedes the real reduction in capital value. Thereby funds are released for new investment. Financing from depreciation accounted for nearly half (!) of the total financial requirements of producing enterprises, on average, in the last decade. Financing out of retained earnings was a source of 5% to 10% of the yearly financial demands of producing enterprises.

This figure is particularly high when compared with Anglo-Saxon standards. Under German law, stock corporations may retain half of their profits without justifying them to their shareholders, who are primarily interested in dividends. Additionally, profits are determined virtually without the effective control of shareholders.

The high share of internal finance is less critical in the housing sector and those producing enterprises which are totally owned by their managers. Even here, however, a distortion emerges since internal finance costs are kept artificially low; elsewhere in the economy these subsidies have to be paid. This general cost-of-capital subsidy for enterprises may be justified by positive external effects (i.e., on the labour market) of real investment. However in stock companies, whose managers do not own the enterprise, the high degree of internal finance raises another problem. On the one hand, managers do not have a special self-interest to put funds into real investments with maximum internal yield because effort would exceed reward. On the other hand, no external market can extract financial funds from these enterprises with low internal yield because internal finance is so dominant. Windfall profits[3] of stock companies not owned by their managers are regularly invested in low-yielding projects. In contrast, in self-owned enterprises,

---

[3] Windfall profits, which are accidentally emerging cheap sources of transitory and permanent financing, easily lead to misallocation of funds: an often-cited example are windfall profits which were passed to oil-producing enterprises in the wake of the 1970s oil-price shocks. These profits were persistently invested in low-return projects (e.g., investment in low-return Canadian shale).

managers invest these low-cost internal funds in maximum-yield projects for reasons of self-interest.

The supporters of the current legislation, which guarantees accelerated depreciation, easy funding from pension provisions, and a high share of retained earnings and transfers, refer to the "long-termism" which results from high internal funding: enterprises would have a secure long-term source of finance and are therefore more likely to carry out long-term investments, and especially risky investments, than enterprises which rely on external funding. External funding implies uncertainty of future financing, since no one knows how financial investors will judge opportunities in different enterprises and hence how they will allocate their funds. Proponents further argue that the current legislation may even prevent some unnecessary bankruptcies, since bad news about the companies in a critical situation would not release a "run" on liabilities of the company.

Even if all these arguments are granted, the extent of internal funding of German enterprises must be judged as too high. Such a financing structure may have been justified in the immediate post-war period when proper capital markets were lacking. But since the 1960s it has produced a "closed-shop" economy, with negative effects on the long-term development: too little of the capital formation has been valued by external markets and could well have been misallocated. In other economies with lower self-financing quotas, long-term and risky projects have been financed by external funds through special institutions (long-term credit banks, venture capital markets). On the whole, high internal funding cannot be considered a success factor in German post-war growth. In particular, some privileges of large stock companies such as subsidised funding via pension provisions, high direct transfers and the easy retention of earnings may be coming to an end.

5.2.3. Finance from external sources

5.2.3.1. Finance via credit markets

The credit market still dominates German external corporate finance. Bank loans accounted for approximately 25% of total business finance in 1990–93 (in comparison, securities accounted to only 6%; see Table 5.2-3). In the years to 1992 (the latest figures available), 54% of all liabilities of the non-financial sectors were incurred in unsecured form, of which 50% consisted of liabilities to banks. Only 30% of the liabilities were secured. The rest consisted of intra-sectoral liabilities and liabilities to foreigners. The acquisition of assets of the non-financial sectors consisted, to a large part, of bank deposits (1990–92: 31%); including deposits at other financial intermediaries, this ratio reaches 42%. In contrast, the acquisition of secured financial assets by all non-financial sectors amounted to approximately 29% of all acquired assets (Table 5.2-4). These figures reflect the dominance of non-market financial intermediation in general and the significance of banks in the intermediation process in particular.

There are behavioural and institutional reasons for the dominance of credit over capital in German external finance: there is a bias in favour of preserving enterprises (even those which are not profitable) and an aversion against instability and speculation which act against market valuation of enterprises. On the capital supply side, the ideal of total protection of creditors implies that bank deposits are preferred to securities. The resulting lack of capital market depth relative to international standards adds to volatility, which is especially disliked by German financial investors. On the capital demand side, a huge share of German enterprises in the small- and medium-sized range do not qualify for capital markets. Finally, there is the traditionally close relationship between enterprises and banks (*Hausbankbeziehung*) and also between private households and banks, both supported by the universal banking system.

External finance via credit markets has contributed to German post-war economic success. The financing of small businesses via bank credit is especially efficient as the bank loan includes financial advice, which is very helpful to small enterprises. The high ratio of credit finance conforms to German circumstances.

5.2.3.2. Finance via capital markets

(a) Immediate post-war period

The establishment of a German capital market was not really successful until the early 1980s. In the immediate post-war period, the bond market had been constrained by two factors. On the one hand, enterprises and public authorities financed themselves largely from internal sources rather than externally from the credit or capital markets. Public authorities were able to rely on tax revenues. Business found external financing via capital markets unattractive because of the excessive protection of creditors which raised the cost of capital. Consequently, the small share of external financing was almost exclusively funded by bank loans. On the other hand, there were also problems in bringing financial surpluses to the bond markets. For potential bond market buyers, confidence in long-term securities had been undermined by the currency reform of 1948. There were uncertainties about future inflation and the development of the capital market.

The bond market was gradually made more attractive for the investor by the creation of an Issuance Co-ordination Committee (1957) and the liberalisation of interest rates (1962). It was not until the beginning of the 1980s, however, that the bond market reached a volume which was comparable to OECD standards. Since then, yearly non-financial sector investment in bonds has amounted to approximately 20% of the total investment (Table 5.2-4).

The equity market had to be revived as well. The capital shortage on the stock market existed for the same reasons as that on the bond market. In addition, there was a substantial aversion of investors against the high volatility of share

Table 5.2-3 Capital formation of enterprises, including housing (selected numbers for producing enterprises in parentheses) and its financing

Position share in %	1950/ 1959	1960/ 1964	1965/ 1969	1970/ 1974	1975/ 1979	1980/ 1984	1985/ 1989	1990/ 1993
I. Capital formation of enterprises								
Gross capital formation	88.7	90.9	87.8	85.5	83.6	83.4	82.8	72.0
Fixed assets	n.a.	84.1	80.8	81.6	80.0	84.1	81.1	73.0
Stocks	n.a.	6.7	7.0	3.9	3.6	-0.7	1.7	-1.0
Acquisition of financial assets	11.3	9.1	12.2	14.5	16.4	16.6	17.2	28.0
Total capital formation	100	100	100	100	100	100	100	100
II. Finance of enterprises								
Internal resources	61.0 (66.6)	61.8 (65.9)	63.4 (65.9)	54.9 (56.0)	61.8 (67.6)	58.5 (63.7)	71.3 (70.7)	60.7 (59.2)
Saving (net retained earnings)	n.a.	21.8 (26.0)	15.2 (18.7)	1.1 (4.7)	-5.2 (5.4)	-13.9 (-5.7)	-0.3 (7.2)	7.7 (1.3)
Capital transfers (net)	n.a.	7.7 (3.3)	9.9 (3.4)	12.8 (5.1)	16.8 (7.1)	16.5 (7.2)	15.1 (6.1)	
Consumption of fixed capital	n.a.	32.4 (36.6)	38.4 (43.8)	41.0 (46.2)	50.2 (55.1)	56.0 (62.2)	56.6 (57.4)	53.0 (57.9)
Incurrence of liabilities and issuance of shares	39.0 (33.4)	38.2 (34.1)	36.6 (34.1)	45.1 (44.0)	38.2 (32.4)	41.5 (36.3)	28.7 (29.3)	39.3 (39.7)
Long-term	29.4	30.5	28.1	34.1	32.0	31.4	24.9	32.8
Bank loans	20.5 (17.0)	17.7 (10.9)	15.9 (11.5)	18.8 (14.8)	20.0 (12.5)	18.8 (10.3)	16.2 (11.9)	19.4 (17.8)
Building and loan association /insurance enterprise loans	3.1	4.0	4.7	6.1	5.2	5.1	1.0	0.5
Sale of bonds	1.6	1.5	0.5	1.2	-0.2	0.4	1.3	2.9
Issue of shares	1.9	2.5	2.0	1.4	1.5	1.4	2.3	2.9
Liabilities against employees (provisions for retirement)	n.a.	1.2 (1.7)	1.2 (2.8)	2.0 (3.9)	2.8 (4.6)	3.2 (3.4)	2.5 (3.2)	n.a.
Other liabilities[a]	2.3	3.7	3.8	4.6	2.8	2.5	1.7	6.9
Short-term	9.6	7.7	8.5	11.0	6.2	10.1	3.8	6.5
Bank loans	n.a.	5.3	6.5	7.4	3.7	5.7	1.8	4.2
Other liabilities[a]	n.a.	2.4	2.0	3.7	2.5	4.5	1.9	2.3
Total finance	100	100	100	100	100	100	100	100
Finance from internal sources in % of gross capital formation	68.7 (78.1)	68.1 (75.8)	72.2 (79.9)	64.3 (71.0)	73.9 (87.2)	70.2 (83.1)	86.2 (92.0)	82.8 (86.1)

- Differences in sums due to rounding; since 1992, including the new Länder -
a) Mainly to foreign countries.

Source: Deutsche Bundesbank, Sonderdrucke der Deutschen Bundesbank, No. 4; Summary of Financial Accounting of the German Bundesbank 1982-91; 40 Jahre Deutsche Mark, Monetary Statistics 1948-87; Monthly Report of the Deutsche Bundesbank, calculations and estimations of Ifo Institute

Table 5.2-4 Acquisition of financial assets and incurrence of liabilities of domestic non-financial sectors (selected numbers for private households in parentheses) by type of investment and loan

Position share in %	1960/ 1964	1965/ 1969	1970/ 1974	1975/ 1979	1980/ 1984	1985/ 1989	1990/ 1992	Stock at end 1992
I. Acquisition of financial assets								
Total long-term	59.5	58.0	51.9	58.4	59.7	57.7	63.6	59.5
Funds placed with banks	22.2 (12.9)	22.4 (23.2)	18.2 (22.7)	18.1 (20.5)	12.4 (12.5)	10.5 (9.6)	4.4 (4.8)	12.2 (12.5)
Time deposits	14.2	8.3	7.0	11.4	11.8	8.4	4.1	8.2
Saving deposits (with agreed notice)	8.0	14.2	11.1	6.8	0.6	2.1	0.3	4.0
Funds placed with building and loan associations	4.8	5.6	5.6	4.6	2.3	-0.2	0.8	2.3
Funds placed with insurance enterprises	8.0	8.9	8.3	10.6	13.8	16.0	11.8	11.6
Acquisition of bonds	10.7 (11.6)	7.0 (8.3)	7.1 (12.8)	11.9 (14.0)	15.2 (21.3)	18.1 (22.8)	23.1 (32.5)	15.7 (20.9)
Acquisition of shares	3.2 (3.5)	5.2 (4.5)	2.7 (1.0)	2.9 (0.7)	3.4 (0.5)	1.9 (1.2)	5.3 (-0.5)	5.9 (5.2)
Other claims[a)b)]	10.6	8.9	10.0	10.3	12.5	11.4	18.1	11.7
Total short-term	40.5	42.0	48.2	41.6	40.3	42.3	36.4	40.6
Funds placed with banks	32.6 (40.4)	35.7 (34.9)	37.6 (32.9)	32.5 (32.1)	28.2 (27.0)	26.5 (27.2)	26.7 (26.7)	29.1 (28.1)
Currency and sight deposits	14.7	12.5	16.1	12.1	10.9	11.2	14.2	12.5
Time deposits	1.1	6.7	10.9	4.8	8.4	7.6	13.0	8.4
Saving deposits (at statutory notice)	16.8	16.5	10.6	15.7	8.9	7.7	-1.6	8.3
Acquisition of short-term bonds	-0.1	0.2	1.9	0.0	1.7	-1.6	2.1	0.8
Other claims[a)b)]	8.0	6.1	8.6	9.1	10.4	17.4	7.6	10.7
Total assets	100	100	100	100	100	100	100	100
II. Incurrance of liabilities and issuance of shares								
Total long-term	80.6	78.6	77.2	87.4	81.0	90.0	79.3	83.1
Bank loans	49.9	48.0	46.3	57.3	44.0	49.7	36.9	45.4
Building and loan association insurance enterprise loans	9.9	11.2	12.0	9.7	9.7	2.8	3.4	7.2
Sale of bonds	6.0	4.4	4.4	8.3	9.2	26.3	25.7	14.7
Issue of shares	5.5	4.4	2.6	2.4	2.3	5.3	4.0	4.8
Other liabilities[a)b)]	9.3	10.5	11.9	9.8	15.9	5.9	9.2	11.8
Total short-term	19.4	21.4	22.8	12.6	19.6	10.0	20.7	16.9
Bank loans	13.5	15.9	15.6	8.1	11.4	5.2	14.8	11.4
Sales of money market paper	0.0	1.0	0.4	0.4	0.5	0.0	1.2	0.5
Other liabilities[a)]	5.9	4.5	6.8	4.1	7.0	4.8	4.8	4.9
Total liabilities	100	100	100	100	100	100	100	100

- Differences in sums through rounded figures; figures for West Germany only -
a) Against foreign countries.
b) Retirement provisions of enterprises included c) Additionally: claims against insurance companies included.

Source: Deutsche Bundesbank, Sonderdrucke der Deutschen Bundesbank, No. 4; Summary of Financial Accounting of the German Bundesbank 1982-91; 1960-92, calculations of the Ifo Institute prices. The government tried populist measures like privatisation which led to widespread share-holding by the people (*Volksaktionäre*). This undertaking was unsuccessful, and most problems of the German equity market still exist today.

(b) Since the 1960s

Although credit relations have always dominated the German financial system, the share of secured financial contracts increased throughout the post-war period. This was in line with the world-wide trend towards securitisation (shift of financial flows from credit to capital markets). The share of securities (including stocks) in all financial assets acquired by the non-financial sector increased from just over 10% in the 1960s to well above 20% in the period 1985–92 (Table 5.2-4). The same trend may be observed on the liabilities side of the non-financial sector: here, the share of credits in secured form increased from 10% in the 1960s to nearly 30%. The secured loans were almost exclusively granted by private households to the government and to banks. Enterprises were not involved. The sharp rise in the volume of securities since 1990 is due to the massive increase in government debt as a consequence of German re-unification; government bonds were in large part absorbed by domestic private households.

The bond market today is certainly the most important part of German capital markets. In terms of turnover it has become significant by international standards. The strength of the German bond market has become obvious in the exceptional situation of the financing of German unification: bond issues tripled from DM 70 billion in the 1980s to DM 220 billion since 1990 (without sharply rising interest rates). The success story of the German bond market is based on the general preference of long-term financial contracts, relatively modest market regulation, strong participation of the government as an issuer and the support of the Bundesbank.

The low degree of regulation has become a special advantage for the German financial system in general. The most important factors of the liberal framework are the universal banking system and the early abolishment of interest rate ceilings. The remaining liberalisation of the German capital market took place during the last ten years.

The federal government, which is responsible for most of the public debt, has raised the attractiveness of the bond market through various reforms. By shifting from the credit to the bond market at the beginning of the 1980s, public authorities have contributed to the establishment of a deep, efficient bond market. Since 1985 the federal government has launched new securities with different maturities and interest due dates. In 1986 foreign banks were admitted to the underwriting syndicate for federal securities, increasing the investment groups already at the time of issuance. From 1991 on, government securities have been traded via the electronic exchange system IBIS. The attractiveness of the bond market has been enhanced by the addition of a futures market (Deutsche Terminbörse, DTB) in 1990, on which bonds with different maturities (five, ten, thirty years) are traded.

In addition, the activities of the Bundesbank have contributed significantly to the success of the German bond market. It supported an interest rate constellation in favour of the bond market by holding short-term interest rates at relatively low levels. The Bundesbank has also played the role of a market maker itself rather than relying on other players (as, for example, the Bank of England, which conferred the obligation of market attention to the discount houses). Its success is reflected in the relatively low volatility of German bond prices.

However, financing via the bond market is confined to the public authorities and the banks (1993: ca. 60% and 40% of all issues, respectively). German enterprises have shied away. Although some disadvantages of corporate bond financing have been abolished, some unfavourable fiscal treatment and tedious listing procedures remain an obstacle for enterprise issues.

The equity market is rather small by comparison. One reason is supposedly that the conservative German investor dislikes speculation. But there is more to it than this. The yield on equity investment has been only slightly above that of bonds in the entire post-war period, failing to compensate for the higher risk. After tax, the unattractiveness of equity investment was somewhat reduced because interest income from bonds was subject to capital income tax, whereas capital gains from equities were tax-exempt (although dividend payments and speculative capital gains were taxable).

From the view of enterprises, too, finance via the stock market has been unattractive. In general, the incentive for companies to tap the equity market is in any case limited for relatively high financing costs. Small- and medium-sized companies—the most prominent size in Germany—frequently avoid broad investment circles, because of additional publicity costs and the need to share control. Furthermore, the business organisation in the form of a private limited company (GmbH) has some legal and fiscal advantages, so that few firms are established as joint stock companies. As a consequence, today's capitalisation of the stock market in relation to GNP amounts to only 20% in Germany, compared to 90% in Japan and 80% in Great Britain. And only 500 of the 2,400 stock companies are listed on German stock exchanges.

The most important deficiency of the German equity market has not been abolished: the lack of transparency. Opaque accounting methods and a legal framework that allows cross-stockholding amongst corporations without any obligation of public disclosure[4] does not foster private investors' confidence. For a long time, the lack of insider trading rules, which define the facts and the penalties of insider trading, also reduced the general attractiveness of the equity market. With the installation of the Insider Code on 1 January 1995, this deficiency no longer exists. But the German universal banking system will still be subject to suspicion of superior information even after the introduction of such a rule.

---

[4] Since 1 January 1995, the possession of over 5% of an enterprise by a stock corporation must be made public.

In Germany, private households have not been able to benefit from high stock yields seen commonly elsewhere, and enterprises have not had access to an additional source of funds. This development must be blamed on specific mistakes of financial market policy. The stock market has not been a factor of success in post-war Germany.

The short-term capital market acts mainly as an exchange for inter-bank central bank money, and serves the banks' refinancing at the Bundesbank. (Recall that only in this narrow delimitation is the market defined as "the money market" in Germany.) The inter-bank market for central bank money balances liquidity shortages and surpluses, which appear as a consequence of transitory (tax payment date, minimum reserve requirements) and structural differences in bank balances. Inter-bank trade is usually done via credit. In contrast, the trade between banks and the Bundesbank usually takes place in secured form, mostly with re-purchase agreements but also with some short-term public securities.

By international standards, the German short-term capital market has always played an insignificant role. Responsible has been the Bundesbank, which wanted a narrow short-term capital market in order to increase the power of its instruments and permit the maintenance of "long-termism". This is why it opposed the development of this market; only since 1991 has there been a market for non-bank short-term issues (DM commercial papers). This market has since reached a notable turnover, especially in the high-interest phase between 1991 and 1993.

The share of treasury bills in the total public debt is very small at approximately 2%. Moreover, these securities are not traded on an exchange. The volume of these securities meet more the requirements of monetary policy rather than the demands of capital market participants. With the Bundesbank as the fiscal agent of the government, the conditions in this market are unlikely to change. Some capital market participants, however, have hoped for some time for improved conditions on the short-term capital market through the issuance of "Bu-Bills", high-volume periodical issues of public securities.

Though the development of the short-term capital market has been quite limited, it is exactly its limitation that has to be judged a success factor of German financial market policy. It has contributed to the substantial long-term orientation of German finance and real investment.

5.3. Comparative Summary of Factors of Production: Capital

There are both differences and similarities between Japan and Germany in terms of the role of capital as a factor of production. The following comparative analysis examines these differences and similarities from such perspectives as the importance of own funds, the role of indirect financing, the dominance of banks and the level of capital market development.

5.3.1. Importance of own funds

Appraisal of own funds is one of the more interesting areas in which differences are visible. Though both countries recognise the importance of own funds per se, they appear to view the role of own funds differently in the context of economic development. Up until the oil-shock period, most Japanese companies sought to improve their net worth ratios in the belief that low levels of highly stable, internally generated funds would be a constraint to growth. In Germany, meanwhile, the growth bottleneck was perceived conversely as deriving from the conservatism associated with abundant own funds. Given that the scale of corporate owned funds is not necessarily linked to economic growth, this difference in viewpoints suggests that there is also a need to focus on the intrinsic characteristics of own funds itself.

5.3.2. The role of indirect financing

One process that is virtually identical in both Japan and Germany is the linkage of accumulated domestic capital to fixed investment by private companies, which has spurred economic growth in both countries. Indirect financing, primarily in the form of bank lending, has played an important part in this process. One feature of indirect financing is that it allows policy authorities a certain degree of control over the distribution of funds. In Japan, for instance, several government-related special financial institutions were set up and proved themselves effective as sources of financing for large-scale capital investment projects and credit for small-to-medium-sized businesses. In fact, under regulated interest rates and low-interest rate policy, Japanese banks were able to allocate the funds regardless of the rate of return on them. In contrast, banks in Germany had to pay heed to controlling the cost of funds because interest rates had been deregulated from the immediate post-war period. Despite this fundamental difference, indirect financing predominated in both countries. This situation was attributable to the existence of policy incentives for direct financing rather than to the degree of headway towards financial deregulation per se. In the United States, for example, under the environment of deregulation of interest rate in the 1970s, there occurred a money shift into the highly developed capital market of that country.

5.3.3. Power of banks to dominate and control

Another characteristic shared by Japan and Germany is the strong dominance that banks exercise over the business community in general. A feature of the situation in Japan is the formation of industrial conglomerates around core bank(s) under the main bank system. Similarly, under the universal bank system in Germany, banks wield even more influence over the business community than is the case in Japan. The sources of this dominance differ, however. In Japan, bank dominance depended on the monitoring and regulation of the money and capital markets by the authorities concerned, and that dominance has been weakened by the financial deregulation process. On the other hand, German banks have been free from such control by the authorities, and their powers of dominance have been nurtured over the years by a preference among individuals and corporations alike for the security afforded by bank deposits, and by corporate reliance on their advisory abilities. German corporate management has thus remained heavily dependent on the abilities and policies of their main banks. For this reason, as pointed out in the conclusions concerning Germany, the German approach has not always been effective. The fact that banks do not always exercise self-regulation is apparent from the processes that led to the formation and subsequent collapse of the Japanese bubble economy of the late 1980s. Germany is no exception to this rule.

5.3.4. Importance of capital markets

Another interesting feature shared by Japan and Germany is the slow development of their capital markets compared with the steady growth of their indirect finance markets, which were driven chiefly by bank lending. It appears this was attributable to a lack of government interest in the cultivation of capital markets. For example, there was little enthusiasm for the development of secondary markets, which are vital to the growth of bond markets, because of the possibility that the expansion of secondary markets could reduce the effectiveness of financial policies implemented by the central bank. Under fixed-exchange rate or managed-float systems, any distortion of the relationship between the long-term interest rate and the short-term interest rate, which is the direct financial policy tool, could obviously be expected to put considerable pressure on the exchange rate. Also, the weight of capital markets in total financing operations was relatively low in both countries. Although this was attributable in large measure to the conservative attitudes of the citizens of both nations, to some extent it also reflected a lack of awareness about the risk associated with financial and capital market instruments.

5.3.5. Conclusions

The above comparative analysis shows that capital played a significant role in fostering the growth of both the Japanese and German economies. The relationships between capital and economic growth in the two countries were not always identical, and there appear to have been considerable differences reflecting their respective characteristics. The following two factors are cited as the most important conditions under which capital can contribute to economic growth.

First of all, the amount of capital must be above a certain threshold level. From the viewpoint of stability, domestic funds will be far more important than foreign funds. Of course, that may no longer be as true as it once was, since the international trend towards financial deregulation that emerged with the 1990s has effectively removed many of the major distinctions between foreign and domestic funds. Nonetheless, the experience of both countries still underlines the importance of domestic capital, considering such factors as exchange rate risk, the desire for security in private savings, and the competitive advantage of indirect financing institutions in the domestic marketplace.

The second factor is that the indirect financing frameworks provide an effective means of harnessing capital for economic growth through capital investment in priority industries. However, several conditions must be met before this mechanism can function. First, government budgets must be basically in balance and not excessively dependent on the issuance of government bonds. Second, the relationship between the long-term interest rate and the exchange rate must be severed, and there must be no significant distortion between the long-term rate and the short-term rate, which is a policy tool. However, both of these conditions have ceased to apply in Japan and Germany.

Japan and Germany have both grown into financial superpowers. Given that the financial deregulation process can be expected to move forward and extend beyond their national borders, the governments, companies, and citizens of both countries are likely to face the challenge of accommodating and adapting to that trend. On this point, it has to be understood that both countries now face immense difficulty in maintaining their own unique systems, and that their citizens—as suppliers of capital—are adopting an increasingly internationalised perspective on their investment options, and furthermore, companies no longer have unconditional access to abundant capital. As market conditions increasingly take on the same qualities at home and abroad, the extent to which environments can be created to attract capital is likely to become an important question for government policy-makers.

6. Factors of Production: Labour

6.1. Japan's Factors of Production: Labour

6.1.1. Positioning of labour

Japan's labour force is known for its homogeneity and superior skills, as well as for strong company loyalty resulting from the lifetime employment system. Descriptions such as these are indicative of the importance of labour as a factor in Japan's economic success. However, the relationship between Japan's economic development and its labour force is far from uniform and has changed with each passing era. It is important to recognise the flexibility with which the Japanese employment system has adapted to change. This chapter examines the structure and characteristics of the Japanese labour force and evaluates its role in the growth of the Japanese economy.

6.1.2. Trends in the Japanese labour force

6.1.2.1. Quantitative assessment

Japan's population growth rate remained high with an average of 2.9% per annum in the first five years of the post-war era. This was the period when the so-called "baby boomers" were born. The population growth rate subsequently declined gradually, but it began to rise again as Japan entered its high-growth period. By the early 1970s, when the baby boomers were reaching marriageable age, it had recovered to 1.3%. However, the rate of increase has declined consistently since the time of the first oil shock, and by the early 1990s it was down to just 0.3%.

These population dynamics are reflected in the labour population, which grew by an average of 1.5% per annum until the time of the first oil shock. This high growth rate was largely attributable to an abundant supply of young workers. By 1970 the percentage of workers in the 15–24 age group was in excess of 20% (Table 6.1-1). However, the supply of young workers subsequently began to shrink as a result of a declining birth rate and an increase in the percentage of people entering higher education. Since 1980, the percentage of workers in the 15–24 age group has hovered at the low end of the 10–19% range. The resulting shortage of young workers has been offset by the entry of women into the labour market. The female working population declined temporarily immediately after the first oil shock but then began to grow and has been expanding at a faster pace than the male work force since 1980. The main reasons for this increase in the female labour force are the expansion of the young working population and a rise in the percentage of workers aged between their late thirties and early fifties. The latter factor has led to an increase in the number of part-time workers (people employed for less than thirty-five hours per week). In 1960 part-timers accounted for only 6.3% of the total employment in the non-agriculture sector. The percentage soared after the first oil shock, and by 1993 it had reached 18.2%.

6.1.2.2. Qualitative evaluation of the labour force

Japan's compulsory education system was extended to include secondary school (junior high school) by the revision of the Fundamentals of Education Act in March 1947. As a result, the basic standard of education rose rapidly in the early post-war period. The level of advanced educational standards can be gauged from the percentage of people entering higher educational institutions. In fiscal 1950, 42.5% of students entered senior high schools. The percentage rose rapidly during the 1960s, reaching 82.1% in fiscal 1970. The admission rate for universities and junior colleges climbed sharply during the 1960s and 1970s, from 10.3% in fiscal 1960 to 37.4% in fiscal 1980. The university and junior-college admission rate for female students has been rising since 1980, but the overall rate of increase has remained gradual (Table 6.1-2).

The number of students taking industrial courses at senior high schools almost tripled from 237,000 (9.2%) in 1955 to 624,000 (12.3%) in 1965. And Japan's economic industrialisation policy was also reflected in the number and percentage of university students taking science and engineering courses, which reached 326,000 (24.2%) in 1970. These trends reflected industry's demand for skilled workers and engineers as a result of the industrialisation strategy adopted by Japan in its high-growth period.

Table 6.1-1 Young labour force and part-timer ratio[a)b)]

- % -

Year	Young labour force	Part-timers
1960	23.4	6.3
1970	21.5	6.7
1980	12.4	10.0
1990	13.1	15.2
1993	13.5	18.2

a) Young labour force in total labour force; part-timers in total non-agriculture employment.
b) Young labour force of 15-24 age group; part-timers working for less than 35 hours per week.

Source: Management and Co-ordination Agency, Annual Report on the Labour Force Survey

Table 6.1-2 Ratio of higher education

- % -

	Senior high school			University and junior college		
F.Y.	Total	M	F	Total	M	F
1950	42.5	48.0	36.7	n.a.	n.a.	n.a.
1960	57.7	59.6	55.9	10.3	14.9	5.5
1970	82.1	81.6	82.7	23.6	29.2	17.7
1980	94.2	93.1	95.4	37.4	41.3	33.3
1990	94.4	93.2	95.6	36.3	35.2	37.4
1993	95.3	94.2	96.5	40.9	38.5	43.4

Source: Ministry of Education, Report on Basic Survey of Schools

The content of Japanese education was uniform and standardised, and priority was given to memorisation rather than creativity. Japanese education contributed significantly to post-war economic development in terms of producing a homogeneous labour force with a high level of knowledge, but this standardised approach was also responsible for the inability of workers and engineers to develop creativity.

6.1.3. Employment structures of the labour force

6.1.3.1. Employment situation

Japan's unemployment rate has remained consistently low by international standards since the high-growth period. After hovering around the 1% level in the high-growth period, the full unemployment ratio climbed as the economic growth rate declined following the first oil shock. Yet even then it remained below 3%. Apart from the low level of overall unemployment, Japan's unemployment situation is also characterised by high jobless rates among young people (15–24) and those in higher age groups (55–64), and by the similarity of unemployment levels in these two categories. An analysis of unemployment rates for males in different age groups shows that unemployment has increased among young workers and those in the higher age groups, particularly since the first oil shock, and that unemployment rates in both groups hovered around 5% in the 1980s.

Also significant is the Japanese practice of maintaining excessive work forces in the name of lifetime employment. This phenomenon is manifested in the so-called "internal unemployment" within companies, which appears to have worsened after the collapse of the bubble economy, and is now estimated at between 500,000 and 2 million. Assuming the true figure to be 1.5 million, this type of quasi-unemployment would be similar in extent to the level of full unemployment in 1993. On this basis, Japan's unemployment rate, including internal unemployment, would be around 5%, or double the official figure. Recently, however, companies have become unable to support internal unemployment, and surplus workers are now joining the ranks of the unemployed.

6.1.3.2. Employment structure by industry

Changes in sectoral employment patterns reflected the industrialisation of the Japanese economy and the transition to a service-based economy. In 1950, 48.5% of workers were employed in primary industries (agriculture, forestry and fisheries), 21.8% in secondary industries (mining, construction and manufacturing) and 29.6% in tertiary industries. During the high-growth period, the primary sector's share declined sharply whilst the shares of the secondary and tertiary sectors increased. By 1975 the percentages were 13.8%, 34.1% and 51.8%, respectively. The upwards trend in the secondary sector's share of employment ceased after the oil crises because of the rationalisation efforts in manufacturing industries, but the share of the tertiary sector continued to rise. In 1990 the ratios were 7.1%, 33.3% and 59.0%, respectively. The fact that the secondary sector has continued to retain over 30% of workers even after the oil crises indicates that manufacturing is still the backbone of Japanese industry. In contrast, the share of the manufacturing sector however has been declining in both absolute and percentage terms, owing to the collapse of the bubble economy and the excessive appreciation of the yen.

6.1.3.3. Self-employment ratio

In 1955, a decade after the end of the war, 56.5% of all employed people were self-employed (including family workers). The ratio declined gradually after the start of the high-growth period and fell below 30% by 1980. By 1994 it declined even further to 18.9%. The reason for the decline in the first half of the high-growth period was a fall in the absolute number of people employed in agriculture and forestry. In the second half, the absolute number and percentage of self-employed people in agriculture and forestry declined only marginally (to the low end of the 90% range), while there was a marked drop in the percentage of self-employed people in industries other than agriculture and forestry. The percentage of self-employed people in industries other than agriculture and forestry has fallen from 34.5% in 1955 to 21.5% in 1975 and 15.2% in 1993. This decline is attributable to the conversion of self-employed people into employees resulting from the growing role of companies as the Japanese economy grew.

6.1.4. Labour productivity

Japan's labour force has displayed very high productivity. During the high growth period, the growth rate of labour productivity (GDP basis) reached an extremely high level of 9.6% per annum (Fig. 6.1-1). During this time, demand expanded rapidly, and there was massive capital investment. Demand, capital and technology all contributed to a dramatic rise in labour productivity. Although the growth rate of labour productivity declined as the economic growth rate fell in the wake of the oil shocks, its pace remained higher than in other developed countries.

An analysis of differences in labour productivity according to company size shows that the ratio between large companies with more than 500 employees and small- and medium-sized companies with 1 to 29 employees in manufacturing industries has remained virtually unchanged at 1:2 since 1970. However, this gap is much larger than in Europe and North America. Large companies' share of the total number of employees has fallen from 26.5% in 1970 to just over 23% in the 1980s, and there has been a corresponding rise in the shares of middle-ranked (with 30 to 499 employees), small-to-medium-sized, and petty companies. This trend occurred because large companies increased their labour productivity by reducing employment after the oil crises, whilst the other group increased labour productivity by expanding employment.

Differences in labour productivity according to company size are paralleled almost exactly by differences in wage levels. Wage levels in small-to-medium-sized and petty companies have remained at around one-half of levels in large corporations. A comparison of full-time wages for different classes of manufacturing companies shows that the ratios have changed little since the high-growth period—a ratio of 100 for large companies, 60–70 for small-to-medium-sized companies, and 50–60 for petty companies. Like the gap in labour productivity, the wage gap in Japan is much larger than in other developed countries.

Fig. 6.1-1 Trend in labour productivity

Note: Labour productivity = GDP at 1985 prices / Total employment

Sources: EPA, Annual Report on National Accounts; Management and Co-ordination Agency, Monthly Report on the Labour Force Survey

6.1.5. Changes in the labour market

This section examines changes in the Japanese labour market in each period through comparisons between companies as the demand side and the labour force as the supply side (Table 6.1-3).

6.1.5.1. Post-war reconstruction period (1945–1954)

During the post-war reconstruction period, the need for labour was limited. A drastic reduction in industry's production capacity occurred due to war damages, and the demand for labour was extremely low. In addition, large numbers of soldiers returning to the labour force created a labour surplus. As indicated by the sectoral shares of employment, this surplus was absorbed by the agriculture sector.

6.1.5.2. High-growth period (1955–1972)

During the high-growth period, a simultaneous high-growth phase in the world economy was reflected in the Japanese economy in a prevailing trend

Table 6.1-3 Phases of development and labour force

Phases	Demand	Supply	Matching	Result
Post-war reconstruction period	Primary industry Heavily damaged production facilities	Mainly demobilised soldiers	Excessive labour absorbed in farm work	Low productivity
High-growth period	Skilled labourer Low-wage labour for mass production	Young labour force with homogeneous level of skill and education	Lifetime employment Seniority-based wage system Enterprise union	High productivity High quality
Post-oil crisis	Planning ability Low-wage labour	University graduates Part-timers	Decline of trade unions Collapse of lifetime employment system Shorter work hours	Higher value-added products
Low-growth and super-high-yen period	Creative and development-type skills	Homogeneous Higher education	Collapse of seniority-based wage system Wage system based on ability	Low-growth

towards mass production and mass consumption. In this environment, companies needed a homogeneous supply of low-cost workers with reasonable skill levels. This need was met when large numbers of people from the first post-war generation began to graduate from a uniform and homogeneous compulsory education system. Another source of employees was the shift of agricultural workers and self-employed people into company employment. As a result, the trend towards nuclear family living was accompanied by an increase in the percentage of women staying at home, which caused the percentage of women in the work force to decline.

6.1.5.3. Post–oil crisis (1973–1990)

After the oil crisis, companies needed workers with higher skill levels and the ability to adapt to changes resulting from advances in processing technology as Japanese industry grew more sophisticated and its international status rose. At the same time, changes in the structure of the working population meant that the growth rate of the young labour force declined, and companies were no longer able to rely on supplies of young, low-cost workers. On the supply side, the university admission ratio was rising, creating a supply of workers who were better equipped to cope with a wide range of situations. At the same time, housewives were beginning to move into the labour market as household finances came under pressure from housing loans, the purchase of durable goods, the rising cost of education and other factors. On the other hand, rises in Japan's economic level were accompanied by increased worker pressure for the reduction of working hours. As a result, the five-day week has become the norm, especially in large corporations, since the late 1980s. This trend has been aided by policy efforts to reduce total annual working hours to levels in other developed countries.

6.1.5.4. Low-growth and super-high-yen period (1991–1995)

Since the collapse of the bubble economy in the early 1990s, the Japanese economy has faced the need for another transition in its industrial structure. The high wages of senior workers under the seniority-based wage system became a fetter for companies during the high-yen recession, and it became difficult to maintain the lifetime employment system. The result was large-scale unemployment in higher age groups, as companies sought to survive by hiring low-cost part-timers. Under the circumstances, companies have begun to seek personnel with creative and development-type skills. However, there has been a consistent decline in the rate of increase in the number of young workers educated under the traditional homogeneous education system, and there has been little change in the structure of the labour force. In addition, the female labour force has started to shift from temporary to long-term employment.

6.1.6. Characteristics of Japanese-style employment

6.1.6.1. Lifetime employment system

Under the lifetime employment system, people spend most of their working lives with a single company and reap the benefits of long-term service through the retirement bonus system. The system gained wide acceptance during the high-growth period, when it was used to retain workers. The foundation of the system was a seniority-based wage structure, in which young workers were employed at low wages, and senior workers, who needed more money for their children's education and housing payments, were paid high wages. The lifetime employment system enabled companies to develop the human resources they needed through in-house education. It also helped to foster company loyalty in workers. Workers accepted the system on the understanding that their jobs were guaranteed for life. However, lifetime employment was provided mainly by middle-ranked and larger companies, and it was not always formalised in smaller companies, which account for one-half of company workers. The high-growth period, which was an essential condition for the lifetime employment system, came to an end with the oil crisis. Thereafter workers increasingly sought the raising of retirement ages to reflect rising average life expectancies, but it became increasingly difficult for companies to maintain the lifetime employment system in its traditional form. After the oil crisis, the system gradually began to change as large companies adapted to this phase with new measures affecting middle-aged and older employees, including wage reductions and secondments to affiliated small- and medium-sized companies.

6.1.6.2. Seniority-based wage and promotion

The system of seniority-based wage and promotion complemented the lifetime employment system. Under Japan's pyramid-shaped employment structure, wage levels were determined not by ability but by age, and, generally, people of the same age would receive the same wage. Age and experience were emphasised when promoting workers within companies, and mid-career recruitment was not often adopted by large companies. Under the seniority-based wage and promotion system, directors and executives were chosen from amongst employees through repeated promotions, and it was extremely unusual to appoint outsiders to these positions. However, it has became increasingly difficult for companies to maintain seniority-based wage and promotion system in a low-growth environment characterised by an increasing emphasis on skills.

6.1.6.3. Enterprise unions

In Japan, labour unions in private-sector industry are organised mainly in company units. In addition, most unions have a policy of co-operating and harmonising with management, and it is not unusual for former union committee chairpersons to become company directors. A characteristic of enterprise unions is the tendency of the labour movement to be defined by company management considerations. Specifically, there is a strong tendency for labour-management wage bargaining to be kept within limits defined by company performance. The belief that worker benefits would increase with the improvement of company performance actually strengthened worker solidarity within companies, thereby helping to underpin company management.

A high percentage of smaller companies have no unions, however, and Japan's total unionisation ratio is low. In addition, the percentage of workers belonging to labour unions has been declining since the first oil crises. The estimated membership ratio has fallen from around 35% in the late 1970s to 24.1% in 1994. This drop in union membership has been accompanied by a decline in the role of unions in company management. The gradual reduction of the negotiating power of labour unions is apparent from the fact that the number of spring wage round struggles and the number of participants in those struggles have been falling since the mid-1970s.

6.1.7. Role of the labour force in Japan's economic growth

The labour force has contributed to the growth of the Japanese economy in a number of ways. First, it has supplied workers to meet the changing needs of industry in each successive era. However high the quality of a work force, it will not function properly unless it is able to satisfy the prevailing demand in each era. The post-war educational reforms led to the supply of low-cost, high-quality young workers. In addition, science and engineering education was expanded in line with Japan's industrialisation strategy, and the university admission rate also rose dramatically. When Japan experienced a shortage of low-cost younger workers after the oil crisis, the labour market supplied part-time workers. There has thus been a virtuous circle between the direction of economic development and rising educational standards, and changes in the shape of the labour force.

Second, the dual structure of the labour force between large companies and small-to-medium-sized companies has provided the flexibility needed to absorb the impact of economic shocks. Wage differentials based on company size are found in other countries and are not necessarily unique to Japan. In Japan, however, middle-ranked companies have functioned as divisions of large companies in terms of both production and costs through their role as subcontractors. This sharing of roles enabled Japanese manufacturers to respond flexibly to the oil and high-yen shocks through cost cutting and other measures. It also gave them an edge in process technology, particularly in such forms as the "design-in" system. The dual structure of the labour force and the strong links between the two structures were the keys to the potential of the Japanese labour force.

Third, the labour force has functioned well as an adjustment mechanism between supply and demand. For example, the labour share of the manufacturing sector has remained low at around 30%, enabling companies to retain a high level of internal reserves to be used for capital investment. The adjustment functions of the past, however, are now gradually starting to show signs of system fatigue. Lifetime employment, seniority-based wages and promotion, and other adjustment mechanisms have become less flexible with the decline in the economic growth rate since the oil crises owing to the institutionalisation of these systems themselves. Japan has yet to develop adjustment mechanisms to meet its needs in a low-growth period.

Fourth, company welfare systems were extremely important to workers because Japan's national social security system was not developed until the second half of 1970s. Company-based welfare systems were even supported by government policy. Moreover, since company-based welfare pensions, housing loans and other components of the welfare system were linked to years of continuous service, they made job-hopping disadvantageous to workers. They thus appear to have had the effect of improving labour productivity by fostering company loyalty and helping to bind workers to single companies for a lifetime.

When considering the future of the relationship between economic growth and the labour force, we need to focus on the major changes that are occurring in the role of labour. From the quantitative perspective, labour input is expected to decrease owing to the aging of the population, a declining birth rate and the reduction of total working hours. In qualitative terms, the standard of labour quality required in the domestic market will be much higher as a result of the overseas shift of manufacturing production bases and inflows of low-priced imported goods. Moreover, advances in such areas as computer technology are leading to changes in the qualitative requirements for white-collar workers. The key to economic growth in the future will therefore be the ability to improve the quality of the labour force and to secure workers capable of creativity and development-type activities. Neither companies nor workers have yet established systems to train human resources of this type.

6.2. Germany's Factors of Production: Labour

6.2.1. Overview of the labour market

During the five post-war decades, the German labour market has rarely been in equilibrium. The reconstruction period of the 1950s was characterised by both a tremendous inflow of workers from East Germany and a rapid employment increase. At the end of the 1950s, a fifteen-year period of buoyant growth was followed by significant labour shortages in almost all sectors of the economy. The "golden age" of the 1960s saw unemployment rates falling to very low levels—an experience which German workers had not had for more than half a century. The shock, however, came in the early 1970s. The breakdown of the Bretton Woods system of fixed exchange rates and the oil crises reversed the climate on the German labour market dramatically. In the course of two recessions—the first in 1973–75 and the second in 1979–82—unemployment rose to the levels of the early 1950s and decreased only slightly in the following boom periods. During the twenty-year period since 1975, neither employment policy nor the labour market itself was able to remove the growing labour surplus. German unification in 1990 brought an additional burden to the labour market. Restructuring of the economy of the new Länder made more than one third of jobs redundant.

Most interestingly, labour market institutions remained fairly unchanged in the face of the growing labour market imbalances during the post-war period. The scope of labour market regulation was extended by tariff agreements regulating not only wages but a broad range of contractual issues. This occurred independently of public authorities. Government regulation was extended as regards social security, employment and labour market policy. Finally, much of the labour market regulation was developed by the courts, including the European courts.

Increasing the density of labour regulations was an expression of the social market economy, as Ludwig Erhard called his economic approach. Putting the burden of social responsibility on the free marketeers was the basis of the social consensus between workers and entrepreneurs. Furthermore, it is regarded as the basis for rapid productivity growth, innovative activity and political stability. The German labour market model thus relies on stable and long-lasting labour contracts rather than short-term labour adjustments. Long-term efficiency of workers is preferred to short-term re-allocation of labour input. Flexible labour adjustment within firms is given priority over adjustments by way of the labour market. Investments in training and profit sharing are the necessary conditions of such a model.

The persistence of high unemployment, however, has exerted serious pressure on the specific German industrial relations approach. The negotiating partners are faced with decreasing rates of organisation on both sides. The thicket of labour market regulations appears to be an obstacle to flexible adjustment. The preference for further improvements in social security, which is already at a high level, is decreasing. The political debate, therefore, is concentrating on new room for manoeuvring, on new forms of employment, and on flexibility of the labour market in general. As there is a trade-off between flexibility and efficiency, a new optimal solution has still to be found.

6.2.2. Labour force

6.2.2.1. Population and labour participation

The growth of the labour supply was supported by both continuous population growth and slowly increasing average participation rates (Table 6.2-1). As far as population is concerned, 81 million people resided in Germany at the end of 1993, 12 million more than in 1950. The two parts of Germany, however, developed differently. The rapid decline of the population in East Germany—which led to the construction of the Berlin Wall in 1961—accounted for the major portion of population growth in the western part during the 1950s. Approximately 3 million people moved to the west during this time. In the 1960s and early 1970s, the stop of migration from east to west caused growing labour shortages in West Germany. New workers came from southern Europe. Between 1961 and 1993, 20 million foreigners immigrated to western Germany, 14 million of which returned to their home countries. The number of foreign residents increased from 690,000 to 6.7 million. Moreover, 2.6 million ethnic Germans living mainly in eastern European countries immigrated to Germany—many of them after 1985. Population growth was dominated by immigration whilst the number of German residents started to decline after the baby boom of the 1960s.

The slow increase of labour force participation from 46% in 1950 to 49% in 1993 indicates little of the significant change in employment behaviour. There were three major trends. First, the strong increase in female labour participation. The percentage of women in the labour force in the age brackets between 25 and 55 years is now 20% to 25%, higher than at the beginning of the 1960s. Close to 70% of women in this age group are gainfully employed. Second, participation rates of young people aged less than 25 have declined owing to increased participation in higher education and longer training periods. Third, fewer older

Table 6.2-1 Population and employment
(Germany)

Year	Population (million)	% share of population			
		Labour force	Employed	Unemployed	Inactive
1950	46.9	46.6	42.6	4.0	53.4
1960	55.4	47.8	47.3	0.5	52.2
1970	60.7	44.2	44.0	0.2	55.8
1980	61.6	45.4	44.0	1.4	54.6
1990	63.3	48.0	45.0	3.0	52.0
1991	80.0	49.0	45.6	3.3	51.0
1994	81.4	47.5	42.9	4.5	52.5

Note: 1950-90 West Germany, 1991-94 eastern and western Germany.

Source: Federal Statistical Office, Ifo Institute.

people are at work, given the more generous early-retirement schemes. In contrast to the West, labour participation of women in East Germany was traditionally high, and women are now being squeezed out of the labour market because of high unemployment.

The labour force in West Germany had two periods of rapid growth during the 1950s and in the second half of the 1970s. Of the total 40 million labour force, presently 32 million workers belong to the western German labour force and 8 million to the labour force of eastern Germany. Owing to lower immigration, future growth is expected to be much lower than during the last twenty years.

6.2.2.2. Education and vocational training

Traditionally, the German educational system has been based on general education (primary, secondary and tertiary education) and a dual system of vocational training. General education splits at the level of secondary education into various types of full-time education (*Gymnasium*, *Realschule*, *Hauptschule*) of which the *Gymnasium* leads to university education together with some other types of vocational colleges. The dual system is the combination of company-based training and part-time education in vocational schools. Full-time education is compulsory for nine years, part-time education in the dual system for an additional three years.

The structure of the German educational system has remained largely unchanged despite reforms of the secondary and tertiary education, and the dual system. Major changes, however, are discernible in education and training participation. The number of young students with university entrance qualifications rose from 11% in 1960 to 33% in 1993. Moreover, at all levels of general education and vocational training, a switch to longer and more sophisticated types of schooling can be seen. Female participation in education and training has increased considerably. Much of this was at the expense of apprenticeship training in the dual system. In 1991, 55% of the population held an apprenticeship degree, 9% a vocational college degree, and 9% a university degree. Twenty-seven percent of the population did not participate in vocational or professional training. The new Länder are characterised by an even higher share of people with vocational training.

Much of the increase in education and training participation can be explained by general societal trends which are characteristic of all industrialised countries. In addition, the deterioration of the labour market situation during the 1970s considerably promoted investment in education and training. Labour markets switched to demand-dominated markets during that time, and education and training became a key factor for the competition among workers for vacant positions. Beyond general education and vocational training, participation in continuing education increased significantly. The supply of skilled labour was able to satisfy demand in general. Moreover, companies made use of the increasing supply of skilled labour by adjusting labour organisation and squeezing out the less-trained workers.

6.2.3. Employment growth

After the creation of seven million new jobs during the 1950s, employment experienced a long period of slow growth in West Germany until the middle of the 1980s. The dynamics of the European single market and of German unification were then able to initiate a new phase of job creation until 1992. This was stopped by the recent recession. Available forecasts are reluctant to predict a further job growth period in the next five years.

6.2.3.1. Employment shifts amongst industrial sectors

West Germany has followed the general trend towards the service industries (Fig. 6.2-1), albeit much more slowly than other industrialised countries. Owing to the manufacturing traditions of the pre-war period, the technical experience and the broad dissemination of technical knowledge amongst workers, post-war Germany was able to regain rapidly its former competitiveness in manufacturing, particularly in the manufacturing of investment goods. Much of the employment growth during the 1950s is to be attributed to additional jobs in manufacturing industries. The move towards service-sector employment started in the early 1960s. However, it was not until the 1980s that the transition to a service economy gained full

Fig. 6.2-1 Trend in employment

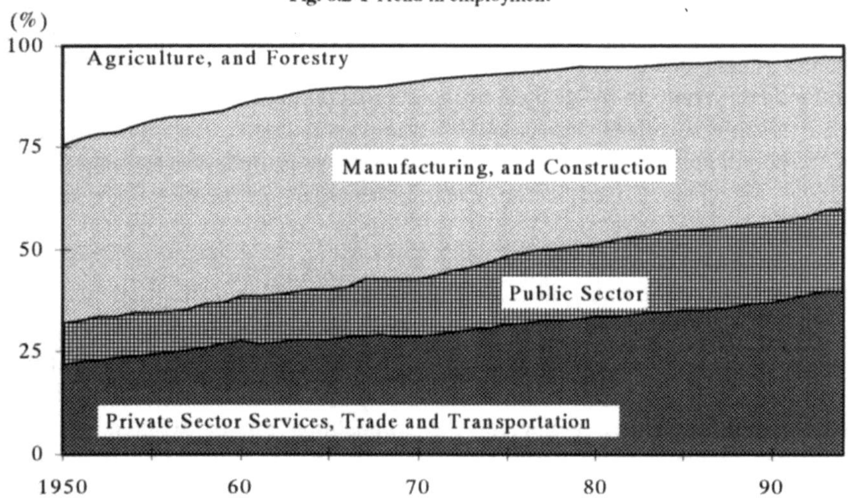

Source: Federal Statistical Office, Ifo Institute

momentum. This late development can be explained partially by the strong specialisation of the West German industry, its favourable competitiveness and its export-based strategy. This position was continuously jeopardised since the 1970s by continual exchange rate revaluation, new competitors on the world markets and high domestic wage levels. During the 1980s manufacturing companies, therefore, changed their strategies, e.g., by making production networks international and by outsourcing services. As a result, employment in manufacturing declined and service-sector employment was fostered. By 1993 the secondary sector (including manufacturing, construction and energy) accounted for 37% of total employment, market services for 40% and public services for an additional 20%. This has been a significant change since the early 1960s, when the secondary sector employed 48% and the tertiary sector as a whole 38%. The share of agricultural employment declined continuously from 14% in 1960 to 3% in 1993. Employment structures in the former GDR were characterised by high shares in agriculture and manufacturing and very low shares in services. After unification, employment patterns adjusted rapidly to western standards with a significant decline in agricultural and manufacturing and a shift towards market services.

6.2.3.2. Change in occupational structures

Among employed workers, the share of white-collar workers increased from 17% in 1950 to 46% in 1993. In contrast, blue-collar workers experienced a relative decline from 49% to 36% of total employment in the same period. This indicates a substantial shift in labour organisation and job content, which is more precisely reflected in the occupational structures of employment. Closely linked to the decline in manufacturing employment is the diminished importance of most production-oriented occupations, such as craft workers, plant and machinery operators, and unskilled jobs, whilst the proportion of administrative, service and professional occupations has increased. In addition to the sectoral shift in employment, there have been significant organisational changes within the sectors. Production-oriented activities were the major target of labour-saving techniques to increase productivity. Until recently, labour saving techniques were much easier for mass production of commodities than for services. The spread of information technologies, however, is presently altering this trend. Many administrative activities are now the main targets of rationalisation.

The shift of employment towards professional and service activities is nevertheless expected to continue. Relocation of production in manufacturing, which is now occurring on a world-wide scale, will further reduce blue-collar jobs. Specialisation in product development, marketing and distribution will foster professional activities.

6.2.3.3. Trends in self-employment

Until the end of the 1970s self-employment in West Germany followed a declining trend. The share of self-employed workers was halved from 16% to 8% in 1993. Even more pronounced was the decline in family workers from 15% to 1.5% in the same period. The major determinant of this decline was the reduction of employment in the agricultural sector. In addition, family workers changed their legal position by becoming employees with better access to social benefits. But the reduction in self-employment was also due to the concentration of enterprises in manufacturing and retail trade in particular. Many of the small manufacturing companies founded in the reconstruction period were absorbed by larger companies. Similar trends were evident in retail trade. During the 1980s, however, the compensating forces gathered sufficient momentum to change the trend. The dynamics of the private service sector opened new opportunities for small companies. The reorganisation of big companies into holdings of small firms contributed in a similar way. Since the beginning of the 1980s, therefore, the number of self-employed workers has increased slightly and is expected to continue in the future.

6.2.4. Labour market after World War II

6.2.4.1. Reconstruction period (1945–1960)

With the country destroyed, disorganised and burdened with the inefficiencies of a barter economy, it took some time for production and labour to achieve a higher level of productivity. During the initial post-war years, hidden unemployment was high and job motivation was low. The starting point of the recovery was the currency reform of 1948, which removed excess money supply and liberalised the majority of markets from administrative regulation.

Initially, the labour market situation was seriously burdened by the growing inflow of refugees from the former German territories. Unemployment rates shot up to more than 10% in West Germany. In the course of reconstruction, however, immigration contributed positively to the recovery. Immigrants did not only create a potential for market expansion but also contributed to a productivity increase with their high level of skills and industrial experience. Moreover, immigrants were highly mobile. The bottleneck for job creation was capital shortage, which was alleviated by repair work and reconstruction. The dynamics of the post-war investment cycle, however, came from growing markets, rising productivity and rising profits.

There was no interference in profits from wage increases. Owing to a very moderate trade-union wage policy, unit labour costs declined. Productivity increases were continuously underestimated in wage negotiations. The political power of trade unions was weak and the inferior economic situation was taken into consideration in the wage negotiations between trade unions and employers. Thus unemployment rates declined rapidly.

6.2.4.2. Labour shortage (1960–1973)

By 1960, the labour market situation switched from unemployment to labour shortages. With the exception of the recession in 1967, the number of vacancies exceeded the number of unemployed persons considerably. Now, growth was restrained by the lack of labour rather than the lack of capital. Immigration policy endeavoured to reduce the existing gap by attracting workers from southern Europe. This was all the more necessary as immigration from the GDR came to a halt with the construction of the Berlin Wall.

The inflow of foreign workers helped to maintain the specialisation of the German economy in manufacturing. Many of them filled the vacancies in industrial plants and in the construction sector. Domestic workers moved to services. Foreign workers took the unskilled and low-paid jobs whilst domestic workers were attracted by skilled activities. Thus the employment of foreigners became an integral part of the labour force.

During the 1960s, wage increases remained low and unit labour costs were stable. This contributed to profit growth and a considerable shift in the functional income distribution towards capital incomes. During the student revolt at the end of the 1960s, the desire for change became an issue of public debate, and workers started to fight for higher wages with illegal strikes in 1969. The period of wage moderation was replaced by a phase of aggressive wage policy. This coincided with the revaluation of the D-Mark.

6.2.4.3. Rising unemployment (1973–1993)

The world-wide recession following the oil-price shock and the contraction of profits created a radical change in the west German labour market. Labour demand was restricted and unemployment rose, bringing the previous years of employment expansion to an end. For several years after the 1974–75 recession, there was a debate as to whether the sharp rise of unemployment was owing to Keynesian easing of demand restriction or to the inflexibility of the labour market as regards wages and labour mobility. The persistence of unemployment during the 1970s and the cyclical shock at the beginning of the 1980s revealed that the German labour market system lacked the flexibility to cope with the unemployment problem.

Much of the political reaction to rising unemployment was concentrated on the reduction of labour supply. Restrictive immigration policy was used to limit the inflow of foreign workers. Early retirement schemes were developed to reduce unemployment amongst older workers. Education and training was promoted to improve the integration of young people. In the course of the 1980s, however, the positive effects of these measures on unemployment were more than compensated by a new wave of immigration from the east and by rising labour participation of women.

Wage policy reacted to rising unemployment by entering a new path of moderate negotiated settlements which even allowed for declining real wages in periods of recession. However, the scope of wage adjustments was not enough to reduce unemployment significantly. Trade unions concentrated on working time reductions to redistribute the limited amount of labour.

During the second half of the 1980s, employment increased considerably owing to the expansionary effects of the European single market and German unification. The unexpected rise in employment was stopped by the recession in the early 1990s, and future employment prospects for the second half of the 1990s remain limited.

6.2.5. Characteristics of the German labour market

6.2.5.1. Industrial relations: centralised wage negotiations and co-determination

There are no codified labour market laws in Germany. The Constitution, however, guarantees the free organisation of workers and employers. This includes the freedom to regulate wages and working contracts by tariff agreements. Only the basic framework for labour contracts, working hours, safety issues and co-determination (*Mitbestimmung*) is regulated by law. Similar to the Anglo-Saxon countries, a substantial part of legal regulation was developed by the courts.

Even if the workers' and employers' organisations only represent a portion of their constituency, their impact on labour contracts is dominant. The German system of wage negotiations is highly centralised and in practice results in a very narrow range of wage settlements.

One of the key features of the German labour market system is the co-determination which was regulated by law in 1951 (*Mitbestimmungsgesetz*) and 1952 (*Betriebsverfassungsgesetz*). These laws give the workers the right to be represented in the supervisory boards of large companies, to establish works councils in all companies, to receive regular information on the financial situation of the company, and to approve management decisions concerning personnel. In spite of continuous debates on these laws, co-determination has become an integral part of management practice and has significantly reduced the potential of internal conflicts between workers and employers.

6.2.5.2. Labour market flexibility: internal versus external adjustments

Given the density of labour market regulations, co-determination and the limited flexibility of wages, German companies were not able to follow an American style of hire and fire practices. They were forced to develop long-term strategies for their labour force, and they successfully took advantage of the opportunities included in such strategies. On the basis of long-term labour contracts, companies invested in human capital, avoided internal job demarcation in favour of flexible internal adjustments of job content, and rejected seniority rules. Flexibility was sought out internally rather than externally by high fluctuation rates of the staff.

Whilst such a strategy contributed to the efficiency of staff, its shortcomings became obvious in the face of rapid structural and technological change. The room for manoeuvring appeared limited in the face of the rapid devaluation of technical know-how and the volatility of market conditions. Reaction periods were too long to be at the forefront of technical progress in some key areas like information technology. Nevertheless, these technologies were successfully applied in the more traditional areas of German innovation.

There is a trade-off between short-term flexibility and long-term efficiency of the labour force. The selection of the long-term efficiency strategy by German companies was not only due to labour regulations but also to the profitability of such a strategy. Based on the skill level of the labour force, companies were able to approach more sophisticated, high-value-added markets which provided high profit rates. The income effects were positive. The major problem of this strategy was the limitation in volume of these high-value-added markets. The employment effects were much lower than the income effects. Moreover, this strategy is now coming under pressure from outside as an increasing number of countries are about to take the same approach. Thus the high-value-added markets will be seeing more competition.

6.2.5.3. Labour market policy: Social benefits and working-hour reductions

The price of the long-term efficiency strategy obviously was the exclusion of part of the labour force from the labour market. Employing only the best workers, companies did not provide a sufficient number of jobs for less-skilled, disabled or simply less-motivated workers. Furthermore, the demand for less-productive workers was limited by stable wage relations between skilled and unskilled labour.

The necessary political reaction to the exclusion was to strengthen the welfare net for the unemployed and to restrict labour supply. By financing social benefits through non-wage labour costs, a vicious circle was opened which increased labour costs in the course of rising unemployment and thus created further unemployment.

Another important area of adjustment to the limited amount of labour demand was working-hour reduction. By 1950 average weekly working hours were at the level of forty-eight hours. By 1980 a reduction to forty hours was achieved. During the 1980s the trade unions worked for further cuts with a major breakthrough in 1984. For the second half of the 1990s the thirty-five-hour week is the new target. While working-hour reductions rank high amongst the workers' preferences, they have helped little to solve the unemployment problem. Much of the reduction in working hours was compensated by increases in productivity instead of increases in employment.

6.3. Comparative Summary of Factors of Production: Labour

There are a number of interesting contrasts in the role of labour in Japan and Germany. These differences relate to such aspects as the labour market, employment systems and policies, and the characteristics of labour unions.

6.3.1. Labour market

The high-quality labour force made a major contribution to post-war economic development in both Japan and Germany. Japan's technical secondary school system and Germany's vocational education system both played a particularly important role in the growth of the manufacturing sector. However, there were significant contrasts between Japan and Germany in terms of the actual supply and demand of labour. Both countries possessed abundant supplies of labour during the immediate post-war reconstruction years. In the 1960s, however, Germany faced a labour shortage that eventually became a serious bottleneck to economic growth. After shifting into a slow-growth phase in the 1970s, it then found itself facing an enormous labour surplus. As a result, the unemployment rate has remained high since the beginning of the 1970s. Japan was supplied with the required amount of labour at each stage of economic development and rarely experienced economic bottlenecks resulting from labour crunches. Labour surpluses did not emerge until after the collapse of the bubble economy.

As a result, Japan's unemployment rate has remained extremely low by international standards. These divergent labour market patterns reflect differences in the pace of the economic growth, and in the change in industrial structures in the two countries. Following the oil-shock period, Japan registered real economic growth almost four times higher than the rate of growth in its labour force, and its service sector began to expand from the 1970s onwards. Germany's real economic growth rate reached only two times the pace of growth in its labour force, and there was only limited growth in its service sector. These contrasts between Japan and Germany have had a major impact on employment policies in both countries.

6.3.2. Employment systems

Both Japan and Germany have systems based on long-term employment. In Japan, lifetime employment became the norm because of the need to secure young workers at low wages. In Germany, the shift to long-term employment resulted from the reinforcement of labour regulations under a social market economy. In both countries, the efficient utilisation of labour under long-term employment systems became an important priority. Considerable emphasis was placed on in-house training and education, and long-term strategies emphasised the improvement of labour productivity. As a result, employment adjustment was made internally through the relocation of workers between work places and other means, rather than externally. Job-hopping became rare, and a system evolved under which most workers spent their entire working lives with the same company. Though Japan and Germany both have systems based on long-term employment, there are also clear differences between the two countries. Japanese employment practice is based on the regular hiring of new graduates as untrained workers. In Germany both labour and management have restricted the employment of untrained workers. This difference appears to be one of the reasons for the difference in the vitality of the German and Japanese economies. Another problem in the German labour market is the mobility of labour due to the high unemployment rate. There are lessons here for Japanese companies, which have been burdened with high levels of internal unemployment since the collapse of the bubble economy.

6.3.3. Labour unions

There are considerable differences in the systems under which labour unions operate in Japan and Germany. Labour unions in Japan are company based. Since work conditions at a given company are largely shaped by business performance, labour-management relations tend to be co-operative. However, only a small percentage of labour unions at the small-company level are organised. For that reason, working conditions vary widely between small and large companies, even within the same sectors of industry. In Germany, unions are organised in accordance with industry categories. Consequently, work conditions tend to be much the same for all workers in a given occupational field. What is more, German unions tend to have immense bargaining power because workers are able to participate in management through labour committees established by law. Yet despite these differences in systems, German unions are very similar to their Japanese counterparts in practice in the sense that they emphasise co-operative labour-management relationships rather than confrontation as a means of improving working conditions or ensuring job security. This approach to labour-management relations appears to have had a positive impact on economic growth.

6.3.4. Employment policies

Japanese employment policies have basically been tied to government measures to stimulate the economy. That is to say, the government has long sought to create jobs and boost wages through the use of fiscal programmes to stimulate demand. In Germany, the government has done nothing to stimulate demand, and employment policies have focused exclusively on the provision of unemployment compensation. There are also contrasts in company-based employment measures. Germany's anti-recession policy gave priority to securing jobs and sought to regulate the supply of labour through such measures as the reduction of working hours and the implementation of job-sharing arrangements. Though companies in Japan have also made efforts to trim working hours, chiefly through cuts in overtime, their objective was to achieve the same result in shorter work time to revive their earnings through the reduction of unit labour costs. Also, the "dual structure" of Japan's labour force is manifested in the fact that small-to-medium-sized companies have long served as a kind of safety valve by absorbing redundant workers from larger companies. Furthermore, efforts to reduce working hours in Japan have emphasised the alleviation of the problem of extreme overwork. This difference appears to reflect the fact that the expansion of demand is regarded as a natural trend in Japan, whilst in Germany downturns in demand are seen as a structural issue.

6.3.5. Conclusions

The first lesson that can be learned from the foregoing analysis is that shifts in the production structure ultimately demand adjustments in the employment structure. In the export arena, Japan and Germany are two of the most competitive countries in the world. Yet companies in both countries are shifting their production operations offshore under pressure from a global downtrend in prices and dramatic increases in the value of the yen and the Deutsche Mark. They also face restructuring in white-collar occupations owing to the information revolution. Both Japan and Germany will need to find ways to shift surplus labour from the domestic manufacturing sector and into the service industries. Though Japan's service sector is more developed at present than Germany's, there has been little deliberate effort or policy measures to expand employment in the service sector in order to take up the slack from manufacturing industries. Stable long-term employment, which in the past contributed to the success of both countries, has now become an obstacle to growth, and it will be necessary to develop employment structures that reflect present changes.

The second lesson is that careful consideration needs to be given to the suitability of employment policies. Given that employment problems are one of the deeper fundamental problems of both countries, the employment policies which are employed to overcome those problems should reflect the economic structure of the country concerned. The measures used to secure jobs need not be uniform. And as pointed out in the Ifo and SIR studies, long-term and short-term remedies are likely to differ in content. Labour is an important economic factor, and the performance of employment policies has a major impact on the economic system as a whole. Long-term approaches must be appropriate, and short-term measures must not be used as a substitute for long-term approaches.

7. Factors of Production: Technology

7.1. Japan's Factors of Production: Technology

7.1.1. Trends in Japanese technology

During the initial phase of the high-growth period, Japan relied heavily on technology imported from the West. As the Japanese economy began to grow, Japan gradually developed its own technology, particularly in the area of applied technology. However, the development was not uniform for all products, and while some Japanese technology progressively gained acceptance in world markets, there were also cases of technology developed from the outset to target world markets. In this chapter we will examine the structure and characteristics of technological development in Japan and the role that it has played in the growth of the Japanese economy.

7.1.1.1. Introduction of foreign technology

Japan's technological development in the post-war period was driven primarily by the introduction of foreign technology. This was partly because Japan's old facilities were almost entirely destroyed during World War II, with the result that it was easier to import advanced technology from other countries. The number of items of foreign technology introduced increased rapidly during the 1960s, reaching 2,007 in fiscal 1971 (Fig. 7.1-1). During the 1970s the figure hovered around the 2,000 level, but it began to increase again in the 1980s. The increase during the 1980s occurred, however, principally in the area of software for computers and other electrical and electronic products, and if software is excluded, the number of technology items actually introduced began to decline in the 1980s. This shows that whilst Japan has improved its technological competitiveness at the hardware level, it has lagged behind in the area of software.

7.1.1.2. Trade in technology

The international reputation of Japanese technology can be assessed to some extent from the balance of trade in technology (hereinafter referred to as the "balance of trade"). Japan has been a net importer of technology since fiscal 1970, when the balance of trade statistics first became available. The ratio of the value of

Fig. 7.1-1 Technology imported to Japan

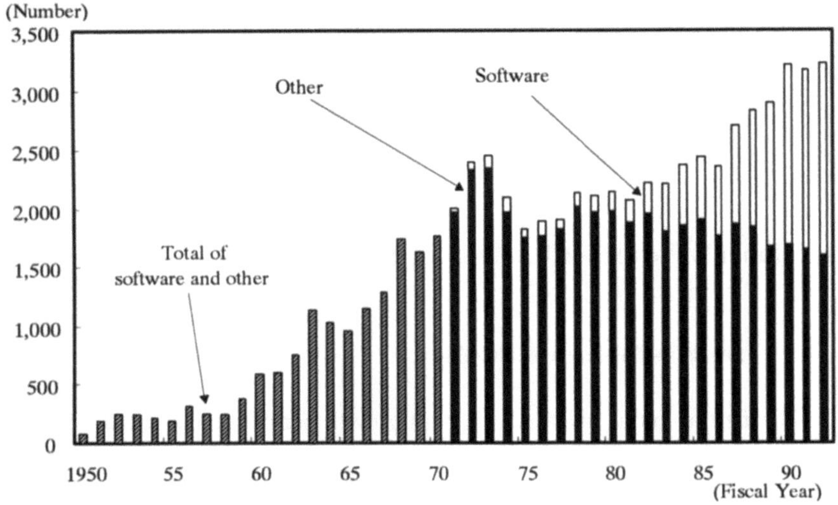

Note: The number before 1970 includes software.

Source: Agency of Science and Technology, Indicatiors of Science and Technology

exports to the value of imports[1] (hereinafter referred to as the "trade balance ratio") generally remained in the 0.2–0.3 range in the early 1970s. The ratio began to rise gradually in the late 1970s, primarily because of an increase in technology exports, but it has remained static at around 0.6 since the late 1980s. The analysis of the trade balance ratio[2] on an industry-by-industry basis shows that most industries were net importers in the early 1970s, but that the highly competitive iron and steel, general chemical and chemical textile industries began to achieve ratios in excess of 1.0 in the mid-1970s. In the 1980s the automobile and pharmaceutical industries also became net exporters of technology with trade balance ratios above 1.0. Between the late 1980s and the 1990s, the trade balance ratios of the automobile and iron and steel industries continued to rise, but that of the general chemical and pharmaceutical industries remained at around 1.0. The ratios for the telecommunications and electronic industries have remained at around 0.5 since the late 1980s. Trends in the balance of trade in technology have thus generally reflected the evolution of Japan's industrial structure. A survey of the regional distribution of the technology trade since the late 1970s shows that Asia and the West have been the markets for 40–50% of exports, whilst around 70% of imports have come from North America and 30% from Europe. As indicated by these

1 Adjusted trade balance ratio based on statistics compiled by the Management and Co-ordination Agency.

2 Unadjusted trade balance ratio based on statistics compiled by the Management and Co-ordination Agency.

figures, Europe and North America have remained net exporters to Japan. Overall, Japan is still a net importer of technology, and the main cause of the up-trend in its trade balance ratio is the expansion of net exports to Asia, with which Japan enjoys a comparative advantage in technology. It would be reasonable to conclude that Japanese technology is still not up to European and North American standards.

7.1.1.3. Gauging technology levels

(a) Number of researchers

In fiscal 1960 Japan had 1.5 researchers (0.9 company researchers, 0.6 university researchers) per 1,000 of population. Thereafter the number increased dramatically, particularly in science and engineering fields, reaching 2.8 (1.7 company researchers, 1.1 university researchers) in 1970, 4.6 (2.9 company researchers, 1.8 university researchers) in 1980, and 6.7 (4.6 company researchers, 2.1 university researchers) in 1990. A comparison with other advanced countries shows that Japan's ratio in 1980 was lower than that of the United States (6.0) but higher than those of Germany and France. It is estimated that Japan was virtually on a par with the United States by 1990.

(b) Number of patents

In 1970 21,400 patents were registered in Japan. The 1993 total was 3.6 times higher at 77,300. An analysis of trends in individual categories shows that chemistry, metallurgy, textiles, processing, control and transportation account for a large share of patents registered in Japan and that in recent years there has also been an increase in the share of those in physics. Japan's share of international patents in major countries reached approximately 20% in 1992, which is indicative of a gradual rise in the international standard of Japanese technology. In the 1980s Japan was the only major nation (excluding the United States) whose share of patents obtained in the United States was exceeded by its share of references to patents obtained in the United States. This also provides evidence of the rising international status of Japanese technology (Fig. 7.1-2).

(c) Size of private-sector R&D

In the 1970s, Japan's expenditure on research and development (including defence expenditure, hereinafter referred to as R&D expenditure) to GDP was similar to that of the United Kingdom and France at around 1.9%, but lower than those of the United States and Germany (Fig. 7.1-3). Japan rapidly overtook the western nations during the 1980s, and by 1992 its ratio was 3.0%, compared with 2.6% for the United States, 2.6% for Germany and 2.4% for France. The main cause of this up-trend in R&D spending was the growth of private-sector R&D expenditure. By the 1990s, Japan's expenditure in non-military areas was

Fig. 7.1-2 Relative indicator of patent in the US

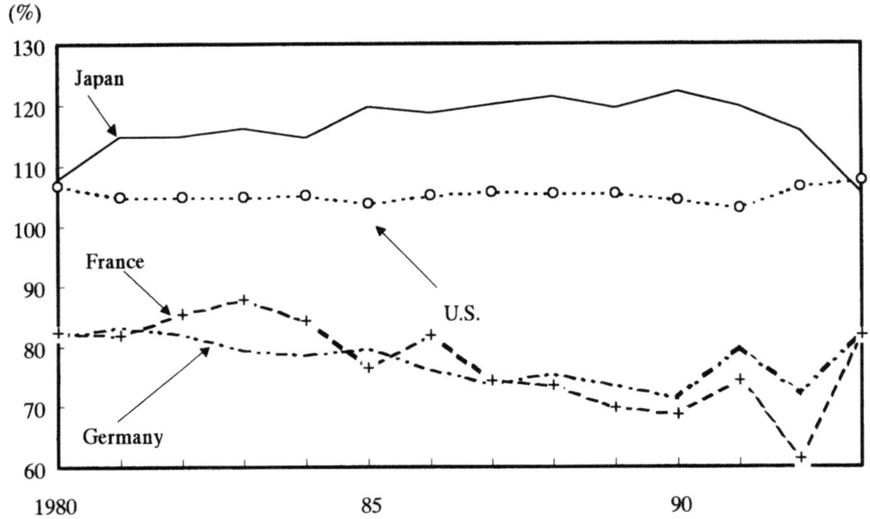

Note: Relative Indicator = Share of patent referred / Share of patent obtained
Source: Agency of Science and Technology, Indicators of Science and Technology

Fig. 7.1-3 Level of R&D expenditure by country

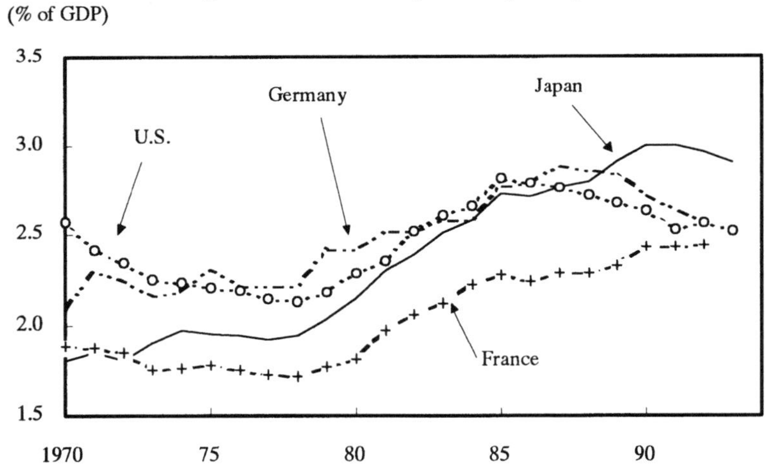

Source: Agency of Science and Technology, Indicators of Science and Technology

significantly higher than that of other countries as a ratio of GDP. Between fiscal 1970 and fiscal 1993, private-sector R&D expenditure by Japanese manufacturers increased 11.1 times. Expenditure by the chemical, iron and steel industries rose by factors of 8.9 and 7.8 respectively, compared with increases of 13.3 times and 13.7 times in the areas of electrical machinery and transportation equipment. These R&D expenditure figures reflect the shift in the centre of gravity of Japanese industry.

7.1.2. Technological progress

7.1.2.1. Post-war reconstruction period (1945–1954)

Japan's post-war technological progress started basically from the pre-war level. Prior to World War II, Japan had maintained a reasonable level of technology by international standards, particularly in military-related fields such as shipbuilding. However, during World War II, Japan's industrial capacity was increasingly devoted to military purposes with the result that it fell significantly behind other countries in technologies for non-military purposes and consumer goods. During the post-war reconstruction period, investment was concentrated in the heavy and chemical industries, but a shortage of funds hindered the importation of foreign technology, and this investment did not give any big influence to the development of technology.

7.1.2.2. High-growth period (1955–1972)

As the world entered the era of mass production and mass consumption, it became essential for Japan to import technology that would enable it to reduce costs and achieve merits of scale, such as the Ford system. Companies aggressively introduced the frontier technology from overseas whilst working to expand their production facilities and integrate their production processes. Japan's own technological standards began to rise gradually, owing to deliberate efforts to develop human resources in science and engineering fields. Home-grown technology was almost limited to enhancements, however, and Japan still relied on other countries for development-type technology. Even so, Japan was beginning to produce revolutionary applications from imported technology, such as the transistor. Meanwhile, the technological standards of small- and medium-sized companies were improving as manufacturers in the processing and assembly industries began to establish integrated parts supply systems with their subcontractors. This process laid the foundations for the subsequent evolution of the Japanese-style production development system.

7.1.2.3. Oil-crisis period (1973–1980)

The resources limitations imposed by the oil crises forced industry to review its mass-production technology and focus on energy-conservation technology. Japanese industry also began to demonstrate its superiority in the enhancement and application of technology in order to develop compact, lightweight, high-quality manufactured goods in keeping with the characteristics of the Japanese market. Japanese skill in the enhancement and application of technology also helped to improve competitiveness in processing technology.

7.1.2.4. Post–oil crisis (1981–1990)

Industry was forced to shift to small production runs of large product ranges in order to adapt to a global trend towards diversified market preferences. The impact of this change on Japan's technology mix was reflected in the application of advances in the technologies of information, telecommunications, and computers to the development of flexible manufacturing systems (FMS) based on computer numerically controlled (CNC) machine tools. Manufacturers further enhanced the competitiveness of their product development technology by introducing computer integrated manufacturing (CIM), which linked development and production directly to market trends.

7.1.2.5. Low-growth period (1991–)

After the collapse of the bubble economy, markets began to demand low-priced goods. Japan's technology mix, which has focused on the value added of manufactured goods since the 1980s, has not yet been adapted adequately to this shift.

7.1.3. Institutional factors behind Japan's technological development

7.1.3.1. The US market

The first reason for Japan's technological development was the existence of a vast and technologically advanced market in the United States. With the United States as its main export market, Japan was eager to acquire advanced technology, and its technology strategy was based primarily on the rapid commercialisation of advanced US technology. Since the 1980s, Japan has been particularly successful in acquiring and commercialising the latest US technology ahead of other countries. This has enabled Japan to achieve world leadership in high-technology industries.

7.1.3.2. Multiple leading manufacturers

The second factor was the existence of multiple leading manufacturers in each sector of industry. This situation spurred fierce competition to develop new technology. However, competition tended to produce applied product technology, such as additional functions or improved ease of use, rather than innovative technology.

7.1.3.3. Japan's technology policy

The third factor was government policy. During the high-growth period, the government provided a certain amount of protection for companies that imported foreign technology. It also limited imports of foreign manufactured goods. Companies that introduced new technology were thus able to achieve high profit ratios in Japan, enabling them to channel profit into such areas as applied technology. After the oil shocks, however, the influence of the government's technology policy gradually waned with the liberalisation of markets for manufactured goods and with the growth of outside competition. Financial assistance in such forms as R&D subsidies became more significant.

7.1.3.4. National enthusiasm for technology

The fourth factor is Japan's history as a technology-oriented nation owing to its lack of resources. Its enthusiasm for the absorption of Western technology was further strengthened by its entry into world markets as a latecomer to the capitalist world. In the pre-war period, this environment led to the development of original technology. As discussed below, however, Japan's technological development since World War II has focused primarily on applied technology.

7.1.4. Characteristics of Japanese technology

7.1.4.1. Development of multiple skills

In line with its industrialisation policy, post-war Japan deliberately developed human resources in science and engineering fields. In addition, Japanese companies trained production process workers with multiple skills by ensuring that each worker experienced multiple tasks and processes. This approach facilitated the rationalisation of production processes. Training in multiple skills also gave workers the ability to adapt flexibly to changes in production processes.

7.1.4.2. Subcontracting system

Japanese manufacturing industries are based on a pyramid structure of primary, secondary and tertiary subcontracting. This structure is not simply a system for supplying parts, and it is based on powerful links that extend to the integration of production processes and cost structures. The subcontracting system has enabled manufacturers to develop extremely flexible production processes. However, subcontractors have frequently paid the price for rationalisation and cost reduction due to their relative weakness.

7.1.4.3. Emphasis on applied technology

Development expenditure accounts for a large share of R&D spending in Japan. However, Japanese technology has been strongly market-oriented since the high-growth period, and the characteristics of the Japanese market are reflected in the priority that has been given to the development of compact, multifunctional products. This emphasis on applied technology proved extremely beneficial when market needs began to diversify in the 1980s. Some observers believe that Japan's overall technology mix is moving even further towards applied research in recent years.

7.1.4.4. Design-in system

Japanese-style technology-development systems are frequently based on the "design-in system", whereby parts manufacturers participate from the product planning stage. This method enables finished product manufacturers and parts manufacturers to absorb each other's technology, and end products are enhanced by the resulting concentration of technology.

7.1.5. Evaluating the role of technology in economic growth

The first role played by technology in Japan's economic growth relates to the destruction of outmoded facilities during World War II. This facilitated the introduction of advanced technology from overseas. In other words, the fact that only the software elements, such as technicians, survived meant that conditions were right for the establishment of a technology base for mass production in the high-growth period.

The second role of technology relates to the matching of technology developed in Japan's unique market environment to world market needs. Technological innovation in the post-war period was based on the new paradigm of an expanding market for consumer durables. There was explosive growth in the markets for durable goods, such as cars and electrical products. Japan also experienced dramatic growth in the market for consumer durables, owing to the rapid trend towards nuclear family living and company employment. However, the scope for the importation of foreign products was limited by the small size of Japanese housing and by income levels that were low by international standards. Manufacturers were also under pressure to produce high-quality goods because of a strong tendency on the part of Japanese consumers to demand products that were high in quality relative to their prices. For these reasons, Japanese manufacturing technology tended from the outset to be strongly market-oriented, and energy was channelled into applied technology and commercialisation technology. The technology used to produce Japanese-style goods matched an increasing demand in world markets for compact and high-quality products in the low-growth environment of the post–oil crisis period. However, it is important to recognise that a significant number of companies had always targeted world markets in their approaches to technology development. These companies have expanded their world markets in new fields since the 1980s.

The third role of technology was in the development of an extremely flexible production structure. The training of multi-skilled workers, the existence of the subcontracting system and technical linkage within and between companies and at the industry level all contributed to the establishment of systems that were able to respond flexibly to changes in market demand trends. These systems were not limited to advances in process technology, and in the 1980s they flourished as product-development technologies based on FMS and CIM. Japanese manufacturers achieved an overwhelming technological edge in such areas as numerically controlled (NC) machine tools and facsimiles.

The fourth role of technology relates to the exclusive emphasis of Japanese industry on those areas of non-military technology in which it excelled. It is important to recognise that Japanese technology was decisively inferior to that of the West in areas such as aviation and petroleum mining. In general, the existence of areas of inferiority has a limiting effect on economic growth. However, the expansion of free trade means that it is sometimes better from the perspective of growth to rely on transfers from other countries, such as through imports, in fields that involve vast development costs and in which one has a comparative technological disadvantage, as was the case in the aviation and oil-field development industries. In this sense, Japan's economic growth actually benefited from the stance of Japanese industry not to adopt a head-on approach to technology development in omni-directional fields, and from its overwhelming comparative disadvantage relative to Europe and North America in areas where Japanese industry did not excel.

The key factors influencing the future relationship between economic growth and technology are likely to be the extremely rapid pace of technology transfers and the rapid global trend towards technology standardisation. Japan no longer enjoys a monopoly over Japanese-style technology, including its production methods, owing to the transfer of production operations to other countries, coupled with dramatic changes in approaches to process technology as a result of the revolution in information and telecommunications technology. From this perspective, it becomes apparent that Japan will need to prepare for the next generation by aiming for a higher dimension of technology.

7.2. Germany's Factors of Production: Technology

Economic growth in industrialised countries is in essence the spread of a system of production based upon the increased application of science as an organised system of tested knowledge (Kuznets, 1968). The post-war period has seen this trend accelerated. Germany has succeeded in building a system of fundamental and applied research, e.g., Max-Planck and Fraunhofer institutes, which has influenced technological progress and industrial expansion by utilising to a remarkable extent the opportunities afforded by modern technological and social innovations.

7.2.1. Economic impact on German technology

7.2.1.1. Introduction of foreign technology and product-cycle trade

The United States was the world leader in introducing major innovations throughout the post-war period until the end of the 1960s. An OECD study credited the United States with 60% of the 110 significant innovations introduced into the world economy during the period 1945–68. The same study credited Germany with fourteen basic innovations (OECD, 1970). US companies enjoyed an absolute advantage in commercialising inventions in the 1950s and 1960s, operating in the world's largest and most affluent domestic market. Innovations were introduced at home; new products (and processes) were then exported to other countries. But these successful exports motivated manufacturers in other countries, notably in Germany and Japan, to acquire the necessary technology to produce the same or similar products. The result was that the trade advantage shifted from the United States to these countries, as postulated in the product-cycle theory of trade (Vernon, 1966).

Germany, backed by foreign investment of US enterprises, became an active importer of innovations originating in the United States and elsewhere, a fact clearly reflected in the net deficit position in technology trade. The royalties at the beginning of the 1960s, including payments for patents, licences and know-how, had a ratio of exports to imports of 0.3. The technological balance of payments shifted to about 0.5 in the mid 1970s. This rate was stable for Germany until the mid-1980s (OECD/DSTI Data Bank). However, with regard to the German figures one has to take into account the "hidden" profit-transfers of foreign enterprises to their parent companies, which seem to be not negligible but cannot be estimated. However, technology acquisition is not a mere act of borrowing; it requires a great deal of adaptive R&D and product, as well as production engineering. Hence, the massive importation of technology led to growth in domestic R&D.

7.2.1.2. Strong R&D orientation

Germany's R&D activities expanded very fast in comparison with other industrialised countries until the end of the 1970s. Emphasis on R&D and technology was a significant characteristic of the so-called economic miracle. An estimation of the rate of advance in technological knowledge on a comparative basis for several industrial countries was made by John W. Kendrick. His estimates, rough as they may be, demonstrate that Germany and Japan expanded the "real

R&D stocks" much faster than other major countries over the period 1960–79 (Kendrick, 1981).

World War II brought about a "wilful destruction" and not a "creative destruction" in the sense of J. A. Schumpeter (1947), providing Germany with the opportunity to build brand-new plants incorporating the latest industrial arts on a massive basis. The dismantling of plants even proved a blessing, because it led to an increase in Germany's productivity and power to compete (Wallich, 1955). After the war, Germany was immediately confronted with international price and technology competition. However, it became a substantial net exporter of merchandise, with trade surpluses larger than those of any other industrialised countries, particularly in recent years. Germany began a period of trade surplus in the early 1950s, whilst Japan did so in the early 1960s. The undervalued currency vis-à-vis the dollar also assisted a trade-triggered transfer of technology. Therefore, companies were able to develop price competitiveness quickly for their products manufactured with imported technologies, whilst US originators of new products were all the more induced to invest overseas or to license their technologies, because their overvalued currency penalised exports but subsidised the transfer of production overseas.

7.2.1.3. R&D and trade-surplus orientation

German manufactured products, notably capital goods, have traditionally been known as dependable, high-quality products, and trade prowess has been built on technological progress in export industries. This strong export orientation can be interpreted as a "modern version of mercantilism" (Schmitt, 1979; Vines, 1980). The profitability of overhead research-and-development expenditures increases as it is spread over a larger volume of output. Hence, protection in the domestic market alone is not adequate; to be efficient it must extend to export markets, and a trade surplus that increases incentives to invest in R&D at home will similarly offer more incentives to purchase advanced techniques and equipment developed overseas (Johnson, 1974).

7.2.1.4. Social and political impact on technology

(1) Post-war period until 1970

(a) Social tolerance of high-technology orientation and market concentration

Even after full employment with an unemployment rate of 0.7% in 1962, the trade unions exercised moderation in wage claims, whilst at the same time output went on rising much faster. The combined effect was a low rise in labour costs per unit of output, and hence a low rate of price increases. Thereafter, the trade unions came to regard annual increases in real wages of up to 8% as normal and began to be more ambitious in their claims (Hallett, 1973). A surplus needed for both the capitalisation of new industries and the finance of R&D was extracted from growth in labour productivity based on capital-intensive production plants with a high degree of mechanisation and automation.

The comprehensive reforms for democratisation introduced at the hands of the Allied Forces left the country in a state of extreme social flux. There was no strong vested interest group except the industrialists, who were assigned the task of restoring production so as to provide employment and economic security for their war-ravished nation, with all the necessary assistance from the government. On the whole, a monopolistic or oligopolistic pursuit of business interests was socially tolerated or even encouraged. Oligopolistic structures and high economic concentration became its key features with the re-emergence of large, powerful enterprises. The public, including labour unions, acquiesced in the pro-business orientation of their government.

The pro-business environment that existed was conducive to both the introduction of modern technology and the exploitation of scale economies. German entrepreneurs vied vigorously with each other in acquiring the best possible technology. It was altogether a relatively easy matter for German companies to adopt advanced technology, for their technological capacity, already high before the war, advanced further through wartime research and was ready to be mobilised again after the war. All that was needed was an economic incentive in the framework of competition. The German economic policy that gave free rein to private entrepreneurship created an ideal environment in which R&D-based industries could come into existence and flourish. In the mid-1960s, Germany exhibited a very high ratio of concentration; the top twenty enterprises alone accounted for more than 60% of R&D expenditures.

(b) Acquiescent trade unions and technological adaptability

In the early post-war years, some trade union leaders continued to advocate militant, anti-capitalist philosophies and sought to establish a fully state-controlled economy. But later the trade unions themselves came to accept the social market economy and paid more attention to satisfying the immediate needs of workers, such as the provision of housing. The country's strike-free record tends to underscore this (Vogl, 1973). The existence of industry-based trade unions allowed employers to reallocate their workers to different jobs within the firm (job rotation) "almost without union question" (Macrae, 1966). In addition, the widely practised apprentice system (on-the-job training) was focused on recruiting young people fresh from schools and training them as skilled employees. This practice represented an institutional innovation or social technology.

The introduction of capital-intensive modern technology entailed significant changes in production methods, skill requirements, pace of work, workshop organisations, and many other aspects of corporate production, invariably affecting workers' welfare. This impact multiplies when an assortment of advanced techniques are simultaneously adopted on a massive scale. So far as the 1950s and early 1960s are concerned, industry in Germany experienced relatively little resistance from labour unions against the adoption of new techniques.

In the late 1950s, fears of technological unemployment surfaced not only in Germany but also in other industrialised countries (Schelsky, 1957; Pollock, 1957; Buckingham, 1961). Empirical studies investigated the impact of technical progress on growth and employment (Ifo, 1962). Trade unions paid more attention to the ambivalence of new technologies for employment. On the one hand, productivity-oriented wage disputes were used as a rationalisation whip to increase payment of workers; on the other hand, rationalisation agreements were concluded to solve individual social problems of technologically redundant people. This strategy was seen as an adequate response to the positive and negative impact of technical progress on the labour market until the mid-1970s.

(2) Altered technological environment from the 1970s onwards

(a) Social and economic constraints

At the end of the 1960s social constraints emerged, increasingly restricting the free rein given to industrial expansion under the pro-business, growth-oriented policies of the government. A new era of group pluralism had arrived; labour unions grew militant, asserting their rights at the workplace. With a serious shortage of labour, a condition that led to an inflow of migrant workers numbering a couple of million throughout the 1960s, German workers became more demanding in their negotiations for higher wages, better fringe benefits and for their rights to participate in management (Scholz, 1981).

The industrialists' paradise was nearly lost in the early 1970s (Hallett, 1973). The government thereafter grew more interventionist in curbing the power of business and promoting labour unions' interest by legislating a series of new laws. These developments invariably imposed new constraints on, and interfered with, the pace of technological progress, for management now had to consult with labour representatives about the introduction of new machinery and production techniques.

In 1978 an unprecedented labour dispute was carried out by the unions in the mechanical engineering and printing sectors. The decrease of employment in these sectors was mainly explained by the "job-killing" effects of micro-electronics and data processing. Empirical investigations on the potential labour market impact of these new technologies for the 1980s were not able to identify positive growth and employment effects on balance, taking into account the general innovation conditions in Germany (Prognos, Mackintosh, 1979; Ifo, 1980).

There emerged one factor, however, that forced Germany to emphasise R&D in search of new technology: it was the need for industrial restructuring in order to meet both the challenge of competition from the newly industrialised countries (NICs) at home and in the export markets, and the imperative to reduce dependency on overseas energy resources (Scholz, 1977). Developing countries were eagerly looking for industrial technology on both commercial and official-aid bases. This kind of demand could only be met if the industrialised countries upgraded their overall industrial structure by discarding low-value-added, labour-intensive manufacturing sectors (Scholz, 1982). This called for a creation of new technology-intensive industries into which the resources released from the shrinking sectors could be absorbed.

(b) Governmental framework for R&D efforts

In the first two decades of the post-war period, the German government funded research through the Ministries of Education and Science in general; the technological development of nuclear power was promoted by a special ministry in the 1950s and 1960s. In the 1970s, the government became more determined than ever to assist directly technological progress in the private sector. It abandoned its hands-off policy and grew increasingly pro-interventionist. The Federal Ministry for Research and Technology (BMFT) was created in 1972. It restructured the direct funding of private R&D activities with regard to small- and medium-sized enterprises in the mid-1970s. It is thus interesting to note that the creation and growth of new industries were assisted by the active involvement of the BMFT in R&D, whereas upgrading of existing old industries was managed by the Ministry of Economics.

In the 1970s science and technology policy was decentralised to a significant extent at the regional level. Governments of the Länder allocated a larger sum of money to promote science and technology than did the federal government (Bund). The Länder have traditionally been highly supportive of research at universities, a fact well reflected in a very high ratio of basic research in Germany's total research efforts: in 1977, for example, basic research accounted for 22.3% of total research efforts in Germany, 12.7% in the US, and 16.2% in Japan (Japanese Science and Technology Agency, 1981).

(c) Orientation of public R&D funds

The rationale for the shift of R&D policies in the 1970s towards interventionism was the economy's confrontation with competition and labour market problems, the oil-price shock and rising social needs. It was politically accepted that the search for new technologies on the part of the private sector alone was not sufficient. In a new age of uncertainties, business profits seemed to be so unpredictable that the firms' financial strength and willingness to undertake new ventures were hampered. These arguments have in the past been frequently used in calling for an intervention by government in the areas of research and technology, but they were now finally accepted as relevant arguments in view of the appearance of serious structural problems confronting the German economy (Scholz, 1977)

The R&D promotion of the German government was strongly oriented towards a strategy of structural change. This goal was a logical choice in view of Vernon's product-cycle theory of trade. It took into account the changes taking place in the structure of the international division of labour, changes brought about primarily by the export-oriented development of NICs, but also by Japan's rise to industrial power. However, in contrast to Japan, the industrial targeting policy that was the driving force in Germany was not an active or vision-oriented one. It was more reactive with regard to current and expected structural problems. An industrial policy, targeting a long-term orientation of economic and social needs, did not seem to be in line with a liberal market system. Although the German Minister for Research and Technology was promoting R&D-based new technologies which could help to restructure the economy, the (liberal) Minister of Economics did not change the innovation conditions in general.

In the late 1970s, the budget of governmental R&D funding was DM 9.1 billion. The uses of technology-promotion expenditures displayed the following structure (BMFT, 1980):

- Securing of energy and raw materials supplies, mainly basic nuclear research	23.3%
- Maintenance of external security, mainly military research	18.9%
- General research promotion and basic research	16.5%
- Transport and traffic technologies	7.5%
- Space research and technology	7.1%
- Electronics and other key technologies	6.0%
- Information technologies and technical communication systems	5.0%
- Environmental engineering	5.3%
- Others	10.4%

R&D programmes targeting higher efficiency and competitiveness comprise about 40%. However, most of them were linked to national infrastructural needs, e.g., energy and telecommunication systems. A direct R&D support of enterprises was only significant in these industry sectors.

In the 1980s the German government proclaimed and followed a more market-oriented research and technology policy, pronouncing the principle of subsidiarity as an important general guideline. On the one hand, this was a necessary condition with regard to the Commission of the European Communities, which had to agree on each programme of member countries linked to private R&D activities. The Commission wanted to prevent R&D funding from being used as a national instrument stimulating unfair competition. On the other hand, a broad spectrum of programmes was developed by the European Commission itself, promoting co-operative R&D projects of European companies.

German unification made it necessary to restructure fundamentally the R&D landscape of the former GDR. In 1994 the Ministry of Research and Technology (BMFT) and the Ministry of Education and Science were (re)integrated. This step was politically justified by the need for a new orientation of science and technology in the future.

Already in the past, the BMFT had promoted the technology-transfer process between know-how producers in science and research and above all small-to-medium-sized enterprises.

For many years there has also been a broad spectrum of technology transfer institutions at the universities, other R&D institutes and at the regional level. Thus, no real institutional gap exists between know-how producers and potential users. However, the question whether the R&D orientation at universities and publicly financed institutes really fits the needs of enterprises remains unanswered. It is still unclear whether this will lead to a new orientation in the German R&D landscape in the future. Taking into account the ongoing controversial discussion on industrial policy and targeting innovation, one cannot see that there will be any important initiatives to change the innovation conditions in Germany in general (Scholz, 1995).

7.2.2. Industrial R&D and innovation activities

7.2.2.1. Importance of R&D policy and innovation regulation

Technological innovations do not only need R&D, but also activities in engineering, design, patents, licences, production, and market preparation. These innovation activities are the conceptual framework of the Ifo Innovation Survey which was introduced in 1979 on an annual basis. For German industries, R&D accounts for about one-third of all innovation expenditures on average. About 90% of all industry-related R&D expenditures are financed by the companies themselves. Therefore, governmental funding probably did not have an important economic impact on the direction of technological development in Germany in general. However, where there are political interventions and regulations affecting technological developments that stimulate innovation processes, their impact cannot be overlooked.

Already in the 1960s, German enterprises in the mechanical engineering industries developed highly mechanised and automated production systems, e.g., industrial robots. However, at this time their use in production was economically inefficient in view of the availability of relatively cheap and qualified foreign workers. Later on, the innovation and diffusion of such technologies were hindered by labour union intervention, the unions arguing that these would intensify unemployment problems. Politically, the BMFT promoted production technologies aimed at the "humanisation of labour impacts" and ran into controversy with labour unions because of these technologies' "rationalisation impacts". However, in the 1980s German enterprises such as those in the automobile industry were forced to introduce industrial robots, NC machinery and highly automated flexible production systems to be internationally competitive.

Another example is the technological development in electronics and telecommunications. The micro-processor was seen as a "job killer" in the 1970s by labour unions. Political conflicts, intensified by the results of controversial findings of technology assessment studies, can now be identified as important innovation barriers in telecommunications, e.g., for the Deutsche Bundespost, with negative repercussions for the German electronics industries in general. Although the BMFT promoted research and development also in other infrastructural sectors, such as nuclear power and new traffic systems, German enterprises were, and are now, heavily confronted with technology acceptance problems by the public.

7.2.2.2. Innovation strategies

R&D which does not have a medium- or long-term impact on technological innovations on the market is unsupportable from an economic viewpoint. German enterprises in general follow this rule. Technological progress has been achieved in a highly competitive environment: fierce competition amongst domestic firms and relentless international competition. Although the government was increasingly involved in promoting R&D to open up new technological frontiers, it was the private enterprises that vigorously stepped up technological efforts to remain competitive in their markets.

Overall trends like global technology and the globalisation of markets were actively emulated by German enterprises. With regard to the impact of technological innovation on international trade patterns, there was a strong structural shift in the post-war period. A comparison of the exports of technology-intensive manufacturers with total exports in OECD countries between 1966 and 1983 reveals that the share dropped from 27% to 25% in the US, from 17% to 15% in Germany, whilst it increased from 8% to 19% in Japan (Kelly, 1977; Sachverständigenrat, 1984). These figures also demonstrate the strength of Japanese companies in entering the world market in the field of high technologies. The high-tech landscape has become a very complex one with respect to multi-disciplinary R&D activities and international co-operation. Multi-national companies have used their patent and know-how basis to build strategic alliances, e.g., in the field of micro-electronics. The development of new generations of components and information systems has become so R&D intensive and their innovation costs are so high that even a powerful single firm cannot afford them in view of the risks of new innovation systems.

It is unclear whether the politicisation of innovation activities of private companies really has had a negative impact on technological development in Germany. In all industrialised countries, there is a growing awareness of the environmental and social impact of new technologies. The non-acceptability of technological innovations by political parties and part of the public could be interpreted as a reaction against the social implications of these innovations and the search for alternatives. This view is in line with historical experience: important technological innovations have always been closely linked with social innovations. In summary, the political management of R&D and technology in Germany has been carried out not so much with a narrow focus on the science and technology policy as such, but rather as part and parcel of the overall industrial policy to create a macro-economic environment conducive to technological progress. That is what J.A. Schumpeter described in 1947 as conditions for "creative destruction".

7.2.2.3. Innovation conditions in the 1990s

The question of whether technical progress will be able to solve problems with respect to the labour market and social needs must also be addressed (Scholz, Wolff, 1981). Whether it will be possible to compensate for the labour-saving influence of technological and social innovation is still an open question (Matzner, Wagner, 1990). Currently, environmental problems that already exist or that may have a negative impact in the future are highly important in influencing the development of technology in Germany. But the controversial discussion of these problems in Germany should not be given more weight than is due. The standing of Germany in world-wide technology competition is not as poor as followers of this discussion may assume. The high level of exports and the appreciation of the D-Mark against the dollar are economic indicators which show that German industries are producing goods with a strong world-wide demand.

With regard to the 1990s, it must be taken into account that after the unification of Germany the post-war experience has been used to consolidate, restructure and modernise the former GDR without an international fund like that of the Marshall Plan after World War II. In this respect, the German economy had and has to solve problems which the US and Japanese economies are not confronted with. However, there is an innovation potential in the eastern part of Germany with a broad promise for the future. The growing competition with low-wage countries in central Europe will have structural effects on the German economy as a whole, which cannot be solved without an innovation strategy based on new technological opportunities in the future.

7.3. Comparative Summary of Factors of Production: Technology

Several key factors must be taken into account when comparing Japanese and German technology. These include technology imports in the pre-war and post-war eras, the relationship between technology and employment, the scientific and technological strategies of companies, and the government's science and technology policy.

7.3.1. Pre-war technology levels and post-war technology imports

Both Japan and Germany boasted high standards of technology before the war. In both countries, the industries that were to become the core of post-war economic development enjoyed considerable international competitiveness before the war. In this sense, technological development before and after the war was not a discontinuous process. Yet it was the introduction of the then most advanced level of sophistication of a developing technology from the United States that enabled post-war technological development to proceed in both Japan and Germany. Though both nations possessed outstanding technology before the war, it would have been difficult for them to press ahead with technological development in the post-war period without the large-scale importation of technology. Of particular interest is the fact that both Japan and Germany emerged from the war with the basic structure for the acceptance and development of imported technology still in place. This was because the war did little damage to key industries, such as iron and steel, with the result that the infrastructure for technological development was to some extent still intact, and because engineers returned home from the war.

7.3.2. Relationship between technology and employment

The relationship between the introduction of new technology and employment in Japan contrasts sharply with that in Germany. In Germany there was strong apprehension that the introduction of new technology would reduce employment opportunities. For this reason, labour unions were tolerant of the introduction of new technology during the high-growth period but resisted it from the low-growth period onwards. In Japan, on the other hand, the introduction of new technology was viewed as a requisite for reinforcing corporate competitiveness in a fiercely competitive domestic market. This perception gap reflects the difference between Germany's industry-based labour unions and Japan's enterprise unions. In Japan, resistance to the introduction of new technology was also mitigated by the dual assumption that markets would continue to expand and by the fact that employment was guaranteed to some extent under the lifetime employment system. In both Japan and Germany, the actual introduction of new technology was accompanied not by the wholesale replacement of work forces but rather by in-house re-deployment and the improvement of technical abilities through on-the-job training.

7.3.3. Scientific and technological strategies in the business sector

In both Japan and Germany, R&D expenditure accounts for a large portion of technology-related expenditure. This has been the driving force behind the advancement of technology in both countries. In Japan, however, R&D expenditure has been channelled primarily into applied research, whilst in Germany spending has focused on basic research. This difference enabled Japanese products to make inroads into a wide range of markets between the 1960s and 1980s, a period characterised by the expansion of world markets for durable consumer goods and the diversification of consumer preferences. During the same period, German products displayed tremendous competitiveness in specific areas, such as chemical products and automobiles. Conversely, it has now become apparent that once market scale reaches a certain level, it becomes difficult to develop the technology for a new generation of products under a system geared to applied technology, as is the case in Japan. This situation is indicative of differences in approaches to technology in the two countries. Japan has expected technology to play the dual roles of product advancement and the creation of new markets (rather than new technology), and has sought to succeed in both areas whilst Germany has tended to specialise in product advancement.

7.3.4. Government science and technology policies

The Japanese government announced at an early stage in Japan's economic development that it intended to promote science and technology. However, this policy focused primarily on basic research, whilst applied research, the forte of Japan's manufacturing sector, was pursued mainly by private corporations. Setting aside the question of whether the government's science and technology policy contributed to growth, the policy clearly provided a future vision for technology. In Germany, science and technology policy did not begin to play a significant role until the 1970s. It appears that support for science and technology has taken more concrete forms than in Japan, including the provision of subsidies by state governments. Although the concern of lagging behind in high-tech fields is apparent, the German government's technology policy seems to have failed to provide a new paradigm for technology in private sector.

7.3.5. Conclusions

Technology has played a positive role as a driving force for economic growth in both Japan and Germany. However, there are sharp contrasts in the direction of technological development in the two countries. In Japan there has been an increasing emphasis on market-oriented technology, especially applied technology. Although this approach has not been successful on all fronts, it has helped to raise levels of technology in many product areas. Moreover, Japanese workers are keenly aware that the development of technology is indispensable in a fiercely competitive market environment. Yet Japan has lagged far behind other countries in the development of basic technology. In contrast, Germany has excelled in basic technology and become extremely competitive in specific areas such as the chemical industry. There has been a strong tendency amongst workers to view new technology as a threat to job opportunities, however, and this apprehension has hindered the development of high-tech and leading-edge technology.

The lesson that can be learned from this analysis is that the direction of technological development is not unrelated to market trends, and that proper attention must be paid to the relationship between technology and other production factors such as labour. In view of the fact that R&D expenditure targeted towards next-generation products is expected to balloon in the future, both Japan and Germany will need to achieve a proper understanding of the positioning of their industries and discover directions for technological development that reflect that positioning.

Part III

Economic and Social Policies and Corporate Systems

8. Fiscal and Monetary Policies

8.1. Japan's Fiscal and Monetary Policies

8.1.1. Definitions of fiscal and monetary policies

The four ultimate objectives of macro-economic policy based on fiscal and monetary policies are (1) economic growth, (2) the securing of employment, (3) price stability and (4) the equilibrium of international balance of payments. The balanced attainment of these goals enables a country to achieve sustained economic development. Under a market economy, the distribution of funds through the economy as a whole is essentially left to the financial and capital markets. However, in order to maintain stable macro-economic conditions, the government must play a role that complements market mechanisms. For this reason, the boundary between the public and private sectors has continually shifted in accordance with the level of economic development and the internal and external economic environment.

In this context, monetary policy is defined as the control that the Bank of Japan exerts over interest rates and the money supply. Through monetary policy, it is possible to implement short-term economic adjustments, whilst ensuring the appropriate growth of the money supply and maintaining the stability of the currency and credit systems. Fiscal policy has three roles. First, it is used to make economic adjustments based on the government's judgement. Second, it is used to distribute resources to the public sector, such as through the development of social capital. And third, it is used to redistribute income through the tax system, subsidise, etc.

8.1.2. Evolution of Japan's fiscal and monetary policies

8.1.2.1. Post-war reconstruction period (1945-1954)

(a) Post-war reconstruction policies

During the post-war reconstruction period, fiscal policy played a major role in rebuilding the Japanese economy from the destruction left at the end of World War II. In 1947, the government moved to alleviate production bottlenecks by introducing the "Priority Production System", under which resources were allocated on a priority basis, primarily to the coal and iron and steel industries. The price-differential subsidy system and the Reconstruction Finance Bank were important policy tools for the implementation of this system.

Under the price-differential subsidy system, the government held down the prices of basic commodities, such as iron and steel, coal and ammonium sulphate, by setting official prices. Price-differential subsidies were paid by the government to offset the difference between these prices and production costs. However, the prices of basic commodities in this period were 30-40% above the official prices, which meant that the cost of price adjustment was enormous. The Reconstruction Finance Bank, which was established in 1947, provided finance to key industries, such as iron and steel, coal, electricity and fertiliser, for their equipment. It was funded from government investment funds and government-guaranteed bond issues by the Reconstruction Finance Bank underwritten by the Bank of Japan.

However, the fiscal deficit widened as a result of the government's positive fiscal policy. In addition, shortages caused by the post-war confusion and the high level of the money supply, owing to massive government bond issues implemented to raise war funds, led to a plunge into hyperinflation.

(b) Dodge Line and recovery to pre-war economic levels

In 1949 the United States sent to Japan J.M. Dodge, who rebuilt the fiscal system and implemented a balanced budget with surplus. Under the Dodge Line, price-differential subsidies and other types of subsidies were drastically reduced, and new lending by the Reconstruction Finance Bank was effectively halted. Inflation subsided rapidly as a result of these measures, but the reaction caused an increasingly serious deflationary shift. On the revenue side, the framework of the Japanese tax system was established in 1949 under the Shoup recommendations. The system was based on the direct-taxation system, centreing on income and corporation tax, and it has continued to form the basis for the present Japanese taxation system.

It was the special demand generated by the Korean War that brought the economy out of the recession triggered by Dodge's deflationary measures. However, in 1951 the domestic economic situation again began to deteriorate as a result of the armistice in the Korean War and a global economic recession. The government responded to this situation by shifting from a stance of totally balancing revenue and expenditure to one that gave priority to economic expansion. In the area of fiscal loans and investment, the government sought to diversify channels for the supply of funds and increase the amount of funds available through measures that included the establishment of the Japan Development Bank in 1951, which was to take over the role of the Reconstruction Finance Bank.

8.1.2.2. High-growth period (1955-1972)

(a) Fiscal policy

Fiscal expenditure expanded during the first half of the high-growth period, particularly in the areas of public works and social security (Fig. 8.1-1). Fiscal investment and loan plans showed double-digit annual increases and contributed to the development of industrial infrastructure through government-affiliated financial institutions such as the Japan Development Bank. This expansionary trend in expenditure was accompanied by annual reductions in income taxes and by the implementation of special tax measures to encourage capital investment. However, the impact of these policies on fiscal resources was offset by the expansion of tax revenue due to high economic growth, and the government was thus able to maintain the balanced-budget principle in its fiscal policy.

During the second half of the high-growth period, the government switched to a Keynesian stance of discretionary fiscal policy in response to the 1965 recession. In order to bridge a revenue shortfall, "deficit-covering bonds" worth ¥260 billion were issued in fiscal 1965 under special fiscal legislation. In the following year, "construction bonds" were issued under a provision to Article 4 of the Fiscal Policy Law. From that time onwards, fiscal policy would remain dependent on government bonds. However, the level of dependence remained at around 10% from the late 1960s until the early 1970s, thanks to the relatively steep growth in tax revenue owing to high economic growth. As in the 1950s, Japan was able to maintain a "small government" situation.

Fiscal policy in the second half of the high-growth period was characterised by an increasingly corrective role, including the rectification of growth-related distortions as well as the improvement of social welfare systems. Funds were distributed to agriculture and small-to-medium-sized business through subsidies

Fig. 8.1-1 Increase in general accounts, and fiscal investment and loan plans

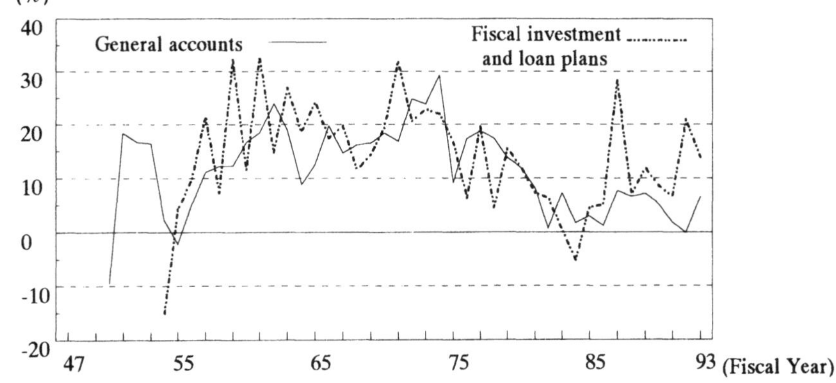

Source: MOF, Financial Statistics

and to backward areas through local government tax allocations. The government thus made active use of the income-redistribution functions of fiscal policy.

Participants in the Smithsonian Conference of December 1971 agreed to a reduction in dollar parity values, and the value of the yen was set at 308 to the dollar. The government responded to the recession caused by this rise in the value of the yen by easing its monetary policy. However, this triggered excessive liquidity and failed to bring about an economic recovery. The government then turned to aggressive fiscal measures based on the use of government bond issues. This caused a rapid increase in fiscal expenditure and dependence on government bonds, as well as triggering inflation. As a result, the real GNP growth rate for 1971 was just 4.3%, equivalent to about one-half of the levels recorded during the high-growth period.

(b) Monetary policy

Like fiscal policy, monetary policy during the high-growth period also gave priority to economic growth. During this period, the so-called "stop-and-go policy" was adopted, and the monetary policy was conducted with a yardstick set at the level of international balance of payments, or more specifically, the level of foreign-exchange reserves. Whilst this policy measure was reflected in a consistently low rate of increase in wholesale prices, the economic growth rate and the rate of increase in consumer prices fluctuated widely from year to year. Nonetheless, this approach enabled Japan to achieve a high rate of economic growth of about 10% on average (Fig. 8.1-2).

Fig. 8.1-2 Increase in commodity prices

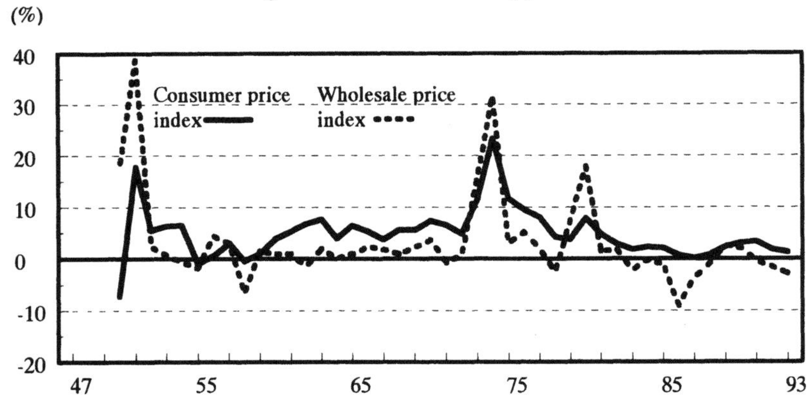

Note: 1951-1988, at market prices in 1985
1989-1993, at market prices in 1990
Source: BOJ, Price Indexes Annual; Management and Co-ordination Agency, Annual Report on the Consumer Price Index

One of the monetary policies employed during the high-growth period was the maintenance of "artificially low interest rates". The policy was implemented through an interest-rate structure under which a ceiling was imposed on deposit rates through the establishment of Bank of Japan guidelines within the scope of the Temporary Interest Rates Adjustment Law and the lending rates set autonomously by the banking industry. An artificially low interest rate is one that is lower than the level that would probably be set by the market in response to supply and demand. The low cost of capital in this period meant that companies were able to invest aggressively in plant and equipment. Since the regulated interest-rate system caused the demand for funds to exceed supply, it also became a policy mechanism for rationing credit to exporting industries and key industries that made a high contribution to growth, such as iron and steel and petrochemicals. In addition, it was used to protect financial institutions with weak credit capacity through the use of regulated interest rates to secure interest spreads.

Day-to-day financial adjustments were effected through the lending policy of the Bank of Japan. In addition, "window guidance" was frequently used to control the growth of lending by individual private-sector banks.

In order to supplement private-sector banks, government-affiliated financial institutions, such as the Japan Development Bank and the Export-Import Bank of Japan, supplied funds on a prioritised basis to industries that were important to economic growth, whilst loans to other sectors were provided by specialised monetary institutions, such as the Small Business Finance Corporation, with a view to achieving balanced economic growth.

The effective functioning of these monetary policies was attributable to the fact that the financial system during the high-growth period was based on indirect financing. An analysis of sources of funds during this period shows that corporate internal reserves were low, whilst the savings of individuals, who were the suppliers of funds, were small and scattered. In addition, the securities market was not functioning adequately. As a result, there was a shortage of funds to meet a burgeoning demand. Yet the efficient supply of the low-interest funds needed for large-scale capital investment in heavy and chemical industries was vital to economic development. An indirect financing system based primarily on banks appears to have been the most effective approach to the efficient allocation of funds as the unbalanced financial structure lacked balance between demand for and supply of funds.

8.1.2.3. Oil-shock period (1973-1984)

(a) Fiscal policy

After the first oil shock, fiscal policy in the 1973-75 period was characterised by the curbing of growth in public-works expenditure as a counter-measure against inflation. However, the government continued to expand social security spending, with the result that there was continued growth in fiscal expenditure. Since Japan's social security system was based on the premise of high economic growth, this increased expenditure was reflected in an expanding fiscal deficit when the economic growth rate decelerated after the oil shock.

It became clear that the economy would not return to the expansionary performance of earlier years after the first oil shock, owing to a vicious circle of surplus savings and inadequate investment. The government responded by implementing an aggressive fiscal policy based on supplementary budgets funded by bond issues between fiscal 1975 and fiscal 1979. As a result, the real economic growth rate remained at around 5%, whilst dependence on bonds soared to 34.7% in fiscal 1979, creating the biggest-ever fiscal deficit in Japan's history (Fig. 8.1-3).

The fiscal crisis was further exacerbated by pressure on Japan to adopt an aggressive fiscal-management stance, since Japan was registering a current account surplus at a time of global economic recession. During the Bonn Summit of 1977, Japan and Germany came under particularly intense pressure to act as "locomotives" to pull the world economy out of recession. Japan responded by adopting an aggressive fiscal-management stance based on deficit-covering bond issues.

In 1981 the government set a target of "fiscal reconstruction without tax increases". The government sought to realise this goal through administrative reforms based primarily on the privatisation of the National Railways Corporation (JNR) and Nippon Telegraph and Telephone Public Corporation (NTT), and through fiscal reconstruction based on the so-called "ceiling system" and "hidden borrowing".

The ceiling system is a method for curbing expenditure growth by setting specific ceilings based on percentages of the previous year's allocation for individual ministries and agencies at the budget compilation stage. In fiscal 1982 a zero ceiling was applied, allowing no increase in expenditure, and between fiscal 1984 and 1987 minus ceiling was adopted. Hidden borrowing is a method of

Fig. 8.1-3 Rate of reliance on bond issues

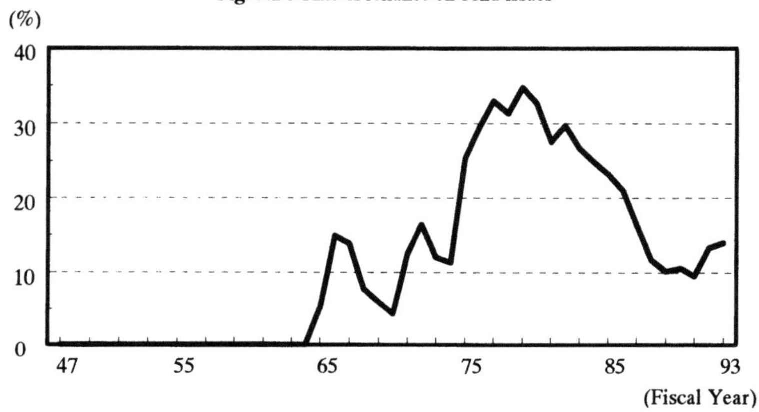

Source: MOF, Financial Statistics

postponing transfer payments that central government is required to make to the local governments and social security funds. By using these methods, the government was able to reduce the fiscal deficit in the general government account, which encompasses central government, the local governments and social security funds, to 0.8% of GNP by fiscal 1985.

(b) Monetary policy

The money supply thus increased dramatically between fiscal 1971 and 1973. It was in this environment that the first oil shock in the autumn of 1973 caused crude oil prices to quadruple. Wholesale prices surged by 15.6% in 1973 and by 31.4% in 1974. In April 1973 the government signalled a change in its monetary policy by raising the official discount rate. However, this was not enough to eliminate the liquidity surplus, and it would take another two years to bring inflation under control.

The lessons learned during this period prompted the Bank of Japan to change its monetary policy framework. Price stability was identified as the ultimate goal of monetary policy, and the money supply rather than interest rates became the main priority in terms of medium-range targets. In 1978 the Bank of Japan began to publish money supply outlooks and to implement policies that would bring the prevailing money supply situation closer to the outlooks. This shift in the policy parameters was a reflection of strong public demand for measures to stabilise consumer prices, since the rate of increase in national incomes had declined whilst the balance of national savings was continuing to rise. It was also based on experience gained at the time of the first oil shock, when Germany and Japan, which adopted price-stabilisation measures, had emerged from inflationary recession ahead of other developed economies.

When OPEC tripled crude-oil prices in 1979, triggering the second oil shock, the Bank of Japan quickly raised the official discount rate in order to prevent home-made inflation driven by opportunistic price increases.

As a result of the policy shift in its framework, the range of fluctuation in the money supply shrank between 1975 and 1985, and the money supply growth rate declined (Fig. 8.1-4). This curbed the inflation rate, and the real economic growth rate remained relatively stable, albeit at one-half of the level recorded in the high-growth period. Monetary policy thus contributed to economic stability.

8.1.2.4. Stable growth period (1985-1993)

(a) Fiscal policy

September 1985 saw the establishment of the Plaza Accord, the main purpose of which was to correct an overvalued dollar through co-ordinated intervention on foreign-exchange markets. The result was a rapid rise in the value of the yen against the dollar, causing the Japanese economy to plunge into recession. The

Fig. 8.1-4 Change in money supply

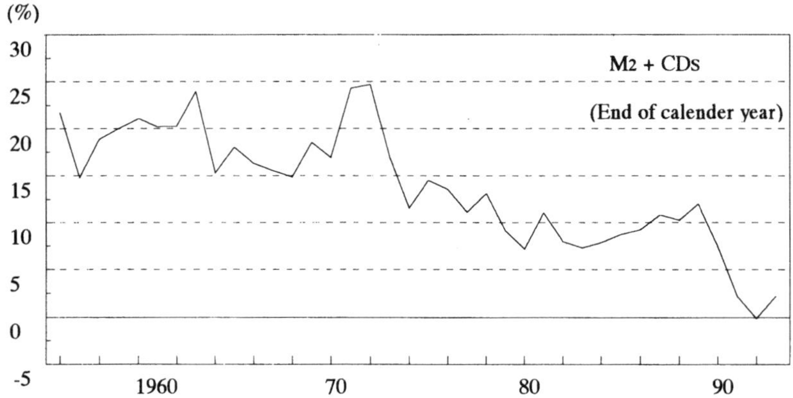

Note: M2 + CDs = Cash currency in circulation + Deposit money + Quasi-money + Certificate of deposit

Source: BOJ, Economic Statistics Annual

Louvre Accord of February 1987 called on governments to bring exchange rates to appropriate levels through closely co-ordinated intervention, and Japan came under strong pressure to expand domestic demand. At this time Japan was still in the process of fiscal reconstruction, but the government implemented large-scale economic stimulation packages amounting to three trillion yen in 1986 and six trillion yen in 1987. The government also adopted an extremely relaxed monetary policy based on the maintenance of low interest rates and a high money supply growth rate. This caused capital investment to expand, whilst the stability of the consumer price index, owing to the beneficial effect of the high yen, triggered an unprecedented upsurge of consumer spending. The result was a domestic demand-led economic upswing that lasted from fiscal 1987 to fiscal 1990. This period was later referred to as the "bubble economy" period.

In fiscal 1990, deficit bond issues were reduced to zero due to the increase in tax revenues based on economic expansion. However, the amount of outstanding public bonds remained the highest amongst the developed nations at ¥190 trillion (at the end of fiscal 1993). Since tax revenue can be expected to stagnate with the shift to a low-growth economy, the government is now searching for administrative and fiscal restructuring strategies that will avoid rigidification as part of preparations for an ageing population.

In 1991 the economy plunged into recession as a result of capital stock adjustments and the collapse of the land and share price bubble. The official discount rate was cut seven times, starting in July 1991, and the government also sought to stimulate the economy by increasing public investment through emergency economic measures four times and totalling ¥45 trillion. Japan's economic performance bottomed out in October 1993, but the recovery process has been feeble and slow.

(b) Monetary policy

After the Louvre Accord, efforts were made to prevent a collapse of the dollar through interest rate cuts in surplus countries like Japan and Germany and through interest rate hikes in the United States. These measures helped to stabilise the dollar. However, as a result of maintaining an extremely low official discount rate of 2.5% as part of international policy co-ordination, the money supply growth rate in Japan remained above 10% for three straight years between 1987 and 1989.

This stimulated the trading of land, shares and other assets, leading to so-called "asset inflation". This increased the ability of companies to raise more funds through bank loans and equity finance at a time when capital investment was expanding. It also caused an upsurge of speculative land investment and the use of "financial engineering" or sophisticated investment mechanisms involving shares, money trusts and so on, thus eventually leading to the formation of the bubble economy.

The Bank of Japan shifted to a tight money stance in 1989. In order to prevent an inflationary trend after the outbreak of the Gulf crisis in August 1990, it raised the official discount rate to 6.0%. The market reacted strongly to this move, and by August 1992 share prices had fallen by 63% from their December 1989 peak. There was also a reactionary downturn in land prices in Tokyo, Osaka and other major cities. After reaching the peak in September 1990, the prices fell by more than 40% and have continued to fall in March 1995. This massive decline in asset prices, brought about by the bursting of the bubble, resulted in latent losses for the financial institutions providing financial support for companies engaged in financial engineering and speculative land transactions.

8.1.3. Role of fiscal and monetary policies and its evaluation

8.1.3.1. Achieving economic stability and avoiding unemployment

A retrospective analysis of the post-war history of fiscal and monetary policies in Japan shows that, during the high-growth period, a balanced fiscal policy and a stop-and-go monetary policy caused economy to achieve high growth under its own steam. In the period after the second oil shock, stable economic growth was maintained through a mixture of fiscal retrenchment and monetary policies designed to curb inflation through control of the money supply.

There were also three periods when fiscal and monetary policies failed to work effectively. The first was the initial phase of the post-war reconstruction process. The second was the period between the Nixon shock and the first oil shock. And the third was the late 1980s. During these periods, discretionary fiscal and monetary policies geared towards economic expansion not only failed to produce the desired outcome, but also triggered side effects including prolonged inflation and deteriorating balance sheets. When fiscal and monetary policies were managed according to specific rules under certain environmental conditions, they contributed to economic stabilisation. When they were managed discretionarily, however, their effectiveness was severely limited.

An analysis of movement in the full unemployment rate shows that Japan achieved full employment during the high-growth period, but that unemployment increased in step with the deceleration of economic growth after the first oil crisis. After that, however, it stabilised at a low level, since the economy remained on a growth curve. Companies also worked to ensure stable employment, with the result that unemployment never became a major economic problem in Japan.

In terms of their economic adjustment role, fiscal and monetary policies generally performed well after the war, aided by the vitality of private-sector business and self-help efforts to adjust to environment changes.

8.1.3.2. Price stability

Price stability was seriously compromised during two periods in post-war Japan. The first was during the hyperinflation phase of the post-war reconstruction process, and the second was during the inflationary phase triggered by excessive liquidity after the first oil crisis. The rate of increase in wholesale prices remained consistently low during the high-growth period, but consumer prices continued to show relatively steep upward movement. Further, the rate of price increases rose only slowly during the late 1980s, but the prices of land and shares rose and fell sharply.

From the viewpoint of price stability, sometimes it is necessary to accept a certain level of inflation as the cost of high economic growth. The Japanese government learned from past policy errors and its monetary policy generally represented an appropriate response to a changing economic environment. However, monetary policy was less effective when it was targeted not towards price stability but towards other goals such as the stimulation of economic activities or the stabilisation of the exchange rate. This suggests that there was a limit to the independence of the Bank of Japan as the central bank and that its ability to implement appropriate measures at the appropriate times was compromised by the government in pursuit of short-term policy goals that were not related to prices.

8.1.3.3. Improvement of social capital

Fiscal policy has also played a role in the improvement of social capital. Until the high-growth period, this role was manifested in the supply of funds to key industries, the repair of damage to Japan's national land, and the improvement of industrial infrastructure. From the second half of the high-growth period onwards, the emphasis shifted to the allocation of resources to depressed areas such as outlying regions and rural communities and to the improvement of the living environment through the development of housing and sewers.

After the first oil crisis, however, the implementation of policies designed to correct economic growth distortions produced negative effects at a time of decelerating economic growth. In other words, these policies were partly responsible for fiscal deficits, and they also turned subsidies into vested interests. In flow terms, considerable amounts of money were channelled into the improvement of social capital. Despite this, Japan continued to lag behind other countries in terms of the level of its social capital stocks that have a direct impact on the lives of its people.

The role of fiscal policy as a tool for the redistribution of resources and income thus has been changing in accordance with the demands of each successive period. However, it has not always functioned effectively, owing to revenue limitations and the increasing rigidification of the expenditure structure.

8.1.3.4. International balance of payments

Under the fixed exchange-rate system, Japan sought to balance its international accounts through a stop-and-go policy. Although the current account shifted into deficit after the first and second oil crises, the trend from the late 1960s onwards was towards an expanding current-account surplus, driven by the improving international competitiveness of Japanese industry. After the transition to a floating exchange-rate system, monetary policy was used to counteract the recessionary impact of the high yen. The government turned to financial easing as a means of compensating for the decline in demand that resulted from the appreciation of the yen, but excessive relaxation jeopardised economic stability after the first oil shock and again during the bubble-economy period of the late 1980s. Under the floating exchange-rate system, the role of monetary policy in adjusting the international balance of payments and the exchange rate has been limited to symptomatic treatment.

In the 1980s, the government sought to remedy the cumulative expansion of its current-account surplus by using fiscal policy to restructure the economy towards dependence on domestic demand instead of external demand. However, progress towards structural adjustment was limited by fiscal reconstruction and by a lack of leadership on the part of politicians.

Fiscal and monetary policies thus functioned effectively as tools for the adjustment of the international balance of payments during the high-growth period. After the oil crises, however, the government continued to give priority to quantitative economic expansion. Economic countermeasures were used to support existing domestic industries, and it was not possible to achieve a transition in Japan's economic structure.

8.2. Germany's Fiscal and Monetary Policies

8.2.1. Fiscal policy

8.2.1.1. 1950-1965: Phase of reconstruction and economic recovery

During the reconstruction phase in Germany, the state was primarily concerned with rebuilding and improving the public infrastructure, but it also made efforts to support the economy by means of improved tax incentives. Businesses were granted shorter-term depreciation allowances to help build up the private capital stock more quickly. To create room for this expansive growth policy, the public sector had a more negative than positive influence on private consumption. This, however, did not prevent government debt policy from having a fundamentally pro-cyclical orientation at the beginning of the 1960s.

8.2.1.2. 1966-1975: State and demand management

With the strong upswing in the economy in 1966 and especially after the 1967 recession, public perceptions of the role of the state changed. In 1967 the Law for Promoting Stability and Economic Growth was passed, which provided the state with the legal foundation and concrete approaches for a growth-oriented economic policy, with public debt policy in the foreground. According to Section 1 of this law, all government action must be in keeping with the requirements of economic equilibrium. Particular sections of this law refer to the anti-cyclical debt operations necessary for reaching this goal, with the requirements being directed not only at the federal government but also at the Länder and municipalities. An economic council was made responsible for co-ordinating deficit spending amongst the levels of Germany's federal system. The law also contains provisions for a debt ceiling.

On the basis of this legislation, the federal government and the Länder pursued an anti-cyclical budget policy which had an expansive effect on the economy in 1967 and a restrictive effect in 1969. This anti-cyclical debt policy, which, strictly speaking, should have been continued in the public sector until the early 1970s, gave way to a more pro-cyclical policy. The reason for this change was especially the clearly pro-cyclical behaviour of the municipalities, which, at all levels of government, received larger tax revenues during the upswing phase. Whereas the federal government and the Länder used these increased revenues to reduce the debt, the increased financial leeway of the municipalities led to debt expansion.

8.2.1.3. 1976-1981: Structural deficit and the limits of government economic management

As a result of the first oil crisis in 1973 and especially because of the 1975 tax reform, tax revenues grew only moderately in comparison to the growth at the beginning of the decade. At the same time, the state recorded the highest deficit to date, caused less by the business situation than by structural aspects. In the following years, government's main concerns were to consolidate the budget and to improve the taxation structure to bring it in line with economic- and growth-policy requirements. In other words, fiscal policy was to be used more strongly as an instrument of growth policy. On the spending side, a mid-term state investment programme was started in 1977, and on the revenue side, a tax reform in 1977 was to strengthen private investment propensity in the medium term. This was a clear indication that fiscal policy was taking on a supply-side orientation. At the same time, however, the question was raised of whether the state was still able to provide growth-policy stimulus in light of the strongly increased national debt.

8.2.1.4. 1982-1989: Supply-side orientation of government policy

The years 1982 to 1985 were marked by consolidation of the public budget. In this period, the so-called structural deficit declined strongly, with both the positive economic situation and the deliberate consolidation measures having been responsible. Thus, spending cuts, especially social spending, were effected: for example, child benefits were reduced as were housing supplements, federal subsidies for social security, student grants and maternity benefits, to mention only a few.

From the mid-1980s, self-sustaining growth set in. Since growth rates in government spending were lower than the growth of nominal GNP, the public sector share in GDP was reduced. Consolidation efforts took place mainly in the federal budget, whereby the federal budget's share of total government' spending declined. The political upheaval in 1989 had considerable repercussions everywhere, and especially on the previously successful consolidation policy of the government.

8.2.1.5. 1990-1995: Fiscal policy in the wake of unification

Since 1990, fiscal policy has been dominated by German re-unification. As a result of unification costs, government deficits rose at an unusually strong pace. To finance the additional spending in the new Länder and also to provide economic assistance for Eastern Europe and to help finance the Gulf War, tax increases were implemented at the start of the 1990s: an income tax "solidarity" surcharge (later rescinded but re-introduced in 1995), increase in petrol tax, insurance tax hike, and a rise in contribution rates to various social insurance forms. Despite the dampening effects of these tax increases, the public sector has generated expansive effects, on balance, which have also benefited the economic situation in western Germany because of increased demand in the new Länder.

After the deficit in the public budget reached its high point in 1993—in absolute terms and as a proportion of GDP—significant reduction was achieved in 1994. This consolidation, however, came at the expense of strong tax increases. The burden of taxes and social charges is expected to be 44% in 1995. For the coming years, the primary task of government will be to reduce this burden on the private sector, which, however, will only come about very slowly because of the strong financial needs the state still has: continued large-scale funding for the new Länder, financial assistance for Eastern Europe, and contributions to the European Union.

The planned tax reductions for 1996 come in the wake of the decision of the constitutional court (*Bundesverfassungsgericht*) to grant tax exemptions on subsistence incomes. With the planned corporate tax reform, the government is seeking to contribute to the attractiveness of Germany as an investment location. In light of these plans and the priority still assigned to consolidation, there must be a clear limitation in the rise of spending. Only in this way can the tax burden be lowered, especially since the second stage of the statutory nursing-care insurance contains a rise in the contribution rate from 1% to 1.7% in mid-1996. In realistic terms, it can be expected that the government spending rate in 1996 will only be slightly less than in 1995.

8.2.2. Assessment of monetary policy

8.2.2.1. History

Post-war German monetary policy begins with the currency shift introduced by the Allies on 21 June 1948. This currency reform had a major impact on the development of the German economy, being later assessed as one of the single success factors of monetary policy (see Section 3.2.1). Before the currency shift, a two-level central banking system was institutionalised, with the central banks of the Länder (LZB) owning their co-ordination body, the Bank of the German Länder (BdL). The German Bundesbank as successor of the BdL with its own legal status was not introduced until 1957. With the appointment of the German Bundesbank, the central bank system was transferred into a centralised system.

Shortly before German reunification, there was a second currency reform in the eastern part of Germany. On 31 July 1990 the currency formerly valid in East Germany, the *Mark der DDR*, was replaced by the D-Mark. This currency shift has had less powerful consequences for pan-German economic development. The effects have been perceptible only in East Germany, and even there they have been exceeded by non-monetary interventions in the economy.

In its external relationship the German currency was always strongly attached to foreign currencies. This integration has always been of exceptional importance for the external and also for the internal value of German currency, and must thus be stressed at the outset. Two main currency standards shaped the history of German monetary policy. Under the supervision of Allied forces, the D-Mark was brought into the world-currency standard of Bretton Woods. This fixed exchange-rate regime was constructed as a dollar standard by treaty; all other currencies had to guarantee parity to the US dollar and thus accept US monetary policy. Deviations from the fixed US dollar parity in this standard were only allowed in times of "serious irregularities". From 1948 to 1973, the D-Mark remained in this fixed exchange-rate standard.

Even after 1973, the German currency never obtained total detachment from other currencies. Since then, the D-Mark has fixed exchange rates only to other European currencies. To begin with, the D-Mark was integrated in the so-called "currency-snake", a fairly loose standard of European currencies of different compositions and with frequent parity variations. Since 1979, the D-Mark has participated in the more strictly regulated European Monetary System (EMS). The EMS is a regime of fixed exchange rates which originally had currency bands of 4.5% in which exchange rates could fluctuate bilaterally. On 1 August 1993 the currency bands were expanded to 30%. Formally symmetrical intervention obligations of central banks with currencies under downwards or upwards pressure initially lead one to expect the EMS to become an average standard between the hard and soft currencies. But practical pressures led the EMS to be established as an asymmetrical hard-currency standard oriented on the D-Mark. The D-Mark established itself as the anchor currency in the EMS that other currencies had to adjust to, just as the currencies in the Bretton Woods system had to adjust to the US dollar.

The post-war development can be divided into four periods in which monetary policy was confronted with different external conditions and different specific problems. In the 1948-59 period, monetary policy attained solid internal equilibrium (stability of prices) and external equilibrium (fixing to the US dollar parity). This was promoted by a rigid monetary policy in the country of the currency anchor, the United States. Even with slightly uneven exchange rates, the external value of the D-Mark was maintained.

In the period from 1960 to 1973, the conflicts to which German monetary policy was exposed assumed ever-growing proportions; monetary policy was in a difficult situation, since internal stability did not match external stability. A tight monetary policy gave rise to current-account surpluses and above all to interest rate–induced capital-account surpluses. Both factors caused a balance-of-payment surplus and upwards pressure on the D-Mark. This jeopardised external stability and thus the adherence to the dollar parity. Internal and external stability excluded each other more and more. In the course of these problems, which existed in other European countries as well, the Bretton Woods system collapsed in spring 1973. The Bundesbank attained, for the first time, control over the circulation of money sufficient to stabilise internal goals.

From 1973 to ca. 1990, the course of monetary policy was in the first instance determined by internal factors, that is by repeated occurrences of distribution conflicts. The Bundesbank, by means of its tight monetary policy, at least gained control of the inflation rate. On the external side, monetary policy was increasingly less troubled for the moment. This was mainly caused by installing flexible exchange rates amongst the three large currency blocs: the EMS bloc, the dollar bloc and the yen bloc. With flexible exchange rates, the pass-through of foreign shocks to the German economy could be mitigated.

In the period from 1990 to the present, German monetary policy has had to deal with challenges of a rapid development on financial markets: less stable money demand now makes monetary aggregates more volatile and hence less useful for monetary policy. Monetary aggregates in Germany had functioned for years both as very good indicators and targets for monetary policy. Currently, they cannot fulfil this function very well. In addition, prices of financial assets, interest rates, and above all exchange rates are fluctuating more strongly than ever before.

8.2.2.2. Politics of monetary authorities

(a) Independence of the Bundesbank

The independence of the Bundesbank contributed to the goal of achieving price stability. But the Bundesbank's independence has led at various times to a lack of assistance in achieving growth and employment goals.

The independence of the Bundesbank was already ensured when its predecessor, the BdL, was founded by the Allies, and the Bundesbank remains one of the most independent central banks in the world (Table 8.2-1). The success in controlling inflation guaranteed by the Bundesbank's independence is incontestably impressive. The following conditions guarantee the wide-scale personal and institutional independence of the Bundesbank from the political system.

- The statutory task of "safeguarding the currency" (Bundesbank Act, Sec. 3) internally and externally, with a priority for internal safeguarding.
- The detachment of government debt financing. For the Bundesbank it is even prohibited to buy government debt for reasons of financing the budget deficit. The most important source of inflation has thus been eliminated.
- The appointment procedures of Central Bank Council members. It guarantees independence of senior Bundesbank members from political influence. The Council consists of up to eight (currently seven) Bundesbank directors and the LZB directors. The potential directors of the Bundesbank are proposed by the federal government, but not until they have passed the hearings before the Central Bank Council are they confirmed.

The Bundesbank has often been urged to participate in supporting growth and employment policies. Such demands are made on the basis of Section 12 of the

Table 8.2-1 Independence of central banks

Country	Index of central bank independence[a)]	Average of yearly inflation[b)]
Switzerland	0.68	3
West Germany	0.66	3
United States	0.51	5
Denmark	0.47	7
Canada	0.46	6
Britain	0.31	7
France	0.28	7
Sweden	0.27	8
Italy	0.22	11

a) The range of this index, which is constructed by the author of the source, is from zero (minimal independence) to one (maximum independence).
b) Inflation is measured as a yearly geometric average during the 1980s and is rounded to the nearest full percentage.

Source: A. Cukierman: Central Bank Strategy, Credibility and Independence, Cambridge, MIT Press

Bundesbank Act, according to which the Bundesbank "must support the general economic policy of the government". They are always based on the link between low interest rates and the revival of economic activities. Three key examples in which demands were placed on the Bundesbank from various quarters to lend stronger support to economic policy illustrate the differences in these conflict situations.

- In his "Gürzenich Address" in October 1950, Chancellor Adenauer demanded that the Bundesbank turn away from its preceding restrictive policies (increase of the discount and Lombard lending rates of 2 percentage points to 6% and 7%, respectively). In his opinion this monetary policy was the death sentence for economic growth. In retrospect, we can see how the politicians grossly underestimated the economic forces.
- In 1966, the stricter policies of the Bundesbank (increasing the discount rate from 3% to 6% without any direct danger of inflation) was one of the reasons for the following serious recession, whose total economic cost has been assessed at DM 30 billion.[1] After rapid interest-rate reductions, the economy recovered quickly, but the recession led to a change in government.
- In 1980 to 1982, the Bundesbank sharpened the restrictive course it had been following. The long-ensuing phase of high short-term interest rates, in which real short-term interest rates were much higher than in the 1970s, led to a long phase of stagnation. This time as well, the phase of the monetary-policy braking manoeuvre coincided with change in the government, which had

---

1 This amount was estimated by the German Council of Economic Advisors (*Sachverständigenrat*) in its 1967 expertise, No. 83, Bonn 1967. It strictly opposed monetary tightening.

been insisting on a rapid easing of monetary policy. In this period the Bundesbank probably applied the brakes excessively.

There were certainly many more such situations in which the Bundesbank regularly pursued a restrictive course against the wishes of the government and also against the wishes of other economic policy players. The results were in some cases better and in some cases worse, in terms of all goals laid out in the Stability Law. This makes an assessment of Bundesbank independence more difficult, despite the successes in controlling inflation.

In any case, the Bundesbank has gained over time an additional degree of freedom in economic policy by means of its independence and the implementation of what it regards as an optimal monetary policy (which in retrospect may have been too restrictive in some instances). If monetary policy had been the domain of government, the short-term decision-making horizon would have led to a more frequent monetary expansion to stimulate the economy.

(b) Demarcation dispute between the government and the Bundesbank

The demarcation dispute that exists between the exchange rate policies of the Ministries of Economics and Finance respectively and the monetary policies of the Bundesbank is one of the less successful chapters of German post-war monetary policy. On the one hand, the conflict is institutionalised in articles 88 and 73/4 of the German constitution, which assign legislative competence for external relations of the currency to the federal government. On the other hand, the Bundesbank—with its wide-scale independence—is responsible for measures to safeguard the (internal) value of money according to Section 3 of the Bundesbank Act.

This potential for conflict became particularly clear in the period from the end of the 1960s to the beginning of the 1970s. As described above, in this period the fixed Bretton Woods D-Mark parity and the exchange rate required to keep the price level stable (which should have been higher) drifted more and more apart. Maintaining the D-Mark parity was the expressed wish of every government in power, which made increasingly stronger demands for changes from the Bundesbank.

Prior to exchange-rate adjustments, strongly *dirigiste* measures of various economic policy-makers were used ever more frequently. Monetary policy was frequently torn between expansionist policies for stabilising exchange rates and contractive policies for stabilising price levels. This stop-and-go produced friction in and of itself. In addition, a package of measures was implemented in order to avoid the flow of foreign currencies into Germany and to soak up domestic liquidity: a ban on the payment of interest on deposits by non-residents (later substituted by a coupon tax for non-resident deposits), tax increases on exports, tax concessions for imports, and the banks' assumption of liquidity-binding papers. Such measures were introduced ever more often and at shorter intervals with upwards pressure on the D-Mark. The allocative friction which resulted from the stop-and-go monetary policy, the arbitrary jumps in exchange rates, and the interventions in capital markets were finally determined by the stubborn refusal of the government in power to adjust exchange rates to the low-inflation conditions in Germany. The adjustments of exchange rates themselves which were at last undertaken were only compromise solutions that were insufficient and taken too late; often this led to even stronger foreign-exchange inflows to Germany.

For the 1980s, with the D-Mark tied to the EMS fixed exchange-rate system, one could also expect the exchange-rate adjustments to lead to similar confusion, resulting in similar foreign-exchange turbulence due to the conflicts of interest between the Bundesbank and the government in charge. However, the potential for conflict was reduced by shifting powers from the government to the Bundesbank. Responsibility for exchange rates, theoretically inseparably bound to monetary policy, was thus also empirically shifted to the Bundesbank. The co-existence of two inter-dependent yet autonomous institutions—the Bundesbank and the Ministry of Finance—that had contributed to instability developed over time to a shifting of power from the Ministry of Finance to the Bundesbank.

8.2.2.3. Politics of the monetary process

(a) 1948 monetary reform

Monetary reform in Germany was an undisputed success. Prior to this reform, Germany had the problem of monetary overhang, i.e., money in circulation exceeded, at regulated prices, the circulation of goods. Money was neither able to fulfil its function as a medium of exchange nor its function as a store of value, since the accepted bank note did not guarantee the acquisition of goods at the designated price. The direct exchange of goods, with its accompanying deficiencies, was the result. There were three measures that could be implemented to eliminate this deficiency: a termination of price controls, an eradication of a portion of the old currency, or the introduction of a new currency in which (with approximately constant prices) old money is converted to a limited amount of new money. The first alternative would have had the great disadvantage of touching off a new phase of monetary policy, with high price increases that could have been a starting point for a wage-price spiral. This path was pursued in the former Soviet Union with precisely these results. The second alternative would have necessitated a phase of restrictive monetary policy in order to soak up a portion of central bank money. In this phase, deflation and high interest rates would have resulted. Deflation and restrictive monetary policy would have caused major uncertainties and distortions.[2]

A new currency was thus the most sensible solution. But this option also had its disadvantages: the new currency led to redistribution as a result of the varying

---

[2] Deflation at the beginning of the 1930s led to a hoarding of money, which in turn was a reason for the world-wide depression.

exchange rates for different assets, on the one hand, and between flows and stocks, on the other. The redistribution effects were dampened somewhat by the *Lastenausgleich* (equalisation of burdens)—the first of its kind after a currency reform—and by the low level of assets compared to pre-war levels. The success of the currency reform was due not only to the way it was implemented but also to support from other policy areas: with the deregulation of prices and legislation that reflected a commitment to a market economy, an environment was created in which monetary policy could make its contribution to the economic miracle that followed. The success of monetary policy in this period is best demonstrated by the surge in growth and employment that occurred once the functioning monetary system was introduced.

(b) Medium-term-oriented money supply policy

A particular success of the Bundesbank's policy was the seizing of the initiative after the release of exchange rates in 1973. At that time, wage demands and price increases spiralled up together so that the Bundesbank had to sharply apply the brakes. In order to prevent the necessity of applying such shock-like counter-measures, since 1974 the Bundesbank has always announced at the beginning of each year an inflation target of 2%. This inflation target is accomplished with a target growth rate for the money supply, which takes into consideration expected medium-term productivity increases and fluctuations in demand for money. The Bundesbank based its proceedings closely on the theoretical monetarist concept, according to which the development of the monetary supply is closely connected with that of price levels in the medium and long run. A modest money supply target should then only ensure a moderate growth range for prices. The concept of announcing and running modest medium-term money supply growth effectively prevented the recurrence of such high inflation rates as in 1973. In particular, price expectations, which trigger wage-price spirals, were stabilised at low levels.

Since the beginning of the 1990s, the application of this concept for monetary policy has become more difficult. Monetary aggregates do not exhibit a close synchronisation with prices any more because money demand has become more volatile. To begin with, German re-unification triggered some shifts amongst monetary assets, because eastern Germans reallocated their portfolios from standardised savings accounts to more flexible alternatives. Additionally, the unstable demand for money was—and still is—a result of ongoing globalisation of financial markets, which allows shifts of financial assets across national borders and across currencies easily. Finally, the variable German money demand can be traced back to certain financial innovations which were introduced in Germany in this period, with some delay in international comparison. The last two causes of volatile monetary aggregates will remain and become even more dominant. Thus, the Bundesbank needs to look for alternative concepts that will in future guarantee a stabilisation of inflation expectations and at last produce low and stable inflation rates.

(c) Moderate regulation of the financial sector

The modest intensity of financial sector regulation clearly has to be judged as a success factor of monetary policy. The most important events in the liberalised German financial market are the liberalisation of interest rates for both loans and deposits in 1967 and the starting of the process of D-Mark convertibility in 1958. Both measures were installed quite early in an international context. Monitoring costs of the regulations and expensive strategies to overcome regulations in capital markets or foreign-exchange markets were avoided. Additionally, the universal banking system that is common in Germany operates with less regulation than a separated banking system.

An activist promotion of financial markets was also far from the Bundesbank's thoughts. At times it wanted to prevent many elements of financial innovation from entering German financial markets for reasons of diminishing effectiveness of monetary policy. Presumably, the Bundesbank underestimated the welfare effects arising from financial innovation. It gave too much weight to the control of monetary policy and not enough to the development of financial markets. But for other reasons as well, a surge of financial innovation was not necessary: fairly liberal rules for financial market participants, tax legislation that did not charge capital markets too much, moderate interest rate volatility by international standards, and a German capital market which is conservative on the investor side.

International competition for financial products—especially via Euromarkets—increased pressures on the Bundesbank to allow financial innovations on German financial markets. Since 1985, the Bundesbank has had a more open attitude to financial innovation. In the first place, bonds with variable interest rates and zero-coupon bonds were allowed (1985); they were followed by some short-term securities (such as certificates of deposits and commercial papers since 1986 and 1992, respectively) and extended futures and options markets (since 1990). Finally (1994), money-market funds were allowed, and very long government securities (30 years) have been promoted and introduced by the Bundesbank.

8.3. Comparative Summary of Fiscal and Monetary Policies

8.3.1. Fiscal policy

The roles of fiscal policy are (1) social infrastructure development, (2) discretionary measures to stimulate the economy, and (3) the redistribution of income. One common feature of fiscal policy in Japan and Germany is the use of social infrastructure development during the post-war reconstruction period to lay the foundations for economic development.

Japan was beset by a capital shortfall in the first half of its rapid-growth phase. For that reason, fiscal policy was based on the principle of a balanced budget. High economic growth was achieved through the self-sustaining expansion of capital investment, which was in turn achieved through efforts to raise the savings rate. In the second half of its rapid-growth phase, Japan continued to pursue rapid economic growth, but it also began to improve social welfare systems and correct the distortions caused by rapid growth. This led to the adoption of a Keynesian approach based on the management of total demand.

In 1967, Germany enacted its Law for Promoting Stability and Economic Growth, thus establishing a framework for growth policies based on the issuance of government bonds. During recessionary periods, this framework called for government bond issues and the implementation of Keynesian demand-expansion policies. In practice, however, Germany followed a pro-cyclical set of fiscal policies tuned to the business cycle with the result that budget expenditures climbed during periods of expansion and contracted during recessions.

In the slow-growth phase of the post–oil shock period, stagnating tax revenues left both Japan and Germany saddled with structurally rooted fiscal deficits. In Japan, the established doctrine of achieving fast economic growth driven by expansion-oriented fiscal policies was coupled with the new objective of building a welfare society. As a result, expenditures ballooned. In Germany, fiscal policy was actively used as a means of spurring economic growth with the inevitable result that the government became increasingly dependent on bond issues.

Germany sought to deal with its fiscal troubles through a drastic restructuring of its existing expenditure structure, including major cuts in social security spending. In Japan, however, vested interests prevented any change to the existing structure of fiscal spending, and the government instead sought to curb expenditure by applying the so-called "ceiling system" to budget estimates submitted by each government ministry and agency. This approach, coupled with an expansion-driven rise in tax revenue, helped to reduce Japan's dependence on government bond issues. The entrenched structure of fiscal spending itself remained in place, however.

Starting in the late 1980s, the need for international harmonisation began to place constraints on Japanese fiscal and monetary policies. To some extent, this situation reduced the flexibility of government policy and compromised its appropriateness. The achievement of policy co-ordination and economic stability in an era of economic globalisation will be a key challenge for policy-makers in the years ahead. Japan already has over ¥200 trillion in government bonds outstanding, and its population is now aging faster than that of any other developed countries. It will therefore be necessary to consider an optimal sharing of roles between the government and the private sector in order to boost economic vitality, whilst keeping the tax and social-insurance contributions burden at an appropriate level.

The challenge for German fiscal policy is the reduction of the fiscal deficit stemming from unification.

Next, we review the relationship between the government and the market economy in Japan and Germany. In Japan, the evolution of that relationship has gone through a number of stages. The post-war reconstruction phase was a period of economic restructuring efforts by the government and GHQ. In the early years of the rapid-growth phase, the relationship was characterised by an emphasis on small government and fast growth led by domestic demand in an environment of artificially low interest rates. During the latter half of the rapid-growth phase and up to 1980, the economy's dependence on government spending began to rise again. In the period since the 1980s, efforts have been made to limit the government's role through fiscal restructuring and moves towards deregulation. The centre of gravity for the roles of the government and private sector in the Japanese economy has thus shifted in accordance with Japan's stage of economic development. In Germany, the government's role appears to have been limited by specific rules. That is why the government has implemented unpopular policies, such as tax increases and social security cuts.

8.3.2. Monetary policy

The consistent aim of German monetary policy has been to maintain the stability of the D-Mark exchange rate. To that end, the Bundesbank has been accorded substantial independence from government influence. Though this arrangement has not always yielded favourable results in terms of stimulating the economy, it has contributed to stable economic growth through the stabilisation of domestic commodity prices. However, at times it has been difficult to achieve the dual objectives of exchange-rate stability and domestic price stability, since tight monetary policies tend to push up the value of the currency. This policy conflict was a particularly serious problem for Germany from the 1960s until the introduction of the floating exchange-rate system in 1973.

The goals and tools of Japanese monetary policy have shifted from time to time under varying economic conditions. Until the start of the rapid-growth era, Japan employed a stop-and-go policy designed to avert a deficit in its balance of payments. This led to the stabilisation of wholesale prices. In addition, a policy of keeping interest rates artificially low provided increased incentives for capital investment, whilst facilitating the supply of funds to key industries. Following the oil shocks, the Bank of Japan sought to stabilise prices by managing the money supply. As these examples attest, Japan was able to achieve its policy objectives whenever its monetary policy was based on a strictly defined set of rules. However, whenever monetary policy incorporated anti-recession or exchange-rate measures designed to deal with external shocks, such as those resulting from the shift to a floating-rate system, or the sharp uptrend in the yen following the Plaza Accord, it typically produced such side-effects as high inflation or assets price spirals.

Innovative financial technology is being introduced in both Japan and Germany. In addition, growth in the scale of their financial and capital markets relative to the real economy has stoked speculative activity, thus confronting policy-makers with the task of steering an increasingly difficult policy course.

8.3.3. Evaluation of fiscal and monetary policies

Economic growth and stability appear to be two of the ultimate goals shaping fiscal and monetary policies. However, there are sharp contrasts between Japan and Germany in terms of their policy responses in these areas. In general terms, whereas Japanese policies have been growth-oriented, German policies have been targeted towards stability.

In effect, Japanese policies have basically favoured strong economic growth, regardless of whether the emphasis at a given point in time has been on small government or wide discretionary intervention in private-sector economic activity by the government or the central bank. Yet the successful policies have been those that depended on the self-sustained growth potential of the private sector rather than on discretionary measures. Policies designed to stabilise the economic system have not always functioned effectively. For example, policies introduced to offset the distortions faced by industrial sectors and social classes left behind in the race for economic growth eventually led to institutional rigidity due to the formation of vested interests. These policies also resulted in the imposition of an increasingly heavy fiscal burden by a social-security system designed for an environment of rapid economic growth. Another consequence was an unwillingness to accept tax increases even during periods of protracted budget deficits. These weaknesses appear to be a manifestation of inadequacies in the functioning of democratic policy-making processes in Japan.

Germany has in principle allowed economic activity to be governed by market mechanisms, and the main policy emphasis has been on anti-inflation measures. Though this approach has yielded a certain measure of success, Germany has been plagued by relatively high levels of unemployment since the oil shock period. Policies focusing primarily on economic stability have been less effective in terms of achieving dynamic economic development through transitions in the country's industrial structure.

9. Competition Policy

9.1. Japan's Competition Policy

9.1.1. Competition policy and conditions for market competition

Although Japan has a market economy framework, the government has imposed direct and indirect restrictions on the conditions that govern competition in the market in order to give priority to Japan's efforts to catch up with the West. Fig. 9.1-1 shows the structure of competition policy in Japan. Industrial policy, trade policy restrictions on direct foreign investment in Japan, etc., will be reviewed in detail in chapter 11.

Japan's Anti-Monopoly Act was introduced in 1947 under the democratisation policy of the occupation administration (GHQ) and was modelled on the Anti-Trust Law of the United States. However, pressure from industry and the Ministry of International Trade and Industry (MITI), which were aiming at improving Japan's international competitiveness, resulted in the inclusion of exceptional provisions, such as toleration of cartels and other competition-limiting behaviours.

In addition, the government has employed direct regulation in areas where market failures are anticipated. First, infrastructure sectors, such as electric power, gas, water supplies, telecommunications and railways, are subject to regulation, given the tendency for natural monopolies to develop owing to the scarcity of

Fig. 9.1-1 The structure of competition policy in Japan

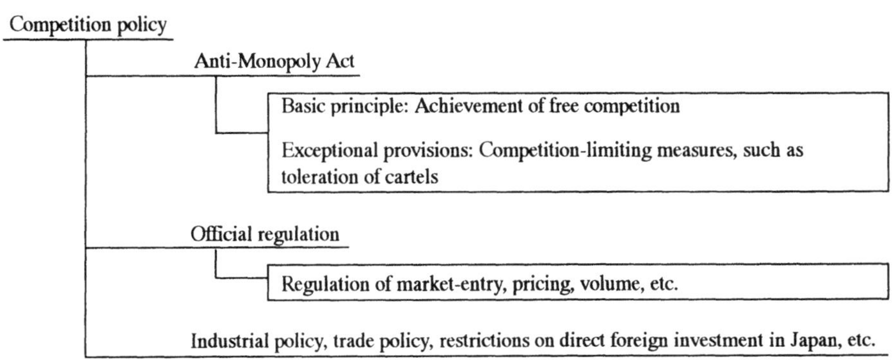

resources and the potential for economies of scale. Next, the financial sector has also remained subject to regulation because of the need to maintain order and discipline within the financial system and to prevent information providers from abusing their superior position. Laws limiting competition have also been enacted with the aim of protecting and fostering small- to medium-sized enterprises in such fields as transportation, retailing and construction. In 1990, areas subject to official regulation accounted for 41.8% of value added and covered a wide spectrum of activities. Sector-wise, whilst only 14.1% of the manufacturing industry is regulated, almost 100% regulation prevails in such non-manufacturing industries as construction, finance, insurance, securities, electric power, gas, water supplies, transportation and telecommunications. Regulatory instruments in these industries, which control such factors as number of offices or outlets, business hours, products to be handled, entrepreneur qualifications, and volume of supply are designed to limit competition through licence, permission, approval, etc. Whilst official regulation has played a positive role by helping to avoid unemployment, it has clearly allowed low-productivity industries to survive for many years in Japan's industrial structure.

It is possible to identify a number of characteristics of competition policy in Japan. First, a wide range of exceptions are allowed under the Anti-Monopoly Act, including cartels and resale prices maintenance. Second, fines and penalties imposed under the Anti-Monopoly Act are minimal. Third, the law is operated primarily through administrative procedures implemented by the Fair Trade Commission, which has a wide range of discretion. Japan's anti-trust policy has thus been administered with flexibility in order to avoid increases in social costs. In addition, the government has implemented competition-limiting policies, such as industrial and trade policies and restrictions on direct foreign investment in Japan, in order to strengthen Japan's international competitiveness. However, this does not mean that markets have always been harmonious, and there has been cut-throat competition even in markets isolated by government policy. In other words, the framework for market competition has been effectively determined by exceptional provisions under the Anti-Monopoly Act, and by official regulations and industrial policy.

9.1.2. Structure of Japanese anti-trust policy

The Anti-Monopoly Act, which is designed to prohibit private monopolies and ensure fair trading practice, has furnished the institutional framework for competition policies in Japan. Certain provisions of the law were relaxed in 1949 and 1953, but in 1977 it was reinforced to reflect lessons learned after the first oil shock, when Japan experienced rampant inflation. It was moderately strengthened again in 1991 as a result of talks under the Japan–US Structural Impediments Initiative.

The agency responsible for enforcing the provisions of the Anti-Monopoly Act is the Fair Trade Commission (FTC). In order to exclude political influence and ensure sustainable and stable conduct of its affairs, the FTC is under the prime minister's jurisdiction as an external bureau of the Prime Minister's Office. It is able to carry out its duties on the basis of its own discretionary judgements. The FTC's actual enforcement method is characterised as indirect intervention, which is designed to restore a competitive market environment through administrative measures that eliminate illegal activities.

The provisions of the Anti-Monopoly Act focus on three areas. First, there is the prohibition of private monopolies. Specific measures in this area, which relate to the prohibition of corporate behaviour limiting competition, include the regulation of mergers and share ownership, and the prohibition of holding companies. Second, there is the prohibition of unfair restrictions on trade, primarily through the regulation of cartels. Third, there is the prohibition of unfair trading methods, which are divided into six categories: unfair discrimination of other entrepreneurs, trading under unfair price; unfair solicitation for and unfair enforcement of trading with the client of a competitor; trading under terms and conditions that unfairly constrain the activities of a trading party; unfair use of one's own position in trading; unfair interference of the trading of a competitor; and unfair solicitation for a disadvantageous act.

The evolution of Japan's anti-trust policy began with establishment of the Anti-Monopoly Act in 1947. This was followed by the backsliding of competition policy through the relaxation of the Anti-Monopoly Act between 1948 and 1976. Between 1977 and 1990, competition policy was promoted through the reinforcement of the Anti-Monopoly Act. And from 1991 up to the present, competition policy has been further reinforced as a result of the Japan–US Structural Impediments Initiative. The government has thus been fluctuating between the easing and tightening of competition policy through repeated amendments to the Anti-Monopoly Act.

9.1.3. Evolution of Japan's anti-trust policy

9.1.3.1. Enactment of the Anti-Monopoly Act (1947)

The pre-war organisation of Japanese industry effectively limited competition. First, four major *zaibatsu* (financial combines or conglomerates)—Mitsui, Mitsubishi, Sumitomo and Yasuda—dominated finance, heavy industry and most other key industrial sectors. By the end of World War II (1945), companies affiliated to these four *zaibatsu* accounted alone for as much as 24.1% of the total capitalisation of all companies in Japan. Second, cartel relationships spanned a broad cross-section of Japanese industry. The onslaught of the Great Depression in 1929 led to the formation of cartels, especially by major firms. In 1931 the government responded to this situation, providing a legal basis for cartels through the establishment of laws to control key industries and legitimise industrial partnerships. Third, giant trusts created through corporate mergers enjoyed monopolies in the iron and steel, paper, and electric-power industries. The managed economy of the war years took shape in this structural climate.

As part of its post-war economic democratisation measures, GHQ moved to dismantle the *zaibatsu* by banning holding companies. In 1947, it outlawed private monopolies by establishing the Anti-Monopoly Act, which was designed to ensure fair trading and prevent the resurgence of the *zaibatsu*. The law contained a number of stringent measures. First, cartels based on price or quota arrangements became illegal in principle. Second, the government was given the power to order the break-up of giant corporations in order to prevent the expansion of business capacities. Third, restrictions were placed on ownership of corporate stock, interlocking directorates and mergers.

These measures drew strong criticism from industry. There was concern about the establishment of the law so soon after World War II, when Japan was still in a state of economic exhaustion. There was also deep suspicion that the Anti-Monopoly Act, which was introduced as part of occupation policy, was designed to weaken the Japanese economy. The institutional framework for competition policy in Japan was thus created by the forced introduction of a competition policy under external pressure. The combination of this factor with the cartel-based structure of Japanese industry in the pre-war era appears to have been responsible for the dual emphasis on conciliation and competition that has characterised Japan's post-war industrial organisation.

9.1.3.2. Retreat from competition policy through the relaxation of the Anti-Monopoly Act (1948-1976)

The government needed to dispose of the vast quantities of shares that it had accumulated through the break-up of the *zaibatsu*. In 1949, therefore, it amended the Anti-Monopoly Act to ease the provision that in principle prohibited companies from holding shares in other companies. It also replaced the licensing system for corporate mergers with a system based on prior notification.

The recession that set in after the Korean War led to increased pressure from industry for the easing of restrictions on cartels. When the peace treaty took effect in 1952, the government took the opportunity to revise economic statutes that had been put in place during the occupation years. In 1953 it moved to relax restrictions under the Anti-Monopoly Act. The provision restricting price- and quota-based cartels was repealed, and an approval system was established to allow the formation of recession cartels and rationalisation cartels. Recession cartels would limit production volumes, capacity, sales volumes and prices during business downturns, whilst rationalisation cartels would enable companies to rationalise their activities by limiting the quality and specifications of products and areas of production. In addition, the restrictions on share ownership, interlocking directorates and corporate mergers were also relaxed. For example, the limitation on share ownership in financial institutions was raised from 5% to 10%.

In 1953, the government introduced a special statute placing export industries and the smaller business sector beyond the scope of the Anti-Monopoly Act. This was a compromise between the industrial policy goals of export promotion and business stability in the smaller business sector, and the Anti-Monopoly Act's insistence on the maintenance of an order based on free competition.

From 1954 onwards, the government established a series of industry laws that provided special exemptions to the Anti-Monopoly Act. These were intended to facilitate structural adjustment in mature industries such as fertilisers, coal and textiles, whilst fostering growth industries in the machinery and electronics sectors (Fig. 9.1-2).

Though these measures resulted in the relaxation of the Anti-Monopoly Act, few recession or rationalisation cartels were formed. This was partly because administrative guidance was used frequently to advise major companies to retrench their operations.

In 1950s corporate mergers were instigated primarily as a means of business diversification by companies with historical, personnel and resource links within the same *keiretsu* (corporate groups). In particular, these mergers led to the re-conglomeration of former *zaibatsu*-affiliated trading houses. In general, however, the level of merger activity remained low for two reasons. First, to exploit wage differentials characterising different corporate scales, it was more advantageous to form *Keiretsu*, in which smaller business partners served as subcontractors. Second, the rapid expansion of the domestic market at a time when foreign trade and investment were still regulated meant that companies were more strongly motivated to expand their own facilities.

In the 1960s, however, Japan began to move towards the liberalisation of foreign trade and investment. In this context, the Ministry of International Trade

Fig. 9.1-2 Number of Anti-Monopoly Act exemptions by category of business laws

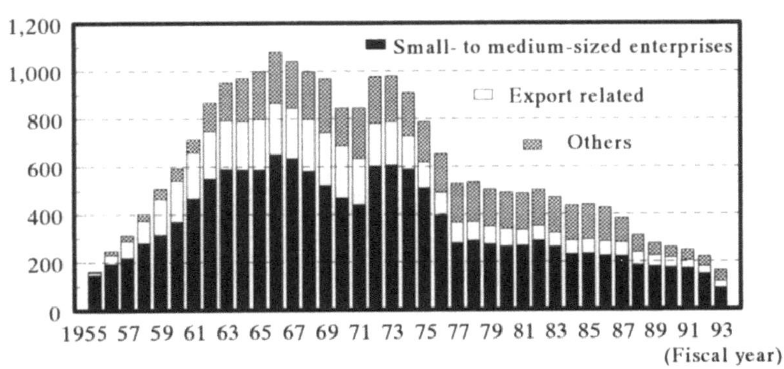

Source: Fair Trade Commission, Annual Report of the Fair Trade Commission (1994 ed.)

and Industry (MITI) began to advocate corporate mergers as a means of bolstering international competitiveness and avoiding wasteful duplication in the areas of capital investment, R&D investment, and offshore business ventures. This led to a series of large-scale mergers during the latter half of Japan's high-growth period, including the merger of Mitsubishi Zosen; Shin-Mitsubishi Heavy Industries and Mitsubishi Japan Heavy Industries to create Mitsubishi Heavy Industries in 1964; the creation of Nissan Motor in 1966 through the merger of Nissan Jidosha with Prince Motor; the merger of Nissho with Iwai Sangyo into Nissho-Iwai in 1968; and the formation of Nippon Steel through the 1970 merger of Yawata Steel and Fuji Steel. In the 1960s and beyond, the level of corporate mergers remained high at around 1,000 cases each year (Fig. 9.1-3).

In the high-growth period, the formation of rationalisation cartels enabled companies, especially in materials-type industries, to avoid excessive competition during recessionary periods. During economic upswings, on the other hand, bullish demand forecasts encouraged companies to invest aggressively in plant and equipment in order to pursue economies of scale as a means of bolstering their international competitiveness. As a result, despite the relaxation of the Anti-Monopoly Act, rapid economic growth created market conditions that remained relatively conducive to competition throughout the high-growth period.

9.1.3.3. Reinforcement of the Anti-Monopoly Act (1977-1990)

Illegal cartels proliferated in the confused climate of sky-rocketing prices, having been formed in the wake of the first oil shock. This situation led to the passage of amendments designed to strengthen the Anti-Monopoly Act in 1977. First, the FTC was given the power to force companies to transfer part of their business operations and to implement other necessary measures in order to restore

Fig. 9.1-3 Mergers approved since 1947

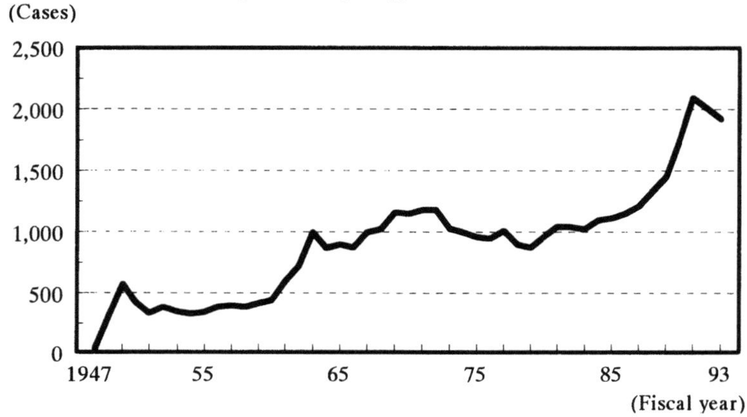

Source: Fair Trade Commission, Annual Report of the Fair Trade Commission (1994 ed.)

competition in areas where an oligopolistic situation developed into monopoly, causing competition to stifle. Second, a new system of punitive surcharges was put in effect to give force to existing provisions banning cartels. Third, the FTC was given the authority to demand explanations in the event of concurrent price hikes in oligopoly-dominated industrial sectors. And fourth, the ceiling for share ownership by financial institiutions was lowered from 10% to 5%.

9.1.3.4. Further reinforcement of competition policy as a result of Japan–US SII talks (1991-)

In the late 1980s, Japan's trade surplus began to expand conspicuously, leading to criticism that its domestic market structure was closed and lacked transparency. During the Japan–US talks under the Structural Impediments Initiative (SII), which started in 1989, Japan was urged to make a number of changes in its competition policy and market practices. First, there was a call for the formulation of guidelines for business practices in the distribution sector. Second, the United States sought action over exclusive trade practices, including stronger enforcement of the Anti-Monopoly Act, the enhancement and expansion of the FTC's investigation system, an increase in punitive surcharges and the introduction of criminal penalties for violations of the Anti-Monopoly Act, and the reduction of exemptions from the Anti-Monopoly Act. Third, on the issue of *keiretsu* affiliations, the United States called for the establishment of guidelines on inter-company dealings.

As a result of the SII talks, the FTC came under pressure to enforce the provisions of the Anti-Monopoly Act rigorously and to ensure transparency in the application of the law. Amendments passed in 1991 increased punitive surcharges against cartels from 1.5% to 6.0%. In addition, guidelines were published for the application of the Anti-Monopoly Act in relation to distribution and trading practices. In 1993, fines for corporations and other entities that acted against restrictions on private monopolies and unfair trading practices were increased from ¥5 million to ¥100 million.

The government is currently overhauling the system of exemptions under the Anti-Monopoly Act.

Some exemptions under the Anti-Monopoly Act are no longer necessary, whilst others are hindering efforts to meet consumer needs. The basic philosophy guiding the present review of these exemptions is that they should be abolished in principle. In the area of resale price maintenance systems, the government plans to cancel all product designations by the end of fiscal 1998.

9.1.4. Evaluation of competition policy

The anti-monopoly policy introduced during the post-war reconstruction period laid the institutional foundations for the development of Japanese industry.

The separation of ownership and management through the dissolution of the *zaibatsu* transferred business leadership into the hands of young managers who adapted aggressively to the competitive market environment, created through corporate splits resulting from the deconcentration of excessive economic power and through the establishment of the Anti-Monopoly Act. The relaxation of the Anti-Monopoly Act in 1953 led to increased share ownership of business corporations, the formation of *keiretsu* (affiliations) by upper-ranked companies, and a rise in share ownership of financial institutions. These changes transformed the structure of business concentration in post-war Japan into a system based primarily on interlocking shareholdings. They also led to the formation of corporate groups in place of the pre-war *zaibatsu*. These corporate groups provided a way of spreading risk at a time when Japan's economic base was still fragile.

An analysis of subsequent developments suggests that, whilst anti-monopoly policy was not always in the forefront of economic and industrial development processes in Japan, it played a positive role as the ultimate means of maintaining competition in Japan's industrial structure. Whilst the competitive environment in Japan differs from the ideal conditions of perfect competition in the US, it appears that Japan has managed to create its own competitive conditions based on the achievement of a balance between competition and conciliation through confrontation between the FTC and MITI/industry. In terms of actual competition in the marketplace, this flexible policy stance has been paralleled by the intensification of competition in markets that were subdivided by a variety of competition-limiting policies. This situation has had the effect of stimulating consumer-oriented innovation.

However, this combination of flexible competition policy and severe market competition merely served to promote growth, whilst Japan was striving to catch up with the industrialised countries of the West. If the Japanese economy is to open up new industrial frontiers, it will be necessary to restructure industrial organisations and structures to facilitate market participation and withdrawal from markets on the basis of market principles. Moreover, the rapid globalisation of business activities will require the international harmonisation of rules and the establishment of equal competitive footing in all advanced industrialised economies.

Market competition can stimulate business innovation and provide the driving force for dynamic change in Japan's industrial structure. To achieve this outcome, Japan will need to ensure that its markets remain competitive through a multi-faceted approach to competition policy, primarily through the Anti-Monopoly Act.

9.2. Germany's Competition Policy

9.2.1. Relation between competition theory and competition policy

A system of competition can orient itself around two primary goals: individual freedom and economic efficiency. These two goals are closely related to each other, depending on the concept of competition. German competition law is oriented more on the protection of individual freedom (Hayek, 1969) than on market results or overall economic goals. The individual is to be protected from restraints of competition which could lead to restrictions on or elimination of individual freedom of action.

The shaping of the German system of competition was strongly influenced by economic principles. Since, despite major advances in competition theory, there is still no consistent, self-contained and practically applicable competition "theory", one refers to so-called "principles" of competition. Thus the paradigm of perfect competition, whose realisation was regarded as increasingly unrealistic, gradually gave way to that of "dynamic competition" (Heuß, 1980). According to this, monopolies, which have patent protection and are limited in time, are regarded as necessary in order to induce pioneering feats from innovating entrepreneurs (following Schumpeter). However, this conception also has its weaknesses.

Further important changes in the arrangement of the system of competition were also caused by the increasing rejection of the theory of "ruinous competition" in cases of production with falling marginal costs. This theory influenced German legislation into the 1950s. Since it became evident, however, that falling marginal costs are usually associated with very different patterns of cost behaviour, the number of proponents of the theory of ruinous competition vanished all the more (Schmidt, 1993).

These changes in theoretical conceptions have opened up completely new fields for competition policy especially with regard to necessities following deregulation and privatisation of natural monopolies. A discussion of these problems, however, is beyond the scope of this chapter. The same applies to a presentation of EU competition law, which has been strongly shaped by Germany (Mestmäcker, 1987). Space is also not sufficient for a discussion of protectionism, subsidies, taxes and competitive conditions in the labour market, which are also part of a system of competition.

9.2.2. Competition legislation in Germany

The main pillars of the German system of competition are the following laws, all of which have been amended to fit contemporary requirements.

- The Law Against Restraints of Competition, also known as the cartel law or anti-trust law, is the most important competition law in Germany. In Section 4, this legislation will be treated separately.
- The Law Against Unfair Competition forbids in Article 1 all behaviours that are *"contra bonos mores"*. Where violations occur, "desistance or compensation can be demanded". Examples of behaviour *contra bonos mores* are misleading information and deception. This law is the oldest, notable German competition law. Its version of 1909 is still largely in force today. It remains extremely important in actual court decisions, but since it has not yet been possible to present a comprehensive catalogue of behaviours that are *contra bonos mores*, it has remained in an area that leaves judges great leeway.
- The Rebates Law of 1933 stipulates which rebates are allowed and which are not. Its goal is to increase price competition and market transparency by prohibiting a proliferation of various rebates. For this reason, cash rebates of 3% on final products and bulk discounts are only allowed, if they are "customary" in trade or commerce. In general they can be granted to bulk purchasers. Rebates cartels, however, were not forbidden, since it was assumed that they do not hinder market transparency.
- The Bonus Regulation of 1932 forbids at all stages in the economic process the granting of so-called "secondary goods". Excluded from this are only "low-value promotional items". Bonuses would lead to a distortion of price competitiveness due to the impenetrable mixing of primary and secondary items.
- Patent Law also affects competition by providing temporary protection of intellectual property. New ideas or inventions are made into tradable goods and safeguarded against imitation via copyright and industrial intellectual property protection. Patent law also has a long history. The American constitution contained provisions for patent protection, and similar arrangements were introduced in Europe two years after the French Revolution. Thus, already in 1883 the first international agreement was reached (Paris Accord), also binding for Germany, which to the present day has increased in scope. An important milestone in this process was the establishment of the European Patent Office which began its work in June 1978.
- Trademark, Design Patent and Utility Model Laws are also aimed at protecting intellectual property with similar regulations as in patent law.
- Foreign trade legislation is also particularly important for competition (Görgens, 1969). Economic history has shown that there is a close connection between import tariffs and cartels. This is clearly demonstrated in Germany after the transition from free trade to the policy of protective duties (1879) under Bismarck, which created the prerequisites for a rapid spread of cartelisation.

9.2.3. History of the Law Against Restraints of Competition

9.2.3.1. Before World War II

The Law Against Restraints of Competition was not passed until 1957 and took effect on 1 January 1958. It has a very long history (Kartte, Holtschneider, 1981). As the right of free trade was introduced in Germany (Trade Regulation Act of 1869) and association bans and trading privileges were abolished, many believed that the creation of monopolies and cartels that would restrict the freedom of trade was unrealistic. When they arose, nevertheless, they were considered the unavoidable consequences of freedom of contract, and efforts were made to combat their excesses (e.g., "exorbitant exploitation") by use of existing laws; some also proposed placing them under government supervision. During economic crises, however, the government frequently assisted cartel formation by means of tax concessions (structural crisis cartels). The toleration of cartels was also promoted by the conviction that they were to some extent useful in protecting firms from excess production; socialists also favoured cartels in the belief that they would facilitate the socialisation of the economy. Not until 1923 was the state given the power to control the abusive practices of cartels in the form of an ordinance against the misuse of economic power.

After the Nazi seizure of power, Germany experienced a phase of increasing compulsory cartelisation. Cartels were legally prescribed, which also forced the so-called "outsiders" to become cartel members. At the same time, the authority of the Reich Ministry of Economics in controlling the economy was constantly expanded, reaching its pinnacle in 1939 in the so-called "Cartel Settlement Decree" which deprived the cartels of their actual tasks and placed them directly under the "Organisation of the Enterprise Sector" of the Nazi regime. Cartelisation had namely advanced to such a point that cartels in their traditional form were no longer necessary to direct the economy. This had major consequences for competition policy after the war.

9.2.3.2. After World War II

After the war, Germany developed very strict anti-trust laws for several reasons. First of all, the Allies issued military ordinances that were clearly influenced by American anti-trust laws. The basis was Section III, Item 12 of the Potsdam Declaration of 1945, which stated: "At the earliest practicable date, the German economy shall be decentralised for the purpose of eliminating the present excessive concentration of economic powers as exemplified in particular by cartels, syndicates, trusts and other monopolistic arrangements". In 1947, relatively similar laws were decreed in the three Western occupation zones on the decartelisation of the German economy.

With increasing East-West tension came a new orientation in American security policy; combating large enterprises was now subordinated to the rapid reconstruction of German industry. The leading principle of competition policy was thus the assurance of free enterprise activities.

It would be wrong, however, to see the Americans as prime movers in anti-trust policies, even if they were intensely disliked by big industry and their associations. Firstly, the socialists and liberals agreed that something had to be done with the large armament monopolies that had worked together closely with Hitler, and, secondly, the basic concepts of the Americans on the link between freedom and competition were shared by a number of influential German jurists and economists of the neoliberal school which had stood in strong opposition to fascism. In their numbers were Eucken and Böhm, who as politicians took an active part in post-war legislation. Neoliberalism held that competition tends to be eliminated by cartels and monopolies in a completely free market economy. Only a strong state can ensure competition.

Individual elements of the neoliberal school, such as the theory of perfect competition, were later pushed into the background. Whereas the Competition Act of 1957 was still oriented on this concept, the subsequent amendments of the Act were based on the model of workable competition (kantzenback, Kallfass, 1981). This led in part to contradictory formulations amongst economists.

Because of the influence of the neoliberal school, German jurisprudence succeeded in further developing the American-inspired anti-trust laws beyond the original post-war occupation framework. After much controversy over whether a misused regulation was to be preferred to a ban on cartels, the Competition Act was passed in 1957 and took effect in 1958.

The then Minister of Economics, Ludwig Erhard, a strong proponent of the Competition Act as the "Constitution of the Market Economy", strongly resisted big industry headed by the Federation of Industry (BDI), which preferred a principle of co-operation instead of a principle of competition. Since, however, this argumentation was not informed by the lessons to be learned from the Third Reich, the influence of the BDI was weakened. Nevertheless, the opponents of the Competition Act succeeded in introducing numerous exceptions.

9.2.4. Main content of the Law Against Restraints of Competition

9.2.4.1. Anti-trust regulations

According to the Competition Act, cartels are banned in principle. Exceptions and special regulations apply especially to the Federal Railway, the Federal Post Office, banks, insurance companies and farms. In these exceptional cases, a distinction is made between cartels that must be reported and those that require permission.

The cartels that must be reported include: condition cartels, rebate cartels, standardisation cartels, as well as export cartels. Condition cartels establish terms of business, delivery and payment, including cash discounts. Rebate cartels regulate a uniform system of granting rebates. Standardisation cartels contain agreements on the use of uniform norms. Because of their rationalisation effects, they are even considered to be desirable. If the cartel officials do not express their objections within a specified period of time, they are considered approved.

Cartels that require permission include: structural crisis cartels, rationalisation cartels, export and import cartels with domestic impact, and cartels that the Ministry of Economics may permit "if in exceptional cases the limiting of competition is necessary for predominant reasons of the economy as a whole and the public interest" (Article 8, Competition Act). Structural crisis cartels are cartels that enable an industry in a structural crisis to adjust its production, according to plan, to reduced demand. Rationalisation cartels are meant to improve the performance of an enterprise. This can also be achieved via specialisation of production (so-called specialisation cartels). Import and export cartels can only be approved if they have no major influence on the domestic market. The admission of cartels that require permission is always limited in time, unless the Ministry of Economics specifies otherwise.

9.2.4.2. Ban on vertical restraints of competition

Agreements with the purchaser of goods that refer to resale to a third party and that prescribe terms and conditions or prices are not allowed. This applies, for example, to retail price maintenance. Here, too, there are exceptions: publishing houses' products like books and newspapers as well as branded articles.

The Competition Act has been amended five times (Kartte, Holtschneider, 1981). The amendments deal with intensification of competition or ordinances that make it easier to take action against illegal practices in courts of law. This development is an evolutionary process in which court decisions have played a major role.

The first amendment of 1965 made it easier for small- and medium-sized firms to cooperate in order to improve their performance and to strengthen themselves in their struggle against larger firms (*Mittelstand* cartels). The reasoning was that an oligopolisation would intensify competition. The Cartel Office, however, can refuse to permit *Mittelstand* cartels if they restrain competition. This amendment also gave the cartel authorities the right to levy fines in cases of anti-trust infringements.

The second amendment of 1973 contains many new features. It intensified the control of abusive practices over market-dominating companies by setting up a narrower definition of the criteria for market domination. Retail price maintenance was forbidden for branded articles. Its place was taken by non-binding price recommendations that are subject to the Cartel Office's control of abusive practices.

A necessary change was the introduction of merger controls. Whereas market domination by a cartel power was not allowed, it was still possible to achieve market domination via the joining of two companies. With this amendment the

Cartel Office was given the authority to forbid mergers if they establish or strengthen market domination. If, however, the company can demonstrate that the merger will lead to an improvement of competitive conditions that will offset the disadvantages of market domination, then the merger must be approved. Analogous to the general clause of the anti-trust law, the Ministry of Economics has the right to permit exceptions in the "general public interest".

Moreover, a Monopoly Commission was established consisting of five independent economic experts. Their task is to prepare an expertise report every two years on developments in enterprise concentration. If the Minister of Economics intends to approve a merger, he must consult the Commission beforehand.

The third amendment of 1976 strengthened merger controls with regard to the press in order to maintain the freedom of information. It also placed smaller mergers in the area of the press under the control of the Cartel Office.

The fourth amendment of 1980 brought numerous intensifications, of merger controls. Also, the control of abusive practices over market-dominating companies was sharpened by the introduction of farther-reaching criteria. The discrimination of small firms, due to buyer concentration of power, was covered by more precise criteria. Also, the control of abusive practices over the utility industry (gas, water, electricity) was intensified for more effective consumer protection.

The fifth amendment of 1989 again strengthened the instruments of merger controls, especially with regard to concentrations in trade. Moreover, special provisions in exceptional cases were strongly limited. The burden of proof in legal proceedings because of a supply boycott were changed in favour of the plaintiff.

9.2.5. Critical appraisal of competition policy

Doubtlessly, the introduction of the Competition Act was the most important milestone in the creation of successful competition policy. Germany received the strongest anti-trust laws in Europe (Mestmäcker, Möller, Schwarz, 1987). The fact that the Federal Republic had liberalised more than 90% of OECD imports by 1954 helped ensure that immediately after the war, an internationally competitive industry was established that made Germany in the 1950s the country with the highest export growth rates in Europe. This strongly assisted the economic catching-up process (Görgens, 1969).

Despite this success, the numerous exceptions to the Competition Act must be criticised. They are also questioned by most experts of competition theory (Tuchtfeldt, 1978). Particular criticism has been aimed at structural crisis, specialisation and rationalisation cartels. Since it is precisely the task of competition to achieve on-going rationalisation, it is very dubious why this should succeed better via a limitation of competition.

It is of particular note, however, that legislators, with the introduction of merger controls in the second amendment to the Competition Act, took account of the fact that the greatest dangers to competition came from increasing instances of concentration and less from other types of restrictions to competition.

The right of the Minister of Economics to allow exceptions for cartels and mergers proved to be less disquieting. Since the concept of "overall economic interest" cannot be operationalised, an endless amount of cartelisation for political reasons was feared. However, hardly any use has been made of this regulation, since it was realised that economic-policy problems cannot be solved by cartelisation. In the few cases where this did occur, public discussion was so heated that their actual importance was greatly overestimated (Monopolkommission, 1994).

The sanctions available to the Cartel Office were also successively improved and intensified. This applies particularly to cases involving monopoly profits, where fines can be imposed up to three times that of the additional proceeds. The Cartel Office has made frequent use of this provision.

In 1990, 87 cases (including new ones) were pending. The Cartel Office wrapped up 56 cases. In 12 cases fines were imposed, 2 cartels were forbidden and 42 cases were suspended.

The following table shows that the ban on cartels has largely fulfilled its task. Only relatively little use was made of the permissible exceptions. If we delete from the 239 existing cartels the export, *Mittelstand*, standardisation, rebate and condition cartels, the number of questionable cartels from a free-market point-of-view is considerably reduced.

Also with respect to concentration, German anti-trust laws seem to have had an effect. Fig. 9.2-1, prepared by the Monopoly Commission, shows the market share of the largest 3, 10 and 100 enterprises in manufacturing and mining from 1977 to 1991. It suggests the conclusion that, with the exception of a slight increase in 1987, concentration has not intensified on the whole.

Table 9.2-1 Types of cartels in Germany from 1958 to 1993

Cartel type	Number of cartels since 1958	Number of effective cartels in 1993
Rebate and condition cartels	114	49
Structural crisis cartels	2	0
Standardisation cartels	16	6
Rationalisation cartels	61	10
Specialisation cartels	122	33
Mittelstand cartels	118	96
Purchasing cooperatives	1	1
Export cartels	127	42
Import cartels	2	0
Special cartels	4	2
Total	567	239

Source: Federal Cartel Office, 1994.

Figure 9.2-1 Market share of the largest 3, 10 and 100 enterprises in manufacturing and mining

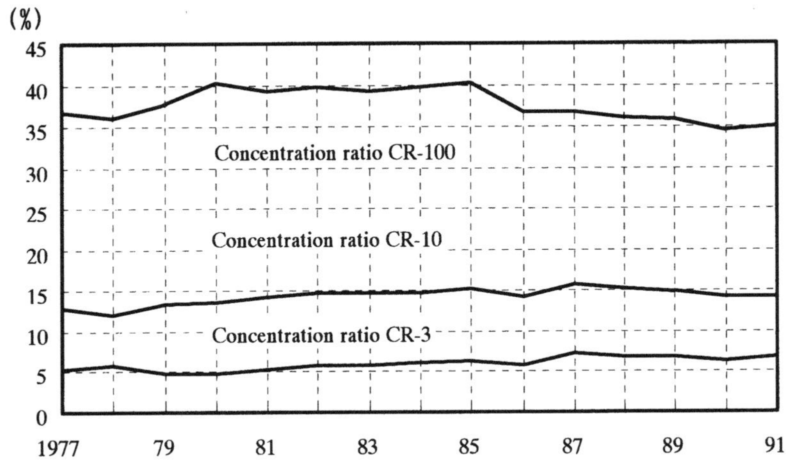

Note: Enterprises in former territory of the Federal Republic, the new Länder not included.

Source: Federal Statistical Office. Dept. IV C, Special Compilations for the Monopolies Commission, 1979, ff.

9.3. Comparative Summary of Competition Policy

9.3.1. Differences

In the postwar period competition policy has been implemented in Japan under the 1947 Anti-Monopoly Act, and in Germany under the 1957 Competition Act. Both the Japanese and German economic systems are based on the principle of free-market competition under these laws. Another common feature is the existence of regulations that allow the approval of cartels as exceptions to these laws. Although both Japan and Germany have similar legal frameworks, there have been major differences in the actual methods used to implement competition policy, and in the competitive environment in their markets.

Germany has pursued competition policy as part of its efforts to create a market environment that would encourage competition. In Germany, cartels with the potential to serve a useful purpose have been tolerated, provided that it was possible to avoid the monopolisation of markets. The law prohibiting the restriction of competition has so far been amended five times, whilst numerous court rulings have led to a gradual tightening of the regulations from perspective of promoting market competition. Changes include the facilitation of procedures to eliminate unfair trading practices by companies that dominate their markets, and controls on mergers that would reinforce market domination.

Japan's Anti-Monopoly Act was originally even stricter that the US Anti-Trust Act. However, industry and the Ministry of International Trade and Industry (MITI) have exerted considerable influence on the law as part of their efforts to strengthen Japan's international competitiveness. The result has been fluctuation between tighter and looser regulation of competition. Moreover, the actual environment for market competition has been determined not by the principles set down in the Anti-Monopoly Act, but by exceptions to the law, other government regulations, and policies that were adjusted flexibly according to the level of industrial development. In this sense, the institutional framework for Japan's competition policy was less consistent than that established in Germany.

9.3.2. Reasons for differences in competition policy

These differences between competition policy in Japan and Germany appear to reflect differences in traditional thinking on market competition.

Germany established a law regulating business transactions as early as 1869. Apart from a period during the Hitler era, when the government adopted policies designed to promote market concentration, it has traditionally maintained the principle that business transactions should be unrestricted. This philosophy was applied consistently, and even the formation of monopolies and cartels was regarded as the inevitable consequence of the freedom to enter into contracts. The post-war law prohibiting the restriction of competition was the result of a directive from the occupying forces. However, ito was the existence of support within Germany that enabled the government to introduce the strictest competition regulations in Europe. Two circumstances within Germany contributed to this outcome. First, people recognised the need to break up the military monopolies that had worked closely with Hitler. Second, German lawyers and economists, who had strongly opposed fascism, advocated the American concept of free competition.

In Japan, the *zaibatsu* (conglomerates) occupied a central position in the market in the pre-war era. Furthermore, the Great Depression of 1929 led to the widespread formation of legally sanctioned cartels, creating an industrial organisation that tended to limit competition. Japan's Anti-Monopoly Act was introduced under the authority of the post-war occupation administration (GHQ) as part of its economic democratisation policy. In this sense, the concept of market competition has not always been accepted as a consistant rule in Japan.

9.3.3. Influence of competition policy on market competition

Germany adopted an extremely tough competition policy in order to prevent the concentration and monopolisation of markets. In the pre-war period, cartels were frequently formed for political reasons, and it was feared that market competition would be limited. However, it gradually became clear that cartels did not hold the answer to economic problems, and subsequently the escape clause that allowed the government to tolerate cartels was rarely used. In order to survive in fiercely competitive markets, German companies began to pursue strategies of product differentiation based on high product quality. The international competitiveness of German companies can be attributed to the combination of this approach with superior technology.

In Japan, the dissolution of the *zaibatsu* resulted in the separation of ownership and management, which led to the emergence of a new generation of managers, and to determined efforts to adopt to the shift towards competitive markets. These changes were responsible for Japan's economic development during the post-war reconstruction period. Competition policy during the high-growth period and beyond combined a tendency towards cartel formation inherited from the pre-war industrial sector, with a market competition structure that had been imposed through external pressure. As a result, Japan's industrial organisation took on the dual characteristics of co-operation and competition. Multiple companies competed fiercely for the same markets in an environment that combined flexible competition policy with severe market competition. Market vitality was enhanced by the resulting drive to cut prices through economies of scale and production-process innovation. Bureaucratic intervention and guidance prevented the strong from overpowering the weak during periods of overheated competition or recessions. This market system, under which business risk was ultimately borne by the government, functioned effectively whilst Japan was working to catch up with the advanced industrialised nations of the West.

Table 9.3-1 A Comparison of competition policy in Japan and Germany

	Japan	Germany
Basic philosophy	Flexible restriction of competition	Consistent promotion of competition especially by liberalising imports
Business sector competition strategy	Competition amongst equals price competition ↓ Promotion of price competition	Strong price competition amongst domestic and foreign companies
Market competition	Normal: Excessive competition Ultimate: Relief through cartel formation	Workable competition

10. Trade and Capital Transaction Policies

10.1. Japan's Trade and Capital Transaction Policies

10.1.1. Background of Japan's trade and capital transaction policies

The short-term purpose of trade and capital transaction policies is to maintain the equilibrium of the international balance of payments. The medium- to long-term goal is to protect and nurture domestic industry. For Japan, which is poorly endowed with resources, it was necessary to ensure the effectiveness of domestic economic policies and regulations by separating domestic and foreign markets so as to achieve economic development in an environment characterised by shortages of foreign currency. Yet Japan's return to the international community naturally implied an obligation to maintain the free-trade system. From 1960 onwards, therefore, Japan's trade and capital transaction policies were targeted at a phased liberalisation process that took account of trends in the competitiveness of Japanese industry. This shift was spurred in part by external pressure.

Trade and capital transaction policies can be divided into four areas: (1) export promotion policy, (2) import control policy, (3) inwards direct investment restriction and (4) external direct investment restriction. Japan promoted exports primarily through the structured implementation of industry policies. These policies were designed to enhance the international competitiveness of industries by imposing certain limitations on free competition, which is the spirit of the market economy system. Import control was achieved, during the post-war reconstruction phase, through the strict regulation of import volumes by means of a foreign currency allocation system. After 1960, imports were controlled primarily through tariff policy.

The primary purpose of capital transaction policy was to protect and nurture domestic industries. This was achieved through the restriction of inwards direct investment. Whilst preventing foreign companies from participating directly in Japanese markets, the government promoted the introduction of foreign technology, thereby improving the competitiveness of Japanese industry. The restriction on direct overseas investment helped to keep Japanese capital in Japan.

This chapter analyses import control policy and restrictions on inwards direct investment, with particular emphasis on their role in the protection and development of Japanese industry.

Fig. 10.1-1 Japanese trade and capital transaction policies

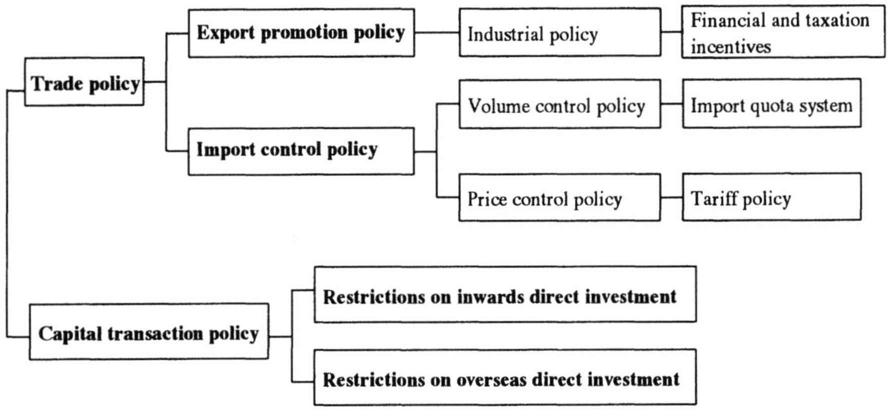

10.1.2. Evolution of trade and capital transaction policies

10.1.2.1. Transition from closed to open economic structure (1947-1959)

The framework for foreign trade in the post-war period was formed through the enactment of the Foreign Exchange and Foreign Trade Control Act in 1949. Most import transactions were subject to an approval or quota system, and imports not considered essential or urgent were strictly restrained. Further, foreign capital inflows were banned in principle under the Foreign Capital Law of 1950. On the other hand, technology contracts and loans required for economic development were aggressively introduced. The government, meanwhile, implemented a number of programmes to promote exports. Tax-related incentives included tax deductions for export-derived income, additional depreciation for export-related facilities, and overseas market development reserves. These systems provided a direct incentive to export, since exporting led to reduced taxes. Financial measures privileged trade finance, such as export advance. Other measures included the introduction of an export insurance system and the collection and distribution of information through the Japan External Trade Organisation (JETRO).

Japan rejoined the international community in 1955 with its formal entry into the General Agreement on Tariffs and Trade (GATT). As its economy grew, it came under increasingly intense foreign pressure to liberalise its economy. From 1960 onwards, it began to respond to that pressure by gradually phasing in policies for the liberalisation of foreign trade and capital transaction, thus initiating a transition from a period of strict curbs on imports to an open economic structure. Table 10.1-1 outlines Japan's post-war trade and capital transaction liberalisation process.

The evolution of Japan's trade and capital transaction policies since 1960 can be divided into three periods: (1) the transition to liberalisation in the high-growth period (1960-72), (2) the completion of liberalisation in the oil-shock years (1973-79), and (3) the period of counter-measures against trade friction in the stable-growth period (1980-94).

Table 10.1-1 Trade and capital transaction policies in post-war Japan

Phase of Development year / month	Developments
Closed economy	
1947 /8	Resumption of private-sector trade
1949 /4	Establishment of unified trade exchange rate ($1 = ¥360)
/12	Enactment of Foreign Exchange and Foreign Trade Control Act
1952 /8	Membership of IMF
1955 /9	Formal membership in GATT
Transition to liberalisation	
1960 /6	Sweeping liberalisation of import restrictions (trade and foreign exchange liberalisation master plan)
1963 /2	Promotion to GATT Article 11 status
1964 /4	Transition to IMF Article 8 status and membership in OECD
/5	Start of GATT Kennedy Round (concluded in June 1967)
/10	Achievement of import liberalisation rate of 92.8%
1967 /7	First capital transaction liberalisation package
1968 /6	Expanded liberalisation of technology inflows
/7	First stage of tariff cuts (1,910 items) under Kennedy Round
1969 /3	Second capital transaction liberalisation package
/10	Decision to liberalise 55 residual import restrictions
1970 /9	Third capital transaction liberalisation package
1971 /4	Liberalisation of capital transaction in automobile sector
/8	Fourth liberalisation package, Announcement of the new US trade policy ("Nixon Shock")
/12	Smithsonian Agreement (yen lifted to ¥308/dollar)
1972 /1	Signing of the Japan-US Agreement on textiles Liberalisation of technology inflows
Completion of liberalisation	
1973 /2	Yen switched to floating exchange-rate system
/5	Fifth capital transaction liberalisation package
1974 /8	Liberalisation of foreign investment in computer industry (50% ownership ceiling)
/12	IC manufacturing (100% ownership allowed) and information-processing industry (50% ownership ceiling)
1975 /2	Real start of GATT Tokyo Round (concluded in December 1979)
/6	Liberalisation of foreign investment in retail sector
/12	Liberalisation of foreign investment in computer industry (100% foreign ownership allowed)
1976 /4	Information-processing industry (100% foreign ownership allowed)
Coping with trade friction	
1980 /12	New Foreign Exchange Control Law enacted (liberalisation of external capital transactions, in principle)
1986 /1	Removal of import tariffs in 146 agricultural items and 1,703 industrial items; reduction of remaining tariffs by 20% in principle
1990 /4	Removal or reduction of import tariffs on 1,008 industrial items
1991 /4	Liberalisation of orange and beef imports
1992 /4	Liberalisation of orange juice imports
/12	Final accord under Uruguay Round

Source: Kousai, Teranishi, ed., The post-war economic reforms of Japan (partially revised by SRI)

10.1.2.2. Transition to liberalisation (1960-1972)

In 1960, the Japanese government unveiled a master plan for the liberalisation of trade and foreign exchange. In the following year, it moved to improve the tariff system and replaced its "positive list" of items free from import constraints with a "negative list" formula, under which imports were free from control, in principle, and only exceptions were listed. Liberalisation measures during this period included the replacement of quantitative restrictions with a price-driven adjustment mechanism based on tariffs. This meant that trade barriers still remained in place. Specifically, the government sought to protect growth-promising industries in Japan by introducing a progressive tariff structure that imposed higher import tariffs on high-value-added consumer goods than on raw materials. By August 1963 these measures had raised the liberalisation ratio to 92%, compared with 40% in April 1960.

In a period when the industrialised nations were moving towards trade and capital transaction liberalisation, Japan became a GATT Article 11 nation in 1963, and gained IMF Article 8 status in the following year. These terms are applied to member nations that have liberalised imports and other current account transactions and do not use import quotas or foreign exchange restrictions to carry out balance of payments adjustments. Japan had thus abandoned its foreign-exchange budget system, under which imports were restricted through the rationing of foreign currency for each import item, and only volume-based restrictions remained in place. At the same time, it had achieved OECD membership, signifying its real emergence as a developed nation with an open economy.

As a result of multi-lateral tariff negotiations under the Kennedy Round (1964-67), the leading industrialised nations moved in concert to lower their import tariffs by an average of 35%. Japan also continued to reduce its tariff barriers. Since trade liberalisation under the Kennedy Round focused primarily on manufactured goods, it helped to boost Japan's exports. After the conclusion of the Kennedy Round, Japan moved towards the abolition of residual import quotas between 1969 and 1972. However, the focus of industrial policy had shifted from the achievement of balance of payments equilibrium through import restrictions, towards an increasing emphasis on the improvement of international competitiveness through the protection of domestic industries. As a result, imports of synthetic fibres, machine tools and computers were not liberalised until after 1970.

Japan's admission to the OECD in 1964 also brought an obligation to liberalise foreign investment (direct overseas investment in Japan). This policy shift, which commenced somewhat later than trade liberalisation, began in July 1967 with the announcement of basic guidelines for the liberalisation of direct inwards investment. However, the range of sectors targeted for liberalisation was extremely limited, and most sectors in which foreign firms had shown interest remained subject to case-by-case screening procedures. This drew a strong negative reaction from other countries.

During the trade and capital transaction liberalisation process, Japan also held bilateral textile talks with the United States over a three-year period from 1969 to 1971. These talks were symbolic as a harbinger of future trade friction between Japan and the United States. Negotiations over an international agreement to limit exports of wool and synthetic fibre products to the United States broke down repeatedly. Because of the importance of its relationship with the United States, Japan capitulated amid US threats to introduce import surcharges, import restrictions and other measures, and an agreement was signed in late January 1972. Thereafter, trade friction between Japan and the United States spread to other areas, including iron and steel, machine tools, semiconductors, automobiles and automobile parts.

For Japanese companies, which had been insulated against competition from foreign products and foreign-owned companies within Japan, the shift to a liberalisation stance meant a transition to an environment in which they were exposed to serious full-scale competition. Yet the basic philosophy underlying Japanese trade and capital transaction policies was strongly oriented towards the fostering of industries through the improvement of their international competitiveness by means of policy that restricted imports in order to enable domestic companies to secure markets and benefit from economies of scale. Initially, liberalisation was seen as a price that Japan had to pay from the perspective of international co-ordination in order to be accepted back into the international community. Accordingly, subsequent liberalisation measures were implemented gradually, taking into account specific circumstances, and always against a backdrop of foreign pressure.

10.1.2.3. Completion of liberalisation (1973-1979)

Despite the yen's revaluation from ¥360 to ¥308 against the dollar and despite the shift to a floating exchange-rate system, Japan continued to register steady growth in its trade surplus. This led to the intensification of foreign pressure for trade liberalisation and import expansion. Japan responded by gradually liberalising imports and foreign-exchange controls and lowering tariff rates. The notion that free trade was preferable began to take root.

The abolition of import quotas for manufactured goods was completed during this phase. In April 1968, 122 items were subject to import restrictions. By 1975 this total had been reduced to 27 items, including only one mineral item (coal) and four manufactured items. The main manufactured items covered by import liberalisation measures in this period included antibiotics, colour film, automobile engines, integrated circuits, computers and computer peripherals.

Even after the conclusion of the Kennedy Round, Japan continued to implement a tariff policy that called for tariff reductions. In December 1972, it cut tariffs on processed farm products and mining and manufacturing products by a uniform 20%. That move lowered Japanese tariff rates significantly and also rectified their progressive tariff structure somewhat. Further, as an outcome of the

Tokyo Round of multi-lateral trade talks (1973-79), the leading industrialised countries cut their import tariffs on mining and manufacturing products to an average of approximately 33%, that is, to two-thirds of their previous level. Japan reduced its tariffs by an average of almost 50%. With these major tariff reductions, the focus of trade negotiations shifted from tariff to anti-dumping restrictions, subsidies and other non-tariff barriers.

The liberalisation of foreign direct investment in Japan lagged significantly behind trade liberalisation. A second capital transaction liberalisation package was executed in March 1969, and a third in September 1970. The automotive sector was fully liberalised in 1971, with implementation of a fourth liberalisation package for a shift to a negative list approach. A fifth liberalisation package brought full liberalisation in all sectors, except agriculture and fisheries, mining, petroleum, leather-goods manufacturing, and retailing. The computer sector was fully opened in December 1975, almost ten years after capital transaction liberalisation had become the focus of debate. This delay reflected fears that mergers and acquisitions by foreign capital could affect emerging industries or sectors with the potential to trigger ripple effects in related industries.

10.1.2.4. Coping with trade friction (1980-1994)

By the 1970s, Japan had largely completed the task of liberalising foreign trade and capital transaction. The 1980s, however, were a time of escalating trade tensions between Japan and the United States, including pressure for Japan to implement voluntary export restraints in such areas as colour television sets, automobiles, machine tools and semiconductor chips. The rapid expansion of the US current account deficit and Japan's current account surplus after 1983 heightened tensions between the two countries significantly. A feature of trade friction in the 1980s was the emphasis on processed and assembled products, such as automobiles and machine tools. These were areas in which Japan had enhanced its international competitiveness during the gradual liberalisation process.

Japan's policy response to trade friction followed three basic patterns. First, when the expansion of imports from Japan triggered legal action in the United States under the Anti-Dumping Code (iron and steel, semiconductor chips, etc.) and the Trade Acts (automobiles, machine tools, etc.), Japan responded by introducing voluntary restraints on export volumes and export shares. Second, Japan implemented various measures in response to US charges under the GATT concerning market access for US products (agricultural goods), and also in response to bilateral negotiations in such areas as telecommunications and supercomputers. Third, Japan sought to satisfy US demands for further improvement in market access during the Structural Impediments Initiative talks. The scope of trade tension between the United States and Japan has expanded to include not only matters relating to competitiveness in individual sectors, but also issues concerning the structure of the Japanese economy. This change reflects growing protectionist sentiment since the 1980s, particularly in the US Congress, resulting in a shift of trade policy from "equality of opportunity" to "equality of achievement" within a fair trade relationship.

Japan has already decided to switch to a tariff basis for all agricultural items as a result of the December 1993 GATT Uruguay Round accord. Japan now has the lowest average import tariff rate of any leading industrialised nation, and it has removed almost all of its restrictions on foreign direct investment in its domestic industries. On this basis, it has achieved more progress towards trade and capital transaction liberalisation than any other developed countries. Yet, as a matter of fact, there are still informal non-tariff barriers, including *keiretsu* transactions amongst corporate affiliates, trading practices and collusive bidding. This situation, together with an expanding gap between domestic and foreign prices due to the appreciation of the yen, is reflected in growing domestic and overseas pressure for measures to pry open Japan's closed markets.

10.1.3. Assessing Japanese trade and capital transaction policies

The evolution of Japanese trade and capital transaction policies was thus characterised by gradual progress towards import liberalisation in response to strong foreign pressure and by somewhat slower progress towards capital transaction liberalisation. During this process, Japan sought to protect and nurture promising domestic industries by restricting imports. It also encouraged export industries by providing subsidies, tax breaks, and low-interest financing from government-affiliated financial institutions. This policy approach resulted from a deep-rooted reluctance on the part of industry and the Ministry of International Trade and Industry (MITI), which feared that capital transaction liberalisation would be tantamount to a second coming of the American "Black Ships" that had forced Japan to open its ports in the nineteenth century. The gradual pace of trade and capital transaction liberalisation from 1960 onwards helped to ease competitive pressures from overseas. Within Japan, however, it stoked fierce competition and strongly motivated firms to invest in plant and equipment, and to develop new technology. Ultimately, liberalisation thus made a major contribution to the establishment of a foundation for Japanese industry and to the improvement of its international competitiveness. In other words, instead of protecting depressed domestic industries, Japan's import control policy appears to have played an indirect role in the promotion of exports by helping to foster growth industries.

In retrospect, however, it also appears that the gradual pace of liberalisation had the effect of stifling competition with foreign products in the domestic marketplace and helped to increase the complexity and tenacity of Japan's distribution systems and trading practices, particularly in the manufacturing sector. In this sense, Japan's approach had a negative effect by leading to the formation of market trading practices that appear opaque and closed to other nations.

10.2. Germany's Trade and Capital Transaction Policies

Exports were undoubtedly one of the driving forces of post-war German economic development. Their share both in GNP and in world exports grew rapidly during the 1950s. In the list of leading world exporters, already in 1953 Germany had assumed third place behind the United States and Great Britain. In 1960 it was in second place behind the US as the world's strongest exporter.

Amongst the numerous factors contributing to German industry's rapid return to international markets are not only the high demand elasticity of the German economy and the flexible response to special consumer needs, but also the ability and willingness to accompany exports of industrial equipment with services in the form of organisation, development, training and education, and a tight web of repair services. Another important factor is that trade policy in the Federal Republic of Germany was guided from the very beginning by the economic philosophy of the *ordoliberal* school of economic thought: German policy-makers realised at an early stage that opening their own markets was a prerequisite for success in the international market. By the end of 1954, 92% of private-sector imports had been liberalised (Giersch et al., 1992).

10.2.1. Import policy

10.2.1.1. Return to the world market in the 1950s

In November 1949, the German government again assumed responsibility for its foreign trade policy. Prior to this, foreign trade had been centralised and almost totally subject to quota restrictions. The Allies needed time before they were ready to grant the German economy re-entry into international trade relations. Since the beginning of 1947, the Joint Export-Import Agency (JEIA) was responsible for the conducting of foreign trade. It supervised and controlled imports and exports, and negotiated bilateral quota systems with roughly fifty countries by 1949.

In light of the virtually complete control of foreign trade, customs played a minor role in the trade policy of the first post-war years. The so-called Bülow-Tariff of 1902[1] was still in effect and greatly in need of revision. What was necessary was a change to an *ad valorem* tariff and a classification of products according to the Brussels nomenclature of 1948, especially since West Germany sought membership in GATT and was required to take part in the Torquay GATT tariff reduction round. Work on the new tariff schedule, which was begun in the autumn of 1949 by a tariff committee appointed by the West German government, continued also during the GATT negotiations. The new tariff schedule went into effect on 1 October 1951. The tariff reductions negotiated in Torquay had already been incorporated. Nevertheless, the duties of the new tariff rate were about 30%

---

[1] Named after Bernhard Heinrich, Fürst von Bülow, German chancellor from 1900 to 1907.

higher than the Bülow Tariff (Giersch et al., 1992). Estimates placed West Germany in a middle position between the high-tariff countries such as Great Britain, France and Italy and low-tariff countries such as Belgium, the Netherlands, Sweden and Switzerland. The Federal Republic joined GATT in 1951 and since then has been subject to the most-favoured-nation principle, from which it in turn profited in GATT-member markets.

In the course of the 1950s, West Germany implemented several unilateral tariff reductions, the first of which came already in 1951. Five more substantial cuts occurred between 1955 and 1957. The goal was the stabilisation of domestic price levels. From 1951 to the beginning of 1958, the average tariff level for imported industrial goods was lowered from 16% to 9.6% (Giersch et al., 1992). Tariff reductions differed according to industry. Industries with weaker growth retained relatively high customs protection.

In the area of quantitative import restrictions, first liberalisation steps were undertaken at the end of 1949. At the beginning of November, the member states of the Organisation for European Economic Cooperation (OEEC) agreed to reduce import quotas by 50% within six weeks. In the following years, West Germany implemented import liberalisation more rapidly than the other OEEC countries. In August 1952, about 80% and at the end of 1954 about 90% of all private imports from OEEC countries were liberalised. On average for all OEEC countries, the degree of liberalisation at both points of time was 65% and 83%, respectively (Giersch et al., 1992). Thereafter, the quotas were reduced in small steps: in September 1956 a liberalisation degree of 91.5% was achieved, and by mid-1958, 94%. The agricultural sector remained the most protected (85.4%). In the manufacturing industry, only 2% of imports remained subject to quotas.

The rapid integration of German industry in the world economy took place in the 1950s under the fixed exchange-rate system. The fixed rate of DM 4.20 for one dollar was made in September 1949 in the context of a general devaluation of European currencies vis-à-vis the dollar. In light of higher inflation rates in most large international trading countries, Germany quickly gained a competitive advantage over foreign competition thanks to the stability of its currency. The large influx of foreign currency in the 1950s presented major problems for German monetary policy (see chapter 8.2 on monetary policy).

After 1951, West Germany gradually introduced D-Mark convertibility, at first for payments in the trade of goods and services and only within the European Payments Union. After April 1954, D-Mark convertibility was introduced for other countries, insofar as they were not in the dollar area. Not until the end of 1958 was convertibility for the dollar area introduced (as in most other OEEC countries) on current-account transactions.

With the establishment of the European Economic Community (EEC) in 1958, a new phase of tariff reductions was introduced. However, the first two intra-EEC tariff reductions of 10% each on 1 January 1959 and on 1 July 1960 was not expressed *de facto* in tariff reductions for many products, since they had already been included in the economic-policy tariff reductions of mid-1957 (the reference period for the intra-EEC tariff reductions was 1 January 1957). The first adjustment to the future joint external tariff of the EEC marked a temporary interruption of the long trend of declining tariffs in West Germany. Since the West German tariff level was below the future EEC external tariff, on average, this first adjustment step meant a slight tariff increase for West Germany vis-à-vis third countries.

10.2.1.2. 1960s: Normalisation and completion of the EEC customs union

In the 1960s, growth in the German economy proceeded at a more moderate pace, and the growth of German foreign trade also normalised. It was the decade of dramatically growing exports and current-account surpluses. Neither the 5% D-Mark revaluation at the beginning of the decade nor the taxation measures at the end of 1968, which placed a 4% tax on exports and provided import tax relief of 4% and 2%, nor an additional D-Mark revaluation in October 1969, was able to stop or slow down this process.

EEC trade policy was marked by the gradual dismantling of internal tariffs and quantitative trade restrictions amongst the six member states. Eighteen months ahead of schedule, on 1 July 1968, the customs union was complete. Nevertheless, there were still trade barriers that prevented the free exchange of goods between the six EEC member states. Technical, administrative and taxation regulations prolonged the segmentation of national markets. These restrictions were particularly felt in the high-tech and service areas as well as in public-sector procurement. Although the EC Commission had already drafted a programme for removing these barriers in 1968, it took twenty-five years for the January 1993 "completion of the single market". Moreover, according to Article 115 of the EEC Treaty, interruptions of free EEC internal trade were possible when divergent national quotas for imports from third countries were circumvented by means of trade diversion within the EEC and when this caused "economic difficulties" in one or more member states. (Owing to the liberalisation of intra-EC trade, imports from third countries could enter a country with a higher degree of restriction via a country with lower restrictions to an extent far above the import quotas of this restrictive country vis-à-vis the third country.) West Germany seldom made use of this article.

An easing of tariffs on goods from non-EEC states followed the two GATT rounds in the 1960s. The Dillon Round (1961-62) led to a 20% external tariff reduction in the EEC; the Kennedy Round (1964-67) brought about a further reduction of 35% to 40% in the industrial area. This more than compensated for the rise in tariffs on German imports in the wake of the gradual introduction of joint EEC external tariffs (by 2 percentage points, up to 11% by 1964). When the Kennedy Round reductions had been implemented in 1972, EEC external tariffs were an estimated one-third below the 1958 West German level (Giersch et al., 1992).

10.2.1.3. 1970s: Trade policy, EC expansion and new competitors in the world market

The 1970s began with strong currency turbulence—which diverse international initiatives by central banks were not able to calm—finally leading to the abolition of the dollar purchase obligation in March 1973. This marked the end of the fixed exchange rates of the Bretton Woods regime. From then on, currencies could move freely vis-à-vis the dollar. The EC decided on a joint floating against the dollar and maintained stable currency relations amongst the member states (European currency snake). Up to the establishment of the European Monetary System in 1979, this first attempt at a monetary union in the EC experienced stormy years. From 1973 to 1979, the upwards valuations of the D-Mark on the dollar amounted to 44%, compared to a 36% average for 18 industrial countries.

After the completion of the Customs Union in 1968, the EC assumed responsibility for foreign trade policy vis-à-vis third countries. Now the Council of Ministers, acting on recommendations from the Commission, took decisions on foreign trade measures regarding third countries. The EC authorities, however, did not always make full use of their powers, since the member states, to some extent, continued to pursue their national trade policies. The most noticeable examples are the bilateral voluntary trade limitations that individual member states concluded with third countries on auto imports. Other examples are the differing national import quotas in a number of industries. National trade policy was especially dominant in economic relations with the state trading countries and with Japan, Korea, Hong Kong and Taiwan.

With the EC accession of Great Britain, Ireland and Denmark in 1973, tariff reductions vis-à-vis these countries were gradually implemented. In the 1972 Free Trade Agreement between the EC and EFTA, tariff reductions for commercial goods were continued for the remaining EFTA members, so that in 1977 the tariff divisions within Western Europe were overcome.

In 1972, in line with the last implementation phase of the Kennedy Round, EC external tariffs were again lowered, amounting to an average rate of only 7.3%. On 1 July 1971, the EC was the first industrial region to implement the proposal of the 1968 UN world trade conference (UNCTAD II), which called for easing the market access of developing countries by granting tariff preferences (General System of Preferences—GSP). An easing of tariffs was granted especially for processed and manufactured industrial products. Agricultural goods were only gradually included in this process (Dicke, Wieczorek, 1987).

In the 1970s—in parallel with GATT negotiations on additional tariff reductions (Tokyo Round, 1973 to 1979)—there was an increasing tendency to revert to non-tariff trade restrictions: so-called voluntary restraint agreements, anti-dumping measures and subsidies.

10.2.1.4. 1980s: Further lowering of external EC tariffs and growth on non-tariff protectionism

In the 1980s, as a consequence of the Tokyo Round, a further gradual reduction of external EC tariffs amounting to 30% was achieved. The EC implemented the new tariff already at the beginning of 1985, three years earlier than originally planned. The average EC tariff level now amounted to about 5% on average; tariffs above this average still prevailed for textiles, paper and pulp processing, and for road vehicles (Dicke, Wieczorek, 1987).

With the EC accession of Greece (1981) as well as Spain and Portugal (1986), the German economy could take advantage of additional trade concessions.

As in most regions of the world, the instrument of non-tariff trade barriers took on increasing importance in EC trade policy. The share of imports affected by these measures increased by 18% from 1981 to 1987, according to the UNCTAD calculations (UNCTAD, 1988). (The increase in the US for the same period was 23%.)

In West Germany, non-tariff trade barriers were employed to a lesser extent than in the EC, on average. In 1983, 12.4% of imports were subjected to non-tariff trade restrictions compared to an EC average of 22.3%. France led EC countries with 57%. Quantitative import restrictions (import quotas) were hardly used in West Germany (Dicke, Wieczorek, 1987). Emphasis was placed on voluntary trade restraint and import monitoring measures. West Germany was second only to Denmark in its limited use of import restrictions allowed in Article 115 of the EEC Treaty.

The degree of protection was and still is industry specific. The strongest protection (via external protection or subsidies) is given to coal, iron and steel, aerospace, shipbuilding, textiles, clothing, and, to a lesser extent, consumer goods such as glass or paper products. The capital-goods industry—with the exception of aerospace and shipbuilding—receives relatively little protection or support. This pattern of protection in Germany has remained virtually unchanged since the mid-1970s (Weiss, 1988).

10.2.2. Export promotion

Export promotion includes all measures aimed at increasing a country's exports. The instruments used can be directed at individual companies, such as favourable conditions for export financing, export loan guarantees, or tax relief on exports. General or "horizontal" export promotion includes government assistance in obtaining information on export markets and various forms of support in entering these markets. Exchange-rate policy is also a part of government export support policies.

In light of the continuously high export and current-account surpluses, for many years the West German government saw no need to promote exports. This situation changed after the mid-1970s, with increasing calls from German industry for stronger government support. The main reasons were the deterioration of international price competitiveness due to the strong real D-Mark revaluation and the appearance of new suppliers in the international division of labour, especially from Southeast Asia, which placed strong competitive pressure on the old industrial countries, including Germany. Alongside standard competitive factors such as high productivity, flexible adjustment to consumer desires, and general shifts in demand structure, new factors such as international marketing, a high level of information on individual markets, and financing conditions gained importance.

10.2.2.1. Company-specific (direct) export support instruments

(a) Export financing

The rise in export share and the shifts in exports towards capital goods has considerably increased the financing pressure on businesses over the course of time. The conditions for financing external trade and export credit insurance have become important competitive factors. In West Germany, the traditional view is that export financing is a matter for commercial banks. Thus, the extent of active government lending policy is limited. According to the OECD, in 1974 only 1.2% of all German exports and less than 5% of exports to state trading countries were supported by public-sector funds (Juhl, 1978). Over the course of time, there has been little change in these proportions.

The institutions entrusted with the granting of low-interest loans are the *Ausfuhrkreditanstalt* (AKA) and the *Kreditanstalt für Wiederaufbau* (KfW) (cf. BMWi, *Exportfibel*, Bonn, 1993). Whereas the AKA finances medium- and long-term business transactions with durations of one to four and one to ten years, the KfW concentrates on long-term loans with a minimum duration of eight years as a rule (in the meantime reduced to four years). The KfW especially finances exports of capital goods. The interest rate applied depends on the minimum lending rate in OECD guidelines. Exporters' self-financing ratio—a low-interest loan is not granted for the total amount—is relatively high. At the KfW, it is at least 15% and can rise to 50% depending on the amount of the loan. At the AKA, the self-financing ratio is between 10% and 15% for A-ceiling and 30% for B-ceiling loans.

In an international comparison of major industrial countries, German firms in the 1970s were especially at a disadvantage vis-à-vis the US, Great Britain and France. There was less of a disadvantage vis-à-vis Japan. The disadvantage lay above all in the relatively high self-financing share and the higher costs this involves, the lower total quota for low-interest funds, and in the fact that—in contrast to other countries—fixed interest rates were only granted for long-term loans.

(b) Export credit insurance

In Germany, Hermes and Treuarbeit Deutsche Revision are responsible for implementing government guarantees for foreign-trade loans. Foreign-trade financing via the AKA or KfW must be backed up by state credit insurance, i.e. by federal government guarantees. In assuming these risks, a differentiation is made between private foreign enterprises ("export credit guarantees") and business with foreign governments and public organisations ("guarantees"). The differences lie, above all, in the rate of the premiums, which are about a third lower in the case of transactions with foreign firms than they are for transactions with foreign governments. Both economic and political risks are guaranteed, usually both together. The self-financing share in cases of loss amounts to at least 15% for economic and 10% for most political risks.

A comparison of export credit insurance in Germany with those in other industrial countries is hardly possible because of the great number of differing conditions (Juhl, 1978).

(c) Exchange-rate insurance

To insure exchange rates on long-term export transactions, which is difficult to realise in foreign-exchange markets, the German government introduced a state exchange-rate insurance in 1972. The institutions charged with the operations are Hermes and Treuarbeit Deutsche Revision. The duration of the loans must be at least two years, since the exchange rate risk can only be insured after a lead time of two years. Whilst the scheme only applies to the US dollar, the British pound, and the Swiss franc, other convertible currencies are eligible only if the exporter is in a position to present *prima facie* evidence that the export treaty would fail if not concluded in this currency. For currencies of EC member countries (British pound excluded), an exchange-rate insurance cannot be given at all. The premium amounts to 0.7% a year. The exporters are compensated for exchange-rate losses if these losses go beyond 3% of the insured exchange rate.

10.2.2.2. Horizontal (indirect) export promotion measures

State export assistance in Germany also focuses on providing information on foreign markets. The participation of German firms in international fairs and exhibitions is also assisted by the assumption of certain costs, amongst other things.

(a) Information on foreign markets

Especially small- to medium-sized enterprises view difficulties in information acquisition as a competitive disadvantage in foreign markets. The German government assists information acquisition primarily via three institutions:

- the Federal Foreign Trade Information Office (*Bundesstelle für Außenhandelsinformation*),
- German embassies and consulates,
- Chambers for foreign trade (*Außenhandelskammern*).

The Federal Foreign Trade Information Office was established in 1951 as a division of the Federal Ministry of Economics. With the help of a world-wide network of correspondents, it compiles practical information on all areas relevant to foreign trade on an industry and country basis. Its main publication is the journal *Nachrichten für den Au ßenhandel*. More in-depth information is provided in regular supplements.

The economics divisions of German embassies and consulates also provide information, consulting and the arrangement of business contacts.

The government also supports the chambers for foreign trade, although this assistance is small in comparison to the contribution made by chamber members. The chambers for foreign trade provide information on law, regulations and other official conditions in foreign countries. They also provide individual information and consultation in initiating and executing business transactions.

(b) State aid for participation in foreign trade fairs and exhibitions

The participation of German firms in international fairs, exhibitions and German industrial exhibitions abroad is also assisted by the German government. Official trade fair participation is primarily in the form of information stands, special exhibits and in joint-enterprise exhibitions. For the latter, federal funds are granted to firms to lessen the costs of exhibition space (BMWI 1993, *Exportfibel*). In addition, there is comprehensive technical and organisational support to help especially small- to medium-sized firms participate in foreign trade fairs.

Exhibitors from the new German Länder receive special assistance. For their first trade fair appearances, they can receive a 50% reduction in participation fees. They also qualify for travel, transport and advertising subsidies.

In recent years, the German Länder have also begun to support firms interested in exporting.

10.2.2.3. Other instruments that can contribute to export promotion

Exchange-rate policy, the assistance of foreign investment, and development aid policy can also promote exports. The under-valuation of the D-Mark has already been discussed.

Foreign investment can support and promote exports if they, for example, improve the service performance of the exporting country or serve as a door-opener for exports from a firm's own or other industries. There is no clear proof that the federal government gives special assistance to foreign investment or capital exports (Juhl, 1978). It is difficult to estimate the importance of the conclusion of investment assistance contracts, the offer to assume guarantees for political risks, concessions in the context of the developing country tax code, or the possibility of qualifying for business establishment loans from European Recovery Programme (ERP) funds, to which the German government frequently refers (Juhl, 1978).

Export assistance can be engendered by development aid in two ways: by fixing a relatively high share of delivery-linked loans and by linking development aid and subsidised export credits. This low-interest mixed financing is especially practised in Great Britain (Beyfuß, 1983). In Germany, this instrument has only recently been used on a large scale: development aid for selected developing countries can be supplemented by funds from the KfW at a 1:4 ratio (*Handelsblatt*, 8.8.1994). Aid linking was already reduced in the 1970s by the German government to about 5% of total development aid.

10.2.3. Liberalisation of foreign direct investment in Germany

In the first post-war years, international capital transactions were subject to foreign-exchange controls. Initially, foreign investments in Germany and overseas investments by Germany residents were not permitted. First steps of liberalisation were taken in the early 1950s. As of 1952, foreigners were allowed to acquire marketable domestic securities and property from blocked accounts. For all other forms of foreign investments in West Germany, approvals were still necessary on an individual basis. For Germans, the acquisition of marketable foreign securities was not possible at this time; for all other investments abroad, individual approvals were required.

The favourable development in the balance of payments during the 1950s led to further liberalisation of currency regulations. Already in 1956 and 1957, bans on capital transactions were the exception and unrestricted transfers the rule (Bank Deutscher Länder, 1957). At the beginning of 1957, foreign investments in West Germany were allowed when conducted by using liberalised capital mark accounts (Libka Mark). Permission was still required for the acquisition of holdings of domestic firms, as well as the establishment of branch offices and production facilities in Germany, if more than DM 500,000 per year was invested. Domestic firms were allowed to invest up to a value of DM 3 million annually without requiring permission.

The next major liberalisation step took place in 1958. As of 1 July 1958, the import of capital was largely possible without permit. The so-called liberalised capital mark (Libka Mark) was abolished. Direct investments by foreigners in Germany as well as the acquisition of real estate were possible without any permission (Deutsche Bundesbank, 1958). Likewise, restrictions were lifted for the acquisition of domestic securities by foreigners as long as the purchase was in freely convertible currency. For only partially convertible currencies there were still some restrictions. German investments abroad were now also possible without permits.

With the replacement of the Allied monetary statutes by the Foreign Trade Law of 1 September 1961, West German capital transfers with other countries were fully liberalised (Deutsche Bundesbank, 1962). This was also the situation that prevailed in the following decades.

10.2.4. Assessment

10.2.4.1. Import policy

From its beginnings—excluding the intermezzo of trade restrictions during the Korean War—German trade policy was aimed at reducing trade restrictions. In the 1950s this was primarily an autonomous goal. Since the end of that decade, it was connected with EEC and GATT membership, even though tariffs were temporarily raised vis-à-vis third countries in relation to the gradual introduction of the joint EEC foreign-trade tariffs. As a whole, liberal German trade policy can be assessed as having contributed to a large extent to the rapid re-integration of the German economy into the international division of labour.

In 1969, the European Community assumed responsibility for trade policy, although some scope remained for national trade policy decisions. Some EC countries used the scope for trade restrictions to a much larger extent than Germany. But also here a few industries exposed to strong international competition remained covered by some form of protectionism. The trade policy decisions of the EC Council of Ministers tended to be guided by the interventionist economic policies of France. Thus, for some product groups, EC foreign-trade policy was clearly protectionist. Nevertheless, for EC trade policy as a whole, the label "Fortress Europe" does not apply. The EC has accepted new members and has concluded association agreements with Eastern European countries. Free-trade agreements have been negotiated with countries of the former Soviet Union (Baltic states), and there are partnership and co-operation agreements with Russia and Ukraine. With the United States and Japan, the EC has established an ongoing—and institutionalised—dialogue on the reduction of structural trade barriers.

As in the past, however, the opening of the EU market for areas still protected today, i.e., "sensitive" industries for which rapid growth in supply pressure from Southeast Asia and Eastern Europe is expected, will progress slowly. In these areas a return to protectionism can always be expected, from which the German economy will also be affected.

10.2.4.2. Export assistance policy

An assessment of the German export assistance system is fraught with difficulties. The differing provisions of the individual assistance measures makes an international comparison exceedingly difficult. At the end of the 1970s, German firms complained loudly about their handicaps vis-à-vis other countries. Studies from this period (Juhl, 1978; Beyfuß, 1983) confirm this impression. "On the basis of numerous individual conditions, it can in fact be demonstrated that other industrial countries provide stronger export assistance than Germany" (Juhl, 1978 [own translation]). Firms at the time put forward a number of demands that the German government was not willing to meet in light of its stabilisation and liberal economic goals (subsidiarity principle). Thus, the German export-assistance programme was never a part of overall economic policy. Whereas an integrated, strategic assistance approach is visible in France or Sweden, for example, the situation in Germany is characterised by a loose co-ordination between public- and private-sector assistance agencies.

At the beginning of the 1990s, German industry's appraisal of the export assistance system evidently changed. In a parliamentary hearing in mid-June 1990, representatives of major federations and several large firms were largely of the opinion that the German assistance system was basically good and needed, at best, only marginal improvement.

10.3. Comparative Summary of Trade and Capital Transaction Policies

10.3.1. Comparison of trade policy

Exports spurred economic development in both Germany and Japan. However, a historical survey of changes in trade policy suggests that, although both countries have participated in the GATT free-trade system, the principles and management of their policies have differed significantly. Germany has generally applied the principle of free trade, applying protectionist measures only on an exceptional basis to industries that lacked international competitiveness. In Japan, on the other hand, trade was gradually liberalised in the period between 1960 and the mid-1980s in response to pressure from other countries for improved access to Japanese markets. Japan's trade policy has been targeted towards the improvement of international competitiveness through export promotion measures rather than towards the protection of crumbling domestic industries. For this reason, imports expanded little even after trade was completely liberalised, and Japan formed a growth-oriented trade structure under which only exports expanded.

The difference in policy approaches can thus be traced to differences in the conditions that prevailed at the start of post-war economic development in the two countries. Japan, which was a less-developed capitalist nation at the time, made catching up with advanced Western countries its national goal, and it sought to avert the structural balance of payments deficits that had occurred during the initial phase of economic development. To achieve these goals, it adopted policies designed to foster internationally competitive industries. Germany needed to

Table 10. 3-1 Comparison of Japanese and German trade policies

	Japan	Germany
Policy principle	• Principle of gradual free trade	• In general, principle of free trade with exception of protectionism
Export policy	• Export financing and tax-incentive benefits • Strategic industrial policy	• No conspicuous export promotion policy
Import policy	• From quantitative restrictions to tariff policy • Passive tariff reductions to foster domestic industries	• From quantitative restrictions to tariff policy • Active tariff reductions to open domestic markets
Background views	• Advancement of industrial structure for reinforcement of international competitiveness of industries	• Establishment of international horizontal division of labour against the background of tremendous international competitiveness • Stabilisation of domestic prices

maintain close trade ties with European countries in order to achieve co-existence and co-prosperity with them. It has maintained the international competitiveness of its industries by promoting international horizontal divisions of labour, whilst opening up its markets to cheap imports in order to maintain the stability of domestic prices.

10.3.2. Comparison of capital transaction policy

Capital transaction policy in Germany was completely liberalised in 1961. Japan initiated its capital liberalisation programme in 1967, but the scope of liberalisation was limited to just a few industries. Capital liberalisation programmes were subsequently implemented in four gradual stages, but it was not until 1976 that total liberalisation was achieved in all but four industries. There was thus a time lag of about fifteen years between the liberalisation of capital in Japan and Germany. As a result, Japan was transformed into a market with extremely high barriers to entry by foreign companies. This transformation was attributable to several factors, including the fact that Japan had already made the transition to a stable-growth period. Other factors included a distribution system and business practices that other countries criticised for being closed, as well as excessively competitive markets, excessive government regulation and high land and stock prices. The appreciation of the yen since the late 1980s has brought higher import ratios for such items as non-durable consumer goods and labour-intensive consumer goods, but the expansion of imports is being impeded by a lack of direct investment from overseas.

10.3.3. Trade and capital transaction policies and economic development

An examination of Japan's trade and capital transaction policies in the half-century since the end of World War II reveals that these policies bore fruit from the standpoint of economic development through export promotion. Whilst Japan has raised its profile in world markets and built a massive current-account surplus, however, it has experienced frequent bouts of economic friction with other countries. On the domestic front, although export industries have attained high productivity, the productivity of the distribution sector, which is protected by regulations, and other tertiary industries remains low. This in turn is causing the gap between domestic and overseas prices to widen. Although Japan has become an economic superpower in macro-economic terms, the Japanese people feel little sense of affluence. Moreover, the continuing appreciation of the yen, which has reached the 80-90 range against the dollar, has caused a serious decline in the international competitiveness of leading Japanese industries, such as automobiles and electrical appliances. If these conditions persist, efforts to counter the effects of the high yen through the expansion of offshore production and sourcing can be expected to accelerate further, leading to heightened concern about the so-called "hollowing-out" of industry as industries that enjoy strong international competitiveness move their production operations out of Japan. To avoid such a scenario, Japan will need to reinforce the international competitiveness of its industries whilst expanding imports through the easing of regulations in order to open up domestic markets.

In Germany, the government has protected such industries as coal, iron and steel, shipbuilding and textiles. However, Germany's commitment to free trade has led to the formation of a trade structure under which markets for trade items are symbiotically shared by neighbouring developed countries. One reason for this situation is the powerful non-price competitiveness of German industrial products. In particular, Germany has achieved strong international competitiveness in traditional processing and assembly industries, such as machinery, and in industries in which economies of scale can be achieved, such as chemicals. In future, newly industrialising economies in Asia, Eastern Europe and elsewhere are expected to become increasingly competitive in these sectors. Germany will thus need to improve its siting conditions and investment environment by reducing the heavy tax burden on corporations and curbing both labour costs and social-policy expenditure. In addition, German industry will need to take an active stance in areas in which multiple industries are merging, such as electronics, information and communications, and in markets that offer higher profits and value added. Germany's commitment to free trade has yielded its greatest economic benefits in an environment in which Germany enjoyed powerful international competitiveness. However, Germany will need to ensure that such success does not hinder industries from developing business activities that are in tune with current industrial trends.

11. Industrial Policy

11.1. Japan's Industrial Policy

11.1.1. Japan's industrial policy system

The level and method of government intervention in industry have changed in various ways in accordance with the stage of economic development and the competitiveness of industry. As shown in Fig. 11.1-1, Japan's industrial policy is divided into structure policy and organisation policy based upon its goals. Further, its instrument is classified into direct intervention and instructive guidance.

Fig. 11.1-1 Japan's industrial policy goals and instruments

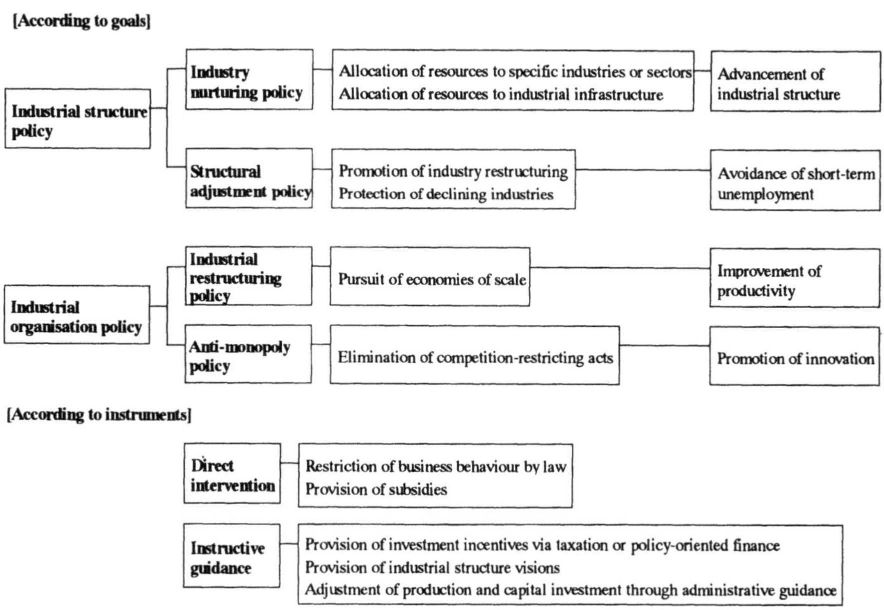

11.1.2. Evolution of industrial policy in Japan

11.1.2.1. Post-war reconstruction period (1945–1954)

(a) Direct intervention policy

Immediately after the end of World War II, production in Japan was severely depressed due to outdated and obsolete production facilities and difficulty in procuring raw materials. In particular, there were grave shortages of iron and steel and coal, which are essential basic materials for industry. The government sought to overcome this bottleneck by introducing the so-called "Priority Production System" at the end of 1946. This system called for labour, capital, food, imported raw materials such as crude oil and other resources to be allocated to the production of iron and steel and coal. This approach was designed to boost production through the reciprocal exchange of products between these two sectors for a period of between six months and one year, after which the benefits of this production growth would be progressively allocated to other priority industries in order to raise the overall level of industrial production (Fig. 11.1-2).

The Reconstruction Finance Bank was established in January 1947 to provide financial support for the Priority Production System. The government also provided indirect support for the system by paying price-support subsidies to bridge the gap between production prices and official prices. In 1947, the first year when this system was initiated, production of ordinary steel reached 740 thousand tons and that of coal 29,340 thousand tons, resulting in an annual increase rate of mining and manufacturing industries at 22.7% and 33.3% in 1948, as compared to

Fig. 11.1-2 Priority production system

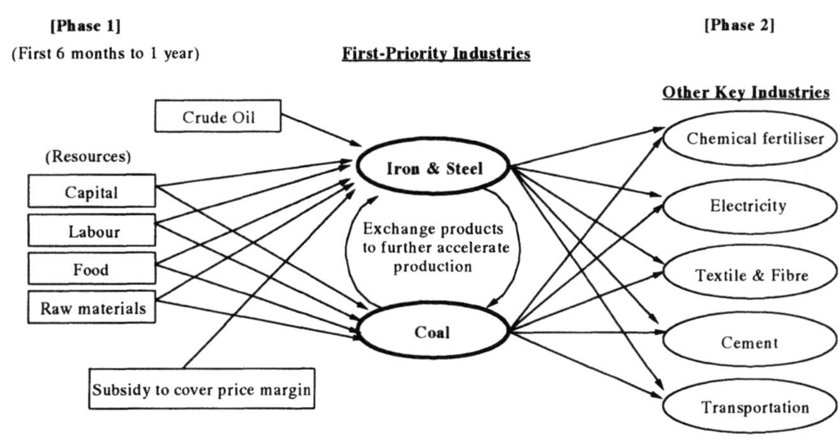

Note: Necessary capital provided mainly through the Reconstruction Finance Bank

the level of previous year. The Priority Production System was thus by and large successful.

However, government investment in the Reconstruction Finance Bank was not sufficient to cover the level of funds required. For this reason, funds were raised through issues of reconstruction finance bonds, most of which were underwritten by the Bank of Japan. In addition, funding for price-support subsidies consumed at least 20% of general account expenditure, making it the largest single item of government spending. These expansionary fiscal policy triggered hyperinflation. Joseph Dodge, who arrived in Japan in 1949, sought to remedy this problem by developing a fiscal retrenchment policy that became known as the "Dodge Line". To all intents and purposes, the activities of the Reconstruction Finance Bank were suspended just three years after their inception.

The Japanese government also employed various forms of direct intervention in industry. In 1946 it took direct control of the allocation, distribution, production and shipment of scarce materials under the Temporary Materials Supply and Demand Adjustment Act. Import volumes and capital transactions also came under direct government control, following the establishment of the Foreign Exchange & Foreign Trade Control Act and the Law concerning Foreign Capital. Since the importation of foreign machinery and the introduction of overseas technology were indispensable for the rationalisation of plant and equipment, the regulation of foreign exchange and foreign capital provided an important means of selecting specific industries at a time when foreign currencies were in short supply.

(b) Industrial rationalisation policy

A number of industrial rationalisation plans were implemented in the 1950s. Examples include the First Steel Industry Rationalisation Plan, the Coal Mining Industry Rationalisation Plan, the Petrochemical Industry Nurturing Policy, the Five-Year Plan for the Development of Electric Power Resources, and the Planned Shipbuilding Scheme. One factor contributing to these developments was the rising international competitiveness of Japanese companies under an exchange rate of ¥360 to the US dollar, which was set under the Dodge Line.

Policy tools included accelerated first-year depreciation for rationalisation investment, additional depreciation over three years, and exemption from import duties for key items of machinery. Policy-oriented finance was provided for the iron and steel, coal, shipping and electric-power sectors under the treasury loans and investments scheme. Between fiscal years 1953 and 1957, subsidies to the shipping industry in the form of assistance with interest payments on shipbuilding loans amounted to ¥10.3 billion.

The outcome of these industrial rationalisation policies varied. Rationalisation succeeded in the iron and steel industry, but not in the coal industry. In the electric-power sector, siting problems led to a shift from hydroelectric power to thermal power generation. Nevertheless, the government's policy direction was appropriate for the post-war reconstruction period in the sense that it sought to nurture industries that offered economies of scale and had wide-ranging linkages with other industries.

To provide financial support for small- to medium-sized businesses, the government established the People's Finance Corporation in 1949, and the Small Business Finance Corporation in 1953. It also created the Credit Guarantee Association (1953) to guarantee loans from private financial institutions. Laws established to protect small- to medium-sized businesses included the Small- to Medium-Sized Company Stabilisation Act (1952), and the Department Store Act (1956).

(c) Assessing industrial policy

During the early post-war reconstruction period, the Japanese government used direct intervention in the allocation of resources as a means of nurturing industries with the potential to form a base for economic growth. No institutional basis had been established for market mechanisms, and the government's direct-intervention policy can be regarded as emergency measures. The effectiveness of the policy was attributable to the private sector's readiness to tolerate government intervention due to its experience of a regulated economic system for a prolonged period during the pre-war and wartime periods. The effectiveness of the policy was further enhanced by public awareness of the urgent need for industrial reconstruction because of the large number of potentially unemployed people in the agricultural sector.

The aim of industrial rationalisation policy, implemented from the 1950s onwards, was to foster internationally competitive industries through discretionary support for technologically superior companies within each industry. Even though the Dodge Line had transformed Japan from a regulated economy into a free-market economy, Japanese companies still lacked the resources to withstand the risks that accompanied rationalisation investment. Government assistance contributed to the restructuring process by reducing these investment risks. The government did not directly select the companies to be targets for rationalisation. Instead, it used market mechanisms through preferential tax breaks and policy-oriented finance. This approach accelerated competition amongst companies, which in turn enhanced the effectiveness of rationalisation.

11.1.2.2. High-growth period (1955–1972)

(a) Industry development policy

Industry rationalisation through facility modernisation and the introduction of technology continued even in the high-growth period. Specific measures during this period included the Synthetic Fibre Nurturing Five-Year Plan, the Petrochemical Industry Nurturing Policy, and the Second Steel Industry Rationalisation Plan. The government also sought to assist processing and assembly industries by passing the Machine Industry Promotion Temporary Measures Act in 1956 and the Electronics Industry Promotion Temporary Measures Act in 1957. In addition, rationalisation cartels were approved with the aim of transforming small- to medium-sized machinery manufacturers, which suffered from low productivity owing to their small size, into medium-scale specialised manufacturers.

The government provided incentives for introduction of foreign technology as a means of nurturing the automobile and electrical machinery industries. However, the level of support provided through the taxation system and treasury loans and investments was low compared with other industries. By the late 1950s, both of these industries had become highly profitable and were achieving self-driven growth, and the contribution from industrial policy was not great.

As part of its industry-support policy, the government allowed special depreciation of rationalisation facilities. It also allowed companies to establish non-taxable reserves for overseas market development and losses on overseas investment. In addition, policy-oriented finance was provided through the Japan Development Bank, the Export-Import Bank of Japan, the Small Business Finance Corporation and other institutions. Electric power, gas and water utilities and the transportation and telecommunications sectors accounted for over 60% of lending by the Japan Development Bank, indicating that policy-oriented finance played a greater role in the development of industrial infrastructure than in the fostering of specific industries (Table 11.1-1).

A variety of subsidies were provided for advanced R&D, including Important Industrial Technical Research and Development Expense Subsidies, Electronic Computer Development Promotion Expense Subsidies, and Small- to Medium-Sized Business Technical Improvement Expense Subsidies, etc. However, the

Table 11.1-1 Industry shares of lending by the Japan Development Bank
- %; ¥ billion -

	1965	1970	1975	1980	1985	1990
Electric power/gas/water	36.4	21.6	20.0	32.5	43.9	42.7
Transportation and telecommunications	34.2	43.1	33.7	24.0	22.5	26.1
Mining	8.5	6.0	2.4	1.2	1.3	0.5
Chemicals	7.0	6.2	6.8	4.8	3.9	3.3
Petroleum refining	0.2	1.8	5.8	5.5	3.7	2.8
Machinery	4.2	4.3	3.8	2.6	2.2	3.1
Real estate	0.2	2.6	6.3	8.6	6.7	5.6
Services	3.7	5.5	6.1	5.5	4.5	5.8
Others	5.6	8.9	15.1	15.2	11.4	10.1
Total	100.0	100.0	100.0	100.0	100.0	100.0
Balance of lending	9,273	17,051	33,412	50,120	76,092	94,673

Source: BOJ, *Economic Statistics Annual*

scope of these schemes was extremely limited, and the amounts provided were small.

(b) Structural adjustment policy

From the high-growth period onwards, the use of councils to make policy decisions became the norm. In 1963, the Industrial Structure Investigation Council presented a vision of industrial structure for the 1960s, in which it advocated "the development of heavy and chemical industries" as a means of raising the ceiling for the international balance of payments and thus achieving high economic growth. At ten-year intervals, the Industrial Structure Council has presented policy suggestions as to the industrial structure considered most desirable under prevailing economic conditions. A very common theme in all of these plans down to the present day has been the need to promote the advancement of Japan's industrial structure as a means of maintaining high economic growth under the free-trade system.

(c) Industrial restructuring policy

Small-scale operations and excessive competition were cited in this period as weaknesses in Japanese industry. There were calls for industrial restructuring as a means of achieving orderly competition, whilst maintaining economies of scale. This shift was attributable in part to increasing moves by companies to strengthen their international competitiveness through mergers, tie-ups and the formation of groups.

In 1963 and 1964, the Ministry of International Trade and Industry (MITI) sought to enact the Special Industry Promotion Temporary Measures Act to promote the restructuring of industry in both the public and private sectors. Under this law, MITI would have had the power to intervene directly in designated industries to bring about centralisation and establish oligopoly. MITI's goal was the internal adjustment of industry through a system of co-operation between the public and private sector, based on consultation amongst the bureaucracy, industry, the financial sector and academia. The legislation was vehemently opposed, however, by the financial sector and industry for fear of bureaucratic control, and the bill was not passed.

The concept survived in the form of the Public–Private Sector Co-operation Round Table Conference, which used policy guidance without any clear legal basis to adjust prices, production and capital investment in materials industries, such as iron and steel, oil refining, petrochemicals, synthetic fibres, pulp and paper. This adjustment process focused on performance indicators, such as industry shares or rankings in terms of production value, and efforts were made to maintain fairness within each industry. Although these policies, which were designed to maintain order in industry, prevented the formation of monopolies, they also led to fierce competition amongst multiple companies of similar size.

In 1961 MITI came up with a plan to concentrate automobile manufacturing into the hands of three companies specialising in mass-produced vehicles, luxury cars and mini-cars respectively. The automobile industry strongly opposed this idea, and MITI's plan ended in failure.

In addition to these efforts to strengthen competitiveness, the government also sought to remedy growth distortions in the smaller business sector and agriculture, forestry and fishery by means of financial measures. A wide variety of industry policies were implemented during this period.

(d) Assessing industrial policy

Industrial policy during the high-growth period was characterised by a transition from the regulatory and direct-intervention approach of the post-war reconstruction period to policy based on instructive guidance. The effectiveness of these indirect, co-operative policy appears to have been enhanced through information sharing and the formation of industry structure visions by the bureaucracy and private sector. In terms of policy instruments, policy-oriented finance and preferential taxation both played important roles as pump-priming tools, and market mechanisms were used to the fullest extent. In this way, the scope for discretionary government decisions concerning the allocation of resources in industry was minimised, thereby avoiding government failures.

Examples of industrial restructuring policy include the adjustment of capital investment in the petrochemical industry through government–private sector co-peration and the merger of Yawata Steel and Fuji Steel to form Nippon Steel. Government intervention appears to have been accepted when it coincided with interests of private-sector companies. On the other hand, despite the failure of industry adjustment measures, the improvement of the automobile industry's international competitiveness shows that the existence of multiple companies of a similar size at a time when demand was expanding rapidly in both domestic and overseas markets had the effect of stimulating innovation and driving industry development. The role of industrial policy was thus not especially significant in such a case.

11.1.2.3. Oil-crisis period (1973–1984)

(a) Industry restructuring policy

In 1978, the government enacted the Specified Depressed Industry Stabilisation Temporary Measures Act to assist industries affected by structural recession as a result of the oil shock. Under this law, assistance was provided to electric furnace steel manufacturers, aluminium refiners, synthetic-fibre manufacturers, shipbuilders, chemical fertiliser manufacturers, cotton and chemical fibre spinners, and cardboard manufacturers. In addition to employment counter-measures, including financial support and employee training, the government also legalised the use of recession cartels to scrap surplus plant and equipment. Although 95% of target for the adjustment to facilities was decided at a high level, most facilities affected were either simply mothballed or closed down, and there was very little actual scrapping of facilities. This is why Japanese industry was again burdened with the problem of surplus capacity after the second oil shock.

In 1981, the government established the Specified Industrial Structure Improvement Temporary Measures Law with the aim of eliminating surplus capacity. The aluminium refining, chemical fibre, chemical fertiliser, paper and cardboard, and petrochemical industries were designated as structurally depressed industries. The law promoted the joint disposal of surplus capacity and also encouraged the improvement of productivity through the development of technology and the concentration of business activities.

(b) Structural adjustment policy

In 1971, the Industrial Structure Council presented their trade and industry policy for the 1970s, the vision of which called for a shift in the structure of industry away from heavy and chemical industries and towards the development of knowledge-intensive industries. The new vision proposed the nurturing of R&D-intensive industries, including such areas as integrated circuits, computers and industrial robots; advanced assembly industries, such as aircraft and NC machine tools; and data-processing industries. In 1978 the Specific Machine & Information Industry Promotion Temporary Measures Law was enacted to provide increased support for the development of the IC, computer and aeronautics industries.

In its trade and industry policy for the 1980s, the government aimed to build a creative, knowledge-intensive industrial structure around a core of frontier technology fields. Specifically, the policy focused on technologies that Japanese industry could develop itself without having to rely on the introduction of technology from overseas, such as biotechnology, new materials, new energy sources and other next-generation industrial technologies, as well as leading-edge fields such as fifth-generation computer technology. After the oil shocks, the government encouraged the development of alternative energy sources and energy conservation. It also took a more aggressive approach to environmental pollution controls.

(c) Industry nurturing policy

Research and development by R&D associations attracted considerable interest as a means of fostering industries in this period. Several private companies would establish joint research institutes and assign research personnel. The government encouraged this approach by providing subsidies to cover 50% of research and development expenditure.

A well-known example of this approach was the VLSI Technical Research Association, which was active between 1976 and 1979. This group was one of the few successes under this policy, however. Its goal was the development of large-scale integration, high-speed semiconductors for use in domestically manufactured computers. The five participating firms were Fujitsu, Hitachi, Mitsubishi Electric, NEC and Toshiba. The association helped to advance basic research in such fields as micro-processing, crystallisation, design and device technology, thereby laying the foundations for the Japanese semiconductor industry. Research carried out by private companies also played a major role, and thus the contribution made by government policy was not especially great.

(d) Assessing industrial policies

During the oil-shock period, the focus of industrial policy shifted from the allocation of resources to the key industries of the high-growth period, to the nurturing of high-tech industries, energy counter-measures and to the restructuring of structurally depressed industries. The government also continued to assist small- to medium-sized companies through tax breaks and preferential financing. Market mechanisms were used to the full in industrial policy, and where market failures were anticipated, counter-measures were taken accordingly. Reasons for this change included the improvement of the international competitiveness of Japanese industry during the high-growth period, and the government's inability to maintain tax breaks and preferential financing for specific industries due to a ballooning fiscal deficit.

This shift in the goals and instruments of industrial policy was appropriate in light of environmental changes and Japan's level of economic development. However, government policies actually played only a small role in the extraordinary growth achieved by processing and assembly industries. In addition, adjustment policy targeted towards structurally depressed industries prevented improvements in the overall efficiency of those industries by allowing weak companies to survive. For this reason, it is difficult to give a positive appraisal of the role played by industrial policy.

11.1.2.4. Stable-growth period (1985–1993)

(a) Industrial policy goals and instruments

The government implemented an action programme to improve access to the Japanese market over a three-year period starting in 1985. Significant improvements were made in standards and approval systems that were deemed to be institutional non-tariff barriers. A comprehensive import expansion package implemented in fiscal 1990 resulted in the reduction of tariffs on 1,008 industrial products.

Since 1985, the government's research and development policy has led to the establishment of international joint-research schemes and the implementation of global R&D projects, such as the Human Frontier Science Programme.

In its trade and industry vision for the 1990s, the Japanese government has maintained its basic stance of maintaining an environment in which market mechanisms can work properly. At the same time, the government is implementing an industrial policy based on four perspectives: (1) improving national living standards, (2) giving priority to socio-economic efficiency rather than economic efficiency, (3) achieving international harmony in industrial activities and (4) laying the foundations for long-term development.

The central issue for current industrial restructuring policy is deregulation in such areas as distribution, information and telecommunications, housing, and finance and securities. There is a national consensus on the need to establish an environment for the creation of new businesses and companies and for the revitalisation of the economy, and the government is contemplating policy that would result in the elimination of economic regulations in principle. However, it has so far been unable to implement effective measures because of bureaucrats' resistance and the business sector's stubborn protection of vested interests.

(b) Assessing industrial policy

The focusing of the international competitiveness of Japanese industry in the machinery industries is appreciated in terms of the efficiency of allocation of resources. As a result, productivity gaps between export-oriented industries and non-manufacturing industries protected by the regulations are further widening. In addition, the problems incurred by the closed Japanese market and the existence of domestic and overseas price differentials are currently emerging. Japan's two-tier industrial structure is, therefore, no longer acceptable, either domestically or internationally. In addition to the traditional approach of adding value to the industrial structure, industrial policy in the stable-growth period also needs to focus on the perspectives of international co-operation and the international harmonisation of rules. In addition, there is now considerable pressure for policy that will bring qualitative improvements in national living standards. At present, however, the Japanese government is merely reacting passively to external pressure, particularly from the United States, and industrial policy is failing to provide leadership for the solution of structural problems.

11.1.3. Role of industrial policy in Japan's economic development

The distinctive feature of Japanese industrial policy is not, as is often said, government–private sector co-operation to foster strategic industries, but rather the use of multiple measures to promote industrial development and stabilise industrial systems. Moreover, Japanese industrial policy is not enforced unilaterally from above, but is rather presented as visions for the structure of industry after a consensus-building process based on close information sharing amongst the government, industry and academia through various councils.

During the high-growth process, Japan's industrial development proceeded contrary to the principle of comparative advantage, as described in traditional trade theory. Although the initial conditions for economic development were characterised by a comparative advantage in labour as opposed to capital or technology, Japan took up the challenge of building an industrial structure based on industries which possessed a potential comparative advantage. The visions developed through co-operation between the government and the private sector in order to make this "leap forward" had the effect of reducing business risk. In addition, these policies could be put into practice by the fact that these visions were not merely forecasts, but rather concepts of an ideal situation. Yet these industrial policies would probably not have been possible without the existence of model industrial structures in the form of the developed countries of Europe and North America and without suitable external conditions, such as access to the United States as an export market for Japanese goods.

Whilst industrial policy cannot be regarded as the driving force for economic growth, on the whole they have played a positive role in the creation of market mechanisms that stimulated the vitality of private-sector companies at each stage of economic development. The provision of direct industrial subsidies has been used mainly in the agricultural sector. However, industrial policy since the high-growth period has not been implemented through strategic and deliberate acts by the government, but rather through a repeated trial-and-error process involving the government and the private sector. In other words, Japanese industrial policy can be described as a "product of interactive conflict" between the Japanese government, which has been firmly convinced of the need to intervene because of the immaturity of the economy and industry, and the business sector, which has pursued free competition.

11.2. Germany's Industrial Policy

Industrial policy can be defined in at least two ways. In the narrower definition it is merely a conglomerate of interventionist measures, most of them directed at specific industries. More broadly defined, it includes policies to promote investment, to develop infrastructure, for the training of workers, for the legal framework and the like, and is often subsumed by the term *Ordnungspolitik*, i.e., policy that sets the framework for an industrial order.

In post-war Germany, those industrial policies that were of a general nature have been sensible. An investment-oriented taxation system, supplemented with specific programmes for small- to medium-sized enterprises and cautiously applied investment-based regional aid contributed to West Germany's economic success.

Sector-specific policies, however, have always been a mixture of general laisser-faire in most industries and heavy intervention in some. One certainly cannot argue that since these interventions are exceptions, they do not matter. In

1989, almost 6% of GDP was spent on subsidies, with just four industries (together contributing less than 10% to national income) receiving more than half of it.

It is the protected industries that were of fundamental importance in the 1950s. This chapter will argue that contributing to the economic miracle were policies that were by no means passive and in some respects even fairly interventionist. These policies, however, were not abandoned when they should have been. Indeed, they turned out to be impossible to jettison for a variety of political and politico-economic reasons. Subsidies continued to rise, reaching new peaks every year until 1984. A plethora of well-organised and powerful vested interests had emerged almost unnoticed. As will be demonstrated, early interventionist policies played an important role in enabling these vested interests to influence the government in later years and hamper future growth. With different policies in the 1950s, early successes would have been less spectacular, yet long-term growth might have been enhanced.

11.2.1. Beginning of German industrial policy

After some initial disagreement in the late 1940s, a consensus emerged for the establishment of a liberal social market economy. This was exemplified by the reforms of 1948 which introduced a new currency and abolished price controls in the majority of industries. Monopolies and cartels that had dominated the German economy since the late nineteenth century were dissolved under British and American pressure.

With regard to industrial policy, the centrepiece of government legislation was the generous tax concessions to investors. Introduced in stages from 1948 onwards, they helped channel funds into investment rather than consumption. Investors were allowed to enter initial depreciation into their balance sheets which far exceeded normal wear and tear, a method that became known as "accelerated depreciation." There was also a continuous incentive to modernise: as a consequence of increased initial depreciation, only minor depreciation could still be claimed when the machines grew older. Indeed, the legislation proved so successful that it was retained and later copied by other countries. In addition, small- to medium-sized enterprises (SMEs) were given special investment aids such as interest-free or reduced-interest loans or even direct grants, measures that became known as *Mittelstandspolitik* (SME policies). Though indiscriminate tax incentives were the rule, *Mittelstandspolitik* certainly played a major role in preventing the pre-war monopolies and cartels from re-emerging.

The federal government also proved very successful in the provision of infrastructure: modern transport and telecommunication networks were built, schools and universities reopened. The training of workers was regarded as crucial for economic success and soon returned to pre-war standards.

Nevertheless, the system initiated in the late 1940s and early 1950s was quite distinct from what libertarians would describe as a truly free market system, and four industries in particular were subject to sectoral intervention.

Agriculture: The satisfaction of people's basic needs such as food and drink has always been viewed as a special task that ought not to be left to markets alone. Following the severe post-war food shortages, providing enough food for everyone at reasonable prices was a top priority. Thus, in 1948, price controls for basic foods were not abolished along with other consumption goods. Farmers were paid subsidies as compensation.

When in the early fifties world market prices for basic foodstuffs fell substantially and settled well below the artificially low domestic prices, government interference in agricultural markets was by no means abolished. Instead, the old idea of self-sufficiency suddenly regained prominence: duties were levied on food imports to keep domestic prices artificially high, thus subsidising farmers at the expense of consumers and encouraging them to increase production. Worse, the government even agreed to buy whatever agricultural surplus might emerge at a pre-determined price. This system was fully established by 1955 and later became the basis for the European Community's Common Agricultural Policy (CAP) set up in 1961.

From a moderate point of view, there was certainly nothing wrong with price controls on food in the late 1940s. However, the system relied on the payment of subsidies to farmers, and, under the influence of the agricultural lobby, the abolition of subsidies turned out to be impossible even as early as 1952, when economic and social policy justifications for market intervention ceased to exist.

Small wonder that future reform attempts were doomed from the outset and that the European Community's CAP, initially modelled alongside the German system, became a constant source of general mistrust in European institutions. Any reform of CAP was virtually impossible.

Coal, Steel and Energy: The "bottleneck industries," coal and steel in particular but also heavy industry in general, were widely regarded as the key industries in their time. As in the overall economy, there was obviously a huge desire for new investments after the destruction of the war, the dismantling of industries by the victorious powers, the influx of refugees, and the partition of the country, which deprived West German companies from suppliers and subsidiaries in the East.

Since investment requires properly functioning capital markets and nothing of the sort existed at the time, there was plenty of scope for government action. The Investment Aid Law required all other industries to make payments into a fund from which investments in the so-called bottleneck industries were to be financed. No government funds were involved, however.

Coal mining, steel and energy were regarded as short of capital but long in importance, not least because by now the Cold War had reached a new peak following the Korean crisis, and autarky was regarded as crucial. Thus certain industries were favoured directly at the expense of others, and it is no coincidence that coal and energy continued to be subsidised and heavily regulated during later years—during booms and recessions—both by the German government as well as by the European Union and its predecessor, the European Coal and Steel Community (ECSC). The development in the steel industry has been somewhat different. The ECSC treaty established a comparatively free internal market (though import restrictions were retained) but allowed for heavy intervention in the event of a so-called steel crisis. But it was not until the late 1970s that such a crisis was to emerge and strong intervention was to begin.

Interestingly, however, one of the most important causes for the malfunction of capital markets was not eliminated until early 1953. It was not until then that the Law for the Encouragement of Capital Markets came into force, deregulating them by abolishing a hitherto existing interest rate ceiling on corporate bonds. But this was too late. Even today, corporate bonds play only a surprisingly minor role in German corporate finance (although there are also other reasons for this.)

Investor-friendly tax legislation was of central importance but it was not everything. Nor was the provision of infrastructure, the promotion of small- to medium-sized enterprises or the training of workers. Certain types of subsidisation and regulation, whether retained or newly established, were certainly not to the economy's disadvantage in the rebuilding phase. When circumstances changed, however, they turned out to be highly resilient when they should have been abolished. What is more, even though economic policy remained on the whole market oriented, the amount of regulation and subsidisation was to increase over the decades to come.

The basis for this development was created in the early days of the West German state.

11.2.2. From the 1960s to the 1980s

Throughout most of the 1960s things went smoothly. Apart from a brief recession in 1966/67, which was quickly overcome, the German economy consolidated, with industrial policy continuing along the lines established earlier.

It was argued above that even the sectoral interventions in the 1950s were generally reasonable, taking into account the economic situation of the time. Now, with rebuilding more or less completed and macro-economic conditions favourable, the golden opportunity had come to abolish measures which had served a good purpose but were now becoming superfluous, if not harmful.

This opportunity was lost. The governing Christian Democrat/liberal coalition, in power continuously since 1949, suffered a loss of reputation after a number of incidents. In 1966 it was replaced with a grand coalition comprising both main parties, a constellation that was even less able to discontinue sectoral interventions since it had even more interest groups to satisfy. Short-termism prevailed.

11.2.2.1. Crisis and recovery

Recession hit Germany following the oil-price shock of 1973. Unemployment rose to levels hitherto unknown, the inflation rate accelerated, and for a brief spell in 1975 GDP growth even turned negative.

Heavily protected industries of the 1950s had by now lost much of their former importance. Shrinking continuously, recession hit them particularly hard. Industries such as steel, but also the Federal Railways and shipbuilding, suffered badly. Coal mining gained initially, but when oil prices came down again during a continuing recession, the situation worsened. The government, by now a coalition of Social Democrats and liberals, felt obliged to take action. Since the main losers of the recession had not only been heavily protected but also employed a large section of the Social Democrats' traditional clientele, interventions turned out to be of considerable size. Yet they remained confined to a mere handful of industries (Tables 11.2-1 and 11.2-2). And subsidies have remained high ever since. Even though the subsequent recovery and concern over the level of government spending brought some reductions from 1984 onwards, pre-recession levels have never been reached again (Fig. 11.2-1).

11.2.2.2. Coal mining

With long-standing protection, the difference between German/European coal prices and those on the world market rose continuously. A system of import duties combined with subsidies for national coal producers, originally established to make Europe independent of energy imports, resulted merely in ever-increasing inefficiency. From 1968 onwards, the government took over 10% of investment costs. In 1974 the *Kohlepfennig* was introduced: electricity producers, mainly public enterprises, were required to use German coal for energy production. In compensation, they were allowed to levy a surcharge on electricity bills, the so-called *Kohlepfennig*. Six years later, in 1980, they were made to sign what became known as the *Jahrhundertvertrag* (century pledge), a contract conserving the *Kohlepfennig* practice until 1995 and requiring electricity producers to buy 40.9 million tons (about two-thirds of total production) of domestic coal each year.

But even though subsidies have been increasing ever since and have reached new record levels every year, there is some hope that market forces will in the end gain the upper hand: employment in mining has been declining continuously and will probably continue to do so, and recent subsidies have often been directed at coal conversion rather than production.

11.2.2.3. Agriculture

The picture in this sector resembled that of coal and steel. Initial goals of self-sufficiency had long been fulfilled several times over. Yet subsidies continued. Farmers are a traditionally strong clientele for centre-right parties, similar to what heavy industry workers are for the left. Nevertheless, as with coal and steel, subsidies reached new peaks almost every year, although the importance of the agricultural sector declined. Recently, there have even been some embryonic programmes of payments to farmers in exchange for ceasing to grow certain types of grain, a promising attempt to be discussed later in more detail.

Table 11.2-1 Share of all subsidies paid (%)

	1973	1979	1981	1984	1985	1987	1989
Agriculture, forestry and fishing	18.2	17.7	15.7	16.3	17.8	19.3	18.5
Coal mining	2.9	7.1	5.8	4.8	4.3	8.4	9.3
Railroad transport	14.6	15.0	12.8	11.2	11.6	11.2	11.4
Housing	19.4	19.0	21.4	19.5	18.9	18.2	16.0
Total	55.0	58.8	55.7	51.7	52.7	57.1	55.1
All enterprises	100.0	100.0	100.0	100.0	100.0	100.0	100.0
All enterprises except housing	80.6	81.0	78.6	80.5	81.1	81.8	84.0
Regional aid	13.2	9.6	11.6	10.2	11.5	11.7	12.5

Source: Joint compilation of subsidies by the German Economic Research Institute and the Federal Statistical Office

Table 11.2-2 Subsidies per gross value added (%)

	1973	1979	1981	1984	1985	1987	1989
Agriculture, forestry and fishing	39.4	54.0	47.2	52.4	65.2	78.0	60.4
Coal mining	22.9	73.1	47.7	43.4	37.1	95.1	124.9
Iron and steel	1.4	1.9	4.2	16.3	15.3	2.8	3.3
Shipbuilding	11.8	19.5	34.8	24.5	23.1	12.0	20.4
Aircraft and spacecraft manufacture.	22.4	19.9	18.5	14.2	14.4	11.2	18.4
Railroad transport	74.4	114.7	92.8	99.0	95.6	101.6	105.2
Housing	22.1	22.1	21.4	21.6	16.8	15.4	12.0
All enterprises	7.5	8.3	7.6	9.0	7.6	7.4	6.5
All enterprises except housing	6.5	7.2	6.5	7.8	6.8	6.6	6.0
Subsidies as % of GDP	6.3	6.8	6.3	6.7	6.4	6.1	5.5

Source: Joint compilation of subsidies by the German Economic Research Institute

Fig. 11.2-1 Subsidies in West Germany 1973–1989

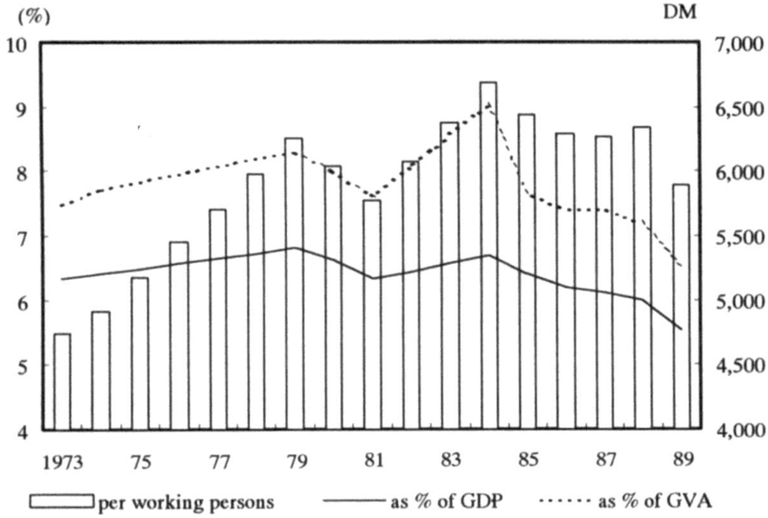

Note: Interpolation for 1975-1978 and 1982/83
GVA: Gross Value Added

Subsidies per industry 1989

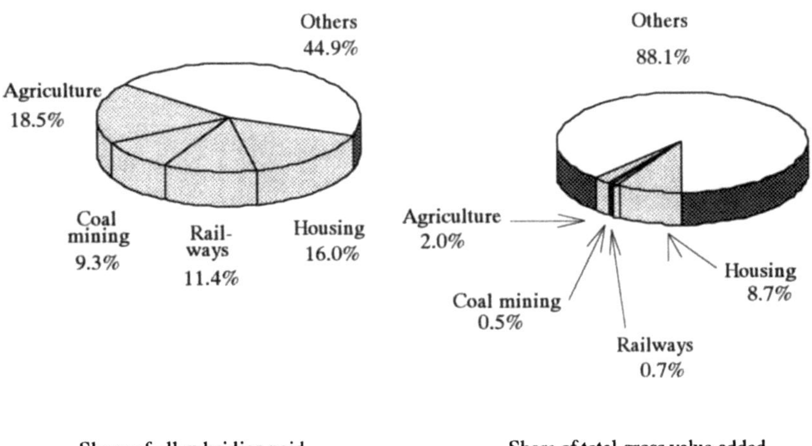

Source: Ifo Institute

11.2.2.4. Other industries

In the 1950s, the German government had occasionally come to the rescue of a large company that had run into difficulties due to management errors, BMW being the most famous example. But when the banking sector was fully developed in the 1960s, this practice eventually stopped. The near-bankruptcy of electrical-equipment manufacturer AEG and, recently, the MG (Metallgesellschaft) disaster, for example, were resolved without government help.

11.2.2.5. Old and new subsidies, policies towards other industries

Sectoral industrial policy did not deal exclusively with just a few crisis branches, even though these have received the bulk of all subsidies. In the 1950s, one of the main reasons for protecting steel and coal was their crucial importance for the country's well-being. Much the same arguments became fashionable in the 1970s and 1980s in support of subsidisation of new and rising industries. Whereas subsidies for coal and steel were now officially justified as a means of smoothing their decline, the new rising stars received public money to accelerate their development. Increasingly, subsidies were paid to high-tech industries: aircraft and spacecraft construction, but also nuclear energy and small amounts for all those developing new technologies.

In 1970 the governments of Germany, France and Spain decided to build a European civil aircraft industry (more or less from scratch), and thus enter a market which had hitherto been dominated by the American companies Boeing and McDonnell-Douglas. In 1976 the first Airbus planes were sold. Even though Airbus' market share has by now reached almost 40%, heavy subsidisation—especially for R&D—is continuing. In terms of opportunity costs, there are still major doubts whether building European aircraft really makes economic sense.

The Airbus programme has been justified along similar lines as that of heavy industry subsidisation in the 1950s: the dependence on foreign countries was to be reduced, and, due to market imperfections, a European aircraft industry, though eventually profitable, would initially be unable to raise enough funds on the capital markets. The first argument is essentially political, though rather doubtful in view of the fact that foreign aircraft manufacturers are competitors rather than members of a cartel: there is no powerful foreign monopolist who exercises market power. But the second one is most certainly flawed: even though corporate bonds are still of minor importance in Germany, capital markets have come a long way from the difficulties of the early 1950s.

Essentially, the main beneficiaries of the Airbus are foreign countries which can now buy cheaper aircraft due to increased competition.

11.2.2.6. Role of the European Community

By the beginning of the 1960s, the European Union, or the European Economic Community (EEC) as it was called then, had taken over much of the responsibility for the heavily regulated industries. Interventions into markets for coal, steel and food became the European Community's main activity. The Treaty of Rome (the EEC's founding document) contained a number of clauses banning market interventions by national governments, but on a European level they were still allowed and national governments were granted a number of exceptions. And they made wide use of them, especially in coal mining, the subsidisation of which was eventually taken over by national governments completely. Under the auspices of the European Community, coal mining, agriculture and steel continued to receive vast and ever-rising amounts of subsidies or were at least heavily regulated.

For national politicians, general European responsibility for subsidies proved quite helpful: the Community could always be blamed for unsuccessful policies, whereas credit for apparent "successes" remained with national governments. "Europe" was blamed for butter mountains and the like, but national politicians took credit for policies improving the income of farmers.

11.2.2.7. Regional policy

Whereas most subsidies have always been directed at specific sectors (and still are), there were also regional aid programmes administered by the federal states. In Germany, regional aid traditionally focuses on investment. Though generally successful, with the economy maturing subsidies increasingly led to a "prisoner's dilemma" situation in which the investor would go to the state bidding the highest bonus. To end such practices, better co-ordination was essential. Thus, from 1968 onwards a new regional aid programme was set up which was to be administered jointly by federal and state governments. As before, regions that were considered to have fallen behind were to be granted special investment subsidies. Together with a similar programme run by the European Community, its main aim was the levelling of living standards within the country or within the Community, whilst preventing different states or countries from competing for investments by means of subsidies. During the 1970s and 1980s, regional aid amounted to roughly 12% of all subsidies paid. This is more than what was received by the federal railways or the coal industry, but less than that given to agriculture.

In Germany, regional aid worked reasonably well. It might have been better targeted, and occasionally investment aids merely resulted in the transfer of a business from one village to another in close vicinity or the establishment of capital-intensive industries without promoting employment, but in general results were quite acceptable. One of the main reasons for this positive result may be the German voting system: both federal and state assemblies are elected under proportional representation. Thus any incentive to direct funds towards marginal constituencies (rather than to where they are most urgently needed) is largely reduced. With first-past-the-post, as in Britain or America, sensible regional aid programmes would be almost impossible.

To summarise, the liberal economic framework established in the 1950s was generally retained. Nevertheless, the level of intervention increased until 1984 and was consolidated thereafter, following economic recovery and concerns over the level of government spending. Apart from high-tech promotion, regional aid and *Mittelstandspolitik*, subsidies remained on the whole confined to a mere handful of industries with two common characteristics: those continually subject to intervention and those of crucial importance in the 1950s but declining ever since (Fig. 11.2-2).

There are initial indications, however, that a redirection of subsidies to promote industrial and agricultural conversion is taking place: employment in heavily subsidised industries is constantly decreasing.

11.2.3. Unification

After German unification, an unprepared federal government was suddenly confronted with the problem of rebuilding the decrepit East German economy. There was ample opportunity for government intervention and subsidisation, and the West German experience of the 1950s could be drawn upon.

Fig. 11.2-2 Contribution to GDP of selected industries

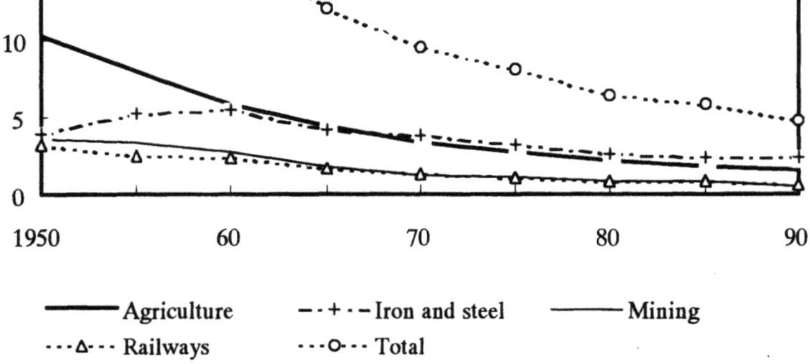

11.2.3.1. Subsidies in the east

In the aftermath of unification, intervention turned out to be of rather limited scope: industrial policy was fairly passive and by no means directed at retaining old industries. Wage subsidies were discussed, but the idea was quickly abandoned. Private consumption, however, was subsidised considerably and at a very early stage by means of the currency union.

A large part of German transfers to the east serves distributive rather than allocative purposes. But public money devoted to industrial and structural policies also plays a major role. As in West Germany in the 1950s, the focus is on infrastructure and the promotion of investment.

The improvement of east German infrastructure has become a major concern. So have investment policies: tax breaks for investors in the east have been substantial, the government has agreed to take over part of investment costs, and interest-reduced loans have been offered for small- to medium-sized enterprises.

Privatisation has become the other major issue. State-owned enterprises dominated the East German economy. In 1990 the so-called *Treuhandanstalt* (THA) was founded and put in charge of their sale, which was more or less completed by the end of 1994. During this process it became ever more obvious that a large section of the east German economy could not be privatised. The THA had to decide whether to subsidise the firms concerned or to close them down. In general, it opted for the latter.

This was a policy which made perfect sense. A contrary policy of traditional subsidisation of declining industries with positive short-term effects would have made the government more popular. But after the first all-German election, it felt secure enough to carry out its eastern strategy: policies applied were reasonable from an economic point of view but extremely unpopular amongst the east German population.

Yet the strategy appears to have worked. The government won the second all-German election in October 1994, albeit narrowly, not least because government popularity in the east has slowly begun to recover.

Refraining from widespread subsidisation of declining eastern industries has certainly been made easier by the lack of powerful interest groups (and the existence of declining western industries, still able to muster political support and eager to get rid of unwanted eastern competitors). The current state of public finances played an important role as well. Thus, the sheer size of the task had positive effects, and western self-interest may have reduced western living standards initially, but will lead to long-term gains.

This is not to say that the government's eastern strategy is beyond criticism from an economic point of view. For example, the integration of East Germany into the Federal Republic meant that its whole set of regulations, accumulated over a period of more than forty years, will now be applied in the east. Rather than abolishing certain West German regulations, they are now being applied in an even larger area. These regulations also include western property rights legislation.

Private property is certainly an important factor in allowing an economy to thrive. But the concept was applied so extensively that people deprived of their property during the communist years are now entitled to reclaim it, a law that has become a major impediment to investment and thus to economic recovery in the east. Recently, however, some modifications in this law have been made.

There are also exceptions to the general restraint in subsidising declining industries: eastern shipyards have been modernised with vast amounts of public money, which in turn has led to new cries for subsidies from their western competitors; and such demands are usually fulfilled.

11.2.3.2. Signs of reform in the west

In March 1991, the newly appointed Federal Economics Minister threatened to resign unless subsidies were cut by ten billion D-Marks within the year. Although this endeavour failed, some small subsidy cuts were achieved. But this initiative, led by a publicity-conscious politician, who later resigned for other reasons, indicates that public opinion on subsidies has changed. Its limited success also reveals how strong organised resistance still is.

The state of public finances following unification is of great concern to the German electorate. Although public spending is not dramatically high in international comparison, it far exceeds levels considered unacceptable in the mid-1980s. Following the experiences of 1923 and 1945-47, it is no surprise that many Germans regard financial stability as a crucial goal. Thus the current situation is one of those rare occasions when politicians may learn to take the concerns of the silent majority seriously.

Subsidies have moved into the centre of public attention. In the past, declining industries have always been protected by means of import restrictions and subsidies. Their basically unsuccessful products were to be made more competitive by subsidising production or encouraging rationalisation. Now, conversion has gained prominence. Increasingly, subsidies are paid to encourage the abandonment of old industries rather than their mere rationalisation: farmers receive payments when they cease growing crops, coal miners are retrained and later work elsewhere. And the number of employees in declining industries continue to dwindle. This gives rise to the hope that subsidisation will also decrease eventually for sheer lack of the number of businesses which can receive them.

And there are other reforms: the Federal Railways are being privatised and run like a private company. There is hope that efficiency gains will eventually make them independent of state aid.

11.2.4. Conclusions

In post-war Germany, those industrial policies that were of a general nature have always been successful: investor-friendly tax legislation, the provision of an adequate infrastructure, sound vocational training and a reasonable university education, a fairly liberal legal system and the promotion of competition have become the cornerstones of industrial policy. Special programmes intended to encourage additional investment in economically backward regions (regional policy) as well as investment aid specifically directed at small- to medium-sized enterprises reinforce this generally positive evaluation.

But on a sector-specific level, German industrial policy has always been a combination of laisser-faire in most industries and heavy intervention in some. In the majority of industries the government has shown restraint, perhaps with the exception of occasionally very *dirigiste* trade rules. Interestingly, those few heavily protected industries have always been the same, during booms and recessions, during periods of structural change and more tranquil periods.

The development of state intervention shows what lasting effects initial decisions can have. Once established, subsidies prove almost impossible to abandon and lead to ever new interventions. Organised interests thrive in a regulated market; lobbying is fostered.

Sectoral policies of the 1950s accelerated economic growth and have thus to be regarded as acceptable. But in the 1960s, when most of the legislation ought to have been jettisoned, the government failed to do so. It was in a weak position at the time, and interest groups had already grown powerful. As a consequence, when crisis loomed in the 1970s, intervention increased drastically. Its main focus was the preservation of by now un-competitive industries rather than the establishment of new ones. The ailing industries of the 1970s turned out to be those which were protected (and economically important) in the 1950s.

One important lesson can be learned from this pattern: however reasonable subsidies and regulations may be initially, eliminating them when the time has come will always be extremely difficult if not impossible. Thus, technological policies started in the 1970s have to be administered with great caution. The same applies to subsidies in eastern Germany.

However, due to the state of public finances and western self-interest, subsidisation in eastern Germany has been quite cautious, apart from the currency union. Public funds have gone primarily to infrastructure and the promotion of investment, which is certainly a sensible policy. Federal subsidies have even been slightly reduced, with a beginning shift from traditional goals to conversion in industry and agriculture-trends which are likely to continue.

11.3. Comparative Summary of Industrial Policy

11.3.1. Differences

The frameworks for industrial policy in Japan and Germany are fundamentally different. Germany has in principle pursued a laisser-faire, non-interventionist industrial policy. The provision of subsidies has been the exception rather than the rule, and subsidy payments have been limited to declining industries or to high-tech industries considered to be important to the national interest. The principles underlying German policy were moulded into a clear-cut set of rules, and government intervention in industry was eliminated as far as possible. The Japanese government, on the other hand, has intervened directly or indirectly in a number of ways and in all industrial fields in an effort to achieve specific policy goals, such as the enhancement of the industrial structure and the improvement of international competitiveness. Its approach to intervention has been finely tuned through the use of such methods as the gradual introduction of market principles according to the stage of industrial development, and the establishment of a policy consensus with the private sector. This approach has been reflected in the maintenance of close ties between the government and private business, with both the government and private enterprise working co-operatively towards economic development. This situation is epitomised in the term "Japan, Inc."

Divergent policy ideologies appear to have played a major role in these fundamental differences. After much debates during the late 1940s, German policy crystallised around the concept of building a social market economy, and industrial policy was positioned as a measure to complement market mechanisms. In Japan, catching up with the industrialised West became the national objective, and the country shifted in stages towards a growth-oriented market economy. When shortages of steel and coal became a bottleneck to growth during the post-war reconstruction period, the government instituted a priority production system that funnelled intensive capital investment into the country's steel and coal industries. During the rapid-growth period that followed, financial support for industry was provided in the form of investment-oriented tax incentives under the Special Taxation Measures Act, as well as policy-based financing from the Japan Development Bank, the Export-Import Bank of Japan and other governmental financial institutions. These policies can be characterised as tools to induce resources allocation through the use of market mechanisms rather than as the provision of funds to specific industries and companies on the basis of the government's policy judgements. In the post–oil shock period, Japanese industrial policy has begun to complement private-sector activities, such as the presentation of industry visions or the adjustment of industry structures through administrative guidance.

Table 11.3-1 Comparison of industrial policy in Japan and Germany

	Japan	Germany
Policy vision	• Economic development on a par with the West	• Creation of social market economy
Immediate policy goals	• Advancement of industrial structure • Improvement of international competitiveness	• Complementing market mechanisms
Policy instruments	• Government financing • Investment-oriented tax incentives • Industrial restructuring and consolidation • Providing vision of industrial structure	• Payment of subsidies • Ordnungspolitik • Non-intervention enabling market mechanisms to function • Investment-oriented taxation system

11.3.2. Similarities and lessons

As the preceding comparison of industrial policy shows, government intervention has been much more intensive in Japan than in Germany. Nonetheless, it is possible to identify several policy similarities that have contributed to industrial advancement.

First, policies for the development of industrial infrastructure and the early cultivation of sectors that are important to a wide spectrum of other industries, such as steel and chemicals, contributed to the establishment of the economic base in both Germany and Japan. There is a stage at which policy-based support can play an effective role in industries that benefit from economies of scale or that have a strong spill-over effect into other industries. It should be noted, however, that the strategic policies used in Japan to cultivate specific industries were effective only until the end of the rapid-growth period. The subsequent development of industry was driven by market competition.

Second, policies based on excessive government intervention in specific industries did not always succeed in either Japan or Germany. In Germany, for example, the government intervened directly in the coal, steel and energy industries in the belief that it would be too difficult for companies in these sectors to use the capital market to raise the enormous sums of investment needed. National security concerns, meanwhile, led to the payment of agricultural subsidies. Whilst government support may have been well justified at the outset, once implemented such measures led to the formation of special interest groups to protect vested interests, with the result that it subsequently became difficult to reduce or eliminate support measures. Adequate attention should be paid to these tendencies. In Japan, the steel and chemical industries were restructured in an effort to improve their international competitiveness. Whilst demand for the products of these industries continued to expand rapidly, it was possible to maintain a balance between competition and co-operation. However, their international competitiveness is now being eroded by decelerating market growth and the industrialisation of Asian countries. In the automobile sector, a MITI concept calling for the concentration of the industry into three companies was derailed by industry opposition. However, it appears that international competitiveness has in fact benefited more from fierce competition amongst large numbers of companies. In other words, international competitiveness has risen in industries in which industrial policy has failed or in which the level of industrial policy intervention was low.

Third, both Japan and Germany provided policy-based support to the high-tech industries that would form the next industrial frontier during the shift to moderate economic growth after the oil-shock period. In Germany, subsidies were provided for development projects in the aviation and nuclear energy fields. These subsidies were of questionable value in terms of the opportunity costs, however. For instance, it would appear that the benefits derived from the establishment of a European aviation industry accrued largely to foreign countries, which were able to purchase airliners more cheaply thanks to the resulting increase in competition. In Japan, the government provided support for the cultivation of research- and development-driven industries such as integrated circuits, computers and robotics, as well as for high-tech assembly industries such as aviation and numerically controlled machine tools. It also staged a development-oriented drive for alternative-energy technology and energy-conservation technology. Though these industrial policies deserve high marks for their role in helping to set the course for industrial development and providing future visions of the country's industrial structure, they have not been very effective in terms of cultivating new high-tech industries.

Viewed in their entirety, the Japanese and German experiences suggest that industrial development has benefited most from policies designed to harness market mechanisms. In Germany, policies have consistently been based on market mechanisms. In Japan, policies of direct government intervention in the allocation of industrial resources were instituted only during the post-war reconstruction period. During the rapid-growth period and thereafter, Japanese industrial policy was primarily designed to guide or complement market trends. To be sure, active government assistance may occasionally play a vital role in cultivating new industries during the early stages of economic development, when the market mechanism has yet to function adequately, or when intensive allocations of resources are considered essential. However, interventionist industrial policy cannot be expected to have a perpetually beneficial impact on industrial growth and development; instead, it appears to be capable of eliciting little more than a pump-priming effect at best. Thus the best industrial policy is non-intervention, enabling market mechanisms to thrive and to lead to an optimum allocation of resources.

12. Social Policy

12.1. Japan's Social Policy

12.1.1. Concept and scope of social policy

The concept and scope of social policy varies in accordance with circumstances in individual countries, including their historical backgrounds and political, social and economic systems. In general, the term encompasses the following aspects:

This chapter deals with social security policy, which contributed to the stabilisation and improvement of living conditions during Japan's post-war economic development, and education policy, which played an important role in human resources development.

12.1.2. Social security policy

The scope of social security in Japan is generally defined in terms of the classifications contained in Recommendations on the Social Security System,

Fig. 12.1-1 Concept and Scope of Social Policy

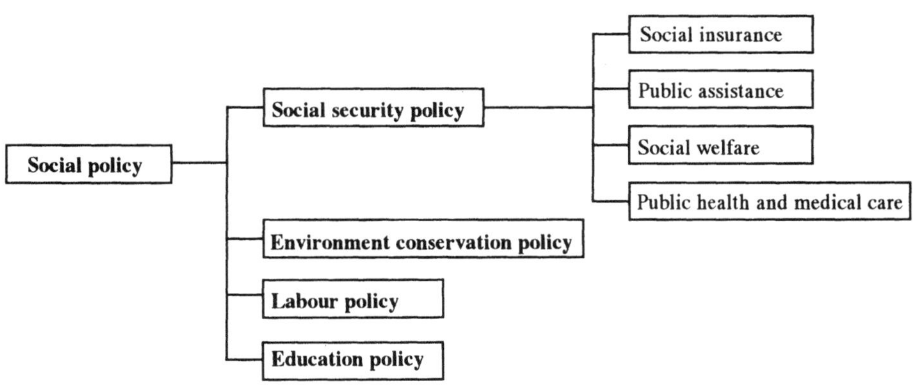

which was submitted to the Japanese government by the Social Security System Council in October 1950. In its narrow sense, social security consists of social insurance, public assistance, social welfare, and public health and medical care. Social insurance can be further divided into health-care insurance, pension insurance, workers' compensation insurance and employment insurance. Today environmental conservation is regarded as part of a broadly defined social security.

For the sake of convenience, the period from the end of World War II up to the present will be divided into four periods. These are (1) the post-war reconstruction period (1945-59), when the social welfare system was formed, (2) the high-growth period (1960-72), when the social welfare system was expanded, (3) the low-growth period (1973-80), when the social welfare system was modified, and (4) the period since 1981, which has been characterised by a re-evaluation of the role of the state and an increased emphasis on self-help.

12.1.2.1. Socio-economic change and the evolution of the social security system

(a) Formation of the social welfare system (1945-1959)

Before and during World War II, Japan had a two-tier public relief system, consisting of a general relief programme, which provided support for the aged and the mentally and physically handicapped, and a military assistance programme, which provided pensions and relief for ex-soldiers and the war bereaved. Although this system was managed by a number of different state agencies, it was similar in nature to a charitable operation and cannot be regarded as a social security system in the modern sense.

The immediate post-war period was a time of enormous social disruption for Japan. Its population of seventy-two million included many who had lost their families, their homes and their jobs because of the war, as well as five million demobilised soldiers and repatriated civilians. The first priority for Japan's post-war government was to restore order so as to free the people of Japan from this environment of chaos and distress.

Most of the government's policies were implemented under the direction of the occupation administration (GHQ). The social security system was no exception. In February 1946, GHQ issued a "Memorandum on Social Relief," in which it set down three principles: (1) non-discrimination and equality, (2) public responsibility (separation of public and private interests) and (3) assurance of minimal living expenses (non-limitation of relief expenditure). These principles became the basic and governing principles of welfare policy in post-war Japan. They were later embodied in the old National Assistance Act of September 1946, the Child Welfare Act of December 1947, and the Disabled Persons Welfare Act of December 1949, which were collectively known as the "Three Welfare Acts". A new National Assistance Act was enacted in 1950, establishing the right to survival as expressed in Article 25 of the Constitution. Further, the Social Welfare Services Act was enacted in 1951.

The spread of social insurance in Japan was interrupted by the war. After the war, the system was rebuilt under the guidance of GHQ, and in 1947 Japan began to formulate a structured system with the promulgation of the Unemployment Insurance Act and the Workmen's Compensation Insurance Act. The "Recommendations on the Social Security System," which was submitted to the government by the Social Security System Council in 1950, identified social insurance funded by individuals as the core of Japan's social security system. Public assistance, social welfare, public health and medical care were accorded a supplementary role in relation to social insurance.

In line with this policy, in 1958 the government totally revised the National Health Insurance Law, which dated from pre-war times. The amended law took effect from January 1959. In the same year, the National Pensions Act was promulgated as the basis for the pension system. The formal framework for universal national insurance and pensions was now in place; thus Japan had made the transition from a social security system based primarily on national assistance as a form of remedial relief to a system based primarily on the use of social insurance to prevent poverty.

(b) Expansion of social welfare (1960-1972)

The Ikeda cabinet, which took office in 1960, announced an "income-doubling plan" that was to have a dramatic effect on Japan's economic development. Labour safety and sanitation were ignored, however, during the high-growth period, and many workers were forced to work long hours for low wages. Poor working conditions were responsible for numerous worker accidents. The government responded to this situation by improving and strengthening the Worker's Compensation Insurance Act of 1947. In 1960, a compensation system was introduced for people suffering from long-term injury or illness. After major changes in 1965, the system became mandatory for all workers.

Economic growth was paralleled by the increasingly serious livelihood problems of weaker members of society, such as the disabled, the aged, children and fatherless families. The government addressed these problems by promulgating a series of laws as part of its efforts to improve social welfare. The Mentally Handicapped Persons Welfare Act was passed in 1960, followed by the Aged Persons Welfare Act in 1963, and the Child and Maternity Welfare Act in 1964. Social welfare was thus based on a framework of six welfare laws.

The ageing of society became a particularly important issue during this period. The 1960 Health and Welfare White Paper referred to the need to establish comprehensive countermeasures based on national perspectives. It identified a need for improvements in the three areas of income compensation, health maintenance and social welfare. The aforementioned Aged Persons Welfare Act was based on this policy, as was the decision in 1972 to provide free medical care for people aged seventy and older.

(c) Modification of the social security system (1973-1980)

The Japanese government declared 1973 as the first year of a new era in welfare. However, the oil shock struck in the autumn of that year, triggering problems that included hyperinflation and a chain of business failures. Efforts to curb spiralling prices through measures to restrain total demand pushed the economy into recession, and in 1974 the real economic growth rate was predicted to slip into negative figures. This economic deceleration was also responsible for a revenue shortfall, necessitating a major review and reduction of spending. Not even social security and welfare, which were characterised by extremely rigid spending patterns, were spared from this process. This was the time of reviewing and debating the so-called "high-welfare, high-cost" concept.

The review process began with efforts to secure funding for the rising cost of medical care. The amendment of the Health Insurance Act in 1977 enabled the government to levy special insurance premiums on bonuses. In addition, the government moved away from free medical care for the aged, which was one of the provisions of the Aged Persons Welfare Act. Under the Aged Persons Health Insurance Act, which was passed in 1982, the aged were required to pay a part of expenses for medical care.

During the high-growth period, the government made a number of improvements to the Unemployment Insurance Act of 1947, including the expansion of its scope, increases in the amount of benefits and an extension of the period over which they could be paid. However, it was becoming increasingly difficult to keep pace with change merely through amendments to the law, and in 1974 a new Employment Insurance Act was established. In addition to the provision of income compensation for the unemployed, the new law also incorporated a number of employment assurance mechanisms, including safeguards against job losses, employment promotion measures and skill development systems for workers. The old Unemployment Insurance Act was thus repealed.

(d) Rethinking the role of the state—increased emphasis on self-help (1981–)

In March 1981, the government established the second ad hoc Commission on Administrative Reform. Its first report, which was submitted in July of the same year, reflected the harsh economic realities of the period after the two oil crises. In the report the Commission identified the expansion of expenditure on social security and education as the reason for the government's fiscal crisis. It advised the government to maintain appropriate levels of welfare for those truly in need, but to give the greatest possible encouragement to the traits of the nation that fostered the qualities of self-sufficiency, self-help and self-responsibility. The report also urged the government to avoid excessive intervention, which would work against these qualities. The Commission saw the development of a vigorous welfare society as the key to curbing social security expenditure. On this basis, it advised the government to reduce the state's share of expenditure in this area, to emphasise self-help efforts and to review medical services, pensions and welfare. The purpose of these reforms was to reduce the state's fiscal burden in national livelihood-related areas and increase the contribution from beneficiaries, whilst at the same time revitalising business activity. Amongst the specific steps taken to reduce social welfare expenditure was the introduction of charging for medical care for the aged (1982) under the aforementioned Aged Persons Health Insurance Act. In 1984, the government made major changes to the Health Insurance Act in order to provide tighter screening of medical consultation fees. It also introduced flat rate charges that required insured persons to meet 20% of the cost of treatment for themselves and 30% of the costs of treatment for dependent relatives. The National Pensions Act was amended in 1985, and the Welfare Pensions Act and the Mutual Aid Association Act in 1986. These amendments had the effect of increasing the premiums paid by the public. They also simplified the public pension system and corrected problems, whilst reducing the level of benefit payments as part of efforts to correct imbalances between systems. Other moves included the reduction of the state's share of livelihood assistance expenditure and the cost of measures in this area (1985-89), a shift from gap reduction to level balancing as the basis for calculating livelihood assistance standards (1984), a transition to a policy emphasising home-based welfare without solving pending problems with income, medical care and housing guarantees, and a review of all subsidies for social welfare-related activities. This rapid sequence of changes had the effect of easing pressure on central government finances by shifting the burden to individuals and local authorities. There can be no doubt that it represented a retreat from the social security system that had been built during the post-war era.

12.1.2.2. Trends and issues affecting social welfare

Japan's post-war social security policy began, under the direction of the occupation administration, with the positioning of social welfare as a means of guaranteeing the people's right to survival. The need for improvements to the pension system increased, in subsequent years, owing to changes that included the concentration of population in major cities, an expanding trend towards nuclear family living, a decline in the self-employed population and an increase in the number of people in employment. From the 1980s onwards, socio-economic development and rising living standards were paralleled by trends that necessitated the modification of Japan's basic approach to social security, including cost increases resulting from a declining birth rate and the growth of the aged population, coupled with an increasingly tight fiscal situation. However, this qualitative transition in social security was driven solely by fiscal factors, and no

Table 12.1-1 Trends in social security payments
- ¥ billion -

Fiscal year	Social security payments	Ratio to national income	Medical care	Pensions	Other items
1965	1,603.7	6.0%	913.7 (57.0)	350.8 (21.9)	339.2 (21.2)
1970	3,523.9	5.8%	2,075.8 (58.9)	854.8 (24.3)	593.3 (16.8)
1975	11,672.6	9.4%	5,688.1 (48.7)	3,886.5 (33.3)	2,098.1 (18.0)
1980	24,604.4	12.3%	10,658.2 (43.3)	10,470.9 (42.6)	3,475.3 (14.1)
1985	35,644.0	13.7%	14,155.0 (39.7)	17,017.0 (47.7)	4,472.0 (12.5)
1990	47,112.2	13.7%	18,213.3 (38.7)	24,248.5 (51.5)	4,650.3 (9.9)

Note: 1. Figures in ( ) represent percentages of total.
2. "Other items" include miscellaneous assistance, allowances, expenditure and payments.
Source: Ministry of Health and Welfare, Health and Welfare White Paper; Economic Planning Agency, National Economic Statistics.

efforts were made to obtain a national consensus about the scope and content of social security, and the apportionment of the cost.

Social security payments began to increase steadily as a percentage of national income from around 1980 onwards, although there has been little change in the ratio over the past decade. A breakdown of social security payments shows that, over the past two decades, the improvement in national living standards has led to a halving of the percentage of expenditures for livelihood assistance, public health and sanitation, and relief measures for unemployment. Meanwhile, the growth of the aged population has resulted in a continuing increase in the demand for pensions. Since 1990, pension payments have accounted for over one-half of all social security expenditures (Table 12.1-1).

From now on, the expenditures on social security in such areas as medical care and pensions will inevitably increase due to the aging of Japan's population, thus calling for an urgent review of the scope and content of welfare and insurance payments. Despite the efforts of the Ministry of Health and Welfare to present a vision for welfare in the twenty-first century during the controversy over a proposed increase in the consumption tax in 1994, the level of national debate remained shallow.

12.1.3. Education policy

12.1.3.1. Evolution of education policy in Japan

(a) Education in pre-war and wartime periods

Even before the Meiji Restoration in the mid-nineteenth century, there were a variety of educational facilities, for example: temple schools, schools operated by feudal clans, private teaching institutions, and Shoheizaka schools operated directly by the Shogunate government. None of these facilities can be characterised as public educational institutions, however. The establishment of a modern education system in Japan began with the promulgation of an educational system by the Ministry of Education in 1872. The educational system was not based on the Confucian philosophy of the Edo period but rather on the perspectives of modern western philosophy, such as individualism and pragmatism. The system was designed to foster equality amongst the four-class system of Japanese society (samurai, peasants, artisans and merchants) by providing a single-track structure of elementary, secondary and higher education for all citizens. However, the government's grandiose plan to introduce an eight-year system of compulsory education was not backed by fiscal means, and no provision had been made for the necessary school buildings, teaching materials and teachers. Thus for fear of imposing a heavy economic burden on the public, as well as of failing to meet regional needs, the system was abandoned when the Education Ordinance took effect in 1879.

Pre-war education policy and the framework of the pre-war school system were formed by a series of school ordinances in 1886 and the Imperial Rescript on Education in 1890. Elementary, middle and normal schools and imperial universities were established under a nationalist education policy, and by 1918 girls' high schools, vocational schools, professional schools and higher schools were added to the system.

By the late 1920s, school education was becoming increasingly military in character, and school subjects were amalgamated and modified to meet the needs of the war effort.

(b) Building a democratic education system (1945–1950)

By the end of the war, the education system ground to a virtual halt and ceased to function effectively. Under the occupation administration, the demilitarisation of education, religion and other cultural activities was the responsibility of the Civil Information and Education Section (CIE). In October 1945, CIE began to eliminate militarism from post-war Japanese education by issuing four major directives. First, the wartime education system would be abolished and replaced. Second, teaching staff would be screened for suitability, and undesirable persons would be purged from the profession. Third, the Shinto religion would be separated from the state, and Shinto education would be abolished. Fourth, teaching of Japanese ethics, history and geography would be terminated, and related teaching materials would be collected and destroyed.

In March 1946, an American educational mission invited by GHQ conducted a comprehensive inspection and survey of the Japanese education system. The subsequent report of this mission resulted in the total reform of education in Japan and became the basis for Japan's post-war education system. Key areas covered in the report included (1) basic principles for educational reform (the provision of educational opportunities in accordance with the abilities and aptitudes of the individual, the exclusion of uniformity and standardisation), (2) language reform (the total elimination of *kanji* and the introduction of the Roman alphabet), (3) educational administration at elementary and secondary levels (the decentralisation of authority, the establishment of boards of education, the introduction of the 6-3-3 school system, the establishment of compulsory education, the introduction of co-education), (4) educational methods (the correction of uniform teaching methods, the introduction of social studies), (5) adult education (the establishment of evening classes, the popularisation of open classes, the establishment of more libraries), and (6) higher education (emphasis on freedom of research and the autonomy of universities, the expansion of opportunities for higher education).

The Fundamentals of Education Act, which was promulgated in 1947 in line with Japan's new Constitution, defined basic principles of education, including the aims of education, equality of opportunity, compulsory education and co-education. These principles guided the subsequent establishment of junior and senior high schools, new-system universities and junior colleges, and the promulgation of ordinances relating to teaching and instruction.

(c) Backlash against post-war reforms—tightening of controls (1951–1959)

The democratic education system, established after World War II, showed strong American influence. The 1950s saw the emergence of conservative and reactionary tendencies in response to increasing international tensions sparked by the outbreak of the Korean War. There was a growing backlash against previous developments from around the time of the 1951 San Francisco Peace Treaty. This resulted in the reinstatement of several school subjects, including ethics, Chinese classics, geography and history, and in the resumption of textbook screening system. These changes were prompted by fears that the post-war education system would lead to a loss of patriotism and a decline in respect of discipline and order.

In 1951 the Advisory Committee on the Amendment of Government Ordinances, installed as one of the Prime Minister's private advisory groups, stated in its Report on the Reform of Education System that whilst the educational reforms implemented in the post-war period had contributed to the establishment of a democratic education system, many aspects of the changes were not in keeping with actual conditions in Japan. The Committee, therefore, called for the establishment of a more rational education system. The Central Commission on

Education, which was established in 1953 as a private advisory group for the Minister of Education, formulated a series of measures that included restrictions on union and political activities of teachers belonging to the Japan Teachers Union, the abolition of public elections for the board of education, and the tightening of textbook screening. These measures created a stronger framework for government control of education.

(d) Emphasis on education policy as part of economic policy (1960–1983)

In the early 1960s, the income-doubling plan launched by the Ikeda cabinet triggered a number of major changes in education policy. The plan called for the raising of skill levels as an aspect of economic policy, identifying the quantitative expansion and qualitative improvement of Japan's resources of scientific and technical personnel and skilled workers as the most important priorities during the term of the plan. Thus education moved in step with economic growth during the ensuing years. In 1960, the Subcommittee on Education and Training under the Economic Council produced a report on the role of long-term education planning in relation to the income-doubling plan. This report emphasised the need to improve and expand upper-secondary education in an era of technological innovation, as well as the need to link general education and basic specialised education with technical education. This growing commitment to co-operation between industry and academia gave industry a bigger voice in education. Economic growth, meanwhile, brought a rapid increase in the percentage of students proceeding to senior high school, and there was increasing pressure from parents and teachers for all children to be admitted to senior high school.

As in the 1960s, education policy continued to be implemented as a part of Japan's economic growth policy in the 1970s. The role of universities and graduate schools was reviewed, and the need for co-operation between industry and academia was emphasised. This period also saw the diversification of upper-secondary education and the establishment of numerous vocational schools in response to calls for the promotion of scientific and technical education. From around 1978 onwards, symptoms of distortion in education began to emerge throughout Japan, such as home and school violence (including "bullying" cases), and refusal to attend school. These were manifestations of the harmful effects of an excessive emphasis on entrance examinations and of competition based on statistical deviation value of test results.

(e) Adapting to social change (1984–)

In 1984, the ad hoc Commission on Education was established to advise the then Prime Minister, Y. Nakasone. In the period to 1987, it produced four reports in which it defined basic directions for education reform, including (1) the principle of respect for individuality, (2) transition to a lifelong education system and (3) preparation for the information society. It also advocated specific measures, including the simplification of the textbook system, the improvement of teacher quality and the use of private-sector resources to fund education. The backlash against the post-war reforms implemented between the 1950s and the 1970s continued in the 1980s. The direction of these policies has been determined in an atmosphere of contention between pressure for tighter control of education and pressure for liberalisation and increased flexibility.

12.1.3.2. Education's contribution to economic development—problem areas

In view of public education's influence on the development of human resources for the labour market, it seems reasonable to conclude that the introduction of compulsory education up to junior high school level and the standardisation of the content of education in the post-war period provided abundant, homogeneous human resources with high quality, becoming one of the driving forces for the industrial development in Japan. Japan's literacy rate is high, and the high standard of education in Japan is apparent from the results of international surveys of mathematical and scientific education conducted by the International Association for the Evaluation of Educational Achievement (IEA). Higher education began to expand rapidly in the 1960s, and the number of individuals in the work force with advanced degrees increased. In addition, advanced scientific and mathematical education increased worker flexibility in response to productivity improvements and frequent technological innovation. These factors formed a foundation for economic growth. By producing a uniform supply of homogeneous human resources, education made an extremely effective contribution to Japan's post-war reconstruction and its process of catching up with the West.

As far as economic prosperity is concerned, Japan has caught up with the West. However, Japan's economic prosperity now depends on its ability to build a highly creative economic society, capable of producing innovative and original concepts and new ideas. Businesses no longer want uniform, homogeneous work forces and are instead seeking individuals with originality, creativity, imagination, international perceptions, and the ability to discover and solve problems.

The declining popularity of science and changing attitudes to employment amongst young people are reflected in predictions of shortages of technical personnel and researchers. In addition, it is becoming increasingly difficult for universities to function effectively as centres for original research and human-resources development, because of delays in improving research facilities and the deterioration of research environments. This situation is reflected in fears of a relative decline in research capabilities, the emergence of imbalances between industry and academia, and the loss of talent through the brain drain.

The present education system is unable to cope adequately with these problems and is not functioning properly as a mechanism for producing creative human resources and leaders. Clearly radical reforms are needed.

Table 12.1-2 Education continuance rate
- (%) -

	Senior high school admittance	University (undergraduate) admittance
1960	57.7	8.2
1970	82.1	17.1
1980	94.2	26.1
1990	94.4	24.6

Source: Ministry of Education, Basic Survey of Schools.

Table 12.1-3 Numbers of researchers
- by type of organisation -

	Companies	Universities
1960	42,938	59,409
1970	94,060	99,413
1980	173,244	161,910
1990	313,948	205,509

Source: Management and Co-ordination Agency, Report on the Survey of Research and Development.

12.2. Germany's Social Policy

12.2.1. Social security system

12.2.1.1. Historical roots of social policy

Social policy in Germany must be assessed in a wider scope of historical evolution which is closely linked to industrialisation. At the beginning of the nineteenth century, the feudalistic agricultural system came to an end with the "privatisation" of large amounts of land property. This was not only the beginning of the creation of a market economy but also the destruction of the distributional system which had existed since the Middle Ages. The social security that was provided by monasteries and feudal land owners was reduced with the fading economic power of these classes. The emerging new industrial class of capital owners was not able and not willing to take over social responsibilities. The creation of the industrial society thus was accompanied by the impoverishment of large parts of the former agricultural workers who now worked in factories. The demotion of handicraft work by industrial production added further problems. Moreover, mass migration from the eastern parts of Europe to the new industrial centres in the west created high unemployment rates, and the growing population added to excess labour supply.

Social policy started in 1839 with the prohibition of child labour. However, it took a further thirty years until the capitalist system in Germany was willing to accept a minimum of social responsibility. In 1869 the first health and safety laws for industrial workers were passed. In 1883 health insurance was introduced, followed by the introduction of accident insurance and pension funds shortly thereafter. This was preceded by a long-lasting political and social struggle from which the German trade unions emerged. By the beginning of the twentieth century, the trade unions had 1.7 million members, and they continued to expand during the following decade. But it was not until before the end of the German monarchy in 1918 that free trade unions were legally accepted. From then onwards, the trade unions grew not only in membership (10 million by 1919) but their political influence became significant:

- The freedom of collective bargaining between trade unions and employers associations was legally confirmed in 1918.
- Co-determination was first introduced in 1920 and allowed workers' representatives to take responsibility for the common economic and social aspects of workers and employers.
- Social care for youth and other non-working people was extended by a social welfare law (1922).
- The foundations of labour market policy were created by the introduction of unemployment insurance and public placement services (1927).

Many of these achievements were endangered by the world crises at the beginning of the 1930s. Moreover, most of the democratic elements of public social policy were cancelled during the Nazi regime. Nevertheless, much of the foundations of social policy in Germany was created during the interwar period.

12.2.1.2. New social constitution (1946–1960)

During the post-war decade, social policy in Germany was focused both on combatting poverty and unemployment in the reconstruction phase and on creating a new democratic constitution of public social policy. During the early post-war years, the need for social care was enormous: 40% of the population were widows and orphans, refugees or disabled people who urgently needed help. Overcoming the deficiencies in housing, nutrition and health care were the most important activities. Many of the social problems, however, disappeared with rapid economic growth, increasing construction activities and achieving full employment by the end of the fifties.

Most importantly, many of the fundamentals of social policy were created during the post-war period. The basic idea was the social market economy, which combined the freedom of entrepreneurial decisions with social responsibility. In a very general way this idea became constitutional. Moreover, the freedom of collective bargaining became a constitutional right. Thus, income policy was to be regulated by the social partners, i.e., labour and management, rather than by the government. The role of the government was confined to redistribution of income via social insurance. But even this area was subject to self-administration by the social partners.

One of the major steps was the introduction of a new type of co-determination (*Mitbestimmung*) in 1952, which was extended to public services in 1955. Beyond creating the right of workers' representatives to participate in economic and social decisions of the management of companies, this law was seen as the first step to a democratic constitution of companies. The introduction of co-determination was highly controversial. Other important laws introduced the payment of child benefits for families, the payment of housing and saving premiums, and the access of farmers to pension funds. Income and wealth redistribution thus became an integral part of public social policy. Moreover, social policy concentrated on protection of workers against lay-offs, on the working conditions of young workers and on maternity protection.

12.2.1.3. Creation of the welfare state (1960–1985)

The 1960s and 1970s were characterised by the extension and refinement of social policy, whose aim was the creation of the welfare state. Linking pensions to economic growth, paying wages during illness and a more extensive rehabilitation plan were all not new, but made social policy more comprehensive. In 1961, a social welfare law was passed which targeted the elimination of poverty by introducing subsistence-level support. In 1969, a labour promotion law was introduced which created a new framework for labour market policy, including unemployment insurance. In 1972 and 1976, co-determination was extended. In 1979, maternity leave was financially supported by public budgets. Early retirement was promoted and additional pension funds were established by companies.

Taken together, social benefits accounted for one third of GDP in 1975. In 1960 the share of social aid was one-fourth. Most of the money was spent for pensions (38%), health (33%) and families (13%). Unemployment absorbed 7% and the promotion of housing and saving 6%. The rest was dedicated to a variety of specific measures.

12.2.1.4. Quest for "lean" social politics (1985–1995)

Slow growth and high unemployment set new limits to the extension of the welfare state, which led to a continuous search for the restriction of social expenditures from the mid-1980s. Whilst a great majority of the population expected public institutions to continue the welfare policies, its financial limits were all the more obvious (Fig. 12.2-1). One of the first steps was the law to consolidate labour promotion in 1985. This law introduced more flexible forms of labour contracts and reduced the protection of workers. However, early retirement was simultaneously facilitated. The second step was the reform of health insurance, which was started in 1988 to reduce the rapid expansion of health expenditure.

Fig. 12.2-1 Increase of social expenditures

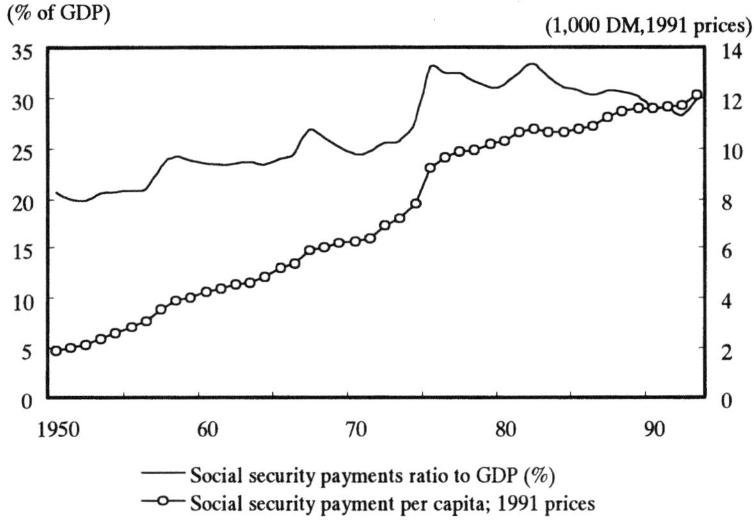

Note: Western Germany

Source: Federal Statistical Office, Ifo Institute

This was continued by a further reform in 1988. A pension reform was set into action to counteract the growing burdens from an ageing population. In view of the additional burdens of German unification, the government was forced to pass a "Consolidation and Growth Programme" in 1993. This programme included:

- the reduction of unemployment benefits from 63% to 60% of former net wages;
- the reduction of subsistence payments for training and retraining to a similar extent;
- the reduction of child allowances;
- the restriction of the illegal use of social benefits.

Total social expenditures decreased in relation to GDP since the mid-1970s and accounted for 29% at the beginning of the 1990s. German unification changed the situation significantly and required a further increase of two percentage points. In addition, a nursing-care insurance was introduced in 1994 to meet the increasing demand for out-patient and stationary care of elderly people.

12.2.1.5. Social benefits

The system of social benefits contains five major parts:

- pension schemes
- occupational incapacitation insurance
- health insurance

- accident insurance
- unemployment insurance

Membership in the public social insurance scheme is obligatory for all employees and partially opened to self-employed persons. Thus 90% of the population is protected by public pension schemes and only 10% depends on private insurance companies.

(a) Public pension insurance

Public pension insurance provides pensions from the age of sixty-five for men and women. It requires insurance premiums for at least sixty months. Early retirement is possible with reduced incomes or in the case of incapacity. The level of pensions is calculated according to the membership period, the level of premiums, and general income levels. The maximum premium is limited to 1.74 times the average wages. Pensions are financed commonly by employers, employees and public budgets. Employers and employees share the total contribution of 19.2% of gross wages. The major burden of public pension insurance is the ageing population. The share of the elderly has already started to grow rapidly during the 1990s, and this trend will continue during the next thirty years. This makes the existing problems of poverty amongst elderly people and the low pension incomes of women even more severe.

(b) Health insurance

Health insurance is also organised publicly. It requires a contribution of about 13% of gross wages, which is also shared commonly by employers and employees. Various measures were undertaken recently to limit the costs. Fixed budgets are available for specific types of health services, and market access is limited. Nevertheless, the health sector remains an area where both social equality and economic efficiency are hardly achieved.

(c) Accident insurance

Accident insurance is targeted to reduce the risks of accidents at the workplace where substantial cost reductions have been achieved.

(d) Unemployment insurance

Unemployment insurance provides benefits to employees for a period of eight months to three and a half years, depending on the age of the unemployed and the previous period of employment. It covers 60% of the previous net income at the minimum. Unemployment insurance is also financed by both employers and employees. The premium is 6.5% of gross wages.

12.2.2. Education and training

Education and vocational training are indicators of the socio-economic development of a society. The degree of wealth and justice, the equality of social and economic opportunities, and the ability to adapt to social and economic change significantly depends on the institutions for education and training.

From a general point of view, we can distinguish four functional levels of the educational and training system:

- individual: to give individuals the opportunity to develop their qualities and characteristics and to live an independent life.
- social: to regulate social stratification by fitting in the individual and by opening prospects of advancement.
- political: to enable citizens to participate in political institutions and decisions.
- economic: to provide individuals with appropriate qualifications and enable them to take part in the economic process.

The multitude of targets makes education and training the key for social evolution.

12.2.2.1. System of general education

One of the constitutive principles for the German system of general education is the cultural jurisdiction of the Länder parliaments. The Länder can develop their cultural policies independently of the federal government.

All the Länder operate their own primary schools (*Grundschulen*) and a tripartite system of secondary schools: *Hauptschulen*, *Realschulen* and *Gymnasien*. Compulsory education begins at six years and ends at eighteen. After finishing primary school—normally after four years, although a later change is possible—the pupils and parents, supported by the advice of teachers, decide on the type of secondary school. From secondary schools, young people go to vocational training (most within the dual system), or to one of the different technical schools or to university.

After a period of economic and social consolidation in the 1950s, a period of expansion of the educational system and of educational participation began in the 1960s. Broader social strata realised that education is a means to social advancement, and increasing standards in many occupations and governmental measurements helped to promote the expansion.

In 1975 and 1976, the number of pupils in the general educational system reached its highest level with more than 10 million persons (without apprentices). Because of demographic reasons, it decreased to 6.7 million pupils in 1989/90. Participation in general education, however, has increased significantly, in particular amongst females.

At the beginning of the 1990s, about 25% of pupils left school with a *Hauptschule* certificate, the lowest level of secondary education. About 36%

achieved a second level (*Realschule*) certificate, and 33% passed the exams to gain access to university education (*Gymnasium*).

Only 6% had no school-leaving certificate. A comparison with the ratio of school leavers of previous generations shows the increasing demand for higher education in Germany.

12.2.2.2. Vocational training in the dual system

The German system of vocational training is often referred to as a "dual system", which characterises the combination of public-run education and company-based on-the-job training.

The German dual system is seen as a model by many educationalists world-wide. Its position in Germany is as strong as ever, and it is regarded as one of the strengths of the German economy. Nevertheless, this system did not always meet with universal acceptance in the history of West Germany.

After 1949, primarily the unions and the political parties close to the unions continued the attempt to introduce a vocational training act on the national level and to standardise the system and performance of vocational training. The employers' representatives, although not a monolithic block, were not in favour of this plan. They were afraid—and this reveals a tradition in the discussion of training regulations—that a greater part of influence could pass from the private enterprise sphere to the public sphere.

The general result of the discussions and debates was that vocational training was recognised as a public area of responsibility, which could not be entirely left to the private economic sector. Vocational training was increasingly considered as part of the general education system, and since reforms were made to the general educational system, vocational training could not be neglected without damage to the whole system.

The concrete result of the controversies was the enactment of the Vocational Training Act (*Berufsbildungsgesetz*) in 1969. Although this law refers only to on-the-job training (schools are under the Länder legislation) and the expression "dual system" is nowhere used, it confirmed the dual system as the German form of vocational training up to the present day. The act requires training to have a curriculum and to be functionally based. Basic non-specialised training is also a part of vocational training. School-based training is recognised as being an integral part of this system. The foundation of the Federal Institute for Vocational Training created a central monitoring and mediating institution.

The German system of vocational training can be characterised as a corporate tripartite system. Both the employers' and the workers' organisations are included in the process of regulation, financing, administration and controlling of training. The government (or governments, keeping in mind Germany's federal structure) delegates, as far as possible, the process of consensus finding to semi-private or private organisations. According to the principles of a market economy, the government only intervenes if markets fail.

12.2.2.3. Human capital investments and the German model

If Germany today is considered one of the world's leading countries in terms of its broad human capital stock and its high living standards, then this is the result of the cumulative effect of a set of economic, social and institutional factors which in the decades since World War II have favoured the development of a high-skill, high-wage, and high-productivity economy. Amongst the factors favouring human capital investments and continuous improvements in economic performance are income distribution rules, a stable wage structure, a capital market environment permitting a long-term investment horizon, macro- and micro-economic employment stability, and a regulatory framework of labour markets encouraging training investments and mitigating the risk of market failure.

A cornerstone of the "German model" and essential factor in accounting for Germany's high-skill strategy is to be seen in the post-war compromise and productivity alliance between capital and labour known as the "modified productivity rule". According to this rule, collectively bargained nominal wage increases would closely follow gains in productivity plus inflation. This has not only foreclosed the option of a low-wage strategy for firms, but has also generated a common interest of both unions and employers' organisations in continuous productivity increases, supported by improvements in general education and training of the workforce.

At the micro-level of individuals, incentives to invest in human capital are ensured by a wage structure which signals clear rewards and has been characterised by a high degree of stability over time. This pattern creates strong incentives for individuals to engage in skills acquisition. From the employers point of view, a stable wage structure has the disadvantage that the relative price of skilled labour (as compared to unskilled labour) declines as general education improves and training curricula become more sophisticated.

Employment stability at both the macro- and the micro-economic level is another important factor encouraging human capital investments. The formation of skills through education, training and practical experience is based on the stability of long-term expectations for both employers and employees. Expected job stability, and clear career and income perspectives linked to training levels are essential in individual training decisions. For both workers and firms, the expected returns on investments in specific human capital strongly depend on the expected duration of employment relationships, which in turn is influenced by macro-economic conditions as well as by the existence of institutional safeguards against dismissals and lay-offs. Reflecting the impact of both macro-economic conditions and micro-institutional arrangements, the average employment tenure of workers in Germany is longer than in most other industrialised countries.

Moreover, aside from involving relatively long "developing times", the returns to human capital investments tend to be far in the future and, therefore, require a long-term investment horizon. Short-term profit constraints may strongly reduce firms' willingness to invest in workforce training and therefore result in under-investment in human capital.

Market failures in workforce training are further minimised by the existence of an elaborate system of unified education and training examinations, marks, and credentials that send clear signals about individual productivity potentials to employers, thus minimising the risk of adverse selection in hiring trainees and workers. Likewise, national standards for training curricula, examinations and certification signal to school-leavers that the skills acquired through apprenticeship training are portable across firms, thereby increasing their willingness to share the costs of training by accepting lower training wages. The specific cost sharing inherent in low training wages, which are negotiated at the industry level by unions and employers associations, in turn, reduces the financial losses of employers if the worker decides to leave after training. Potential disincentive effects resulting from "poaching" of trained workers by non-training firms are strongly reduced by the fact that training takes place industry-wide, and each firm in the industry thus has access to a pool of skilled labour.

The combined effect of these and other factors has been essential in enabling German firms to make the human capital investments required to sustain competitiveness in the face of continuous real wage increases.

12.3. Comparative Summary of Social Policy

12.3.1. Japanese and German Social Policy and Related Issues

Social welfare and education are both pillars of the economic and political systems in Japan and Germany. Diverging significantly in their cultural and historical backgrounds, these two countries both place emphasis on social cohesion rather than individual freedom. The reduction of income divergence in the society and the provision of a skilled labour force emerged as indispensable requirements of a highly productive economic society. This concept sharply contrasts to the path taken in the United States and other countries in the world. Whilst Japan and Germany are presently searching for leaner welfare systems, the United States is debating the extension of social policy. Will this lead to a new "third way" in social politics? This fact indicates at least the need for reforms on both sides, even if the new ways are still to be detected.

12.3.2. Comparison of Social Security Systems

The nucleus of social policy was the start up of industrialisation in both countries. The deprivation of large parts of the workers of their agricultural subsistence created the need for income transfers to the aged and disabled persons. The increasing health risks of industrial production called for protection measures and insurance compensation. The risk of unemployment required a guarantee of minimum income levels. Parallels do exist not only in the origin of social policy but in the further developments. The re-orientation of the societies in both countries towards democratic principles after World War II made social policy an integral part of the new constitutions. Economic growth provided the momentum for the creation of a golden age of social policy during the 1960s. The oil-price shock in the first half of the 1970s rendered many of the former ideas unrealistic. The 1980s made both countries rethink their social systems even if the steps undertaken to revise social protection remain quite different. Not only declining birth rates and increasing shares of aged persons put a heavy burden on the existing social security systems. The extension of social welfare absorbed large parts of public spending and reduced the monetary flexibility of governments. Thus a new consensus on the scope and content of social policy and the appointment of costs is required.

Whilst there are similarities between Japan and Germany, however, their philosophies regarding social security systems have evolved through fundamentally different development stages. The framework for Japan's social security system was created during the post-war reconstruction period. After the high-growth period, Japan sought to become a welfare state, but the deceleration of its economic growth led to the expansion of its budget deficit, prompting a review of the welfare system. During the initial phase of economic development, livelihood support measures were implemented to provide relief to those already affected by problems. The improvement of the welfare system after economic growth had reached a certain level raised the savings rate of society as a whole and accelerated economic growth. However, since the people of Japan have seen the social welfare system as the state's responsibility, there has been a strong tendency towards the formation of vested interests.

In Germany, the immediate post-war era saw the emergence of the concept of a "social market economy" in which enterprises would be required to fulfil their social responsibilities. The government's role in social security has been limited to the redistribution of income through insurance systems. Germany's social security system is thus based on the notion that the state, enterprises and individuals should each bear their own responsibility. This approach has led to the creation of an extensive social security system.

12.3.3. Comparison of Education Policies

Education is a further instrument to create equal opportunities in a society. In the spirit of the European Enlightenment, education was seen as the creation of a new type of equal citizens, being able to participate in the social and political life. Under the dominance of economic welfare goals prevailing today, education is seen as a basic condition for innovation, productivity and of economic growth. The two countries are good examples of how education and training can be used to create an economic potential, and to succeed in international competitiveness by ingenuity and efficiency. Nevertheless, both countries are re-examining their education and training systems at present. The lack of flexibility of the workforce, the danger of declining popularity of science and technology, and the smaller input of young and trainable workers appear as threats to the existing systems. Moreover, the education and training institutions do not seem to adequately cope with the requirements of the future. Thus, educational policy is a further area of debate where new solutions must be found.

The education policies of Japan and Germany differ considerably in terms of the role of education as a mechanism for investment in human resources. In Japan, general education plays an important role at all levels from compulsory to higher education. However, Japanese education places little emphasis on the use of vocational or specialised education to enable students to acquire knowledge and skills that will be of direct relevance in the workforce. For this reason, on-the-job training (OJT) has played an important role in Japan. Today this education system has been criticised as a process that merely mass-produces homogenous human resources who lack creativity. During the high-growth period, however, the system was effective as a means of supplying human resources with a certain level of knowledge, thereby facilitating the creation of corporate organisations targeted towards corporate growth.

In Germany, vocational training forms part of the school system from the compulsory education level onwards. In this way, Germany has created a system under which society as a whole ensures that people are educated and trained to a certain level of skill. This widespread system of vocational education has enabled Germany to achieve high levels of skill and productivity.

The education systems of Japan and Germany are both targeted towards long-term perspectives rather than short-term benefits. In addition to their cumulative effects, however, these roundabout policies have also helped to produce human resources with the ability to adapt flexibly to environmental change. This virtuous circle was made possible by the long-term employment systems of enterprises.

Yet both Japan and Germany are currently reviewing their education and training systems. The present systems are threatened by a lack of flexibility in the workforce, the danger of a decline in the popularity of science and technology, and the shrinking population of young, trainable workers. Moreover, education and training institutions do not appear to be responding adequately to future needs. Education policy is thus an area in which new solutions will need to be found through continuing debate.

13. Corporate Systems

13.1. Japan's Corporate System

13.1.1. Background of Japan's Corporate System

13.1.1.1. Company mix dominated by major corporations

The composition of Japanese corporations shows that middle-ranked firms and small- to medium-sized enterprises with capital of less than one billion yen are predominant in terms of number (Fig. 13.1-1). Most of these smaller companies have developed niche markets and have been operating within the framework of divisions of labour, acting as subcontractors or affiliates under the umbrella of major corporations. Small- to medium-sized enterprises thus occupy an important position in Japan's industrial system. However, judging from the fact that 30% to 50% of the total performance (sales, current profits, etc.) is by corporations with capital of over ¥1 billion, the core of the structure is clearly made up of those large corporations.

Historically, the efforts of the post-war Allied occupation to break up Japan's *zaibatsu* (industrial conglomerates) and purge leading industrialists expanded the scope for new business ventures. The emergence of a new generation of business proprietors had a major impact on the formation of competitive markets. The Japanese economy was reborn in a post-war environment characterised by competition between pre-war companies and new venture companies, such as Sony and Honda. The demand for funds soared as Japan moved into its high-growth period, and corporate groups began to form around banks that had not been dismantled or split up. The high-growth period was the era of heavy and chemical industries, and companies increasingly sought to enhance their international competitiveness through mergers. The establishment of second sections on Japan's stock exchanges in 1961 led to the emergence of a large number of middle-ranked companies, which subsequently achieved rapid growth. The Japanese corporate system, including interlocking shareholding, the main bank system, lifetime employment, seniority-based promotion, and *keiretsu* (corporate grouping), gradually evolved around major manufacturing firms.

Fig. 13.1-1 Japan's company mix (December 1994)

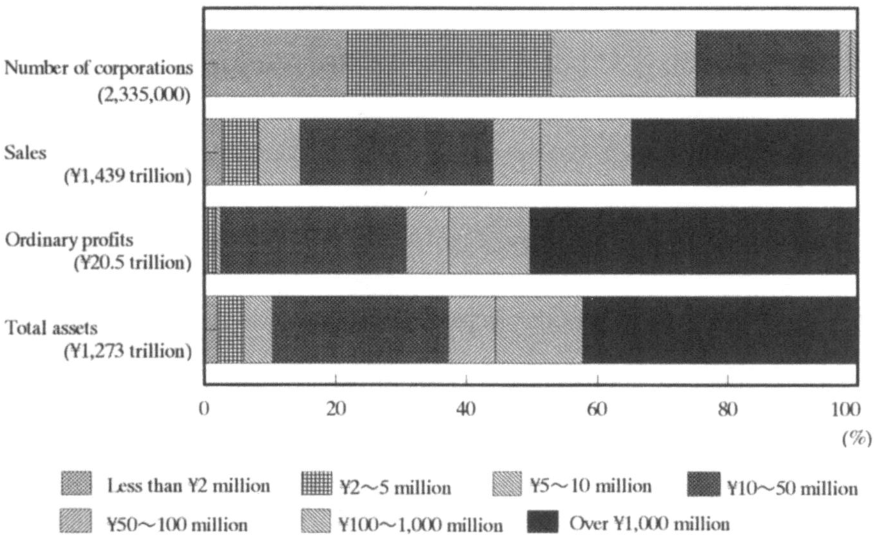

Source: MOF, Annual Report on Statistics of Corporations

13.1.1.2. Formation of growth-oriented corporate system

Japan's economic goal in the post-war era was to catch up with the advanced Western economies. Even though Japan now boasts a GDP that is higher than that of most Western countries, this motivation towards growth remains strongly entrenched. The emergence of growth as a supreme goal of its own gave Japan's corporate system the ability to overcome any circumstantial changes.

Japan's post-war corporate system is based on the centrally controlled systems that were adopted when the Japanese economy was operating on a wartime footing. These systems, which included the co-operation between labour and management and syndicated financing by designated financial institutions, were restructured into a growth-oriented system under the market-based economic principles introduced through the post-war reforms implemented by GHQ. For this reason, the Japanese corporate system has always been a mixture of harmonious elements under governmental control (or guidance) and fiercely competitive elements amongst its constituents.

13.1.2. Japanese corporate governance system

13.1.2.1. Interlocking shareholding structure

Corporate behaviour in post-war Japan has been controlled and defined through interlocking shareholding structure. An analysis of changes in the shareholder mix of listed companies shows that the percentage of shares held by individuals has been continuously falling from around 70% in early post-war years, when most shares were owned by major capitalists, to around 20% at present (Fig. 13.1-2).

This decline was initially triggered by the dissolution of the *zaibatsu* (industrial conglomerates). It has been paralleled by a rise in the percentage of shares owned by financial institutions and business corporations on a reciprocal basis. Banks, insurance companies and other financial institutions owned around 20% of shares until the second half of the high-growth period. However, their slice rose rapidly to around 30% after the liberalisation of direct overseas investment from 1967 onwards. The percentage of shares held by financial institutions rose above 40% in the late 1980s, when an extremely relaxed financial environment caused an upsurge of equity financing. The percentage of shares held by business corporations reached a peak of 27.5% in fiscal 1973 and has again been in a mild downward trend since then. The combined percentage of shares held by financial institutions and business corporations stood at 64.7% in 1993.

Japan's shareholding structure has thus evolved with financial institutions and business corporations having acquired shares, not only for pure investment purposes but also as an extension of their business relationships. Reciprocal share ownership with the financial institutions or businesses with which they deal has enabled companies to keep a high percentage of their shares in the hands of stable

Fig. 13.1-2 Percentages of shares held by each shareholder category

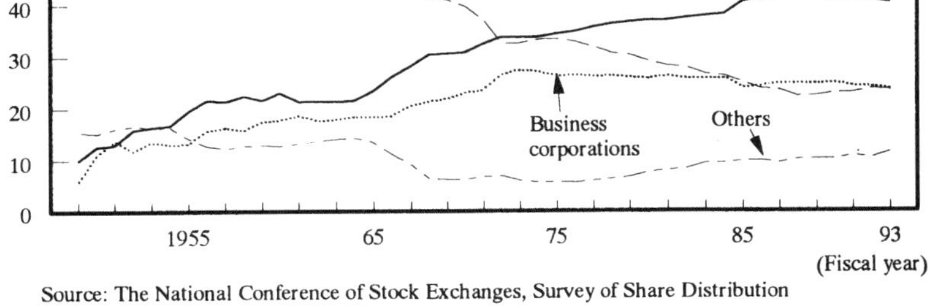

Source: The National Conference of Stock Exchanges, Survey of Share Distribution

and long-term shareholders. Today interlocking shareholding varies between 10% and 40% of outstanding shares, depending on individual cases.

Interlocking shareholders are referred to as "silent partners". Even if they are major shareholders, these silent partners normally exert little influence over management decisions. They also exert little pressure with regard to profit dividends. On the other hand, the high percentage of shares held by long-term shareholders has contributed to management stability and continuity by shielding Japanese companies from hostile take-over bids and enabling management to avoid genuine shareholder scrutiny.

With large slices of their companies' shares in the hands of long-term shareholders, managers were able to make investment decisions based on long-range perspectives. It was thus possible to invest in projects with low earning potential, provided that these would lead to the expansion of sales and market share. Low dividend pay-out ratios enabled companies to increase their internal reserves. This facilitated energetic investment, bringing increased hidden reserves to interlocking shareholders. Interlocking shareholding also played a major role in the expansion of continuous, long-term business relationships between partner companies.

Under this unique shareholding structure, Japan's corporate control system has evolved not as a structure based on "shareholder sovereignty," where pure investors, having acquired shares in the capital market in pursuit of investment earnings, have the strongest voice over the company management, but rather as a structure based on the "community concept," in which company executives seek to distribute profits efficiently not only to shareholders but also to employees, creditors, and customers.

13.1.2.2. Main bank system

In Japan, the role of management scrutineer has been played by "main banks." A company's main bank is a financial institution that ranks high amongst that company's sources of finance and is also one of its leading shareholders. Until the amendment of the Anti-Monopoly Act in 1977, Japanese banks were allowed to own no more than 10% of outstanding shares. Following a transitional period that lasted until the end of 1987, this threshold was lowered to 5%. Main banks maintain comprehensive, long-term business relationships with companies through interlocking shareholding. Frequently they also maintain personnel links, e.g., through the secondment of directors. If a company experiences a financial crisis, its main bank is expected to act as a last resort by leading rescue and rehabilitation efforts.

The origins of the main bank system can be traced back to a system established by Japan's wartime government to enable military suppliers to raise funds through "syndicated lending by designated financial institutions". During the economic confusion that followed the dissolution of the *zaibatsu* in the post-war reconstruction phase, former *zaibatsu* firms were unable to obtain finance. In addition, a stock market slump prevented them from raising funds through share issues. This situation led to increased *keiretsu* financing from financial institutions within each business group.

During the high-growth period, the main bank system was also applied increasingly to transactions with middle-ranked and small- to medium-sized companies.

As Japan moved from post-war reconstruction to rapid economic growth, the main bank system became an effective means of meeting industry's voracious demand for funds. Because interest rates were kept artificially low during this period, excess demand for funds was generated in the bank lending market. In this environment, the main banks became the core of a credit rationing system. It was thus possible to give heavy and chemical industries priority for the allocation of scarce funds, as the Japanese economy moved towards a more advanced industrial structure. Co-operative relationships between the main banks and their client companies brought benefits to both sides: companies enjoyed reliable access to funds, whilst the banks were able to build client bases and gain earning opportunities.

This system of corporate control through the combination of interlocking shareholding under the main bank system sustained a corporate system based on the sharing of risk between shareholders, employees, banks and their clients, whilst relying on continuous business growth. The system was able to function because, until the end of the high-growth period, the combination of capital shortages with a strong demand for investment meant that companies remained heavily dependent on bank borrowing.

13.1.2.3. Formation of corporate organisations

Corporate decision-making in Japan has been based primarily on a bottom-up decision-making system. With this method, agreement is to be reached amongst all parties through a process of approval in stages that begin with those handling the task in question and end with those who have final decision-making authority. Whilst this system has some disadvantages, including slow decision-making and uncertainty about where responsibility lies, it also offers advantages, since the achievement of a shared understanding amongst all concerned through the decision-making process facilitates the smooth implementation of decisions.

A variety of management-control methods were imported from the United States after the war. In the early 1950s, statistical quality-control techniques were introduced into production operations with the aim of improving productivity. During the high-growth period, these techniques were developed and expanded into the productivity-improvement activities, known as "total quality control (TQC)." TQC enabled all employees to participate in management through activities in small groups. It brought productivity improvements by providing a way to utilise the ideas of individual employees and by improving understanding about overall production processes.

The formation of Japanese corporate organisations was thus guided by three principles based on long-term skill formation: an emphasis on consensus formation, the "on the spot" primacy of the manufacturing process, and dedication to group activities. Methods based on co-operation across a wide range of tasks enabled individual employees to maintain long-term perspectives, whilst entire corporate organisations were able to unite in corporate management methods to bring about steady improvement. Co-operation and trust were stressed in the context of human relations within companies, and give-and-take interaction was valued rather than strategic negotiation in zero-sum games. As a result, corporate growth through diversification was achieved primarily through the utilisation of internal corporate resources rather than through M&A activities.

13.1.3. Continuous, long-term relationships amongst companies

13.1.3.1. Production *keiretsu*

Production *keiretsu* (groups) evolved out of relationships between assemblers and parts manufacturers as subcontractors, notably in the automobile and electrical-appliance industries. They are stratified relationships extending to two or even three levels, and over the years these business relationships have been strengthened through such means as interlocking shareholding or the secondment of directors. These systems were able to flourish because the relatively lenient enforcement of Japan's Anti-Monopoly Act enabled companies to discover approaches based on co-operative behaviour.

This approach enabled assemblers to obtain cheaper and better parts by encouraging competition to cut costs and improve quality through the use of a small number of manufacturers to supply them with parts. There were other advantages as well. For example, it was possible to avoid the risk associated with the major investment required for in-house production of parts. Assemblers were also able to reduce transaction costs by using the market, and they could take advantage of the relatively low wages paid by their *keiretsu* firms. There were advantages for parts manufacturers as well. For example, they were able to secure a certain level of demand, which facilitated capital investment. They were also able to base management strategies on long-term perspectives, such as the accumulation of technology through exchanges of information with assemblers.

Even these long-term business relationships are subject to restraints, since the partners can terminate their involvement or make claims. As a result, relationships within production *keiretsu* have become competitive. For example, parts manufacturers in the automobile industry are involved in product development from the very early stages under the "design-in" system, whilst electrical-appliance assemblers encourage multiple-parts manufacturers to compete on price and quality at the time of model changes or the development of new products. These methods prevent subcontractors from becoming complacent under continuous subcontracting relationships.

13.1.3.2. Distribution *keiretsu*

Major manufacturing companies in such fields as automobiles, cosmetics and electrical appliances have formed *keiretsu* of extremely small retailers. Reasons for this approach include not only imbalances in population density and rising land prices resulting from the concentration of population in major cities, but also the protection of small- to medium-sized retailers under the Law Concerning the Adjustment of Retail Business Operating in Large-Scale Retail Stores. Through their distribution *keiretsu*, manufacturers were able to control distribution by means of uniquely Japanese trading practices, such as the setting of standard retail prices, the return of unsold merchandises, and the payment of a variety of sales-linked rebates. In addition to the promotion of sales, the *keiretsu* played an important role in improving after-sales service and in monitoring consumer needs.

13.1.3.3. Expansion of market share as an investment principle

The management goals of Japanese companies are the maximisation of profit and the expansion of corporate scale on the basis of long-term perspectives. These goals evolved out of the need for corporate growth to be able to sustain conflicting systems, such as lifetime employment, seniority-based wages and internal promotion. The maintenance of *keiretsu* business relationships was possible only through market expansion.

As long as high growth could be expected, companies continued to implement forward investment, even when rates of return, the normal criteria for investment, were low. Banks were able to expand their earnings by providing financial support for companies that invested aggressively. They avoided the risk of business failures by taking advantage of interlocking shareholding under the main bank system to supervise corporate behaviour.

As far as areas of investment are concerned, Japanese corporate behaviour has been characterised by a tendency to avoid risk by following the behaviour of competitors in the same business line. This has been reflected in fierce competition to gain even a slight edge in markets for similar products. Whilst individual product markets may be dominated by a small number of manufacturers, the number of companies participating in each market tends to be large, since major companies are strongly motivated to develop full product ranges.

This situation has had the effect of keeping corporate earnings low. Competition amongst similar companies thus helped to maintain a strongly growth-oriented corporate system. It also led to an excessive emphasis on market shares in business behaviour, even to the extent of disregarding costs in the short-term perspective. The result was an over-competitive industrial structure. In foreign markets, these behaviour patterns were manifested in concentrated torrents of exports, which led in turn to trade friction.

13.1.4. Relationship between economic development and corporate behaviour in Japan

These characteristics of the Japanese corporate system and Japanese corporate behaviour contributed in various ways to Japan's post-war development. First, a growth-oriented corporate system made Japanese industry sensitive to shifts in demand (Table 13.1-1). During the high-growth period, domestic demand expanded as investment bred further investment. Through this process, Japanese companies were able to enhance their international competitiveness. When the oil shock struck, Japanese companies developed export markets, whilst slimming down their balance sheets through measures that included the reduction of capital investment and the repayment of debt. With the advent of the stable-growth period, Japanese companies began to stimulate demand by responding to diverse consumer needs through a more market-oriented approach, including the enhancement of value added and the introduction of small-lot production of large product ranges.

Second, because of its emphasis on continuous, long-term relationships, the Japanese corporate system has brought management efficiency improvements through dynamic adaptation to a variety of environmental changes, thereby functioning as a mechanism enabling companies to achieve cyclical improvements in growth and efficiency. The Japanese corporate system coped with the major external environmental changes caused by the two oil crises of the 1970s and the high-yen shock of the late 1980s without any change in its basic framework. This demonstrates the flexibility rather than the rigidity of the Japanese corporate system.

Table 13.1-1 Characteristics of the Japanese corporate system

Corporate system	Japanese characteristics
Corporate control	Interlocking shareholding, main bank system
Management goals	Maximisation of profit, expansion of company size
Employment system	Lifetime employment, seniority-based salaries
Organisational principles	Emphasis on consensus, primacy of on-the-spot production processes, dedication to group activities
Division of labour	Production *keiretsu*, distribution *keiretsu*, networking
Investment behaviour	Dedication to expansion of market share, tendency to follow competitors' behaviour
Corporate behaviour principles	Emphasis on continuous, long-term relationships

↓ ↓

Cyclical achievement of corporate growth and efficiency

This virtuous circle of growth and efficiency improvements was possible because Japan existed under an introduction-type technology paradigm based on a fusion of process innovations with existing technology, and because there was a certain level of domestic and external demand. In other words, Japan was able to base its efforts to achieve world-class economic development on the "second-place" strategy of catching up with the West.

Now that Japan has caught up with the West and emerged as a front-runner, however, Japanese companies are starting to face a variety of problems. First, the business practices and *keiretsu* relationships that helped to form the Japanese corporate system have become the focus of criticism from other countries, which see them as unfair, opaque and closed. Second, whilst the Japanese economy as a whole has achieved high growth, there have been increasingly conspicuous negative consequences. Employees have endured long working hours and separation from their families due to transfers to distant places, and the system also created vast numbers of "company men" dedicated to their official duties at the expense of their entire private lives. Third, the rapid appreciation of the yen has magnified unfairness in the system. For example, major corporations are now exerting excessive pressure on small- to medium-sized subcontractors to cut prices. Fourth, materials-manufacturing industries have lost the ability to overcome their structural dependence on government, due to a chronic supply-demand gap resulting from excessive capital investment. And fifth, a management style based on labour-management co-operation has blurred management responsibilities, and there is concern that the path to corporate self-reform may be closed as a result.

In addition to these problems stemming from the Japanese corporate system, the Japanese business sector is also confronted by the need to create a new corporate system in order to revitalise an economy stifled by a variety of massive and fundamental changes, including the maturation of existing technologies, internationalisation, and the ageing population. Overall, it appears that the traditional Japanese corporate system was able to function effectively under the specific conditions that existed during Japan's economic development phase, but it is now facing the need to make a drastic change.

13.2. Germany's Corporate System

Of the numerous aspects that can be used to cast light on the businesses of a country, only those that are particularly characteristic of the German economy can be examined here. First, the importance of small- to medium-sized businesses (*Mittelstand*) will be presented. This will be followed by an explanation of the main forms of business recognised by German law. In the third section, the German model of co-determination (*Mitbestimmung*) by labour and management will be described. Then, an overview of the ownership structure of German joint stock companies and the special role that banks play in the German economy will be looked at.

13.2.1. Development and structure of small- to medium-sized enterprises

Nearly 90% of the firms in the German business sector are small- to medium-sized enterprises (SMEs). These companies, which comprise the *Mittelstand*, have the following characteristics:

- The company is owned by one person or a group of people who also bear legal liability for the firm.
- The company is directed by the owner or by a manager appointed by the owner.
- The owner assumes all business risks.
- There is no or only slight recourse to the free and organised capital and financial markets.
- A striving occurs for more competitive independence vis-à-vis suppliers and customers.

Even though a large portion of SMEs are important suppliers for large corporations in vehicle manufacturing, electrical engineering or the chemical industry, these owner-operated companies try to avoid becoming too dependent on these corporations. With their own R&D activities and an individual marketing profile, SMEs strive to achieve the necessary scope for autonomous decisions. Their collaboration with both their suppliers and their customers is of limited duration and only affects a few areas of their product range so as not to limit the scope for their own decisions.

The high intensity of technological competition in the German and European product markets has enhanced the acknowledged high economic and technological performance of German SMEs. The numerous domestic and foreign competitors in Germany provide an important environment in which SMEs must test the competitiveness of their own products and services.

The organisational and decision-making structure of SMEs is characterised by:

- short decision-making channels within the company,
- intensive integration of R&D activities in production planning and control,
- high employee flexibility in production and other business activities, and
- a close link between marketing and the other business areas of the company.

In recent years, many SMEs have intensified the incorporation of new technological developments in product and production design in order to maintain and improve their competitiveness. This increased use of new product and process technologies was assisted by the close co-operation between these firms and numerous research institutes in Germany. This co-operation is facilitated by technology-transfer institutes that serve as intermediaries between SMEs and publicly funded applied research institutes. This link to research institutes gives SMEs easier access to new technologies which can be incorporated into their own product spectrum.

The positive performance of many SMEs is also the result of the wide scope of their products and services. Only few SMEs display a high degree of specialisation, which often entails a considerable limitation of their flexibility in decision-making and competition. A broad range of products and services provides SMEs an excellent basis for quick reactions to changes in domestic and foreign markets.

13.2.2. Statutory company forms and corporate governance

The German *Mittelstand* has a pre-eminent role as the economic and technological backbone of the German economy. Although there are some industries dominated by very large companies, which hold large individual market shares, most sectors are characterised by a great variety of small- to medium-sized independent companies which act autonomously and vie for surplus by innovative or differentiating strategies. In this diverse industrial structure there is great scope for differing business strategies, management styles and ownership structures.

Germany has a great variety of statutory company forms for privately owned firms. There are two main categories: *Personengesellschaften*, which are un-incorporated proprietorships and partnerships with unlimited liability, and *Kapitalgesellschaften*, which are limited liability firms. With a total number of 1,803,777 un-incorporated companies out of the total of 2,103,974 legally independent firms and a share of 85.6% (in 1988), the former group presents by far the most widely spread legal form of business organisation in Germany. As these un-incorporated firms create 45.6% of the taxable revenues in Germany, it is obvious that they also carry considerable economic weight. Within the *Kapitalgesellschaften* there are two main categories: *Gesellschaften mit beschränkter Haftung* (GmbHs) and *Aktiengesellschaften* (AGs). AGs are stock corporations which may be publicly traded but need not be. GmbHs may have publicly traded stock but are usually privately held companies with corporate charter restrictions on share trading. The AGs, although far outnumbered by firms in the other categories, are the largest German companies. In 1980, 1,717 AGs accounted for 20.2% of all revenues subject to value-added tax (Federal Statistical Office, 1992).

Since only AGs and some GmbHs have publicly traded stock, market capitalisation in Germany is very low. Whilst the market capitalisation of domestic equity is more than 50% of GDP in the US, the UK, Switzerland and Japan, in 1994 it accounted for only approximately 24% in Germany. Furthermore, with only 665 companies listed on the German stock exchanges in the year 1990, going public in Germany is rather the exception than the rule.

The corporate governance of German incorporated companies is organised through a board system. However, only AGs and GmbHs with more than 500 employees are legally required to have boards. AGs have an *Aufsichtsrat* (supervisory board), a *Vorstand* (management board) and a *Betriebsrat* (works council). The management board is responsible for the conduct of business and represents the company legally vis-à-vis third parties. The supervisory board is responsible for the appointment and the supervision of management. In practice it functions as an advisory body for management. The works council is in charge of the legitimate interests of the companies' employees. Both labour representatives and elected shareholder representatives are legally prescribed members of the supervisory board. Smaller GmbHs and un-incorporated companies need only have boards if they so choose.

In marked difference to the US, supervisory board members in German companies are not liable for management decisions which are detrimental to shareholder interests. The supervisory board is clearly not a forum for carrying out shareholder interests. The legal liability of the supervisory and the management board members is directed at the company as a whole. The interests of the firm are paramount, i.e., the further existence and success of the company in the well-defined interest of all parties concerned: shareholders, labour, management, creditors, customers and suppliers.

13.2.3. Co-determination

Workers' co-determination (*Mitbestimmung*) has a long tradition in Germany, dating back to the phase of early industrialisation. Already in the second half of the last century, several firms voluntarily institutionalised staff representation, giving them tasks which were previously assumed by management. Their activity consisted initially of administration of company social programmes and gradually expanded to consultation regarding employees' personal and social problems. This development was interrupted by the Nazis, as the staff representatives lost their power and the tasks were assigned to a "company leader" in line with the Nazi leadership principle.

After World War II, the earlier tradition was reassumed, as expressed in four important pieces of legislation: the Law of Co-determination in the Coal and Steel Industry of 1951 with many subsequent amendments, the Industrial Relations Law of 1952 which unified 11 post-war Länder industrial relations laws, the Co-determination Law of 1976, and the Federal Personnel Representation Law which adapted co-determination to the working situation of government employees.

The Law of Co-determination in the Coal and Steel Industry only affects firms with more than 1,000 employees, if they are organised as an AG, a GmbH or a mining society. Its most important characteristic is the so-called parity co-determination: the supervisory board consists of equal numbers of employees and stockholders. To prevent stalemates, a neutral member is added with the consent of both stockholder and worker representatives. If agreement is not reached, the candidate is elected at the annual assembly where stockholders are in the majority.

In contrast to co-determination in the coal and steel industry, the Industrial Relations Law of 1952 is weaker, with worker representatives holding only one-third of the seats on the supervisory board.

The 1976 Co-determination Law strengthened the position of employees in large firms, applying to all corporations with more than 2,000 workers. For smaller firms, the 1952 Industrial Relations Law still applies. According to the 1976 Co-determination Law, half of the supervisory board is elected by the workers and half by the shareholders. The shareholders have the fundamental right of appointing the chairman of the supervisory board who casts the deciding vote in stalemates, preventing decisions from being made against the will of the shareholders.

German co-determination legislation views the enterprise as a social and organisational unit in which shareholders and workers have similar and not fundamentally contrary interests. The major principle is the preservation of peace within the enterprise. Conflicts of interest between capital and labour are avoided as much as possible and are tackled in the collective bargaining process.

The works council has participatory and co-determination rights. In accordance with the Industrial Relations Law, management is obligated to inform the works council in detail on everything that is vital to exercising employee rights. This includes enterprise changes such as plant closures, reductions, relocation and mergers. Violations of this regulation can be prosecuted as infringements of law.

The works council's co-determination rights refer particularly to all social and personnel issues, especially to questions directly involved with the organisation of the working place, the regulation of working hours, the distribution of working hours throughout the week, the formulation of general holiday guidelines, etc. The works council has the right to be consulted in matters of personnel planning, new technological equipment, work routines or work procedures. In economic affairs, the council has special rights in the establishment of social plans after redundancies.

Moreover, the works council has a consensus or rejection right in cases of particular individual personnel measures such as hiring, transferring or regrouping. The council must be consulted before any dismissal. Where agreement with management cannot be reached, the industrial tribunal must decide.

Co-determination and the employee participation in firms decision-making processes is assessed as useful and meaningful by both labour and management. The consensual system of co-determination cannot eliminate conflicts, but it has contributed to making a favourable industrial climate one of the most positive factors for Germany as an investment location.

13.2.4. Ownership structure in German public shareholding companies

The aggregate ownership structure in German public shareholding companies can be seen from the *Finanzierungsrechnung* of the Deutsche Bundesbank (Table 13.2.1). The following are the most remarkable characteristics.

- The portions of common stocks held by individuals—at present roughly 19% (including individuals' stocks held by investment funds)—is rather small and

Table 13.2-1 Shareholder structure of German publicly listed companies according to the *Finanzierungsrechung*
- % -

Investors	1960	1970	1980	1990	1994
Private households	30.3	31.3	21.2	20.0	15.9
Investment funds	--	--	--	--	7.4
Corporate sector	40.7	37.4	42.8	39.0	40.2
State	12.0	9.6	8.5	4.4	3.1
Banks	8.0	9.1	11.6	14.0	9.2
Insurances	3.4	4.2	4.8	7.8	13.1
Foreigners	5.6	8.5	11.1	14.8	10.9

Note: Prior to 1994, the shareholder stakes by the different investor groups held in the investment funds were added to the investor groups directly.

Source: Deutsche Bundesbank, *Ergebnisse der gesamtwirtsschaftlichen Finanzierungsrechnung für Westdeutschland; Monatsbericht der Deutschen Bundesbank*

has been continuously falling since the sixties. Within this group, the share of individuals and families acting as major shareholders is far more dominant than the small shareholders' group.

- The single largest group of shareholders is the corporate sector itself. The non-financial corporate sector holds about 40% of all shares in German publicly listed companies. In many cases corporate companies hold the majority shares in other companies. Nearly 85% of companies in Germany have at least one shareholder who owns more than 25% of the company shares. The group of major investors who hold shares exceeding 25% consists mainly of corporate companies, followed by owner families and individuals. This structure illustrates the widely spread holding pattern in the German enterprise system.
- There are also significant amounts of stocks held by banks (9.2%) and insurance companies (13.1%) in Germany. Both investor groups have continuously increased their shares since 1960. Apparently, the holding structure is a widely followed practice in the financial sector as well. Furthermore, banks and insurance companies also have major investment holdings in industrial enterprises, commerce and the services sector. Some large block shareholdings in the larger German companies by German banks, such as Deutsche Bank's Daimler-Benz holding, are well known to the public and are frequently the subject of controversy.
- The two remaining investor groups, the state and foreigners, figure less prominently, though their position might be extraordinarily important in some cases, e.g., the fully foreign-owned subsidiaries in the automotive industry (Ford, Opel) or in petroleum (BP, Shell, Esso, Elf).

Although various types of ownership distribution can be observed, the concentration of ownership in the hands of one investor, whoever it may be, stands out. Of particular notice is the dominant position of a domestic holding company or a family group which holds more than 50% of the shares in practically every second German listed company. The holding structure is widely used in the German enterprise system. Major business lines or company acquisitions are usually held in legally independent, economically dependent subsidiaries or associate companies. Internal growth and M&A-related growth is documented by the increase of company subsidiaries.

The holding-structure system is utilised by virtually all industrial sectors. The big names of German industry, such as Daimler-Benz, Thyssen, Mannesmann, Siemens and Volkswagen, are all holding companies. There are also some huge mixed industrial conglomerates like Veba, RWE and Viag. But the holding pattern is also popular amongst much smaller companies like Freudenberg, Heraeus, Merck and so on. Holding structures can be also found in the tertiary sector, for example in banking (Deutsche, Dresdner, Commerz, Bayerische Vereinsbank, West LB), insurance (Allianz), commerce (Metro, Rewe-Leibrand), and the media (Bertelsmann, Kirch, Burda).

Business expansion by merger and acquisition is legally restricted by anti-trust laws in Germany. If the acquisition of a minority or majority stake in a company or a merger leads to a monopolistic or market-dominating position, the Federal Cartel Office either prohibits such an act or approves it only subject to certain conditions. Such actions by the Federal Cartel Office effectively prevented further industrial concentration in many cases.

13.2.5. Role of banks in German corporate governance

In contrast to the special banking system in other countries (US, UK, Japan), in the German universal banking system banks are allowed to conduct all types of banking business. The German universal banks accept all sorts of short-term and long-term money, they grant short-term credit and also medium- and long-term loans. They are also involved in securities transactions on their own and on their customers' account. As mentioned above, banks are also significant shareholders of many listed companies. In short, banks are retailers, merchants, security dealers and investors. Starting in the eighties, banks branched out into the insurance business, as well.

The banks also have the right to vote in proxy for customers who have deposited shares in bank depots. This right enables the banks to exert influence on the corporate policies of firms, regardless of whether they themselves have financial interests or not.

Notwithstanding the potential accumulation of economic power, the universal banking business system has a number of advantages, though the disadvantages must also not be overlooked. In view of the wide range of services, risks are balanced, making the universal banks less susceptible to crises. Balancing risks means that universal banks are under less pressure to practise an aggressive, i.e.

riskier loan policy. Moreover, the bundling of various banking services has cost advantages as well as providing a denser network of branches. The final advantage is their close contacts to the private sector (Hummel, et al., 1993).

German banks actively participate in the non-financial business world. In particular, they are able to exert considerable control on German companies by placing members on the supervisory boards. At the end of 1988, the private banks held 100 seats in the supervisory boards of 100 of the largest German enterprises. The executive board members of Deutsche Bank alone have seats in 40 supervisory boards of the 100 largest firms in industry and commerce (Herrhausen, 1989).

It is widely assumed that banks through voting right accumulations and the exercising of proxy voting rights play a significant role in the corporate control and decision-making process of publicly listed companies in the absence of active hostile takeover markets. The relationship between banks and industry can be described as an entanglement of loans, holdings and personnel. The role of the German banks in corporate Germany is highly controversial and subject to frequent policy debates.

The proponents of the German banking arrangement refer to a reduction of agency costs when a universal bank acts both as a bondholder and as a shareholder. In general, the bank's commitment to the long-term survival of the company is believed to be significantly higher. Other benefits include monitoring of corporate management and discouraging management from over-investing in assets or collaborating with other stakeholders at the expense of the public stakeholders (Kaen, Sherman, 1994).

The critics point to the principally inherent conflicts when banks have to combine their interest as creditors and shareholders. Since, in addition to their own shareholdings, banks may also act as proxies for deposited shares at the annual shareholders' meetings, critics fear the huge amount of economic power held by banks. Since the banks have intimate knowledge of the sales and profit prospects of the enterprises, the shift of the decision-making process from the enterprises to the banks and the possible uncontrollable concentration of power causes many critics to be apprehensive.

The debate on the power of the banks is fuelled by the difficulties in correctly comprehending the degree of their actual influence on corporate decision-making. For a better understanding, a short assessment of the importance of the German banks in their function as shareholder and creditor is in order.

At the end of the eighties, the ten largest private banks held 0.6% of the nominal capital of all corporations in the non-banking sector, which had declined from 1.3% in 1976 (Herrhausen, 1989). Focusing on the publicly listed companies, the banking share amounted to 9.2% in 1994, as shown above. This share, however, also includes the intra-banking holdings. In any case, in 1990 of 24 of the largest 100 German companies, individual banks or insurance companies held stakes exceeding 5% (Monopolkommission, 1990/91). Moreover, the 9.2% banking share does not take the indirect equity participation into account. In this respect, extreme estimates suggest that the five largest German banks and the two largest insurance companies control, through their direct and indirect stockholdings combined, nearly half of the German stock market. On the other hand, German banks own virtually no stock in small- to medium-sized companies.

Bank lending in the context of external corporate finance, with average gross shares of 18% and net shares of 11% through the period of 1970-1989, is less important than conventional wisdom assumes. Furthermore, the analysis of financing pattern of German companies shows that the control of banks over large firms weakened somewhat over the last decade (Edwards, Fischer, 1994). On the other hand, banks, through their function as creditors, are still able to influence considerably the decision-making of small- to medium-sized companies.

To sum up, the role of German banks in German corporate control is less that of a shareholder than that of a creditor with inside information and the potential to vote ownership interests in the interests of creditors. Hence, banks' considerable influence on companies is mainly directed towards preserving the competitiveness of the firm and protecting the bank's creditor interests in the company itself and in related customer and supplier companies (Kaen, Sherman, 1994). Apparently the positive effects stem precisely from the intense relationship between the German universal banks and trade and industry. Banks can help identify management problems in the financial matters of a company at an early stage, implement timely restructuring measures, and thus prevent insolvency. In many cases, the firms themselves seek out the advice of the banks. In general, however, the firms are interested in good relations with several banks in order to prevent a single bank from gaining too much influence (Hummel et al., 1993).

Through their relationship with enterprises, German universal banks aim at promoting their various lines of business. Besides commercial lending and investment banking, the universal banks are active in international finance, leasing, industrial insurance and consultancy. But above all, the banks themselves regard their industrial and other holdings as a striving for blue-chip, long-term investments to balance their risks and yields in the long term. German banks are less interested in risky projects or high asset growth. This basically conservative position explains why banks tend to support existing structures more than foster an intensification of competition (Hummel, et al., 1993).

13.2.6. Economic development and the German corporate system

Both the post-war economic development and the structural components of the German economy have been shaped by the features of German corporate organisation.

The German *Mittelstand* is certainly the most vital element in the German economy. In the past, its flexibility and dynamism have often been instrumental in overcoming cyclical and external shocks. Because of the financial and technological independence of numerous SMEs, Germany has a wide variety of economic actors with a high degree of decision-making autonomy. Often by pursuing niche strategies, these SMEs have developed an unusually broad range of internationally competitive goods and services.

The German economy's holding system, which is characterised by a high degree of ownership concentration in the hands of corporate companies or owner families, seems to have encouraged long-term investment at the expense of forgoing the benefits of diversification in risk-bearing functions. This goes hand-in-hand with German banks' interests as creditors in preserving firms' competitiveness. Within this structural framework, the larger German corporations have been able to strive for long-term competitiveness, in particular in capital-intensive industries. However, this basically conservative structure has often meant lost development opportunities in new markets and new technologies.

13.3. Comparative Summary of Corporate Systems

13.3.1. Differences

The two studies on the corporate system in Germany and Japan have revealed some differences which certainly stem from diverging traditions and cultural backgrounds.

One obvious difference is the role of small- to medium-sized enterprises. In both countries SMEs are dominant factors in the economy, accounting for the bulk of private-sector employment. However, the *Mittelstand* in Germany, which is rooted in the history of independent artisans, tradesmen and merchants, tends to be more independent than small firms in Japan. German SMEs more often have their own R&D and export activities, distinct market profiles, and depend to a lesser extent on single contractors. This may be due to an earlier development of clusters in the Germany economy which, in turn, have led to a highly specialised segmentation of supply. Small firms in Japan tend to supply simple parts and services as subcontractors or affiliates of major corporations.

Another difference is cross-shareholding amongst corporations. This form of interlocking capital links between firms belonging to a group (*keiretsu*) is typical for Japanese companies and perhaps a distant echo of the pre-war financial/industrial trusts (*zaibatsu*). Japanese companies have profited from reciprocal share ownership with the banks and businesses they deal with by keeping a high percentage of their shares in the hands of stable and long-term shareholders. There are no parallels to cross-shareholding in Germany, even though the role of the corporate sector in German shareholder structure of listed firms is significantly higher than in Japan. Interlocking shareholdings in Japan usually have a low level but may reach 40% of outstanding shares in the aggregate. Participation in Germany quite often exceeds 25% for one single shareholder. This is certainly influenced by the prevalence of holding companies in Germany. The significance of bank shareholdings in Germany is considerably lower than in the case of Japan. However, there may be considerable hidden control potential for German banks through voting rights accumulations and the exercising of proxy voting rights.

Formalised co-determination is a German feature that does not exist in Japan and other advanced countries, although Japanese management more often than not implicitly feels accountable for the interests of its employees. The roots of co-determination in Germany date back to early industrialisation. Large-scale normalisation of co-determination was established by the socio-liberal coalition in the 1970s.

Different market capitalisation, too, may be linked to different traditions in financing. Whereas market capitalisation of domestic equity as a percentage of GDP is above 50% in Japan, it reaches roughly 24% in Germany.

13.3.2. Similarities and lessons

On closer examination, the similarities in the segment of listed corporations show up below the formal level.

Both countries share an important though differently organised role of banks. In Japan, banks are members of the *keiretsu* and have a long-term relationship with firms via their role of management scrutineer, shareholder and through personnel links. In Germany, these long-term relations are created through participation in the supervisory boards. As in Japan, cross-links through loans, holdings and personnel exist. Both in Germany and in Japan there is a kind of concentrated ownership structure in which banks have an explicit or implicit stake, the latter not always visible in the individual bank shareholder ratio. These structures encourage long-term investment at the expense of foregoing the benefits of deversification in risk-bearing functions.

A comparable kind of employee involvement is aimed at co-operative industrial relations and the creation of a common, long-term vision of the company both in Germany and in Japan. In Japan, good labour relations have been fostered by the lifetime employment system, which induces companies to make substantial investments in its employees' training and welfare. The employees have reciprocated by developing a strong loyalty to their company. Japanese "quality control circles" enable employees to participate in management through activities in small groups that have led to productivity gains. The system of co-determination in Germany has institutionalised employees' role as "stakeholders" in their companies and has fostered a co-operative, long-term approach in industrial relations.

In business as well, a long-term orientation prevails in both Japan and Germany, which stands in contrast to the short-termism that prevails, especially in American business. This long-term orientation, reinforced by the involvement of financial institutions and employees, may be one of the important success factors of both economies.

13.3.3. Differences in business growth mechanisms

Although there are similarities between business systems in Japan and Germany, there are fundamental differences in business growth mechanisms.

Because of government regulation and Japanese commercial practices, Japanese companies have engaged in excessive competition in insulated markets. The sources of competitiveness under this type of market competition are strategies based on price reduction through the improvement of production efficiency, and the ability to focus on a market and respond quickly to its needs. Japanese companies have achieved high growth by expanding their market shares.

German companies have formed finely divided niche markets whilst exposed to international competition. They have been able to achieve steady growth by using know-how established under the *Meister* system to supply high-value-added products.

Business behaviour in Japan is characterised by an emphasis on high growth. This contrasts with the tendency of German companies to target steady growth. Whilst the Japanese economy was catching up with the advanced nations of Europe and North America, corporate growth was desirable in the sense that it ensured long-term employment for workers. For this reason, Japanese companies continued to invest heavily whilst tolerating low profitability. This aggressive investment behaviour was sustained financially by the "main bank" system, from the perspective of industrial organisation by subcontracting and affiliation systems, and in terms of government policy by a flexible competition policy. Companies engaging in this type of investment behaviour could reduce their risk by pursuing the same actions as their competitors whilst benefiting from market expansion driven by competition. In this sense, the approach was economically logical.

Because the principle of free competition has been applied so consistently in Germany, companies have normally pursued conservative investment behaviour. This tendency has been sustained at the institutional level by the co-determination system involving management and labour, and by the universal banking system. By dividing up markets amongst themselves, German companies have sought to benefit from higher profitability whilst seeking business stability.

Both Japan and Germany have achieved economic development by pursuing economic logic whilst maintaining a complementing relationship between corporate systems and corporate behaviour.

Table 13.3-1 A comparison of corporate system and behavior in Japan and Germany

		Japan	Germany
Shareholder structure	Major firms	Interlocking shareholding	Holding companies
	Smaller firms	Family ownership	Family ownership
Industrial organisation	Major firms	Cartel structure	Major corporate trusts
	Smaller firms	Subcontracting, affiliation	Free competition
Bank–company relationships		Main bank system	Universal banking system
Management decision-making		Bottom-up decision-making	Co-detemination by management and labour
Position of employees		Labour-management co-operation	Equal partnership of labour and management
Corporate behaviour		Growth-oriented; conformity with other companies	Stability-oriented; formation of own markets

Part IV

Challenges and Responses towards Important External Shocks

14. Oil Shocks

14.1. Japan's Oil Shocks

The two oil shocks that occurred during the 1970s were triggered by an increase in crude oil prices resulting from the reduction of output by oil-producing nations. These sudden external shocks had a major economic impact on Japan, which was almost totally reliant on imported crude oil for its energy. Prices soared due to the increased cost of imported goods, and the economy inevitably sank into stagnation. The purpose of this chapter is to examine the effect of the two oil crises on the Japanese economy, to analyse the response of the government and industry, and also to consider whether or not that response was appropriate.

14.1.1. Outbreak of the oil shocks

14.1.1.1. First oil shock

The first oil crisis began when the Organisation of Arab Petroleum Exporting Countries (OAPEC) suddenly raised its crude oil prices in response to the fourth Middle East War in October 1973. In August 1973 the price of Arabian light was $3.07. By January 1974 it was 3.8 times higher at $11.65. The price increase was accompanied by a gradual reduction in crude oil exports. In Japan the sudden increase in the cost of crude oil triggered rises in both wholesale and consumer prices (Fig. 14.1-1), which were called "frenzy prices."

The impact was compounded by an economic recession resulting from a tight money policy, and the Japanese economy slid into stagflation. Until that time, Japan's economic growth had been driven primarily by mass production and heavy industries, using cheap energy imported from other countries. The oil crisis brought with it recognition that energy was a finite resource and that the supply could easily dry up without warning.

Although the oil crisis was essentially a price shock, it was initially perceived by the public and industry as a supply shock. This misperception triggered speculative behaviour, including the cornering of various commodities. Prior to the oil crisis, the Japanese economy had been affected by aggressive public investment under the Tanaka cabinet's "Theory of Remodeling the Japanese Archipelago". Excess liquidity and an overheated economy were under extremely strong inflationary pressure. The rise in oil prices in this environment caused both

Fig. 14.1-1 Growth trend of commodity prices

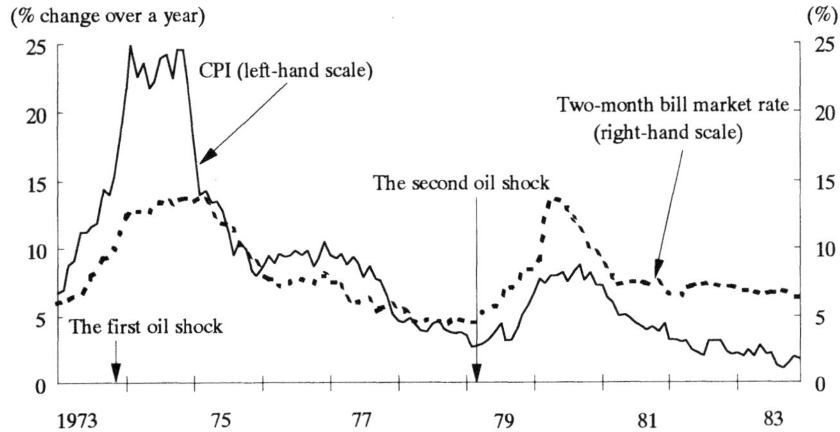

Source: BOJ, Economic Statistics Monthly: Office of the Prime Minister, Monthly Report on Price of Consumer Goods

wholesale and consumer prices to climb sharply. Labour unions were meanwhile able to win large wage increases in the name of protecting their members' livelihood. This combination of imported inflation with domestic pressures caused a steep and generalised uptrend in the prices of goods. The government sought to defuse inflation by tightening its fiscal and financial policies. However, capital investment and consumer spending both fell off sharply, before inflation could be brought under control, and the economy plunged into recession.

14.1.1.2. Second oil shock

The second oil crisis was triggered by the tightening of supply and demand on the world oil market, owing to the reduction of Iran's output of crude oil as a result of the Iranian Revolution of December 1978. The Organisation of Petroleum Exporting Countries (OPEC) took advantage of this situation to raise crude oil prices substantially in several stages during 1979. The official price of Arabian light rose from $12.70 in November 1978 to $24.00 in December 1979 and $28.00 in April 1980.

The second oil crisis can be divided into two phases. The first phase lasted from 1979 to 1980. During this period, the lessons learned during the first oil crisis enabled Japan to avoid "home-made inflation" by maintaining labour share. Corporate earnings did not come under pressure, since wage increases were kept within the range of productivity increases. As a result, capital investment was not adversely affected. For this reason, the situation during the second oil crisis was not as serious as that caused by the first oil crisis, and the Japanese economy was expected to recover quickly, since both private-sector capital investment and exports appeared to be on a steady uptrend. The easing of financial policy was expected to provide an additional boost.

The second phase lasted from 1981 to 1983. During this period the economy entered a deep recession, accompanied by employment uncertainty. Prices stabilised, but a synchronised global recession and the rising value of the yen caused exports to decline. The economic turnaround was slow to materialise, and the recession continued for three years.

14.1.2. Responses to the oil shocks

14.1.2.1. Government's responses

(a) First oil shock

The government's response to the first oil shock focused on price stabilisation. In addition to the establishment and implementation of a price control law, the government also moved to curb total demand through such measures as expenditure cut-backs and a hard and fast financial squeeze. Measures that included the deferment of fiscal expenditures had already been in progress since April 1973 as a part of efforts to cope with an overheated economy. The onset of the oil crisis in December of that year led the cabinet to approve a further tightening of fiscal execution, and the budget for fiscal 1974 was characterised by retrenchment through the reduction of investment-type expenditures. The financial squeeze was tightened in December 1973, when the official discount rate was raised by two percentage points, from 7.0% to 9.0%. The inflation rate remained stubbornly high, however. Until the outbreak of the first oil crisis, massive government bond issues and the revaluation of the yen as a result of the Nixon shock had created an excess liquidity situation. Even before the oil shock, prices were under upward pressure from economic overheating and other factors. Within the government, there was considerable support for the view that the expansion of domestic demand was essential in order to reduce the trade surplus and that a certain level of inflation should, therefore, be tolerated. Prior to the oil crisis, the Bank of Japan had raised the deposit reserve ratio twice and added a total of 2.75% to the official discount rate through four separate hikes. However, the central bank was clearly too slow to adopt a tighter financial stance, and this delay is blamed for transforming imported inflation resulting from higher oil prices into home-grown inflation. The economic counter-measures implemented after the first oil crisis included both financial and fiscal measures.

There were four increases in the official discount rate, which raised the rate by a total of 2.5% over a six-month period beginning April 1975, and the government also implemented four reflationary packages.

(b) Second oil shock

During the second oil crisis, the government and the Bank of Japan made all-out efforts to curb stagflation and avoid home-grown inflation. The official discount rate was raised by a total of 5.5% percentage points in five stages between April 1979 and March 1980. Other measures included strict supervision to prevent companies from implementing sympathetic price increases. At the same time, the government continued to maintain a restrictive fiscal policy stance. Japanese-style income policies were also effective in curbing home-made inflation. That is, the government obtained the agreement of labour unions to reduce spring wage demands in step with reductions in the consumer price index. The Ministry of Labour periodically held informal government-union-employer meetings to exchange information, and evaluate and debate the situation. In this way, unions were guided to exercise restraint in exchange for measures to improve the living environment for workers. The government and the Bank of Japan were firm in their conviction that a recession was an acceptable price to pay in order to curb inflation. However, this perception appears to have been based on the assumption that the recession would be less severe than that which occurred after the first oil crisis, since there were no signs of a downturn in capital investment.

The government probably expected capital investment to play a central role in measures to stimulate the economy after the second oil crisis. In the seventeen months between August 1980 and December 1981, the Bank of Japan reduced the official discount rate by a total of 3.5% in four stages. It also maintained its fiscal retrenchment stance in an effort to repair the fiscal damages caused by massive deficit-covering bond issues. Unfortunately, the government was forced to abandon its relaxed monetary stance early in 1982, when it became necessary to give priority to the avoidance of imported inflation resulting from the weakness of the yen against the dollar owing to a high interest rate policy in the United States. This caused private-sector capital investment and construction investment to stagnate. The government also maintained a retrenchment stance towards fiscal policy. In addition, the slow pace of recovery in the world economy meant that exports were unable to provide the driving force needed to boost the economic recovery. As a result, the adjustment that followed the second oil crisis lasted three years.

14.1.2.2. Industry's responses

Industry responded to the two oil crises by (1) passing on cost increases through prices, (2) reducing costs and (3) promoting energy-saving efforts. However, there were differences in the responses to the first and second crises, and overall it would be reasonable to say that the lessons learned during the first crisis were reflected in a more realistic approach during the second.

(a) Passing on cost increases through prices

During the first oil crisis, the industry raised the prices of goods and services by larger margins than oil prices. However, the pace of wage increases also accelerated, creating a vicious circle in the price environment. In addition, companies accumulated inventories in excess of their needs in anticipation of shortages of raw materials. They also engaged in speculation in anticipation of price increases. However, the government tightened its supervision of price trends, including sympathetic price increases, and ultimately companies became unable to add cost increases to selling prices. This caused a serious decline in business earnings. The resulting sharp rise in labour share subsequently had the effect of curbing capital investment.

During the second oil crisis, only part of the increase in oil prices was added to the prices of manufactured goods. As a result, the price spiral situation that characterised the first oil crisis did not develop, and the effect on business was minimal compared with the impact of the first crisis.

(b) Cost reductions

During the first oil crisis, companies reviewed and cut costs in all areas. Special priority was given to the reduction of fixed costs, such as depreciation, financing costs and labour costs, which had ballooned during the high-growth period. Strategies towards these goals included the curbing of inventory investment and capital investment, and the reduction of borrowing and labour costs. The sharp tightening of monetary policy between 1973 and 1975 was accompanied by a downturn in capital investment throughout the business sector, and companies were forced to adopt slimming-down management policies. The main focus of retrenchment was the reduction of workforce through the reduction of new hiring and the replacement of full-time workers with part-timers.

During the second oil crisis, real wages were held down by keeping the nominal wage increase rate to the same level as the consumer price index or lower, thereby reducing total labour costs. However, the stagnation of consumer spending owing to the decline in real wages, the curbing of government expenditures, the deceleration of exports and other factors were reflected in the prolonged duration of the recession. As was the case after the first oil crisis, companies were eventually forced to cut workforce.

(c) Energy saving

The progress towards energy conservation after the first oil crisis is apparent from the downtrend in consumption of crude oil and energy per unit of real GDP (Fig. 14.1-2). The energy conservation trend was not limited to the simple saving of energy, and the trend also induced capital investment in energy conservation measures. The processing and assembly industries, which flourished after the first

Fig. 14.1-2 Consumption of crude oil and energy per unit of real GDP

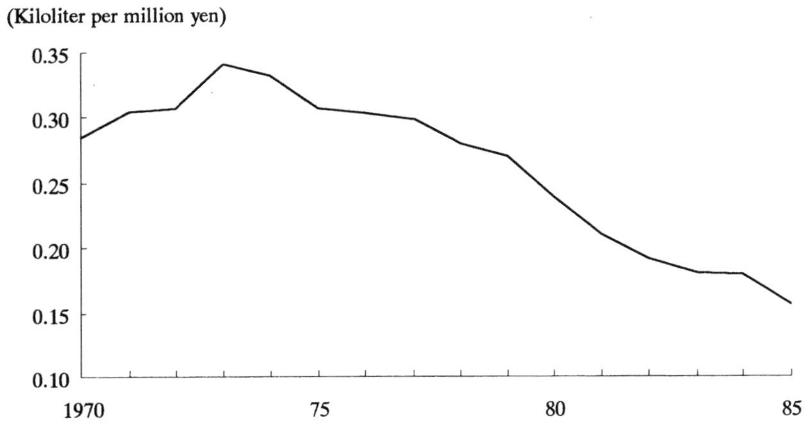

Note: Real GDP is at constant price of 1985.
Estimated consumption (crude oil) = Inventory at the end of previous year + Domestic production + Import – Inventory at the end of year concerned

Source: EPA, Annual Report on National Accounts
MITI, Monthly Book of Production, Supply and Demand of Petroleum, Coal and Coke

oil crisis, began to invest aggressively in this area, partly because of their need to replace facilities in step with the development of new technology.

During the second oil crisis, investment in energy and other resources conservation measures received an additional boost from the availability of surplus funds in hand from business earnings. This type of capital investment was characterised by large-scale spending over prolonged periods in order to achieve major improvements across entire systems. The change in industry's recognition of energy prices as the learning of the first oil crisis thus helped to reduce the impact of the second.

(d) Energy-use efficiency

The improvement of energy efficiency in the period after the first oil crisis was reflected in the growth rate of energy consumption in Japan, which averaged minus 1.4% in the thirteen years from fiscal 1973 to fiscal 1986. By fiscal 1990, energy consumption per unit of production in the manufacturing sector as a whole had been reduced to about one-half of the fiscal 1973 level, bringing improvement in the efficiency of energy utilisation. Among key industrial sectors, there was conspicuous efficiency improvement in the chemical industry, and substantial progress was also made in many other sectors, including iron and steel, pulp and paper, and non-ferrous metals. Analyses by the Ministry of International Trade and Industry (MITI) indicate that the reduction of energy consumption per unit of production in individual industries played a larger role than changes in Japan's industrial structure, such as the shift to industries with low energy consumption in the curbing of energy consumption in the manufacturing sector.

These massive energy-saving efforts reduced the industrial sector's share of final energy consumption from 65.9% in fiscal 1973 to 50.3% in fiscal 1992. Furthermore, energy consumption was reduced by three percentage points in absolute terms over the same period. Investment in energy conservation measures accounted for 3.3% of total capital investment in fiscal 1978. By fiscal 1982 this had risen to 5.7%. Thereafter the ratio tended to decline and fell back to 3.5% by fiscal 1985.

14.1.2.3. Structural transition in industry

The response of the Japanese economy as a whole to the oil crises can be characterised as a structural transition in industry. The two oil crises caused a shift from growth led by energy-consuming industries to growth led by low-energy-based industries.

The first oil crisis brought decline for industries that consumed vast amounts of energy, such as petrochemicals and heavy manufacturing, which had flourished during the high-growth period, and also for energy-related industries and producers of materials, such as ceramic, earthenware and stoneware products, and chemical products. Their place in the limelight was taken by processing and assembly industries, such as electrical machinery and transportation equipment. Industry's efforts were not limited to saving energy, and companies also began to invest in measures combining the reduction of petroleum and energy consumption with the rationalisation of operation based on technological innovation. These efforts began to lead to the creation of new products that embodied technical advances, such as fuel-efficient cars and seamless steel pipes.

This transfer of industry leadership became definite as a result of the second oil crisis. The processing and assembly industries achieved dramatic export growth on the back of a global trend towards energy conservation, and Japanese industries began to attract attention in world markets.

14.1.3. Evaluation of responses to the oil shocks

14.1.3.1. Evaluation of Government's responses

The economic environment was different during the first and the second oil crises, and the government's responses cannot therefore be evaluated under the same criteria. However, some observers attach considerable importance to the government's success in averting stagflation during the second oil crisis, which it was unable to do during the first. Certainly the Bank of Japan deserves praise for its shift from a stance of preventing interest rate rises at all costs to one of tolerating higher rates and for its emphasis on the money supply growth rate from the time of the first crisis onwards. However, if macro-economic policy is also taken into account, the government's response during the second oil crisis appears less praiseworthy. The first crisis was far more serious in terms of the depth of the economic recession, as measured by the economic growth rate and other indicators. Yet because of the prolonged recovery process during the second crisis, the cumulative impact was actually greater than during the first crisis. The adjustment after the second crisis was prolonged not only because financial policy was hindered by external factors, but also because the government was unable to take prompt and flexible action at the fiscal policy level. Whilst it may not have been feasible to take the traditional path of large-scale public-works expenditure, the government would have been able to keep spending at a certain level, whilst implementing measures to replace consumption spending with investment spending.

It is also interesting to compare Japan's policy response with those in other countries. The first oil crisis revealed Japan's vulnerability to situations of this type, and its policy response was not highly regarded in other countries. Yet many overseas observers praised Japan for its success in avoiding a major economic downturn during the second oil crisis. Major industrialised countries that were severely affected by the second oil crisis included not only Italy, which like Japan is heavily dependent on oil imports, but also the United States, which is less dependent. Both the United States and the United Kingdom experienced soaring inflation and plunged into stagflation. Japan's macro-economic indicators, such as the growth rate and the inflation rate, were healthier than those of other countries. Although Japan's success in curbing inflation was a valuable achievement, yet its overall response, including actions during the recovery phase, was not necessarily superior to the responses of other countries. This is because financial policies were constrained by external factors, such as the high interest rate policy of the United States. The 1970s were a time of transition to increasing international linkage amongst major economies, which inevitably limited the usefulness of traditional policy instruments. However, the Japanese government could have adopted innovative policies, such as deregulation, in order to alleviate the supply-side shock.

14.1.3.2. Evaluation of industry's responses

Industry's intensive and thorough response, including energy conservation investment and cost reductions, was generally regarded highly and given credit as the source of Japan's powerful economic adaptability. Although there are some who felt that the response of Japanese industry was nothing special, Japanese companies deserve recognition for maintaining a stronger commitment to energy conservation than their overseas counterparts after the oil crises and for maintaining their earnings by using every available means to cut costs during the second crisis. Japanese industry also managed to reduce labour costs without creating unemployment. This accomplishment reflects the high priority that Japanese companies gave to their responsibilities as employers under a system that put jobs ahead of wages, given the inadequacy of Japan's social security system compared with that of other countries. In exchange for maintaining jobs, companies cut labour costs in other ways, such as the reduction of wage rise rates and the adjustment of long working hours and overtime hours. From the viewpoint of Japan's overall socio-economic system, it is necessary to keep visible unemployment to a minimum. In this context, we should perhaps conclude that Japanese companies took the best possible course during this period.

Also significant is the fact that rising costs spurred companies to seek new paths to survival through the development of new technology. Their adaptation to the oil crisis through cost cutting deserves particularly high praise in view of the subsequent success of Japan's processing and assembly industries in the world markets.

14.1.3.3. Responsse of the Japanese economy as a whole

Some economists take the view that the oil crises marked a turning point for Japan's latent growth rate. However, it is likely that the growth rate would have declined sooner or later because of other factors, such as the emergence of environmental problems or rising raw material prices. In addition, there were already signs of a shift to lower growth in the 1970s, since capital stocks had reached a certain level and the capital coefficient was rising. In other words, whilst the oil crises were one of the triggers of the transition from high growth to low growth, that transition would have been inevitable even without the crises.

It is unlikely that the Japan's high-growth period came to an end simply because of an inappropriate response to the oil crises. In view of the transition to an industrial structure led by processing and assembly industries, high marks could possibly be given to Japan's response to the two oil crises.

14.2. Germany's Oil Shocks

Energy is an important factor of production in all industrialised countries. Oil plays a crucial role for the energy markets because of its price leadership. The oil-price shocks of the 1970s therefore marked both an important shift in the relative prices of production factors and an inflationary push for the industrialised countries. After a short discussion of the resulting price signals in Germany, the reactions of economic policy and the response of enterprises will be presented.

Figure 14.2-1 Relative prices for energy

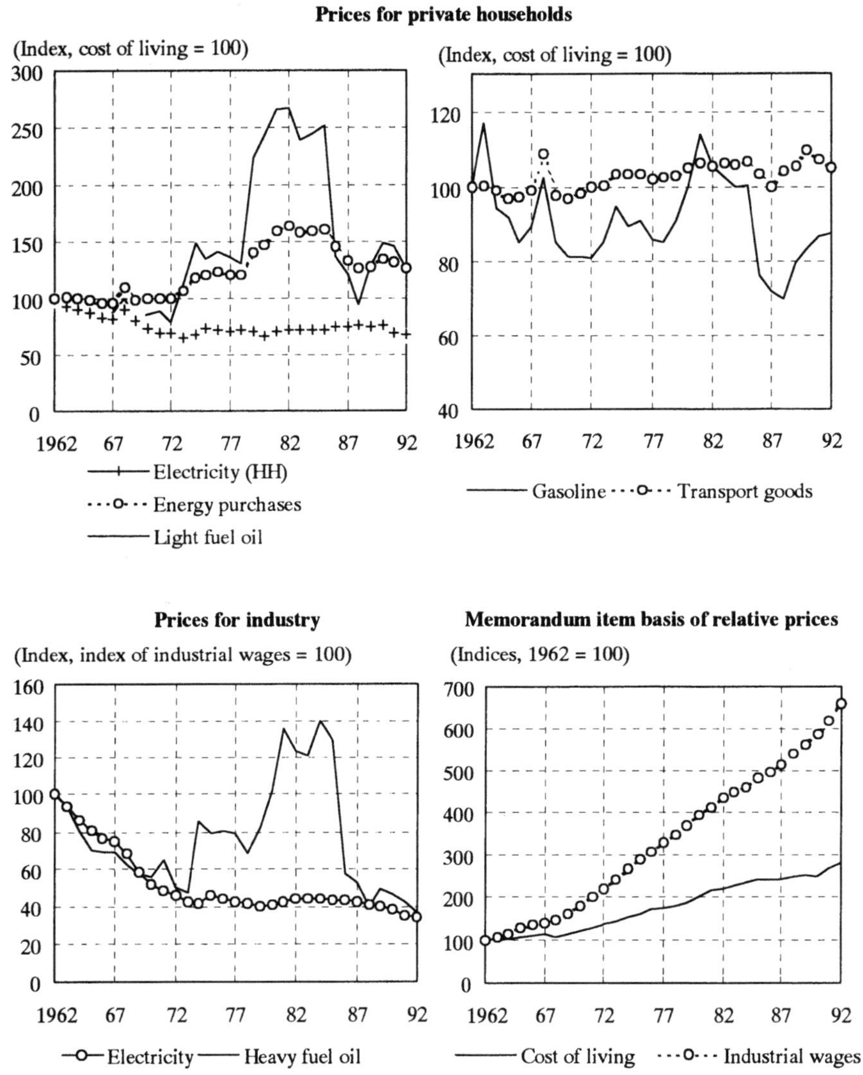

Source: Federal Statistical Office, Arbeitsgemeinschaft Energiebilanzen

14.2.1. Development of the relative prices of oil and energy

Oil is traded in dollars and hence price signals were peculiar for Germany, because the oil price hikes were modified by the development of the D-Mark-dollar exchange rate. On the one hand, owing to the strength of the D-Mark during the 1970s, the increase in the oil price was weaker than in most other industrialised countries. On the other hand, the phase of dollar strength during the first half of the 1980s perpetuated the second oil-price shock (Fig. 14.2-1). After the third "negative" price shock resulting from the collapse of oil prices in 1986/87, relative prices for oil and energy dropped back to the levels of the 1960s or below. Higher relative prices remained only in sectors with a strong increase in energy taxes. The fall in energy prices was accelerated by the phase of D-Mark strength in the second half of the 1980s.

Energy is used for heating purposes, for transport and for creating mechanical power. The price of energy in the latter use can be measured by the price of electricity. The energy price for transport is indicated by the fuel price. As Fig. 14.2-1 shows, only in the case of heating did the oil-price shocks of the 1970s result in a pronounced relative price increase in energy. This is true both for private households and for industry.[1] The relative price of energy for transport purposes was higher than in the 1960s only during a short phase in the early 1980s. The price of cars and of other transport-oriented goods and services increased more significantly. Because of the high share of capital costs, the price of electricity remained inelastic with respect to the fluctuations in the oil price. The relative price of electricity followed a downward trend,[2] encouraging mechanisation and automation.

14.2.2. Policy to encourage adjustments

Supply shocks like the oil-price hikes confront economic policy with two challenges. The first challenge is to avoid the formation of inflationary expectations in the economy with their distorting effects on the allocation of resources. The second task is to facilitate the adjustment of the economy to the new structure of prices and to avoid macro-economic frictions in the course of the adjustment process. Adjustments can be realised in different ways, i.e., by changing

- the distribution of the oil supply by the supplying country;
- substituting oil with other sources of energy;
- saving energy by changing consumption patterns and/or avoiding energy losses;
- increasing the efficiency of energy use by introducing new technologies for energy transformation and storage;
- restructuring the economy towards less energy-intensive industries.

---

1 For private households, the index of the cost of living was used as a yardstick for the general development of prices. For industry, the index of wages seemed to fit this purpose better, because all means of energy saving would imply an additional input of labour necessary to produce the ideas and capital goods to reduce energy consumption.

2 The introduction of improved production technologies allowing scale effects helped to restrain the increase in production costs in this phase.

With the exception of the last point, German economic policy encouraged all these methods of adjustment. An important prerequisite for the efficiency of these measures was, however, to secure true price signals by fighting inflation.

14.2.2.1. Macro-economic policy stance

The danger of an inflationary spiral triggered off by the oil-price shocks arose because of the widely accepted formula for the determination of the increases in negotiated wages, i.e., consumer price inflation rate plus (expected) increase in labour productivity (Sachverständigenrat, 1974). Because of this danger, the Deutsche Bundesbank imposed a tight monetary policy on the German economy after the first and the second oil-price shocks. The phase of monetary tightness was associated with very high interest rates both in nominal and—taking into account expectations of inflation—in real terms. The Bundesbank was encouraged to implement a restrictive monetary policy, because the German economy was in a strong upswing phase both in 1973 and in 1979. But only in 1973/74 did yearly wage increases achieve two-digit levels, which meant a real danger for price stability in Germany. In 1979/80 trade unions and employers had learned their lesson and agreed on comparable moderate wage increases of 5-6% per year. Whereas the recession of 1974/75 was a necessary stabilisation crisis, doubts remain as to whether monetary policy was not too tough after the second oil-price hike and whether the resulting recession of 1981/82 with its permanent negative supply effects was really necessary (Gerstenberger, Hölterhoff, 1984).

14.2.2.2. Sector-oriented policy

German economic policy encouraged the substitution of oil by other resources and the saving of energy by particular sectoral policies. The most important policy was to stabilise the sales of the German coal industry by a special subsidy financed by a duty on electricity sales (*Kohlepfennig*, introduced in 1975) on one hand, and to expand atomic energy as a source of electric power generation, on the other. The so-called Coal-Nuclear Energy Pact had an important social component by stabilising employment in North-Rhine, Westphalia and Saarland, the regions most dependent on coal mining. As a result of this policy, oil was nearly completely substituted by other energy sources in the production of electricity (Bundesregierung, 1986). The creation of district heating systems also received special aid: this policy was directed both at the substitution of oil and at the increase in the efficiency of energy use. Sectoral policies to get rid of energy-intensive industries were not implemented.

Due to the rising opposition against atomic energy because of the diffusion of ecological concern during the 1980s, political consensus on energy collapsed, resulting in a virtual stop in the construction of new atomic energy plants in Germany. As the collection of the *Kohlepfennig* had to be halted after a decision of the German High Court of 1994, this pillar of the policy stabilising German coal mining has also collapsed.

14.2.2.3. Incentives for energy saving and increasing energy efficiency

The German government introduced a host of measures to encourage energy saving and to increase the efficiency of energy use. The variety of measures introduced included (Gerstenberger et al., 1984; Hinz et al., 1992):

- measures to sharpen public consciousness of the problem such as the prohibition of the use of cars on some Sundays in 1974;
- regulations concerning heating and thermal insulation properties in housing and public buildings;
- voluntary agreements with industries, such as the agreement with the German car industry on targets for the reduction of gasoline consumption in cars;
- incentives for R&D oriented towards energy saving, increasing the efficiency of energy production, transformation and storage, and creating new "soft" energy sources like the use of solar energy;
- government aid for investment in systems reducing energy consumption in industry and in the area of housing;
- subsidies for engaging professional advisers in energy-saving questions.

The financial incentives consisted of a variety of measures which could partly be cumulated with other government aid (i.e., in the framework of regional policy). The measures included investment grants, special depreciation allowances, and loans with reduced interest rates (IHK, 1988). Together with the price signals, the financial incentives and the other policy measures affected the behaviour of industry and private households in West Germany to a considerable extent. In the first half of the 1980s, for example, 5-6% of capital expenditures of manufacturing industry were devoted to energy saving (Neumann, 1990). In the energy-intensive branches, energy saving investment reached a share of more than 10%.

German economic policy did not stop at encouraging energy saving and the creation of new energy sources after the oil-price collapse in 1986. The decision to continue reflected different considerations. One consideration was the inherently instable constellation on the oil markets judged from a long-term point of view. Of growing importance, however, were the environmental aspects of energy consumption. The worldwide CO_2 problem with its potential repercussions on the climate and the level of the oceans cannot be solved without a pronounced reduction in the fossil-fuel consumption of industrialised countries.

14.2.3. Impacts on the German economy

14.2.3.1. Macro-economic effects

In Germany, the two oil-price shocks were answered with a restrictive monetary policy and ended in recession: both in 1974/75 and in 1981/82 real GDP dropped by 1%. In both cases capital expenditures were hit most by the resulting squeeze on demand expectations, on the (expected) rate of return and the increase in the user's cost of capital. The decline in capital expenditures resulted in a lower rate of growth of capital stock and, consequently, in a lower number of newly created jobs per year. This was one reason, why after both recessions, the level of unemployment remained significantly higher than at pre-recession levels. The hysteresis phenomena in unemployment, however, also resulted from changes on the supply side of the labour market (Wagner, 1994). Without doubt, the German labour market situation would have been more favourable without the two oil-price hikes or with a more carefully deliberated reaction of monetary policy and wage policy to these challenges. This still holds true despite the fact that the "negative" oil shock of 1986/87 and its purchasing power effects stimulated private consumption in the second half of the 1980s and considerably helped to expand employment in this phase.

With regard to inflation and the clearness of price signals, the restrictive monetary policy was successful. Measured by consumer prices, the rate of inflation was contained below 8% and 7%, respectively, in the two years following the oil-price hike. The external balance deteriorated in both cases because of the sharp increase in import prices. But after both the first and the second oil price shock, the balance on current account remained positive due to the import-curbing effects of the recession.

14.2.3.2. Effects on innovation activity

The combination of an increasing relative price of energy and policy incentives towards energy conservation should trigger off a wave of innovation activity. Measured by indicators based on patent statistics, in most segments of technology oriented towards developing new energy sources and increasing the efficiency of energy transformation and energy use, invention activity actually increased strongly in Germany during the 1970s (Gerstenberger, 1992). The search for new so-called "soft" energy sources like solar and wind energy experienced a boom in Germany and in all industrialised countries. After the peak of relative energy prices in the early 1980s, worldwide innovation activity focused less on energy-oriented issues than during the 1970s. This was also true for Japan, but not for Germany, where the focus of R&D on energy issues continued to increase in the second half of the 1980s. This reflects the more intense discussion of the need to reduce energy consumption for the purpose of environmental protection (CO_2 problem) in Germany.

14.2.3.3. Change in the energy mix

The changes within the system of energy supply induced by the oil-price hikes and the reactions of economic policy to this challenge were dramatic, both with regard to the energy supply by supplying region and by energy source. Whereas 96% of German oil consumption originated from OPEC countries in 1973, this share was reduced to 56% by 1985 owing to the switch to North Sea oil (Bundesregierung, 1986). In addition to the re-orientation to less-risky supplying regions, the share of oil within the German energy supply was reduced considerably during the 1970s and the 1980s (Fig. 14.2-2). The rising trend in the share of oil in primary energy consumption governing the 1950s and 1960s was halted. Because of government aid encouraging the use of coal in electricity generation and in the iron and steel industry, the share of coal was stabilised at a rate of 28%. Thus, the increase in use of natural gas from North Sea and Siberian sources and of atomic energy on the German energy market was fully at the expense of oil as an energy source. The share of oil in primary energy consumption decreased from 55% in 1973 to 41% in 1990. In this phase, natural gas increased its market share by 7.5 and atomic energy by 11 percentage points. Whereas natural gas was a substitute for oil in the thermal energy market, atomic energy and coal replaced it in the production of electricity. The new atomic power plants were used in the area of continuous electricity production. Coal displaced oil in medium-load power plants.

As Fig. 14.2-2 shows, not only the energy mix has changed significantly; overall energy consumption also switched to a markedly different and less steep path after 1973. The change in the growth pattern was most pronounced in final energy consumption for thermal purposes, which has shown a downward trend since 1973 (Fig. 14.2-3). The use of fuel for transport purposes and for electricity achieved only a reduction of the average rate of growth from 8% in the period 1960-73 to 2-3% between 1973 and 1986 (Mayer, 1990). In addition, the demand became more sensitive to business fluctuations. The different reactions by kinds of energy use reflects the diverging trends in energy prices by kinds of use. As shown, only the relative price of energy for thermal uses increased significantly during the phase of the two oil-price hikes.

14.2.3.4. Development of specific energy consumption

The new trend in energy consumption for thermal uses reflects the success of the introduction of better heating systems in private households and improved insulation. The diffusion of these technologies was accelerated by government regulations and financial incentives (Behring et al., 1989). But industry also increased the efficiency of energy use considerably (Karl, 1986). The strongest decline of energy consumption per unit value-added was realised in the basic materials industry, which has an above-average energy intensity because the transformation of materials needs high amounts of energy input. In this part of

Fig. 14.2-2 Primary energy consumption

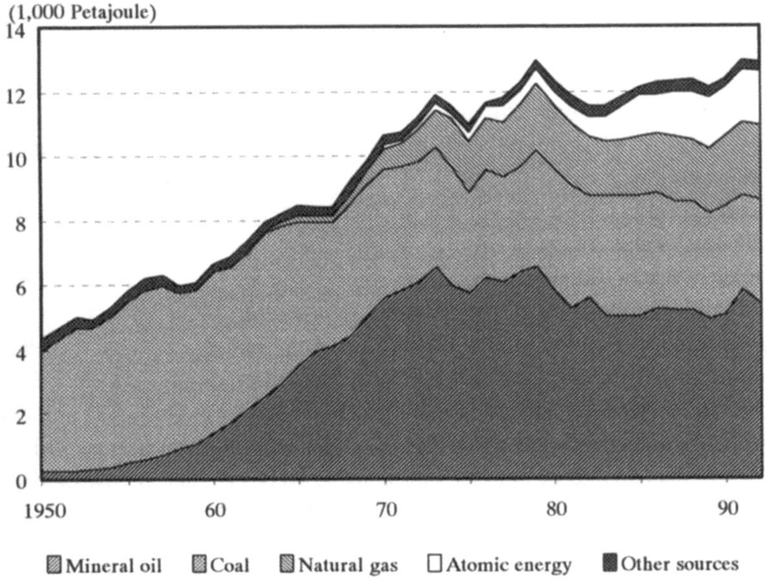

Source: Arbeitsgemeinschaft, Energiebilanzen

industry, the reduction of energy consumption per unit of output was already a topic before the oil-price shocks. After 1973, only the rate of decline of specific energy consumption accelerated by half a percentage point a year (Fig. 14.2-4). In the durable and non-durable goods-producing industries, the oil-price shocks resulted in a downward trend in specific energy consumption in the latter only after some delay. The increase in the efficiency of energy use per year, however, remained significantly higher in the energy-intensive industries. The stronger response to the price shocks in the energy-intensive industries was also confirmed by detailed input-output studies (Ifo, 1980).

Due to the changing pattern in the specific energy consumption in the different sub-sectors, the specific final energy consumption of manufacturing industry decreased by a yearly average of –2.9% in the period 1973-86, compared to –2.1% between 1960 and 1973. Changing patterns in the sectoral transition of industry added only a very small portion to the acceleration, by 0.8 percentage points per year of the declining trend of manufacturing's specific final energy consumption.

The increase in the efficiency of energy use in industry and private households was not fully passed on in the form of a reduction of the primary energy input per unit of GDP, because the energy consumption (including losses) in the energy-producing industry itself increased per unit of output after 1973 (Fig. 14.2-3). The change from a downward to an upward trend in the specific energy consumption in energy production was brought about partly by the necessity to reduce emissions. The intensive use of filter systems caused additional energy input. The new trend is also related to the conventions used to calculate energy inputs for electricity produced by atomic energy plants.

Private transport also responded to the oil-price shocks, both in terms of behaviourial changes and alterations in specific energy consumption (Hahn, Ratzenberger, 1991). Changes in automobile usage, however, were not permanent. The reactions reflected, to a larger extent, the real income and employment effects of the three oil shocks than the price changes themselves. Average fuel consumption per kilometre and year showed no short-term reaction to the changes in fuel prices. Only since 1980 has there been a downward trend, which even accelerated after the drop of the relative fuel price back to pre-1973 levels. The significant delay has to do with the time necessary to substitute the existing stock of cars with new and more energy-efficient models. As the average lifetime of cars is still well above ten years in Germany, the restructuring took several years until measurable effects on the average fuel consumption of all cars in use occurred.

Fig. 14.2-3 Final energy consumption by kind of energy use

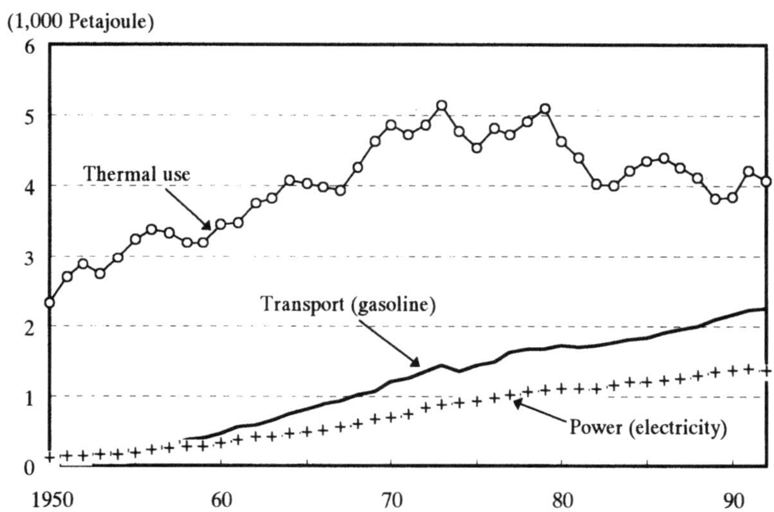

Source: Arbeitsgemeinschaft, Energiebilanzen

Fig. 14.2-4 Trends in energy efficiency

Primary energy consumption per unit of gross domestic product

(Petajoule per million DM GDP)

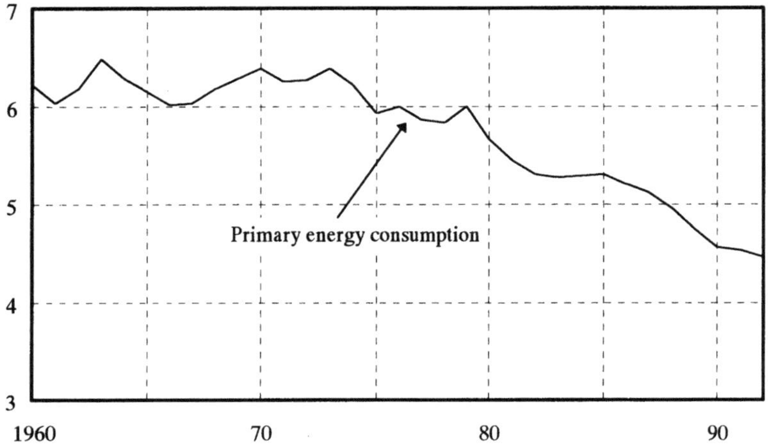

Note: GDP at 1991 prices

Specific energy consumption by industry

Production of energy and basic materials

(Petajoule per million DM value added)

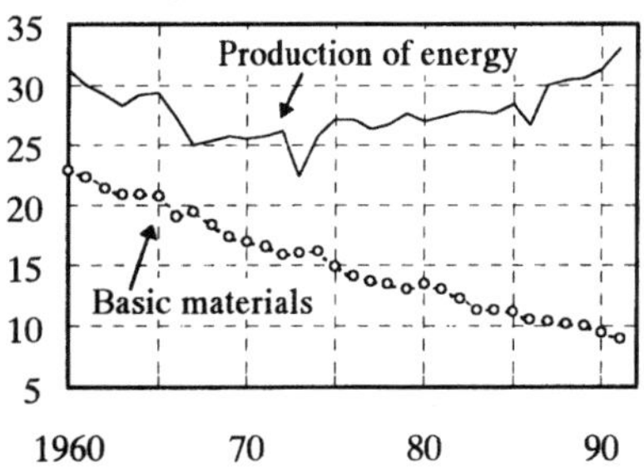

Production of durables and non-durables

(Petajoule per million DM value added)

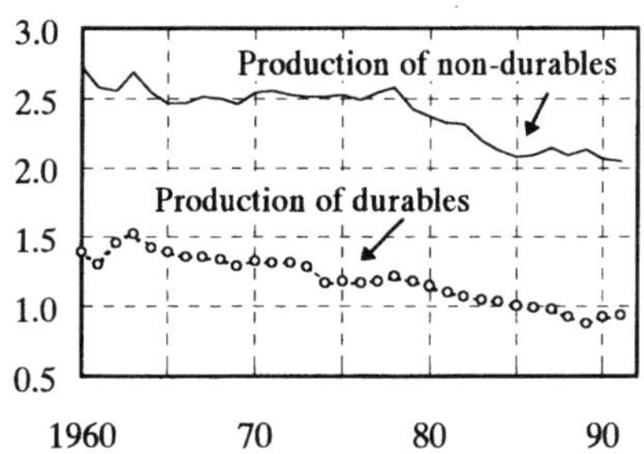

Source: Federal Statistical Office, Arbeitsgemeinschaft Energiebilanzen

14.2.3.5. Impact on sectoral transition

The phase of expensive energy had only limited effects on the pattern of sectoral transition in the West German economy (Gerstenberger, 1988, 1990). The most pronounced changes occurred within the energy-producing sector itself. For coal mining, a reversal of the downward trend was, however, not brought about. Oil-based industries like mineral-oil refining, chemistry, plastics and the rubber industry lost more growth momentum than other industries after 1973 and could no longer create jobs as in the 1960s. Because of the incentives for new automotive technologies, the car industry profited slightly, on balance. The general pattern of sectoral transition in Germany, i.e., expansion of know-how and engineering-intensive areas of industry and of the service sector at the cost of low-skilled labour and energy-intensive industries, was strengthened by the two oil price hikes. Because increasing the efficiency of energy use will continue to be an important target for environmental reasons, the change of structures will remain permanent despite the new phase of cheap energy that began in 1986.

14.2.4. Evaluation

An examination of the reactions of economic policy to the challenge of the oil-price shocks produces ambivalent results. Without doubt, there is a need for better co-ordination between monetary policy and wage policy in cases of external price shocks. However, the German politico-economic system has not been able to create either the broadly accepted rules or the institutional framework to achieve this improvement in harmonising monetary, fiscal and income policies.

The policy incentives to accelerate the adjustments to the energy price signals helped, as a rule, to approach this target. The companies responded on a very broad basis by introducing energy conservation measures and by coming up with new or improved products and services. The financial incentives suffered regularly from free-rider effects, i.e., a substantial part of the energy conservation measures would have been realised without government intervention. The question that must be raised is whether such a rich mixture of regulations and fiscal incentives as applied by the German government was necessary to realise the energy-efficiency gains achieved in West Germany. The answer, however, demands an in-depth comparison of the energy conservation performance of the industrialised countries. Taking into account the lobbying of industry against all forms of energy taxes, the question is whether the government had the choice of applying potentially more efficient policies relying on the allocation function of prices.

14.3. Comparative Summary of Oil shocks

14.3.1. Policy responses

Japan and Germany were in similar positions when hit by the oil-price shocks. In both countries the economy was strongly dependent on oil imports. The price shocks occurred in a phase when both countries were struggling for price stability. This was especially true for the first oil-price hike, when the economy was overheated in both countries. Because of these similarities, there are also parallels in the policy responses.

In both countries, monetary policy was strictly focused on suppressing the inflationary effects of the oil-price shocks. Despite these efforts, inflation rates in both countries peaked after the two oil-price hikes, and the period 1973-82 saw the highest average inflation rate of the post-war period. As labour and management tried to stabilise real wages despite the deterioration of the terms of trade, this conflicting policy constellation resulted in an increase of unemployment—more in Germany than in Japan. This difference is explained only partially by the differences in wage policy adopted in Japan and Germany. In both countries, wage increases had returned to moderate levels already during the second oil-price hike, albeit in Japan the reduction was more pronounced. The poorer employment performance in Germany was also linked to the overvalued D-Mark in the second half of the 1970s and early 1980s. Another factor was the better performance of Japanese industry in utilising the opportunities of micro-electronics.

14.3.2. Reactions to the relative increase of energy prices

Due to the strict anti-inflationary policy stance, in both countries the price signals pointed clearly towards a reduction of oil and energy consumption in business and private households during most of the 1970s and early 1980s. These signals were enhanced by an economic policy aimed at energy conservation and oil substitution, consisting of both regulatory measures and financial incentives in both countries. In Japan these measures were mainly targeted at manufacturing industry whereas in Germany the incentives focused on private households and other small energy consumers, and on the reduction of energy consumption for heating purposes in general. In the process of these struggles, the energy-saving movement produced the new industry of energy conservation.

The very interesting point as to the response to the oil shocks was that the energy-saving movements of the industrial sector accelerated the change of the industrial structure. Particularly in Japan, the industrial structure shifted from so-called heavy and long industry to processing and assembly industry. However, it should be noted that the heavy and long industry had already suffered from its over-capacity before the oil shocks, and the structural change would have happened without the oil shocks. On the contrary, Germany did not experience a dramatic change of the industrial structure. This difference between the two countries seemed to reflect on their directions of industrial development after 1980.

14.3.3. Policy results

This policy stance was successful in both countries, as the following indicators for the changes in energy consumption show. The indicators of the

Table 14.3-1 The efficiency of energy use in 1991

Indicator	Index Value for 1991 (1973 = 100)	
	Japan	FRG (West)
Per-capita data		
Primary energy consumption	119.9	104.0
Oil consumption	88.3	77.7
Final energy consumption	108.4	101.2
Per unit of real GDP (at constant prices) data		
Primary energy consumption	68.6	71.3
Oil consumption	50.5	53.2
Final energy consumption	62.1	69.3

Source: Energy policies of IEA countries, 1993; Ifo Institute calculations.

efficiency of energy use are related both to the development of the population and of economic activity measured by real GDP. As there are considerable lags in the adjustment of companies and private households to changes in the price signals, the efforts to save energy continued also after 1987, when the era of high oil prices ended. Owing to the collapse of the OPEC cartel, the relative price for oil and other energy sources dropped back to the level of the 1960s.

Energy consumption per capita continued to increase in both countries after 1973, albeit at a considerably lower rate than in the 1960s and early 1970s. Only the oil consumption per capita was reduced in absolute terms. Oil as a primary energy source was substituted by natural gas and atomic energy especially in energy production itself and in the manufacturing industry.

Primary energy consumption per unit of real GDP was reduced by roughly 30% in both countries. This implies that Japan and Germany managed to achieve the greatest progress in energy conservation amongst the larger industrialised countries. Especially, industry and private-households sectors succeeded in reducing their energy consumption. In both countries the transport sector has gained in importance as an energy consumer.

Comparing both countries totally, Germany showed higher efficiency in terms of energy consumption per capita and Japan showed higher efficiency in terms of energy consumption per unit of GDP. These results seemed to have been brought about by the policy differences: the main target of energy saving was focused on households in Germany, whereas it was focused on the industrial sector in Japan.

14.3.4. Conclusions

In both countries, the lowering of energy consumption per unit of output in the individual industries contributed more to the increase in the efficiency of energy use than the swing towards less energy-intensive industries. Industries with high energy costs ranked on top of the list of energy savers. The rise in investment in energy-saving technologies thus had a positive outcome in both Japan and Germany.

On the whole, Japan's and Germany's responses to the oil shocks were considerably evaluated. Household and industrial sectors achieved fair success and the lessons of energy saving have been sustained to the present. This is supported by the fact that Japan and Germany have still maintained the position of advanced industrial countries in the world economy, despite the two oil shocks.

15. Exchange Rate Changes

15.1. Japan's Exchange Rate Changes

15.1.1. Exchange rate policy

15.1.1.1. Fixed exchange rate system (1947–1971)

As Japan's occupation administration, GHQ's initial policy goals were the dismantling and demilitarisation of Japan's military infrastructure. The intensification of the US-Soviet Cold War was reflected in a subsequent shift of priorities towards the reconstruction of the Japanese economy. In December 1948, GHQ directed the Japanese government to implement "Nine Principles for Economic Stability." Joseph Dodge was sent to Japan as financial adviser to the Supreme Commander for the Allied Powers (SCAP) to carry out these principles. He developed the so-called "Dodge Line" policy, which was designed to curb inflation through specific measures, including, amongst others, the maintenance of a balanced budget, the abolition or reduction of government subsidies, and the prohibition of bond issues by the Reconstruction Finance Bank.

On 25 April 1949, a fixed exchange rate of 360 yen to the US dollar was established as part of the Dodge Line. This brought Japan into the Bretton Woods system, which identified the US dollar as the key currency. The yen-dollar exchange rate remained unchanged for over twenty-two years until August 1971, when Japan shifted to a floating exchange rate system in the wake of the "Nixon Shock". During this period, Japan never devalued its currency, and imbalances in the international balance of payments were adjusted by means of financial policy. Until the high-growth period, financial squeezes were imposed whenever Japan's foreign currency reserves fell below US$2 billion, which was considered the critical level. When the reserves rose above that level, financial policy was eased. This approach was known as the "stop-and-go" policy.

15.1.1.2. Transition to a floating exchange rate (1971–1994)

From 1968 onwards, Japan began to register surpluses in its international balance of payments, and in September 1969 the Bank of Japan implemented the first monetary squeeze that was undertaken after the war under a surplus balance of payments. The balance of international payments ceiling, which had previously

Fig. 15.1-1 Exchange rate and purchasing power parity (GDP basis)

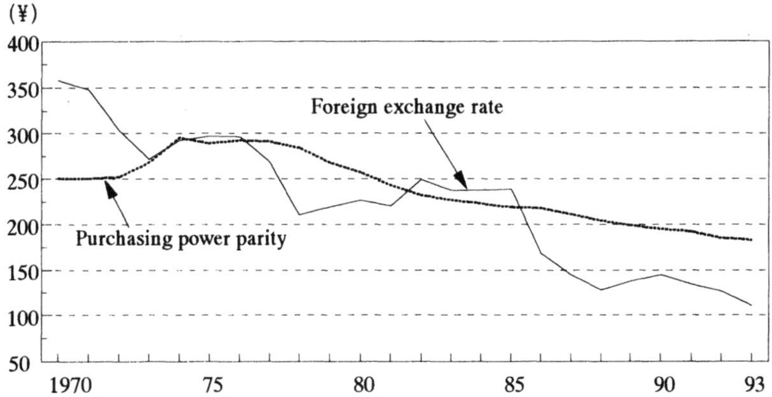

Source: BOJ, Economic Statistics Annual; OECD, National Accounts

limited growth, had thus ceased to exist. The basic reason for the expansion of the balance of payments surplus was a significant improvement in the international competitiveness of Japanese industries, notably iron and steel, shipbuilding and automobiles, owing to the pegging of the exchange rate at 360 yen to the dollar for over twenty years.

In August 1971, President Nixon suddenly announced the suspension of the dollar's convertibility into gold. In December of the same year, the finance ministers of the G-10 nations met at the Smithsonian Institution in Washington, D.C., and reached agreement on a multi-lateral currency parities realignment. The parity value of the yen against the dollar rose by 16.88% to 308 yen. This was the biggest shift amongst the nations participating in the currency realignment, exceeding the 13.57% shift in the value of the D-Mark. Despite these shifts, the United States made little progress towards the correction of its payments imbalance. The excessive accumulation of dollars overseas triggered an accelerating loss of confidence in the dollar, and in 1973 the United States shifted to a floating exchange-rate system. This marked the collapse of the Bretton Woods system, which had sustained the world economy in the post-war era. Since then, the underlying trend in the yen-dollar exchange rate has been towards a stronger yen, reflecting Japan's accumulating current account surplus (Fig. 15.1-1).

15.1.2. Adapting to a stronger yen

15.1.2.1. Transition to a floating exchange-rate system

Even after the transition to a floating exchange rate, Japan rarely used exchange rate adjustments as an economic policy instrument for balancing its international balance of payments. The Japanese government's policy response to the yen's rise after the Nixon Shock in 1971 took the form of intervention to sell yen and buy dollars, coupled with monetary relaxation, an approach that led to excessive liquidity. It was during this rapid uptrend in the money supply that then Prime Minister Kakuei Tanaka adopted an aggressive fiscal stance based on his "Theory of Remodeling the Japanese Archipelago". The situation was compounded by a sudden rise in crude oil prices due to the first oil crisis. The result was rampant inflation called "frenzy prices." A policy over-reaction to the high yen had the effect of prolonging this inflationary phase.

15.1.2.2. Japan's response after the Plaza Accord

The Plaza Accord of September 1985 triggered a steep rise in the value of the yen. The Japanese economy had already passed the peak of its business cycle in June of that year, and the rising exchange rate pushed the economy, especially exporting industries, into recession. In order to overcome the high-yen recession, the government tried to adjust Japan's economic structure by changing the driving force of the economy from export to domestic demand. However, it had adopted a severe belt-tightening budget as part of its fiscal reconstruction efforts. The efforts to stimulate the economy relied heavily on monetary policy as well as exchange rate measures.

The Bank of Japan initially sought to stabilise the yen-dollar exchange rate in the 190 yen range, and in January 1986 it cut the official discount rate for the first time in 27 months by 0.5%, to 4.5%. However, this failed to halt the uptrend in the exchange rate, and the central bank continued to reduce the official discount rate in stages from March 1986 onwards. The Louvre Accord of February 1987 called for the stabilisation of exchange rates at their then existing levels, and Japan cut the official discount rate to 2.5% as part of its policy co-ordination under that agreement.

By October 1986, the economy had already entered a recovery phase. In May 1987, however, the government announced an emergency economic package that included fiscal expenditure amounting to ¥5 trillion and income tax cuts totalling ¥1 trillion. Thereafter, the government maintained an extremely relaxed monetary stance, a situation that continued for over two years until the official discount rate was raised in May 1989, as a precaution against inflation.

This combination of self-sustaining economic recovery with an expansionary fiscal policy and prolonged monetary relaxation led to an unprecedented period of sustained economic expansion, driven by capital investment and consumer spending. However, the timing of fiscal measures was delayed owing to the fact that the government gave priority to fiscal reconstruction, whilst the shift to a tighter monetary stance was delayed by the need to give precedence to international policy co-ordination. This situation led to the forming of a rampaging assets inflation in land and share prices that would have far-reaching repercussions later on.

15.1.3. Adapting to the high yen in industry and business

15.1.3.1. Export drives and the emphasis on domestic demand

The export ratio of processing and assembly industries rose dramatically during the oil-crisis period, reaching 36.9% in fiscal 1985. However, the export ratio declined sharply in fiscal 1986 and has since remained static at around the 30% level (Fig. 15.1-2). When domestic demand slumped during the oil-crisis period, Japanese companies sought to secure earnings through increased exporting. As the yen began to rise from 1985 onwards, however, they focused increasingly on domestic demand. This approach reflected a decline in the price competitiveness of Japanese products, owing to a sustained rise in the value of the yen and to a relative decline in the advantage in terms of their competitiveness based on non-price factors such as catching-up challenges from Southeast Asian countries and the renewed competitiveness of the United States.

15.1.3.2. Enhancing high-value-added product and raising export prices to reflect the high yen

Japanese companies have sought to increase the value-added content of their exports. The trend of export volume index and real export (national accounts basis) shows that export volumes increased by only about 5% on average each year between fiscal 1987 and fiscal 1989 due to the impact of the high yen, but exports in real terms grew strongly by 10-15% during the same period (Fig. 15.1-3). This trend was the result of technological advances in the fields of information technology and electronics, as well as owing to the efforts of iron and steel manufacturers to develop high value-added products to meet the needs of user industries.

The share of capital goods in Japan's total export items has been rising consistently since the high-growth period, reaching 58.7% in fiscal 1993. This change in Japan's export structure reflects the vital importance of Japanese capital goods to production activity in the countries to which these goods are exported. It has helped to alleviate the erosion of Japan's price competitiveness following the appreciation of the yen.

This uptrend in the value-added content of exports is also attributable to the efforts of Japanese companies to pass on the effects of the high yen through higher export prices. A comparison between the rate of increase in the exchange rate and the rate of increase in yen-based export price index between 1986 and 1988 shows that 50-70% of the rise in the value of the yen was added to export prices.

15.1.3.3. Shift to overseas production

In the light of the erosion of their price competitiveness owing to the rapid appreciation of the yen after the Plaza Accord, manufacturers took counter-

Fig. 15.1-2 Export ratios of listed manufacturing industries

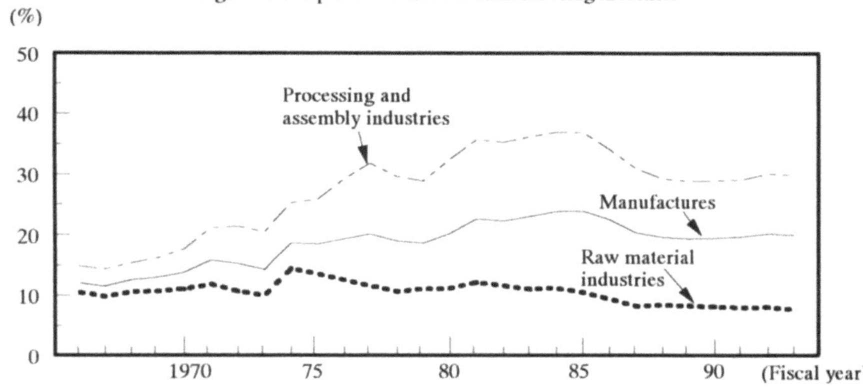

Source: Financial Statement of each organisation

Figure 15.1-3 value-Added content of exports

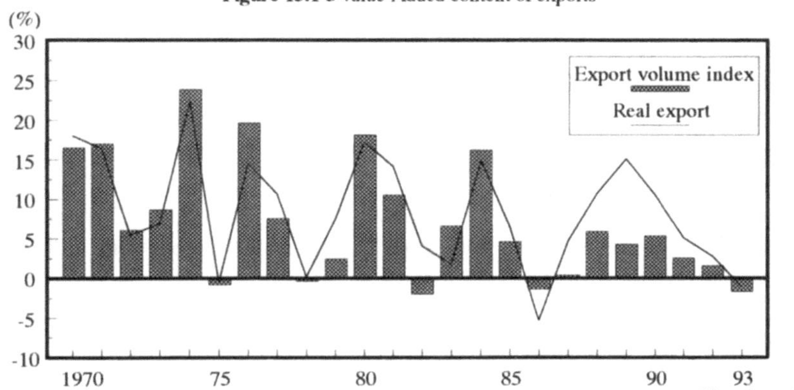

Source: EPA, Annual Report on National Accounts; MOF, The Summary Report on Trade of Japan

measures by shifting their production operations overseas. Much of the direct investment channelled into North America and Europe was targeted towards local market sales, but the purpose of direct investment in Asia was to shift production operations to areas where low-cost labour was available.

Between fiscal 1983 and fiscal 1986, overseas direct investment by manufacturers amounted to around $3 billion per annum, which was similar to the level in the late 1970s. In fiscal 1987, however, investment doubled to $7.8 billion. It rose further to $13.8 billion in fiscal 1988, and to $16.3 billion in fiscal 1989, reaching a level 5-6 times higher than in the early 1980s (Fig. 15.1-4). The growth rate of overseas direct investment has fallen sharply since fiscal 1990 as a result of hovering business earnings. However, the level of investment has remained high, with a fiscal 1993 total of $11.1 billion. The emergence of overseas direct investment as a significant factor in Japan thus dates from about a decade ago.

This trend is reflected in the overseas production ratio (sales of overseas subsidiaries as a percentage of manufacturers' domestic sales). In fiscal 1987, when overseas direct investment began to expand, the ratio stood at 4.0%, and it climbed to 6.4% by fiscal 1993, although it is still less than one-quarter of the ratio for the United States.

During the uptrend in the value of the yen in 1985, there was concern that the shift to overseas production would lead to the hollowing-out of domestic industry. However, the expansion of overseas direct investment in that period was paralleled by an uptrend in domestic capital investment, and no hollowing-out occurred. Reasons for this include the sustained high growth of the domestic economy, led by domestic demand, and the efforts of companies to form international divisions of labour based on levels of value added of products.

15.1.3.4. Business diversification

Industries affected by the maturation of their core activities have turned to business diversification. This is particularly true of the iron and steel industry, which has diversified into such fields as new materials, biotechnology, information and telecommunications, and the leisure industry. However, none of these activities have grown into major areas of business. From 1986 onwards, high share prices prompted an upsurge of equity financing, and there were 2,857 mergers and acquisitions between 1986 and 1989. Not all mergers and acquisitions undertaken with the aim of business diversification were successful.

Fig. 15.1-4 Direct overseas investment by manufacturing industries

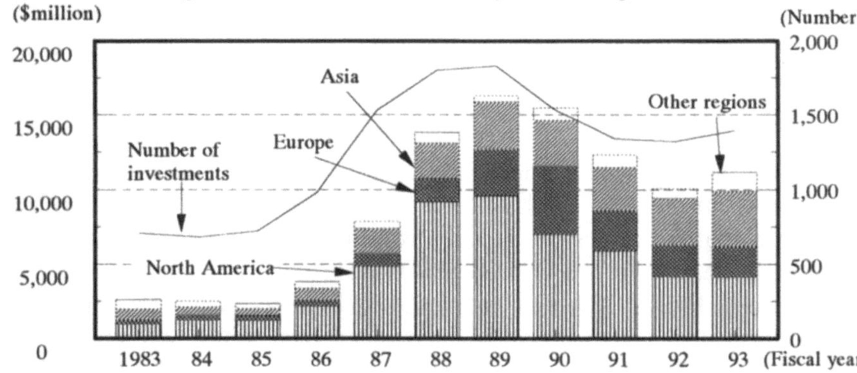

Source: MOF, Foreign Direct Investment

15.1.3.5. Utilising the benefits of a higher yen

Processing and assembly manufacturers have increasingly sought to benefit from a stronger yen by raising the percentage of procuring parts and other requirements from overseas sources. Particularly for companies with high export ratios, this approach has been an effective way of hedging exchange-rate risk by paying for supplies in dollars. In addition, the shift to overseas production has been accompanied by efforts to secure profit margins through increases in the percentage of parts and other requirements procured locally.

Electrical machinery manufacturers are increasingly re-importing consumer electrical appliances produced by their own overseas ventures. Technological advances have led to the packaging of many components, enabling manufacturers to transfer assembly operations to overseas subsidiaries or to employ overseas companies to produce on consignment basis.

Major retailers and general trading firms have, meanwhile, focused on a development-and-import scheme as well as the development of private-brand products. This approach reflects gaps between domestic and overseas prices, as well as improvements in the supply capacity and technical standards of newly industrialised economies. In particular, there has been a conspicuous increase in development-and-importing of products requiring relatively little processing, such as apparel and household goods, and of items that are relatively expensive in Japan owing to government restrictions, such as foodstuffs.

15.1.4. Structural change and the ability of Japanese industry and the Japanese economy to adapt to a high-yen environment

15.1.4.1. Evaluating foreign exchange policies

Although the appreciation of the yen has, in general, a positive impact on improving terms of trade, there has so far been a tendency to focus on the negative implications, including the deterioration of profit margins. This reflects the weighting of Japan's industrial structure towards industries that depend heavily on exports, such as automobiles, electrical machinery and general machinery. For this reason, the Japanese government's basic policy stance on foreign exchange has been to prevent excessive rises in the value of the yen and to stabilise the exchange rate. However, exchange rates are determined by market mechanisms and cannot be easily controlled in the long term by the economic policies of one country. Moreover, the vast size of the foreign exchange market means that there is limited scope for the control of exchange rates through such means as co-ordinated intervention by multiple governments.

In view of this situation, the Japanese government has adopted policies designed to alleviate the impact of the high yen as much as possible through such means as the expansion of public investment and the easing of financial restraints.

However, these approaches have their respective advantages and disadvantages, and have not always worked effectively. It is clear that, in some cases, policies have not only failed to yield the desired results, but have also hindered structural economic reform. It will, therefore, be necessary to improve the efficiency of domestic economic and industrial systems, and enable consumers to enjoy the benefits of a stronger yen through deregulation.

15.1.4.2. Evaluating the response of industry and the business to the high yen

The response of the Japanese business sector to the high yen between 1973, right after the transition to a floating exchange rate, and 1985 was based on corporate strategies employed throughout the post-war era, including the enhancement of product value-added, the improvement of export competitiveness through rationalisation, and the reduction of costs. In the period after the second oil shock (1982-85), the yen weakened against the dollar because of Japan's current account deficit and the high-dollar policy of the Reagan administration. This situation had a positive effect on the export competitiveness of Japanese industries.

Export industries have responded to the appreciation of the yen since 1985 by working to strengthen the export competitiveness of their products. They have also shifted increasingly towards offshore production, leading to the formation of product- or process-based international divisions of labour. Reasons for this approach include the overseas expansion of Japanese companies and the growing industrial potential of Southeast Asian countries.

The exchange rate at which manufacturers can make a profit has risen consistently. In 1994 it reached ¥118.1, compared with an actual exchange rate of ¥102.2 (Table 15.1-1). The break-even point has risen by 75.4% since 1986, compared with a 64.9% rise in the actual exchange rate. The fact that the continuous uptrend in the actual exchange rate has been accompanied by a rise in the break-even point exchange rate reflects the extreme adaptability of the Japanese industry. The efforts of Japanese companies to adapt to a high-yen environment have, however, triggered paradoxical trends, for the resulting improvement of their export competitiveness has caused a cumulative rise in Japan's current account surplus, leading to further rises in the value of the yen.

Table 15.1-1 Break-even point exchange rate in manufacturing industry

- ¥ -

Calendar year	1986	1988	1990	1992	1994
Actual exchange rate (A)	168.5	128.2	144.8	126.7	102.2
Break-even point (B)	207.2	141.1	133.2	126.2	118.1
Difference (A)-(B)	-38.7	-12.9	11.6	0.5	-15.9

Note: 1. Break-even points are based on surveys conducted in January of each year.
2. Actual exchange rates are based on yearly arithmetic averages.

Source: BOJ, Economic Statistics Annual; EPA, Questionnaire Survey of Business Behaviour

The repetition of this "vicious circle" has started to expose distortions in Japan's economic and industrial structure. The persistent efforts of Japanese industry to adapt to a changing environment have caused internationally competitive industries to concentrate their resources efficiently within Japan, resulting in a formation of industrial groups that are vulnerable to rises in the value of the yen. In addition, a widening productivity gap between highly productive export industries and domestic industries sheltered by regulations has created a gap between domestic and overseas prices, and thus the resulting economic structure has made it difficult for consumers to benefit from the merits of the high yen. The efforts of Japanese industry and business to adapt to a high-yen environment have thus produced a distorted result of micro-economic success and macro-economic failure.

Whilst individual companies must work constantly to improve productivity, it will be necessary from now on to move away from the concept of adapting to a high-yen environment, but to focus instead on the development of an industrial structure and corporate systems that can absorb exchange-rate fluctuations efficiently. This will require changes in Japan's domestic economic and industrial structures, including an emphasis on products that offer high earning potential, the development of original products, an increase in the percentage of trade transactions denominated in yen (39.7% of export transactions and 19.2% of import transactions were denominated in September 1994), the quantitative and qualitative expansion of overseas production, and improvements in the efficiency of domestic distribution systems. These changes should enable Japanese companies to become truly competitive as global enterprises.

15.2. Germany's Exchange Rate Changes

15.2.1. Changes in the D-Mark exchange rate

15.2.1.1. Fixed exchange rate system (1949–1970)

In Germany the Allied military authorities fixed the external value of the currency at 3.33 D-Marks to the dollar in 1948. In the 1949 exchange-rate realignment, most European currencies were devalued in relation to the dollar—the D-Mark by 20.7% to DM 4.20 per US dollar. In the following two decades individual currencies, especially the D-Mark, pound sterling and the French franc, were repeatedly subject to pressure to appreciate or depreciate. In the 1950s the D-Mark was considered undervalued. The surplus on current account ran to about 2% of GDP already in 1952 to 1954. But the first D-Mark revaluation did not occur until 1961 and amounted to 5%. Until about the year 1967, the world economy experienced a period without serious currency conflicts. Towards the end of the decade, however, West Germany increasingly became the target of international currency speculation. After an "ersatz revaluation (higher taxes on exports and tax relief on imports)" failed to calm the currency markets, and a strong flow of capital entered Germany at the beginning of 1969, the October 1969 revaluation of the D-Mark was inevitable. It amounted to 9.3%.

15.2.1.2. Breakdown of the Bretton Woods system (1971–1979)

The next major shock to the Bretton Woods system occurred in 1971. In the first half of this year, the international monetary crisis was centred on the dollar and the D-Mark. West Germany was nearly flooded with capital flows from the United States. This led in May to a suspension of the foreign-currency purchase obligation and to a floating of the D-Mark exchange rate. In August of the same year, the convertibility between gold and the dollar was terminated. In the "Smithsonian" exchange-rate realignment of December 1971, the sanctuary defended by the United States for years, according to which the dollar as the key currency in the international monetary system could not be devalued vis-à-vis gold, was destroyed. Against the former gold parity, the dollar was devalued by 7.9%. The D-Mark revaluation over the dollar amounted to 13.6% altogether and 6%, on average, over all other currencies.

In mid-February 1973, the last attempt was made to save the Bretton Woods system via new parity adjustments. The US dollar was again devalued by 10% and the Japanese yen was allowed to float. The members of the currency snake established in April 1972 kept their cross rates unchanged. Soon thereafter, however, the next wave of speculation set in. In early March of 1973, foreign exchange markets in West Germany and many other countries were closed. Several EC countries (Belgium, Denmark, West Germany, France, Luxembourg, and the Netherlands) began to jointly float their currencies against the dollar. Great Britain and Italy, as most other countries, let their currencies float individually.

In the following period of flexible exchange rates, the strong appreciation of the D-Mark continued (Table 15.2-1). After a D-Mark appreciation of 47% vis-à-vis the dollar between 1969 and 1973, this trend continued at about the same rate until the end of the decade. From 1973 to 1980, the appreciation of the D-Mark against the average of eighteen industrial countries was somewhat less than vis-à-vis the dollar. It is noteworthy that these D-Mark exchange rate movements evidently did not suffice to offset the price differences to these eighteen countries: calculations of the Deutsche Bundesbank show a real depreciation of the D-Mark in this period of about 8% (Table 15.2-1).

15.2.1.3. Developments after 1980 (1980–95)

In the 1980s, the D-Mark showed a big swing vis-à-vis the dollar. The dollar's strength during the first half of the decade led to a D-Mark depreciation of nearly 40% and in the second half to an appreciation of the D-Mark of about 80%.

Table 15.2-1 External value of the D-Mark
(% changes vis-à-vis previous period)

Period	Vis-à-vis			
	US dollar	EMS currencies	Average of 18 industrialised countries	
			nominal	real[a]
1969/60	+ 6.2	–	–	–
1973/69	+ 47.5	–	–	–
1980/73	+ 46.5	+ 24.9	+ 36.9	– 8.4
1985/80	– 38.3	+ 21.0	+ 1.6	– 14.7
1990/85	+ 82.1	+ 5.6	+ 20.4	+ 7.3
1994/90	– 0.0	+ 2.8	+ 4.3	+ 5.7
April1995 Dec.1990	+ 13.8	+ 1.4	+ 5.5	+ 5.4

a) In terms of consumer prices.

Source: Deutsche Bundesbank; calculations of the Ifo Institute.

Since the D-Mark's appreciation trend over the other important currencies continued (several EMS exchange-rate adjustments), the average external value of the D-Mark remained largely unchanged from 1980 to 1985. In real terms there was a clear depreciation of the D-Mark (Table 15.2-1).

In 1990 to 1994, the trend for a higher valuation of the D-Mark vis-à-vis the dollar was interrupted. The short-term fluctuations continued, however. With respect to currency relations within the EMS, it is noteworthy that adjustments were more seldom towards the end of the 1980s. The crisis of 1992/93 was countered by expanding the band-widths to 15% in both directions.

In the first months of 1995, the dollar began a new plunge. The appreciation against the D-Mark amounted to 11.8% in April compared with the average of the fourth quarter in 1994.

15.2.2. Policy responses

15.2.2.1. Breakdown of the Bretton Woods system

The death throes of the Bretton Woods system and the concomitant foreign-trade disturbances were the most serious problem for the economic policy in the history of West Germany. The flows of foreign exchange from the United States, attributable both to the inversion in the international interest rate gap as well as the loss of confidence in the dollar, went to a large extent—directly or indirectly—to West Germany. In 1970, total German balance of payments showed a record surplus of DM 22 billion. From January to May 1971, the period of the first major crisis in the fixed exchange-rate system, an additional DM 19 billion was added (cf.

Table 15.2-2). The current account in this period had a surplus of only DM 5.6 billion.

Although the business cycle had long since peaked, the Bundesbank and the German government were forced to adopt further restrictive measures. In mid-1970 the Bundesbank raised its minimum reserve rates. The government suspended the degressive tax depreciation, introduced a surcharge on income and corporation tax, and cut its own spending. With these measures, about DM 24 billion was immobilised; nevertheless, the free liquidity reserves of the banks doubled (Emminger, 1976). The catch-phrase coined at the time spoke of the international monetary markets as an "ersatz government".

The inability of German economic policy to stop the flow of foreign currency led finally to the floating of the D-Mark exchange rate in May 1971. This relieved the monetary policy strain for the Bundesbank, since Germany was no longer the prime target for international capital flows. For a time, monetary flows came to a complete standstill. Complete autonomy, i.e., the opportunity to conduct a purely domestically oriented monetary policy was, however, not regained by the Bundesbank. It remained essential to watch foreign developments so as not to encourage new flows of foreign exchange to West Germany.

Table 15.2-2 Balance of payments in West Germany from 1968 to 1975 (in billion DM)

Period	Current account	Capital account	Total balance of payments[a]
A. Monetary crises 1968/69:			
Jan. 1968 - Sept. 1969	+ 16.9	– 2.1	+ 14.9
Oct. - Dec. 1969	+ 2.4	– 20.5	– 18.1
Jan. 1968 - Dec. 1969 Total	+ 19.4	– 22.6	– 3.3
B. Monetary crises 1971:			
Jan. 1970 - March 1971	+ 5.6	+ 35.3	+ 41.0
June - Dec. 1971	+ 0.7	– 3.3	– 2.6
Jan. 1970 - Dec. 1971 Total	+ 6.3	+ 32.0	+ 38.3
C. Monetary crises 1972/73:			
Jan. - July 1972	– 0.1	+ 19.0	+ 18.9
Aug. 1972 - Jan. 1973	+ 2.7	– 6.4	– 3.7
Feb. - March 1973	+ 1.5	+ 18.8	+ 20.3
Jan. 1972 - March 1973 Total	+ 4.2	+ 31.4	+ 35.6
D. Since the beginning of floating April 1973 - Sept. 1975	+ 40.7	– 37.7	+ 3.0

a) Balance of all transactions (= change of net foreign assets of the Bundesbank without valuation adjustments as a result of exchange rate alterations and without allocation of special drawing rights).

Source: Emminger, 1976

Even after the Washington Realignment of December 1971, the Bundesbank was forced to pursue a foreign trade–oriented monetary policy. The United States loosened its monetary policy for reasons of its domestic economy, causing once again extensive monetary flows from the United States shortly after realignment. In December 1971, and again in February 1972, the Bundesbank lowered the discount rate. At the same time, also in February, the re-discount quota was reduced by 10% and the minimum reserves quota of additional foreign deposits increased to 40%. In March 1972, a cash deposit rate[1] of 40% was introduced on loans taken out abroad. For a time, capital flows abated. In connection with the sterling crisis in June of the same year, the Bundesbank attempted to neutralise the liquidity flowing into Germany by raising the minimum reserves, lowering the re-discount quota and increasing the cash deposit rate. In addition, at the end of June the government made it necessary for foreigners to receive approval before purchasing domestic fixed-interest securities.

These various defensive measures, along with an increase in interest rates in Euro-money markets, led to a flow of foreign exchange out of West Germany from August 1972 to January 1973, which gave the Bundesbank leeway for monetary policy tailored to the needs of the domestic economy. From October 1972 to January 1973, it raised the discount and Lombard rates in several stages.

The next crisis of confidence in international currency parities began at the end of January 1973. The influx of DM 24 billion in foreign exchange into West Germany within five weeks (from the end of January to the beginning of March 1973) led to an enormous over-expansion in domestic monetary circulation. In the first quarter of 1973, the central bank currency supply rose by 12%, the money supply M1 by 16% and M2 by 28% (seasonally adjusted yearly rates; Emminger, 1976).

Immediately after the closing of foreign exchange markets in March, the Bundesbank undertook initial measures to soak up the excess liquidity: the minimum reserve rate was increased substantially. In May, the discount and Lombard rates were raised twice by a total of two percentage points, to 7% and 9%, respectively. The government introduced a stabilisation programme, also in May, which included an 11% investment tax, the elimination of a degressive tax depreciation allowance on equipment spending and a stabilisation levy of 10% on income and corporation tax.

With these measures, the monetary situation was again brought under control. The previous, excessive money supply expansion was largely absorbed. Great success was also achieved in combatting inflation. From early 1973 on, West Germany was able to largely disconnect itself from the international inflationary vortex, which it had become caught up in from 1970 to the beginning of 1973 because of its open, external flank. Since early 1973, the rise in the cost of living again clearly declined beneath that of other countries. In the autumn, the first signs

---

[1] Banks were obliged to deposit 40% of the loans taken abroad at the Bundesbank.

of a turn round in inflation in the direction of stability were visible. These trends, however, were soon overshadowed by the first oil price explosion.

15.2.2.2. After Bretton Woods

After the breakdown of the fixed exchange-rate system, economic policy in Germany was less troubled from the external side than before. The flexible exchange rates mitigated the transfer of foreign shocks into the domestic economy. Economic policy was determined more strongly by internal factors (see Chapter 8.2). Nevertheless, it soon became evident that even when exchange rates were allowed to float freely, full immunity from inflationary trends in other countries was not possible; at best, a direct transfer of inflation from outside could be cushioned. Demand fluctuations in other countries also continued to have an effect on the domestic economy as West Germany became more integrated in the international division of labour. Interest rate policy had by no means become autonomous. Interest rate differences no longer expressed themselves as changes in currency reserves but as exchange rate fluctuations. In certain circumstances, interest rate policies became dependent on the exchange rate.

Especially the continuing downward movement of the dollar exchange rate in the 1970s from the average 1973 value of DM2.66 to DM1.81 in 1980, from which a worsening of the German economy's competitive position on world markets was expected, led the Bundesbank in the second half of the 1970s to abandon its restrictive monetary policy and to buy large amounts of dollars.

The strong rise of the dollar during the first half of the 1980s was more or less accepted without intervention.

In the 1980s, German monetary policy efforts were increasingly directed at international policy co-ordination of exchange rate policies. In the Plaza Accord of September 1985, the over-valuation of the dollar was recognised and a downward correction was termed desirable. If necessary, such a movement of the dollar exchange rate was to be encouraged by close international co-operation. However, the dollar exchange rate had already peaked in March of the same year and sank from an average of DM2.90 in 1985 to DM1.80 in 1987. A further decline in the dollar, and hence a further D-Mark appreciation, was not acceptable to the Bundesbank. In line with the Louvre Accord of March 1987, it attempted to stabilise the dollar exchange rate at the level reached in 1987, undergoing at the same time the risk of stronger inflation in the German economy with the concomitant expansion of the money supply. By the end of the 1980s, the dollar exchange rate was kept at the level of around DM1.80.

The 1990s, which began with a renewed depreciation of the dollar, brought no extreme challenges for German economic policy. The average 1990 dollar exchange rate of about DM1.60 was largely maintained, with fluctuations from year to year, until 1994. The weakening of the dollar since the beginning of 1995 by about 10% led the Bundesbank, after long hesitation, to reduce interest rates, but it was not prepared to intervene on a large scale as in past years.

After the breakdown of Bretton Woods, West Germany still had an intervention obligation for currencies in the "European Currency Snake" and since 1970 for those belonging to the European Monetary System. The EMS confronted German economic policy with momentary problems, but the crises were resolved relatively quickly by a flexible utilisation of the system: several exchange rate adjustments and expansion of the currency widths in 1993 to a 15% bandwidth.

15.2.3. Counter-measures by German industry

15.2.3.1. Intensifying foreign investment activities

In the 1950s, the undervalued D-Mark clearly assisted the exports of German industry. Even the D-Mark revaluation in 1961 had little effect on the favourable German position in international competition. Change was only brought about by the strong shifts in international currency relations in the final phase of the Bretton Woods system; the D-Mark was revalued strongly. In comparison with the currencies of twelve industrial countries, the D-Mark gained about 50% in value from 1969 to 1973. Real appreciation at this time can be assessed at between 20% and 30%. In light of this considerable worsening of German industry's price competitiveness, losses for German exporters were to be expected, even though the non-price competition factors played a great role in German export successes. Experience shows, however, that the price elasticity of demand has risen with the extent of change in product prices.

The Ifo Institute's calculations for 1972 to 1985 revealed a price elasticity of German exports from 1972 to 1985 of less than one. Only exports to the United States and Canada proved to have had price elasticity of more than one (Gerstenberger, 1987). Taking the period from 1980 to 1991, the relatively low price elasticity of German export volume was confirmed (Gerstenberger, 1992). The competitiveness of German industry primarily depends on its position in factors not related to price, such as technological standards, product quality and service-network efficiency. Yet, a relatively low price reaction also leads to sales losses, which are viewed by industries as more or less a problem, depending on the general economic situation.

Estimates based on regression analysis revealed that the adjustment of German exports to real exchange rate alterations extend over more than one year, as a rule. In many markets, reactions take an even longer period. This delayed reaction to price changes expresses the concentration of German exports in the capital goods area, in which production and delivery times are relatively long.

The development of world export shares in the 1970s shows a certain sensitivity of German exports to exchange rates. Compared with the considerable shifts in international price relations to West Germany's disadvantage, the decline of Germany's share in world exports was relatively low (Table 15.2-3). It must be taken into consideration, however, that various factors are responsible for changes in world market shares, which can have cumulative or compensating effects. In the second half of the 1980s, German exporters partially made up for their losses. At the beginning of the 1990s, the world market share of German exports declined again somewhat, but they remained at levels achieved in the second half of the 1970s.

No major negative impact was expected from the D-Mark appreciation in the first half of 1995: the depreciation of the dollar was subsequently corrected somewhat; on average for the currencies of eighteen industrial countries, the D-Mark appreciation amounted to barely 3%. There are indications, however, that exporters reacted by reducing prices in order to overcome the increasingly stronger international competition despite D-Mark appreciation.

Besides intensive efforts to further improve product quality, to increase the flexibility in responding to the changed demand structure and to improve the reaction to special customer wishes, German industry reacted to exchange-rate shifts by heightening foreign investment activity. Because of exchange-rate shifts, production costs in Germany had risen to the top of the international cost rankings. The sums of money invested abroad increased significantly during the late 1960s. For the first time they were higher than direct foreign investment in West Germany.

Since 1973 they have surpassed the foreign investment activity of the 1960s several times over (Table 15.2-3). The share in total investments (foreign and domestic) rose considerably.

The important role that exchange rate alterations played in intensifying German foreign investment in the 1970s is also seen in the outstanding position of the United States as a preferred country for German investment. The D-Mark experienced its strongest appreciation vis-à-vis the dollar. Although German direct foreign investment grew in all larger regions to which German industry exported, the increase was most spectacular in the United States. At the end of 1977, the stock of German direct foreign investment here was higher than in any other country (Hummel, et al., 1996). This preference for the US at this time was not only to maintain market positions, as shown in the fact that businesses began to invest in America, which for them had previously been an unimportant market. After the strong decline in the dollar, it had simply become profitable to invest or produce in the United States.

In the 1980s and 1990s, the trend of increasing foreign investments of German industry continued. Additional motives for foreign investment gained importance, especially the increase of protectionist tendencies in the world economy or the deepening integration of regional markets (European single market 1992). Moreover, the international deregulation trend and the rapid internationalisation of capital markets facilitated the foreign investment process.

Table 15.2-3 Real exchange rate, share in world exports and foreign direct investment of Germany

Period	Real exchange rate development of DM[a)] End 1972 = 100	Share of German exports in world exports in %	German direct foreign investment[b)] in DM billion Total
1962/65[c)]	•	10.6	1,118
1966/68[d)]	•	11.3	1,508
1969/72[c)]	•	12.3	3,062
1973	109.4	12.9	5,638
1974	108.2	11.6	4,530
1975	103.5	11.3	5,227
1976	103.7	11.3	5,056
1977	105.2	11.5	5,094
1978	105.8	11.9	7,993
1979	106.1	11.3	9,563
1980	100.2	10.3	14,155
1981	90.6	9.5	17,433
1982	92.0	10.3	7,316
1983	92.5	10.2	14,263
1984	88.0	9.7	22,108
1985	85.5	10.3	1,848
1986	90.7	12.1	4,093
1987	94.0	12.6	5,251
1988	91.4	12.1	28,686
1989	89.1	12.0	20,079
1990	91.8	12.1	20,900
1991	89.6	11.3	36,208
1992	92.9	11.5	25,722
1993	96.4	(..)	
1994	97.0	(..)	

a) Vis-à-vis eighteen industrial countries. With the weighted average of foreign trade volumes and excluding the differing inflation rates.
b) Changes in investment stock. To 1977: BMWi; after 1978: Deutsche Bundesbank (changes in investment stock at year's end).
c) Annual averages.
d) Value for 1967

Source: Exchange rates: Deutsche Bundesbank, *Monatsberichte*. World market shares: Dresdner Bank, *Historische Reihen*. German foreign direct investment: Deutsche Bundesbank, *Monatsberichte* ("Kapitalverflechtung der Unternehmen mit dem Ausland").

15.2.3.2. German companies' defence strategies

Already in the 1970s, economists and businessmen were increasingly of the opinion that the economy was faced with serious problems not only from the momentous discretionary devaluation and revaluation but also from exchange-rate fluctuations, whether this comes from long-lasting upward and downward movements, as was the case for the dollar exchange rate in the 1980s, or from short-term, almost daily exchange-rate fluctuations. And even in fixed exchange-rate systems the rates are not completely stable. Here, however, the maximum variations are determined by the intervention points or band-widths, and are thus known. In a system of flexible exchange rates, this is not the case, since the central banks are not obligated to intervene in currency markets. Furthermore, it is by no means certain that currency changes will follow the path taken by the economic fundamentals (level of prices, productivity, current account balances, etc.). The ever closer integration of international capital markets as well as the differing speed of price reactions in commodity markets, on the one hand, and in capital markets, on the other, often lead to "overshooting" exchange rates. Many years of experience have shown that the extent and duration of such exchange-rate movements may differ considerably and are thus hard to foresee.

Businesses have used different instruments to react to the increased risk of currency fluctuations, including hedging, diversion of trade flows to regions with more stable exchange rates vis-à-vis the domestic currency, shifting production abroad, abandoning export markets, and adopting a stronger domestic-market orientation. A mailed survey conducted by the Ifo Institute of German industrialists in 1987 produced the following results. The main risk factor is the uncertainty about the length and extent of long-term appreciation and depreciation trends, as was the case for the dollar exchange rate in the 1980s. In comparison, the short-term exchange-rate fluctuations were seen as less problematic. The dominant defence measures were financial safeguards (exchange futures, discounting of foreign-exchange drafts and so-called finance derivatives) and company internal measures (increased own-currency invoicing, enlargement of risk-management personnel).

The predominance of the financial and internal measures are evidence of the considerable efforts made to avoid adverse effects of exchange rate risk on the volume of foreign trade. At the same time, there is evidently reservation towards strategies that have direct effects in the business world. The portion of companies that chose such strategies was relatively small. A strong domestic-market orientation and a preference of sales regions with stable exchange rates vis-à-vis the D-Mark was only practised by 16% and 19% of the firms, according to the Ifo survey. Shifting production facilities abroad played an even smaller role. This strategy tended to be used most by companies that already produced abroad.

The relatively high risk-aversion preparedness of the companies participating in the survey suggests the conclusion that firms sought to prevent or reduce as much as possible the direct negative effects of strong exchange rate fluctuations on foreign trade volume. These defence measures, however, became a cost factor for the firms. By passing on these costs to the customer, the foreign trade volume was possibly affected indirectly, depending on the amount of these costs, at least in areas where supply encountered price-elastic demand. Regression analyses of the Ifo Institute show that these conclusions are justified (Hardy, Herrmann, 1988).

15.2.4. Appraisal

The collapse of the Bretton Woods system created the most serious problems in the history of German economic policy, the first signs of which were visible in 1969. The frequent monetary crises prevented Germany from pursuing monetary and fiscal policies purely oriented around the domestic economy. In Germany the struggle against inflation induced by internal causes was made more difficult and at times impossible. In fact, because of the immense influx of money, which despite monetary-policy counter-measures led to a dramatic liquidisation of the economy, inflationary tendencies were intensified. At the height of the Bretton Woods crisis, the inflation rate in West Germany was 6.9%. Certainly, some of this inflation can be attributed to factors in the German economy. The question of whether economic policy-makers used all possible counter-measures at the time is difficult to answer.

German industry utilised various measures to counter their worsening position in international price competition. To be sure, because of the special product structure, demand for German exports does not react quickly to price changes. This does not mean, however, that in cases of large exchange-rate alterations, especially the extent of those in the 1970s, that positions in foreign markets were also not endangered in advanced and high-technology products. A negative reaction of demand to price increases is to be expected in any case, even if price elasticity has a value of less than one. One of the most obvious reactions of German industry, especially in the 1970s, was an intensification of foreign investment. Moreover, efforts were always made to maintain the non-price competitive position. In competition for innovation, German industry held a strong first ranking in major technology fields in Europe in the 1990s (Gerstenberger, 1992). Mechanical engineering and road vehicle construction are in a technological position to successfully confront competition from abroad. One of the domains Germany dominates is that of environmental technology. Weak areas are in micro-electronics, information and communication technology, and in biotechnology and genetic engineering.

15.3. Comparative Summary of Exchange Rate Changes

15.3.1. Responses to exchange rate fluctuations and the implications for economic structures

The difference in the responses of Japan and Germany to exchange rate fluctuations stems from a disparity in two fundamental economic conditions: the international monetary system of which the two countries are part and the trade structures established by each during their economic development. In 1973, the international monetary system shifted from a fixed exchange-rate system based on

Table 15.3-1 Counter-measures against exchange rate fluctuations in Japan and Germany

	Japan	Germany
International monetary system	Fixed exchange-rate system → Floating exchange-rate system	Fixed exchange-rate system → Currency Snake → EMS (continuation of fixed exchange-rate system in real terms)
Ties with the dollar	Strong linkage between yen and dollar	D-Mark as key European currency
Policy	Measures against high-yen deflation	Anti-inflation measures
Private-sector response	Measures to increase high-value-added industry to alleviate decline in price competitiveness	Price adjustment based on strong non-price competitiveness
Trade system	Improving free trade system	Totally free trade system

the Bretton Woods structure to a floating exchange-rate system. Under the new system, the yen's value has risen relative to the dollar on the strength of Japan's growing current account surplus. Persistent concern about the deflationary impact of the high yen on Japan's domestic economy has led the government to respond to exchange rate fluctuations primarily through counter-measures designed to stimulate the economy, such as the expansion of government expenditure and monetary relaxation. Counter-measures in the business sector have focused on the alleviation of declines in export profitability, owing to the high yen rather than on efforts to reap the benefits of a stronger yen. Until now, there has been little awareness of the fact that exchange rates are determined by market mechanisms that seek to bring about equilibrium in the international balance of payments. Both the government and the private sector have harboured a sense of crisis that is reflected in a tendency to overreact somewhat to the appreciation of the yen.

Even under the fixed exchange-rate system, Germany flexibly revalued the D-Mark in response to changes in its current account surplus. After the collapse of the Bretton Woods system, the D-Mark remained the key currency under the so-called "European Currency Snake", which was in effect a fixed exchange-rate system. For this reason, although the value of the D-Mark has constantly tended to rise, the level of appreciation has been relatively moderate. Partly because of the existence of mechanisms to mitigate the economic impact of exchange rate fluctuations, Germany's monetary policies have focused on anti-inflationary measures.

An analysis of trade structures shows that the sharing of product markets in Europe made it relatively easy for Germany to reap the benefits of a rise in real purchasing power because of the increased value of the D-Mark. Japan, on the other hand, formed a trade structure that was specialised towards automobiles and electrical machinery, and which was primarily dependent on exports to the United States. This trade structure evolved whilst Japan was catching up with the industrialised Western economies. Japan's industrial structure thus performed well in terms of the efficiency with which resources could be allocated for economic growth, but it lacked resistance to the effects of exchange rate fluctuations.

15.3.2. Policy responses

These differences in economic structure were also reflected in sharp contrasts in the policy responses of the two countries after the collapse of the Bretton Woods system. Despite the fact that Germany was heading towards a recession, tight money policies were implemented to prevent the money supply from being swelled by an influx of funds resulting from the inversion of the international interest differential and dwindling confidence in the dollar. In Japan, on the other hand, the maintenance of the yen at 360 to the dollar became an imperative. Aggressive monetary relaxation introduced by the Bank of Japan caused money supply to grow at an annual rate in excess of 20%, which triggered excess liquidity. The result was that Japan did not achieve an economic recovery. The government responded by pursuing expansionist fiscal policies financed by government bond issues. As a result, the Japanese economy was battered by inflation.

Germany's macro-economic policies after the transition to a floating exchange-rate system were determined primarily by domestic factors. In the late 1970s, huge amounts of dollars were purchased as a means of averting a decline in international competitiveness due to the appreciation of the D-Mark. However, Germany has generally limited itself to a passive policy response to exchange rate fluctuations since 1980, even when it was called upon to co-operate in the international co-ordination of exchange rate policies. Japan responded to the appreciation of the yen after the 1985 Plaza Accord by maintaining monetary relaxation over a long period of time, overlapped by ill-timed expansionary fiscal policies. This approach triggered an unprecedented economic boom, but the end result was assets inflation manifested in soaring land and stock prices. The resulting distortion of the economic structure left a huge bill to be paid in subsequent years.

15.3.3. Responses of industry and business

The responses of industry and business to the appreciation in their country's currency are basically the same in any country; the options are quite limited. Yet a comparison of Japan and Germany shows that Japan has responded more dynamically to the yen's appreciation through structural transition. German industry averted a decline in its price competitiveness in the face of the D-Mark's appreciation by gradually lowering prices whilst monitoring long-term exchange rate movements. Since German exports retained their high quality and penetrated niche markets, a downturn in price competitiveness did not immediately lead to a contraction of export volumes. A comparison of current levels of dependence on imports (ratio of imports to GDP) reveals that Japan has a 7% dependence rate against Germany's 22%. Thus, a rise in the value of the currency has a larger downward effect on prices in Germany. In addition, Germany's trade is not heavily weighted towards specific products and countries, which means that the deflationary effect of the D-Mark's appreciation is smaller. Germany's stance was to accept the fundamental premise of a stronger D-Mark and engage in international competition with neighbouring industrialised countries under a totally free trade system. As a result, Germany created a structure that differentiated between domestic and imported goods in accordance with the level of value added.

There has been a strong tendency in Japan to target productivity improvements and the enhancement of the industrial structure. The enhancement of the industrial structure has been achieved through synergy between improvement of the international competitiveness of individual export items and the expansion of the production contribution of industries whose products are highly competitive internationally. In the slow-growth period after the oil shocks, the international competitiveness of Japanese industry was dramatically enhanced through changes in the structure of industry.

15.3.4. Responses to exchange rate fluctuations and economic development

Japan's policy response to exchange rate fluctuations has at times tended to rely excessively on the use of economic stimulation to alleviate external shocks. Moreover, delays in the implementation of such policies sometimes created negative after-effects. On the other hand, at the private-sector level, the efforts of the business sector to reduce production costs and shift to high-value-added products enabled companies to clear the high hurdle of a strong yen and penetrate overseas markets. This in turn propelled Japan's economic development.

German economic policies have emphasised stable expansion rather than rapid economic growth. This stance was supported by an international monetary system with the D-Mark as a key currency, acting as a buffer against exchange rate fluctuations, and by the formation of a complementing trade structure in a geographical environment, which is characterised by the co-existence of multiple advanced industrialised nations within Europe.

The future is expected to bring increasing economic globalisation and a rapid rise in the industrial potential of developing countries. The comparative advantage resulting from the non-price competitiveness of the exports of both Japan and Germany will dwindle, and price competition is expected to intensify in the international market-place. For this reason, it will be difficult for Japan and Germany to continue their reign as export superpowers in the coming years.

Though Germany's exchange rate policies have focused on regional co-operation within Europe, in essence it made a transition to a floating exchange-rate system in response to the revision of the EMS fluctuation margin to plus or minus 15% after 1993. This has started to weaken the old international monetary system.

In the area of trade, other EU countries are distancing themselves from Germany, whilst German companies are shifting their focus to the Eastern European market. This combination of trends is starting to erode Germany's stable trade structure. The negative effects of exchange rate fluctuations, specifically the adverse impact of a strong D-Mark on the German economy, are expected to increase gradually. The problem will be compounded by domestic factors, such as high labour costs.

For the Japanese manufacturing sector, an exchange rate of ¥100 to ¥110 to the dollar is regarded as the profitability threshold. With the exchange rate in the ¥80 to ¥100 range, export industries will face a very tough situation. To cope with this situation, the private sector will need to expand offshore production further and raise overseas procurement ratios. The government's policy response will need to focus on the creation of an industrial structure that is less vulnerable to exchange rate fluctuations through deregulation and the improvement of market access.

16. Environmental Problems

16.1. Japan's Environmental Problems

16.1.1. Evolution of environmental problems

As shown in Fig. 16-1.1, environmental problems can be broadly divided into domestic and global problems. Japan's environmental problems cover a broad spectrum, ranging from traditional industrial pollution caused mainly by business (hereinafter referred to as "pollution") to global environmental problems such as ozone layer depletion.

Fig. 16-1.1 Environmental problems

Domestic environmental problems

- Traditional industrial pollution (air pollution, water pollution, soil contamination, noise, etc.)
- Ecological problems
- Urban and lifestyle-related environmental problems (water pollution caused by domestic wastewater, air pollution caused by automobile exhaust, etc.)

Global environmental problems

- Industry and livelihood-related
  - Energy-related environmental problems (global warming, acid rain, etc.)
  - Non-energy-related (ozone layer depletion, trans-border shipment of hazardous waste, marine pollution, etc.)
- Ecological problems (destruction of forests, desertification, depletion of wildlife)
- Pollution problems in developing countries

Source: MITI, Compendium of the environment, 1994

16.1.1.1. Establishment of a legal framework for victim relief (until about 1972)

(a) Environmental problems

Japan's pollution incidents in the pre-war era date back as far as the Ashio copper mine incident (around 1887) and the Besshi copper mine sulphurous acid gas incident of 1894. In this sense, Japan was a "world leader" in pollution. These problems did not become national issues, however, since they were treated as private law issues between affected residents and the companies responsible for the unlawful activities.

In post-war Japan, priority was given to the development of heavy and chemical industries under the high economic growth policy of the 1950s. As a result, wastewater, smoke and other substances were discharged from factories with little or no treatment. The public was also concerned primarily about the achievement of economic affluence, and there was little interest in pollution problems.

Pollution problems first began to attract the serious attention of the public in the late 1960s, owing to a series of four major lawsuits about pollution-related illnesses (Table 16.1-1). Most Japanese were shocked by the tragic health damage suffered by people as a result of pollution-related illnesses, and critical attention began to focus on companies that had shown total disregard for the health of nearby residents by failing to institute adequate pollution-control measures. This led to the formation of citizens' groups throughout Japan to fight pollution.

(b) Government response

Criticism about pollution issues was directed not only at companies that caused pollution but also at the government's failure to curb irresponsible economic behaviour in the business sector. The struggle to overcome pollution problems was initially led by local authorities. From around 1949 onwards, the

Table 16.1-1 Outline of four major pollution-related diseases

Disease	Location	Cause	Period
Minamata Disease	Minamata City, Kumamoto Prefecture	Methyl mercury	Early 1950s
Itai-itai Disease	Jinzu River basin, Toyama Prefecture	Cadmium	Mid-1950s
Yokkaichi Asthma	Yokkaichi City, Mie Prefecture	Smoke	Late 1950s
Niigata Minamata Disease	Agano River basin, Niigata Prefecture	Methyl mercury	Early 1960s

Source: Environment Agency, The Twenty-Year History of the Environment Agency

Tokyo Metropolitan Government, Osaka City, Kanagawa Prefecture and other local governments began to pass ordinances to prevent pollution and smoke emissions. In 1964, the central government responded by establishing an Environmental Pollution Department in the Ministry of Health and Welfare to study basic issues relating to pollution prevention. However, industry maintained that its ability to pay for pollution-prevention measures was limited, and that anti-pollution measures should be based on policy that emphasised harmony between sound industrial development and protection of the living environment. The government's response was less than aggressive, as evidenced by the content of the Environmental Pollution Prevention Act. This law, which was passed in 1967 as a basic framework for pollution counter-measures, included a provision requiring "harmony with sound economic development."

The intensification of public opinion against pollution prompted the government to shift to a policy of making full-scale efforts to overcome pollution problems, and the provision concerning "harmony with sound economic development" was deleted from the law during a special session of the National Diet in 1970. At the same time, a series of laws were passed to deal with specific pollution issues, such as the prevention of water contamination, sea pollution, air pollution and soil contamination on agricultural land. In 1971, the Environment Agency was established as an administrative agency specialising in environmental matters. In addition, pollution-control regulations were strengthened, and the government also began to enhance relief measures for victims of pollution-induced diseases.

In 1972, the government amended the 1969 Law on Special Measures Concerning Redress for Pollution-Related Health Damage. The effect of the amendment was to introduce the principle of absolute liability for compensation, under which a party responsible for pollution-induced damage was liable to pay compensation, regardless of whether the damage was intentional or owing to negligence. This was followed in 1973 by passage of the Pollution-Related Health Damage Compensation Act, whereby polluters (mainly businesses) would be obliged to compensate pollution victims not only for medical expenses but also for the loss of future income. It was during this period that Japan completed most of its basic anti-pollution measures, consisting primarily of direct regulations based on tough standards targeted towards sources of pollution and a compensation system to provide relief for pollution victims.

A number of pollution-related economic measures were also implemented during this period. For example, low-interest loan systems operated by the Japan Development Bank, the Small Business Finance Corporation and other institutions were expanded to provide support for investment in pollution-prevention facilities. In addition, the government passed the Natural Environment Conservation Act in 1972 and began to work in earnest towards the conservation of the natural environment, including primeval forests.

(c) Business sector's response

Under the economic growth policy implemented from the mid-1950s, the business sector gave priority to the improvement of production efficiency and showed little enthusiasm for anti-pollution measures. Companies showed little concern about the effects of factory effluents of smoke and water on the environment and local residents. Even after the four major pollution lawsuits, industry failed to tackle pollution seriously. This is apparent from the stance of the Japan Federation of Economic Organisations (Keidanren) towards the enactment of the Environmental Pollution Prevention Act, which it regarded as "premature".

However, public environmental awareness was strengthening, and there was also growing acceptance of the "polluter-pays principle" advocated by the OECD, which maintained that enterprises should be responsible for pollution control and the costs of preventive measures. These factors prompted the business sector to move more aggressively against pollution. In 1965 private-sector enterprises invested just ¥29.7 billion in anti-pollution measures. By 1975 there had been a 32-fold increase to ¥964.5 billion. The business sector's commitment to pollution prevention is apparent from a comparison of this growth with the rate of increase in total capital investment by businesses, which increased only five times over the same period.

16.1.1.2. Shift in emphasis from pollution regulation to improvement of living environments and nature conservation (1973–1984)

(a) Environmental problems

Pollution problems were beginning to abate owing to factors that included the effect of pollution-control measures implemented in the late 1960s and early 1970s, and industrial stagnation caused by the two oil crises. On the other hand, rapid urbanisation, lifestyle changes and other forces were reflected in the emergence of urban- and consumption-related environmental problems such as water pollution caused by domestic wastewater, air pollution owing to automobile exhaust, noise generated by day-to-day life, and waste-disposal problems caused by a growing waste output.

As a result, public concern about environmental issues expanded to encompass urban- and consumption-related environmental problems and environmental conservation, in addition to traditional pollution problems. This shift in the focus of public concern was also manifested in lawsuits by citizens. During these years numerous environmental lawsuits were filed, including applications for injunctions against the construction of expressways and garbage-disposal plants.

It was also during this period that the darker side of the Japanese economy began to emerge in the form of distortions caused by rapid economic growth. These problems were exposed by a number of factors, including the development of heavy and chemical industries, motorisation and the concentration of population in major cities. Concern about these distortions led to a public opinion backlash against Japan's preoccupation with GNP.

(b) Government's response

After the mid-1970s, the focus of environmental policy in Japan shifted from pollution prevention to the improvement of living environments and the conservation of nature. This shift resulted from an OECD review of Japan's environmental policy over the previous decade (1967-75). The results of this review, which was conducted in 1976 and 1977, indicated that Japan had lagged behind in environmental measures relating to the improvement of living environments and conservation of the natural environment. In 1978 the government began to work in earnest towards the solution of new problems, such as urban and consumption-related environmental issues. Measures included the amendment of the Water Pollution Prevention Act to enable total-load restrictions on pollutants flowing into bodies of water, and stringent controls on automobile exhaust emissions.

However, many of these problems arose from ordinary social and economic activities, which meant that it was difficult to identify the exact sources of pollution. As a result, it was impossible to address these problems using only the traditional method of direct regulation, which was designed primarily to regulate and control pollution sources. The government, therefore, turned to new approaches, including the promotion of the Amenity Town Plan as a multi-faceted initiative for the systematic development of infrastructure, such as roads and sewers. Unfortunately, these measures had little effect in practical terms.

(c) Business sector's response

Pollution-control investment, which had surged in the late 1960s and early 1970s, declined dramatically in the late 1970s. This was owing in part to the impact of the oil crises, but it also reflected the completion of the cycle of investment in air pollution control hardware. However, this investment played a major role in reducing pollution-induced health damage of the kind that led to the four major pollution lawsuits. Japan gained international recognition by developing pollution-prevention technology that enabled companies to meet the pollution regulations established by the Japanese government, which were said to be the toughest in the world.

There was also progress in the area of urban- and consumption-related environmental problems. The automobile industry led aggressive efforts to develop technologies capable of meeting strict automobile exhaust standards. Whilst these efforts in the business sector made it possible to attain targets per unit, a rapid increase in the total number of automobiles owned in Japan meant that there was no immediate improvement in the overall air pollution problem. Japanese

Table 16.1-2 Overseas pollution incidents involving Japanese companies

Country	Environmental problem	Period
Malaysia	Radioactive thorium pollution	Early 1980s
Indonesia	Lime citrate pollution	Late 1970s
Korea	Hexavalent chrome pollution; Sulphurous acid gas and cadmium pollution	Late 1970s

Source: Japan Federation of Bar Associations, Japanese export of environmental hazards and environmental disruption

companies were, meanwhile, becoming involved in pollution problems overseas, particularly in Southeast Asia (Table 16.1-2).

16.1.1.3. Efforts to address global environmental problems (1985–)

(a) Environmental problems

A business upturn driven primarily by domestic demand sometimes led to urban- and lifestyle-related environmental problems which had first come to the fore in the late 1970s and worsened during the latter half of the 1980s, partly because of an increase in waste volumes resulting from the excessive growth of consumption. The exacerbation of these problems was particularly conspicuous in Tokyo with its increasing concentration of population and economic activities. The alleviation of urban environmental problems there became more difficult because of rising land prices and other factors.

During this period, the increasing sophistication of industry and the advancement of science and technology led to the emergence of pollution problems which were caused by new chemical substances not covered by existing laws and regulations. One example is ground water contamination by trichloroethylene released by semiconductor plants and other facilities. There is also increasing evidence of global environmental problems, including ozone-layer depletion due to chlorofluorocarbons (CFCs), as well as global warming resulting from increased production of carbon dioxide. These problems are reflected in rising public concern about environmental problems and in growing public participation in voluntary initiatives to solve environmental problems, such as through recycling activities.

After its 1976-77 survey of environmental policies in Japan, the OECD stated that Japan was lagging behind in the area of amenity policy. However, the 1992-93 survey resulted in a glowing report stating that Japan had proved it was possible to reconcile environmental policies with economic policies. During the Earth Summit held in Rio de Janeiro, Brazil in June 1992, Maurice Strong, Secretary-General of the United Nations Conference on Environment and Development, praised Japan as a world leader in anti-pollution measures.

(b) Government's response

Efforts to deal with the growing severity of urban and lifestyle-related environmental problems included an initiative to popularise environment-friendly products through the "Eco Mark" system, which was introduced in 1989, primarily by the Japan Environment Association (an auxiliary organisation of the Environment Agency). In addition, in 1991 the government passed the Law for the Promotion of Utilisation of Recycled Resources and amended the Waste Disposal and Public Cleansing Law to facilitate resources recycling and waste treatment. The government also turned its attention to pollution caused by new chemical substances. It conducted research to provide accurate data on pollution levels, and in 1989 it introduced stronger controls on trichloroethylene through measures that included amendments to the Water Pollution Prevention Act.

In the area of global environmental problems, the government moved to discourage the use of CFCs by enacting the Law Concerning the Protection of the Ozone Layer through Control of Specified Substances and Other Measures in 1988. In 1990 the government announced the Action Programme to Arrest Global Warming, under which Japan is working to reduce carbon dioxide emissions. Japan had thus enacted measures even before the 1992 Earth Summit.

Furthermore, in 1994 the government formulated the Fundamentals of Environment Act to serve as a basis for future environmental measures. It also enacted legislation to support a comprehensive approach to a broad range of environmental issues, including urban and lifestyle-related environmental problems and global environmental problems. In addition to traditional methods based primarily on the direct regulations of pollution, the government is also considering future approaches based on economic methods, such as the introduction of an environment tax or deposit system.

(c) Business sector's response

The rapid appreciation of the yen since 1985 has led to aggressive direct overseas investment by Japanese companies. Some companies have been implementing pollution-control measures at their overseas facilities in order to avoid the pollution problems in the communities where they operate. The business sector is also working to alleviate urban and lifestyle-type environmental problems. For example, household electrical appliance manufacturers are introducing parts that can be easily recycled, whilst supermarkets are selling more environment-friendly products.

In the two decades between 1970 and 1990, Japanese companies invested a total of ¥8.5 trillion in anti-pollution measures. Reasons for this investment include the establishment, improvement and enlargement of related laws, and the provision of low-interest finance by government-affiliated financial institutions. However, it also reflects changes in patterns of thinking and behaviour on the part of the companies themselves, partly for fear of being labelled a polluter.

Technologies are being developed to prevent pollution caused by new chemical substances. Waste treatment methods that render trichloroethylene and other chemicals harmless are already coming into practical use. In the area of global environmental problems, major corporations are leading efforts to reduce carbon dioxide emissions. In addition to efforts by individual companies, industry as a whole is making significant efforts to overcome global environmental problems. For example, in 1991, the Keidanren published an eleven-point Global Environment Charter, in which it set down environmental guidelines for the business sector.

16.1.2. Environmental problems and Japan's economic development

16.1.2.1. Economics of pollution

During its high-growth period, Japan strove for economic development with little consideration for the environment. This led to tragic pollution problems, including the four major pollution cases. An independent research group within the Environment Agency (the Study Group for Global Environment and Economics) calculated the cost of health damage caused by three of these cases (excluding the Niigata Minamata disease case), and the cost of preventive pollution-control measures with a view to providing a basis for an economic comparison of the two approaches. In the case of the Yokkaichi asthma problem, counter-measures undertaken after the outbreak at a cost of about ¥14.8 billion limited the area affected and kept the cost of damage down to ¥1.3 billion. However, delays in implementing full-scale measures to cope with Minamata disease and itai-itai disease meant that damages amounted to approximately ¥12 billion and ¥2.5 billion, respectively, which far exceeded the cost of preventive measures, estimated at approximately ¥100 million and ¥600 million, respectively.

The results of this comparison show that losses can be minimised through the implementation of a certain level of anti-pollution measures and that failure to implement preventive measures not only leads to tragic loss of life and health damage but also results in major economic losses.

16.1.2.2. Macro-economic impact of anti-pollution investment

After the four major pollution cases, the business sector began to invest aggressively in pollution-control measures. The Environment Agency has estimated and compared the economic indicators for the decade until 1975 under two scenarios, one in which the private sector undertook this investment and one in which it did not (Table 16.1-3). The comparison shows that the negative effect of the increased cost burden on the heavy and chemical industries as a result of this investment was offset by the positive effect of increased earnings in other industries, such as the pollution-control hardware industry, and that real GNP

Table 16.1-3 Macro-economic impact of private-sector anti-pollution investment

Real GNP	Approx. 0.9% increase
Real personal consumption	Approx. 0.4% increase
Real private-capital investment	Approx. 7.4% increase
Real national current-account surplus	Approx. ¥300 billion decrease
Consumer price index	Approx. 1.2% increase
Wholesale price index	Approx. 1.7% increase

Note: 1. Estimate based on the Environment Agency's integrated environmental model.
2. The figures represent percentage or absolute differences between two values obtained from simulations based on the assumptions that the private sector invested or did not invest in pollution control during the decade from 1965 to 1975.
3. The real national current-account surplus is based on 1970 prices. Other results are based on 1975 figures.

Source: Earth Environment Keizai Kenkyusho, The Japanese experience in environmental hazards; Proem to the discource on the industries of an environment-conservation type

under the scenario in which there was investment in anti-pollution measures was 0.9% higher than under the scenario in which there was no investment.

Production of pollution-control hardware was worth a mere ¥34.1 billion in 1966. The rapid growth of the industry is apparent from the fact that by 1975 its output had grown 20-fold to ¥683.1 billion. Investment in anti-pollution measures thus contributed significantly not only to the reduction of pollution damage but also to the development of the pollution-control equipment industry and other new business areas.

16.1.2.3. Evaluating Japan's responses to environmental problems

Initially, Japan showed little enthusiasm for environmental issues. However, growing public concern encouraged environmental counter-measures, with the government setting environmental regulations and the business sector developing new technology and investing in facilities in order to meet those requirements. Whilst Japan's approach was not ideal, it learned from experience and made steady progress towards the development of anti-pollution technology.

On the other hand, dealing with environmental problems involves cost increases for individual companies because of the need to develop environment-related technologies and protection systems. Ultimately these costs are passed on to individual citizens. Despite this cost, however, environmental protection and the creation of an environment-friendly economic system are vital to the achievement of sustainable economic development. From an international perspective, Japan is expected to play a leading role in dealing with environmental problems and must work aggressively to find solutions by applying its experience and technology in co-operation with other nations.

16.2. Germany's Environmental Problems

16.2.1. Major stages of environmental policy in Germany

Germany is one of the most environmentally conscious European countries, with the most stringent environmental legislation and firmest enforcement. The necessity of environmental regulation resulted from the large share of high-polluting industries in the German economy and largely coal-based power generation. Furthermore, large-scale environmental damage, such as the effects of acid rain on the national forests, pollution of the Rhine, radioactive fallout from the Chernobyl explosion, and the public focus on quality-of-life issues called for early environmental regulation. More recently, the urgent need to accelerate the clean-up and ecological modernisation of the eastern Länder (former GDR) provided further impetus.

The first phase of environmental policy in West Germany started in the early 1970s with the formulation and institutionalisation of an independent environmental policy. The impetus for environmental action in this phase was the necessity to ward off dangers quickly and consistently. Because of its reactive nature, the term "fire-brigade principle" is used for this phase.

At the beginning of the 1970s, the German Parliament created a tight network of environmental regulations. In the areas of clean air (Federal Emission Control Act, Technical Specifications for Clean Air, Leaded Fuel Act), water management (Water Management Act, Waste Water Charges Act, Detergents Act), noise abatement (Federal Emission Control Act), aircraft noise control (Specifications for Aircraft Noise) and waste disposal (Waste Disposal Act, Waste Oil Act) as well as in the complex areas of nature conservation (Nature Conservation Act, Federal Species Protection Act, Federal Forest Act), protection from hazardous materials (Chemical Act, DDT Act, Plant Protection Act, Fertiliser Act) and energy conservation (Energy Assurance Act, Energy Saving Act), fundamental regulations were established.

With the onset of recession in the mid-1970s and rising unemployment, criticism was directed in a second phase at environmental policy and the question of the cost effectiveness of environmental policy instruments was raised for the first time. The Council of Experts on Environmental Affairs informed politicians that instead of regulating solutions, a tax on water pollution could save several hundred million marks with the same environmental effect. This was the hour of the Waste Water Charges Act. Initiated in the 1971 environmental programme, this legislation was signed into law five years later and took effect after an additional five years.

The third phase of environmental policy came in 1982/83 with the beginning of the Kohl administration. Almost as a legacy of the Social Democrat/Liberal coalition, a renaissance of regulatory policy arose. The dying forests (*Waldsterben*) necessitated immediate action. Environmental policy-makers thus reverted to their strongest weapon—regulation—in this case the Large Combustion Installations Act. Characteristic of environmental policy under the Kohl administration, however, was the discussion of the employment of market-oriented instruments. "More environmental protection for less money" was the slogan. Mindful of the American deregulation debate, more regulatory flexibility was demanded. Another characteristic was a rapid increase of industry agreements and subsidy programmes, especially at the Länder level.

The fourth phase of environmental policy in the second half of the 1980s was marked by the clean-up of hazardous sites and by a number of environmental catastrophes. Environmental policy-makers made several proposals for ecological restoration and prevention of environmental threats that resulted from insufficient, or subverted, environmental protection. Examples are the special fund of the Social Democrats in Parliament, "Work and Environment", the Urban Clean-up Programme and various proposals for a hazardous site clean-up fund, licensing

Table 16.2-1 Selected federal environmental acts and ordinances

1957	Water Management Act
1962	Detergents Act
1968	Waste Oil Act
1971	Leaded Fuel Act Protection from Aircraft Noise
1972	Waste Disposal Act DDT Act
1974	Federal Emission Control Act Environmental Statistics Act
1975	Washing Agents and Detergents Act
1976	Nature Conservation Act Radiation Protection Ordinance Waste Water Charges Act Energy Saving Act
1980	Chemicals Act Hazardous Incidents Ordinance
1982	Sewage Sludge Ordinance
1983	Large Combustion Installations Act
1986	Hazardous Substances Ordinance Species Protection Ordinance Precautionary Radiological Protection Act Waste Avoidance and Management Act
1987	Origin of Waste Water Ordinance
1988	Small Combustion Installations Act Deposit-Refund Systems for Plastic Bottles Ordinance
1990	Environmental Impact Assessment Act Environmental Liability Act
1991	Prohibition of CFCs Ordinance Packaging Waste Ordinance

Source: OECD.

proposals for waste management of problem substances, amendments to the Environmental Liability Act, and a water subsidy or interest fee.

After years of focusing on industry and systems- and substance-oriented environmental protection, attention was now directed to the consumer. Influencing consumer behaviour by taxes on certain products and by ecological tax reform were the new catch phrases.

In the fifth phase of environmental policy since the beginning of the 1990s, the supranational dimension was discovered. The European Single Market was coupled with a demand for stronger international integration of national environmental polices. Moreover, the international dimension received increasing attention through discussions on climate changes, the ozone problem and on energy and climate tax. With German unification, the question arose as to how to create a German-German "Environmental Union" in view of the differences in economic and environmental systems.

16.2.2. Major environmental policy approaches in Germany

The basic regulatory framework for environmental policy in Germany since the 1970s can be classified as "command-and-control", and is characterised by source- and pollutant-specific standards, generally based on a feasible control technology. Applied to similar sources with low initial abatement costs, this regulatory instrument was relatively efficient at reducing pollution.

In recent years, however, the application of incentive-based environmental policy instruments has been increasing. This shift came about for the following reasons. First, government authorities realise that strengthening direct emissions controls will no longer be effective once current environmental quality targets are met by pollutant-specific standards. Secondly, the ecological consequences of products, waste streams or standard inputs of industrial-production processes defy "end-of-pipe" mechanisms, calling for the use of policy instruments that foster environmentally friendly production and products. Third, the number of chemicals or materials for which environmental controls are sought is steadily expanding; regulation by product has become an increasingly unwieldy task.

The combination of these two patterns—the increasing identification of damaging substances and the recognition of the need to switch from end-of-pipe clean-up to products and processes—has stimulated the search for new approaches. The information/education approach relies on measures that foster the transparency of firms' production and products. The measures include environmental-impact assessments or awarding certificates to environmentally friendly products (environmental labelling). The ultimate instrument is to force polluters to accept liability.

These new regulatory patterns are reinforced by the use of economic instruments, such as user or pollution charges, deposit refund systems, subsidy schemes and tradeable pollution permits. These instruments assign a price to the production or consumption externalities, hence encouraging polluters to curb the damaging activity.

The above-mentioned approaches and innovative instruments such as voluntary self-commitments by industries allow businesses and households to respond flexibly to pollution-reduction requirements, thus yielding savings in pollution-abatement costs and fostering technical innovation.

16.2.3. Achievements in pollution abatement

Remarkable progress has been made in West Germany in dealing with numerous pressing environmental problems identified over the past two decades. Especially in the areas of pollutant emissions from stationary sources, wastewater discharges and municipal waste management, environmental policy objectives have been reached.

The scale of these achievements is even more impressive if compared with the deterioration that would have occurred had nothing been done. In fact, West Germany has achieved a decoupling of economic growth from the flow of several major pollutants. For example, over the 1980s, whilst GDP grew by 23%, air emissions declined by 71% for SO_2 and 35% for particulates. This decoupling is a necessary step towards sustainable economic growth.

Progress on air pollution was triggered by concerns with health risks in certain industrialised areas in the late 1960s, and then in the early 1980s with forest damage (*Waldsterben*). Pollution reduction is partly the result of energy efficiency gains and of the stable or declining shares of coal, lignite and oil as primary energy sources. It also results from national air-management programmes which are aimed at numerous pollutants from a variety of sources. These programmes are mostly based on the use of "best-available technology" and a mix of emission, fuel-quality and product standards. Overall, the air-management programmes have proved to be effective both in achieving environmental objectives and in reducing health risks and improving ambient air quality.

Water pollution abatement and control programmes have followed a similar pattern over the past two decades in West Germany. Considerable investment in the construction and renewal of sewers and of municipal and industrial wastewater treatment plants has led to country-wide purification of wastewater, reducing point-source discharge loadings. The water-management programmes have also proved to be environmentally effective in achieving objectives and improving the quality of surface waters.

Concerning waste management in West Germany, efforts have focused on achieving three major objectives: 1) ensuring that wastes are sent to final disposal with minimum damage to the environment, 2) preventing or reducing waste generation, and 3) enhancing waste recovery, reuse and recycling. Stable total quantities of wastes over the past two decades, increasing recovery rates for industrial wastes since 1977, and the enhancement of environmental quality through rigorous disposal standards and stringent requirements for incinerators suggest that these objectives have been met.

Priorities on the future agenda for environmental policy in Germany (and many other countries) include the control of carcinogens, ground-level ozone, soil acidification, freshwater pollution, nitrogen pollution of waters by pesticides and fertilisers in agriculture, automobile-related emissions, and the protection of sensitive eco-systems, such as forests. Furthermore, severe capacity limits of existing disposal facilities and public opposition to the installation of new landfill or incinerator sites, have resulted in stepping up efforts to increase waste recovery and to reduce waste generation, including the use of charges and subsidies to foster waste prevention and recycling, as well as the use of "eco-labels" such as the Blue Angel. These measures, however, need time to have an effect on the environment, and it is too early to evaluate their cost-effectiveness and their macro-economic effects. Further problems, such as contaminated soil sites, are still subject to research in Germany on remedial technologies and costs.

16.2.4. Economic impacts of environmental protection

16.2.4.1. Spending on environmental protection

Between 1975 and 1991, West German manufacturing industry and the West German government spent over DM 420 billion (at current prices) on pollution abatement (Table 16.2-2). At 1985 prices, this works out to an annual average of about DM 26 billion.

In 1991, about 7,400 out of a total 73,000 manufacturing companies (generally employing 20 or more people) invested in pollution abatement. The average amount per company was approximately DM 880,000, with environmental investments averaging 5% of the overall investment volume (1980: 3.5%; 1984: 4.4%; 1986: 7.4%; 1989: 6.8%). The largest sums were devoted to air quality (ca. 50% of environmental investments) and water quality (ca. 29%).

In various manufacturing sub-sectors, environmental investment as a share of total investment expenditure ranged from 0.8% to 24.9% (1991, for unified Germany). Spending of producers of chemicals (15%), non-ferrous metals and semi-finished products (13.3%) and oil refineries (13%) was well above average.

Compared to other countries' "green spending" quotas, Germany spends generously on environmental protection (Table 16.2-3). Moreover, it is amongst the few countries whose environmental spending/GNP quota has shown slight growth since the early 1980s. Nevertheless, environmental spending accounts for barely 1.6% of GNP. There are many other areas—in particular defence, education and health—where spending is up to five times higher.

The relative magnitude of environmental spending varies widely among different industries. In 1990, spending on environmental protection by utilities and in the mining and quarrying sector amounted to 1.17% and 1.13%, respectively, of

Table 16.2-2 Environment expenditure
(at current prices, in DM million; West Germany)

Year	Manufacturing industry		Government		Total[b)]
	Investment	Operating costs	Investment	Operating costs	
1975	2,480	3,220	4,740	2,980	13,420
1976	2,390	3,620	5,270	3,260	14,530
1977	2,240	3,940	4,860	3,530	14,580
1978	2,150	4,240	5,860	3,900	16,150
1979	2,080	4,680	6,940	4,390	18,090
1980	2,660	5,170	8,060	4,670	20,550
1981	2,930	5,890	7,390	5,120	21,330
1982	3,560	6,490	6,500	5,390	21,950
1983	3,690	6,850	6,030	5,610	22,190
1984	3,500	7,290	5,900	5,930	22,630
1985	5,630	7,820	6,750	6,430	26,630
1986	7,300	8,020	7,540	6,980	29,850
1987	7,710	8,620	7,930	7,510	31,780
1988	8,030	9,430	8,200	7,810	33,470
1989[a)]	7,630	10,440	9,080	8,370	35,520
1990[a)]	7,230	11,230	10,380	9,340	38,180
1991[a)]	6,470	11,960	12,050	10,170	40,640
Total	77,680	118,910	123,480	101,390	421,490

a) Provisional figure.
b) Deviations in totals are due to rounding.

Source: Federal Statistical Office; Ifo Institute calculations.

gross output, compared with just 0.27% in the manufacturing industry. Operating costs for environmental protection amounted to 2.22%, 1.95% and 0.42%, respectively (Table 16.2-4).

16.2.4.2. Environmental policy and industrial location

The assertion that stringent environmental regulations induce businesses to relocate their operations in order to exploit international differences in the costs of environmental protection and thus endanger the future of Germany's industrial base is quite frequently made by German pressure groups, industry and government representatives. However, a number of studies carried out in West Germany came to the conclusion that, in practice, industrial activities are not relocated solely on the grounds of environmental policy but on the grounds of international labour cost and tax differentials, the proximity to markets, and the

Table 16.2-3 Environmental spending: An international comparison

Country	Total spending on environmental protection			Public spending on environmental protection		
	% of GNP					
	1985	1987	1990	1985	1987	1990
Austria	..	1.7	..	1.0	1.0	..
Canada	..	..	1.1	0.7	0.7	0.9
Denmark	..	..	..	0.7	0.8	1.0
France	0.8	1.0	1.0	0.6	0.7	0.5
Germany	1.5	1.6	1.6	0.7	0.8	0.8
Japan	..	1.1	1.1	0.9	1.0	1.0
Netherlands	1.5	1.5	1.5[a)]	1.0	0.9	0.9[a)]
Sweden	..	..	..	..	0.7	..
United Kingdom	1.3	1.5[b)]	1.5	0.7	0.6[b)]	0.4
United States	1.4	1.4	1.4	0.6	0.6	0.6

.. No figures available.
a) 1989.
b) Estimated.

Source: OECD

Table 16.2-4 Cost structure in the manufacturing industry (1990; West Germany)

Sector	Gross output	Investment	Environmental investment	Environmental operating costs	Personnel	Material consumption	Rents and Leases
	DM billion	Percentage of gross output					
Electricity, gas, district heating and water supply	160.7	12.3	1.17	2.22	13.4	11.9	1.7
Mining and quarrying	29.3	7.6	1.13	1.95	44.8	29.5	0.8
Manufacturing industry	1,825.2	5.2	0.27	0.42	25.2	39.7	1.4
-Primary and general producer goods	489.0	5.3	0.62	-	20.4	38.2	0.9
-Capital goods	879.7	5.3	0.13	-	30.1	38.4	1.5
-Consumer goods	251.6	5.6	0.19	-	27.2	40.5	1.8
-Food, drink and tobacco	204.9	4.1	0.13	0.24	12.8	48.0	1.5
Building trade	142.2	4.2	0.06	0.05	38.0	27.2	2.1
-Construction	110.7	5.0	0.06	-	38.1	24.7	2.2
-Finishing and services	31.5	3.1	0.04	-	37.3	35.8	1.6

Note: - No figures available.
Source: Federal Statistical Office; author's calculations.

desire to evade trade barriers and import restrictions. A recent study commissioned by the Federal Environmental Agency (Umweltbundesamt) concludes: "There is no evidence from the past to indicate that environmental policy in the Federal Republic of Germany has, on balance, detracted from the country's appeal as a site for industry" (*Berichte,* 1/93). This is partly due to the existence of various programmes devised to encourage environmental commitment.

Moreover, future harmonisation of environmental legislation will even out international abatement expenditure requirements. The process of harmonising environmental regulations within the European Union has already started, and it can be assumed that, in the long run, continuing environmental deterioration will induce other countries to internalise pollution externalities. Hence, competitive edges from slacker environmental standards will only be temporary.

High environmental standards can even turn out to be a competitive advantage, since the ecological soundness of a site is a crucial factor for attracting well-qualified personnel. Sparse investment in highly polluted regions of the new Länder, such as the areas around Leipzig, Bitterfeld, Halle and Merseburg, exemplifies that inadequate environmental infrastructure and unresolved problems of contaminated sites are major impediments for economic development.

Licensing procedures, legal channels, reporting requirements, sanctions and monitoring activities associated with environmental protection differ considerably amongst industrial nations. German legislators impose a relatively high number of regulations, which can be inhibiting. However, company surveys showed that most licensing procedures take less than six months. In order to cut licensing costs and avoid investment bottlenecks, the federal government intends to simplify administration further, for example with new legislation facilitating land release for residential development.

16.2.4.3. Environmental policy and competitiveness

Environmental technology is one of the fastest growing markets in Germany. In 1991 its annual turnover of about DM 26,000 million was equivalent to 65% of turnover in mining and quarrying, and just less than 13% of turnover in the chemicals industry. The number of companies offering goods and services in the green technology market is up from 1,000 in the early 1980s to 5,000 at present. This development is partly due to the pioneering role which Germany has played in environmental protection.

Observers agree that the prospects for increasing sales are good, as other countries will continue to attach more importance to environmental protection, generating bigger export markets for German industry, particularly in the Single European Market. In addition, billions will be invested in domestic manufacturing facilities over the coming decade, and strong growth in sales of clean technology can be expected in the east of the country.

Germany has been especially successful with its exports of clean technology. In 1990 it was by far the biggest exporter of environmental goods, with a 21%

share of world trade. The United States accounted for 16% and Japan for 13%. One of the major reasons for Germany's success with its green-goods industry is that exacting national policies on environmental protection created an early domestic demand, which ultimately gave Germany a technological edge over its competitors. Through consistent employment of leading-edge pollution abatement technologies, such as flue gas desulphurisation systems to cut down NOx emissions, thermal treatments and biofilters for odour treatment, Germany has acquired a leading position in the field of airborne pollution. The future implementation of the Residual Heat Ordinance will contribute to establishing Germany's lead in the development and production of efficient energy systems.

Thus, the installation of advanced abatement technologies in Germany gave and will give testimony to the technological potential for curbing pollution, encouraging other countries to tighten their policies.

16.2.4.4. Environmental policy and employment

A study commissioned by the Umweltbundesamt (*Berichte,* 5/93) observed that environmental protection leads to job growth: the number of people working in the field of environmental protection grew steadily throughout the 1980s to reach more than 200,000 in 1990 (western Germany). In addition to local governments, the manufacturing industry, the recycling trade, and private and public waste-disposal operations are major employers. The fastest environment-related job growth is being witnessed in the manufacturing industry. In the 1980s the number of people in this sector directly concerned with environmental tasks increased by 60%.

Out of 546,000 jobs which depended indirectly on environmental protection in 1990 (western Germany), some 340,000 were in the manufacture of capital goods and day-to-day environment work. Since these statistics do not include environment-related job-creating schemes, human and capital resources employed for environmental protection in other sectors, and job creating through ecologically oriented energy and transport policy, the total number of jobs must have been considerably higher.

Because of incomplete data and the fluidity of economic transformation in eastern Germany, we only have a fragmentary picture of environment-related employment there. The available data suggests that at least 134,000 work places dealt with environmental protection in 1991; amongst them, 60,000 were established through job-creation schemes.

Estimates for environment-related employment in western Germany in the year 2000 range between 786,000 for a present-trend scenario, which assumes that environmental policy will continue in its present direction (with emphasis on repairing the damage), and a further 100,000 if environmental protection is accorded a greater social priority than at present, emphasising the precautionary principle.

Table 16.2-5 Number of people employed directly in environmental protection (West Germany)

Field of employment	1980	1984	1990
Local and regional authorities	82,655	89,185	103,100
- planning, administrative and executive bodies	25,200	31,000	35,000
- higher education	4,072	4,800	8,000
- sewage, waste, street cleaning	53,583	54,385	53,600
· sewage treatment	21,357	23,560	-
· waste disposal	20,224	18,786	-
· street cleaning	12,002	12,039	-
- parks and gardens	*	*	6,500
Public and private waste management	24,600	26,500	27,200
- public waste management	8,100	8,500	-
- private waste management	16,500	18,000	-
Recycling trade	23,100	3,200	29,980
Other services	2,800	3,500	4,850
- chimney sweeps	2,800	3,500	3,600
- environment consultants, households	*	*	1,250
Manufacturing	22,000	24,600	34,500
Non-profit organisations	2,500	5,000	6,000
Total (listed activities)	157,655	171,985	205,630

* Figures not included.

Source: Berichte 5/93 published by the Umweltbundesamt.

16.3. Comparative Summary of Environmental Problems

16.3.1. Outbreak of environmental problems and responses thereto

During the past fifty years, Germany and Japan have faced similar environmental problems. Both countries experienced substantial levels of ambient pollution in the 1950s and 1960s, caused by the rapid growth of highly polluting industries. In the 1980s, the focus shifted to consumption-related environmental problems such as automobile exhaust and municipal waste. In addition, both countries have had to deal with their contributions to global environmental problems. Responses to these problems by policy-makers of the two countries are to be reviewed in the following sections.

German policy-makers have relied heavily on command-and-control instruments, i.e., policies where the environmental authority specifies regulations for each pollution source or group of sources. The 1974 Federal Emission Control

Act is an example of this approach. In the late 1980s, doubts about the cost-effectiveness and sustainability of direct measures of restraint and the increasing complexity of environmental problems stimulated discussion on incentive-based policy instruments. Although numerous suggestions for the use of market-based instruments have been made, very few have been implemented thus far.

Early Japanese environmental legislation, on the other hand, aimed at enforcing the polluter-pays principle through direct liability rules. The ecological effectiveness of this strategy is questionable, since victims had to prove the polluters' guilt. In general, until the 1970s, Japanese authorities' commitment to business interests allowed environmental regulation only if human health had been or was at risk of being severely damaged. The deletion of the provision of being in "harmony with sound economic development" from the Environmental Pollution Prevention Act of 1967 marked the beginning of a new phase in environmental policy, achieving a stronger orientation towards the prevention principle by reinforcing liability compensation schemes, implementing strict pollution-control or product standards and incentive-based instruments, as well as fostering research on pollution abatement or elimination. This policy mix, with emphasis on research activities and technology transfer, is also being used to address today's global environmental problems.

16.3.2. Qualitative changes in environmental problems and the implications for economic growth

A comparison with the regulatory measures employed during the initial phase of environmental policy shows that German policy-makers were not reluctant to use direct intervention as a way of achieving immediate environmental improvements, whilst Japanese regulatory authorities relied on self-regulation, which had little effect. However, now that environment problems have started to impact on urban living standards, both the German and Japanese governments have moved towards more comprehensive policies. In the business sector, companies have shifted from a stance of paying compensation after environmental damage has occurred, to one based on environmental counter-measures before problems arise. As a result, the Japanese and German environmental regimes are today amongst the strictest in the world. However, Japan gives higher priority to environment-related research and development.

These changes in policies towards environmental issues reflect new awareness of the fact that environmental problems are inextricably linked with economic growth. Current thinking in both Japan and Germany is that pre-emptive measures against environmental problems are cheaper than remedial action after problems have occurred. There is also support for the view that the creation of new business and employment opportunities through efforts to deal with environmental problems outweighs the loss of opportunities due to environmental regulation and can push up growth rates. As discussed in the section on Germany, another reason for the progress made on environmental issues is the fact that environmental regulation has not had the effect of curbing business investment.

16.3.3. Cost-effectiveness of environmental efforts

Overall, both Japan and Germany are working actively to overcome environmental problems. However, there are clear differences in the processes involved. These differences reflect differing perceptions of the economic benefits of protecting the environment. Germany's environmental policy begins with the provision of copious data about business costs resulting from pollution controls, and the impact of such measures on the German economy. Only then does the government point out the positive economic effects of environmental protection, as if to justify its environmental policy. In Japan, the government emphasises the social benefits of environmental protection and the economic benefits of participation in international environment-related markets. This difference in priorities appears to reflect public opinion, especially in the business sector, about green policies. Statements by business groups in Japan, such as the Keidanren's Global Environment Charter, indicate that a consensus has been reached between the regulatory authorities and the business sector on environmental goals. In Germany, companies hit by recession are clearly on the defensive and tend to question the benefits of pollution controls.

16.3.4. Learning from environmental problems

The task for the future will be to raise public interest in environmental issues. In July 1994 Germany established a new recycling and waste law, the ultimate aim of which is to promote recycling. The *Grüner Punkt* system of pre-sorted garbage collection was also introduced in order to ensure that citizens participate in recycling. Japan has meanwhile introduced the Eco-Mark system and a recycling law.

It will be extremely interesting to observe the changes that occur in the Japanese and German economic systems in the future as a result of efforts to deal with environmental problems. Both Japan and Germany have been recently affected by economic downturns and will need to modify their traditional economic systems. Will this situation result in a retreat from environmental efforts? The alleviation of environmental problems clearly has a positive impact at the macro-economic level and in the long-term perspective. However, the short-term cost of environmental protection cannot be ignored at a time when business in Japan and Germany is threatened with declining international competitiveness.

What is clear is the fact that environmental problems have a direct impact on life. Also clear is the need for Japan and Germany, as advanced nations, to take the initiative in this area.

Part V

Development in Selected Industrial Sectors

17. Chemical Industry

17.1. Japan's Chemical Industry

17.1.1. Industry definition

The chemical sector consists of industries whose industrial technologies are similar to or exhibit the characteristics of chemical processing. As shown in Table 17.1-1, this criterion applies to an extremely broad range of industries. This analysis will be focused primarily on the material-type chemical industries or intermediate chemical products industries that have supplied the materials needed by Japan's internationally competitive industries, especially automobile and electrical appliance manufacturing.

17.1.2. Post-war development of the chemical industry

17.1.2.1. Post-war reconstruction (1945–1954)

The production capacity of Japan's chemical sector declined dramatically in the immediate post-war period because of the destruction of production facilities

Table 17.1-1 Scope of the chemical industry

Material chemical industries	Chemical fertiliser manufacturing Inorganic chemical manufacturing (soda, etc.) Organic chemical manufacturing (basic petrochemicals, etc.) Synthetic fibre manufacturing
Processing chemical industries	Manufacturing of processed oil and fat products, soap, synthetic detergents, surfactants, coatings Pharmaceutical manufacturing Manufacturing of cosmetics, toothpaste and other cosmetic preparations Other chemical industries (explosives, etc.)

Source: Management and Co-ordination Agency, Standard Japanese Classification of Industries (October 1993 rev.)

by air raids, the ageing of facilities owing to heavy use during the war years, and the loss of overseas factories in Taiwan, Korea, Manchuria and elsewhere. In addition, shortages of raw materials forced most surviving factories to halt production. In 1945 the chemical sector's output fell to just 17.5% of its pre-war peak in 1939.

In December 1946 the government introduced the priority production system, under which the first priority was given to the coal and iron and steel industries. The chemical fertiliser industry was accorded the next highest priority because of the need to overcome a grave food crisis. Funds channelled into the fertiliser industry between the end of the war and the end of fiscal 1948 reached approximately ¥10 billion, including both capital investment and operating capital, with treasury funds having accounted for ¥8.5 billion of this total. Increased production by the chemical fertiliser industry triggered rapid production growth in other sectors, such as ammonia, sulphuric acid and carbides, and by 1950 the output of the chemical industry had recovered to the pre-war level. In 1951, the government formulated a Three-Year Plan for Economic Self-Reliance. Efforts under this plan resulted in the development of an organic chemical industry based primarily on coal chemistry and electrochemistry.

17.1.2.2. High growth led by materials (1955–1969)

In July 1955, the Ministry of International Trade and Industry (MITI) adopted measures for the development of the petrochemical industry. This policy had three aims. First, the government intended to develop the petrochemical industry in order to provide raw materials for the synthetic fibre and synthetic resin industries, which had grown rapidly. Second, Japan was at this time dependent on imported petrochemical products, and the government intended to replace these with domestic products in order to save foreign currency. Third, the development of the petrochemical industry was seen as a way of enhancing the international competitiveness of Japanese industry as a whole by supplying low-cost petrochemical materials instead of high-cost solid raw materials. Support measures adopted for the petrochemical industry included the prioritised allocation of foreign currency for use in the introduction of foreign technologies, preferential treatment under the taxation system, and policy financing by the Japan Development Bank. The Petrochemical Industry Commercialisation Plan (1955–60) was launched under this policy, and the government authorised the construction of new ethylene centres by four companies, which were primarily of former *zaibatsu* lineage.

Products manufactured domestically by Japanese petrochemical companies quickly replaced imports, and facilities were soon operating at full capacity. Despite this, there was no reduction in imports of primary petrochemical products, such as polyethylene and synthetic rubber. As a result, the petrochemical industry gained a reputation as a growth area, and more and more companies sought to move into the field. Under the Second Commercialisation Plan (1960–65), the government authorised the construction of ethylene centres by five firms, including petroleum companies.

The petrochemical industry also had an impact on existing industries. Under the First Commercialisation Plan, the government adopted a policy of avoiding measures that would have a drastic effect on existing industries. As a result, there was only limited conversion of production methods. However, the policy adopted under the Second Commercialisation Plan sought to reduce product costs and boost supply capacity in existing industries by changing both raw materials and manufacturing methods. Existing chemical industries, such as carbide-based acetylene chemicals, quickly shifted to the petrochemical method. As a result, the use of naphtha cracking fractions in the chemical sector rose from 48.5% at the end of the First Commercialisation Plan in 1960 to 80.9% at the end of Second Commercialisation Plan in 1965. This trend led to the establishment of integrated petrochemical complexes. The petrochemical industry continued to grow through the absorption of existing chemical industries. Shipments of organic chemical products grew steadily from just 13.9% of total chemical sector shipments in 1955 to 20.2% in 1960, 29.0% in 1965 and 35.3% in 1970. Organic chemicals had become a core area of the chemical sector (Fig. 17.1-1).

In terms of the value of the total output of its chemical sector, Japan overtook France in 1965 and Britain in 1966. In 1968 it surpassed West Germany and moved into second place in the free world behind the United States.

Fig. 17.1-1 Trends in the shipment mix of the chemical sector

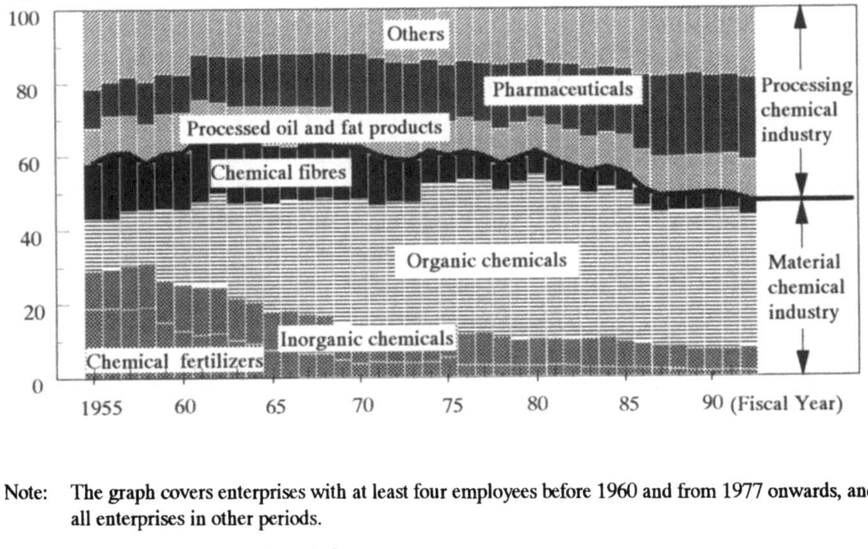

Note: The graph covers enterprises with at least four employees before 1960 and from 1977 onwards, and all enterprises in other periods.

Source: MITI, Table of Industrial Statistics

17.1.2.3. Structural recession in the material chemical industry (1970–1984)

During the second half of the 1960s, it became increasingly apparent that the petrochemical industry would not be able to survive against international competition without ethylene plants that provided annual production capacities of at least 300,000 tons. This awareness was reflected in the construction and planning of giant plants with capacities of 300,000 tons or more, including a 450,000-ton plant built by Imperial Chemical Industries (ICI). In 1967, the government accordingly tripled its annual production standard for the construction of new ethylene plants from the 1965 level of 100,000 tons or more to 300,000 tons or more.

The aims of this move were to make individual plants more competitive and to consolidate capital through the withdrawal or restructuring of inefficient companies. The government's intent was to reinforce the structure of the industry, which at that time included a plethora of companies that were smaller than their counterparts in Europe and North America. For ethylene centre operators, the new standard was a hurdle that had to be surmounted, if they were to avoid wasting their past efforts. They used joint investment and other means to meet the standard with the result that the industry restructuring sought by the government did not occur. Between 1969 and 1972, nine facilities with annual ethylene production capacity of 300,000 tons each were built. Efforts were also made to expand the capacities of ammonia plants to 1,000 tons per day. This trend towards increased capacity in these basic product categories led to the expansion of production facilities for vinyl chloride monomers and other derivative products.

Demand for petrochemical products was, meanwhile, stagnating for several reasons. First, the shift in raw-material utilisation from natural fibres to synthetic fibres had run its course. Second, electrical appliances and other durable consumer goods became widespread. Third, the business cycle had shifted into recession with the end of the "Izanagi Boom," which was the longest economic uptrend of the post-war era. This was reflected in a widening gap between supply and demand in the ethylene market from 1970 onwards (Fig. 17.1-2). In 1972 anti-depression cartels were formed not only for vinyl chloride resin and polyolefin but also for ethylene, which are the basic products of the petrochemical industry.

The decisive factor behind the material chemical industry's transition to a low-growth phase was the 1973 oil crisis. Fictitious demand brought a short-term improvement in the earnings of chemical manufacturers in fiscal 1973 and 1974. However, product price rises driven by the surge in crude oil prices not only caused a decline in domestic demand for chemical products, especially petrochemical products, but also led to a export downturn due to the weakening of international competitiveness. This situation exposed a serious over-capacity problem in the material chemical industry. After the second oil crisis in 1979, the material chemical industry became known as a structurally depressed industry.

In 1978 the government passed the Provisional Law for the Stabilisation of Specified Industries in Recession. This was followed in May 1983 by the

Fig. 17.1-2 Production and ordinary profit of ethylene centres

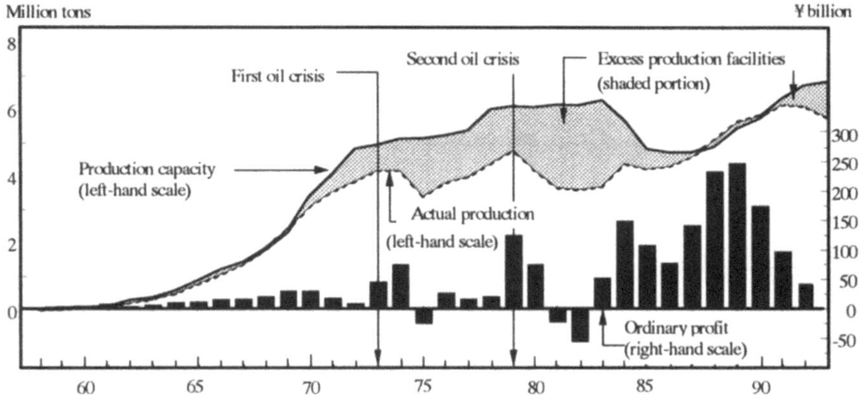

Notes: 1. Production capacity and actual production of ethylene are based on calendar years, and ordinary profit on fiscal years.

2. Ordinary profit is reckoned from the years in which companies commenced ethylene production.

Source: Chemical Economy Research Institute (Japan), Comprehensive Survey of the Chemical Industry; Performance and State of the 50 Major Chemical Companies); Corporate Financial Statements; Japan Petrochemical Industry Association

establishment of the Provisional Law on Structural Improvement of Specified Industries (hereinafter referred to as the "Structural Stabilisation Law"). The purpose of these laws was to reduce the supply-demand gap through the closure or mothballing of small- to medium-sized and obsolete facilities in such areas as ammonia, chemical fertilisers, ethylene, polyolefin and vinyl chloride resin.[1] To prevent excessive competition for sales, joint sales companies[2] were established for vinyl chloride in August 1982 and for polyolefin in July 1983.

Apart from the oil crises, another factor that had a serious adverse impact on the material chemical industry in the 1970s was the emergence of pollution problems in the first half of the decade. From the early 1970s onwards, manufacturers invested aggressively in pollution control measures to overcome the pollution problems that had started to become apparent in the mid-1960s. In the

---

1 In the ethylene industry, for example, facilities were closed or mothballed in proportion to respective market share. Each company was able to select the most convenient basis for calculation from amongst (a) production capacity share, (b) share of actual shipments in the previous year, or (c) share of average actual shipments in the previous three years.

2 These were sales companies set up under the joint ownership of several companies in the same industry for reasons that included not only the avoidance of excessive competition for sales but also the commissioning of production and sales, and rationalisation through product streamlining and other means. They are approved by the Fair Trade Commission.

petrochemical industry, investment in anti-pollution measures reached a peak of one-quarter of the total investment in 1975. This investment, which made no direct contribution to earnings, caused business costs to rise and exerted considerable pressure on profit. However, it also enabled the Japanese chemical sector to achieve world leadership in pollution-control technology.

17.1.2.4. High yen and internationalisation (1985–)

The government sought to boost the economy out of the strong-yen recession that began in 1985 through policies designed to expand domestic demand. The recovery of domestic business performance was accompanied by a gradual improvement in the performance of the material chemical industry, and in 1988 the twelve ethylene centre operators achieved record ordinary profits. This led to the repeal of the Structural Stabilisation Law in 1988.

However, the prospects for major growth in the domestic market today are poor because of several factors affecting demand for material chemical products. First, the domestic market has matured with the completion of the demand replacement process that saw chemical fibres replace natural fibres and plastic products replace metal products. Second, user industries, such as automobiles and electrical machinery, are relocating their production facilities offshore due to the appreciation of the yen. Third, the high yen has enhanced the price competitiveness of foreign products, leading to an increasing flow of low-price imports.

The growth of the Southeast Asian economies is expected to bring growth in that region's demand for material chemical products. Japan's material chemical companies, which in the past developed primarily in a closed domestic market, will now need to cope with two types of internationalisation: competition from foreign products in the domestic market and the offshore relocation of production facilities.

17.1.3. Demand trends

The post-war development of the Japanese chemical sector began with chemical fertilisers, subsequently dominated by coal chemistry until 1954 and by petrochemicals until 1969. The core field since 1970 has been processed chemical products. The development of the Japanese economy has also been reflected in shifts in the main user categories from agriculture (chemical fertilisers), the textile industry (synthetic fibres) and manufacturers of sundry goods (synthetic resins) to the automotive and electrical appliance industries (synthetic resins) and manufacturers of medical products (pharmaceuticals).

An analysis of the shipment mix in 1993 shows that processed chemical products accounted for over one-half in value terms at 54.5%. Pharmaceuticals are particularly important and represent about one-quarter of the total value of shipments. The petrochemical industry accounts for over 40% of shipments of material chemical products (organic chemicals plus synthetic fibres in Fig. 17.1-3).

Fig. 17.1-3 Composition of chemical products shipment (1993 value)

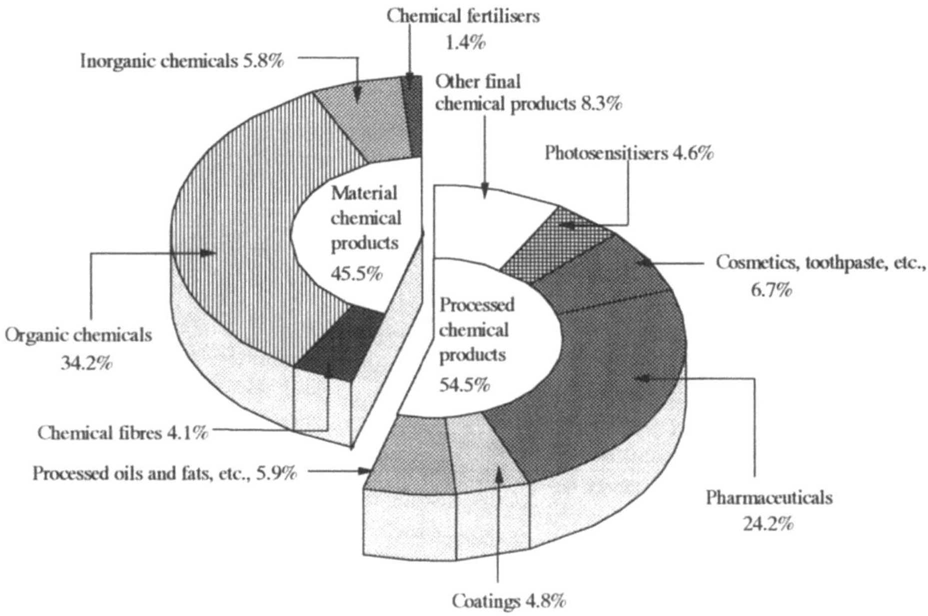

Source: MITI, Table of Industrial Statistics

Exports account only for approximately 10% in value terms, which indicates that the Japanese chemical sector is oriented primarily towards domestic demand. An analysis of import-export balances for each product category (Table 17.1-2) shows that pharmaceuticals is the biggest net importer with \$2.4 billion, and plastics is the biggest net exporter with \$3.9 billion. In regional terms, exports to Southeast Asia exceed imports from that region by \$8.2 billion, whilst imports from North America and Europe exceed exports to those regions by \$6.4 billion. Overall, Japan's trade in chemical products is characterised by net exporting of material chemical products, particularly to developing countries, and net importing of processed chemical products, primarily from developed countries. This pattern reflects Japan's limited research and development capabilities in the area of processed chemical products, such as pharmaceuticals and other items, which means that there are few original Japanese products capable of competing at the international level.

According to MITI's 1991 Input-Output Tables (Extended Tables), the biggest industrial users of chemical products are chemical industries, which account for 30.5% of sales. This is approximately 1.5 times higher than the share of the plastics industry, which accounts for 20.1% of sales. As discussed later, this

Table 17.1-2 Exports and imports of chemical products (1993)
- $million -

	Exports	(%)	Imports	(%)	Difference
By product category					
Plastics	5,610	(27.8)	1,727	(9.6)	3,883
Organic compounds	6,783	(33.6)	5,033	(28.0)	1,750
Pharmaceuticals	1,475	(7.3)	3,923	(21.8)	-2,448
Other chemicals	6,331	(31.3)	7,281	(40.6)	-950
Total	20,199	(100.0)	17,964	(100.0)	2,235
By region					
Southeast Asia	10,103	(50.0)	1,866	(10.4)	8,237
Former Soviet Union and other communist countries	1,292	(6.4)	863	(4.8)	429
North America and Europe	7,500	(37.1)	13,898	(77.4)	-6,398
Latin America	577	(2.5)	669	(3.7)	-162
Other regions	797	(4.0)	668	(3.7)	129

Source: MITI, International Trade White Paper 1994

wide gap reflects the formation of sophisticated divisions of labour within the chemical sector.

17.1.4. Supply system and industry structure

The structure of the chemical industries shows two characteristics. First, companies are smaller than their Western counterparts and operate under more specialised divisions of labour. Second, there is a tendency towards excessive competition in the material chemical industry.

17.1.4.1. Contrasts with the West: Smaller companies and more specialised divisions of labour

In Europe and North America, the concentration of activity that occurred in the 1920s led to the restructuring of the chemical sector into huge oligopolistic corporations. These companies formed a capital accumulation mechanism under which the development and monopolisation of technology led to excess profits that could be invested in research.

On the other hand, the Japanese chemical sector progressed from importing products from the West to the achievement of domestic production through the introduction and imitation of foreign technology. Because the afore-mentioned Western mechanism did not operate, there was little capital accumulation. Furthermore, businesses formed independently of each other in separate categories, such as chemical fertilisers, soda, oils and fats, dyes and coatings, thus bringing about no intersectional capital formation. Because of this background, the chemical industry started the post-war era with a structure characterised by large numbers of companies with little capital accumulation.

The material chemical industry is a facility-intensive field requiring an enormous amount in capital investment. It is also characterised by the co-production of an extremely wide range of derivatives from raw materials, such as naphtha and salts. Each type of derivative requires different facilities and technologies, which means that the production of derivatives involves even greater additional expenditure.

With their limited capital accumulation, individual Japanese companies were unable to afford the huge capital investment required to establish production facilities for a full range of products from basic items, such as ethylene, to various derivatives. This problem was overcome through the centralisation of facilities in complexes that were established by multiple companies, each handling a specific area of production. However, this process did not lead to company consolidation. One reason for this was the fact that the petrochemical industry at that time was considered a growth industry, and each company was determined to maintain its individuality. Another factor was government restrictions on the areas of activity in which companies could become involved.

During the high growth phase, the rapid expansion of domestic markets allowed even small, inefficient companies to survive, with the result that no thought was given to corporate expansion or diversification through company consolidation.

After the material chemical industry went into recession in the 1970s, the government worked to maintain and protect the industry order. This also had the effect of hindering progress towards restructuring, particularly through consolidation.

The situation in Japan is thus characterised by the formation of divisions of labour within the material chemical industry, and also between the material chemical industry and the processed chemical industry. The division of labour between the material chemical industry and the processed chemical industry at the start of the post-war era can be explained by the lack of capital accumulation by individual companies.

17.1.4.2. Excessive competition in the material chemical industry

By the 1960s many companies had entered the material chemical industry. Since the industry, especially petrochemical manufacturers, depended on technology introduced from overseas for its manufacturing technologies, none of the companies involved were able to establish monopolistic positions by means of original patents. Moreover, with ethylene production capacity at 300,000 tons per annum per company, there was an over-supply situation, in which complexes tended to be equipped with uniform production facilities based on the same layout, consisting of a full set of facilities for olefin derivatives but without any other special features. In addition, government protection encouraged aggressive capital investment.

Facility-intensive industries have a basic tendency towards excessive production. The combination of this pattern with the circumstances described above was responsible for a structural tendency towards excessive competition within the material chemical industry. This tendency came to the fore when the supply-demand gap began to widen in the 1970s. Ordinarily, such conditions would lead to the absorption or elimination of uncompetitive companies. However, an industry order that included inefficient companies was maintained through government guidance with the result that excessive competition has continued down to the present day.

17.1.5. Role of industrial policy

17.1.5.1. Introduction of technology and policy support

In the post-war period, the Japanese chemical sector began to develop original organic synthesis technologies. In the area of chemical fertilisers, Toyo Koatsu (now Mitsui Toatsu Chemicals) commercialised urea, whilst in the field of synthetic fibres, vinylon was commercialised by Kurashiki Rayon (now Kuraray) and nylon by Toyo Rayon (now Toray Industries).

Petrochemical technology failed, however, to develop in Japan because of an environment that did not use petroleum as a raw material. The commercialisation of the petrochemical industry thus relied on the introduction of advanced technology from overseas. Companies vied to introduce the latest technology with the result that Japan became known as a trade fair for petrochemical technology from around the world. The government responded to these developments in the chemical sector by aggressively implementing measures to foster the industry. Specifically, the government was to first produce medium- to long-range demand forecasts, then indicate plans for the investment needed to satisfy this demand, set targets for optimum production levels and cost rationalisation and, where business plans were in line with these targets, approve the introduction of technology. Total support was also to be provided, including loans from government-affiliated financial institutions, as well as special depreciation measures and other tax concessions.

This powerful government intervention led to structural dependence on the government, which in turn resulted in an excessively competitive environment where companies raced to invest in facilities and equipment. This was because any company that gained an edge in the race to expand production capacity was able to establish a vested interest that would ensure government protection. Furthermore, because securing access to investment opportunities as a vested interest had become the most pressing management priority, investment was concentrated in raw material operations with the result that it was impossible to shun business risk through diversification strategies, such as expansion into the processed chemical industry.

17.1.5.2. Industry protection policy

The material chemical industry thus became structurally disposed towards dependence on the government, whilst individual companies tended to give priority to vested interests when making management decisions. The government's response to this situation took the form of industrial policies designed to maintain the industry order.

For example, under the First Petrochemical Industry Commercialisation Plan (1955–60), the government guided companies, in principle, to avoid commercialised products that would compete with those of existing industries. Under the Second Petrochemical Industry Commercialisation Plan (1960–65), if a new petrochemical company's production plan conflicted with the production rationalisation plan of an existing company in the same field, the new company's involvement would be limited to intermediate products, and the existing company would be given the role of turning these into final products. Policies during this period were thus designed to encourage expansion and development, including both new and existing chemical companies.

When the supply-demand gap began to widen in the 1970s, the government sought to protect the entire industry, including inefficient companies, through measures such as the establishment of anti-depression cartels and joint sales companies, as well as the passage of the Structural Stabilisation Law. The basic framework for the administration of protection during this period can be found in the 1971 Interim Report of the Industrial Structure Council. This report referred to the vulnerability of facility-intensive industries to problems that prevented them from adjusting supply flexibly in response to price fluctuations, owing to the uniformity of their products, as well as engineering characteristics that required enormous amount of fixed capital. It also stated that because of a possible occurrence of "market failures" in such industries, it was necessary to supplement market mechanisms in some way, such as through capital investment adjustments.

Inefficient companies were able to survive because of the protection of existing chemical industries under the Petrochemical Industry Commercialization Plans, because of the formation of anti-depression cartels and because of provisions in the Structural Stabilisation Law. This situation has hindered the concentration of capital in the chemical industry, which has become known for its confused proliferation of small companies.

17.1.5.3. Evaluation of industrial policy

In the immediate post-war era, the government sought to overcome food shortages by according policy priority to the chemical fertiliser industry. This policy ultimately made a major contribution to the recovery of the chemical sector.

Furthermore, government measures relating to the commercialisation of the petrochemical industry, including the preferential allocation of foreign currency, also led to the saving of foreign currency through the replacement of imports with domestic production, which was one of the goals of commercialisation. Foreign currency used under the First Petrochemical Industry Commercialisation Plan totalled $58 million (¥20.9 billion at ¥360 to the dollar), of which $35 million was spent on technology royalties and $23 million on imported machinery. Foreign-exchange payments thus accounted for one-fourth of the approximately ¥80 billion needed for plant construction, including the introduction of technology. However, this approach yielded foreign-currency savings of about $107 million (about ¥38.5 billion) in 1960, compared with the amount that would have been required if production in that year had been replaced by imports. In addition, price reductions driven by competition amongst numerous companies made a major contribution to the development of other industries, such as automobiles and electrical machinery.

From the long-term perspective, however, it would be difficult to claim that Japan achieved its goal of increasing international competitiveness. Industrial policy relating to the chemical sector hampered the concentration of capital and the distribution of risk through diversification, and the resulting structural tendency towards excessive competition had the effect of keeping profit levels low. That is why even today Japanese companies lag far behind their counterparts in Europe and North America in their capacity to invest in research and development (Table 17.1-3). This situation has been a major obstacle to the improvement of

Table 17.1-3 Comparison of research and development expenditures

Country	Company	R&D investment ($million)		Percentage of sales	R&D personnel
United States	Du Pont	1,040	2,057	6.6	N.A.
	Dow Chemical	547		4.7	7,000
	Monsanto	470		7.0	N.A.
Germany	Bayer	726	1,923	4.6	12,700
	Hoechst	709		4.9	13,500
	BASF	488		3.2	11,000
Japan	Mitsubishi Chemical	137	308	3.5	1,850
	Sumitomo Chemical	117		3.6	1,800
	Showa Denko	54		2.6	1,080

Source: MITI, New Chemistry Developing in the 21st Century

international competitiveness in the material chemical industry. This failure appears to have occurred because the government erred in timing the shifts in its industrial policy from protective fostering to the elimination of protection and the transition to free competition.

17.1.6. Principal factors behind industrial development

Industrial policy in the material chemical industry has left a serious negative legacy for the future development of the chemical sector by hindering the concentration of capital and by causing Japanese companies to lag far behind their counterparts in Europe and North America in R&D investment. However, there is also evidence that the material chemical industry has made considerable progress. For example, Japan's production capacity for ethylene, which is a basic petrochemical product, with 6,770,000 tons is now the second largest in the world after the United States with 21,190,000 tons at the end of 1992.

One key factor behind this development has been a relative decline in the prices of chemical materials compared with other raw materials. This has generated increased replacement demand as users switch from other materials. Another factor is the growth of major users, such as the textile, automotive and household electrical appliance industries. Since the 1970s, the proportion of chemical materials exported has remained at about 10% of production. Whilst this is certainly not high, large amounts of chemical products are also exported indirectly as materials used by the automobile and electrical appliance industries and other industries with high export ratios. The material chemical industry has thus been able to achieve development through the expansion of production in these areas. And although the industry has experienced problems, including its dependence on the government, the biggest factor in its development, needless to say, has been efforts of companies in the industry to meet the needs of demanding industrial users by maintaining and improving quality and by reducing costs.

17.2. Germany's Chemical Industry

The chemical industry is one of the most significant German industry clusters. German firms are leaders in a vast array of chemical and related products, as well as in associated machinery and equipment such as pumps, liquid measurement and control equipment, and even in services such as the engineering and construction of chemical plants. Even the strict definition of chemical industry comprises a very broad range of industry types, as shown in Table 17.2-1. German competitive positions in chemistry are closely associated with those in pharmaceuticals, dyes and synthetic fibres. The chemical industry is thus better described by an analysis of its different components, but for the purpose of international comparisons a short survey of the whole sector is expedient.

Table 17.2-1 Industry definition of chemical industry by statistical systems

Content	International statistics Trade (SITC) Rev. III
Inorganic intermediates	52
Organic intermediates	51
Fertilisers, pesticides	56, 591
Plastics and synthetic rubber	57, 58
Synthetic fibres	
Paints, varnishes and related products	531, 533
Pharmaceutical products	54
Others (adhesives, body care, detergents, tannic acids, explosives, etc.)	532, 55, 592 - 598
Refinement	

Source: UN, Standard International Trade Classification

17.2.1. Post-war development of the chemical industry

17.2.1.1. 1945–1954: Post-war reconstruction

World War II caused the loss of foreign assets and trademarks owned by German chemical companies. Extensive parts of industrial facilities were destroyed or confiscated as reparations; patents and know-how were seized by the victor nations. De-cartelisation of IG Farbenindustrie Aktiengesellschaft[3] and control of production and research activities took place as a part of the surrender conditions. These aimed at a general output reduction to 50% of the pre-war level; production in war facilities for materials such as sulphuric acids, nitrogen and chlorine was reduced to 32% of the 1936 level. Production and research prohibitions were imposed in the areas of nuclear fission, synthetic fuels, synthetic rubber and various other chemical products. These restrictions were loosened only in 1951, and the chemical industry was then able to produce almost anything it pleased.

As a result of these restraints, the German chemical industry fell behind in production and research by several years in comparison to international competitors, especially those in the United States. The German industry's relative

[3] Against the background of increasing trust formations in the United States, the German chemical industry had started to co-operate in communities of interests for the purpose of maintaining international competitiveness in the beginning of the twentieth century. In 1925 an efficient and influential cartel, I.G. Farbenindustrie Aktiengesellschaft, developed from the merger of seventy firms. Within a divisionalised and decentralised organisation, the fundamental principle of competition between the participating firms was retained. At the same time, a supervisory board installed joint procurement and sales organisations, and co-ordinated decisions on investment, acquisitions, market strategies and monetary matters. The cartel had only a share of about 30% of total turnover in the chemical industry, but it comprised the largest chemical companies. The share of exports amounted to almost 60%.

technological backwardness was caused by wartime destruction, the disruption of traditional production relationships (because of the division of Germany), former government policy (relying on the use of abundant supplies of domestic coal in the 1930s and the early 1940s, whilst other nations were already concentrating their research on petroleum-based technologies) and the break-up of IG Farben. Thus the three prime tasks in the immediate post-war period were to rebuild production facilities, to catch up with the new standards of excellence in chemical research and to recapture foreign markets.

The German chemical sector thus had to make a new start, and in the long run disentanglement proved more an advantage than a disadvantage. The German chemical sector had a prestigious standing in the pre-war period, based on groundbreaking chemical research. Prior to World War II, the drive for self-sufficiency in materials elevated the industry to a vital national priority. Though it had lost its technological advantage, there was a new chance in establishing new production facilities, so dismantling the IG Farben proved favourable for further development. The division of this key wartime firm into component parts that were much more rational and competitive proved profitable.

At the beginning of the 1950s, however, plans for changes in the industry were hampered by capital shortages, the still visible after-effects of the war (technological lag, the unresolved break-up of IG Farben) and legal restrictions (on research, production and, because of the tariff policy until 1953, on petrochemical manufacturing). Nevertheless, first successes were gained in the areas of pesticides, packaging techniques, insulation technology and pharmaceuticals. On the basis of pre-war knowledge, the relatively new plastics industry was able to expand quickly.

By 1954 almost DM 3.5 billion had been spent to repair war damages to the chemical industry; in 1955 turnover was about DM 14 billion, 25% of which was exports (Table 17.2-2).

17.2.1.2. 1954–1973: Growth and overseas expansion

West German industrialists who succeeded IG Farben moved quickly during the 1950s and 1960s to replace coal-based feedstocks with petroleum-based feedstocks. By 1961 more than 50% of all organic chemicals in the Federal Republic of Germany were derived from petroleum, up from just 15% in 1950. From 1955 to 1965 the annual production growth-rate of total petrochemicals amounted to about 20% with the highest increases being registered in plastics. In 1957 the West German chemical industry had still produced less than one-fourth of its organic chemicals from petroleum or natural gas. During the following years, however, this situation changed dramatically. The feedstock and technological transformations in the industry continued during the 1960s and 1970s. The percentage of organic chemicals produced from petroleum or natural gas rose to 70% in 1965; in 1970 the proportion rose to 90%. Since 1973 virtually all organic chemical products (95%) have been made from petroleum or natural gas. As a

Table 17.2-2 Key data for West Germany's chemical industry

Indicator	Unit	1950	1960	1970	1980	1990
Employees	1985 = 100	53.6	85.8	110.5	103.0	106.4
Turnover						
Index	1985 = 100	4.7	15.6	33.5	72.4	109.2
Share of manufacturing industries	in %	8.8	9.0	9.4	10.2	10.4
Production						
Index	1985 = 100	7.4	25.4	64.7	91.3	112.4
Real annual average growth rate	in %	20.0	14.4	5.6	– 3.6	2.7
Exports						
Volume	1985 = 100	1.4	8.1	24.1	61.5	109.8
Export ratio	1985 = 100	29.7	51.7	72.0	84.9	100.4
	in %	15.4	26.7	37.2	43.9	51.9
Imports						
Volume	1985 = 100	0.9	6.3	22.3	59.8	119.8
Import ratio	1985 = 100	19.7	37.9	64.7	80.1	106.3
	in %	7.5	14.4	24.6	30.5	40.5
Balance of trade	Million DM	664	3,417	8,673	20,840	31,409
	1985 = 100	2.0	10.5	26.6	63.9	96.2
Domestic demand	1985 = 100	5.0	17.3	36.1	75.2	107.9
Producer prices	1985 = 100	58.5	60.0	54.1	82.5	93.8

Sources: VCI; Federal Statistical Office

result of this transition, West German firms regained a competitive position in international markets. As a part of the industrial tradition of economic self-sufficiency in Germany, the coal-based chemical industry persisted in the face of the apparently overwhelming superiority of petroleum-based processes.

Producing petrochemicals meant that German chemists and industrialists had to begin to think in completely different ways. There were differences in terms of the optimum scale for an industrial plant, with petrochemical plants generally being much larger than coal-chemical facilities. In addition, the reliability of the feedstock supply became a much more difficult issue, because petrochemicals required reliance on overseas sources of oil rather than on domestic coal. It took time to alter habits that had led to the pre-war success, especially when the new alternative did not yet appear suitable for all types of organic chemical manufacturing. In the beginning of the 1950s, acetylene production, at that time the basic plastic component, expanded. Calcium carbide as intermediate stage from coal to plastics was proved to be no longer necessary, thermal cracking of petrol fractions now allowed new production processes. Olefins such as ethylene and propylene then proved to be products with easier access, lower costs and safer handling. In the following years there was a considerable increase in ethylene production. Between 1955 and 1965 ethylene production rose at an average annual growth rate of 34.6% (Table 17.2-3).

The brisk development of motorisation in Europe induced a rising demand for olefin products. Within a few years, coal as a raw material was nearly completely displaced by petrochemical processes; these provided the materials from which—through intermediate stages—plastics, synthetic fibres, solvents, washing agents, lacquer and varnish materials, fertilisers and pharmaceuticals could be derived.

Falling sales prices and rising demands on plastic quality and sophisticated products required steady rationalisation and innovation. In the plastics field, research efforts were reflected in progress in packaging (foils, polystyrene), advances in polymerisation (invention of low-pressure-processed polyethylene) and the development of new materials. Plastic production per capita in Germany rose from 1.8 kg in 1950 to 70 kg in 1972. Different kinds of plastic materials were used in both the building and construction industry and in the automobile, furniture and packaging industries. Capacities and further development for synthetic fibres production were extended, and production multiplied from the late 1950s until the early 1970s.

As a result of permanent research, pigments and dyes as traditional products of the German chemical industry reached international standards, synthetic lacquer resins displaced nearly all natural resins and oils. The pharmaceutical sector could build on the IG Farben foundations and soon gained a leading international position. At the beginning of the 1970s, Hoechst and Bayer ranked amongst the world's top producers in pharmaceuticals. Agrochemicals also utilised pre-war knowledge and took their part in the expanding market. As a consequence of increasing wealth and research efforts, detergents, washing agents and cosmetics showed high increases in the 1950s and 1960s.

Business strategy was aimed at securing a full provision of resources. The breakthrough in petrochemicals led to endeavours in ensuring the flow of oil as raw material. Thus German firms followed two strategies: first, backward integration of upstream industries or the acquisition of refineries (BASF); second, influencing location policy and thereby attracting refineries to the surroundings of already existing production facilities (Hoechst). As a reaction to the precarious situation of raw oil supply during the oil crisis, plans to build company-owned nuclear power plants emerged. The 1973 oil crisis led to heavy competition in the mineral oil market.

During the 1960s, the German chemical industry expanded on a world-wide scale, particularly to the United States, the North Sea countries and South America. The big chemical companies recognised that success required a presence in the US market, the world's biggest market for chemical products. Establishing joint ventures with powerful US firms and acquisition of firms with complementary or substitutive production programmes at the same time meant linking up with established sales organisations. The three big companies' world-wide expansion

Table 17.2-3 Ethylene production in West Germany

Country	Unit	1955	1965	1975
Germany	1,000 tons	35	686	3,360
	Share of Western Europe in %	21.8	35	28
United States	1,000 tons	1,380	4,340	12,000

Source: Teltschik, 1992

Table 17.2-4 Turnover of major West German chemical firms

Company	1955	1970	1985	1955-70	1970-85
	Million DM			Average annual growth rate (%)	
BASF	1,365	10,520	46,610	7.7	4.4
Bayer	1,437	11,129	45,926	7.7	4.1
Hoechst	1,270	11,592	42,722	9.1	3.7
Total	4,072	33,241	135,258	8.2	4.1

Source: Teltschik, 1992

led to steep increases in turnover. From 1955 to 1970 their nominal turnover rose at about double the rate of the following years from 1970 to 1985 (Table 17.2-4).

Thus the chemical industry was one of the most important growth industries in West Germany during the 1950s and 1960s. Despite considerable losses in capital stock and production capacity, and international isolation, it recovered quickly after the early 1950s. Between 1950 and 1970 the chemical industry's average annual growth rate (measured by production growth) reached 11.5% in real terms and thus exceeded the average of the total industrial sector, whose annual average growth rate was 7.3% over the same period. The chemical industry contributed considerably to the positive West German balance of trade. By the 1970s the three large firms, BASF, Bayer and Hoechst, ranked amongst the world's top five chemical producers. Their embrace of petrochemicals thus enabled the organic chemical industry to contribute substantially to West Germany's economic miracle and to the country's continuing economic success.

In 1973 the West German chemical industry had the largest export rate amongst the leading industrial nations with regard to total chemical production. In 1974 the three big IG Farben successors, Bayer, Hoechst and BASF, held the first three places in turnover amongst the Western chemical firms. Their turnover reached DM 58.8 billion or 6.7% of total world chemical turnover.

17.2.1.3. 1974–1982: Business slowdown

When Bayer, Hoechst and BASF had implemented their overseas expansion strategy and economic growth had simultaneously begun to slow down in the late 1960s, a new assessment and allotment of domestic production fields became a necessity. Broad diversification and thus a scattered use of resources had given German firms competitive disadvantages in comparison with US firms, whose strategy was concentration on special activities. Lesser product diversification, a lower vertical range of production and the comparatively homogeneous US domestic market gave comparative advantages to US companies.

German production programmes often comprised a multitude of different products and were—even at the same stage of production—more complicated and in most cases more cost-intensive than American production programmes, which concentrated on similar and complementary products. The lower vertical range of production, which means a lesser degree of product variation at different stages of product treatment, such as the separation of basic chemical products and processed products, created competitive advantages by concentrating on few production fields, whilst German companies kept—and still keep—producing a multitude of products at different stages with different requirements in manufacturing and procurement. Thus the three big German chemical companies held the top rank with regard to turnover, but in terms of profitability return on investment and capital structure, US companies clearly outranked German firms.

In 1973, 90% of the chemical industries' demand for raw materials was met by oil and its derivatives. Thus the drastically rising oil prices in the wake of the oil crisis had serious consequences on competition, leading to a crisis especially in the synthetic fibre industry. The unrestrained expansion of fibre capacities resulted in excess supplies that in combination with the oil crisis had negative effects. Shutdowns of several production facilities were the consequence drawn from this constellation of economic circumstances.

Demand growth also decelerated in the 1970s. This development was connected with some important shifts in the demand structure. In previous years growth had been driven by the steady development of new applications for chemical products. During the 1970s it proved increasingly difficult to find or develop new applications. Synthetic fibres and standard plastics were the most affected sectors. But decreasing sales necessitated reduced production in all parts of the chemical industry. With a capacity utilisation of just 70% and less short-term efficiency, consolidation proved necessary. Investment plans had to be postponed or cancelled.

17.2.1.4. 1983–1990: New challenges and perspectives

From an international viewpoint, the German chemical industry cluster still ranks amongst the most important in the world. It is in first place in exports and third place in turnover. But for some time it has shown the lowest growth rates in

Fig. 17.2-1 Growth rates of West Germany's chemical industry

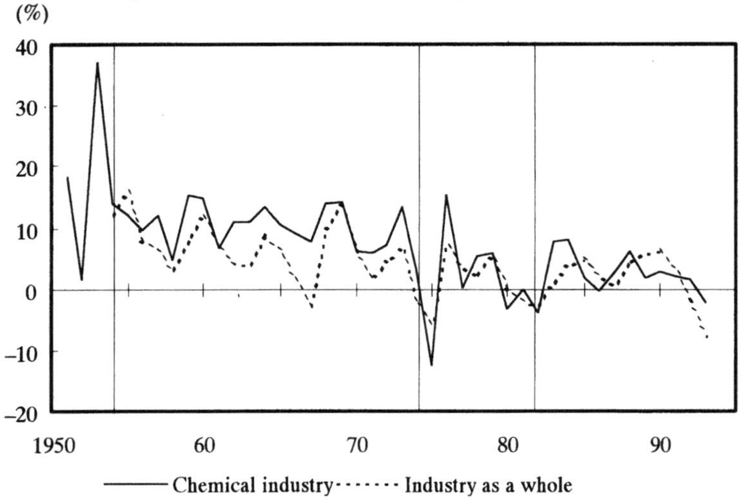

Note: Phases of development as discussed in this section are indicated by vertical lines.
Source: VCI, Ifo Institute

production and productivity amongst all leading chemical-producing nations, as well as significantly lower percentage profits.

The West German chemical industry undoubtedly grew faster than the industrial average up to the end of the 1970s, until change occurred in the early 1980s (Figure 17.2-1). With several years of lower growth than in industry as a whole, chemicals experienced a below-average development during the 1980s. Only from 1992 onwards did the chemical industry come off better than industry as a whole, but considering the fact that these growth rates are negative, the chemical industry can no longer be regarded as the growth industry it used to be up to the 1980s.

Structural change appeared in rudimentary form already in the 1980s. There were major shifts in investment and production structure. Domestic investment was replaced by foreign investment to some degree, and the basic chemical industry's production share of all the industry shrunk as the downstream processing industry grew. The share of all the chemical industry's domestic gross fixed-capital formation decreased from 66.8% in 1981 to 54.8% in 1992. Whilst there was a decline in the production of chemical elements, basic chemicals and intermediate products, production of consumer-related goods such as body- and health-care products increased. Further decreases were registered in chemical products for agricultural and packaging purposes. This appears to be part of the normal structural change within an advancing industrial sector.

At the beginning of the 1990s, minor shifts developed into a major structural crisis. Competition became increasingly global and new competitors from South-east Asia and Eastern Europe emerged. German companies slid into the position of cost-intensive and unwieldy producers. Additionally, the drifting of important downstream industries to Eastern European countries has made the situation more difficult today. With downstream industries such as textiles migrating abroad, demand, for example for synthetic fibres, has been reduced. Production declines were the consequence. Other purchasing sectors such as automotive, electrical and mechanical engineering industry find themselves facing structural change as well, and in the process of relocating their production facilities are also affecting the sales prospects of the German chemical industry.

Besides these economic developments, the chemical industry also faces technological challenges. In the field of basic technology, production processes are available globally today. Qualitative equivalent products can be produced more cheaply in Southeast Asia. Nowadays, competition domains that used to offer advantages are tending to shrink in Germany. Furthermore, the acceleration of world-wide innovation competition in the field of high-tech clearly reveals the chemical industry's weaknesses. This especially involves areas such as biotechnology and genetic engineering, and fields in the important purchasing sectors such as electronics and road vehicles.

In 1981 the German chemical industry spent about DM 6 billion, which was almost 22% of German industry's total R&D expenditures. It thus held second place amongst German industry sectors, exceeded only by electronics. In 1993 these expenditures amounted to nearly DM 11 billion, or a share of 18.2%, putting the chemical industry in the third place behind road vehicles and electrical engineering. The German chemical industry is one of the most research-intensive sectors of industry, but a growing share of R&D expenses is flowing into product cultivation, optimisation of processes, rationalisation and pollution control. Therefore, basic research capacities have been constrained and innovation frequency has decreased. In recent years, production shutdowns have been observed especially in the area of basic chemical production, owing to the growing competitive strength of foreign suppliers.

17.2.2. Market and demand trends

In terms of turnover, the German chemical industry holds the fourth place (after road vehicles, electrical engineering and mechanical engineering) in total German industry. In 1992 German chemical industry accounted for 17.1% of Western industrial countries' total exports in the chemical field, well ahead of the second-place United States and the third-place France, although the German share of world exports was reduced by extensive foreign investment. A sizable export surplus is discernible in all areas of production, amongst which processing specialty products traditionally hold by far the biggest share.

The analysis of export-import balances indicates that the German chemical industry is a net exporter (Table 17.2-5). Pharmaceuticals are the biggest net exporter with DM 4.6 billion, but the next two biggest export branches, plastics and organic compounds, both contribute a considerable share of about DM 4 billion each to the chemical industry's export surplus. The German chemical industry is a net exporter not only reckoned by product categories but also by regions. Three-quarters of trade relations are sited within Western Europe. The globalising competition in the market for chemicals is a serious challenge, but the industry maintains its international competitiveness through extended R&D and innovative product development.

The German chemical industry is closely interlinked with almost every other sector of industry, both as supplier and purchaser. Of total domestic sales, 50% meets demand for intermediate products, whilst the other half consists of genuine final products which again are used in other industrial sectors at a share of more than 80% (agrochemicals, plastics, pigments and dyes). Besides intra-industry sales and sales of consumer goods, three main buyer branches dominate the sales structure. The largest percentage share in sales at 16% is accounted for by the chemical industry itself. It is closely followed by the public-health sector at 13%, consumer goods at 11%, the car industry at 10% and the building and construction industry at 9% (Fig. 17.2-2). Recent years have brought a shift in the demand structure. The shares of the health-care sector (and thus the pharmaceutical industry) and the car industry have grown. Other industries such as textiles have become less important as purchasers of chemical products.

In the course of time, the production structure has shifted slightly towards consumer-related goods. For example, the production share of inorganic basic materials and chemicals decreased to less than half of the 1953 value up to 1993 (Table 17.2-6), whilst the share of consumer products was 1.6 times as high as it was thirty years before. Agrochemicals again lost almost 80% of their production share (Fig. 17.2-3). This development is based primarily on the steady growth of pharmaceuticals, which reached a production share of 20.1% in 1993. Whilst the share of plastic products grew until the 1980s, there was a falling-off in production in later years. Due to a partial market saturation which restricted demand mainly to replacement purposes—in contrast to previous years—the share of plastics and synthetic fibres stagnated or even shrank considerably.

As shown above, the structural crisis of buyer industries and relocation of production facilities to Eastern European or East Asian countries has seriously affected the chemical industry's prospects for domestic production. Besides a growing globalisation of competition, the German market is confronted with increasing imports from Asian and East European countries. With import structures being quite stable, the still increasing share of imports from Asia is widely felt (Table 17.2-7).

Table 17.2-5 Import and export of chemical products, 1992 (Germany)
(Unit: DM billion, %)

	Exports		Imports		Difference
By product category					
Plastics	14.4	(16.5%)	10.6	(18.5%)	3.8
Organic intermediates	16.9	(19.5%)	12.9	(22.6%)	4.0
Pharmaceuticals	11.8	(13.5%)	7.2	(12.6%)	4.6
Other chemicals	44.0	(50.5%)	26.4	(46.3%)	17.5
By region					
Europe, of which:	64.5	(74.1%)	46.5	(81.6%)	18.0
Middle/Eastern Europe	4.3	(4.9%)	1.8	(3.1%)	2.5
Asia, of which:	10.7	(12.3%)	4.4	(7.6%)	6.4
Japan	3.1	(3.6%)	2.5	(4.5%)	0.6
US and Canada	6.6	(7.5%)	5.4	(9.5%)	1.1
South America	1.8	(2.1%)	0.3	(0.5%)	1.5
Other regions	3.5	(4.0%)	0.4	(0.7%)	3.1
Total	87.1	(100%)	57.1	(100%)	30.0

Source: VCI

Fig. 17.2-2 Share of the chemical industry's sales by sector in the domestic market

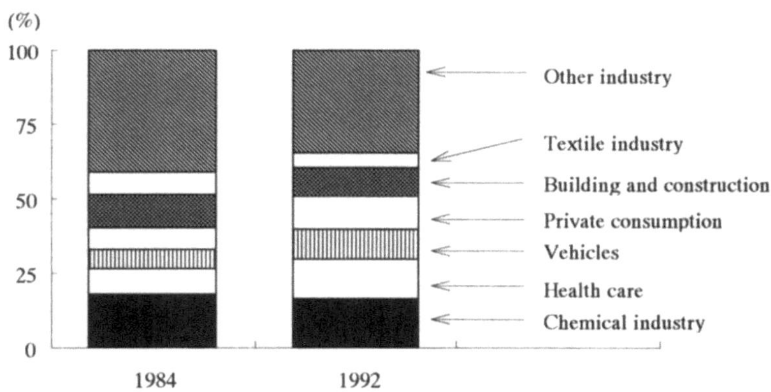

Source: VCI

Table 17.2-6 Production structure of West Germany's chemical industry (shares of nominal production value in %)

Product group	1953	1960	1970	1980	1990	1993
Inorganic intermediates	12.8	11.2	7.8	8.3	7.0	6.1
Organic intermediates	14.9	14.6	14.7	19.7	16.3	14.6
Chemical specialty products mainly for processing, thereof:	52.4	54.5	50.8	45.8	46.8	–
· Fertilisers, plant-protective and pest control agents	10.3	8.8	6.3	5.5	3.4	2.3
· Plastics and synthetic rubber	7.1	12.3	14.4	16.6	17.8	15.5
· Synthetic fibres	8.3	7.5	8.5	4.0	3.4	2.8
· Paints, varnishes and related products	13.0	12.4	12.0	10.1	12.6	11.4
· Adhesives	1.3	1.4	1.2	1.1	1.2	1.3
· Tannic acids, chemicals for construction industry	2.1	2.0	2.2	2.3	2.5	2.3
· Chemical products for construction industry	1.8	1.5	1.0	1.4	1.6	2.1
· Others	8.5	8.6	8.2	7.2	4.3	–
Chemical specialty products mainly for consumption, thereof:	19.9	19.7	26.7	26.2	29.9	–
· Pharmaceutical products	9.3	9.7	12.8	14.4	16.6	20.1
· Soaps and detergents	5.7	4.6	5.4	4.2	3.0	3.1
· Body care	2.4	2.9	4.6	4.2	5.3	6.2
· Chemical products for application in photography	1.5	1.7	1.7	1.5	2.0	2.1
· Chemical products for use in schools and offices	0.9	0.8	1.2	1.2	1.7	1.5
· Others	-	-	1.0	0.7	1.3	–
Total chemical products	100	100	100	100	100	100

Source: VCI; Federal Statistical Office, Fachserie 4, Reihe 3.1; Ifo calculations

Table 17.2-7 Regional structure of German chemical imports

Region of origin	Unit	1960	1970	1980	1990	1993
World	Million DM	2,776	9,881	26,493	53,052	46,615
EU	%	29.1	53.2	66.8	64.8	59.6
Other European countries	%	23.3	15.0	12.6	13.9	16.0
Asia, of which:	%	3.5	3.4	4.8	7.9	9.0
Japan	%	1.0	2.5	2.9	5.0	5.1
United States	%	29.9	18.4	9.3	8.9	10.0

Source: VCI

Figure 17.2-3 Production structure of chemical industry in West Germany

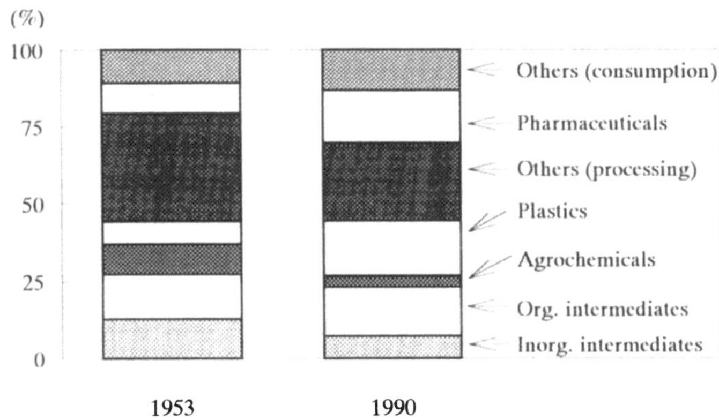

Source: VCI, Federal Statistical Office

17.2.3. Supply system and development trends

The German chemical industry is characterised by three significant competitors of comparable size and prospects. Together they hold a share in the chemical industry's turnover of about 60%. After the war, the IG Farben successors, Hoechst, Bayer and BASF, were once again dominant in the West German chemical industry and extremely powerful in international markets. The three corporations could to some degree act together through the chemical industry's trade association. But the fact that they were legally separate and consequently pursued different and competing interests marked a qualitative change in the structure of the chemical industry in Germany. Rather than tending towards monopoly, the industry is characterised by oligopoly. There are about fifty companies producing in the field of basic chemistry, but only three of them hold an outstanding position with yearly turnovers of over DM 40 billion each. Only four companies are situated in the mid-range of turnover between DM 3 and 15 billion. But 85% of companies range in turnover classes below DM 3 billion.

German rivals actively compete not only for sales but, equally important, for prestige, scientific and technical firsts, and the best personnel. German domestic competition is often not over price but over technology, product performance, reputation and service. In Germany, the top managers of many companies often have technical backgrounds, so technological competition arising from managers' orientation and goals is the impetus of improvement, even when the number of competitors is small.

In Germany, the shortage or absence of locally available raw materials such as coal and oil stimulated the breakthrough in synthetic materials. World War II accelerated such efforts, as shortages were common. Labour shortages and high German labour costs, combined with labour laws that make layoffs difficult, have long been important stimuli to process innovation. The lack of natural factors of production created pressures to move into more technically advanced industries such as the chemical sector. The need to import many raw materials has placed a premium on sophisticated processing. Thus Germany has a long tradition of world-class research in the field of chemistry. Pre-eminence in science and technology gave German firms early-mover advantages.

The return of German firms to respected and active membership in the international business community was a function of the re-achievement of sovereignty by the Federal Republic, but the economic performance engendered in part by re-joining the international community also helped stabilise and increase the power of the West German state.

Of great importance to the post-war chemical industry were the relationships between German firms and their counterparts in the United States and, to a lesser degree, Great Britain. BASF, Bayer and Hoechst were the most active firms and most significant in positioning the West German chemical industry to recapture its former status in technology and markets world-wide. Although in terms of technology the West German chemical industry lagged behind its American counterparts in some important areas, especially in petrochemistry, negotiations on technology transfers and on international co-operation between firms were not one-sided. West German firms had much to offer even to the Americans, and they had a great deal with which to bargain in their business with chemical industrialists in other countries. One of the subjects of technology transfer was German acetylene chemistry, which required hands-on experience and hence was not suitable for a knowledge transfer on the basis of patent licences. Many firms possessed the technological know-how that could secure their long-term competitiveness. One of the most important areas in this context was polyethylene production. German firms were able to deal with their foreign counterparts from a position of surprising strength and to move once again into technologies at the forefront of organic chemistry. The development of processes to produce low-pressure-processed polyethylene allowed them to participate in the polyethylene bonanza. The production process demanded less capital equipment and lower energy, and the product had properties markedly different from those of polyethylene produced by the high-pressure process.

The German chemical industry's surprisingly strong bargaining position so soon after the war was based in part on personal relationships that had remained intact despite the wartime interruption, as well as on some new, energetic personalities in the industry and a number of holdovers from the tradition of research and development at the IG Farbenindustrie AG. The astonishing demand for chemical products was also a factor.

17.2.4. Policy influence

As the German political and economic system is not marked by government intervention on behalf of its industries, the general influence of government policy on the chemical industry is not directly perceptible. In the early post-war years, the German chemical industry benefited from the Marshall Plan. As part of this aid, a technical-assistance programme was arranged which was meant to further European market integration and help Europe to catch up technologically.

The role of economic policy is mainly confined to restraints on the chemical industry in later years. Subsequent to a major shift in public opinion in the late 1960s and early 1970s, strict environmental protection regulations were established which regulated production processes and waste handling. Permission and licensing delays were caused by the increasing density of legal restrictions on production and research. Currently, the implementation of biotechnology and genetic engineering research results are being delayed by legal restrictions. From an international perspective, relatively high corporate tax burdens and labour costs have led to competition distortions. From an economic position, long-term competitive disadvantages in promising production areas may be a result of this short-sighted and restrictive position.

17.2.5. Evaluation

Like other industries, the West German chemical industry was severely affected by the war but recovered quickly in the post-war years. From 1960 to 1973, chemical production in the Federal Republic of Germany increased by more than three times and thus outperformed all other sectors of the economy. The chemical industry performed especially well in export markets, which were essential for the economic miracle. Due to the different stages of development, reconstruction and growth slowed down in some periods, but there was always a rising trend in economic variables (Fig. 17.2-4).

The primary impetus for the recovery of the major West German chemical firms was a combination of influences originating in the pre-1945 period. The forces of continuity—in equipment, technology, personnel and organisation—were, in the main, responsible for the chemical industry's recovery. But the results were not simply a return to the pre-war status quo. The strands of continuity and the recovery they helped bring about formed the preconditions for the resurgence of the IG Farben successors in the 1950s. The resurgence itself, however, was only possible in combination with vital changes within the German chemical industry.

Two changes in the chemical industry stand out above all others. First, the decartelisation of IG Farben left three powerful but competing companies that could pursue their paths to success between co-operation and competition. They have managed to compete vigorously against one another, even in foreign markets, without major crises. Competition amongst these three has stimulated creativity in marketing and technology, but has not caused destructive behaviour. The second major structural change in the large-scale West German chemical industry was the transition from self-sufficiency to dependence. Heavy dependence on foreign markets and supplies came to characterise the industry. The German chemical industry's success in sustaining and enhancing competitive advantage has been fuelled by pressure from factor disadvantages.

Fig. 17.2-4 Development of the chemical industry

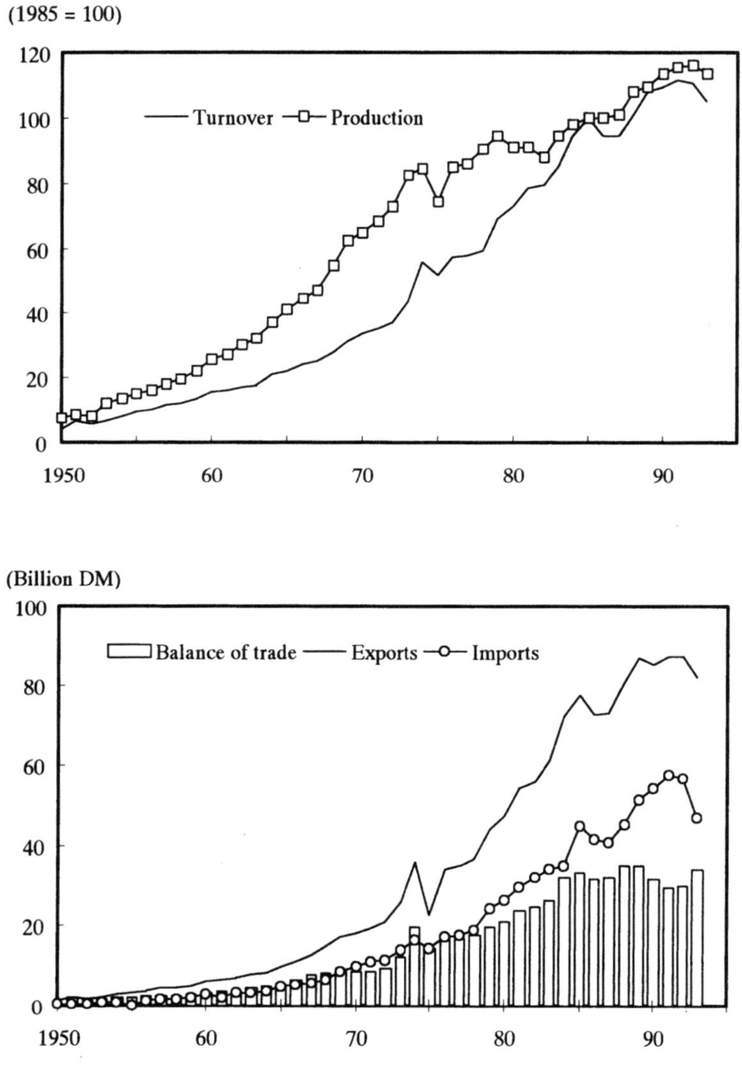

Source: VCI, Ifo calculations

However, one of the most important factors in the success of West German firms in the post-war period was a major technological change: the consistent transition from traditional, coal-based chemistry to modern petrochemical technology. In replacing coal with petroleum as its feedstock, the industry was able to produce goods in far greater quantities than would have been possible using only the traditional sources of coal-based feedstocks. Thus full participation by West German firms in the technological transformation of the international chemical industry was a key factor in West Germany's success from the 1950s to the present.

The main reason for economic success has been scientific research, which also differentiates the chemical industry from most other industries. Unlike heavy industries, the chemical industry was very research-intensive and thus contributed to the impressive West German economic performance in the post-war period. The need to invest enormous sums in research, to gamble on new products, to search continuously for improvements in products and processes requires a risk-taking ability that still challenges the German chemical industrialists today.

A framework of tough regulations and public opinion critical of some new technologies is hampering the industry's progress. Although the firms have responded to these disadvantages and have invested in foreign capacities for basic research, especially in the United States, there remains one crucial question on the perspectives of the German chemical industry: Will it be able to maintain its leading position as a technology leader in spite of domestic difficulties? At least in some areas of genetically engineered products, the German firms' global market share will be below the average of shares in other chemical products' markets.

17.3. Comparative Summary of the Chemical Industry

17.3.1. Industry description

Encompassing a very wide range of products, the chemical industry is a complex industrial branch consisting of a wide variety of sub-branches. On analysis of the sector's portfolio of activities, four types of chemical products and sub-branches can be distinguished.

The first product group is basic chemicals (commodities), which are highly capital-intensive and involve high-volume production. These commodities (fertilisers, polymers, etc.) have direct applications in other sectors (agriculture, plastics processing, etc.) or serve as synthesis intermediates. The key success factor for this sector is cost management.

A sector of growing importance is specialty chemicals, which involve a high degree of human capital investment, such as research and development (pharmaceuticals, etc.) or marketing (body and health care, etc.). The key factor in this sector is innovation.

The third product group is application chemicals, which are produced as a range of goods developed for specific user sectors (paper, leather, office products, etc.). In this field, customer support is of major importance, and this branch of the industry therefore tends to provide services along with its products.

The last product group consists of engineering and fine chemicals, which are typically produced by small- to medium-sized firms, not under their own brand-mark but as intermediates for larger groups, for whom they act as sub-contractors.

The importance of sub-sectors or product groups varies from country to country, but there are some sectors which are of considerable importance almost everywhere: basic chemicals, plastics and pharmaceuticals.

As a key industry providing a variety of intermediate and final products, the chemical industry is able to produce growth impulses. Because of its close intra-industry links, some adjustment pressure of upstream or downstream industries can increase if the chemical industry falters as an engine of growth.

Since the chemical industry's market position is connected very closely to the development of petrochemical processes, the analysis of the Japanese and German post-war chemical industry focuses on the basic chemical industry's development, which has laid the foundations for the economic performance of several downstream industries such as pharmaceuticals and plastics.

17.3.2. Industry development patterns in Japan and Germany

The analyses of the development of Japanese and German chemical industries show that they followed similar patterns with respect to structure of production, demand and purchasers. Both chemical industries went through the same stages. Coming from fertilisers and coal chemistry and moving on to genuine petrochemistry, demand structure now emphasises derived and processed products such as pharmaceuticals and plastics. Both industries reached high growth rates in the first post-war decades (Table 17.3-1) which indicated that they were perfect growth industries, but they faced crises in the early 1970s, when the post-war demand boom ebbed and the first oil crisis pushed feedstock prices. But at the same time, a comparison clearly indicates evident differences between German and Japanese realities and developments.

Whilst Germany was competitive in foreign markets through early technological research efforts and therefore could show a high export ratio, the Japanese chemical industry remained reliant on imports over a long period, both with respect to products as well as to technology. Thus the German chemical industry was able to reach international competitiveness much earlier.

This may be a result of the differing structures of the respective industries. The Japanese chemical industry was characterised by a large amount of small

Table 17.3-1 Average annual growth rates 1960 -1974

	Chemical industry	GNP
West Germany	9.7 %	4.6 %
France	7.4 %	5.7 %
Great Britain	6.0 %	2.9 %
United States	8.0 %	3.8 %
Japan	12.0 %	10.0 %

Source: Teltschik, 1992.

companies. The German chemical industry, however, had kept some of the huge pre-war organisation, so that a few oligopolistic market participants could serve a big market without losing incentives for competition. Because of different company sizes, the possibilities for capital accumulation and risk diversification, and therefore the potential for research and development, varied quite a lot.

With regard to company size, the Japanese market structure was established or preserved by MITI policy measures. In general, Japanese government policy in the first post-war decades focused on the chemical industry, which was considered a key industry supporting the development of other industries and thus was heavily promoted. Under MITI measures the Japanese chemical industry was able to grow rapidly, but powerful government intervention created some dependence in companies which adapted to investment and product programmes promising protection. The government tried to induce structural change by funding large-scale production sites. The Japanese firms—small by international standards—launched joint initiatives to set up common production facilities. In contrast, the German chemical industry was not able to rely on massive government support and although they had to face risks, they had the advantage of being completely free in their decision-making.

17.3.3. Present situation in Germany

In the early 1990s the chemical industry, especially in Western Europe, entered a stage of re-orientation because structural weaknesses clearly emerged. To preserve competitiveness, extensive structural measures had to be taken. The industry in future will be determined by globalising competition, the growing importance of Asian countries, the emerging of new competitors in opening markets such as China and Eastern Europe, a concentration of suppliers especially in pharmaceuticals, and the further shortening of innovation cycles, whilst R&D continues to grow more and more complex and costly in several production fields.

Germany alone accounts for more than 25% of the chemical industry within the European Union and clearly reflects the assets and limitations of the European chemical sector. There are strong companies with wide product variety and integration, but they have difficulty in following more innovative paths. Higher factor costs than elsewhere intensify the complicated competitive situation, which is additionally burdened by the required modernisation of chemical plants in eastern Germany.

The growth potential of the German chemical industry is far from exhausted and it is one of Europe's strongest sectors. However, owing to high factor costs, Eastern European competitors and a somewhat lesser commitment to innovation (especially in biotechnology) in comparison with the United States and Japan, it is expected that the international position of Germany will be slightly eroded. But in general, German companies are harvesting the fruits of restructuring schemes, such as concentration on a few promising fields, helped along by healthy economic conditions such as strengthening demand and a partial recovery of prices in 1994.

17.3.4. Present situation in Japan

The chemical industry in Japan is facing the problems connected with the opening of its internal market under international political pressures and a reassessment of the value of domestic products on the part of domestic customers. Besides the strong yen, the problem is more of a structural one of oversupply and excessive competition. Japanese firms have sought to compete in nearly every possible product area, and this has resulted in the production of small quantities of minor products and multiple deliveries that push up costs. The result can be booming imports, currently 10% of the domestic market, but which could take over 20% or even 30% of the market soon. Re-organisation and re-structuring are therefore key issues in Japan, too, and it seems that some companies are already cutting excess capacities through mergers and acquisitions. In chemicals, Japan has not played the role it has in other product sectors, but it can be expected that Japan's share will grow in the next few years, probably by concentrating on certain products.

Owing to its structural peculiarities, the Japanese chemical industry has focused on the domestic market and on intermediary goods intended for the electrical industry, automotive industry, etc. In these markets there has been strong competition which is advantageous for downstream industries.

As a result, the industry has been affected by the appreciation of the yen, inducing client industries to re-locate production. The Japanese chemical industry has to follow this development or to shift strategies towards R&D. A growing number of patent applications indicates the latter.

Despite less extensive export orientation, which led to competitive disadvantages in the past, the Japanese chemical industry has compensated with innovations (Table 17.3-2). In 1990 its share of world inventions amounted to 21.9% and therefore clearly outranked the West German chemical industry. As the largest market for chemical products the United States still held first place. To be

Table 17.3-2 Competitive position of producers in the market for chemical products (shares in %)

Country	Shares of OECD exports 1990	Shares of chemical exports in the country's total exports	Shares of world inventions[a)]
Germany (West)	17.4	11.0	17.7
Japan	6.0	4.9	21.9
US	13.9	11.3	35.2

a) Inventions with patent applications in at least two countries.

Source: OECD Statistics, EPIDOS/INPADOC, Ifo Institute

innovative, companies have to bear risks and dispose of sufficient capital stocks. True, industrialists in the United States are generally considered to be less averse to taking risks, but it seems that the Japanese chemical industry has become aware of these factors and will begin to move into new markets.

17.3.5. Industry outlook

World-wide there was and continues to be a trend towards larger companies with extended possibilities for R&D, and a great number of mergers and acquisitions have taken place on the basis that larger entities are in a better position to withstand international competition, at least in the commodity sectors. Because of company size, the top chemical firms are mostly Western Europe and American.

The lengthy process of restructuring is still topical and most firms are heading towards re-specialisation and a new approach to the market. The re-direction of production is primarily a switch from low-value-added products such as basic chemicals to specialised high value added, such as pharmaceuticals. The latter combine high value added with low sensitivity to business cycles.

From a qualitative viewpoint, two major changes are altering the orientation of activities in the chemical sector. First, biotechnology has the potential for allowing raw materials other than petroleum to be used and could in some cases replace chemical engineering techniques, thereby paving the way for a vast field of innovations, in particular genetic therapies. Second, the increased importance of ecological concerns is modifying the competitive landscape for various products, whilst also encouraging producers of chemicals to provide new products and services.

18. Steel Industry

18.1. Japan's Steel Industry

18.1.1. Industry Definition

The manufacturers that make up the Japanese steel industry can be classified, in accordance with their production methods, into blast furnace operators, electric furnace operators, rolling-mill operators and so on.

Electric furnace operators are further subdivided into ordinary steel makers and special steel makers, whilst rolling-mill operators are classified into re-rolled steel makers and other types of rolling-mill manufacturers. There are also steel processors, who take the sheet steel and rods produced by blast furnace and electric furnace steel works and process them into galvanised sheet, tin-plate sheet, pipes and other products.

The Japanese steel industry is thus composed of a variety of steel manufacturers and processors. This analysis will focus on blast-furnace steel manufacturers, which led post-war growth and development of the industry.

18.1.2. Post-war development of the steel industry

18.1.2.1. Post-war reconstruction (1945–1960)

Immediately after the end of World War II, there were only three operational blast furnaces left in Japan. Crude steel production in 1946 was 650,000 tons—barely 10% of the pre-war peak (Fig. 18.1-1). At the end of 1946 the Japanese government drew up plans for the gradual reconstruction of the war-ravaged steel industry under the "Priority Production System", which called for initial priority to be given to the recovery of coal and steel production. As a result, production of crude steel recovered to 6.78 million tons by fiscal 1951, about ten times the level in the immediate postwar period.

In 1950 Nippon Steel was broken up into two companies, Yawata Steel and Fuji Steel, under a policy adopted by the GHQ with the aim of eliminating excessive concentrations of economic power. However, production moved into high gear following the outbreak of hostilities on the Korean Peninsula in the same year. Thereafter, the Japanese steel industry went through two rationalisation

Fig. 18.1-1 Crude steel production (Pig-iron equivalent)

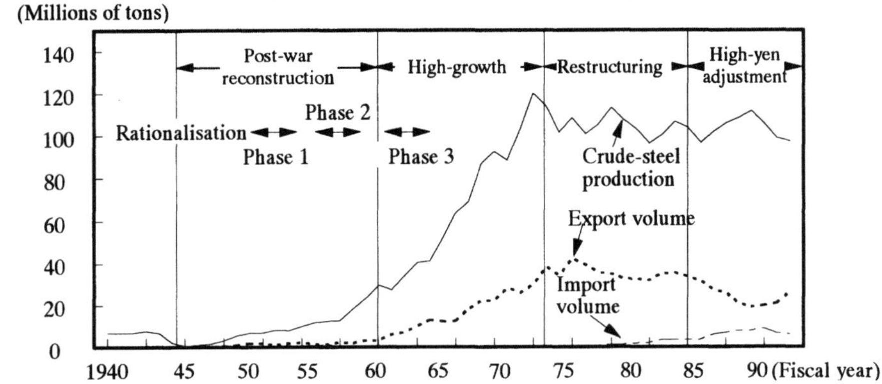

Source: Committee on Iron and Steel Statistics, Handbook for Iron and Steel Statistics

phases (1951–55 and 1956–60), resulting in the establishment of integrated production systems. The Japanese government assisted this process with support measures, including the provision of low-interest loans through the Japan Development Bank. Mass production under integrated production systems boosted crude steel output, which by fiscal 1953 had recovered to its pre-war peak of 8 million tons. By fiscal 1960, Japan was the world's fifth largest producer of crude steel with an output of 23.16 million tons.

18.1.2.2. High-growth period (1961–1973)

The first two rationalisation phases were followed by a third (1961–65), which resulted in the construction of large-scale integrated steelworks in coastal locations. The industry also began to export steel aggressively in order to earn the foreign currency needed to pay for imported iron ore, coal and other basic raw materials. By fiscal 1961 Japan had overtaken the United Kingdom to become the world's fourth largest steel producer, and in fiscal 1964 it moved into third place ahead of West Germany with an output of 40.5 million tons. In 1973 crude steel production peaked at 120 million tons. Having achieved excellent productivity and quality, the Japanese steel industry established itself as a key industry in Japan, and steel become known in Japan as the "rice of industry", meaning indispensable materials or necessities for industry.

18.1.2.3. Restructuring (1974–1984)

The oil crises had a major impact on the Japanese steel industry. Demand for steel fell as Japan's economic growth decelerated, and rising fuel prices drove up production costs. The steel industry faced other problems in the form of growing trade friction with the United States, as well as criticism over environmental pollution at home. The industry responded by implementing rationalisation plans, including the closure of surplus facilities and the reduction of employee numbers and the introduction of low-cost, energy-efficient production systems. The government meanwhile introduced industry support measures to encourage rationalisation using electric furnace operators producing ordinary steel. As a result, the Japanese steel industry was able to maintain and even strengthen its international competitiveness. Crude steel production was affected by the slump in domestic demand and declined after peaking out in fiscal 1973. This was followed by repeated rises and falls over the next several years until production reached a new peak of 106.5 million tons in fiscal 1977. In fiscal 1980 Japan became the world's second biggest steel producing nation after overtaking United States, which was unable to compete with Japan's export offensive.

18.1.2.4. Adapting to the high yen (1985–1994)

After 1985 the Japanese steel industry came under pressure from a rapidly appreciating yen. Faced with slackening domestic demand and a decline in exports and export profitability, the Japanese steel industry was forced into a new round of restructuring, and steel manufacturers turned to diversification. Although they achieved moderate success with ventures in such areas as chemicals, engineering, ceramics and LSI chips, none of these activities grew sufficiently enough to rank alongside steel making as core areas of business. As the Japanese economy experienced a bubble economy from 1987 onwards, steel manufacturers relaxed their rationalisation efforts and began reinvesting in their existing facilities. Since 1990, however, the industry has been hit by further rises in the value of the yen and by economic recession and has been forced anew to restructure its over capacities and workforce, as well. Crude steel production fell to 96.4 million tons in fiscal 1986, before recovering to 100 million ton level in fiscal 1987. Since fiscal 1991, it has remained below 100 million tons.

18.1.3. Demand trends

18.1.3.1. Contributions from domestic demand and exports

An analysis of demand trends in terms of orders received for ordinary steel shows that, during the post-war reconstruction period, the average annual growth in demand for steel was a 35.3%. A breakdown of the factors contributing to this demand statistic reveals that domestic demand was responsible for 31.5 percentage points, while exports were responsible for the remaining 3.8 percentage points (Fig. 18.1-2).

Fig. 18.1-2 Contribution of domestic and overseas demand to orders for ordinary steel

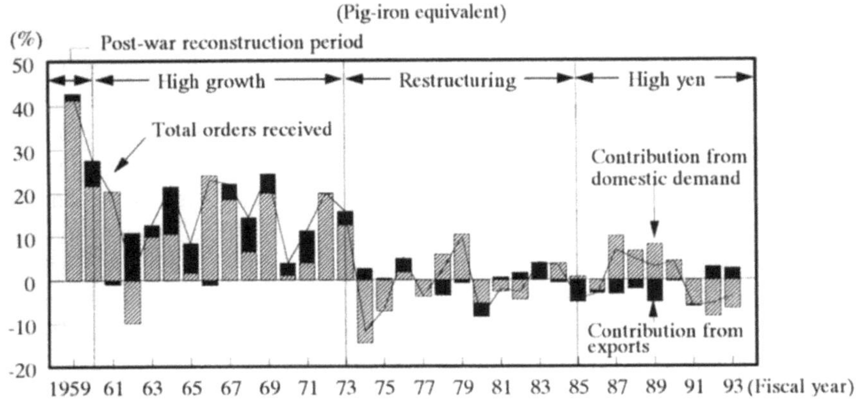

Source: Committee on Iron and Steel Statistics, Handbook for Iron and Steel Statistics

During the high-growth period, demand for steel grew by an average of 15.3% per annum, which was significantly higher than the economic growth rate. The contribution of domestic demand to this growth averaged 10.7 percentage points, reflecting the development of heavy and chemical industries. The improvement of the industry's international competitiveness was meanwhile paralleled by a rise in the growth contribution from exports, which averaged 4.6 percentage points.

In the subsequent restructuring period, the oil crises caused demand for steel to slump into negative growth averaging 1.2% per annum. The deceleration of the Japanese economy was reflected in domestic demand, which made a negative growth contribution averaging 1.2% per annum. The contribution from exports remained static because of the impact of voluntary restraints on export to the United States.

Demand for steel has remained flat in the high-yen adjustment period. The average annual growth contribution from domestic demand rose to 0.8% after 1987, primarily because of the bubble economy, whilst the average annual growth contribution from exports fell to minus 0.8%, owing to the appreciation of the yen in 1985 and since 1990.

18.1.3.2. Domestic demand trends

Domestic demand trends in each industry sector can be gauged from estimates of consumption of ordinary steel. The construction industry has consistently accounted for 40–50% of domestic steel consumption. The number two ranking in terms of steel consumption passed first from shipbuilding to industrial machinery and then to automobiles, reflecting changes in Japan's industrial structure (Fig. 18.1-3).

18.1.3.3. Export trends

An analysis of trends in export destinations for Japanese ordinary steel reveals that exports to North America increased from just a few percent of total exports in the 1950s to over 50% in the mid-1960s. However, North America's share subsequently began to decline, and by 1993 it had fallen to below 10% (Fig. 18.1-4). Exports to Southeast Asia, which had accounted for more than 50% of total exports during the 1950s, fell to less than 30% in the mid-1960s. They began

Fig. 18.1-3 Estimated shares of ordinary steel consumption by demand sector

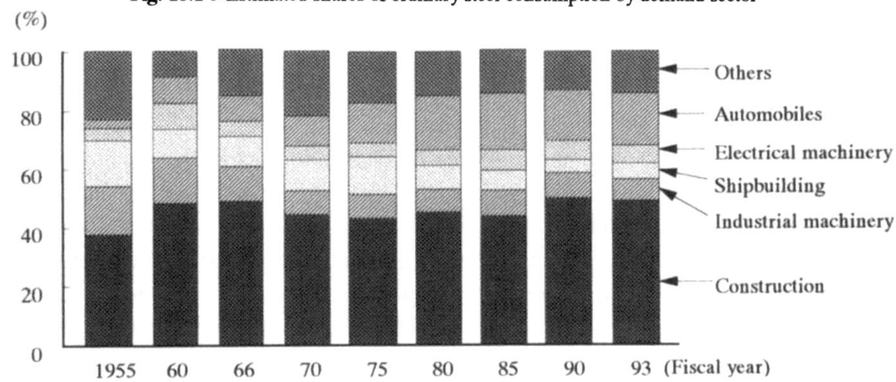

Source: Committee on Iron and Steel Statistics, Handbook for Iron and Steel Statistics

Fig. 18.1-4 Market distribution of ordinary steel exports (by volume)

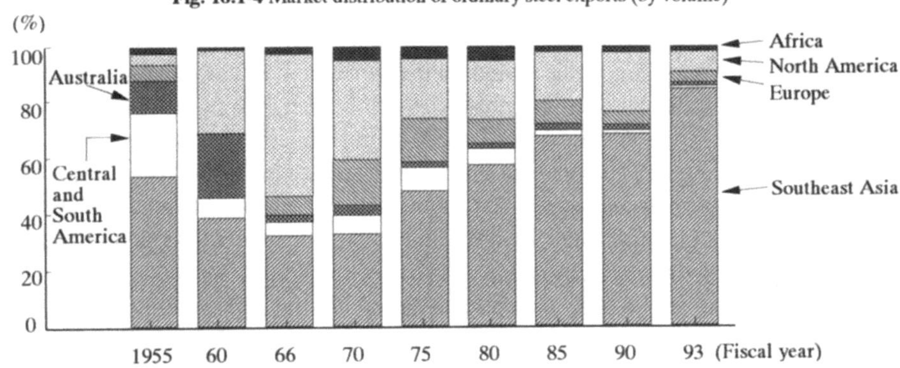

Source: Committee on Iron and Steel Statistics, Handbook for Iron and Steel Statistics

to increase dramatically in the 1970s and by 1993 had risen to over 80%. The 1970s were thus a period of transition when Southeast Asia replaced North America as the main export destination for Japanese ordinary steel.

This change is attributed to the escalation of trade friction between Japan and the United States. In the 1960s the US steel industry faced a sudden upsurge of competition from Japanese industry. Unable to compete on either price or quality, US manufacturers could not halt a rapid increase in imports from Japan. Trade friction between Japan and the United States intensified in the late 1960s, and moves to restrict imports gathered momentum. In 1969 the Japanese steel industry introduced the first voluntary restraint system on exports to the United States. In 1972 it was forced to implement a second voluntary restraint system.

18.1.4. Supply system and the structure of the industry

18.1.4.1. Construction of large-scale integrated steelworks in coastal locations

In the process of implementing three rationalisation plans, the Japanese steel industry built under government guidance a mass-production system based on large-scale integrated steel works in coastal locations. During the first rationalisation plan (1951–55), the industry concentrated on the repair of existing steelworks and the modernisation of rolling mills. Investment in ordinary steel production leapt from ¥42 billion during the three years of the initial plan to ¥128.2 billion over the revised five-year period. This was post-war Japan's first large-scale investment in industrial modernisation. To facilitate the implementation of the rationalisation plan, the government provided low-interest finance through the Japan Development Bank and established a special foreign currency lending facilities in the Bank of Japan under the foreign currency allocation system. It also introduced foreign funds through World Bank loans for the first time in the post-war era.

In 1950 Kawasaki Steel, which was then a privately owned open-hearth steel maker, adopted a unique strategy by announcing plans to build Japan's first integrated steel works. Since this plan would require capital investment far greater than the capital of a small open-hearth steel manufacturer, it was strongly opposed by the Bank of Japan and integrated steel manufacturers. Concerned about its future without being able to carry out upstream processes in its own blast furnaces, Kawasaki Steel pushed ahead with the plan. It thus became the first of several open-hearth steel manufacturers to move into integrated steel production. As a result, the second rationalisation plan (1956–60) was characterised not only by capital investment of the type undertaken during the first phase but also by an emphasis on the introduction of large-scale blast furnaces, LD converters and continuous hot-rolling mills, and on the development of integrated production capabilities at existing plants. Total investment in ordinary steel production facilities reached ¥545.9 billion, 4.5 times higher than under the first rationalisation plan. Steel production capacity also rose sharply, from 11.28 million tons at the end of 1955 to 28.19 million tons at the end of 1960.

During the third rationalisation plan (1961–65), priority was given to the construction of large-scale integrated steel works in coastal locations, equipped with computer systems of the latest model. Investment in production facilities for ordinary steel during this period totalled ¥859.2 billion. The coastal locations of the large-scale integrated steel works enabled steel manufacturers to establish mass-production systems, based on low-cost imports of high-quality raw materials and as a result to establish the world's best standards in productivity as well as in quality.

A number of new steel works were built, including Kawasaki Steel's Chiba works, Sumitomo Metal's Wakayama works, Kobe Steel's Nada works, Yawata Steel's Tobata works, and NKK's works at Mizue. By the end of 1965, steel output had risen to 53.26 million tons, 1.9 times higher than the level at the end of 1960.

18.1.4.2. Introduction of foreign technology

Capital investment under the three rationalisation plans enabled the Japanese steel industry to take advantage of world-class technical innovation by aggressively importing machinery and technology from overseas. During the first rationalisation plan, the industry modernised its rolling mills by replacing its outdated pull-over mills with continuous rolling mills (hot-strip mills). About 60% of the new machinery was imported. There was also considerable importation of facility operation technology, and in 1951 Yawata Steel and Fuji Steel began to introduce continuous rolling-mill operation technology.

Under the second rationalisation plan, the importation of machinery decelerated whilst technology imports doubled. The most obvious example was the LD converter method, which provided approximately ten times more steel-production capacity than the old open-hearth method. Japanese manufacturers made their own improvements to the LD converter method, which was introduced by Yawata Steel in 1957 and by NKK in 1958. During the high-growth period, Japanese steel works phased out their open-hearth furnaces and replaced them with enhanced LD converters. Several factors contributed to the demise of the open-hearth method, such as the problem of ensuring a steady supply of scrap iron, which was the basic raw material for open-hearth furnaces, and the instability of scrap iron prices, as well as high fuel and construction costs. Japanese steel manufacturers competed with each other in this period for introducing the hot-strip mill, another revolutionary technology equal to the LD converter, because this technology improved the productivity of rolling processes. As a result, Japan became the world's second-biggest nation possessing such mills after the United States.

These innovations not only helped the Japanese steel industry to achieve world leadership in productivity and quality, but also stimulated shipbuilding, machine manufacturing and other assembly and processing industries to invest in the modernisation of their own production lines. New technology also ensured reliable supplies of intermediate goods to the construction and civil engineering industries.

From the post-war reconstruction period through to the high-growth period, production by converters rose from 3.7% of total production in fiscal 1950 to 80.8% in fiscal 1973, whilst that of open-hearth furnaces fell from 80.7% to just 1.5% during the same period. Steel production using open-hearth furnaces effectively ceased in the late 1970s. The production share of electric furnaces remained fairly constant at 15.7% in fiscal 1950 and 17.8% in fiscal 1973.

18.1.4.3. Securing stable supplies of basic raw materials

The development of integrated production facilities by the Japanese steel industry has been paralleled by its efforts to secure stable supplies of basic raw materials. The Japanese steel industry learned a bitter lesson by experiencing major problems during World War II. Although only 20% of its facilities were damaged during the war, its import routes for iron ore and coking coal from China were totally cut off, leading to a dramatic decline in production. After the war, however, the GHQ fortunately permitted the importation of fuel oil and Sakhalin coal in 1947, and in the following year, Japan was allowed to import coal from the United States and Canada, and iron ore from China. Japanese steel manufacturers were, meanwhile, concluding their own long-term purchase agreements with overseas producers of basic materials and expanding their supply routes to include Malaysia, the Philippines, Africa and South America. Australia became a particularly important supplier for Japan, because its proximity meant lower transportation costs. By locating their large-scale integrated steel works in coastal areas as well as by building special-purpose bulk cargo ships, Japanese steel makers were able to lower transportation costs and to establish stable supply systems for low-cost raw materials.

18.1.4.4. Cost reduction and energy conservation

The rise in energy prices following the oil crises caused the management priorities of Japanese steel manufacturers to shift from the improvement of facility productivity through mass production to cost reduction and energy conservation through process improvements. Measures introduced by the industry included oil-less operation, the recovery of waste gas and heat from converters, the use of continuous casting, and the automation of control systems. As a result of these efforts, the Japanese steel industry succeeded in maintaining world leadership in facility productivity and quality. Continuous casting technology, which was introduced from the United States in 1955 by Sumitomo Metal, played a particularly important role. This revolutionary technology brought dramatic improvements in facility productivity, since it eliminated the need for blooming during the steel production process. It was used increasingly after the oil crises, and by 1980 the proportion of steel produced by means of continuous casting in Japan was the highest in the world at 60%, compared with 45% in West Germany, and by 1983 the ratio had climbed to 90%.

18.1.4.5. Improvement of value added

After the oil crises, the focus of production in the Japanese steel industry shifted from general-purpose products to high value-added items, such as thin sheet and surface-treated sheet steel. The uptrend in the value added of steel can be gauged from movement in the real value of steel prices (fiscal 1971=100), which rose rapidly after the second oil crisis to peak at 125.6 in fiscal 1982. After 1985, the appreciation of the yen caused the index to fall back to its fiscal 1971 value in fiscal 1987. However, in fiscal 1991 it had recovered to 122.3, comparable to the fiscal 1982 peak (Fig. 18.1-5). One reason for this movement is the fact that the Japanese steel industry responded to declining demand by switching to business strategies based on quality rather than quantity, at a time when processing and assembly industries, such as the automobile industry, needed high value-added steel products to cope with the environmental changes that arose after the oil crises.

18.1.4.6. Exports and licensing of technology

The decline in demand for steel after the oil crises also had an impact on the aggressive exporting activities of the Japanese steel industry. During the high-growth period, priority was given to exporting as a means of earning the foreign

Fig. 18.1-5 Steel prices (real value)

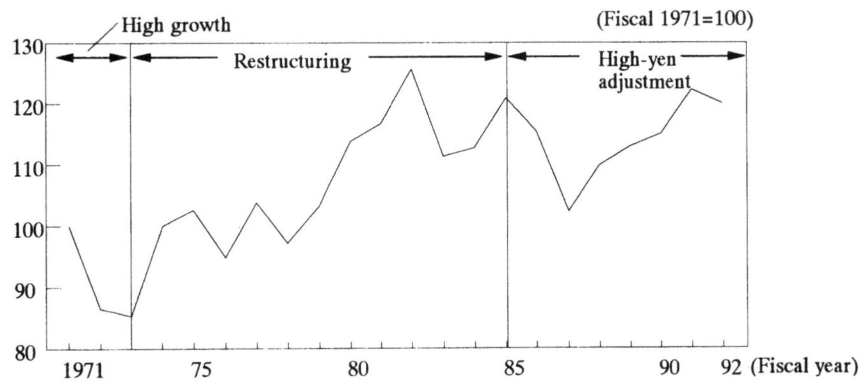

Note: Steel price (¥/ton) = (Value of shipments of manufactured goods, etc. / Volume of crude steel production) / Wholesale price index

Sources: MITI, Table of Industrial Statistics; Tekko Shinbun, Yearbook of Iron and Steel currency needed to import basic raw materials. Japanese steel manufacturers steadily expanded their export volumes by providing unrivalled quality and by adhering strictly to delivery dates. Foreign markets thus contributed as much to the industry's development as the domestic market. After the oil crises, however, the Japanese steel industry was forced to introduce voluntary export restraints. As a result, the focus shifted from exporting to licensing of technology and the acquisition of equity stakes in foreign companies. The process began with NKK's acquisition of a stake in a US company, National Steel, in 1984. This was followed by the establishment of a number of joint ventures by Japanese steel manufactures.

18.1.4.7. Separation of production and distribution

The Japanese steel industry improved efficiency in the field of distribution by establishing a unique system, the most important feature of which is the total separation of production and distribution operations. In the Japanese steel industry, the importation of basic raw materials and the sale of steel products are generally handled by general trading firms (*sogo-shosha*) and specialised trading companies. Direct trading of steel is limited to railway companies and some government and public agencies, with sales to these groups accounting for only about 5% of total steel shipment volume. Steel is sold through general and specialised trading companies in two ways: direct deliveries to large- and medium-volume users and sales through specified agents (secondary wholesalers) to small-volume and regional users. Depending on the end users' requirements, steel sold through general and specialised trading companies may be processed by shearers, slitters and other processing companies before final delivery. The Japanese steel industry has established a division of labour involving steel manufacturers, trading companies, processors and specified agencies, and encompassing all aspects of production and distribution, from the importation of basic raw materials to the distribution and delivery of steel. This system has brought many benefits, including fine-tuned sales activities, strict adherence to delivery dates and the improvement in value added. It has been highly praised by end users both in Japan and overseas.

18.1.5. Role of industrial policy in industry development

18.1.5.1. Industrial policy in the post-war reconstruction period

Industrial policy in the post-war reconstruction period focused initially on leading the Japanese steel industry quickly towards recovery through the "Priority Production System". The focus then shifted to the development and protection of the industry. Through two rationalisation plans, the government guided the industry on prices, production volumes and capital investment, and provided the driving force for the development of integrated production facilities. The separation of Nippon Steel, which was a semi-governmental integrated steel

Fig. 18.1-6 Manufacturers' shares of crude-steel production

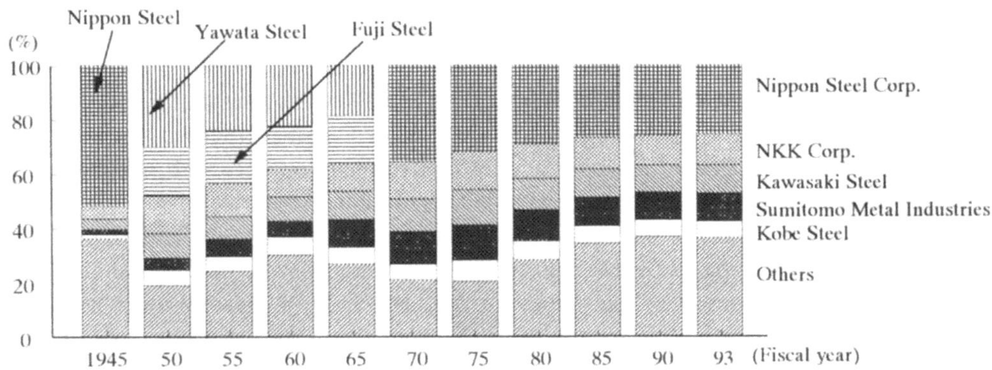

Notes: 1. Nihon Seitetsu was broken up into Yawata Steel and Fuji Steel in 1950. In 1970 Yawata Steel and Fuji Steel merged to form Nippon Steel Corp.
2. Electric-furnace steel producers are included in "Others".

Sources: Japan Iron and Steel Federation, Survey of Iron and Steel Statistics

manufacturer, into two private corporations (Yawata Steel and Fuji Steel) in 1950 spurred a shift to integrated steel production by open-hearth steel manufacturers. It also transformed the cooperative market of the pre-war steel industry into a competitive market, consisting of three front-runners (Yawata Steel, Fuji Steel and NKK) and three latecomers (Kawasaki Steel, Sumitomo Metal and Kobe Steel).

The consistent priority for industrial policy during this period was the development and protection of the industry through direct government intervention. This approach made a major contribution to the establishment of an industry base and the subsequent transition to a competitive market (Fig. 18.1-6).

18.1.5.2. Industrial policy in the high-growth period

Industrial policy in Japan's high-growth period provided the driving force for the development of large-scale integrated steel works in coastal locations under the third rationalisation plan. The low productivity of US manufacturers had the effect of stimulating exports to the US market, and Japan emerged as one of the world's biggest steel-producing nations. Within a short time span, the Japanese steel industry was hit in 1965 by the deepest recession of the post-war era. Industrial policy during this period called for the merger of companies, the sharing of facilities through rotated or joint capital investment, and the government also sought to tighten its guidance on prices, production volumes and capital investment. However, since industrial policy after the second rationalisation plan was based on administrative guidance, which had lesser power of compulsion, the government was unable to prevent the three front-runners and the three latecomers from competing for market share. Recognising the limited effectiveness of its industrial policy, the government placed its hopes for the restoration of industry order by the leadership of Nippon Steel, which was formed in 1970 through the merger of Yawata Steel and Fuji Steel. The merger went ahead despite a negative recommendation by the Fair Trade Commission in 1968. As a result, the focus of government policy towards the Japanese steel industry shifted from a competitive market to a co-operative market made up of five manufacturers with integrated production facilities and Nippon Steel as industry leader.

Industrial policy in this period made a major contribution to the international standing of the Japanese steel industry. The declining power of administrative guidance meant, however, that hopes for the restoration of industry order were placed in the leadership of Nippon Steel. This approach helped to restore order as far as prices, production volumes and capital investment were concerned, but it also led to a sudden shift towards co-operation within the industry.

18.1.5.3. Industrial policy since restructuring

Industrial policy since the restructuring period has focused on adaptation to a post-oil crises environment through rationalisation, cost reduction and energy conservation. This approach has made a significant contribution to the maintenance and enhancement of the Japanese steel industry's international competitiveness. Of particular importance was the establishment of anti-depression cartels under the Specified Recession Industry Stabilising Temporary Measures Law (1978) and Specified Industry Structure Improvement Temporary Measures Law (1983) for electric-furnace steel makers, whose price competitiveness was eroded by rising electric power charges. The price competitiveness of electric-furnace steel makers was rapidly restored thanks to the subsequent stabilisation of crude oil and scrap iron prices. Industrial policy during the bubble economy that began in 1987, however, allowed steel manufacturers to suspend rationalisation efforts. As a result, the Japanese steel industry has been forced to undertake another round of rationalisation owing to further rises in the value of the yen and the onset of economic stagnation since 1990.

Whilst industrial policy encouraged restructuring and contributed to the maintenance and reinforcement of international competitiveness during this period, the increasing shift towards cooperation in the Japanese steel industry since restructuring has prevented the completion of the rationalisation process. This has clearly had a negative impact on the industry's development, including stagnant and lukewarm efforts for restructuring.

18.1.6. Key factors behind industry development

18.1.6.1. Receptiveness to technical innovation

Industrial policy provided the driving force for the development of the Japanese steel industry during the post-war reconstruction period. It also played a significant role in the industry's development in the subsequent high-growth period, enabling Japan to maintain and enhance its status as one of the world's leading steel-producing nations. Industrial policy was not the only factor that helped the Japanese steel industry to achieve the growth unequalled in any other countries. Another key factor was the industry's ability to assimilate new technology. Technical innovation has brought a wide range of benefits to the Japanese steel industry, including not only the improvement of facility productivity, but also stable access to basic raw materials, increased value added and the improvement of user services. These achievements can be attributed to the fact that the Japanese steel industry was able to make effective use of existing production facilities, which suffered only light war damage, and technology accumulated from the pre-war period, whilst introducing foreign technology. The industry's subsequent development thus benefited from its possession of facilities and know-how, enabling it to assimilate the world's most advanced technology.

18.1.6.2. Vitality of private enterprise

A second factor behind the industry's success is the vitality of private enterprise. This is typically demonstrated by the role played by Kawasaki Steel, a privately owned open-hearth steel manufacturer, in the post-war reconstruction period. Despite strong opposition from integrated steel manufacturers and the Bank of Japan, Kawasaki Steel built Japan's first integrated production steel works, thereby stimulating other open-hearth manufacturers to establish integrated production systems. Yawata Steel and NKK, meanwhile, led the aggressive introduction of foreign technologies during the same period, such as LD converters and hot-strip mills, and subsequently pioneered the spread of those technologies in Japan. This commitment to aggressive management on the part of private-sector companies can be traced to the vigorous entrepreneurial spirit that emerged in Japan's post-war steel industry, thanks to the post-war split of Nippon Steel and the outbreak of the Korean War. The powerful entrepreneurial spirit of business proprietors in the steel industry played an important role in the industry's development.

18.1.6.3. Flexible adjustment to environmental change

A third factor that has contributed to the success of the Japanese steel industry is the industry's ability to adapt flexibly to environmental change. In the post-war reconstruction and high-growth periods, the industry used imported technology and machinery to create integrated production systems suited to Japanese conditions through the construction of plants in coastal locations. As a result, Japan became the world's most powerful steel-producing nation. Since the restructuring period, the Japanese steel industry has adapted to the environmental changes caused by the oil crises by promoting energy conservation and cost-cutting, increasing the value added of steel, and forming relationships with foreign companies based on the supply of technology or the acquisition of equity stakes. These efforts have enabled the industry to maintain an industry structure based on five integrated manufacturers with integrated production facilities. This has been achieved despite the sometimes negative impact of industrial policy, and can be attributed to the ability of the Japanese steel industry to overcome various problems by adapting flexibly to changing conditions and environments. The efforts of companies to cope with changes have thus contributed to the industry's development.

18.2. Germany's Steel Industry

18.2.1. Industry definition

The steel industry is traditionally described as one of the key industries of an economy. In the industrialised countries, however, it is increasingly losing this role to new high-tech industries such as micro-electronics. However, if one considers the fact that around half of the types of steel on the market are newer than six years old (Vondran, 1995a), steel can still be seen as a modern and innovative product.

Because of its membership in the European Coal and Steel Community (ECSC) and the European Union (EU), an investigation into the German steel industry must also take into account the European context. Therefore, this chapter will apply the distinction used by the European Commission (cf. Commission of the European Communities, 1991), which in contrast to the usual German and international definition does not include the manufacture of tubes. According to this definition, "the steel industry encompasses steel production from raw-materials processing to the production of finished and final rolled-steel products" and "covers the operations of coke manufacture, ore preparation, pig-iron processing in blast furnaces, steel processing from pig-iron in converters, steel processing from scrap in electric furnaces, continuous casting and/or hot rolling of semi-finished products, hot rolling of long and flat products, cold rolling of flat products, and metal and organic coatings".

18.2.2. Important periods in the growth and development of the German steel industry

Over the entire period under investigation from 1945 to 1995 the German steel industry has lost a great deal of importance within the economy as a whole. The reasons for this are to be found in particular in the fact that on the one hand, manufacturing industry has become less significant in comparison with the service sector and, on the other hand, the steel industry has become less significant within the manufacturing industry. This can also be seen from the fact that in the forty years between 1950 and 1990, the proportion of manufacturing jobs accounted for by the German iron-and-steel-producing industry fell from 4.6% to 2.5%, and its share of turnover fell from 6.2% to 2.7%.

18.2.2.1. 1945–1960: Reconstruction phase

Immediately after the end of World War II, steel companies were placed under the direct control of the Allies because of their great importance to industry and the wartime economy. Recovery from the consequences of war was constrained until around 1950 by means of dismantling and output limitations (maximum crude steel production of 5.8 million tons), which were later relaxed somewhat. In addition, the Allies weakened the productive capacity of the German steel industry by restructuring the previously seven groups into twenty-three unit companies in order to break up the traditionally integrated structures linking the raw material base, steel production and steel processing. This created considerable inefficiencies. On 23 July 1953, France, Belgium, the Netherlands, Luxembourg, Italy and the Federal Republic of Germany founded the ECSC, which in the future was to exert a decisive influence on the German steel industry. As a result, the deconcentration measures already implemented could gradually be reversed and capacity restrictions lifted.

Although the German steel industry steadily expanded since then—in 1954 production returned to the pre-war level—in the period from 1950 to 1960, imports of some types of steel were necessary to meet the constantly rising demand resulting from the extraordinarily strong growth in demand for capital goods during the Federal Republic's "economic miracle". During this period, the German steel industry can clearly be characterised as a supplier's market. Its growth rates were higher than the economy as a whole. The reconstruction phase ended at the beginning of the 1960s.

Between 1947 and 1960, production of crude steel rose from around 3 million to over 34 million tons, with the German share of world crude steel production reaching a post-war record of 9.8% in 1960 from a starting point in 1947 of 2.3% (Table 18.2-1, Fig. 18.2-1). Capacity was utilised to a high level; at the same time the numbers employed rose sharply to over 417,000 (Fig. 18.2-2). The post-war peak of 420,568 was reached in 1961. Since then, employment has been dropping almost continuously.

Figure 18.2-1 Production and capacity of crude steel

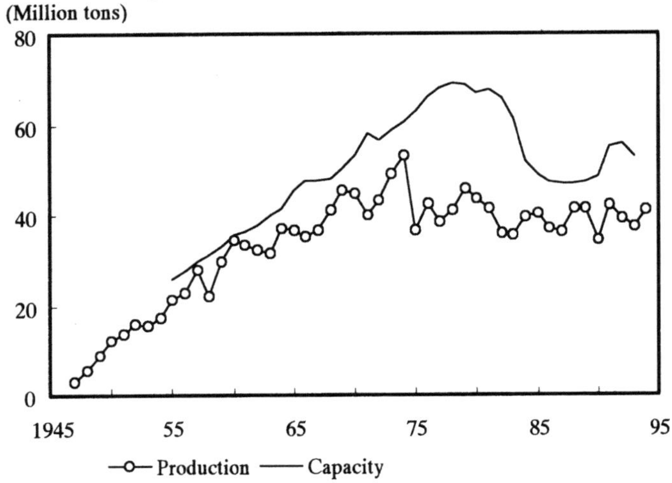

Source: EUROSTAT

Fig. 18.2-2 Employment and capacity utilisation

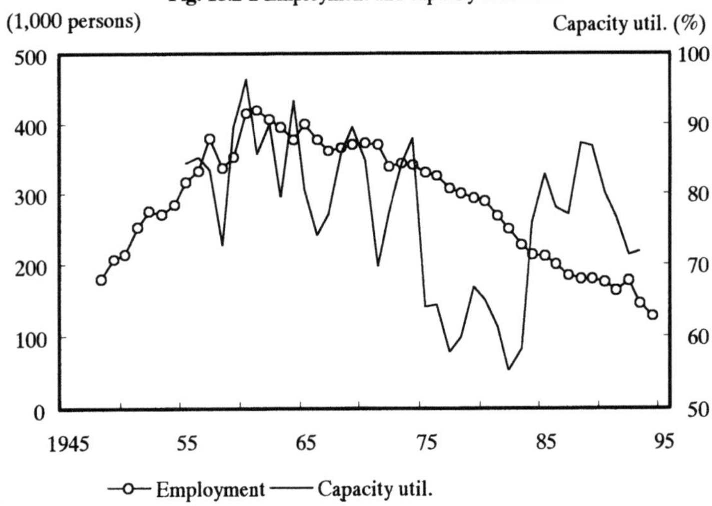

Source: EUROSTAT, Wirtschaftsvereinigung Stahl, Ifo calculations

18.2.2.2. 1961–1974: Expansion phase

Because of the enormous investments in the 1950s, the German steel industry was able to catch up in the early 1960s with the international leaders in terms of technology, and it achieved a significant position among the countries of the ECSC.

Nevertheless, because of less demand for capital goods between 1961 and 1967, the industry recorded significantly lower rates of growth and was tending towards stagnation. As a consequence of rapid expansion of capacity, the level of utilisation dropped (Figs. 18.2-1, 18.2-2). Companies reacted to this by modernising their production capacity and rationalising, so as to be able to hold their own on the world market in spite of the increasing competition from traditional receiver countries. Between 1961 and 1967 crude steel production grew by only 9.8% to 36.7 million tons. The numbers of employed persons fell to around 361,000 and the share of the world market dropped to 7.4% (Table 18.2-1, Figs. 18.2-1, 18.2-2). Japan overtook German crude steel production in 1964.

In contrast, the period 1968–74 saw growth of boom proportions. After the first recession in the Federal Republic there was a clear economic upturn, bringing with it increased demand for capital goods, motor vehicles and construction work, thereby sharply increasing the consumption of steel. Stimulated by the boom, the high profits, and positive forecasts for steel consumption up to the year 2000, producers expanded production and invested in new processes (oxygen steel, continuous casting). At the same time, obsolete plants were shut down. At the height of the world-wide steel boom in 1974, the German steel industry reached a peak production of 53.2 million tons (Table 18.2-1, Figs. 18.2-1, 18.2-2), which represented an increase in crude steel production since 1967 of almost 45%. At 7.5%, the 1967 share of the world market was just exceeded. Employment, however, fell further to under 344,000.

18.2.2.3. 1975–1987: Crisis phase

As a consequence of the first oil crisis, the economy went into a deep recession in 1974 and 1975. This recession dragged the steel industry down with it, as demand amongst purchasers dropped, ending the steel boom of the post-war period. What at first had been seen as a temporary slump in demand soon turned out to be the beginning of a structural change and thus of the steel crisis, for demand also reduced as a result of improved qualities of steel, the great technological progress in the production and use of steel, and the enhanced potential for substitution with materials such as plastics, aluminium, ceramics, etc. At the same time, pressure from imports grew because of the increasing number of steel-producing countries, and exports proved more difficult. Within just three years crude steel production in the Federal Republic fell by over 26% to below 39 million tons. At the same time, however, capacity increased further (1977: 67.7 million tons), because of, amongst other things, positive forecasts of demand, so that capacity utilisation fell and overcapacity increased (Fig. 18.2-1). For this reason, the German steel industry saw itself forced to adapt its capacity. By the end of the 1970s, a gradual recovery of the steel market was taking place before a return to recession in 1980. As a consequence, the EC considered it necessary to declare a state of manifest crisis, as provided for in the ECSC Treaty, in order to regulate the market. Compulsory minimum prices and production quotas were set.

This was accompanied by an increase in national and EC subsidies, tolerated by the EC on the condition that production capacity be reduced.

In the period from 1983 to 1987, strong demand for capital goods brought about a marked stabilisation of the German steel industry, albeit from an obviously lower starting point. The restructuring measures introduced also played a part in this. The reduction of overcapacity was actually only tackled from 1982 with massive shutdowns, and it continued until 1987 in an effort to close the still wide gap between production capability and demand (Fig. 18.2-1).

Since 1975, German crude steel production has hovered around 40 million tons per year. The reduction in employment, which was observed as early as 1962, did not at first accelerate after the beginning of the recession, since this was viewed as a cyclical phenomenon (average 1974–80: –2.9%). From 1980 a markedly higher annual drop in employment was seen (average 1980–84: –7.0%; 1984 level: 215,453). Between 1974 and 1987, the world market share of German crude steel production dropped from 7.5% to 4.9% (Table 18.2-1, Figs. 18.2-1, 18.2-2).

18.2.2.4. 1988–1995: Stabilisation phase

In 1988, the last of the EC crisis measures were discontinued and companies could once again act more freely on the steel market. After the end of the re-unification boom in 1992, the former West German economy went into recession, which also affected the steel industry. It was necessary to close down and privatise the partly and very obsolete production sites in the new *Länder*. Since 1993, decisions have been taken to shut down over 5 million tons of crude steel capacity and 3.5 million tons of rolled steel capacity. Since the end of the recession in 1994, an almost boom-like development has been evident. Plants have been nearly fully utilised, prices are rising and job losses are expected to be lower than in previous years.

Job losses have slowed since 1992. The rate of loss between the years 1993 (–33,424) and 1994 (–17,756) dropped dramatically, and by the end of 1994 only 127,433 people were still employed. The world market share of German crude steel production dropped only slightly between 1988 and 1993, from 4.9% to 4.8% (Table 18.2-1, Figs. 18.2-1, 18.2-2).

18.2.3. Trends in steel market demand

Basically, there are three observations to be made on the demand side of the German steel market.

Since steel is a basic commodity, demand is indirect and determined primarily by the evolution of the gross national product or industrial production. Demand behaves in a very cyclical way. According to Wienert (1986/87), steel consumption in the OECD countries remained static during the period 1960–86 whilst industrial production increased by 3%; each percentage point increase (decrease), however, increases (decreases) steel consumption by 2%. Rahmeyer (1992) also states that since the beginning of the 1970s growth has been decreasingly steel-intensive.

Since the end of the reconstruction phase, demand for steel has shown a below-average evolution in comparison with overall demand. The following factors can explain this phenomenon: on the one hand, the importance of the steel-consuming sectors has reduced; on the other hand, steel has been used in a more efficient way thanks to improved production and processing methods, so that specific consumption of steel, i.e., the steel content in steel products, has dropped (self-substitution). Moreover, steel has been replaced by other materials (plastics, concrete, light metal, etc.).

In past decades there has been a clear trend away from structural steel towards flat steel. In 1947 the ratio of structural steel to flat steel was still two to one, whereas today it has reversed to approximately one to three. Within the flat steels group the importance of heavy plate has decline, whilst that of thin sheet has increased. This is due in part to the decline in shipbuilding and the increase in significance of the automotive industry.

18.2.3.1. Domestic demand

The evolution of domestic demand for steel can be seen from the level of apparent consumption (Table 18.2-1).[1] These almost quadrupled between 1950 and 1974. This strong expansion came about, above all, because the rebuilding of war-torn Germany (and Europe) was very steel-intensive, and growth was strong in precisely those industries in which steel is the crucial material (e.g., the automotive sector, consumer durables, mechanical engineering, shipbuilding). After the slowdown in the growth of the steel industry in the first half of the 1960s, which was caused by the less rapidly expanding demand from the capital-goods industry, the favourable cyclical trend brought about stronger demand for capital goods and motor vehicles after the recovery from the German recession in 1966 and 1967, so that demand for steel once again moved ahead strongly. The reasons for the drop in demand following the first oil crisis were partly cyclical, but demand for steel also declined because of a drop in the rate of investment. In the period from 1983 to 1990, demand for steel fell in sectors such as construction and shipbuilding, which were heavily affected by cyclical and structural changes. At the same time, the steel industry had to adjust to new demands from customers, for example in connection with just-in-time production.

Changes in the way demand was shared amongst the various manufacturing industries in the period 1960–91 can be seen in Table 18.2-2 and Fig. 18.2-3. It can be seen that the importance of vehicles and metal goods increased sharply, that the share of wire and bright drawing, cold rolling and forming increased slightly and

---

[1] Apparent consumption is defined as crude steel production plus steel imports less steel exports, plus or minus changes to the level of stock held by dealers and producers.

Table 18.2-1 Key numbers of the evolution of the German steel industry 1947–1994

Year	Crude steel production	Crude steel capacity	Crude steel utilisation	Share in world market	Apparent consumption	Imports (in crude steel weight)	Import share	Exports (in crude steel weight)	Export share	Total employees*
	1,000 tons	1,000 tons	%	%	1,000 tons	1,000 tons	%	1,000 tons	%	
1947	3,060			2.3						**180,291
1950	12,121			6.3	11,512					236,218
1955	21,336	25,300	84.3	7.9	22,874	3,421	15.0	2,483	11.6	313,277
1960	34,100	35,335	96.5	9.8	30,184	4,958	16.4	7,944	23.3	417,328
1965	36,821	45,530	80.9	8.0	33,800	6,869	20.3	10,286	27.9	398,991
1970	45,041	53,100	84.8	7.5	44,196	10,805	24.4	11,907	26.4	374,428
1974	53,232	60,415	88.1	7.5	43,004	9,916	23.1	21,801	41.0	343,995
1980	43,838	66,924	65.5	6.1	41,453	12,707	30.7	18,372	41.9	288,228
1995	40,497	48,952	82.7	5.6	40,103	12,507	31.2	18,227	45.0	213,957
1988	41,023	46,828	87.6	5.3	42,517	13,863	32.6	18,269	44.5	181,410
1990	38,434	48,131	79.9	5.0	42,936	15,938	37.1	17,545	45.6	174,992
1994	40,837	***52,295	***72.0	***4.8	41,210	16,391	39.8	18,813	46.1	127,433

* German definition (including steel tube industry)

**1948 ***1993

Source: EUROSTAT; Wirtschaftsvereinigung Stahl; Ifo calculations

Table 18.2-2 Evolution of the share in apparent steel consumption by sector (in %)

Sector	Year				
	1960	1970	1980	1990	1991
Wire and bright drawing, cold rolling and forming	18.0	20.0	22.0	21.5	20.0
Steel tube industry	12.0	12.0	13.5	10.0	10.0
Forging	2.5	2.5	2.0	2.0	1.5
Mechanical engineering	9.0	8.0	8.5	9.0	9.0
Vehicles	7.5	10.0	12.5	13.0	13.0
Metal goods	18.5	18.5	18.0	22.0	23.0
Structural steelwork	10.0	9.0	7.0	6.0	7.0
Shipbuilding	3.0	3.0	2.0	1.0	1.5
Electrical engineering	3.0	3.5	3.0	3.5	3.5
Building and civil engineering	9.0	7.0	6.0	4.5	5.0
Other industries	7.5	6.5	5.5	7.5	6.5

Source: Wirtschaftsvereinigung Stahl

that the steel tube industry, structural steelwork, and building and civil engineering sectors lost importance as steel customers.

Up to 1960 steel imports were still of secondary importance. However, there was an almost continuous increase in foreign steel supplies from the 1952 level of under 7% of supplies to the market, reaching 24% in 1970, 31% in 1980 and 40% in 1994 (Table 18.2-1, Fig. 18.2-4). The main supplying countries throughout the period were the ECSC or EU countries, in particular, France and the Benelux countries; their share dropped steadily, especially in favour of third countries in Europe. The increasing imports into Germany in the first half of the 1960s were the result above all of increased Japanese involvement. In the 1990s there has been a drop in imports from EU countries, whilst following the fall of the Iron Curtain supplies from eastern Europe have increased sharply, and their share of total imports has correspondingly increased at the expense of the EU countries.

18.2.3.2. Exports

Exports are the second factor determining demand for steel and one which has grown in importance during the period under consideration. In 1965 they crossed the threshold of 10 million tons of crude steel weight (Table 18.2-1). During the years 1961–67, export markets in Asia were increasingly lost to Japan. Between 1966 and 1974 German steel exports more than doubled. In the crisis years from 1977 to 1983 the increase in exports had a compensating effect on demand for steel. The main destination countries remained those of the EC and the United States. In the following years foreign demand continued to play an important part in determining overall demand. Both the volume and the share of

Fig. 18.2-3 Share in apparent steel consumption by sector (in %)

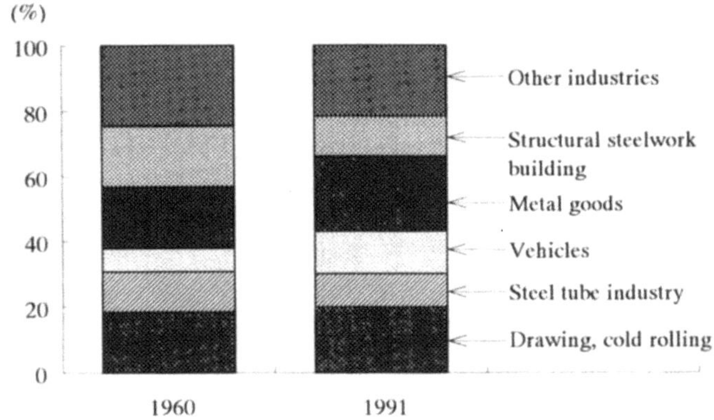

Source: Wirtschaftsvereinigung Stahl

Fig. 18.2-4 Exports and imports

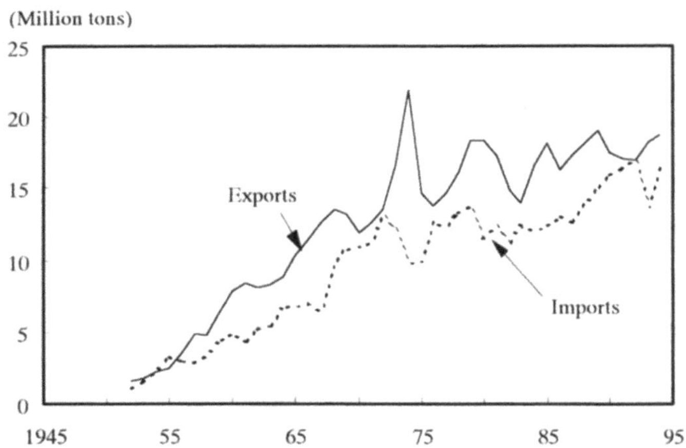

Source: EUROSTAT

exports increased. Above all, exports to the United States (in spite of protectionist measures), and in recent years to China, increased sharply.

Although world-wide the traditional steel producers (but above all Japan) expanded their capacity sharply in the post-war period and some developing and newly industrialising countries built up their own steel industry, thereby actually worsening the export potential of the industrialised countries, exports steadily grew more significant for the German steel industry. The export share rose from 10% of total crude steel production in 1952 to 46% in 1994. The simultaneous very sharp rise in the share accounted for by imports (from 7% to 40%) indicates increasing international specialisation. Overall, however, it can be said that there has been a reduction in Germany's traditionally high trade surplus in steel over the last ten years (Fig. 18.2-4).

18.2.4. Supply system

Steel works were traditionally situated near coal and iron ore deposits. In Germany, the Ruhr and the Saarland are the traditional centres—both of which have coal deposits. Further locations are close to the former iron ore extraction sites (Siegerland, Peine-Salzgitter, Upper Palatinate). Today, however, it is no longer the raw material deposits that are decisive in the choice of location, but the location of the steel customers. Because customers were already located near steel producers in Ruhr, the Saarland and in the Peine-Salzgitter, they remain good steel sites today. Since World War II, a few new mini–steel works have also been set up on coastal sites and in southern Germany. By far the largest proportion of German steel production takes place in fully integrated iron and steel works (pig-iron, crude steel and rolled steel).

18.2.4.1. Development of the supply system during the different periods

World steel production in the post-war period was concentrated almost exclusively (95%) in North America and Europe (United Nations, 1989). In Germany at the beginning of 1946, of the forty blast furnaces in the Ruhr only eight were operational, as a result of wartime destruction. Crude steel production in 1946 totalled less than 3 million tons (22 million tons before the war). The steel industry of the Ruhr was particularly badly affected by the dismantling.

As a consequence of the rectification of the Allies' de-concentration measures made possible by the founding of the ECSC, in the early 1960s larger groups had joined forces around August-Thyssen Hütte, Rheinische Stahlwerke, Mannesmann, Klöckner-Werke, Hoesch Werke, Dortmund-Hörder-Hüttenunion, Krupp and Klöckner (cf. Schafmeister, 1993).

Against a background of optimistic demand forecasts for steel in the early 1960s, steel companies began planning their capacity on the basis of peak demand in order to be able to react flexibly to increases in demand (cf. also Rahmeyer, 1992) As a result, and because of the tendencies towards stagnation, overcapacity arose. In 1966, in order to avoid a price war, every one of the thirty German steel producers combined to form the four rolled-steel groups that were set up as regional cartels to fix prices and quotas with the aim of co-ordinating decisions on investment, production and sales, and stabilising prices and revenue. Thus for the first time, the German steel industry was reacting to demand on the basis of close co-operation. The contracting out of rolling work facilitated a comprehensive shutdown and scrapping of plant. The rolled-steel groups were replaced by the so-called rationalisation groups in 1971. These too amounted to a cartel governing price and volume, although they were expanded to include joint purchasing of raw materials and the possibility of quota exchanges and specialisation. Rolled-steel groups and rationalisation groups were indeed able to halt the collapse in prices, but there was still a need for further rationalisation. (cf. Schafmeister, 1993).

Thanks to the modernisation and rationalisation measures taken from the mid-1960s, the German steel industry found itself in a relatively good position at the beginning of the crisis. Because of the previous steel boom, which led to forecasts of a further increase in demand, the capacity of German steel works continued to increase up to 1978. As this was the case across Europe, fierce competition broke out for the steadily dwindling EC steel market. Concealed price competition used to secure market share led to a reduction in the effectiveness of the national cartels. For this reason, international production agreements were signed in the context of the DENELUX and EUROFER cartels (formed in 1976). The German steel companies used this time to adjust their product range and concentrate on attractive steel products in the area of thin sheet and high-grade steel. With the economic downturn, the collapse in prices, and rising energy and raw material costs in 1980, the member companies increasingly failed to comply with the cartel agreements. As a consequence, the cartel collapsed and the EC saw itself forced to declare a state of manifest crisis. From then until the end of the 1980s, it was the EC that was crucial in determining the further evolution of the German steel industry. Since then it has been intervening less.

18.2.4.2. Input factors

The two most important raw materials for steel production are iron ore and coal or coke. Iron ore had traditionally been produced in the Federal Republic (in particular around Salzgitter), but the quantity was never sufficient to meet demand. The tapping of overseas deposits at the beginning of the 1960s, which were very rich in iron and could be extracted by open-cast mining, led to a change in the supply structure of iron ore imports. In 1950 Sweden was still supplying almost the total import requirement, whereas today it lags far behind Brazil and is just ahead of Canada and Australia, with a vastly reduced share. German iron ore extraction has all but ceased because of quality and price disadvantages.

The traditional link between coal extraction and steel production in the German steel industry was called into question when German coal became increasingly expensive in comparison with the world market, and other forms of energy (fuel oil, natural gas) were being used more and more. The steel companies sold their pits to Ruhrkohle AG, which was founded in 1968, but in the so-called *Hüttenvertrag* (iron and steel industry agreement) they undertook to buy their coal from Ruhrkohle AG. It is true that they received government aid as compensation for a price that was high by world market standards, but this could not fully make up for the cost disadvantages of German coal. In spite of the purchase obligation, imports of overseas coal and overseas iron ore increased because of the drop in shipping rates in the 1960s. In 1950, coal imports were still coming almost exclusively from the Saarland, which at that time still belonged to France, whereas in 1960, the United States was already in the lead, and in 1993 most coal supplies came from South Africa, Poland and Australia.

18.2.4.3. Technology

With the investment surge in the 1950s, the German steel industry was able to catch up with the international leaders. From the mid-1950s, the main focus of investment switched from general re-construction to the construction and expansion of modern and efficient hot wide-strip rolling mills in order to be able to meet the enormous increase in demand from the automotive and capital-goods industry for high-quality thin sheet. This concentration of investment was continued in the 1960s, but the cold rolling mills were also expanded. At the beginning of the 1970s, the investment activity switched to oxygen steel and continuous casting as well as the automated control of steel works. Since 1975, investments have mainly been made to rationalise and modernise steel works for new technologies and processes, and to accelerate the introduction of established technologies. From 1983, the steel industry concentrated above all on the introduction of new processes in high-quality thin sheet (cf. Schafmeister, 1993).

The technical progress in the steel industry during the post-war period was characterised by two process innovations: oxygen steel and continuous casting. Up to the mid-1960s the German steel industry was dominated by the Thomas and the open-hearth processes (Table 18.2-3). 1957 saw the introduction to Germany of the oxygen steel-making process, which because of its technological superiority became the leading production process from the 1970s onwards. The essential advance in this process lay in a greatly reduced cycle time, a considerably lower use of energy, lower investment and better steel quality. Hence throughout the world the Thomas and the open-hearth processes were steadily replaced by the oxygen process. The German steel industry was level with the average pace of change in the EC, but about ten years behind Japan (Schafmeister, 1993). In comparison with other countries, Germany has only a small share (1993: 23%) of the electric steel process, which is used above all in the so-called mini–steel works.

In the area of steel-casting technology, too, there was an important new technological development. From the mid- 1960s interrupted ingot casting was replaced by continuous casting. This happened relatively quickly and at the same pace as in Japan. This made it possible to achieve enormous productivity gains. The first plant went into operation as early as 1958. In 1993 this technology had a share of 95% (Table 18.2-3).

Table 18.2-3 Evolution of the shares of steel production processes in the Federal Republic of Germany 1947-1993 (in %)

Year	Thomas process	Open-hearth process	Electric steel process	Oxygen steel-making process	Continuous casting
1947	39.3	59.2	1.6	0.0	0.0
1950	42.8	55.3	1.9	0.0	0.0
1955	42.5	53.2	4.3	0.0	0.0
1960	43.9	47.2	6.4	2.5	0.0
1965	29.5	42.9	8.5	19.1	2.1
1970	8.1	26.3	9.9	55.8	8.3
1974	3.0	17.5	10.8	68.8	19.4
1980	0.0	6.7	14.9	78.4	46.0
1985	0.0	0.0	18.5	81.5	79.5
1990	0.0	0.0	17.7	82.3	91.3
1993	0.0	0.0	23.1	76.9	94.6

Source: Schafmeister (1993); Wirtschaftsvereinigung Stahl; Ifo calculations

18.2.4.4. Enterprises

As Rahmeyer (1992) states, it is not possible to adapt production capacity continuously to meet fluctuations in demand because of technically determined indivisibility and rigid links between production plants in the steel industry. Because of this, and because of high exit barriers, slumps in sales bring about a drop in capacity utilisation and lead rapidly to price wars and heavy losses. For this reason, too, there is a tendency in the steel industry towards horizontal and vertical mergers between enterprises, so as to achieve economies of scale (heating and energy links between iron and steel works and coal pits, rationalisation and modernisation to reduce production costs). Thus an initial wave of mergers took place after the ECSC Treaty came into force in 1953, removing, amongst other things, the inefficiencies that had come about as a result of the de-concentration measures. A series of mergers also took place in the Federal Republic of Germany in the 1960s and 1970s.[2] As a result of this, but also as a result of closures, the number of German steel producers fell between 1975 and 1986 from sixty-three to forty-three. The process of concentration is also seen in the fact that in the mid-

2 For example, in 1969 Salzgitter AG took over Ilseder Hütte; Thyssen combined its tube production with Mannesmann and in 1973 took over Rheinstahl AG; Klöckner-Werke AG bought Eisenwerk-Gesellschaft Maximilianshütte mbH in 1976 (cf. also Oberender, Rüter, 1989; 40f.). In the late 1970s Arbed-Saarstahl AG was formed with Federal government support from a re-organisation of the three Saarland steel companies, of which two were on the brink of collapse (Wienert, 1983; 265).

1970s twenty companies produced more than 80% of the crude steel, whilst at the beginning of 1985 this proportion was shared by only seven companies (Eckart, 1988). German steel industry companies differ fundamentally from those of other countries in that—apart from Salzgitter AG which has been privatised in the meantime—all were in private hands.

Between the mid-1960s and the late 1970s it is possible to observe two strategies, which will be demonstrated here using the example of two companies that adopted these strategies most consistently. The Thyssen Group diversified by taking over competitors or various divisions of competitors and by establishing and expanding downstream processing to become a large complete supplier (Schafmeister, 1993). The Mannesmann Group developed by expanding tube production and eliminating other divisions to become a special supplier, but also diversified itself by expanding plant construction. Since the 1980s practically all suppliers have also implemented a strategy of diversification to spread and reduce risk by investing in the promising area of telecommunications and software. In a world-wide comparison, the largest German steel companies Thyssen (10.7 million tons) and Krupp-Hoesch (7.9 million tons) ranked 7th and 17th respectively in 1994 (Vondran, 1995b). The next largest German companies were Preussag, Klöckner and Saarstahl.

In spite of the high concentration of companies in the German steel industry vis-à-vis other sectors of the economy, an international comparison shows it to have below-average concentration. Whilst large companies have been formed with production volumes in excess of 10 million tons in Japan and the United States, this level has only been reached in Germany by the Thyssen Group. This also has to do with the reluctance of German steel companies to give up their independence. For this reason even the intended mergers did not take place, for example the two mergers planned in the early 1980s which would have led the Ruhr and Salzgitter steel companies to form two large groups. Krupp and Hoesch only merged in 1992. Moreover, since then Krupp-Hoesch and Thyssen have been collaborating in the production of high-grade steel, tin plate and electric sheet.

18.2.5. Role of national government and of European Coal and Steel Community (ECSC) policies in industrial development

The steel industry has always been characterised by government regulation. The reasons for this have to do with military and industrial concerns, and prestige. A further cause for political intervention resulted from difficulties experienced when capacities were removed in times of crisis. Such overcapacity arises because of technical indivisibility, a cost structure with a high proportion of fixed costs, only slight differences in efficiency between the companies, uncertainty about the future evolution of demand, and the specific nature of the inputs used (cf. also Deily, 1988).

For the German steel industry there are two regulatory bodies: the federal government and the ECSC. The role of the ECSC will be described first, because its regulations also inform German policy on the steel industry.

18.2.5.1. Role of European Coal and Steel Community (ECSC) policy in industrial development

The essentially free market–oriented ECSC Treaty that became effective on 23 July 1953 enabled the Federal Republic to throw overboard the conditions imposed by the allies. The prohibition of discriminatory practices in merchandise movements between member states plays a decisive role in this treaty. However, the High Authority set up under the ECSC Treaty also has extensive powers of intervention to eliminate market co-ordination.[3] These include the regulation of prices and quantities, freight, transport charges and purchase conditions, the sales organisation as well as powers of intervention in investments and in research and development.[4]

The first intervention in the European steel market took place in 1963 in the context of the tendencies towards stagnation and excess supply of the early 1960s, which led to a drop in prices and concealed price competition (the granting of illegal discounts, the sale of perfect products as second-class quality). The aim was to stabilise prices, amongst other things, by more rigorous checking of compliance with list prices by the ECSC companies and the imposition of a quota for cheap imports from the COMECON area. In 1972 such a quota was also imposed on Japanese steel imports in order to limit the effects of the comparatively weak competitive position of the European (and German) steel industry, which was caused predominantly by technical factors.

However, the European steel market up to the mid-1970s could still be described as competitive, if also partly regulated (cf. Rahmeyer, 1992). With the arrival of the steel crisis, the EC at first held back from intervention in the steel market and—apart from external trade regulations—left it to the companies in the EUROFER cartel to introduce measures to solve the crisis, including a voluntary quota system. The renewed slump in demand for steel from 1980 led to the

---

[3] The free-market orientation manifests itself in the prohibition of import and export duties and of volume restrictions on merchandise movements, discrimination with regard to prices and delivery conditions, special assistance by member states, and practices which restrict competition by carving up markets, e.g., cartels (cf. Rahmeyer, 1992; 255). Some deviations, which are to become more significant later, are provided for, however, in the form of direct and indirect market intervention (cf. Rahmeyer, 1992; 256). Indirect market intervention includes information, financial assistance for investment programmes, and measures to achieve price transparency and for narrowly fluctuating list prices. Direct market intervention (time-limited import restrictions and time-limited determination of production quotas and minimum prices) are provided for in cases of manifest structural crisis to prevent the formation of a cartel amongst the companies.

[4] The powers of the High Authority of the ECSC were transferred to the European Commission in 1967 with the founding of the European Community (EC).

collapse of the EUROFER cartel. Thereupon the EC Commission felt compelled to declare a state of manifest crisis in accordance with Article 58 of the ECSC Treaty. Minimum prices and production quotas were set for all European steel producers to avoid ruinous competition, and a rigid monitoring system was set up to prevent concealed price competition. Imports from third countries were limited by means of duties, quotas and voluntary agreements to restrict supplies.

In the crisis years national subsidies grew (above all in Great Britain, France, Italy and Belgium). This was tolerated by the EC, although such subsidies were forbidden according to the ECSC Treaty. The EC Subsidy Codex for Steel, which since 1981 had continuously been waived, permitted time-limited national subsidies for the steel industry on condition that production capacity was reduced in order to achieve the modernisation of plant, which was more profitable over the long term, and the closure of plant that could not survive.[5] Following the recovery in demand after 1987, production quotas and minimum prices were removed, and subsidies were only paid for research and development, for investments in environmental protection and for closures.

18.2.5.2. Role of national government policies in industrial development

In the 1950s. the German federal government pursued a neo-liberal industrial policy: the state concentrated on the creation and securing of the necessary economic framework, but otherwise held back. With the onset of stagnation tendencies in the steel industry in the early 1960s, German industrial policy also became more interventionist in order to overcome corporate crises and to rebuild competitiveness, but also to pursue regional and social policy goals (volume of subsidies 1960–1970: approximately DM 2 billion). The emphasis was on loan guarantees for investment projects for which market finance was difficult to obtain.

From the mid-1970s there was substantial government intervention both in the Federal Republic and in the European Community in order to facilitate a reduction of the existing overcapacity. Whilst in the crisis years from 1975 to 1979 the countries of the European Community paid out a total of over DM 24 billion in subsidies, and between 1980 and 1985 almost DM 83 billion, the Federal Republic was very restrained in this area (1975–79: DM 0.9 billion; 1980–85: DM 6.3 billion). When in late 1977 two of the three steel companies in the Saarland were on the brink of collapse, it supported a rescue plan based on a pooling of production.

In 1981 and 1983, as a consequence of the maintenance subsidies which were being paid by other EC member states and which distorted competition, the federal government decided to provide support worth around DM 3 billion for the restructuring of the German steel industry in the period 1983–85 as part of the

---

5 By 1985 it was thus possible to reduce hot-rolling capacity within the ten EC member states by 32 million tons.

Stahlprogramm (steel programme).[6] As a result, the measures aimed at restructuring and adapting capacity were implemented more quickly, and the competitiveness of the German steel industry was improved. In addition, the federal government set up an R&D programme for the period 1982–85 with a fund of DM 500 million. With the *Stahlstand orteprogramm* (steel locations programme) (1982–90) and the *Sonder programm zur Schaffung neuer Arbeitsplätze außerhalb der Montanindustrie* (special programme for the creation of new jobs outside the coal, iron and steel industry) (1989–93), the government encouraged the creation of replacement jobs at steel locations in (future-oriented) industries with the aid of regional investment subsidies, and provided assistance with severance programme costs and with social provisions for former steel industry employees who were unsuccessful in finding a new job (cf. Rahmeyer, 1992).

18.2.6. Main factors in the development of the German steel industry and future prospects

18.2.6.1. Main factors in the development of the German steel industry

a) Evolution of demand

A damper was put on the development of the German steel industry, at the latest from the beginning of the steel crisis in 1975, by the contraction of steel-intensive industries (shipbuilding, mining, etc.), which occurred simultaneously with the advance of sectors consuming less steel (chemicals, data processing, services), by the development of higher-quality, lighter steels (self-substitution), and by substitution with other materials such as plastics, light metals, ceramics and concrete. As a result, the industry lost importance within the economy.

b) Technology

Important technological innovations were (jointly) developed in the German steel industry, such as the oxygen steel-making process, continuous casting and also the casting of sheet steel close to final dimensions. Because of the rapid introduction of new technologies it was possible, from the re-construction phase onwards, to catch up again with the international leaders and hold this position. As a result, enormous increases in productivity were possible. In general, the companies of the German steel industry were successful in adapting to the structural change in the sector by modernising and rationalising. Furthermore, the development of new applications for steel on the basis of improved processing and consumption characteristics opened up new markets.

---

6 Of this, DM 1.2 billion was set aside for investment subsidies and the remaining DM 1.8 billion for structural improvement measures (research, creation of replacement jobs, financial support to assist redundant employees with re-training, etc.).

c) Intervention and regulation

If intervention by the federal government and the ECSC or EC ensured that some steel companies survived at times of crisis, the criticism must also be made that many problems were not solved and that, on the contrary, it helped create and perpetuate overcapacity. By the setting of minimum prices, production quotas and the granting of subsidies, the shutdown of inefficient capacity was impeded (Rahmeyer, 1992). There are many who claim that only with the ending of government restrictions on competition was it possible for the steel industry to emerge from its structural crisis (cf. e.g., Oberender, Rüter, 1989).

d) Mergers

An essential reason for the problems of the German steel producers lay in their reluctance to merge with each other to achieve a cost-efficient plant size. Even when mergers failed because of the desire of companies to remain autonomous, at least at times of crisis they recognised the need for close co-operation to reduce capacity and to rationalise (e.g., rolled-steel groups, Rationalisation Groups). However, the medium- and long-term definition of an effective policy for the sector proved difficult.

e) Diversification

The diversification strategy adopted since the 1980s by practically all suppliers proved very successful. By investing in the promising area of telecommunications and software, they were able to spread risk and thus become more independent of fluctuations in the steel market. This advantage was put to use in the last steel crisis in the early 1990s, when it was possible to offset part of the losses on steel against other sectors.

18.2.6.2. Future prospects

Major changes are to be expected on the supply side in the next few years, as small electric-steel works, which use scrap as their raw material, increasingly put pressure on the traditional large steel works (cf. Wienert, 1993). This must be seen in connection with the introduction of the casting of sheet steel close to final dimensions—a German development—which, in comparison with traditional processes, is estimated to require 40% less in terms of investment costs, 80% less in terms of labour costs, and 50% less in terms of energy (Vondran, 1995a). Consequently, highly productive, flexible, smaller plant will take the place of the larger, inflexible units that were only cost efficient when working at high levels of capacity utilisation. These small flat-steel works will be set up either as subsidiaries of the large works or by outsiders. For this reason, it is to be expected that a considerable concentration will take place amongst the remaining large steel works, since otherwise the necessary high-capacity utilisation will not be achieved. As the electric-steel works achieve a labour-productivity rate which is two to three times higher than the traditional oxygen steel works, the pressure to reduce jobs will increase rather than decrease.

In future, there will be increased co-operation between the steel industry and the industries it supplies. There are several reasons for this development. On the one hand, this will allow risks to be contained, whilst profit margins become ever finer. On the other hand, with customers adopting just-in-time production, logistical co-operation is becoming increasingly important. Moreover, the increasing demands made by customers with regard to dimensional stability, surface quality, strength, deformability and corrosion resistance require the development of made-to-measure steels (Schafmeister, 1993). This is why it will also be necessary to increase the pace of steel research. With the new steels that are being developed it will also be easier for the German steel industry to hold its own in the world steel market, which will prove increasingly difficult with uniform tonnage steels.

Over the longer term, the prospects for the German steel industry are good. A precondition for this is fair competition within the EU and on world markets, and the removal of the competitive distortion caused by subsidies particularly within the EU. But it is also necessary to eliminate structural overcapacity (around 30 million tons in the EU and around 5 million tons in Germany; Vondran, 1995a) and to reduce the numbers employed. In the case of exports, loss of ground in world markets is anticipated in future as new steel-producing countries, which of late also produce higher-quality steels, have the advantage of lower wage costs and fewer environmental restrictions. Moreover, in all probability the pressure from imports from central and eastern European countries will continue (Wienert, 1993).

Thus in future, the German steel industry will again face major problems. Given the speed of innovation, however, it is necessary to contradict the often expressed opinion that the steel industry in Germany is a dying industry. It will not, however, regain its earlier importance.

18.3. Comparative Summary of the Steel Industry

In the discussion of the German and the Japanese steel industries, the analysis was carried out on the basis of the definition of the steel industry as steel production from raw-materials, processing to the production of finished and rolled-steel products.

18.3.1. Difference in development processes

In Japan and the Federal Republic of Germany, many of the steel mills were destroyed at the end of the war, and in Japan the raw-material supplies were cut off. A prime necessity for Japan was thus to secure raw-material supplies from abroad. This was not a problem for the Federal Republic with its own coal and iron resources. The obligation to use domestic coal supplies, however, later became a competitive disadvantage, owing to the higher costs in comparison with coal on the world market.

Since the steel industry is an important basic industry in a national economy, the expansion of steel capacities in both countries was of decisive importance. Whereas up to the mid-1970s this industry expanded gradually in Germany, expansion in Japan proceeded at a swift pace since the late 1950s. For both countries, the steel industry provided an important basis for post-war recovery and made a vital contribution to the enormous growth of the Japanese economy and to the German economic miracle. Over the years, the steel industry's importance declined in both countries as a result of substitute materials and the strong growth of other industries (e.g., automobiles, electrical industry, services).

In the early 1960s, large, integrated steel mills were built in coastal locations in Japan, assisted by low-interest government loans. Thus Japan created new standards for economical, integrated steel mills and also touched off extensive new construction and modernisation in Europe (Franz, 1988). In the Federal Republic, however, the domestic raw-materials supply led to the modernisation of existing facilities which remained inland, close to raw materials.

Since the early 1960s, the competitiveness of the German steel industry declined in comparison with Japan. This was also evident in the fact that German steel exports to Asia shrank as Japanese manufacturers took over these markets, shifting the focus of their exports from North America to Asia. The results of the international weaknesses of the German steel industry especially vis-à-vis Japan in the critical years of 1975 to 1987 were cushioned by the high degree of protection in the EC market.

In the critical years up to the mid-1980s, the German steel industry was hit much worse than the Japanese industry. The strategy for overcoming the crisis was similar in both countries. Rationalisation efforts (especially eliminating excess capacities, introducing energy-saving and cost-efficient production facilities) were undertaken. Also, the production share of higher-value-added steel products was increased, for which growing demand was generated from the automobile industry and other steel-processing industries.

18.3.2. Role of technology in industrial development

A key success factor in both countries was the technology employed. Especially in the Japanese steel industry, innovations from all over the world were quickly introduced. This fact is generally regarded as the main reason for Japan's successful development at a high level of production and technology. The implementation of new open-hearth production techniques (e.g., the replacement of the Thomas and Siemens-Martin procedures by the oxygen steel-making process) was much faster than in the Federal Republic or the United States—also because of government co-ordination and financial support. Since such a co-ordination of investment activity was lacking in the Federal Republic, activities aimed at locational questions were also less focused, less unified and more hesitant than in Japan. As a result, the cost structure of German steel producers was less favourable, which also found expression in a reduced competitiveness vis-à-vis the Japanese steel industry.

After the post-war reconstruction of the steel industry, Japan and Germany soon had the most modern production facilities in the world, although the advantages of both countries over competitors were gradually reduced. The German steel industry's modernisation advantage vis-à-vis its competitors in Europe (especially France and Italy) increasingly declined, especially as a result of differing national subsidy practices and the distortions this causes in competition.

Whereas the German steel industry achieved and defended its leading position by developing or contributing to the development of new processes (e.g., oxygen steel and continuous casting), the Japanese industry adopted and developed these new processes quickly and in a co-ordinated manner.

18.3.3. Role of industrial policy in industry development

In both countries, government regulations played a decisive role in post-war developments in the steel industry. This is not surprising, since the steel industry in all countries was and is an object of strong political interest. Quite clear is the leading role of the Japanese government, which protected and assisted the steel industry throughout the post-war period with classical measures such as regulating prices, production output and investment, with anti-trust policies, and also with re-organisation and financial support. In Germany, the state did not assume such a leading role in the steel industry. The measures taken by the ECSC, EC and the German government were less a result of a co-ordinated effort of all firms than the initiative of individual producers, who, however, were not able to find solutions for excess capacities or structural problems.

There is an important difference in the way industrial policies are shaped in both countries. The German model always fluctuated between the liberal avoidance of interference and politically motivated intervention (cf. Schafmeister, 1993), and attempted, as a rule, to operate with incentives instead of regulations. In Japan, producers were forced to perform or suffer the withdrawal of assistance. Since the mid-1980s, the West German government also began to attach conditions to its subsidies. In Japan, too, there were fluctuations in industrial policy towards the steel industry. Immediately after the war and the destruction of the pre-war structures, the Japanese government, under pressure from the United States, gave strong support to the re-construction and modernisation process aiming initially for a competitive market. In the course of the 1960s, the model became that of a co-operative market. This was only successful, however, when demand for steel was rising. The steel crisis then revealed the rigidity that this model fostered. Industry policy measures in Japan and Germany also delayed the re-organisation of the steel industry and contributed to a perpetuation of difficulties by safeguarding many non-competitive steel companies.

An important negative factor in the post-war development of the German steel industry must also be seen in this connection: the unwillingness of enterprises to merge with each other to achieve a more cost-efficient enterprise size. This stands in contrast to the successful merger of Yawata Steel and Fuji Steel to form Nippon Steel in 1970.

18.3.4. Vitality of private enterprise and industry development

A Japanese success factor that must also be relativised is the vitality of private enterprise. Individual producers develop their strategies in growing dependency on industrial-policy provisions, also, for example, with regard to the introduction of new technologies. An exception is the initiative of Kawasaki Steel in establishing an integrated steel mill in 1950.

Despite all difficulties, the steel producers of both countries have reacted flexibly to changes in demand, as seen in the diversification strategy in recent years. Whereas the German enterprises have moved into the areas of telecommunications and software, the Japanese producers have found new areas of business in chemistry, engineering, or ceramics.

In light of increasing environmental regulations, steel's ability to be recycled into high-quality products will give it advantages in competition with substitution materials such as plastics, light metals, ceramic or concrete. In both countries, however, further rationalisation measures and job reductions will be necessary to solve structural problems. Moreover, present conventional blast-furnace mills will face increasing competition from smaller electric-furnace steel works when the new technology of the casting of steel close to the final product dimensions has been perfected for industrial use.

19. Machine Tool Industry

19.1. Japan's Machine Tool Industry

19.1.1. Defining the machine tool industry

Machine tools are machines used to cut, grind, shear or forge metal products into their intended shapes by removing unwanted material. Because processing methods vary so widely, there are many different types of machine tools. They can be grouped, according to the United Nations industry categories (SITC), into cutting machine tools, which include milling machines, lathes and other metal cutting machines, and shaping tools, such as presses, which shape products without cutting away any material (Fig. 19.1-1).

In Japan, the term "machine tool" has a narrower definition and is applied only to lathes and cutting tools. Presses and other shaping tools are classified as secondary metal-processing machines. A third category encompasses large presses, including those manufactured in-house by shipbuilders. Since each type of machine is manufactured by different types of companies, they are covered by separate industry organisations. Cutting tools account for only 0.9% of total machine production in Japan. However, the high technical standards of cutting machine tools, including their processing speed and precision, have had a major impact on the quality and productivity of other manufactured goods, including dies and machinery parts.

The following analysis focuses primarily on the impact of these factors on the development of metalworking machine tools (cutting tools), the international competitiveness of which has improved dramatically since the introduction of numerical control (NC) technology.

19.1.2. Evolution of the Japanese machine tool industry

Japanese machine tool (cutting tool) industry was founded on technology introduced from Europe and the United States. The improvement of the industry's international competitiveness, primarily through the development of NC machine tools, has been reflected in the growing value of its output. The industry's evolution can be divided into the following four stages (Figs. 19.1-2, 19-1.3).

Fig. 19.1-1 Classes of machine tools and their definitions

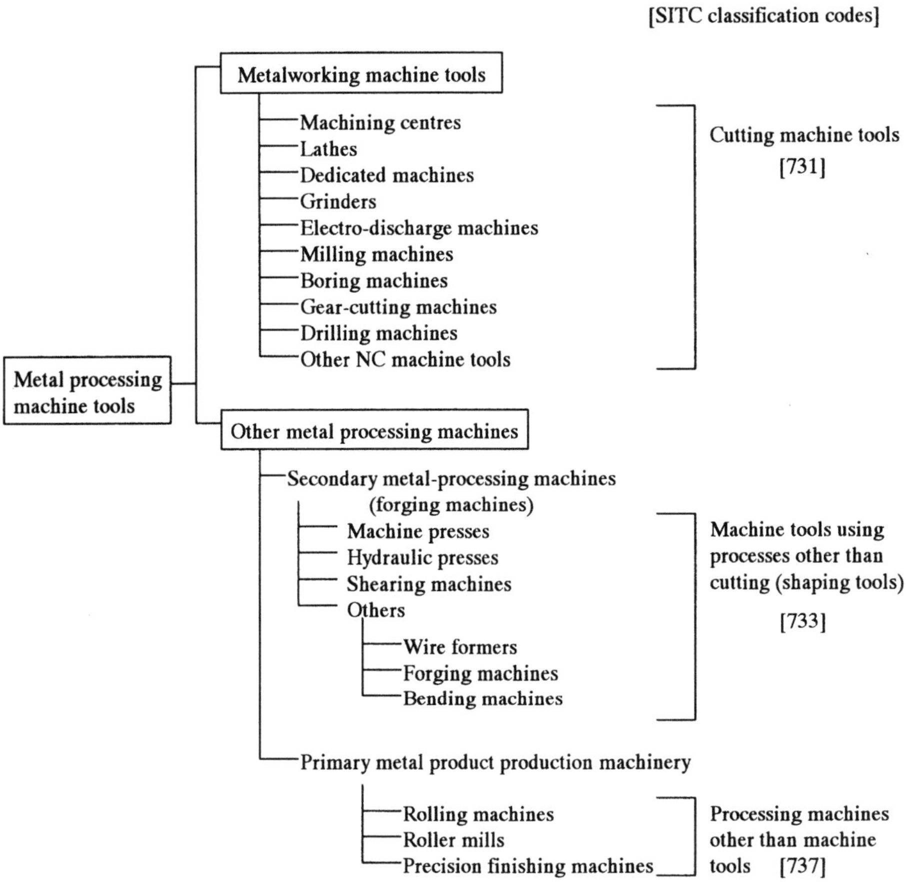

Note: Machining centres: These use boring, milling and drilling machines to carry out multiple processes in a single operation.
Lathes: These cut away the outside surface or drill and bore spinning cylindrical or disc-shaped materials.
Dedicated machines: These are used to process specific products.
Grinders: These grind material by means of grindstones.
Electro-discharge machines: These employ electrical melting to process material that is difficult to cut.
Milling machines: These use rotating, toothed, cylindrical cutters to plane, curve and cut slots.
Boring machines: These bore out the inside of a drilled hole to a prescribed diameter and tolerance.

Sources: Japan Machine Tool Builders' Association, Survey of Machine Tool Statistics; Japan Forming Machine Association, A Summary of Forming Machine Statistics

Fig. 19.1-2 Trends in the development of the machine tool industry (cutting tools)

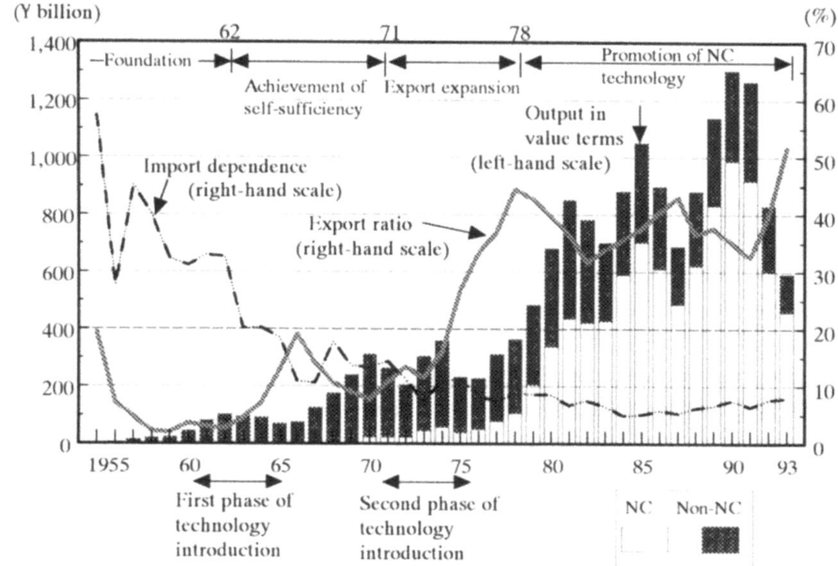

Source: Japan Machine Tool Builders' Association, Survey of Machine Tool Statistics

Fig. 19.1-3 Trends in numbers of manufacturers and employees and output value per employee in the machine tool industry (cutting tools)

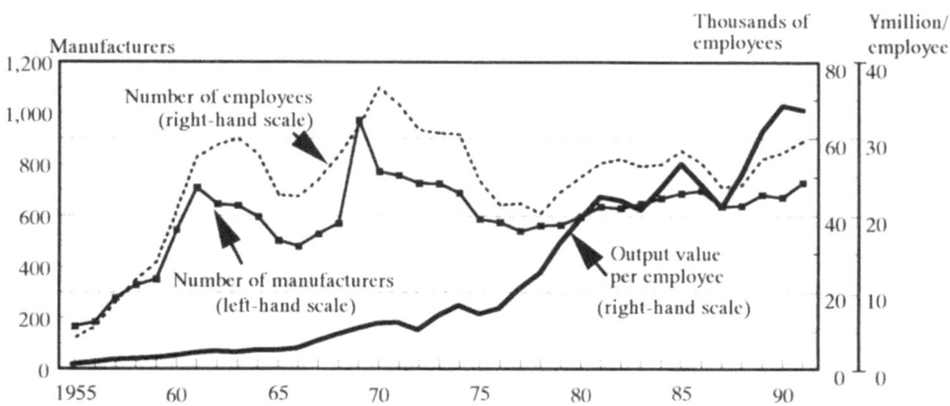

Source: MITI, Tables of Industrial Statistics

19.1.2.1. Building the foundations (1945–1962)

From the end of World War II until 1962, imported tools accounted for over 30% of the Japanese machine tool market. It was in this environment that Japanese machine tool manufacturers began to lay the foundations for full-scale production. In the war years, over four hundred machine tool manufacturers operated under government control. After the war, the number of machine tool manufacturers decreased sharply because of the loss of military demand, the flooding of the market with used machine tools, and the importation of foreign products. By 1950 there were only thirty-two manufacturers left.[1] The Japanese government sought to foster machine tool manufacturers by providing subsidies for the development of prototypes and by preferential tax treatment, such as special depreciation systems. Capital investment boomed during the high-growth phase that occurred between 1955 and 1962. The number of machine tool manufacturers quadrupled, whilst the number of people employed in the industry increased seven-fold. The value of machine tool production (mostly ordinary machine tools and lathes) increased by a factor of twenty-seven.

19.1.2.2. Achievement of self-sufficiency (1963–1971)

Between 1963 and 1971, Japan moved towards self-sufficiency in machine tools as domestic manufacturers began to gain a slice of domestic demand in competition with imports. Domestic demand for machine tools dropped sharply between 1963 and 1966 owing to a capital investment adjustment. During this period, Japanese machine tool makers used technology introduced from Europe and the United States to widen their product ranges. Demand for machine tools soared between 1966 and 1971, thanks to the expansion of the Japanese automobile and industrial machinery sectors. The number of people employed by machine tool manufacturers reached a peak of 70,000 in 1970. The value of production reached ¥312 billion, and the increase in supply capacity was reflected in a decline in dependence on imports, which fell from 32.6% of the market in 1962 to 11.6% by 1971.

19.1.2.3. Export expansion (1972–1978)

The period between 1972 and 1978 brought considerable improvement in the industry's international competitiveness. Dependence on imports declined from 11.2% to 8.8%, whilst the export ratio soared from 13.4% to 44.4%. The recession brought on by the Nixon Shock in 1971 and the first oil crisis in 1973 caused a

---

1 After the end of World War II, ninety Japanese machine tool makers with annual production capacities of 10,000 units or more were ordered to surrender their machine tools for use in reparations. The reparation designation was later cancelled, and used military machine tools were released into the market.

major decline in the number of Japanese machine tool manufacturers and in the number of people employed in the industry, both of which fell by 30% and 45% (by 1977 and 1978 respectively) compared with the records set in 1970. Despite this downturn, the industry continued to introduce NC technology, and in value terms production of NC machine tools increased from 12.0% of total machine tool production in 1971 to 29.4% in 1978. As domestic demand stagnated, manufacturers began to expand their exports of NC machine tools, especially to the United States. By 1978 the export ratio had soared to 41.2%.

19.1.2.4. Promotion of NC technology (1979–1993)

Between 1979 and 1993, the contribution of NC machine tools to the total value of machine tool production climbed from 29.4% to 77.3%. The expanding use of NC technology in a growing range of machine tools was reflected in the increasing sophistication of NC machine tools, the principal type of which was the machining centre.

By 1981 Japan had overtaken the United States to become the world's leading producer of machine tools and was starting to experience trade friction with both Europe and the United States. Europe introduced monitoring of Japanese tool imports in 1986, and in 1987 Japanese machine tool manufacturers adopted a system of voluntary restraints on exports to their main export market, the United States. From the mid-1980s onwards, Japanese machine tool manufacturers stepped up their establishment of offshore manufacturing bases, which led to decelerating growth in the value of exports. From 1986 onwards, Japan's "bubble economy" led to increased reliance on domestic demand, and the market soared to a peak of ¥1,303.4 billion in 1990. The bursting of the bubble and subsequent protracted recession caused the value of machine tool production to fall, and by 1993 it had slumped to 55% of its 1990 peak. This decline was even greater than that experienced during the oil crises.

19.1.3. Demand trends

19.1.3.1. Domestic market trends

Table 19.1-1 traces trends in machine tool orders by different industries. The biggest user of machine tools is the general machinery industry, which accounts for 30-50% of total orders, followed by the automobile industry (20–40%). These two machinery industries have consistently accounted for around 80% of total machine tool orders.

Domestic demand for machine tools has been driven by the buoyant capital investment of Japanese machinery manufacturers. Fig. 19.1-4 shows trends in capital investment by the main machinery manufacturing industries (1955=1). Between 1966 and 1970, when Japan was moving towards self-sufficiency, the

Table 19.1-1 Domestic demand: orders and industry shares (%)

	1955	1960	1965	1970	1975	1980	1985	1990	1993
Domestic demand (¥ billions)	3	50	42	185	98	421	697	1,039	323
Machinery manufacturers	80.8	85.6	78.3	87.8	83.3	94.6	79.0	73.5	78.6
General machinery			34.4	43.8	53.1	42.6	40.6	41.9	36.3
Automobiles			27.9	28.8	16.5	39.3	25.8	28.7	28.7
Electrical equipment			5.5	6.2	5.1	5.5	6.1	5.9	6.9
Precision machinery			6.0	4.1	3.6	4.1	5.1	3.5	3.8
Shipbuilding			4.4	4.9	5.0	3.1	1.5	1.6	2.9
Iron and steel industry	2.6	11.0	4.1	5.1	6.1	1.5	1.3	1.4	2.2
Metal products			6.5	3.8	5.0	2.5	4.4	3.4	4.6
Others	16.6	3.4	11.2	3.4	5.5	1.3	15.3	21.7	14.7

Source: The Thirty-year History of Motherly Machinery

automobile industry and other sectors sought to improve their international competitiveness through large-scale capital investment. There was a particularly sharp rise in investment by the general machinery industry, which has a high proportion of small- to medium-sized companies. This sudden increase in demand for capital goods at a time when reliance on imports was rising stimulated the growth of Japanese machine tool manufacturers.

Since the late 1970s, Japanese machinery industries, notably the electrical machinery and automobile industries, have invested aggressively in automation. Two main factors were responsible for this trend. First, the Nixon Shock and the first oil crisis created an increasing need for productivity improvements at the processing and assembly stages. Second, rising wage levels caused labour costs to increase relative to capital costs. Manufacturers, therefore, began to replace manually operated machines by installing NC machine tools, which could operate for extended periods of time. In 1980, 95% of all machine tool orders were placed by machinery manufacturers, with the automobile industry alone contributing 39%. From 1980 onwards, manufacturers were increasingly installing industrial robots[2] as well as NC machine tools. Together with NC machine tools, these devices called "mechatronics" made an important contribution to factory automation. This trend towards investment in automation technology was driven by the strategies adopted by Japanese manufacturers of automobiles, electronics and precision machinery, which sought to increase their market shares by quickly starting up new production lines and using the benefits of mass production to reduce prices. As a result, machine tool makers came under increasing pressure to improve production efficiency and shorten delivery time.

---

2 Industrial robots consist of manipulators, which hold and move materials in the same way as a human arm, and control systems.

Fig. 19.1-4 Trends in capital investment by machinery manufacturers

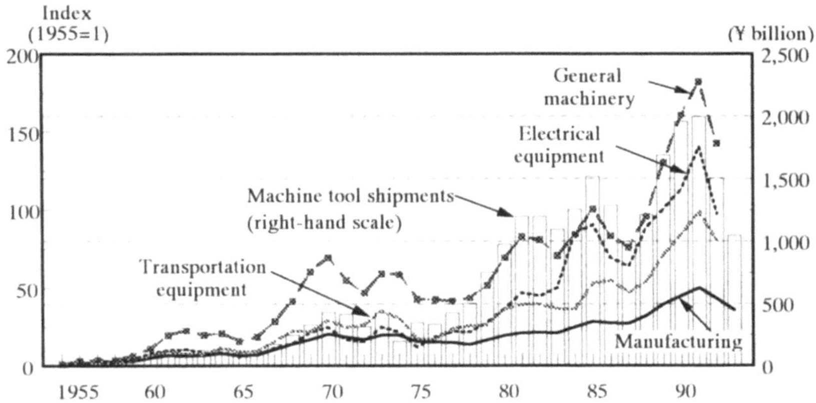

Notes: 1. Capital investment figures are nominal.
2. Figures are indexed (1955=1).

Sources: EPA, Annual Report on National Accounts

In the mid-1980s, Japanese automobile and electrical appliance manufacturers turned to frequent model changes as a means of stimulating consumer demand in these areas. This created a need for machine tools capable of producing a wide variety of items. NC machine tools were systematised with industrial robots and other equipment, and by the mid-1980s they had evolved into the core components of FMS (Flexible Manufacturing System) and FMC (Flexible Manufacturing Cell)[3] technology. By 1993 Japan's industrial robot workforce was by far the biggest in the world, accounting for 60.2% of the world total of industrial robots in operation. The former Soviet Union was a distant second with 10.6%, followed by the United States with 8.2%, Germany with 7.2% and all other nations with 13.8% (based on a survey by the International Federation of Robotics).

19.1.3.2. Trends in overseas markets

During the foundation-building stage, machine tool exports were dominated by cheaper models that were exported mainly to developing countries. The value of machine tools exports to developed countries began to increase in earnest in the late 1970s, when NC machine tools emerged as the main export category (Table

[3] Flexible manufacturing systems (FMS) are the systems designed to handle small production runs of large product ranges without human intervention. Generally, such systems consist of NC machine tools, industrial robots, automatic transportation systems, automatic warehousing systems, automatic inspection systems, and central computer control systems. The main components of FMC are NC machine tools and industrial robots.

Table 19.1-2 Trends in machine tool exports and market distribution (%)

	Export value (¥ billions)	Share of NC machines	Export Destination					
			US	West Germany	UK	Korea	Taiwan	Others
1955	0.7		0.1	0.0	0.1	1.0	0.0	98.9
1960	1.6		1.6	0.0	0.0	2.2	5.0	91.2
1965	9.0		19.6	1.0	1.7	2.3	5.3	70.0
1970	24.1	2.5	16.0	3.9	2.0	5.6	0.3	72.2
1975	61.6	13.1	22.8	4.0	4.0	13.3	0.3	55.7
1980	296.6	64.1	36.0	7.6	4.9	4.2	10.1	37.2
1985	395.0	72.1	42.8	7.2	3.8	7.1	2.1	37.1
1990	455.8	81.6	28.8	11.2	4.0	13.5	4.0	38.5
1993	306.1	78.5	31.7	6.8	0.5	13.3	2.0	45.8

Sources: News Digest, The Thirty-year History of Motherly Machinery

19.1-2). Between 1975 and 1980 the value of exports surged from ¥61.6 billion to ¥296.6 billion, which is equivalent to an annual growth rate of 36.9%. Over the same period, the contribution of NC machine tools to total machine tool exports expanded from 13.1% to 64.1%. The percentage of machine tools exported to the United States increased from 22.8% in 1975 to 36.0% in 1980, whilst Germany's share rose from 4.0% to 7.6%.

The success of the Japanese machine tool industry in opening up markets in the developed countries was attributable above all to Japan's leadership in the introduction and mass production of low-cost machines based on NC technology. In the United States, on the other hand, NC technology was used mainly in high-end machine tools designed for use by military suppliers, such as aircraft manufacturers. Europe was reportedly slow to introduce NC tools because of the leadership that it had gained in machine technology, owing to its master toolmaker–based mechanical engineering system. A second reason for the success of Japanese machine tool manufacturers was their ability to offer accurate delivery and superior after-sales service. US machine tool companies, on the other hand, had stabilised their operations during the late 1970s, when US demand expanded resulting in large order backlogs. This situation was reflected in a gradual lengthening of delivery times. Spurred on by the expansion in US demand, Japanese machine tool makers enhanced their after-sales service systems by assigning staff permanently to US sales companies, which they had been establishing since the 1960s. This strategy of commitment to customer needs gradually enabled Japanese machine tool makers to establish a foothold in the US market.

In 1977 US machine tool manufacturers began to criticise the rising tide of Japanese imports. Sharp increases in imports of Japanese machine tools started to cause trade friction with both the United States and Europe. European countries introduced monitoring in 1986, and in 1987 Japan implemented a voluntary restraint agreement covering exports to the United States. Japanese manufacturers were meanwhile starting to establish overseas production operations in earnest, particularly for NC lathes, machining centres and electro-discharge machines. In this way, they were able to lower the US-bound proportion of machine tool exports from 42.8% in 1985 to 31.7% in 1993, whilst Japanese manufacturers' share of the US market in terms of value remained virtually static, falling from 24.6% in 1985 to 22.7% in 1993.

19.1.4. Supply systems and industry structure

19.1.4.1. Product characteristics

By establishing mass-production systems, Japanese machine tool manufacturers were able to produce NC machine tools, particularly multi-purpose machine tools, at prices low enough to widen the market for NC tools to include small- to medium-sized companies. Fig. 19.1-5 shows trends in the wholesale price indexes of NC lathes, lathes, NC milling machines and milling machines. From the early 1980s, there was a rapid decline in the prices of both types of NC machine tools. By 1993 NC machine tools accounted for 77.3% of the value of all machine tools produced in Japan. High-performance NC lathes and machining centres, which accounted for 23.1% and 24.0% respectively, represented about 50% of the total value of Japan's machine tool output. Dedicated machine tools for use by

Fig. 19.1-5 Trends in the wholesale price index of NC machine tools

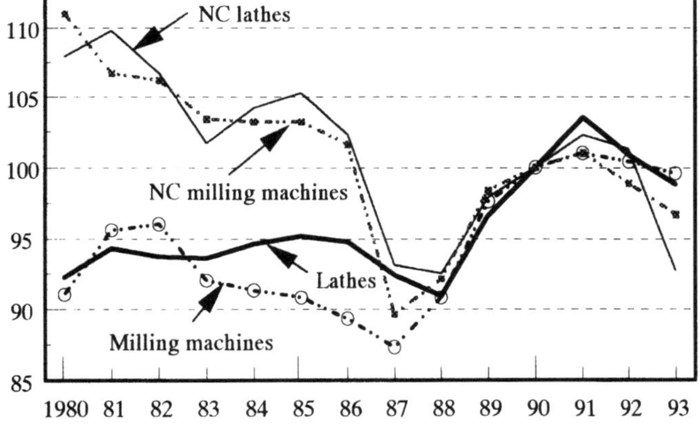

Source: BOJ, "Price Indexes Monthly"

automobile makers and other manufacturers also accounted for a significant share of 17.1%. Meanwhile, users requiring machine tools for super-high-precision processing, such as grinding machines and gear cutters, remained dependent on imports from Switzerland and Germany.

19.1.4.2. Industry structure

The characteristics of machine tools and the wide variety of metal processing needs are reflected in the structure of the machine tool industry. Some 600 machine tool manufacturers are crammed into a small market that even at its peak was worth only ¥1.3 trillion. Of these companies, 70% have three hundred or fewer employees, making this an industry dominated by small- to medium-sized companies. Yet there are also twenty companies with a capital of ¥10 billion or more that are members of Japan Machine Tool Builders, Association. These companies, which are mostly global concerns involved in the production of NC lathes and machining centres, account for 44% of the industry's output (in value terms). Based on the statistics of the Association, production per employee in a manufacturing company with a capital of less than ¥10 billion was ¥15 million per annum, whilst this was ¥24.2 million at a company with a capital of ¥10 billion or more. This indicates that the productivity of big corporations is 1.6 times higher than that of smaller companies, due to mass production and advanced equipment. According to *American Machinist* magazine, fifteen of the world's top twenty-five machine tool manufacturers (ranked in terms of 1993 sales) are Japanese companies.

Around 40% of employees of Japanese machine tool manufacturers are directly employed in company factories, where they acquire production skills through on-the-job training. Workers are trained in multiple skills and deployed to various processes. They are frequently moved amongst areas of work, including processing and assembly, finishing, process control and design. This approach lowers the barriers between different kinds of work and creates a system that can adapt flexibly to new technology.

Machine tool manufacturers also make active use of process subcontracting. An estimated 5,000 primary subcontractors with at least 35,000 secondary subcontractors handle casting, component processing and assembly. In addition, machine tool makers often buy NC controllers, hydraulic devices, servo-motors, ball screws and other key components and materials from outside sources. These components account for 72.1% of total purchasing costs, which in turn account for 45.6% of the materials cost of machine tool manufacturers.

NC devices are purchased from a specific manufacturer. This situation arose because FANUC (formerly a part of the data-processing equipment manufacturer Fujitsu) was able to establish a monopoly by introducing NC technology from the West ahead of other manufacturers and by developing and mass producing devices based on that technology. As a result, Japanese machine tool manufacturers became dependent on NC devices manufactured by FANUC, which controls approximately 50% of the world market. Unlike US and European companies, which turned to in-house production, Japanese machine tool manufacturers were spared the cost of developing their own NC devices. They also benefited from declines in the prices of NC devices owing to the increasing use of semiconductors and from user confidence resulting from the standardisation of specifications.

Since any company in Japan could easily source NC devices and other high-tech components, there was a rapid influx of new companies into the market. This led to price competition as manufacturers strove to rationalise their production processes.

19.1.4.3. Introduction of the latest model technology

Since the 1970s Japanese machine tool manufacturers have continuously invested in the latest equipment and technology. The installation of state-of-the-art facilities has allowed them to rationalise machine tool production and shorten delivery time. Since the 1980s, machine tool manufacturers have aggressively introduced FMS technology, which combines machining centres with industrial robots that handle transportation and assembly. This has enabled them to shift to 24-hour production. When demand slackens, however, manufacturers are often forced to lower their prices drastically in order to maintain operating rates.

19.1.4.4. Distribution systems

Before World War II, machine tools were distributed chiefly through direct sales. After the war, distribution via trading companies became the norm. As the sales volumes of domestic manufacturers expanded, specialist importers began to act as agencies for those companies. Later, general trading companies also entered the machine tool market. During the recession in 1965, the government provided subsidies for instalment sales with the aim of encouraging capital investment by small- to medium-sized companies. Unfortunately, the spread of the instalment sales system led to deterioration in the cash-flow positions of machine tool manufacturers, which were structurally prone to excessive competition. As a result, manufacturers became increasingly dependent on finance from trading companies. The extremely important role played by agencies and trading companies in the market is apparent from the fact that machine tool manufacturers, more than 50% of whose sales volumes are handled by agencies and trading companies, now occupy the majority share of 57% of the total.

During the late 1970s and the 1980s, the direct sales system pioneered by Yamazaki Mazak System spread through overseas markets. This resulted primarily from three factors. First, US dealers in Japanese machine tools were often traders in used machinery. Second, Japanese machine tool manufacturers were unable to use their own brands. Third, the establishment of local sales companies was essential because of the difficulty in obtaining information and providing service.

19.1.5. Role of industrial policies

19.1.5.1. Industrial policies in the early foundation-building period

A variety of support measures with various purposes were implemented during the foundation-building phase of the Japanese machine tool industry. The first of these was the Corporate Rationalisation Promotion Act (fiscal 1952), which targeted thirty-two industries, including automobile manufacturers and machine tool manufacturers. Measures included a specially recognised depreciation system, which allowed accelerated depreciation of 50% of the value of new plant and equipment in the first year. The government also introduced the Machine Tool Import Subsidy (fiscal 1952), which provided subsidies for one-half of import payments for machine tools required by domestic machine tool manufacturers. Another government measure was the Machine Tool Prototype Subsidy System (fiscal 1953–55), which provided subsidies covering one-half of the estimated sales price of newly developed machines. This system, which was applied to sixty-four machines produced by twenty-eight companies, played a significant role in fostering domestic machine tool manufacturers. Other measures included the Machine Instalment Credit Insurance Temporary Measures Act (1961), under which the government provided financial subsidies to encourage small- to medium-sized companies to install machine tool by facilitating the use of instalment payments systems.

19.1.5.2. Industrial policies during the ensuing years

It was between fiscal 1956 and fiscal 1970 that industrial policy was used most actively as a means of countering the effects of trade and capital liberalisation. The Ministry of International Trade and Industry (MITI) formulated its three-phase Machine Tool Manufacturing Industry Rationalisation Basic Plan, which was based on the Machinery Industry Promotion Temporary Measures Act (fiscal 1956–60, 1961–65 and 1966–70). The aim of this plan was to develop a machine tool industry that could avoid excessive competition and achieve economies of scale by adjusting production categories to create a structure based on specialist production. The plan established supply and demand targets, rationalisation goals and capital investment plans, and defined appropriate levels of production for each type of machine tool. Policy finance was provided by the Japan Development Bank and the Small Business Finance Corporation under the Facility Modernisation Designated Machinery Finance system. The Ministry advised manufacturers to cease production of machine tools if they controlled less than 5% of the industry market for those items or if the products in question accounted for less than 20% of their in-house production. Industry organisations formed their own arrangements in response to this plan. In 1966, ten groups were formed, and efforts were made to adjust machine tool production within each group. However, this approach proved ineffective, owing to the lack of competing products in each group, and the group system was abandoned during the 1966–70 economic expansion. From 1961 onwards, a 15–25% tariff was applied to imported machine tools as a trade liberalisation measure. This was low compared with the tariff on imported automobiles, and the level of competition with imported machine tools remained relatively high. The liberalisation of capital transactions in 1970 triggered an upsurge of technology tie-ups with foreign manufacturers. The result was a major improvement in the technology standards of Japanese manufacturers.

19.1.5.3. Later industrial policies

Measures under the Machinery Industry Promotion Temporary Measures Act were later continued under the Specific Electronics and Specific Machinery Industries Promotion Temporary Measures Act (1971–78) and the Machine Information Industry Promotion Temporary Measures Act (1978–85). NC machine tools were eligible for investment promotion measures implemented during recessions, including the Specially Recognised Depreciation System for High-Precision Machine Tools (1976), which allowed special depreciation of 25% of the purchase price, and the Investment Promotion Taxation System (1978), which allowed 10% of the purchase price to be deducted from corporate tax.

19.1.5.4. Evaluation of industrial policy

In retrospect, it is apparent that industrial policy towards the machine tool industry was successful in the sense that it helped to foster Japanese machine tool manufacturers, primarily by encouraging modernisation during the industry's foundation-building period and the subsequent drive towards self-sufficiency. For example, although machine tool manufacturers were able to use only 60% of the grants available under the Machine Tool Import Subsidy system as a result of the impoverished state of the industry, a total of twenty-six machines were imported from the United States and Europe by ten manufacturers. Furthermore, the government's efforts to create an investment environment conducive to the modernisation of machinery industries through tax breaks and other measures led to an upsurge of capital investment that benefited the machine tool industry both directly and indirectly. However, production adjustment measures designed to strengthen the structure of the machine tool industry failed to realise the government's aims to establish a production structure based on specialised companies and to consolidate the types of machines produced. This was because the policy was limited to the establishment of targets. Yet in the long-term perspective, fierce and unrestricted competition amongst large numbers of companies ultimately brought improvement in the international competitiveness of the industry.

19.1.6. Main factors contributing to the development of the industry

The main reason for the growth of Japanese machine tool manufacturers was their leadership in the commercialisation of general-purpose NC machine tools. The ease with which Japanese manufacturers were able to introduce this new technology can be attributed to two factors. First, the practice of frequently shifting employees amongst different areas of activities encouraged flexible factory systems. Second, there was the presence of FANUC as the leading specialist producer of NC systems. The rationalisation of production through the continuous introduction of the latest technology, such as FMS, also made a major contribution to the machine tool industry's ability to develop low-cost NC machine tools. The price competitiveness of Japanese machine tool manufacturers was further enhanced by their ability to work interactively with small- to medium-sized companies, which also possessed advanced processing technology, through the outsourcing of parts and the subcontracting of processes.

The need for labour-saving measures in the post–oil crisis environment led to the increasing use of NC machine tools by Japanese manufacturers, including not only major corporations but also small- to medium-sized companies. In addition, Japanese users are extremely demanding about the precision and efficiency of the capital goods they use in their production processes. This characteristic reflects fierce competition, particularly amongst automobile and electrical machinery manufacturers, to increase market share through the rapid start up of production lines and through price reductions made possible by mass production benefits. This environment strengthened the competitiveness of Japanese machine tools in terms of both price and non-price factors, including delivery time and after-sales service. More recently, the sophistication of NC machine tools has received a further boost from the development of systems capable of small-lot production of large product ranges, which are vital to the diversification of manufactured goods, and to product differentiation strategies.

Fierce competition at the processing and assembly stages has forced Japanese machine tool manufacturers, which are mostly small- to medium-sized companies, to pursue strategies that closely reflect user needs. This situation has enhanced the ability of Japanese NC machine tools to compete internationally in both price and non-price terms.

19.2. Germany's Machine Tool Industry

19.2.1. Overview

19.2.1.1. Product programme

Traditionally, the German capital-goods industries have always been highly competitive in respect of quality standards and technology. One major underlying factor explaining this strength is the qualification of the workforce, the so-called "dual education system" of apprenticeship on the shop floor and classroom education in natural and engineering sciences. In combination with the high social status of engineers—compared with other nations'—many German companies' strategies have been centred around technical issues.

Within this context, the technological orientation of the machine tool industry is typically German. The companies have a strong position in the supply of special-purpose machines, such as finishing and gear-cutting machines, customised machinery and engineered systems, e.g., transfer lines, FMS and FMC.

Simultaneous with the increasing share of engineered products, the importance of forming machines has grown. In the early 1950s it accounted for 25% only, but it reached an all-time high of 36% in 1994 and will continue to remain higher than 30%.

19.2.1.2. Machine tool industry's importance within the German manufacturing industries

In Germany about three-quarters of production is delivered to capital-goods industries and most of the remainder to other manufacturing industries. Because of the specific machining and engineering know-how, the industry is indispensable for their clients.

The design of automated production lines is one important task of computer-aided manufacturing (CAM). Its full integration into other companies' functions (CIM) has been achieved by inter-linking the production planning system (PPS) and computer-aided design (CAD) with computers that supervise the flow of the production.

In spite of this importance, the weight of this industry compared to the rest of manufacturing industries is low. The machine tool firms contributed only 0.5% to the overall production in 1994. In 1960 the contribution accounted for 1.6%. The reason for this tendency lies in emerging new products, e.g., robotics, computers, etc., in the capital-goods markets (Fig. 19.2-1).

Fig. 19.2-1 Machine tool production and demand

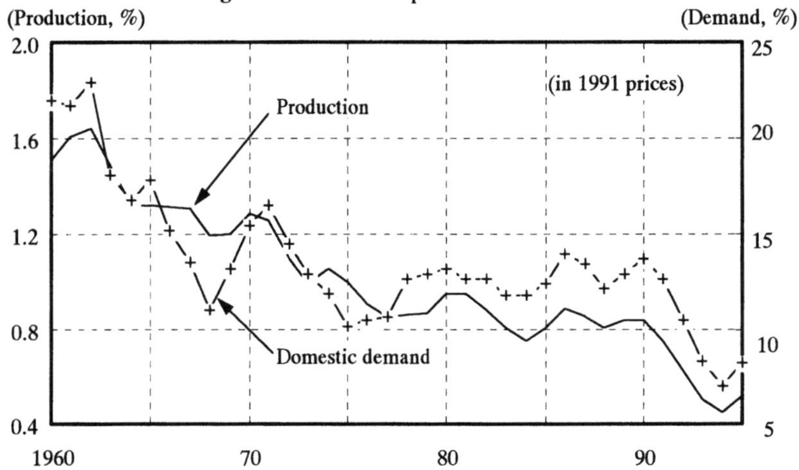

Source: Federal Statistical Office; VDMA; Ifo Institute

19.2.2. Important stages in the post-war period

19.2.2.1. Reconstruction period (1948–1960)

The dissolution of the Third Reich and the formation of various occupation zones posed serious questions for the future of Germany. The eastern parts that had a share of 50% of German machine tool production were lost to the Soviet Union, Poland and the German Democratic Republic, created under Soviet protection. The following analyses focus on the development of the Federal Republic up to 1991; thereafter, they comprise reunited Germany.

Up to 1948 the production of machine tools was totally forbidden. Thereafter, the constraints were loosened. In 1948 West German machine tool production reached DM 120 million, and new order bookings indicated growth. During the following years, exports grew strongly as a consequence of the boom induced by the Korean war. Up to 1952 the export ratio increased to 50%, which was the average level up to the mid-1960s. As a result of the influx of know-how from East Germany, the industry succeeded in becoming a full-hand supplier during the first half of the 1950s. Thus, the import ratio was low at around 10% and remained at this level up to the mid-1960s (Fig. 19.2-2).

Fig. 19.2-2 Import and export of German machine tools

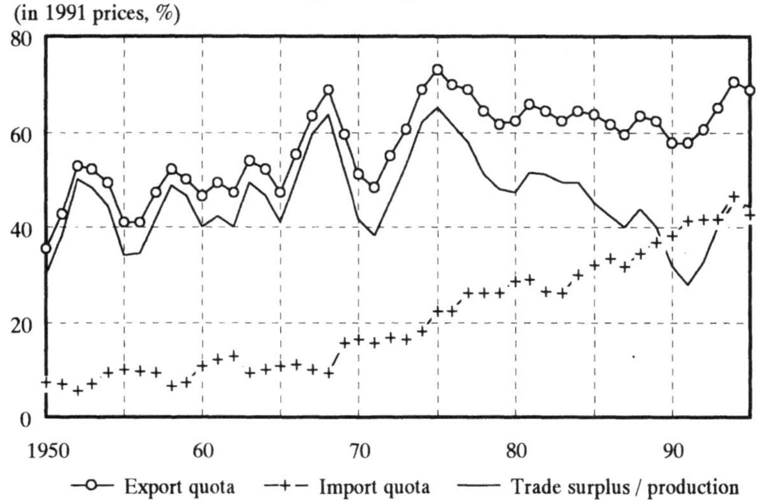

Note: Export quota = exports / production
Import quota = imports / consumption

Source: VDMA; Ifo Institute

19.2.2.2. Final stage of reconstruction after World War II (1961–1971)

The expansion of the German economy was caused by internal reconstruction and external demand. The latter was induced by a growing international competitiveness, based on a cheap but well-trained labour force, engineering know-how, and perpetuated by economic framework factors. Because of low inflation rates and a strong growing productivity, the D-Mark tended to become undervalued in a system of fixed exchange rates despite several appreciations.

Within this environment, machine tool companies invested heavily in the expansion of domestic production, and a growing number of foreign workers were recruited. The development peaked at the beginning of the 1970s, foreign employment reached a share of 8.5% of the total workforce, and the investment ratio, i.e., the investment expenditure for machinery and equipment as a percentage of value added, gained an all time high of 12.5%.

In the late 1960s, the first time in the post-war period, foreign machine tool suppliers were able to increase their shares in the German market significantly. The import ratio surpassed 15% in 1970 and continued to increase. Simultaneously the export ratio that had reached an excessively high level of 70% in 1968 shrank to about 50%. In retrospect, both of these developments indicate a changing pattern in companies' behaviour.

Table 19.2-1 Key data of the German machine tool industry

Variables	DM million[a]	Real average annual growth rate in % [b]				
	1991	1950-60	1961-71	1972-83	1984-90	1991-95
Production	15.9	13.8	3.6	-2.3	4.2	-7.5
Exports	9.2	16.9	4.0	-0.2	3.0	-5.4
Imports	4.7	16.1	7.8	0.1	14.6	-9.1
Domestic demand	11.4	12.1	3.8	-3.9	8.8	-11.1
Indicators		Average of the period in %				
Export ratio		46.4	53.6	63.4	61.6	62.2
Import ratio		8.3	12.5	23.1	32.8	40.9
Trade surplus[c]		41.5	46.9	52.4	42.6	36.1

a) West Germany.
b) West Germany, beyond 1990 total Germany.
c) As a percentage of German machine tool production.

Source: VDMA, VDW, Ifo Institute

19.2.2.3. Internationalising markets (1972–1983)

Up to the end of the 1960s the German machine tool industry tended to be a full-line supplier, highly competitive in technology and price. Its price competitiveness diminished with the end of the Bretton Woods fixed exchange-rate system and a more aggressive wage policy of the trade unions. Additionally, the former strong productivity growth did not continue (Fig. 19.2-3) The companies focused more on the manufacturing of technologically advanced machinery. To remain full-line suppliers, a growing share of low-end products was procured from foreign firms.

In the early 1970s German firms provided 22% and 35% of world-wide production of machine tools and world trade respectively. The contribution to the world output shrank only slightly, whilst the share of world trade continuously shrank until the mid-1980s and stabilised at around 25%. Both of these reductions were caused by emerging new competitors. Nevertheless, the export ratio grew until the mid-1970s, and since then has been fluctuating at around 65%. Foreign suppliers continuously gained market shares in Germany throughout the period, and the trade surplus—as a share of machine tool production—started to declined after the mid-1970s (Fig. 19.2-4).

19.2.2.4. Bright investment climate in manufacturing industries (1984–1990)

After a severe recession in 1982/83, the subsequent recovery ended a decade of dampened investment activity. The upward trend peaked in 1990. Several causal factors have been identified: the necessity to replace outdated machinery and equipment procured during the investment boom at the end of the 1960s, the

Fig. 19.2-3 Labour productivity of the German machine tool industry

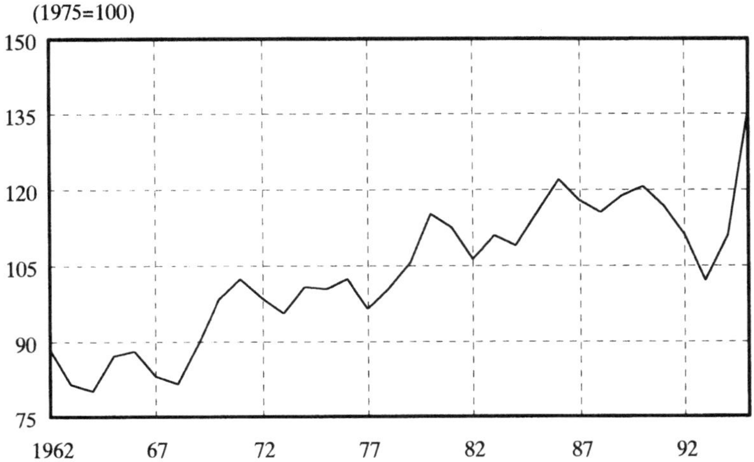

Source: VDW, Ifo Institute

Fig. 19.2-4 German key data in the global machine tool business

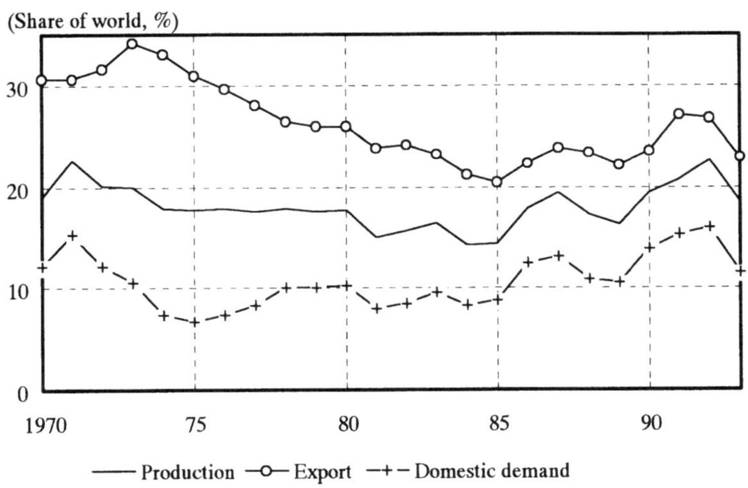

Source: American Machinist, Ifo Institute

availability of new automation techniques, and companies' initiatives to prepare for the Single European Market.

During the early 1970s the dissemination of numerically controlled machine tools started, but their share of all machine tools had run up to only 17% in 1981. After 1981 dissemination accelerated, and up to the end of the decade the share of NC machines reached nearly 60% and approached the saturation point (Fig. 19.2-5). Additionally, high-speed processing, non-mechanical machining, multi-purpose machinery and FMS/FMC were disseminated during that time.

The bright investment climate was not a German phenomenon only; nearly all West European countries enjoyed a similar development. The German machine tool industry with its close trade relations to European countries experienced a strong growth, and its share of world-wide production and international trade grew until the early 1990s up to 22% and 27%, respectively.

19.2.2.5. Merging of east and west German machine tool industries (1991–1995)

At the beginning of the 1990s, many European countries suffered the most severe recession in the post-war period, and investment expenditure slumped. Because of unification, the recession was delayed somewhat in Germany. But the machine tool industry was unable to prevent a reduction of exports already in 1991. The appreciation of the D-Mark in 1992 and 1993 worsened the situation.
Manufacturers of standard machines in the cutting machine tool area were hit harder by the recession than others. Some important manufacturers went bankrupt and a major reshuffling took place. The share of cutting machine tools in the production of all machine tools shrank from 70% to 63% within a couple of years. But retrospection indicates a continuing trend towards long-term shrinkage that had

Fig.19.2-5 Dissemination of numeric controls (Share of NC machines)

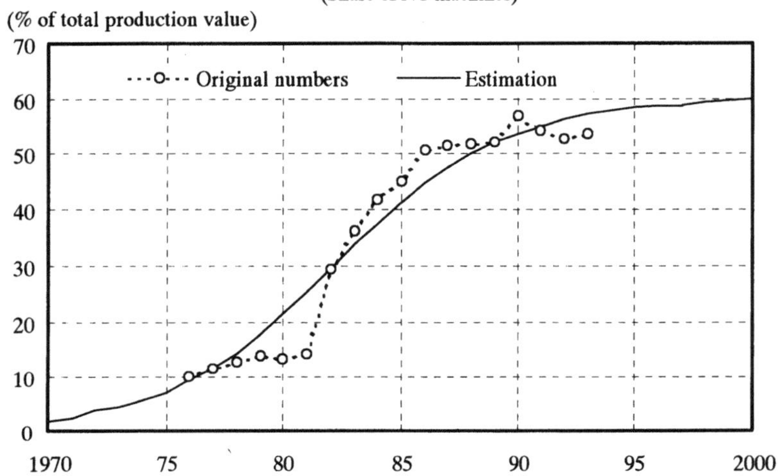

Source: VDW, Ifo Institute

only been halted by the effects of the dissemination of NC technology (Fig. 19.2-6).

In 1991 the east German machine tool industry contributed about 8% to total German production. Although it had been one of the most important suppliers of manufacturing technology in the former Eastern Bloc, much of the production equipment and processes were out-of-date. Many plants were shut down in recent years. In 1994 this trend had come to an end, and currently the framework conditions of east Germany provide a more competitive environment.

19.2.3. Demand side

19.2.3.1. Domestic market

Most of the demand for machine tools comes from capital-goods industries. The automotive industry is in the lead with about one-third, second in this ranking is the electrical products industry, comprising engineering and durable consumer products, followed by mechanical engineering with about one-fifth. Steel forming and metal structure manufacturing have only a share of 5% each of total domestic demand. The machine tool demand of the aerospace industry is of minor importance by volume, but its high technological requirements provide an important technological pull.

Although the German machine tool industry has always been strongly dependent on exports, domestic demand has affected the orientation of the product programme. The industry's competence in machining big parts has been positively influenced by the importance of clients in heavy industries. Precision machining,

Fig. 19.2-6 Share of cutting machines

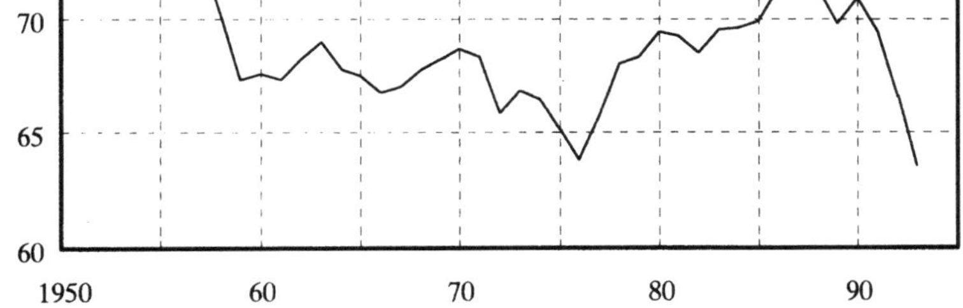

Source: VDA, Ifo Istitute

such as grinding and gear cutting, is required by the capital-goods industry for the manufacturing of high-performance production machines.

The poor status of German manufacturing industries in electronics, specifically consumer electronics, has resulted in only moderate demand for machines suited to high-precision machining of extremely small parts. This explains the relatively weak position of the German machine tool industry in this market segment.

19.2.3.2. Foreign markets

Shortly after the foundation of the Federal Republic, the German machine tool industry was successful in foreign markets. Major demand came from Western Europe, which ordered about 70% of total exports throughout the 1950s. The reconstruction of Western European production facilities provided the environment for growth. During this period, eastern Europe—traditionally important for German firms—was a difficult market due to the restrictions of the cold war (Fig. 19.2-7).

Already during the late 1950s the importance of Asian markets grew, and the focus of German exports to Western Europe tended to decline. In 1960 the machine tool deliveries to Asia ran up to nearly 20% of total machine tool exports, and since then have been staggering around 10% to 15%. The most important single markets have been Japan and the Peoples Republic of China. Both of these markets boomed during the late-1980s and have stimulated exports into this region once more.

Fig. 19.2-7 German export of machine tools (Major destination share)

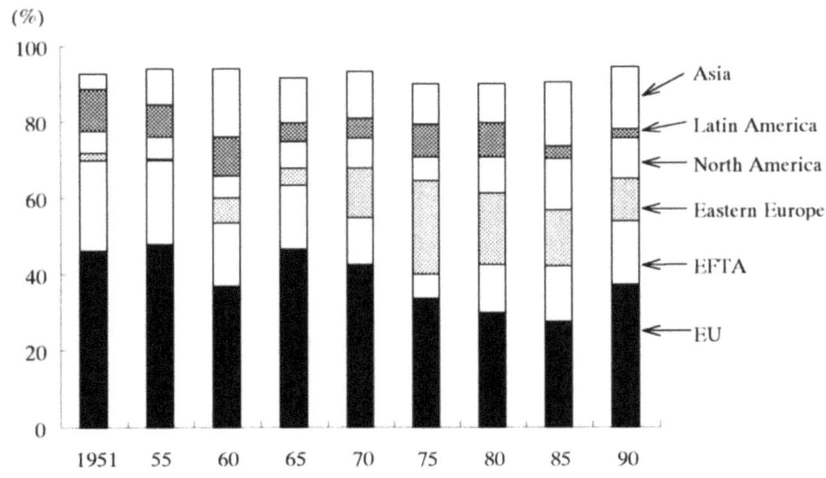

Source: VDMA; Ifo Institute

Exports to European countries comprise a broad product programme, whilst deliveries to overseas markets are bound above all to special machinery. This means that German firms' global approach is linked to comparative technological advantages. Therefore direct investment, as a strategy to substitute exports for local production, has been of less importance for German firms than for Japanese competitors.

19.2.4. Supply side

19.2.4.1. Characteristics of German machine tools

In addition to Swiss firms, German manufacturers have succeeded in supplying machine tools requiring special machining know-how, especially in finishing and gear-cutting processes. Their know-how in the machining of extremely big parts, such as the machining of ships' diesel-engine crankshafts, gives them a leading edge in world markets.

In the area of engineered automated systems, the industry has become an important supplier of know-how to client industries. The demand of the automotive industry is of special importance for the manufacturers of transfer lines and FMS/FMC.

19.2.4.2. Industry structure

In terms of company size and ownership, the machine tool industry is typical for the so-called German *Mittelstand* (middle-sized companies). The average number of employees per company is 215. The majority of independent firms are controlled by one or only a few owners. Traditionally these are committed to the long term and pursue corresponding strategies. But their basis for financing is rather limited, because they do not have broad access to capital markets and are often linked to one bank only, the so-called *Hausbank*. During the past decades a shift towards joint-stock companies has taken place, and some independent companies disappeared in the course of acquisitions by competitors and by mergers.

Centres of gravity for the machine tool industry are North-Rhine Westphalia and Baden-Württemberg, both closely linked to the automotive industry, and in eastern German Saxony.

In comparison with other European countries' machine tool industries, German firms are large. However, analysis by size shows that the structure is homogeneous. There are no German firms which dominate the industry in terms of size and market share, as in Japan, and only a few extremely small firms exist, as in Italy and Japan, that have difficulty operating as independent companies.

19.2.4.3. Management strategies

Traditionally, German companies are driven by technology. Often engineers and even university professors are members of the executive or supervisory board and responsible for the development of companies' strategies. There are some family-owned, medium-sized firms that have become world leaders in market segments.

In the sector of standard machinery this orientation has proven not to be very successful. Although these firms gained shares in overseas markets during the 1960s and 1970s, especially in the United States, they never launched adequate market strategies. These firms remained vulnerable because of only commanding low market shares and by being dependent on cross-border deliveries.

During the early 1980s, most German machine tool manufacturers started to renew their production technology by launching FMS/FMC equipped with robots. These activities continuing throughout the decade were not only instigated to reduce costs, but also to accumulate experience with advanced automated systems. The assembly of machine tools remained a predominantly labour-intensive process and the automation of warehousing was of minor importance, because even in the area of standard machinery batches are too low for efficient use.

In response to the developments of the early 1990s, machine tool manufacturers have strengthened their efforts to reduce production costs by subcontracting and purchasing standardised components. There are some opportunities to reduce disadvantages especially in the manufacturing of standard machines. For castings and other non-key components, central eastern European suppliers have gained importance.

In the late-1980s, German machine tool firms enjoyed growing profits, with shares of total turnover at about 4% on average for the industry. With regard to the then booming demand, this percentage was too low and indicated an insufficient financial performance. Thus, the recession of the early 1990s induced heavy losses.

19.2.4.4. Distribution

In the domestic market, direct sales to customers are of major importance, above all in customised machinery markets. Many firms have their own representatives and bureaus for after sales services. Others use agents with exclusive distribution rights. Machine tool trading companies are of minor importance only.

Many machine tool suppliers have their own distribution organisations in other European countries that provide direct market access. Otherwise, distribution subsidiaries are of importance only in the US market. Whilst in the past companies tried to open up foreign markets independently, currently a growing number of joint ventures are being launched.

19.2.5. Framework conditions and the government's industrial policy

19.2.5.1. Social partnership

A special feature of the German labour market is the Law on Collective Wage Bargaining. Negotiations are undertaken by representatives of the industries' employer associations and their counterparts, the industries' unions. This situation has led to relatively low wage-differentiation compared with other countries.

This environment helped foster a consensus which offset the opposing interests of employers and employees throughout the reconstruction period. Since the 1970s wage bargaining has become tougher; what was an advantage turned out to be a burden because of inflexibilities in adjusting to the highly different and changing requirements of firms. Machine tool manufacturers have had to focus more and more on markets where they enjoy comparative advantages. Strategies for cost reduction have been set in motion by outsourcing labour-intensive production to other countries.

German unification has helped to improve flexibility in the labour market. In the east, wages are lower, working hours are longer, and more companies are not participating in collective wage agreements, which stimulates intra-German competition. Nevertheless, the German machine tool industry must focus more and more on the manufacturing of special machinery and subcontract a growing share of non-key parts and components to foreign firms.

19.2.5.2. Competition policy

Competition is an important prerequisite for the functioning of the market mechanism. It is an impediment to the companies' objective to maximise profits. As long as market access is open, monopolists and innovators are followed by others, and there is a permanent stimulus for pushing developments for new products and processes.

The watchman of the liberal German market system is the Federal Cartel Office (Bundeskartellamt), which has the express task of ensuring competition. Any activities that curb competition can be forbidden. Companies' agreements on the assignment of categories of products to different companies, such as proposed by the Japanese MITI, would be prohibited in Germany. Even in emergency cases, the Cartel Office thoroughly investigates the impact of mergers on competition. For example, in the case of the direct competitors Maho and Deckel, considerable time passed before both stumbling firms were allowed to merge.

19.2.5.3. Industry associations

Employers' associations provide advantages, especially in the case of an industry of medium-sized firms. Associations do not only act as representatives and lobbies. They are also in charge of logistic support for member firms and coordinate common activities. The German Machine Tool Association (VDW) is a prototype of such an organisation and was created at the end of the nineteenth century.

During the early 1950s, the Association launched activities to improve access to foreign markets, one of which was the co-ordination of a joint European initiative for a common exhibition, the so-called EMO. Another important field of activities lies in the organisation and co-ordination of research and development. Already in 1951 the Association started to support universities. The traditionally close and fruitful interrelations were revived and expanded continuously.

Machine tool firms have also worked together in basic R&D (*Gemeinschaftsforschung*), partly funded by government ministries.

19.2.5.4. Research and development

In the early 1960s, the VDW monitored the development of numeric controls in the United States and prepared its own research. Before the 1970s, these machines were of minor economic importance only. In the early 1970s, publicly funded schemes for research into electronic data processing in the manufacturing industries, especially machining and designing of products, were launched, with machine tool industry participation. Since then, publicly funded schemes for R&D in German firms have been expanded at the level of the EU, the federal government and the German Länder.

In spite of all the efforts in Germany and in other European countries, electronic companies were not able to provide numeric controls in the late 1970s that were comparable in price and technology with those of Japanese producers. This was a major handicap, and German firms had to relinquish shares in highly expansive markets. In the late 1980s the situation stabilised, and the Japanese lead in this technology has been eliminated.

With regard to machine tool innovations, German firms are world leaders based on the number of domestic and foreign patent applications. Second in this ranking is the United States followed by Japan (Fig. 19.2-8). Considering the size of German industry, which is much smaller than the Japanese, this indicates an extraordinary effort in R&D. In relation to turnover about 6% is spent on R&D.

There is a focus in German R&D on the mechanical sciences, including high speed machining. In new technologies, such as in ceramics, metal coating and controls, German firms are not far ahead. There is a relative weakness in new technologies that has been typical for German manufacturing industries.

19.2.5.5. Assessment

The machine tool industry in Germany is integrated in a highly developed international division of labour. This has resulted in the procurement of more simple machinery from abroad and of non-key parts from Southern or Eastern European companies. The domestic division of labour is predominantly focused on

Fig. 19.2-8 Inventions in machine tool technologies

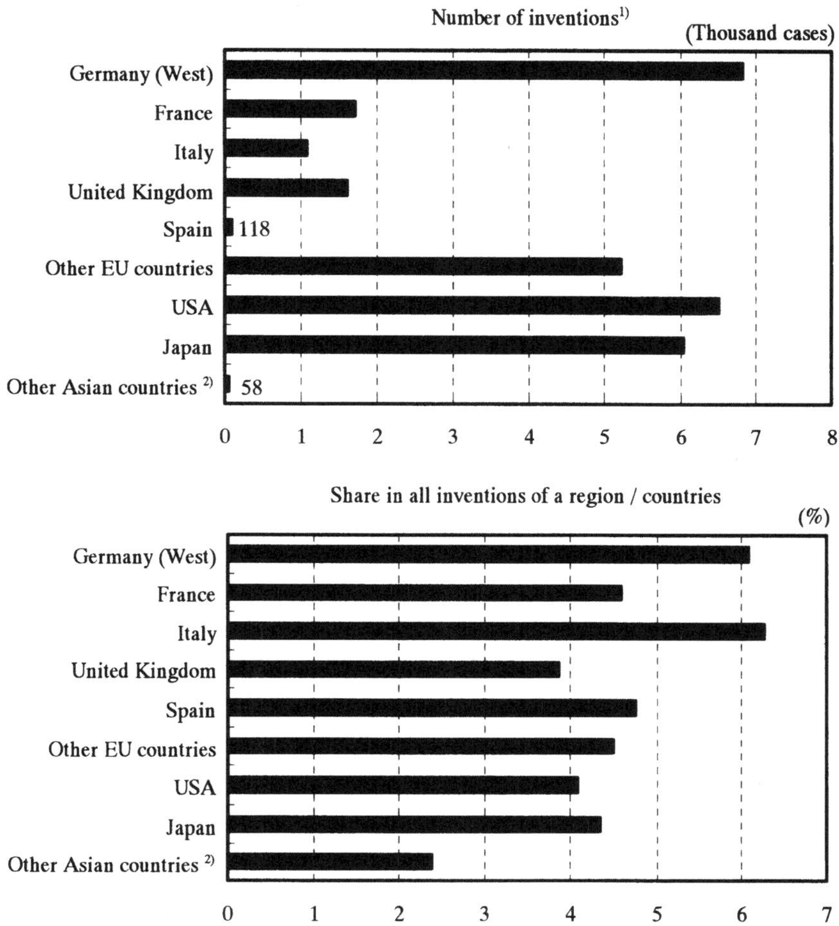

Note: 1) Patent applications in more than one country between 1982 and 1989
2) People's Republic of China, Korea, Malaysia, the Philippines, Singapore, Taiwan, Thailand

Source: Inpadoc; Ifo Institute.

high-tech components. This situation is an effect of the relatively homogeneous labour market that supplies qualified but not cheap labour.

There are many suppliers in the machine tool market with overlapping product programmes. The predominantly medium-sized firms have not tended to develop towards big firms with high market shares. This situation is due to the structure of ownership, but also to difficulties in financing growth strategies. Furthermore, activities affecting competition would have been thoroughly investigated by the cartel agency. In addition, the structure of the industry has been stabilised by a non-standardised supply of preliminary products that hampered an evolution of volume markets and provides an explanation for the weakness in standardised machines.

19.2.6. Major success factors and prospects

19.2.6.1. Specialisation

The German machine tool industry has focused on engineering sciences and has a strong international position in areas of specific processes. This orientation is in line with comparative advantages of Germany in global competition. A sufficient number of well-educated engineers is supplied by universities, and there are highly reputed research institutes for the execution of basic R&D.

Emerging competitors from the NICs, suffering bottlenecks from a lack of qualified engineers, focus on standardised machinery. Thus, these countries make the most efficient use of the scarce input "engineer". NIC competition is especially strong in standardised machinery markets and poses a problem for industrialised countries' firms because of their limited price competitiveness. For German firms this problem is less serious.

Nevertheless, totally abandoning markets for standard machines would endanger the long-term existence of the German machine tool industry, owing to the connections between standardised and special machinery. High-volume output eases the funding of basic R&D that can be utilised for all kinds of machine tools, and some components for machine tools must be manufactured in high numbers.

19.2.6.2. R&D efforts

The German machine tool industry is know-how driven, and many firms are concentrating in areas in which they have a leading edge in technology. These specialising companies are global players, although many of them are medium-sized and family-owned.

Other firms are working in the area of manufacturing systems. They develop machines and FMS/FMC for specific production purposes. These firms are dedicated to specific applications or to one industry. They have gained more and more know-how in production processes and have become indispensable for client industries that are reducing their own production planning staff.

The latest available technologies are thoroughly evaluated before being used as the basis for innovation. German firms are averse to risk-taking and fear that advanced technologies could endanger the quality and reliability of their machines. This cautious approach is not only true for the machine tool industry but for most German industries. The disadvantages of German firms caused by the late adoption of NC techniques have diminished, but another new technology may become important that once more will be utilised too late and pose a further threat to the industry.

19.2.6.3. Internationalisation

During the reconstruction period, German firms enjoyed the advantage of a growing European demand. With the 1957 Rome Treaties the basis for the European Economic Community was laid, and German machine tool firms became European players with an average market share of 18% in member countries. Production sites and distribution networks were established.

Overseas markets were of minor importance only, and exports were not promoted by strategic investments. Above all, independent agencies were designated as footholds for sales and services. One exception was the United States, the most important foreign market apart from France. Some German machine tool companies have set up their own production sites and distribution agencies. Nevertheless, the market penetration has remained low in comparison with the Japanese competitors that entered the United States market later on.

Because of the focus on Europe, the growth potential for the German machine tool industry is low. This is true for industrialised Western European countries but also for Eastern Europe. The successor states of the former Soviet Union will continue to be troubled economically and the Central Eastern European countries will only enjoy a modest recovery. Thus, the German machine tool industry has to increase its access to overseas markets, especially to those of the Asian Pacific Rim.

19.3. Comparative Summary of the Machine Tool Industry

The machine tool industry is small and its contribution to the value added of all of the manufacturing industries for most industrialised countries is less than 1%. Nevertheless, it is of major importance for manufacturing firms' process innovations.

Generally speaking, a machine tool is defined as a "self-creating" machine. A more specific definition is based on use: machine tools are designed to machine metal and so-called new materials, such as ceramics, whereas woodworking machines are explicitly excluded.

Based on the type of machining, there are two broad product groups: cutting and forming machine tools. The first group accounts for about three-quarters of the world production and the second accounts for the rest.

The major groups amongst cutting machine tools—tools that remove chips from the workpiece—are lathes, milling, boring, drilling, grinding and gear-cutting machines. Further subgroups are machining centres that combine different operations, e.g., milling, drilling and finishing operations.

The machine tool industry also supplies flexible manufacturing systems/cells (FMS/FMC) that are used for the automatic machining of complete parts. These systems consist of several NC-controlled machine tools, handling equipment (e.g., robots), workpiece storage and a host computer. A specific kind of FMS is the transfer lines purchased by the automotive industry.

The major groups amongst forming machine tools—defined as tools that reshape massive or sheet material—are presses, hammers, forging, bending and shearing machines. As in the case of cutting machines, automated manufacturing systems are available, e.g., transfer presses for car bodies that combine several machining steps within one integrated system.

Machine tools for non-mechanical machining, such as electrical-discharge machines/electro-chemical machines (EDM/ECM) and laser-cutting machines assumed growing importance during the 1980s.

Machine tools are a category of capital goods that are indispensable for factory automation. But advanced automated processes require more and more complementary input, such as handling, transport and warehousing equipment, so computers and software have enjoyed a greater demand than that for machine tools. Thus, the relative importance of machine tools has shrunk in nearly all industrialised countries. The share of machine tools in total manufacturing output has shown a long-term, declining tendency for Germany and Japan.

19.3.1. Industry's post-war situation

A comparison of the German and the Japanese industry indicates that German firms regained competitiveness much earlier during the post-war period. They succeeded in supplying a comprehensive product programme during the early 1950s and simultaneously gained shares in foreign markets. Germany enjoyed price competitiveness due to low domestic inflation rates; productivity gains and stable exchange rates perpetuated these advantages. These framework conditions were favourable for investment in domestic plants.

During this period, the lack of self-sufficiency in the Japanese economy made it dependent on machine tool imports. MITI launched initiatives to reduce this dependency, amongst them a proposal to restructure the machine tool industry. Firms were encouraged to focus on their core business, resulting in an efficient use of scarce resources, economies of scale and limited competition. Although this initiative was not welcomed by the industry, its structure was changed in the long term. It is noteworthy that this proposal contained elements closely related to US management theories aimed at firms operating in standard machinery markets.

Since the early 1970s, the price competitiveness of Germany has worsened, owing to, amongst other factors, a tougher wage policy, higher inflation rates and the appreciation of the D-Mark under a flexible exchange-rate regime. In combination with a homogeneous labour market, German firms relinquished production of low-tech products, and deepened the international division of labour.

The importance of foreign firms in the domestic market grew, whilst dependency on foreign demand remained high.

During the early 1970s, the Japanese economy reached self-sufficiency in the supply of machine tools and started its triumphant advance in the world market. Important underlying factors were standardisation and NC technology. Above all, FANUC's strategy of striving to become a market leader in numeric controls by supplying technologically advanced, low-priced electronic/electrical packages induced machine tool manufacturers to evolve from medium-sized to volume suppliers, a tendency that was encouraged by the MITI initiatives mentioned above.

19.3.2. Export strategy

Japanese firms pursued a two-fold strategy in opening up Asian and North American markets: exports and direct investment. This has given them direct market access and has made them less vulnerable than their German competitors. The Japanese activities in Western Europe were less important in the beginning, but accelerated during the latter half of the 1980s. Frictions have risen in the course of growing market penetration, but voluntary restraint agreements and monitoring bodies have not been able to stop Japanese success.

In Germany, as in other European countries, the development of numerical controls was delayed, and there was no firm that pursued a strategy comparable to FANUC's. In all of Europe, four major players and many smaller firms were competing on the market with a multifarious supply hampering the utilisation of economies of scale. In addition to suffering from a technological gap, German/European firms were not price competitive. In the course of the 1980s they caught up technologically, but in terms of prices they were not competitive until the early 1990s—partly caused by the appreciation of the yen and partly by the supply of advanced and simultaneously low-priced numeric controls.

19.3.3. Structural differences

In the machine tool industry both the German as well as the Japanese companies tend to be medium-sized. Most firms are independent and do not belong to a group or *keiretsu*. Whilst the size structure of the German industry is homogeneous, in Japan it is dominated by several firms that are overwhelmingly big and highly competitive in standard machinery markets and have become global players. The funding of their dynamic growth was easier than it would have been for German firms because of better access to financial markets. In addition, there are numerous small firms in Japan that utilise extremely cheap labour on the domestic market and work as subcontractors for final machine manufacturers. These firms have been of importance for the high price competitiveness of the entire Japanese machine tool industry. In contrast, German firms have few opportunities to procure low-priced preliminary products from domestic subcontractors.

19.3.4. Corporate strategy

German firms have utilised comparative advantages in the area of engineering to succeed in international competition. Companies' strategies are driven by technology. Machine tools for special machining operations, machining of extremely big parts, and systems have been of major importance. This orientation is also linked to the strength of German manufacturing industries in capital goods, especially mechanical engineering.

The strategic orientation of Japanese firms is marked by an application of US management techniques and provides one explanation for their success. The firms that were successful in the area of standard machine tools in Japan pursued thorough price reduction of NC machine tools through mass production and increasing the efficiency and effectiveness of the production process.

The readiness to apply new technologies is another important characteristic of the Japanese machine tool industry and is partly due to framework conditions different from those in Germany. Japanese firms' clients stimulate R&D. For instance, precision machining of small parts is required by the highly successful Japanese electronics industry.

19.3.5. Policy differences

German economic policy has been marked by liberalism, although since the early 1970s some elements of industrial policy have been introduced, above all in the area of R&D. Political interference has always provoked criticism, but in the area of new technology research specific initiatives were introduced to close the gap to the United States and Japan, albeit with limited success. The competitiveness of German machine tool firms was above all acquired by exposing themselves to functioning markets and using comparative advantages.

In the past, guidance and protection were at the centre of Japanese industrial policy, and initiatives for the strengthening of the machine tool industry's competitiveness were launched. This has changed over time, and industrial targeting has become more or less a co-ordinating process. MITI acts as a mediator for firms, determining important areas for basic research and defining joint projects. In combination with the market requirements, new technologies have achieved high priority.

In Germany there is strong competition between domestic and foreign machine tool suppliers in most of the market segments. Predominantly foreign companies use independent agencies as distributors. In Japan the situation is quite different. Since self-sufficiency has been reached, foreign suppliers are only of importance if no adequate domestic supply is available. This is partly due to stiff competition amongst domestic standard machinery manufacturers, but also to the structure of distribution. A great number of independent agencies, working predominantly on a regional basis, makes it difficult for foreign companies to gain a broad market access.

The German and the Japanese machine tool industry focus on different areas, but in the area of standardised machine tools direct competition will continue. Although German firms have lost market share, they are currently increasing their efforts in these markets. If they succeed, long-term perspectives are bright; otherwise the industrial cluster will be weakened, synergies will be lost, and firms will suffer losses, even in the German machine tool industry's domain markets of specialised machinery.

Japanese firms will be facing the challenge of emerging competitors from the NICs in standardised machines—a challenge intensified by the yen's appreciation. The advantages of low-wage labour in Japan have disappeared and a structural change in production is necessary. Relocation is one option, but the necessary adjustment is hampered by capacities installed during the late 1980s. Owing to the regional orientation of exports and the close links to the electronics and airplane industries, the growth perspectives are better than for their German counterparts.

20. Automobile Industry

20.1. Japan's Automobile Industry

20.1.1. Definition of the industry

Passenger cars, trucks and busses are generically called "automobiles;" passenger cars are further subdivided into ordinary cars, small cars and light motor vehicles. The criteria used for classifying passenger cars in Japan are shown in Table 20-1.1.

In this chapter the history of the automobile industry and the factors contributing to its growth are examined with the primary focus placed on standard passenger cars. Every automobile is assembled from some 20,000–30,000 parts, which are made by numerous parts manufacturers from a wide variety of materials. In late 1993, 910,000 people were directly engaged in manufacturing automobiles, and if employees in such sectors as materials and parts as well as sales and servicing are included, the number would increase to over three million. The total production in terms of value amounted to ¥21 trillion for the automobile manufacturing industry during 1993, and ¥42 trillion with the peripheral industries for parts and materials included. Automobile exports (including parts and motorcycles) were worth $76.8 billion for 1993, or 21.3% of total exports. Statistics such as these are indicative of the importance of the automobile industry to the Japanese economy.

20.1.2. Industry development after the war

20.1.2.1. Forming the industry basis (1945–1964)

(a) Post-war reconstruction

The Japanese automobile industry began to develop as a result of subsidies and other assistance from the government, which had become aware of the military importance of automobiles during World War I and the Manchurian Incident of 1931. Yet in 1936 Japan produced just 1,000 units of standard passenger cars. During World War II, automobile manufacturing was designated a strategic industry subject to government management under Japan's centrally controlled

Table 20.1-1 Classification of passenger cars in Japan

	Displacement	Width	Height	Length
Light four-wheel cars	Less than 660cc	Less than 1.4m	Less than 2m	Less than 3.3m
Small cars	660～2,000cc	1.4～1.7m	Less than 2m	3.3～4.7m
Ordinary cars	Over 2,000cc	More than 1.7m	Over 2m	Over 4.7m

wartime economy. Production facilities were devastated by air raids, however, and by the end of the war capacity had fallen almost to zero.

The post-war development of the automobile industry began when the government gave approval for truck production in September 1945 and passenger car production in August 1947. The main manufacturers were Toyota, Nissan and Isuzu, all of which initially focused on truck production. Manufacturers faced a temporary crisis during the deflationary crash triggered by the introduction of the "Dodge Line" in 1949. They rapidly recovered under the impetus of the special demand generated by the outbreak of the Korean War in 1950.

(b) Introduction of foreign technology

In 1954 the government tightened restrictions on automobile imports in order to promote domestic production. Thereafter, Japanese manufacturers began to introduce technology aggressively under tie-ups with foreign manufacturers. Nissan, Isuzu and Hino commenced production of compact passenger cars under technology tie-ups with Austin, Rootes and Renault respectively, and Mitsubishi Heavy Industries began domestic production of jeeps under a technology-assistance contract with Willys of the United States.

(c) Fostering of related industry

In 1955 the Ministry of International Trade and Industry (MITI) announced a guideline plan for nurturing a "people's car", selecting a single automobile manufacturer in a position to produce it on a large-scale basis. Whilst it ended in failure, the scheme did give each automobile manufacturer impetus to develop a compact car.

The Machinery Industry Furtherance Temporary Measures Laws enacted in the same year, aimed at supporting and fostering the machinery industry, amongst others, plus general industry and the parts industry, contributed to nurturing the primary parts manufacturers and building up the foundation of the division of labour within the industry.

20.1.2.2. Growth period led by domestic demand (1965–1972)

(a) Growth of motorisation

The high-growth period brought a virtuous circle in which rising income levels boosted consumers' purchasing power, leading to the expansion of consumer demand. This environment, together with the construction of expressways, triggered a rapid motorisation trend in Japan. As the market expanded, Toyota, Nissan and other manufacturers began to build new plants one after another in order to increase their supply capacity. Passenger car production surged dramatically from 20,000 units in 1955 to 700,000 units in 1965.

(b) Strengthening international competitiveness

As Japan began to shift to a more open system through trade and capital liberalisation and other changes, manufacturers were confronted with the need to improve their international competitiveness. In 1961 MITI presented a concept calling for the formation of Japanese manufacturers into three groups. Whilst this plan ended in failure, it fostered a sense of crisis amongst manufacturers, by encouraging production rationalisation and triggering fierce competition in both quantitative and qualitative terms. The resulting improvements in cost and performance enhanced the industry's international competitiveness.

This situation also encouraged mergers and tie-ups. Nissan merged with Prince, whilst tie-ups were formed between Toyota and Hino, Toyota and Daihatsu, Nissan and Fuji Heavy Industries, Mitsubishi and Chrysler, and Isuzu and GM.

20.1.2.3. Growth period led by export (1973–1980)

The outbreak of the first oil crisis in the autumn of 1973 had a major impact on the Japanese automobile industry, and output of passenger cars plummeted from 4,471,000 units in 1973 to 3,932,000 units in 1974. Production quickly recovered, however, and by 1980 an output exceeded seven million units. In the same year, Japan overtook the United States to become the world's leading automobile producer, with a total output of all vehicles having surpassed 11 million units. The main reason for this up-trend was the expansion of exports to compensate for sluggish domestic demand. Exports increased from 1,087,000 units in 1970 to 5,967,000 units in 1980, owing to the development of fuel-efficient, low-pollution, high-performance compact vehicles with a lower price than the European cars for export to the United States, the world's largest automobile market, at a time when crude oil prices were rising in the wake of the oil shock.

20.1.2.4. Expanding overseas production (1981–1985)

The expansion of Japanese automobile exports to the United States caused the performance of the US automobile industry to deteriorate. This led to serious unemployment problems and mounting criticism of Japan, subsequently escalating into Japan–US trade friction. From fiscal 1981 onwards, Japanese manufacturers sought to alleviate this problem by introducing voluntary export restraints. The ceilings imposed under this system were progressively raised from 1,680,000 units per annum during 1981–83 to 1,850,000 units in fiscal 1984, and 2,300,000 units per annum during fiscal 1985–86.

Despite these restraints, steady demand for fuel-efficient, small-sized cars in the US market, coupled with strong encouragement from the US which hoped for increases in employment, prompted the Japanese automobile manufacturers to expand their overseas production operations and to increase their sales by scaling up dealer networks and by improving after-sales service, especially in North America. Honda first commenced its local production in the United States in 1982, then Nissan in 1983 and the GM–Toyota joint operation in 1984, followed by various parts manufacturers. The comparative advantage structure changed after the Plaza Accord of 1985, which caused a rapid rise in the value of the yen. The shift to local production accelerated and began to encompass other manufacturers as well.

20.1.2.5. Formation and collapse of the bubble economy (1986–1994)

An extremely slackened financial policy introduced in 1986 led to the formation of an unprecedented "bubble economy" that caused stock and land prices to skyrocket. The resulting assets inflation boosted domestic demand by an average of more than 8%, triggering a high-growth phase. Manufacturers responded to the growth of domestic demand by expanding their production facilities; for instance, both Toyota and Nissan built new plants. However, the subsequent recession, which was deepened by the collapse of the bubble, caused domestic demand for automobiles to peak out in 1990 followed by annual declines for the next three years in succession. This was the worst long-term downtrend in sales during the post-war era. The market finally began to show signs of recovery with the emergence of replacement demand in 1994. However, there is now concern about the "hollowing-out" of the domestic industry, as manufacturers aggressively expand their overseas production to reduce costs in the face of export restrictions and the appreciation of the yen.

20.1.3. Supply system and industry structure

As outlined below, the Japanese automobile industry has a number of distinctive features different from the European and North American industries.

20.1.3.1. Competitive co-existence of numerous manufacturers

In Europe and North America, there is an oligopolistic situation where a few manufacturers have gained dominance through a long history of mergers and other changes. In Japan, eleven manufacturers (eight passenger car makers, three truck makers) co-exist in competitive relationships.

20.1.3.2. Vertical pyramid structure linking assemblers and parts manufacturers

Japanese automobile assemblers rely more heavily on outside suppliers of parts compared with their US and European counterparts. Assemblers and parts manufacturers are linked vertically in pyramid structures, with assemblers at the top supported by primary, secondary and even deeper layers of parts suppliers (Fig. 20.1-1). Parts manufacturers in Europe and North America, on the other hand, are highly independent in general and extremely businesslike in their dealings with assemblers. In Japan, parts manufacturers generally tend to rely on automobile assemblers, to which they are closely linked through *keiretsu* (affiliation) relationships.

Each assembler has a co-operative organisation of affiliated parts manufacturers, such as Toyota's *Kyoho-kai* and Nissan's *Takara-kai*. However, these relationships have changed in recent years. Assemblers are striving to reduce costs by procuring low-cost parts, regardless of the affiliations or nationalities of suppliers (optimised procurement), whilst parts manufacturers are endeavouring to reduce their dependence on their parent companies by expanding their sales to non-group assemblers. These and other trends are transforming the traditional links into increasingly dry and businesslike relationships.

20.1.3.3. Manufacturer-dominated group sales

Like parts manufacturers, Japanese automobile dealers are affiliated to assemblers (Fig. 20.1-2). Dealers are supplied with models determined by their assembler and are given exclusive rights to specific territories. In theory, dealers could sell other assemblers' cars without prior consultation, but in practice, they sell only cars manufactured by the assembler to which they are affiliated. Dealers and the affiliated assembler thus form a community bonded by a common destiny.

This system was modelled after the one originally established by GM in the United States. Today, American dealers and assemblers operate on a more businesslike basis without affiliation structures, and dealers have sufficient independence to deal with assemblers on an equal footing.

Japan's exclusionary *keiretsu* sales system worked well when sales were expanding, but in times of stagnation it eroded the earnings of dealers by preventing them from getting rid of high-volume, low-margin trading structures. Dealers affected by the stagnation of sales over the past few years are increasingly turning to sales of imported automobiles to enhance their product line-ups. Changes are inevitably occurring in the traditional system of *keiretsu* sales, partly because of overseas criticism regarding the exclusivity of the system.

Fig. 20.1-1 Pyramid structure of assemblers and parts manufacturers

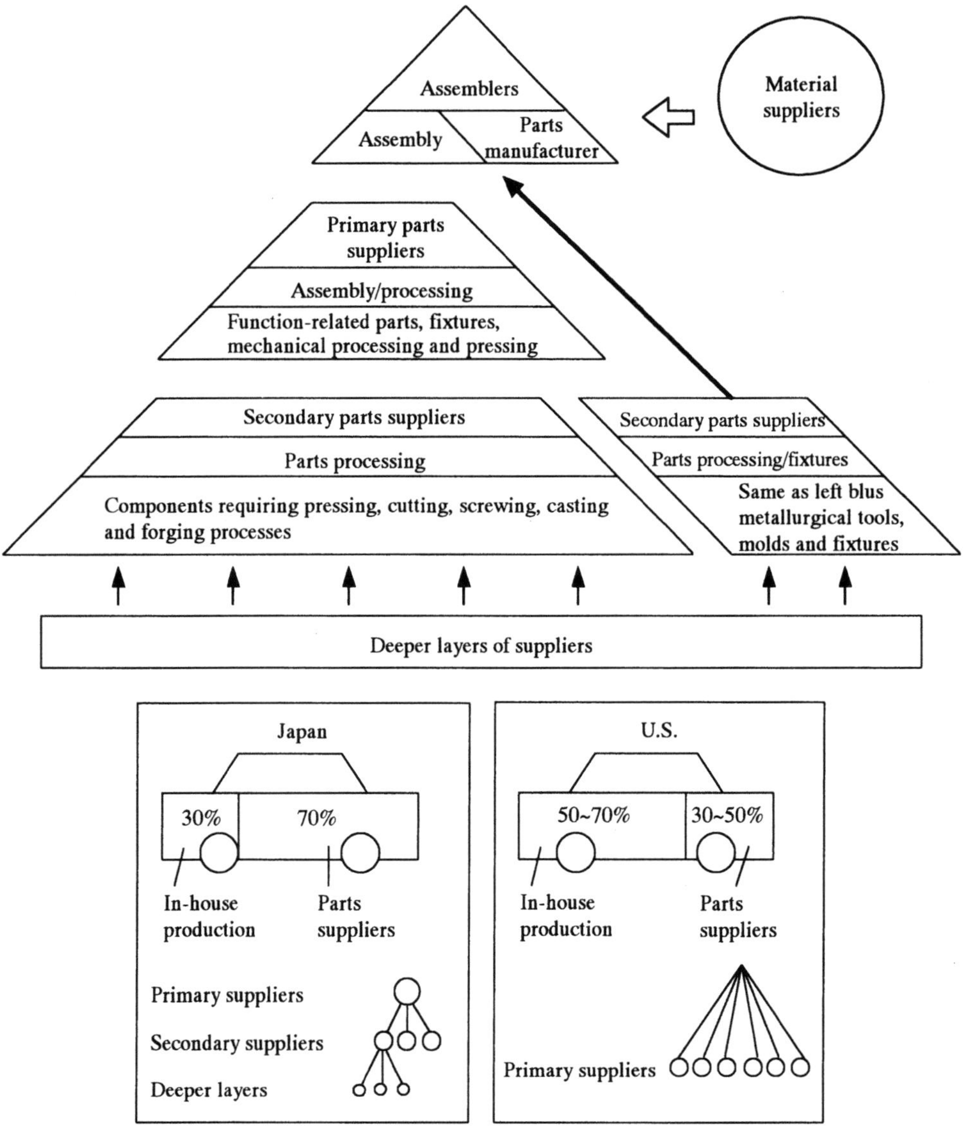

Source: Japan Automobile Manufacturers Association, JAMA Report No. 58

Fig. 20.1-2 Distribution system of domestic passenger cars

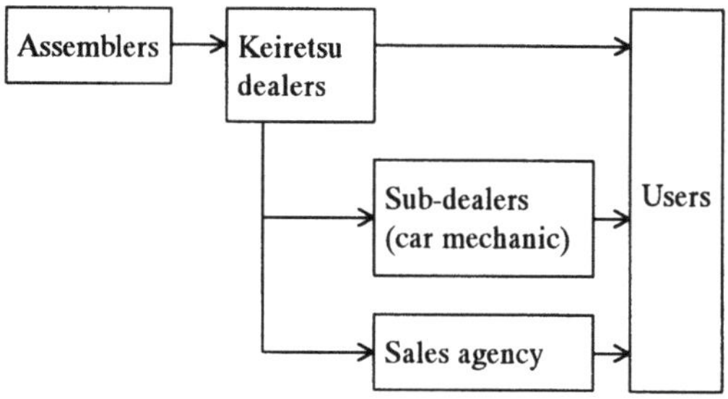

20.1.4. Role of industrial policy in industry development

20.1.4.1. Various protective and fostering policies

The rapid growth achieved by the Japanese automobile industry over such a short period of time during the post-war reconstruction was attributable in part to a succession of government measures to protect and nurture the fledgling industry. In that period, the Japanese automobile industry was not considered viable because the technology then employed was too far behind European and US standards. MITI, however, regarded the development of an automobile industry as vital to the advancement of Japan's industrial structure and argued that the automobile industry should be aggressively supported as a future strategic industry.

Amongst the main industrial policies implemented by the government, there were protective measures, such as extremely high import duties and commodity taxes, particularly on compact cars (1954); the postponement of liberalisation of automobile imports (1960); the limitation of buyers of imported vehicles to hire car firms and media organisations (1954); and the restriction of foreign investment in Japan.

The measures adopted to foster the industry included the designation of the automobile industry as one of thirty-two key industries under the industry rationalisation policy (1952); the announcement of the plan to develop compact car manufacturing by selecting one manufacturer to produce a "people's car" (1955; this met with fierce opposition from the industry and did not materialise); and the announcement of the plan for a grouping concept to enhance the international competitiveness of the Japanese automobile industry by integrating passenger car manufacturers into three production groups (1961; this also did not materialise but accelerated rationalisation of the industry).

20.1.4.2. Evaluation of the industrial policy

Air raids and other events left the Japanese automobile industry with zero production capacity at the end of World War II. The industry's postwar development began with truck production by Toyota, Nissan and Isuzu. However, there was a massive technology gap between Japanese manufacturers and leading manufacturers in the West, and the industry could not have achieved self-sufficiency without the introduction of technology from European and American manufacturers. Without government protection and support, the domestic market would inevitably have been dominated by Western manufacturers, as was the case in the pre-war era. Although the people's car concept and the grouping concept could not be implemented, they had the effect of hastening the development of passenger cars and promoting mergers and tie-ups.

Thanks to government protection and support, the Japanese automobile industry was able to consolidate its business base and enhance its international competitiveness during the 1960s. This was reflected in vehicle exports totalling more than one million units per year in the 1970s.

20.1.5. Main factors of the development of the industry

The efforts made by MITI and other governmental organisations during the infancy of the Japanese automobile industry played an important role in its subsequent growth into one of the world's leading industries. Even more important, however, were the entrepreneurial spirit and determination of individual automobile manufacturers to catch up with European and American manufacturers through steady efforts to expand their activities and improve quality. In this section an analysis will be made of the factors that enabled the Japanese automobile industry to achieve world leadership despite its status as a latecomer.

20.1.5.1. Competitive industrial structure with numerous manufacturers

As described earlier, the structure of the Japanese automobile industry has evolved through fierce competition amongst eight passenger car assemblers. In addition to Toyota, which is the clear leader in terms of product ranges and selling power, there are also middle- and low-ranked manufacturers that can survive only by maintaining a competitive edge based on unique technology and specialist fields. This competitive situation contributed to quality improvements by stimulating manufacturers to improve their technology and develop new products.

20.1.5.2. Establishment of the Japanese-style lean production system

Mass production (the Ford system) has been the basis of automobile production throughout the world ever since Ford commenced production of the

Model T in 1908. Japan's automobile sales market was still small in the 1950s and 1960s, however, and demand was extremely diverse. The task confronting automobile manufacturers in that period was to establish systems capable of efficient, large-range, small-lot production. The first company to attempt this task was Toyota, which created its own unique production system through a process of trial and error. The result was the "lean production system", which is also known as the "Toyota production system" (Fig. 20.1-3). A variety of schemes have been incorporated into this system, including the just-in-time method, the *kanban* method, automation, and the standardisation of production. Goals included the minimisation of intermediate inventories, the elimination of mass production of rejects, the reduction of processes and process workers, and the facilitation of production adjustment through small-lot production. In addition to these production-related efficiency measures, Toyota also introduced quality control (QC) circle activities that involve all workers in efforts to improve quality and operations (Fig. 20.1-4). Toyota began to introduce the system in 1955, and by 1963 it was firmly established in all factories. The system subsequently spread to affiliated parts manufacturers and even to other assemblers, leading to the improvement of the Japanese automobile industry as a whole. A steady flow of ideas and innovations from this source, together with the co-operation of parts manufacturers, brought further improvements in quality and productivity. The mass-production system used in Europe and America was designed to reduce costs through merits of scale. Its weakness was its inability to adapt flexibly to changing technology and markets. The Toyota production system was developed by adapting this system to Japanese conditions. It proved extremely effective in responding to the expansion of demand and the diversification of consumer needs, whilst reconciling the improvement of quality with the improvement of productivity (Fig. 20.1-4).

The statistical report on labour productivity by the Ministry of Labour shows that the working hours involved in producing one passenger car unit was shortened to a third during the period from 1966 to 1980 through the increased productivity (Fig. 20.1-5).

20.1.5.3. Close co-operation between assemblers and parts manufacturers

As mentioned earlier, the Japanese automobile industry is based on a stratified pyramid structure with assemblers at the apex, supported by successive layers of parts manufacturers. Assemblers support affiliated and co-operating parts manufacturers in various ways—including the secondment of personnel, technical guidance and financial assistance. This support enables assemblers to procure high-quality, low-cost parts with perfect timing ("just-in-time" system). Parts manufacturers, on the other hand, participate in the development of new models from the initial stages ("design-in" system) and strive to meet the expectations of the affiliated assembler by improving quality and reducing costs, and, in return, they can rely on a steady flow of orders. This approach led to the formation of close, long-term relationships between assemblers and parts manufacturers. It was the determined efforts on both sides of this relationship that enabled the Japanese automobile industry to achieve international competitiveness—based on the high quality, low price, fuel efficiency, low pollution and other characteristics of Japanese automobiles.

Fig. 20.1-3 Toyota Motor's production system

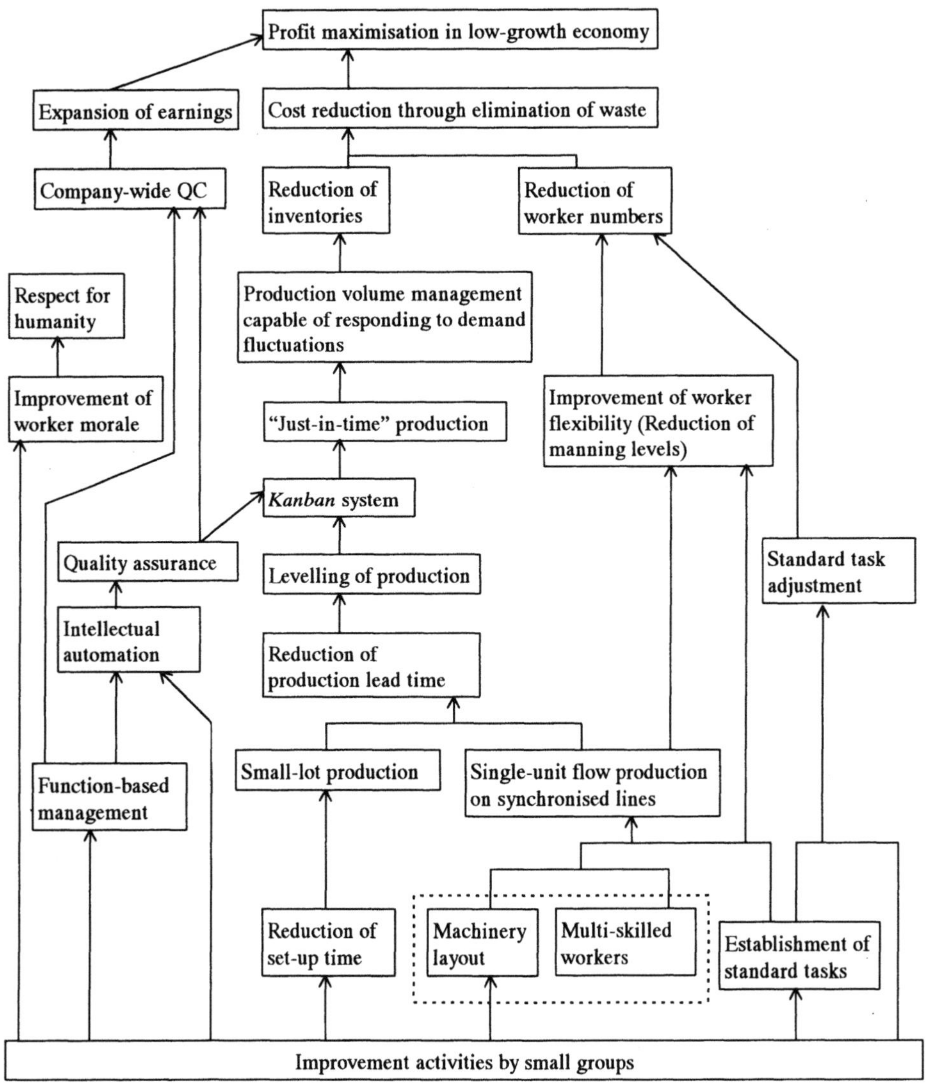

Source: Monden, New Development in the Toyota Production System

Fig. 20.1-4 Labour productivity indexes of automobile industry in Japan, US, and West Germany

(Man-hour basis, 1975=100)

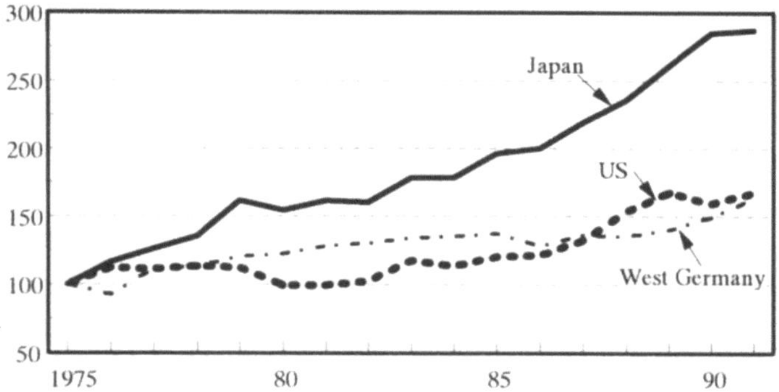

Source: Japan Productivity Centre for Socio-Economic Development, International Comparison of Labour Productivity

Fig. 20.1-5 Working hours directly involved in producing one passenger car unit

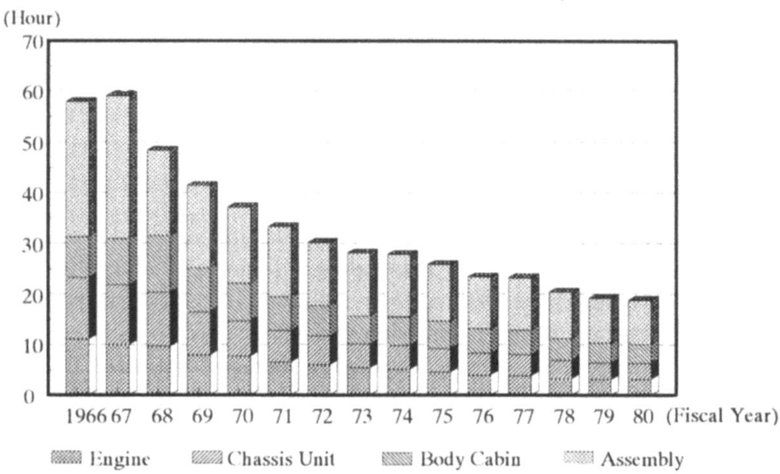

Source: Yonekawa, et al, The Post-war Japanese History of Corporate manegement, vol 2

The improvement of the industry's international competitiveness resulted from the existence of large numbers of excellent parts manufacturers and suppliers of raw materials. Japanese parts manufacturers are not limited to operating as subcontractors to assemblers. The so-called "design-in" manufacturers carry out their own design work and play an important role in product development by presenting plans and proposals to assemblers. Many of them have gained international reputations for product quality and supply parts to European and American manufacturers as well. Automobiles are manufactured from a wide range of raw materials, including iron and steel, rubber and plastics. The manufacturers that supply these raw materials in Japan are amongst the best in the world in terms of product quality. Japan's excellent manufacturers of parts and raw materials are fully able to meet the expectations of automobile assemblers, and their contribution helps to enhance vehicle quality at the final assembly stage.

20.1.5.4. Stable labour relations

Japanese management is based on the "three sacred treasures" of enterprise: unions, lifetime employment and seniority-based wage systems. These three factors have enabled Japan to maintain extremely stable labour relations. In the automobile industry, the deflationary crash triggered by the implementation of the Dodge Line in 1949 brought financial crises for many automobile manufacturers, and companies were forced to cut production and lay off workers. This led to frequent labour disputes, the most famous of which were the Toyota strike of 1950 and the Nissan strike of 1953. After these bitter experiences, labour relations began to stabilise, and labour and management were soon working together to improve productivity and quality. The formation of enterprise unions led to the establishment of the prior-consultation system, which helped to build mutual trust between labour and management, and facilitated production adjustments or transitions to new production systems.

20.1.5.5. Adaptability to problems facing the industry

In the past, the Japanese automobile industry has survived a number of crises with the help of some luck: it expanded exports during a slump in the domestic market; it developed fuel-efficient, low-pollution vehicles in response to the oil crises and tougher exhaust emission standards; and it shifted to overseas production in response to export restrictions, the appreciation of the value of the yen and other changes. Thus, automobile production in Japan has been continuously expanding throughout fifty years of the post-war period without a noticeable break, and most manufacturers have been able to co-exist and thrive together.

However, from 1990 onwards, the environment surrounding the automobile industry has been undergoing a dramatic change, and the industry now faces a number of problems that are even more difficult. First, the maturation of the domestic sales market is reflected in decelerating growth and a widening supply-demand gap. Second, export profitability and price competitiveness are deteriorating, owing to the rapid appreciation of the yen. Third, the domestic industry is being "hollowed out" by the shift to overseas production as a means of substituting export. Fourth, the introduction of tougher environmental and safety standards is causing costs to escalate. Fifth, as a result of having responded to users' needs for higher-grade and more diversified cars during the bubble economy period, car manufacturers are now equipped with a high-cost production system. Sixth, the industry is facing a new threat in the form of aggressive inroads made by imported automobiles, the sales of which are expanding because of massive price cuts and the development of an increasing number of models designed for the Japanese market (right-hand steering wheel, compact size, etc.).

In future, the industry will need to cope with these problems in order to survive. The fate of each manufacturer will depend on successfully overcoming these problems. It is likely in some cases that the industry will go through major changes, including industry restructuring and winnowing out of some manufacturers.

20.2. Germany's Automobile Industry

20.2.1. Definition and positioning of the sector

20.2.1.1. Definition and composition

The automobile industry can be defined in a narrow and in a wide sense. In a narrow sense it includes only the manufacturing of motor vehicles (passenger cars and commercial vehicles) and of motor vehicle chassis and engines. The product group "commercial vehicles" comprises vans and trucks, road tractors, motor buses and special-purpose motor vehicles (e.g., fire-fighting vehicles, crane trucks, ambulances). Not included are agricultural tractors. With regard to the European sector classification (NACE), this narrow definition corresponds with NACE group 351. In this study, the sector within this definition is called the Motor Vehicle Industry.

In a wide sense, the sector also comprises the manufacturing of parts, accessories and special bodies for motor vehicles and of motor-drawn trailers and caravans. In this wider sense the sector is referred to as the Automotive Industry. In the European classification it represents NACE class 35. The differentiation of the parts included in the sector's definition is somewhat problematic. In the German statistical system, electro-technical parts, car accumulators, gauges and instruments, tires and seat frames, for example, are not included in the product group "parts for motor vehicles". On the other hand, typical products included in this group are gearboxes and transmissions, clutches, steering systems, radiators, braking equipment, shock absorbers, heating systems and air-conditioning equipment, exhaust systems, engine parts, etc.

Furthermore, in the German statistical system, an additional, super-ordinate sector definition is of considerable importance. This sector is called the Road Vehicle Industry and comprises, besides the automotive industry, some small

Table 20.2-1 Composition of the West German road vehicle industry
- Production 1990 -

Product group	DM billion	Percentage of (1)	(2)	(3)
Passenger cars	114.97	82.8	58.9	55.7
Vans and trucks	15.05	10.8	7.7	7.3
Road tractors	3.46	2.5	1.8	1.7
Buses	3.01	2.2	1.5	1.5
Motor vehicle engines[a)]	2.34	1.7	1.2	1.1
(1) Motor vehicle industry	138.83	100.0	71.1	67.3
Trailers[b)]	3.92	-	2.0	1.9
Bodies[b)]	5.70	-	2.9	2.8
Parts and accessories[c)]	46.77	-	24.0	22.7
(2) Automotive industry	195.22	-	100.0	94.7
Motor cycles	0.43[d)]	-	-	0.2
Bicycles	1.05	-	-	0.5
Parts for cycles	0.72	-	-	0.3
Other vehicles[e)]	0.55	-	-	0.3
Repair of road vehicles[f)]	8.27	-	-	4.0
(3) Road vehicle industry	206.24	-	-	100.0
In addition:				
Electro-technical parts[g)]	13.09	-	-	-
Accumulators[g)]	0.89	-	-	-
Gauges and instruments[g)]	1.49	-	-	-
Seat frames[g)]	1.24	-	-	-

a) For sale (exports, replacement, etc.). b) Including parts thereof. c) For motor vehicles; excluding electro-technical parts, accumulators, gauges and instruments, seat frames, etc.
d) Estimate. e) Trailers for agricultural purposes, invalid chairs, perambulators, etc.
f) Including painting and transformation. g) For road vehicles.

Source: Federal Statistical Office, *Fachserie 4, Reihe 3.1*

product groups: motorcycles and mopeds, bicycles, parts for cycles, other vehicles (agricultural trailers, invalid chairs, perambulators, etc.) and repair, painting and transformation of road vehicles. This aggregation normally is used for sectoral analysis of the manufacturing industry and for the sectoral disaggregation of the German national accounts statistics. The composition of the German Road Vehicle Industry is shown in Table 20.2-1. In contrast, this definition is not used in the European statistical system.

However the sector is defined, it is clearly dominated by the product group passenger cars (Table 20.2-1). Therefore, in Section 2 and the following, this study focuses on the development of German passenger car manufacture, whereby the term car is used as a synonym for passenger car. Exceptions are made only if the overall context requires a wider view or if the given data base makes it necessary (e.g., in the case of employment or investment data).

20.2.1.2. Domestic positioning

The road vehicle industry is one of the most important sectors of the German manufacturing industry and thus of the overall German economy. In the national accounts statistics, the value added of this sector came to DM 88.7 billion in 1990. This is a 3.7% share of GDP and 12% of the total manufacturing industry, giving the road vehicle industry position three in the ranking of the manufacturing sectors, behind the electro-technical industry (4.0% or 13.1%) and the mechanical-engineering industry (3.9% or 12.7%), two other strong industry sectors that have also contributed to the success of German car production.

Furthermore, the road vehicle industry is the sector with by far the largest intermediate input amongst all manufacturing sectors in Germany. Therefore, measured in terms of gross production value, the road vehicle industry ranks number one within the manufacturing industry (1990: 14.4% of total manufacturing output). That means the road vehicle industry is not only a large manufacturing sector but also has great linkages with other parts of the German economy.

In addition, the road vehicle sector plays an important role in the German foreign trade balance. Although road vehicle imports are high (1990: DM 47.34 billion), the sector's exports are much higher (1990: DM 112.77 billion), resulting in a significant trade balance surplus (1990: DM 65.43 billion). Hence, also regarding the export value and the trade balance surplus, the road vehicle industry holds a leading position within the German economy.

Finally, the road vehicle industry is also of great importance for the German is also of labour market. According to the national accounts statistics, in 1990 the sector directly employed 4.8% of all people with jobs in Germany (11.8% of manufacturing employment). Because of its large intermediate input, the impact of the road vehicle industry on the overall employment situation in Germany is much more significant than the direct employment figures indicate.

20.2.1.3. International positioning

German industry is one of the pioneers of motor vehicle development. Already in 1886 the first operational car was constructed by Karl Benz. But the mass production of motor vehicles was initially introduced in the United States by Henry Ford in the 1920s. In 1937, when 4.8 million cars were manufactured in the United States, German car production reached only a level of 0.33 million units. After World War II, Germany soon became number two in the ranking of the motor vehicle manufacturing countries, displacing the United Kingdom in 1956. This position was kept up to 1966. Thereafter the German automobile industry was

Table 20.2-2 Road vehicle industry in the context of the West German national accounts statistics 1990

Indicator	Units	Sectoral data	Percentage of the	
			total economy	manufacturing industry
Value added	DM (bn)	88.7	3.7	12.0
Gross production	DM (bn)	288.1	4.8	14.4
Exports	DM (bn)	112.8	12.8	17.7
Imports	DM (bn)	47.4	6.6	10.3
Net exports[a)]	DM (bn)	65.4	39.8	36.9
Employment	1,000	1,056	3.7	11.8
Fixed investment	DM (bn)	16.8	3.2	15.9
of which is in equipment	DM (bn)	14.7	6.0	16.5

a) Exports minus imports.

Source: Federal Statistical Office, *Fachserie 18, Reihe 1.3*

surpassed by the dynamically expanding Japanese motor vehicle production, but has kept rank three up to the present.

In 1990, 49 million motor vehicles (passenger cars and commercial vehicles) were produced world-wide, 5 million of which came from Germany. This means the German share of world motor vehicle production came to 10.2% (Japan: 27.6%, US: 20.0%). In Western Europe, Germany is the largest manufacturer of motor vehicles; in 1990 its share was about 32%. In addition, German producers (including the German subsidiaries of General Motors and Ford) also manufacture a large number of motor vehicles in other countries. In 1990 production abroad amounted to more than 1.8 million units (or 3.7% of the world's total). Most of these capacities are located in other European countries, but also Brazil, Mexico and South Africa have significant shares.

In western Germany, 3.2 million new motor vehicles were registered in 1990. This made Germany the largest motor vehicle market in Europe. But compared with the United States (13.9 million in 1990) and Japan (7.8 million in 1990), the German market is relatively small. Nevertheless, Germany still occupies position three in the world-wide ranking of national motor vehicle markets. This position was solidified by German re-unification, which enlarged the German automobile market by about one-fifth.

20.2.2. Development of the sector

20.2.2.1. Pre-war situation

As mentioned above, Germany—like the United States, the United Kingdom, France and Italy—had a fully developed automobile industry before World War II.

Table 20.2-3 Production of motor vehicles in the main manufacturing countries
- 1,000 vehicles -

Country	1960	1970	1980	1990
Japan	482	5,289	11,043	13,487
United States	7,905	8,284	8,013	9,780
West Germany	2,055	3,842	3,879	4,977
France	1,349	2,504	3,378	3,769
Italy	644	1,842	1,610	2,121
United Kingdom	1,811	2,051	1,348	1,566
Spain	56	539	1,182	2,053
Canada	396	1,194	1,374	1,926
USSR/CIS	524	916	2,199	2,134
Total[a)]	15,907	29,109	38,751	48,752
Percentage of total: West Germany	12.9	13.2	10.0	10.2

a) Including other countries.

Source: VDA, *International Auto Statistics 1994;* VDA Yearbooks.

But the situation in Germany was different from that in the main competing countries. Up to the end of the 1920s, Germany had high engineering potentials and comprehensive development capacities, but the production was dispersed amongst a large number of manufacturers (86 in 1924) and to numerous types and models. No strong marketing efforts in the direction of mass motorisation and mass production were present. Because of the well-developed railway system, the high population density, and reduced purchasing power after World War I, the need for a new transportation system was—in contrast to the United States—not of high priority in Germany. Passenger cars were classified as luxury goods to be manufactured in small-scale production facilities. In 1928, production was about 101,700 cars, manufactured by 33 firms and represented by 127 types.

This situation changed after the Nazi takeover in 1933. The automobile sector now became a strategic industry. Not only was supplying the broad population an important goal of the regime, the reduction of unemployment and the military aspects were also a high priority in its political intentions. An important element in this connection was the initiation of the German Autobahn programme. Up to 1938, car production rose to 276,800 units manufactured by twelve enterprises. Volkswagen was intended to carry the mass motorisation process in Germany but could not enter production due to the outbreak of war in 1939. The most important German car manufacturers at the end of the pre-war period were Opel, Auto-Union (DKW, Wanderer, Horch, Audi), Daimler-Benz, Adler, Ford, Hanomag, BMW, Borgward and NSU-Fiat.

20.2.2.2. Post-war reconstruction period (1945–1953)

At the end of World War II, the German automobile capacities were largely destroyed. Initial efforts to reconstruct the German motor vehicles industry were made already in 1945 under the control of the occupation forces. Ford and Daimler-Benz received permission to resume production of commercial vehicles; Volkswagen was able to manufacture some 1,300 cars in 1945 because some of its military production equipment escaped war damage. Daimler-Benz began with post-war car production in 1947 (about 600 units), and Opel and Ford followed in 1948. Together these four companies manufactured about 30,000 cars in 1948.

After these first steps, the stabilisation of the political situation and the establishment of the Federal Republic of Germany, the West German automobile industry recovered very fast. Further, traditional manufacturers re-entered the market (Borgward in 1949, Auto-Union with DKW models in 1950, and BMW in 1952), and car production rose from 104,100 in 1949 to 387,900 in 1953. Already in 1951 the same number of cars was manufactured in West Germany (276,600 units) as in all of Germany before the war.

Thus, up to 1953 the German automobile industry was restored to pre-war capacities in the western parts of the country (about 73% of the German pre-war capacities for car production were located here) and re-established in the framework of the former company structure. Of the leading companies of the pre-war period, only Adler was not able to rebuild its capacities and it disappeared from the market. However, Volkswagen entered the post-war market as an additional major competitor. Both Auto-Union and BMW had lost their main facilities located in the Soviet zone. Nevertheless, both companies re-entered the West German car market by transforming their facilities in West Germany and making use of their traditional know-how.

The first years of the reconstruction phase were not only marked by political restrictions and the lack of purchasing power but also by the scarcity of new equipment and materials. The old machinery had to be repaired and put into operation again. This process and the fast recovery of production was supported by the know-how and the experience of the existing, well-trained workforce and the engineering potential originating from the pre-war period. This skilled workforce and the manufacturing know-how made it possible to extend production volume rapidly when the industrial supply network was back in full operation in the early 1950s. By that time the main plants were prepared for mass production.

20.2.2.3. Post-war boom period (1954–1965)

The reconstruction period proceeded to a period of continuous, strong growth lasting up to the mid-1960s. Without any setbacks, German car production went up to 2.73 million units in 1965. This development was carried by both a rapidly expanding domestic demand and a permanent increase of exports. Germany entered the phase of mass motorisation (supplying private households) backed by a booming economy. Already in 1960 private demand surpassed commercial demand (supplying enterprises and public authorities) for new passenger cars, and in 1965 four of ten households owned a car. Though the competition of other European manufacturers (especially from France and Italy) was already strong, the share of imports reached a level of only 10-12% in the early 1960s, and German products clearly dominated the home market.

In addition, German cars held a strong position on the world market, and German manufacturers were successful not only in Europe but also in the United States and other countries. The German export share (percentage of production) rose from 37% in 1953 to 52% in 1965.

The main product group at that time was composed of the so-called lower-middle-class vehicles (with engines of 1.0 to 1.5*l* piston displacement). On average, more than 60% of the total German car production in this period can be allotted to this group. On the lower end, small and (in the 1950s) very small cars were also developed and manufactured, but they played a minor role. The percentage of total production units of small cars was about 10% up to the early 1960s and declined sharply after 1963. The main manufacturers did not serve this partial market due to low profitability; others disappeared or changed their product programme.

The main trend in the 1960s was to extend the programmes to upper-class vehicles and to concentrate on high quality and high performance. German manufacturers developed the American market for small cars with their lower-middle-class vehicles, based on a high-quality image even in this low-end class. In addition, in Europe German producers were also successful in the higher classes of the car market (upper middle class with 1.5 to 2.0*l* capacity and large cars with more than 2.0*l*).

20.2.2.4. First period of instability (1966–1971)

The following six-year period was basically still a phase of growth but with strong fluctuations and a decline in domestic sales expansion. Germany experienced the first recession in its automobile market in 1967 (new car registrations: –10%) and exports also went down significantly (–11%) that year. The recovery in 1969 and 1970 was strong, but not strong enough to return to the former dynamic growth trend. At the end of the period, German car production came to about 3.7 million units.

The weakening of domestic sales growth was not caused by a slowdown in demand evolution but primarily by a strong increase of car imports. The share of imports (percentage of new registrations) rose from about 12% in 1964 to nearly 32% in 1971. This import surge had two sources: other European competitors strengthened their position on the German market significantly (primarily French and Italian companies), and one German manufacturer began to supply the German market from additional capacities in another European country (a new plant of Ford/Cologne in Belgium started large-scale operation in 1964).

The main reason for the sharp increase in car imports at that time was the fact that the major German manufacturers disregarded the home market for small cars. Thus European competitors had the chance to open the German market at its low end, and they were successful in widening this market segment. But also in the lower middle class, importers gained more and more market shares, whilst German producers concentrated on serving the dynamically growing upper market segments.

Fig. 20.2-1 Car production in Germany

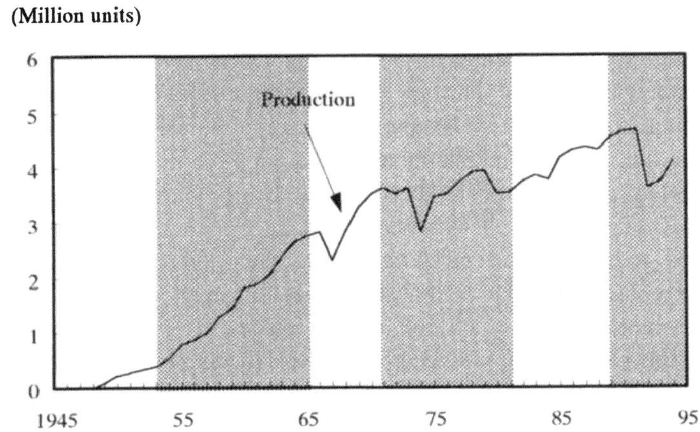

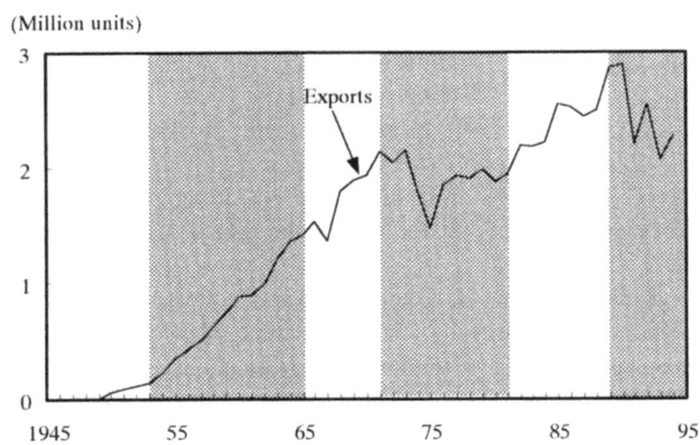

Source: VDA, International Auto Statistics, 1994; VDA, Yearbooks

Table 20.2-4 Car market in Germany (West)

Variables	1960	1970	1980	1990	1994
Car density[a]	Cars per 1,000 population				
	81	230	377	486	502
Market data:	1,000 Cars				
New registrations	970	2,107	2,426	3,041	2,594
of which are:					
Widening	824	1,208	623	543	821
Replacement	146	899	1,803	2,498	1,773
Imports	94	593	764	1,152	934
of which from:					
France	43	290	228	238	213
Italy	41	144	104	152	98
Japan	-	1	252	468	227
Domestic sales[b]	876	1,514	1,662	1,889	1,660
Exports	865	1,947	1,873	2,598	2,270
of which to:					
Western Europe	424	910	1,363	2,026	1,669
North America	226	795	365	299	209
Production	1,817	3,528	3,521	4,661	4,094
Share of:	%				
Replacement[c]	15.0	42.7	74.3	82.2	68.3
Imports[c]	9.7	28.1	31.5	37.9	36.0
Exports[d]	47.6	55.2	53.2	55.7	55.4
Average value[e]:	DM per car at constant 1985 prices				
New registrations	9,770	11,910	14,330	19,450	.
Imports	6,240	8,260	9,880	13,870	.
Domestic sales	10,110	13,270	16,400	22,570	.
Exports	9,650	10,940	14,780	22,320	.
Production	9,890	11,990	15,540	22,430	.

a) Total number of cars in operation per 1,000 population. b) New registrations of cars produced in Germany. c) Percentage of new registrations. d) Percentage of production. e) Average value per car at manufacturer/importer level (excludes gross margin and sales tax).

Source: VDA, *Tatsachen und Zahlen* (diverse yearbooks).

German exports were still running well at that time, although the Japanese competitors started to enter the American market for compact cars and weakened the German position there. In 1971, 2.2 million cars were sold abroad (58% of production): 49% of total exports were destined for Western Europe, 43% to North America (US and Canada).

20.2.2.5. Period of stagnation and turbulence (1972–1981)

The following ten-year period brought some fundamental changes in German car production trends. The 1970s were a turbulent decade for the world economy and for the German automobile industry. The main reasons for this turbulence were:

- the abandonment of the Bretton Woods agreement in 1973 and the changeover to a flexible exchange-rate system resulting in an appreciation of the D-Mark;
- the two oil-price shocks of 1973/74 and 1979/80 and their effects on car demand;
- the emergence of the Japanese automobile industry as a new global market player.

These events caused a setback in German car exports, especially in North America, where the Japanese were very successful in widening their market shares at the expense of Germany in the segment of small cars, due to the lower prices of Japanese cars. At the end of this period, in 1981, German car exports came to about 1.95 million units (9% less than the 1971 level). The percentage of the deliveries to North America of the total German car exports went down to about 13%.

On the home market the situation was different. Each of the two oil-price shocks induced a sharp decline in German car demand. Between these two recessions there was a strong recovery with a peak in 1978. German domestic car sales followed this undulation closely because of the fact that the import share did not continue to increase. This means that German manufacturers were able to stabilise their positions on the home market during this period: the percentage of imports in new car registrations was at the same level in 1981 (30%) as it was in 1971 (32%).

By and large, German car production—measured in units—did not record a growth trend during this period but was characterised by strong variations due to the impacts of the oil-price shocks, superimposing a stagnation tendency because of weak export performance with regard to the American market. Production in 1981 (3.58 million units) was thus below the corresponding figure of 1971. But on the other hand, the upgrading of the production programme accelerated strongly, which meant that the real value per car was much higher at the end of the period (about DM 16,180 in constant 1985 prices) than it was at the beginning (about DM 11,890). On average, the gross production value (at constant prices) of German car manufacturing grew by 2.8% per year during this period, although the number of produced cars fell by 0.3%.

20.2.2.6. Second period of growth (1982–1989)

In the 1980s German car production returned to a stable growth trend. But the strength of this development was—measured in units—significantly weaker than that of the boom period in the 1950s and 1960s.

At first exports recovered. In the United States, German manufacturers returned to the market with their upper class models. This process was supported by the depreciation of the D-Mark in the early 1980s. In addition, German competitors continued to improve their positions in Western Europe and in other parts of the world, even in Japan. The background of this development can be seen in the special German quality image, based on high performance and high-end vehicles, which made it possible to be successful in spite of relatively high prices.

On the other hand, the position of German manufacturers on their home market weakened again: the percentage of imports in new car registrations rose from 30% in 1981 to nearly 36% in 1989. Japanese manufacturers entered the German market as additional players (beginning in 1978/79) and European competitors improved their positions considerably. Therefore, domestic sales could not be enlarged significantly during this period, but were somewhat higher at the end of the 1980s than at the beginning of this decade.

Car production came to about 4.56 million units in 1989, corresponding to an annual growth rate of 3.1% on average in this period. Furthermore, the upgrading process continued in the 1980s and led to a specific value per car of about DM 21,450 (at constant 1985 prices) in 1989. Real gross production value thus grew on average by 6.8% per year from 1981 to 1989.

20.2.2.7. Period of German re-unification (from 1990)

The early 1990s were again a turbulent phase for the German car manufacturers. The domestic market increased significantly as a result of German re-unification in 1990: not only by the enlargement of the market potential (population) by about one-fourth, but also because the car density in the former German Democratic Republic was relatively low and the technological standard of the cars in operation poor, which led to a sharp increase of demand. The buying of a "Western" car was of high priority in the budgets of the people in the new Länder. This demand was initially met by used cars from the former West Germany, leading to an additional boom in new car sales in the western part of the country. But this re-unification boom was short-lived, and already in 1993 there was a drastic setback of the car demand in Germany: new car registrations fell by 18.7% in all of Germany (–18.8% in western Germany). The recovery in 1994 and 1995 was weak because of limited purchasing power primarily due to re-unification costs.

In addition, the international competitiveness of German car manufacturers grew weaker. This process began in 1986 in connection with the repeated appreciation of the D-Mark: German cars became too expensive. In the late 1980s this was compensated by the booming car demand in Western Europe, but after 1990 it became more evident, and in 1993 car exports from Germany declined by 19.1%. German car manufacturers reacted by starting a restructuring process which is still going on. Maximum car production in Germany was reached in 1992 with 4.86 million units. In 1993 it dropped by 22% to 3.8 million cars.

20.2.3. Demand trends

20.2.3.1. Domestic demand

The process of mass motorisation in Germany began in the second half of the 1950s and led to a car density in West Germany of about 500 cars per 1,000 population in 1994, one of the highest in the world. The widening demand (annual increase of total cars in operation) reached a first peak in 1970 (1.2 million units) and a second one in 1978 (1.24 million units). In the first half of the 1980s it fell to an average level of 0.55 million, recovered to 0.95 million in the second half of this decade and went down again to 0.7 million units, on average, in West Germany between 1990 and 1994. The curve of this demand component shows strong short-term variations and follows a declining trend from the early 1970s (Fig. 20.2-2). This trend will continue, as the market is near saturation level.

The other component, the replacement demand, began to grow strongly in the second half of the 1960s, reached a level of widening demand in the early 1970s, and continued to grow by relatively moderate increments. The pre-unification maximum was reached in 1988 (1.92 million units). The unification boom hoisted the replacement demand in western Germany to about 2.8 million units in 1991 because of used car sales to eastern Germany, but the reaction in 1992 let it swing back to 2.2 million, and in 1994 it fell below the pre-unification level (1.8 million). The average lifetime (up to scrapping) of the cars registered in western Germany rose from 8.0 years in 1965 to 11.4 years in 1993, which indicates that the dynamics of replacement demand was somewhat less than that of total demand (new car registrations).

Both components together form the development curve of total demand. In 1953 only 0.25 million new cars were registered in West Germany. Up to 1970 this number increased to 2.1 million units. In the 1970s and the 1980s new car registrations continued to grow, but the intensity of growth was somewhat weaker than in the periods before. Furthermore, the growth trend was superimposed by strong short-term variations, caused primarily by the two oil-price shocks in the 1970s. At the end of the pre-unification period, in 1989, new car registrations in West Germany came to 2.8 million units (after a peak in 1987 of 2.9 million).

As mentioned above, German re-unification led to a boom in the German car market. In west Germany new car registrations climbed to 3.4 million in 1991, and in east Germany an additional 0.7 million new cars were registered (together: 4.2 million units). After this maximum, the German car market slowed down somewhat in 1992 (3.9 million) and collapsed in 1993 in the west and east; together, only 3.2 million new cars were sold in this recession year. In 1994 no recovery occurred, and domestic car demand also remained weak in 1995.

Fig. 20.2-2 New car registrations in West Germany

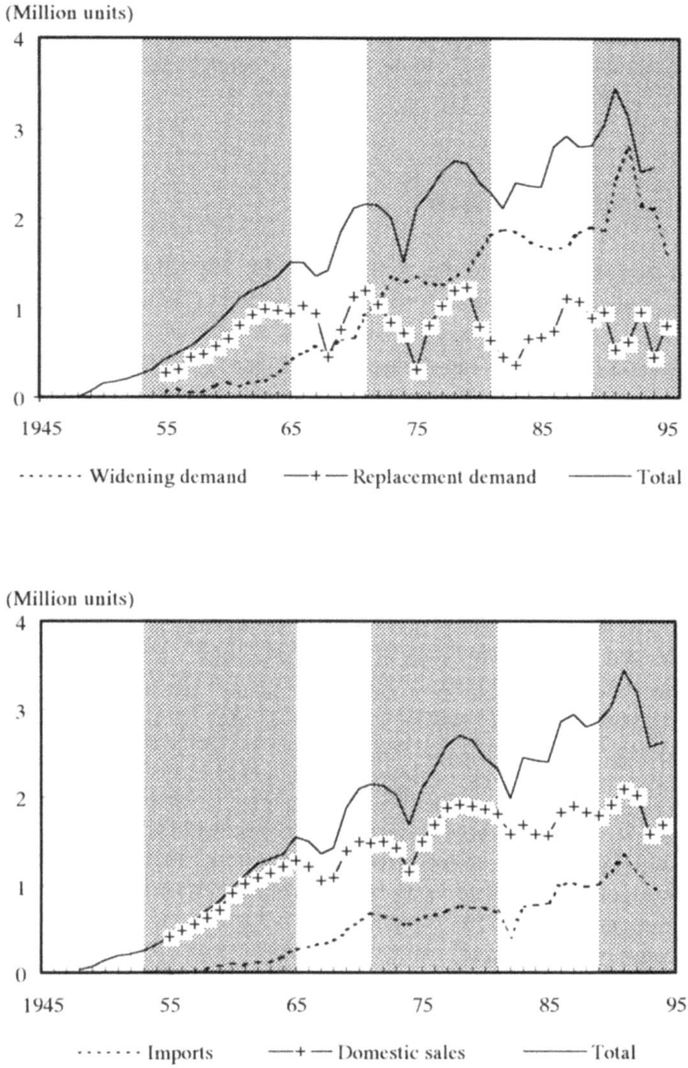

Source: VDA Yearbooks

20.2.3.2. Global demand

The world car market increased strongly during the 1960s: from about 9 million units in the late 1950s it rose to a level of 30 million in 1973. This upswing trend was interrupted in the 1970s primarily because of the impacts of the two oil-price shocks. Beginning in 1983 a new growth period occurred, leading to a level of about 35 million units in 1990.

The demand for German-made cars could not fully match this trend. The German industry's share of the world market was the highest in the early 1960s at about 15%. The percentage went down to about 12% in the mid-1970s and recovered somewhat during the 1980s. In 1990 it reached about 13% but fell below 12% in 1993 and 1994.

20.2.4. Structure of the industry

German car manufacturing stems from the capacities of six independent companies: Volkswagen, Opel, Ford, Mercedes-Benz (Daimler-Benz), BMW and Porsche. The largest, the Volkswagen group, is composed of two trademarks with separate product lines (VW and Audi). Volkswagen, Daimler-Benz and BMW are joint-stock companies, Porsche is a family-owned enterprise, and Opel and Ford are subsidiaries of the large American motor vehicle producers General Motors and Ford. Volkswagen, Opel and Ford focus on large-scale compact and middle-class cars, whereas Mercedes-Benz, BMW and Audi occupy the high-end market segments, and Porsche is a specialist for high-performance roadsters. This market partitioning was largely a result of strategic decisions and market processes. Mercedes and BMW concentrated on the upper end of the market where more profits could be made and succeeded in establishing such a strong image as luxury car makers that competitors experienced difficulties in this market segment. Volkswagen's long-lasting success with the "Beetle" led it to concentrate on the small-car market segment. Mercedes-Benz is also a major manufacturer of commercial vehicles in Germany; Volkswagen produces vans and small trucks; and BMW is the only remaining German producer of large motorcycles.

This is the company structure that has prevailed since the early 1970s. Of the nine traditional producers manufacturing more than 5,000 cars at the end of the pre-war period, six were able to re-establish their activities during the post-war reconstruction period up to 1953: Daimler-Benz (1947), Opel (1948), Ford (1948), Borgward with the three subsidiaries Borgward, Lloyd and Goliath (1949), Auto Union with the product line DKW (1950), and BMW (1952). The seventh of this group, NSU-Fiat, followed in 1956 (Neckar Automobilwerke/Deutsche Fiat). Moreover, Volkswagen entered the scene in 1945 and three other newcomers came onto the market: Porsche (1950), Glas (1955) and NSU-Motorenwerke (1957). Both Glas and NSU came from the motorcycle branch. Thus, in the late 1950s, eleven domestic suppliers (with thirteen trademarks) were present on the German

Table 20.2-5 Car production in Germany (West) by manufacturers
- 1,000 vehicles -

Manufacturer	1960	1970	1980	1990	1994
Volkswagen	787	1,518	1,232	1,509	1,162
Audi	125	317	285	421	355
Volkswagen group	-	1,835	1,517	1,930	1,517
Opel	351	812	787	1,030	964
Ford	193	409	419	595	461
Mercedes-Benz[a)]	123	280	439	574	584
BMW	44	159	330	500	550
Porsche	8	17	29	32	18
Other	186	16	-	-	-
Total	1,817	3,528	3,521	4,661	4,094

a) Until 1989: Daimler-Benz.

Source: VDA, *Tatsachen und Zahlen*

car market. Besides this, about ten other German manufacturers—coming from the motorcycle or commercial vehicle side—appeared for a short time on the car market between 1950 and 1957, but could not sustain their car business for more than several years.

Of the remaining eleven German car producers at the end of the 1950s, the Borgward group encountered financial difficulties and went bankrupt in 1961. The reasons for this were management errors, not a lack of technological or engineering performance: Borgward was well-known as an engineering-oriented enterprise with high development skills. Volkswagen took over Auto Union in 1965 and NSU in 1969 and merged both to form Audi NSU Auto Union (from 1985: Audi) as a second trademark of the Volkswagen group. In 1967 BMW took over Glas, and in 1973 the German subsidiary of the Italian Fiat group (Deutsche Fiat) closed down production.

After these mergers and terminations of production from 1961 to 1973, no more changes in the German car industry structure at the national level occurred.

20.2.5. Role of industry policy

In the German automobile industry competition prevailed and protection was unknown. The industry thrived and financed its own research and development. German industrial policy measures, thus, did not play a role in the history of the automobile industry in the Federal Republic of Germany. German car manufacturers, however, benefitted indirectly from industrial policies of other European countries which restricted car imports: deliveries from Japan were limited first of all in France, Italy and Spain and—to a lesser extent—also in the

United Kingdom and in Portugal. This gave German manufacturers a competitive advantage over their Japanese rivals in these protected markets. These measures, however, are scheduled to cease by the end of the 1990s.

20.2.6. Factors behind the development

The basic strategy of the German car manufacturers was to focus on high-performance and high-quality vehicles. High quality means not only high reliability of the cars and their components but also early introduction of advanced technologies in the different automotive subsystems, both with respect to the functionality and the safety of the vehicles (e.g., ABS braking systems). This car-making philosophy was not only applied to upper-class vehicles but also to compact and middle-class cars. The auto industry is quick to point out that the high performance of German cars, in terms of acceleration, speed, safety and reliability, is put to a daily test on the German Autobahn network, most stretches of which have no speed limits.

With this high-performance, high-quality strategy, German manufacturers have been able to achieve above-average prices on the markets. The global success of the German upper-class and high-end vehicles strengthened the solid image of automobiles made in Germany.

The possibility of maintaining a relatively high price level was essential for the success of German car manufacturers. The German automobile industry has had to cope with very high labour costs and short working hours per employee. Since the appreciation of the D-Mark in 1986, Germany has had by far the highest labour cost level of the major motor vehicles producing countries (Table 20.2-6).

Table 20.2-6 International comparison of labour costs and working hours in the motor vehicle industry

Country	Labour costs[a)] (DM/h)			Working hours[b)] (h)
	1980	1990	1994	1993
West Germany	26.84	41.91	57.06	1,399
France	19.66	26.09	29.49	1,609
Italy	17.73	28.63	27.40	1,315
United Kingdom	14.95	25.05	26.72	1,814
Spain	12.63	27.01	26.82	1,570
United States	24.83	33.13	39.55	2,126
Japan	13.26	26.83	45.47	1,959

a) Including social costs. b) Effective yearly number of hours per worker.

Source: *DA Pressedienst*, 31.1.1995

In view of the fact that the German car market is completely open for imports and more than half of the German car production is sold in other countries, it is evident that the high production costs are the main problem for the German competitive position. Up to the early 1980s this disadvantage was compensated by a relatively high productivity compared with the main European competitors. But the situation has changed during the past ten years as a result of the efforts of the other European producers to improve their positions. Furthermore, compared with Japan, the productivity of the German automobile industry is insufficient.

The weakening of German competitiveness became obvious in the early 1990s, primarily because of Japanese car-makers' upgrading strategy and their improved quality image, along with lower price levels. In the meantime, German manufacturers have reacted with a comprehensive reorganisation of the production process and the management system aimed at improving productivity, price competitiveness and flexibility. In 1993 employment in the German road vehicle industry decreased by 8.7% and in 1994 this process continued (by about – 6.5%).

20.3. Comparative Summary of the Automobile Industry

20.3.1. Historical contrasts

The automobile industries in Japan and Germany underwent a very different historical development. Germany was amongst the pioneers of automobile construction. Know-how in product design and assembly technology, a skilled labour force and a well-developed infrastructure were present even before World War II. Automobile production in the 1950s and 1960s was able to grow dynamically on this foundation, since as a result of the German economic miracle domestic demand for cars and commercial vehicles expanded strongly. The design of German automobiles was oriented to the demands of the domestic market, but these vehicles also proved to be very successful in the world market. This development was an autonomous market process: industrial policy and protectionist measures were not involved, nor was technology transfer from other countries.

In Japan, the industrial structures for the mass production of automobiles were not created until after World War II. In the initial phase, co-operation with European and American companies played a role. Industrial-policy guidance was also attempted in the establishment phase, but in the final analysis it was not very significant for the development of the car industry in Japan. An important factor, however, was that the Japanese domestic market was largely protected by trade policy measures up to the 1970s and also was difficult to penetrate for foreign suppliers because of Japan's distinctive distribution system. Another key aspect was that already in the 1970s the Japanese manufacturers planned their capacities in accordance with a global strategy and adjusted the design of their vehicles to the requirements of the major markets of the United States and Europe. On the basis of a protected domestic market and a global export strategy, Japan developed into the largest automobile producer in the world in the 1980s. This was achieved even though both the US market and the European Community were limited, owing to politically negotiated voluntary-restraint agreements on automobile imports from Japan.

20.3.2. Comparative advantage of automobile industries in Japan and Germany

The strength of German motor vehicle manufacturers lies in their high technological level and high product quality. The range concentrates on vehicles in the middle, upper and luxury categories, and the product volume is marked by a strong increase in the value per vehicle. The weaknesses of the German competitive position are especially in the high price levels. This is the result of higher than average personnel costs and—in comparison with Japan—lower productivity.

In contrast, Japanese manufacturers gained their initial market shares on the basis of low prices in the segments of compact and medium-sized cars. In the course of the 1970s and 1980s, product quality was continuously improved and leading positions were also achieved in this category. Moreover, at the end of the 1980s exports were expanded in the categories of the upper and luxury classes.

The price advantage of Japanese manufacturers over their German competitors was not only due to lower personnel costs but also because of a more efficient organisation of the overall production process. This included important elements such as:

- lean production methods in combination with a system of high-grade quality assurance (reject avoidance), group competence (staff motivation) and constant improvement of the details of the process by utilising the full potential of worker suggestions;
- the pyramid structure of the supplier system with a close linkage between supplier and manufacturer, and differing personnel cost levels at the individual steps of the pyramid;
- very stable labour relations.

German automobile producers have realised in the meantime that they must take measures to strengthen their cost competitiveness. A thorough restructuring process with the goal of raising the level of productivity and flexibility has already been introduced.

20.3.3. Market competition and success factors

An analysis of success factors from the perspective of market competition suggests that the key to success for German manufacturers has been to create niche markets that target specific groups of consumers. The early liberalisation of Germany's domestic markets prompted individual manufacturers to focus on specific types of luxury automobiles, and to enhance their competitiveness in those particular areas. The result was an environment that was not conducive to competition amongst multiple manufacturers. This concentration of products and markets appears to have been the key to the success of the German automobile industry. In Japan, each manufacturer maintains product ranges that cover most consumer strata. As a result, competition within each segment tends to be fierce. In addition, when consumers decide to trade up to a higher grade, manufacturers strive to keep them within their own product ranges. Competition amongst manufacturers is extreme. The success of the Japanese automobile industry can be attributed to the honing of competitiveness in this environment.

However, these success factors tend to be evened out in international markets. In the American market, for example, there are American and Japanese cars capable of competing with luxury German cars, and so there is fierce competition within the same segments. Similarly, Japanese automobile manufacturers find it difficult to capture consumers in the American market by means of the tactics they use in Japan, and are thus forced to base their competition strategies on the products themselves. In this sense, the competitive environments and strategies that have contributed to success in Japan and Germany may become ineffective as a consequence of internationalisation. For this reason, German automobile manufacturers are starting to recognise that they will need to adopt Japanese methods in order to improve their competitiveness. They are already working to improve their productivity and adaptability through in-depth restructuring efforts. At present, the Japanese and German automobile industries are maintaining their status as success industries by virtue of the superiority of their products. Given the resurgence of American manufacturers and the emergence of Asian manufacturers, however, there is no guarantee that their status will remain secure in future.

20.3.4. Outlook for the automobile industry

Automobile manufacturing is still a key industry. However, global market expansion and escalating competition will necessitate changes in traditional German and Japanese strategies. German luxury-car manufacturers are already diversifying into multiple product categories, including economy models. Both Japanese and German manufacturers are also diversifying their production operations. In particular, there has been a dramatic influx of Japanese, American and European manufacturers into the rapidly growing Asian economies. This trend has started to result in the hollowing out of domestic automobile industries in

Japan, North America and Europe. In the long-term perspective, therefore, it is possible that automobile manufacturing will cease to be an industry with the potential to create large numbers of jobs, and that only head-office functions will remain in the home countries of automobile manufacturers. In order to deal with this situation from a national economic standpoint, the automobile industry will need to move towards more sophisticated activities, such as the development of next-generation transportation equipment.

21. Consumer Electronics Industry

21.1. Japan's Consumer Electronics Industry

21.1.1. Definitions

According to the Current Production Statistics Survey, conducted and published by the Ministry of International Trade and Industry (MITI), the items that are directly related to the electrical machinery industry are shown in Table 21.1-1 below.

The analysis in this paper concerns only the items defined as consumer electronics equipment (6) in the above table.

The consumer electronics field includes televisions, video-cassette recorders, video cameras, tape recorders and stereos to stereo headphones, radios, car-stereo systems, loudspeakers, hearing aids and the like.

Furthermore, in Japan, the "consumer electrical appliances industry" is generally considered to span everything from the home appliances of (3) above (refrigerators, washing machines, etc.) and lighting and fixtures (4) to consumer electronics (6) (i.e., audio-visual equipment).

21.1.2. Development of the consumer electronics industry

21.1.2.1. Post-war reconstruction period (1945–1955)

The radio, first domestically produced in 1925, was the mainstay product through this period. In 1955 the firm called Tokyo Tsushin Kogyo, which was established in 1946 and was later to become known as Sony Corporation, placed the first transistor radio on the market, after having licensed patents on transistor technology from the United States. Japan's radio age came into its own with the inauguration in 1951 of private radio broadcasts by Chubu Nippon Hoso. NHK, the national network, had already been airing regular television broadcasts since 1953.

Table 21.1-1 Industries related to electrical machinery

(1)	Static electrical machinery and equipment	Transformers, power converters, capacitors, electric furnaces, etc.
(2)	Switching gear	Make-and-break controllers, switching equipment, circuit breakers, etc.
(3)	Consumer electrical appliances	Heaters, kitchen appliances, air conditioners and other housing-related equipment, etc.
(4)	Light bulbs, wiring, and lighting fixtures	Light bulbs, lighting fixtures, etc.
(5)	Communications equipment and wireless devices	Telephones, exchange equipment, broadcasting equipment, etc.
(6)	Consumer electronic equipment	Video equipment, audio equipment, etc.
(7)	Components and accessories for communications and electronic equipment	Resistors, capacitors, etc.
(8)	Electron tubes, semiconductor chips, ICs	Electron tubes, semiconductors, etc.
(9)	Applied electronics equipment	Computers, PCs, X-ray machines, etc.
(10)	Electric instrumentation	Instruments, measuring devices, etc.

21.1.2.2. Full-blown growth (1956–1966)

During the economy's rapid-growth years, rising incomes and narrowing income disparities effectively gave shape to a mass-consumer market. In 1959, the industry produced ten million transistor radios, one of its leading products. Of that total, nine million units were earmarked for export, primarily to the US market. Around 1955 the penetration rate exploded for black-and-white TVs, which became the driving force of the domestic audio-visual equipment market, and counted as one of the three must-have appliances (or "three sacred treasures") of the era, the other two being washing machines and refrigerators. Towards the end of this phase, many makers had begun gearing up to produce ICs domestically, one of the key components in consumer electronics products.

21.1.2.3. Internationalisation (1967–1972)

Around 1965, colour TVs gained in popularity as one of the three "Cs" (coolers, i.e., air conditioners, and cars, being the other two). Colour TVs in particular were coveted most by consumers and ultimately became the industry breadwinner with the Tokyo Olympics as a springboard. In the meantime, the industry also spawned new demand for component and integrated stereo systems by introducing transistor-based models. Exports of colour TVs and stereo systems to the United States shot up, and in the process bilateral trade contention was pushed to the fore. With a labour crunch at home, encroaching levels of competition from the developing world and a serious new flare-up in trade tensions as background factors, there began a steady industrial drive to set up local-market manufacturing ventures abroad.

21.1.2.4. Transition to moderate growth (1973–1985)

During and after the oil crisis years, pressure to introduce energy-efficient products was not as strong on audio-visual equipment makers as it was on makers of conventional home appliances. Nonetheless, as a measure to counter the business slump, many makers of audio and video equipment rushed ahead with work to automate their production lines. During this period, VCRs for home use emerged as the industry mainstay. Also, manufacturers stepped up their output of colour TV sets, incorporating new electronic-tuner technology chiefly to whip up replacement demand.

21.1.2.5. Measures to counter the high yen (1986–1994)

In order to prevent the strengthened yen from eroding their international competitiveness, many makers have scrambled to transplant their manufacturing operations offshore, especially to other countries in East Asia. However, with no promising new "hit" products yet on the horizon, the domestic industry is facing the looming prospect of a hollowing-out.

21.1.3. Industry's importance to Japan's economic development

Japan's household electric and electronic appliances (including audio-visual equipment) industry posted significant gains during the country's high-growth years and eventually came to be known as a symbol of the era itself. That is to say, the steady stream of new products into the marketplace, the expansion of levels of consumption and the parallel development of the national distribution system all fed and counted as part of the country's rapid economic growth.

The ratio of the shipments (in value terms) of consumer electric and electronic products to private final consumption expenditure (based on GNP) registered its peak of 4.8% in 1962, closely followed by 4.7% in 1969 (Fig. 21.1-1). Despite signs of reaching maturity in the years since, the industry has nevertheless managed to sustain its share of total consumption expenditure at a level of over 2%, essentially by bringing a succession of new products to market and steady efforts at lowering prices (Fig. 21.1-2).

Needless to say, consumer electronics is just as much a research and development–oriented industry as it is a typical processing and assembly trade. Further, firms in the industry tend to run peripheral operations in an extremely broad spectrum of fields, ranging from machinery and basic materials to software. In terms of Japan's overall industrial structure, the consumer electronics industry continues to hold a core position of prestige on a par with the automobile industry.

Fig.21.1-1 Domestic shipments of electric home appliances as percentage of private consumption

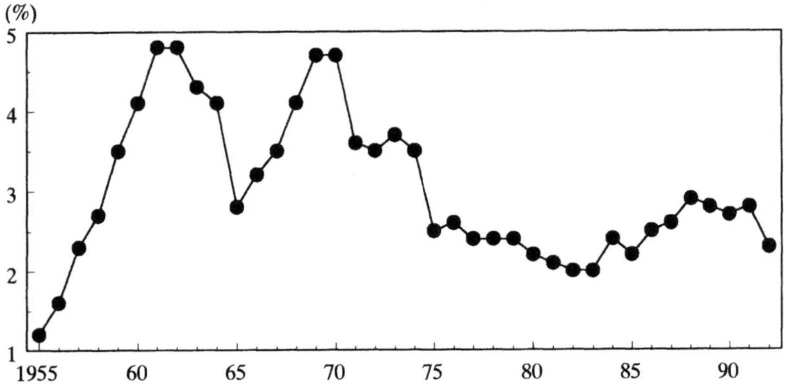

Source: Association for Electric Home Appliances, A Handbook of the Electric Home Appliances Industry

Fig.21.1-2 Trends in production cost per unit

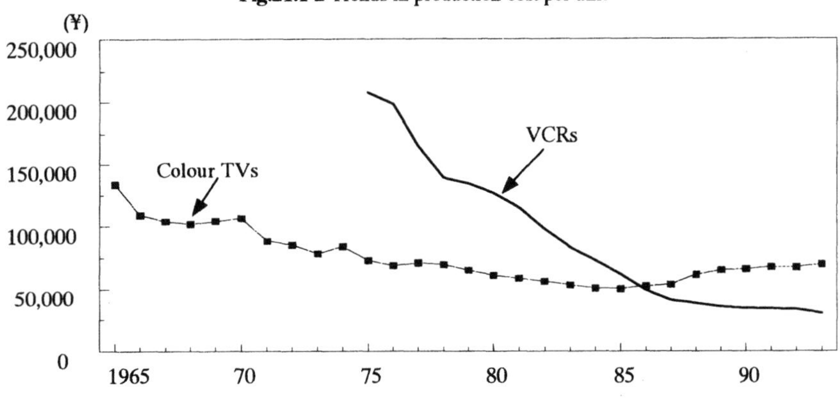

Source: Electric Industries Association of Japan, Consumer Electric Appliances Databook

21.1.4. Trends in demand

21.1.4.1. Trends in the household penetration rate

The household ownership (or penetration) rate for main products in the audio-visual appliances category, which was appraised as the driving force for economic growth in each of the above-mentioned periods, traced a sharp upward curve. This was attributable in large part to the demonstration effect of the "keeping up with the neighbours" psychology so strongly ingrained into Japanese

Fig. 21.1-3 Trends in penetration rates for audio-visual products

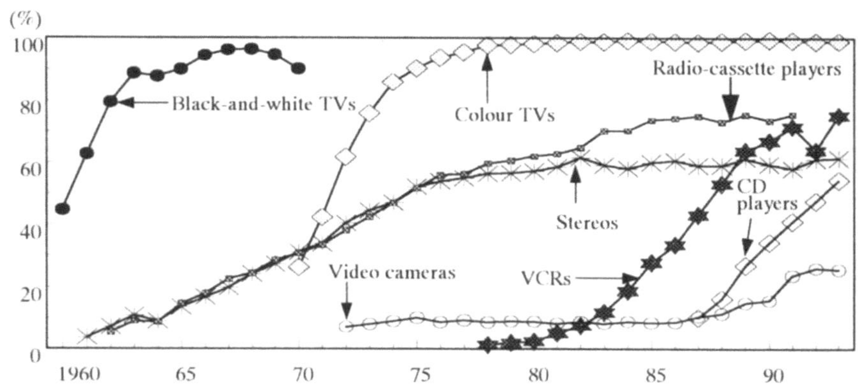

Note: The statistics classification for VCRs was changed in 1992.

Source: EPA, Survey of Consumption Trends

society. Typical expressions of this phenomenon were apparent in the popularity of the "three sacred treasures" of 1955 (namely, black-and-white TV sets, washing machines, and refrigerators) as well as the "three Cs" of 1965 (colour TVs, coolers, and cars). As a trend the household penetration rate for such goods usually takes off at a sharply accelerated pace once it surpasses 30%. For this reason, a product is considered to be moving towards full-scale sales growth when its penetration rate is around the 30% level.

21.1.4.2. Trends in output, exports and imports

In 1955 the combined total output of audio-visual products in Japan measured only ¥24.3 billion in value terms. Over the ensuing decades, however, the industry pushed hard to develop its markets at home and abroad. As a result, in 1985 total output topped ¥4.91 trillion, up more than 200-fold in the space of thirty years.

One of the distinguished features of the Japanese audio-visual appliances industry is that its mainstay products have shifted repeatedly from one item to the next, whilst maintaining average product life cycles. In terms of output value, radio products ruled the market around 1950. Around 1960, black-and-white TVs accounted for the top share, but from the mid-1960s and for some time thereafter colour TVs grabbed and held the lead.

Cassette-tape recorders reigned as the industry's breadwinner at the start of the 1980s, whilst video-cassette recorders (VCRs) furnished the top share of output over much of the ensuing decade. At this moment, it is not clear what will become the mainstay of the future. After the household penetration rate for mainstay

Fig. 21.1-4 Overseas production ratios for major Japanese manufacturers of audio-visual equipment

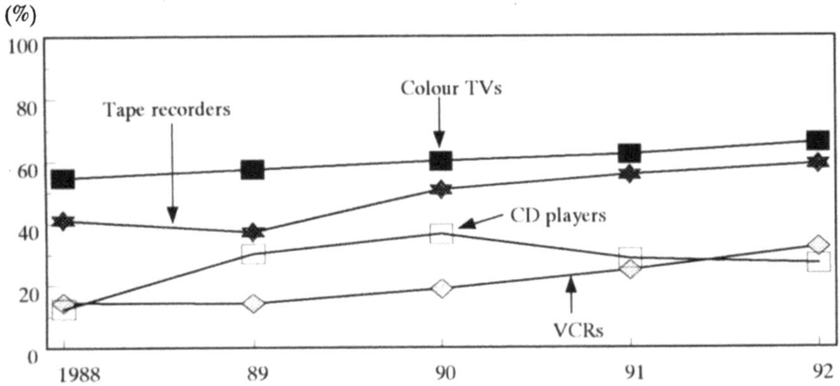

Source: Association for Electric Home Appliances, A Handbook of the Electric Home Appliances Industry

products has gone up considerably and the first round of demand for such products has subsided, there is a tendency for exports to start to pick up rapidly.

However, as a result of the sudden upsurge in the value of the yen beginning in the autumn of 1985, export competitiveness was lost. Thus some important companies began moving their manufacturing bases offshore, triggering a decline in the volume of finished-product exports, which at one point had accounted for over half the industry's total output in value terms.

In recent years, re-imports of finished products from the overseas transplants have been growing at an impressive pace. In fact, an increasing number of audio-visual appliances now have overseas production rates of above 50% (Fig. 21.1-4). What is more, a closer look reveals that not all are produced offshore by Japanese transplants; the number of OEM (e.g., original equipment manufacturing) products from manufacturers in Korea and other nations is also multiplying.

21.1.4.3. Features of demand in overseas and domestic markets

Of the total global demand by product category, shares for VCRs and CD players held by Japanese manufacturers, in output terms, maintain an especially high ratio at over 80%, followed by shares in the 40–50% range for colour TV sets and standard cassette-tape player products.

One of the principal reasons for the success achieved by Japanese makers in markets at home and overseas can be explained by the strategic decision to utilise transistor and IC technologies in their audio-visual products at an early stage, as well as to shift over to compact and portable models. The core technology behind the transistor was developed by Bell Telephone Laboratories in 1947. By 1960 innovations in that technology had led to integrated circuits, comprising transistors, resistors, capacitors, and so on, all on a single chip. During the ensuing years, this evolutionary process gave shape to microprocessors, LSI chips and further to VLSI chips. All these technologies were initially limited to military applications in the United States. In contrast, in Japan makers promptly sought to adopt, assimilate and perfect each new innovation, and then pioneer in its commercialisation, as was seen with Sony's transistor radio in 1955 and Sharp's IC-based calculator models in 1966.

Japanese consumer electronics firms have dominated the domestic market with their absolute competitiveness, and, consequently, competition from foreign-based firms has not presented any serious problems, even though products from overseas transplants of Japanese firms were re-imported. Imported products from Korea and other NIES could not secure an adequate share in the Japanese market.

21.1.5. Industry structures and supply systems

21.1.5.1. Industry structures

Given that barriers to access are by no means high, Japan's audio-visual appliances industry has been characterised by a large number of entrants, all exposed to fierce competition.

The types of businesses active in this market can be categorised roughly into manufacturers of general household electric appliances, general electric machinery, and audio-visual equipment. The appliance makers include such leading world-class firms as Matsushita Electric Industrial, Sanyo Electric, Sharp, and Fujitsu General. The companies in the category of general electric machinery are Hitachi, Toshiba, and Mitsubishi Electric; all three are manufacturers of heavy electric machinery, having moved into the home-appliance business as part of a drive to diversify their operations. Finally, Sony, Victor Co. of Japan, Pioneer Electronic, Kenwood, Aiwa, and Sansui Electric all rank amongst the leading makers of audio-visual equipment. As things now stand, there are virtually no disparities to speak of in the product and manufacturing technologies these companies command. Should one develop a new product, in most cases, the rest will soon follow with versions of their own. Indeed, product differentiation is not a very competitive strategy over relatively long-term periods of more than a year. For this reason, strengths in sales networks or brand recognition easily influence a company's competitiveness in the market. Two companies that excel in these areas are Matsushita Electric and Sony; both produce many products that command top share.

Given the effectiveness of low pricing strategies, all firms in the industry are continually striving to shave their costs to the bone (Fig. 21.1-2). The ability to weather fierce price competition in the domestic market has been reflected as one of their competitive strengths at the international level. Indeed, this would appear to be one of the factors that have supported Japan's strong giants in this field.

Compared with foreign counterparts, Japanese electric machinery makers are considered to out-source a relatively smaller share of the materials and components they demand. This supplies one reason why even larger firms tend to run several plants for the manufacture of a diverse array of products, either in separate locations or all on the premises of a single complex. In this regard, they differ significantly from auto-makers with their huge assembly lines, and steel or chemical manufacturers with their giant equipment and vast facilities. This, coupled with a flexible manufacturing approach, has effectively enabled the firms to shift smoothly and frequently from one mainstay product to the next.

21.1.5.2. Distribution and retailing strategies

Although the last few years in particular have witnessed a steady increase in the volume of consumer electronics sales through volume merchandisers, discount stores and supermarket chains, their share of total domestic sales has traditionally been controlled by the number of authorised dealers which are called *keiretsu* stores engaged primarily in sales of a specific brand.

The drive to establish *keiretsu* networks of affiliated outlets began in the 1960s, when Matsushita Electric, in a bid to break out of a slump in the industry, moved forcefully to consolidate its wholesalers and establish a chain of exclusive retailers. Taking that cue, the other leading companies then pushed ahead also with efforts to consolidate and organise their wholesalers. By the late 1960s, all had completed work to set up their own sales networks.

Once the drive to organise wholesalers was complete, they then set about the task of heightening the share of their brands sold through retailers by employing a rebate system. Currently, consumer appliance retailers in Japan number over 65,000 nation-wide, and most are affiliated outlets of one maker or another. The

Fig. 21.1-5 Trends in electric/electronic appliance sales by type of outlet

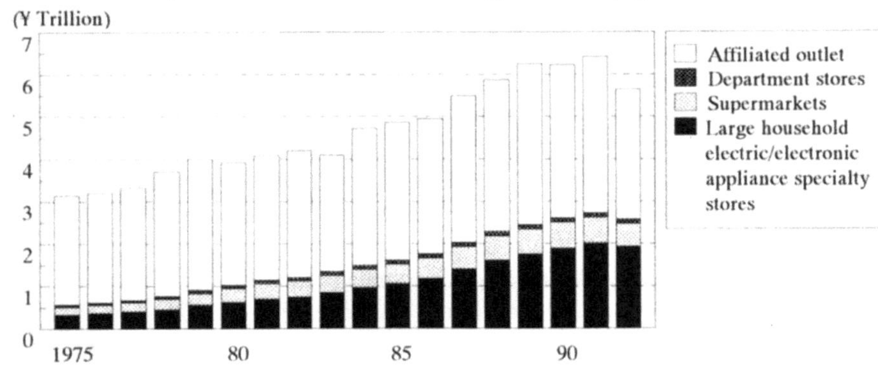

Source: Electric Industries Association of Japan, Consumer Electric Appliances Databook

largest affiliated retail chain is run by Matsushita, with Toshiba in the second-largest slot, followed by Hitachi, Sanyo, Mitsubishi, Sharp and Sony, in that order.

Volume retailers and supermarket chains began expanding their share of consumer appliance sales at a steep pace in the late 1970s (Fig. 21.1-5). Wide-ranging product selections and attractive pricing are the key factors behind this trend. Of late, practically all the affiliated retailers of all groups are undergoing hard times. Consequently, the consumer electronics makers now face the task of overhauling their chain-outlet policies.

21.1.5.3. Product development and marketing strategies

The household penetration rate for most key consumer appliances approached the saturation point around 1975. In response, makers sought to stimulate new and replacement demand by developing items that served new categories of use, or integrated the functions of otherwise separate products. Some examples are given below.

(a) New categories of use: Makers segmented the market further by age groups and categories of use, and developed products for each new segment. Specific examples of this genre include headphone stereo sets and car audio systems.

(b) Functional integration: Makers also tried to promote replacement demand by combining the features of several existing products into one package. For instance, radio-cassette decks integrated the functions of radios and cassette tape decks, whilst tele-video sets combined televisions with VCRs.

21.1.5.4. Move into overseas markets

The shift to offshore production of audio-visual appliances began in 1965 with the start-up of radio plants in Thailand and Hong Kong by both Matsushita and Sanyo. At the time, emerging import restrictions and drives to promote domestic industries in the developing countries were the chief motivating forces.

In the early 1960s Asia was the main target of Japanese direct investment, which in most cases aimed at overseas operations taking advantage of cheap local labour forces.

The early 1970s, however, saw Japanese firms begin a full-fledged thrust to set up offshore production ventures in their key overseas markets, with a view to produce substituting exports from Japan, thus side-stepping new restrictions that had been slapped on local imports. Sony initiated this trend in 1972 when it set up a local venture to produce colour TV sets in the United States. This move into the US market was eventually emulated by Matsushita Electric, Sanyo Electric, Mitsubishi Electric, Toshiba, Sharp, Hitachi and Victor Co. of Japan.

In the 1980s, Japanese makers then began setting up local ventures in Europe and the United States—the big consumption markets—for the manufacture of

VCRs, one product category then facing virtually no serious foreign competition. Later in the decade, the overseas transplants were increasingly characterised by a mixture of motivating forces: for instance, those that capitalised on low-cost labour to produce low-value-added products, or those that oriented themselves inside local consumer markets as part of a bid to develop long-term, stable outlets. They also sought to avoid stoking trade frictions or to escape the pressures of the ever-rising value of the yen.

As one outgrowth of this series of developments, though, the industry has come face-to-face with a hollowing-out trend in its manufacturing bases at home. In the light of the lessons of its past growth and development, an introduction of innovative new products is cited as the most effective strategy for the industry to deal with this problem. At present, however, any tangible image of new products is yet to be revealed.

21.1.5.5. R&D strategies

After the household penetration rate for key appliances had reached the end of its growth cycle, elements of the industry persisted in trying to spark new demand by unveiling an array of new products, new features, and competitive pricing policies. As a result, product life cycles have contracted; the typical pattern now is for the next model to reach the market between six months and a year down the road. This in turn demands that research and development be maintained on a non-stop basis; in addition, given the climate of formidable competition, each manufacturer is under pressure to pursue development work aimed essentially at trimming production costs. This is the basis for the perception of consumer electronics as an industry highly dependent on R&D.

On the other hand, the industry has become horizontally specialised. In fact, it is quite common for a company to use a component supplied by one of its rivals as the most critical part in its mainstay product (e.g., the cathode-ray tubes used in TV sets) instead of producing the item itself.

Also typical is the tendency of most manufacturers to immediately begin work on their own versions of any rival product. The founder of Osaka-based Matsushita Electric once characterised this situation quite well when he commented, "We have a research lab in Tokyo that calls itself Sony."

21.1.6. Role of industrial policy

Protective policies effective during the early formative years were essentially the only element of official industrial policy that actually contributed to the development of Japan's consumer electronics industry. Whilst companies active in the field have since been pitted against each other in a climate of unbridled competition, most have grown and prospered by and large through friendly rivalry and not on the basis of any supportive government policies, per se.

The following were the legislative measures introduced as policy tools, which were considered effective in protecting and nurturing Japan's consumer electronics industry during its early years.

(a) Foreign Exchange and Foreign Trade Control Act (1949)
Comprising a framework for the allocation of foreign exchange, this law sought to restrain imports and protect domestic industries until they could assimilate new technologies from abroad and develop effective levels of international competitiveness.

(b) Law Concerning Foreign Capital (1950)
This measure guaranteed foreign-fund transfers for the payment of royalties and other pecuniary rewards in return for borrowed technologies, and established a system for the licensing of foreign technologies and investment projects in Japan.

c) Law for the Acceleration of Rationalisation of Enterprises (1952)
Designed to foster facility modernisation in critical industrial fields, this measure introduced a special depreciation formula (i.e., depreciation by half the depreciable value of the fixed assets in the initial taxation year) and provided for reduced tax rates or outright exemption from taxes on fixed assets. Further, the tariff on machinery equipments imported for the modernisation were exempted.

(d) Law on Temporary Measures for the Development of the Electronics Industry (1957)
This law had several objectives as a measure aimed at securing and training technical personnel in the field and supporting efforts of domestic manufacturers in the development of new technologies. Basically, it offered subsidies and tax breaks for the establishment of necessary frameworks at universities and research institutes, and for private-sector projects to develop new technologies; it furnished long-term, low-interest funding and tax breaks for work to develop and modernise production and inspection facilities; it encouraged joint projects in specialised manufacturing processes; and it promoted exports along with efforts to stimulate domestic demand.

21.1.7. Main factors for the development of the industry

21.1.7.1. Domestic factors

The very existence of a steadily expanding domestic market can be cited as the factor of primary importance. The demonstration effect, which has its chief basis of support in the strong Japanese penchant for "keeping up with the neighbours", was one of the most critical factors fuelling the market's expansion during the country's post-war era of rapid economic growth. Even today, it still seems to be one of the fundamental motivating factors behind the efforts of consumer electronics firms to sustain a steady stream of new products into the marketplace.

Beyond that, though, is a supply-side factor: namely, the existence of several firms producing practically the same product. That state of affairs has given rise to a flood of model variants, which in turn has stoked the flames of competition, inspired ever-improving standards of quality and performance, and fostered a steady pattern of price cuts in real terms. These developments and the market growth have had a synergistic effect on each other.

In tandem with the technological innovations, improved productivity and market growth, mainstay products were launched one after another, found widespread acceptance and then reached maturity. The drive to spark new domestic demand whilst maintaining this basic pattern of product life cycles is the chief factor behind the industry's growth and trail of successes in the domestic market to date.

21.1.7.2. Overseas factors

On the home front, relentless contention in the arena of product development and the battle to drive down costs armed firms in the industry with a sweeping array of competitive strengths at the international level. The shift to compact and portable audio-visual appliances was based on a pioneering drive to introduce consumer goods that incorporated new transistor and IC technologies. To be sure, that shift was one of the factors propelling Japanese consumer electronics companies to success overseas. However, in that it was aimed at creating products suitable to small living spaces in Japan, this shift could also be termed one outcome of fierce levels of competition in the domestic marketplace.

Fundamentally, the industry owes its success overseas to the existence of a massive and dynamically growing domestic market. The same can be said for practically all other Japanese industrial sectors that have become internationally competitive, not just consumer electronics.

21.1.7.3. Future prospects

Today, the protracted domestic recession and a persistently strong yen are confronting the industry with an unprecedented array of difficulties. Furthermore, as one reward for its efforts to globalise its operations, the industry has come face-to-face with the threat of a hollowed-out manufacturing base at home. Finally, the over-diversification of product lines and excessively short model cycles have surfaced as factors that contribute to cost overruns.

Though the industry has begun exploring practical strategies to deal with its assortment of current woes, the dual trends towards increasingly information-intensive and electronically affluent consumer lifestyles are furnishing it the potential for new growth.

Digital technologies will be the key to efforts aimed at accommodating the increasingly information-intensive society of the twenty-first century. In fact, the market will likely witness a steady stream of digitised consumer electronics products in the years ahead, and it is not at all hard to foresee the debut of entirely new products that completely fuse audio and video with PCs, phones and other data-processing and communications gear. Indeed, that process will likely get a boost from the fact that in many cases, makers of audio and video products in Japan already turn out data processing and communications hardware as well. It is anticipated that Japan's consumer electronics industry will enter a new growth phase in the late 1990s. The next century, moreover, will probably witness the formation of an entirely new leading industry that integrates consumer electronics with industries in data-processing and communications and other electronics fields.

21.2. Germany's Consumer Electronics Industry

21.2.1. Industry definition

Defined according to the SIC (no. 3651), the industry comprises all kinds of radios (including portable and car), TV sets (B&W, colour, portable), VCRs, camcorders, audio equipment (turntables, tape- and cassette-recorders, amplifiers, tuners, CD players, speakers, headphones and microphones) and antennae. Recording material (tapes and cassettes) and recorded media (records, cassettes, CDs; SIC no. 3652) are not included, as producers and market mechanisms differ widely.

21.2.2. Development of the industry

In the 1950s the industry experienced rapid development: its share of production value in manufacturing climbed from roughly 0.5% in 1950 to more than 1% in 1960; it oscillated at about 1% until the late 1970s and then declined again to 0.5% in the 1990s. The share of employment rose even more (from 0.6% to roughly 1.5% in the late 1970s) and showed a similar decline. These outlines of development already suggest a distinction of three different phases of development. Taking further indicators into account, the second phase from 1960 to the late 1970s also emerges. This produces four phases of development which can be classified as follows:

- post-war reconstruction and TV diffusion (–1960),
- demand slowdown (1960–1968),
- increasing internationalisation and colour TV diffusion (1968–1978),
- erosion of market share through low-cost competition (1978–1992).

Table 21.2-1 Reference numbers for consumer electronics

	Year	1950	1960	1968	1978	1992
Indices	(1985 = 100)					
Production	Radio, TV	7	41	45	139	81
	Audio, Video	1	21	33	65	116
	Consumer el.	5	34	40	112	94
Price	Radio, TV	166	145	119	106	93
	Audio, Video	106	98	98	101	90
	Consumer el.					
Export	Radio, TV	0	17	21	85	103
	Audio, Video	0	8	17	31	131
	Consumer el.	0	13	19	61	115
Import	Radio, TV	0	1	7	72	237
	Audio, Video	0	1	5	35	150
	Consumer el.	0	1	6	50	185
Market	Radio, TV	8	37	42	142	159
	Audio, Video	1	11	17	61	138
	Consumer el.	4	24	30	102	149
Quota	(in %)					
Export share in production	Radio, TV	4	28	31	42	86
	Audio, Video	14	38	49	45	-[a]
	Consumer el.	5	30	37	43	96
Import share in market	Radio, TV	1	1	11	31	92
	Audio, Video	3	11	28	57	-[a]
	Consumer el.	1	3	16	38	98
Production share in manufacturing		0.55	1.25	0.91	1.02	0.48
Balances	(DM million)					
Trade	Radio, TV	13	647	586	1 231	– 2 846
	Audio, Video	5	207	315	– 546	– 2 319
	Consumer el.	18	854	901	685	– 5 165
	(%)					
Employment as against period average	Radio, TV	– 6.3	– 3.3	2.3	5.8	– 4.4
	Audio, Video	– 6.6	1.2	0.2	1.4	– 2.5
	Consumer el.	– 6.4	– 1.8	1.6	4.4	– 3.8

[a]: not calculable due to statistical problems.

Sources: ZVEI, statistical reports; Federal Statistical Office: *Lange Reihen zur Wirtschaftsentwicklung*; Ifo calculations

21.2.2.1. Post-war reconstruction and TV diffusion (–1960)

This period can be characterised by overall strong growth of all figures except imports, which remained insignificant in the radio and TV segment and showed moderate growth in the audio equipment segment leading to a market share of 11%. There was only incremental technological change in products which already existed before the war, e.g., radio or audio equipment. As there were many competitors on the market, prices fell considerably in these segments. The rapid growth of the reconstruction period was prolonged through mass distribution of TV sets from the beginning of the 1950s. Here the prices remained stable.

21.2.2.2. Demand slowdown (1960–1968)

The demand slowdown phase during the 1960s reflected the first larger international recession after the war combined with saturation phenomena and a dearth of new products, apart from hi-fi equipment. This is underlined by a further decrease in radio/TV prices and only slight increases in internal and external demand whereas the audio segment shows stable prices and growth in demand and production. Employment continued to increase. So did imports, which gained a considerable share of the German market (on average 16%).

21.2.2.3. Internationalisation and colour TV diffusion (1968–1978)

This period was marked by strong increases in exports and imports as well as a technology push from colour TV diffusion. Strong import competition led to more than doubled shares on the German market. This strong development of imports was amplified by rapid changes in exchange rates: in 1968, 4 D-Marks equalled 1 dollar; in 1969 the rate fell to DM 3.66; in 1971 average rates were down to DM 3.49 and continued to fall to DM 2.01 in 1978. In audio equipment, where the share of imports approached 60%, the trade balance became negative towards the end of the period. Colour TV diffusion led to strong growth in the audio/video equipment segment.

21.2.2.4. Erosion of market share through low cost competition (1978–1992)

This period is characterised by declining production in the radio/TV segment, a falling and finally massively negative trade balance and very strong reductions in employment.

The following sections will seek to analyse the underlying reasons for this development in Germany.

21.2.3. German market and development trends

21.2.3.1. Trends in domestic demand

The German consumer electronics market grew from roughly DM 400 million in 1950 to DM 13.5 billion in 1992. For most of the time, TV-set demand dominated the development: during the 1960s and 1970s it accounted for more than two thirds of demand. During the 1980s its share shrank to slightly more than half in 1992. This development was mainly due to the diffusion of VCRs (which are included in the audio/video equipment segment) and was further influenced by the increasing sales of CD players.

The average yearly growth of demand for consumer electronics at 8.8% per annum was significantly higher than that of wages and salaries in mining and manufacturing (on average 8.1% per annum between 1950 and 1992). The higher growth was stimulated by several factors:

- product innovation,
- changes in household size and
- overall falling prices combined with rising incomes.

The first major influence from product innovation was diffusion of black-and-white TV starting in the early 1950s and levelling off in the 1970s. The household penetration rate peaked at slightly below 80% in the late 1960s. At this time, another push for growth arrived with the introduction of colour TV (penetration rates reached more than 90% in the 1990s). The diffusion of VCRs in the eighties further stimulated demand growth. In 1993, 46% of all households owned one. Though less spectacular, innovations in audio equipment—starting with hi-fi in the late 1950s, audio cassette-recorders in the 1960s, and CD players in the 1980s—also contributed to demand growth. In 1993, 72% of all households had a hi-fi system, 55% an audio cassette-recorder and 35% a CD player.

The reduction of household size and thus an increase in household numbers was another major influence on demand growth. In the early 1960s more than half of all households consisted of three and more persons. In 1992 nearly 60% of all households consisted of only one or two persons (Fig. 21.2-1). Falling prices combined with rising incomes and thus increased spending can also be regarded as a major influence on growth. More than 90% of all households showed net incomes below DM 1800 in 1962. In 1992, their respective share had fallen to less than 15% (Fig. 21.2-2).

Until the late 1960s, German demand was met by production in Germany. A considerable share of the import quota of 16% in 1968 was accounted for by imports from German plants abroad. This share rose to 38% ten years later and grew further. Owing to OEM imports, imports of assembled components, acquisitions of large German firms by foreign companies, and considerable direct investment of Japanese firms—often leading to multiple exports and imports of one commodity in various stages of production—it is impossible to calculate a reliable quota for the end of the period.

In 1968, imports still came mainly from Western Europe: more than 80% of TVs and over 55% of audio equipment. Non-Western European imports prevailed only in the radio segment (Table 21.2-2). Here, Japan held an import share of 42% (its share in TV and audio segments was around 14%).

Ten years later, products from the Far East dominated the import segments of radio and audio equipment. In this period enormous changes in exchange rates had taken place: the D-Mark doubled its value against the dollar between 1968 and 1978. In all segments Japan was the most important foreign supplier on the

German market. Its shares in radio/audio imports lay between 48% (radio) and 62%; in the TV segment the share was considerably lower (21%) and only slightly larger than that of Austrian imports. This was also due to PAL licence agreements, which limited Japanese sales. Other Far Eastern countries already had a considerable share in imports in 1978: 13% in the TV segment (mainly black and white), 22% in the radio segment, and 7% in the audio equipment segment.

Fig. 21.2-1 Changes in household size structure

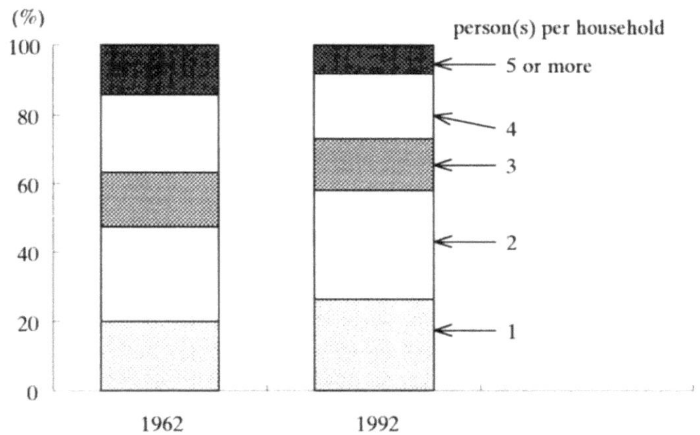

Fig. 21.2-2 Changes in income structure

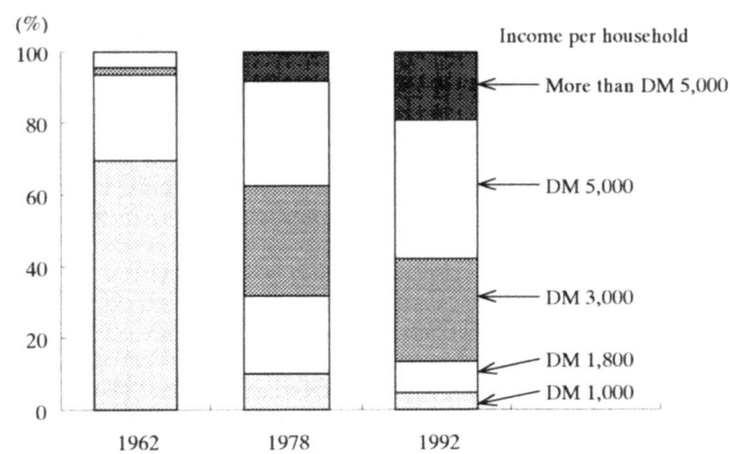

Source: Statis Bund

Table 21.2-2 Regional structure of German imports

Segment	Country/Region of origin		1968	1978	1992
TV	World	DM million	86	715	2,943
	EC	%	80.4	31.1	43.7
	EFTA	%	-	33.1	15.7
	Japan	%	14.0	20.7	5.8
	Far East excl. Japan	%	-	12.9	33.6
Radio	World	DM million	102	1 003	2,394
	EC	%	33.1	18.8	24.1
	EFTA	%	4.7	6.4	1.9
	Japan	%	42.1	47.9	24.4
	Far East excl. Japan	%	-	22.4	48.5
Audio/Video	World	DM million	150	807	2,578
	EC	%	42.0	12.4	18.8
	EFTA	%	13.6	14.4	7.3
	Japan	%	24.9	62.3	46.9
	Far East excl. Japan	%	-	6.9	25.5
	USA	%	17.6	1.7	1.2

Sources: OECD, *Trade by Commodities,* Series C; Federal Statistical Office, *Zusammenfassende übersichten, Fachserie 7, Reihe 1*

21.2.3.2. Trends in importing

The important changes in import structure up to 1992 were due to several factors:

- a further increase of imports from low-cost countries. Far Eastern imports (excluding Japan) reached import shares of between 25% (audio/video equipment) and 50% (radio). Mainland China already held considerable shares in 1992: 7% in TV, 13% in radio, and 4% in audio/video segments.
- a significant reduction of Japanese shares. This was due to tariff and non-tariff barriers (minimum price and self-constraint agreements, mainly in TV and video equipment segments) issued by the EC, which in turn led to Japanese direct investment in (EC) Europe. Increasing EC import shares can be attributed to this development (which was accentuated by several EFTA countries joining the EC).

With growing household penetration rates, most of the products of consumer electronics—apart from high-end audio equipment and to some extent camcorders—became household commodities. This led to changes in the distribution system and in customer appreciation of price. The distribution of consumer electronics products, especially in the TV segment, relied up to the late 1970s on specialised retailers. They not only provided know-how, but also installation (including antenna installation and tuning) and repair services. In exchange for high resale margins, they were closely attached to the national industry. The changing character of products from specialised goods, which necessitated technical advice, to commodities opened other high-volume distribution channels with lower margins, with price becoming the most important factor of competition.

21.2.4. German supply and development trends

21.2.4.1. Changing conditions in the industry

In the post-war period (and up to the 1960s) innovation was mainly driven by sectoral R&D. This gradually changed in the following years. Innovation in consumer electronics became ever more dependent on external R&D in the field of active components. The transition from tubes to semiconductors, and from printed circuits to VLSI chips, deeply influenced consumer electronics and its industrial cluster. The cluster of consumer electronics in the beginning was mainly constituted by transmission bodies (mostly regulated), national programme producers, a specialised distribution chain, and component manufacturers, leaving ample margin for small and specialised producers.

Increasing integration of functions on single chips led from generation to generation to ever increasing potentials for economies of scale. It also reduced depth of manufacturing considerably and allowed at the same time for higher automation of assembly and testing, thus amplifying effects of scale. Large vertically integrated firms—producing components as well as equipment—were able to profit even more from these conditions, as chip costs for small batch producers increasingly made up for important shares in product price. Another effect favouring large, diversified companies is the increasing possibility of using similar technologies in different sectors, e.g., consumer electronics, office machinery or telecommunications like monitors (TV, PC, videophone), CDs (audio, video, CD-ROM) and in quickly growing dimensions of software and standards for coding, compression and transmission of signals. The key segment of the cluster in the 1990s has changed from consumer electronics to software and components.

In turn the developments leading to high-scale production have stimulated high-volume distribution and world-wide marketing of products, thereby increasing the importance of marketing services and decreasing the weight of distribution in the cluster.

Further changes in the cluster were stimulated by liberalisation of transmission. The role of national programmes (and thus also national standards) was diminished by alternative programme sources.

The dynamics of multimedia—integrating computing, communication and consumer electronics—will further change the industrial cluster. A rapidly changing field without prevailing standards might reduce the role of today's large enterprises if there are no national champion policies.

Fig. 21.2-3 Changing clusters in consumer electronics

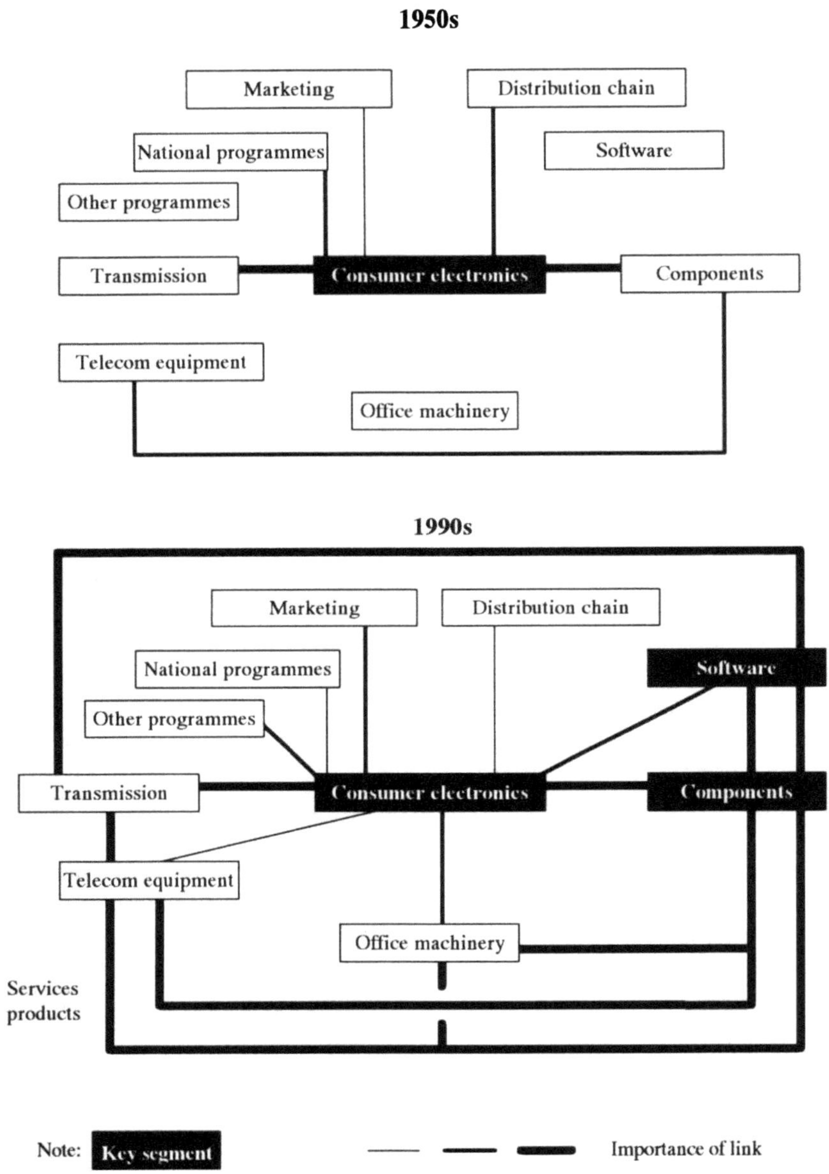

21.2.4.2. German production, markets, and technological position

German production value increased from DM 440 million in 1950 to DM 10 billion in 1978, fell back to roughly DM 8 billion in 1981 and then arrived again at DM 10 billion at the turn of the 1990s. As prices fell, "real" production did not grow after 1978. Employment declined even earlier: it peaked in 1974 at about 118 thousand and fell to 45 thousand in 1992—38% of its highest value.

From the mid-1950s onwards, the TV segment (including related equipment later on) became the driving force of production: by the 1980s TV sets and then TV sets and VCRs accounted for at least two-thirds of German production. Until 1971, black-and-white TV sets were the cash cows of consumer electronics (Fig. 21.2-4); from 1975 to 1986, colour TV sets played that role; from 1987 onwards, they shared it with VCRs. It is interesting to note that colour TV production nearly doubled its output compared to black-and-white TVs, and VCR production seems to have had a significantly shorter cycle with lower output as compared to colour TVs.

Audio production cycles show quite a different picture (Fig. 21.2-5). Until the early 1970s, high volumes were achieved in radio and turntable production. Later, German production did not reach high-volume production—apart from radio equipment for cars—in mass-market segments like audio cassette-recorders or CD-players.

A comparison of production output in selected segments of equipment with the development of the number of plants shows a considerable increase in economies of scale. Whereas, for example, nineteen plants had an average output of 2.2 million units of black-and-white TV sets, thirteen plants produced about 4 million units of colour TV sets, on average. Similar developments can be seen with car radios or other radio sets.

Amongst exports, TV equipment had no dominant role over audio equipment until the early 1970s. From then on, however, TV equipment exports were greater by far than audio equipment exports, indicating here as well as in production an increasing concentration on this segment. Since 1980, the foreign markets became increasingly more important than the home market (Table 21.2-1). The very high export and import quota (of around 100%) probably reflect the problems of trade statistics with multiple exports and imports due to international division of labour.

Until the mid-1960s, there was no significant international trade in consumer electronics. In 1968 Germany exported consumer electronics equipment amounting to roughly one billion D-Marks (which accounted for about 12.5% of world trade; a good position with regard to Germany's share in GNP and population). Already at this time, around two-thirds of the exports went into European countries. Within the next ten years, radio and audio equipment exports saw their shares in world trade halved. This corresponds to the doubled D-Mark/dollar exchange rate in this period and indicates a non-competitive cost structure at the higher D-Mark rates. Export shares in the United States fell sharply. Only TV exports were able to increase their share by four points—by increasing exports more than five times.

Fig. 21.2-4 TV equipment production cycle

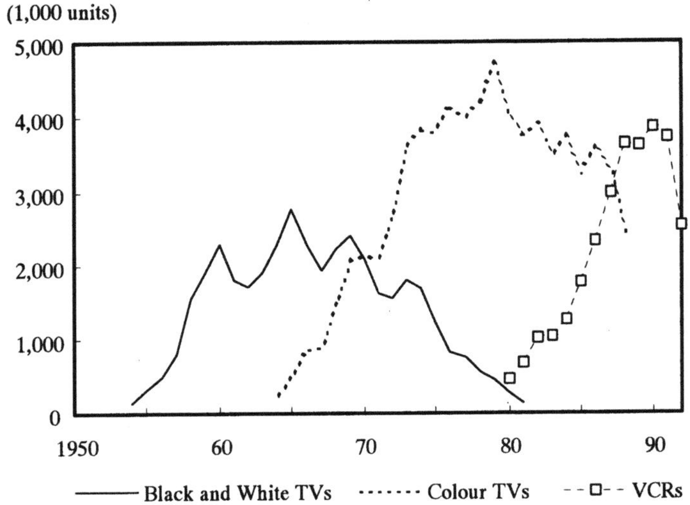

Source: ZVEI, Produktionsberichte; Ifo calculations

Fig. 21.2-5 Audio equipment production cycle

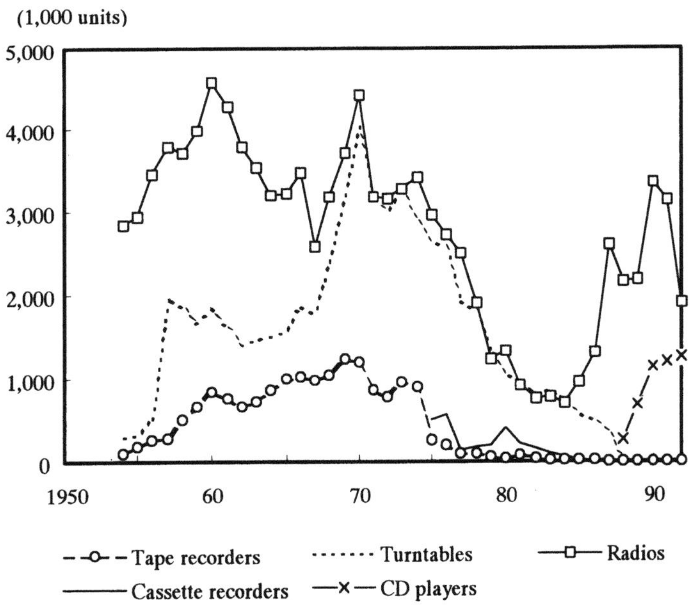

Source: ZVEI, Produktionsberichte; Ifo calculations

Table 21.2-3 Regional structure of German exports

Segment	Country/Region of destination		1968	1978	1992
TV	World	DM million	297	1,634	1,562
	EC	%	35.2	63.8	69.3
	EFTA	%	36.5	19.1	22.1
	non OECD	%	21.4	14.6	8.0
World trade share		%	14.8	18.6	
Radio	World	DM million	324	628	739
	EC	%	44.3	67.8	76.9
	EFTA	%	22.5	20.0	13.3
	non OECD	%	10.8	6.9	6.6
	North America	%	11.8	1.7	1.4
World trade share		%	11.1	6.3	
Audio/video	World	DM million	362	430	1 698
	EC	%	40.1	51.4	83.3
	EFTA	%	20.5	18.8	7.3
	non OECD	%	12.2	13.1	4.5
	North America	%	15.8	11.9	4.2
World trade share		%	12.3	6.3	

Sources: OECD, *Trade by Commodities*, Series C; Federal Statistical Office, *Zusammenfassende übersichten, Fachserie 7, Reihe 1*

Table 21.2-4 Development of German share in international applications for patents (World = 100%)

Segment/Country	1970	1978	1986	1990
Total				
Germany	15.2	11.9	11.3	8.4
USA	35.0	26.3	19.0	20.4
Japan	24.8	38.7	49.6	50.8
Pictorial communication				
Germany	19.8	12.7	13.2	8.6
USA	31.8	24.8	20.7	20.7
Japan	25.8	40.1	43.9	48.0
Cathode-ray tubes				
Germany	10.1	8.6	8.8	3.2
USA	36.7	37.8	26.0	20.8
Japan	22.9	29.6	33.4	33.7
Information storage based on relative movement				
Germany	13.5	9.9	8.5	6.4
USA	42.3	23.4	15.1	16.9
Japan	24.7	42.5	64.1	64.1

Source: INPADOC, *World Patent Statistics*; Ifo calculations

The loss of non-European market share—and thus the increasing concentration of exports on Europe—already indicate losses in competitive position. As a further deterioration of world trade share indicates, the development continued to the end of the selected period. The increase in VCR exports resulted mainly from the production of Japanese plants in Germany.

The loss of competitive position can also be interpolated from an analysis of international activity in patent applications. In total, more than 72,000 international applications for patents were examined. Only international applications were chosen to correct the national bias in propensity to apply. Apart from consumer electronics technologies as a whole, the segments of pictorial communication and cathode-ray tubes (containing the bulk of TV technology) and information storage based on relative movement (containing audio- and video-recording on tape and CDs, but also data storage on flexible and hard disks or CD-ROMs) were investigated more closely.

From 1970 onwards—earlier data on international applications are not available in comparable form—there is a declining trend of German applications in all segments. On average, the German share in international applications worldwide was nearly halved as Germany remained a technological follower in most of the segments. The reduction was especially strong in the TV segment (pictorial communication and cathode-ray tubes). A similar, though less important, decline can be seen in US applications; still, through the shift to electronic components and software, the US was able to maintain its position of technological leadership. In most of the segments, international applications of Japanese origin grew considerably (Table 21.2-3). Korea also gained significant share in the 1990s: on average it held more than 5%, in cathode-ray tubes roughly 22%.

21.2.4.3. Industry structure, enterprises and strategies

In the post-war period, large pre-war firms like AEG, Bosch and Siemens dominated the German market. But there was also a host of new, mostly family-owned firms of which Grundig was the only one to outgrow its medium size. Netherlands-headquartered Philips was the only foreign firm to have a considerable production volume of consumer electronics in Germany. In the 1960s, the picture changed only slightly, with ITT having bought Schaub-Lorenz and Graetz (the consumer electronics units of SEL). Take-overs by foreign firms increased in the 1970s: General Electric acquired a majority holding of Kuba, General Telephone and Electronics received controlling interest in SABA, and Gillette bought Braun (because of its razor business). Two of the medium-sized companies—Dual and Perpetuum Ebner (PE)—started a co-operation and one—Körting—went out of business.

In the 1980s the picture changed decisively: the only medium-sized firms to survive as mainly family-owned enterprises were either antennae firms (Fuba, Hirschmann, Kathrein) or microphone and headphone producers (Sennheiser). In the latter segment also, several smaller firms—like Peiker or Beyer—still exist. There are also a number of niche suppliers in the segment of high-end audio equipment. The mass-market segment of consumer electronics—apart from Bosch and Siemens, which both sell considerable amounts of OEM products—is entirely in foreign hands. Philips purchased Grundig, the biggest German producer; Thomson bought several medium-sized firms and the consumer electronics segment of AEG, but has strongly reduced production in Germany. Japanese firms have mostly set up their own plants to supply the German market. American firms, though important shareholders in the 1970s, sold their stakes and are no longer present.

In order to understand why German firms—though outward-oriented via exports and direct investment—were not able to cope with change in industry structure, a closer look must be taken of the leading players: AEG, Bosch, Grundig, SEL and Siemens.

AEG was still well-placed in the 1960s: its technological position was good, owing to its development of PAL; it was large, diversified and also developed electronic components. But for too long it followed an international expansion strategy of buying many high-risk firms without being able to profit from higher batches. When exchange-rate changes in the 1970s fundamentally altered the competitive situation, this strategy, aimed at outperforming the national competitor Siemens, left no possibilities for strong investment in components and R&D, and eventually led to bankruptcy.

Bosch—except for its car radio business—and Siemens, both large and cash rich, had other centres of interest as exchange-rate changes reduced the competitiveness of German consumer electronic products relatively to Asian products. Thus, the consumer electronics business adapted to the changing situation by selling OEM products. To a certain extent SEL can be seen within this group, as telecommunications was thought to be its core business.

Grundig was the only big firm producing consumer electronics equipment almost exclusively. Relatively early on, Grundig invested in other European countries. The lack of diversification made Grundig more vulnerable to business cycles. Grundig was also dependent on component supplies from other manufacturers, thus losing parts of its core competence when industry structure changed.

The strategy of German firms had the following common elements: no R&D co-operations, production process orientation in rationalisation, and a similar approach to marketing. These strategic orientations were quite different from those of the Japanese competitors. Whereas German firms tried for too long to keep the high-end market segment and stuck to their high-price and segment-by-segment diffusion strategies—thus slowly reaching higher batches and lower prices—their competitors took the risk of developing for a mass entry with low prices and very high batches, skipping possible extra profits from the upper-market segment. Further advantages were achieved by a rationalisation aimed at minimising costs in an integrated logistics system, the choice of high-volume/low-cost distribution and shared R&D projects.

21.2.5. Policy influence

For many years, the political perception of consumer electronics in Germany was marked by its primary features: significant exports, good technological performance (based mainly on PAL technology), high-quality products and low-qualification/low-income jobs. There certainly was no need for political intervention, which in general was seen as the wrong strategy for Germany. When the far-reaching changes in industry occurred, it took some time before they were recognised. The underlying causes were not analysed correctly in the beginning.

Nevertheless, indirect policies may have influenced consumer electronics, and important direct influence was exerted from Brussels. The indirect influences include regulation, competition and R&D policy; the supranational influences include trade and also competition and R&D policy. It is extremely difficult to evaluate policy influences on the sector.

Regulation of broadcasting through the Deutsche Bundespost—a publicly owned monopoly—and programming through, at first, regionally installed monopolies and later by an oligopoly of two public bodies, one of them emitting nation-wide, probably has facilitated the creation of national standards. It may too, also have centred too much attention on the German conditions. Their influence, though, should be seen as weak.

Until the late 1980s, competition policy, especially M&A control, was oriented only towards the German market, though globalisation of markets for consumer electronics was already a fact. This policy allowed mergers normally with a 30% share of the German market (depending on existing concentration). In the critical phase of market concentration, this policy may have discouraged sensible mergers. The effect should not be seen as very important.

German R&D policy had no important direct influence on consumer electronics. The questionable and inefficient allocation of huge R&D funds on atomic energy and computer programmes in the 1960s and 1970s may have sent out the wrong signals for research and academic training. Their influence on research in consumer electronics cannot be assessed.

EC policies for the sector consisted of tariff barriers, self-restraint agreements, minimum price commitments, dumping procedures, and R&D programmes. Their effect certainly was significant to Japanese direct investment in Europe. In Germany it is centred on VCR production. The political intention of strengthening European supply via protection was not achieved. The minimum price commitment led to huge additional profits in Japan, which were in turn used to advance component development. This effect has been negative for the competitive position of European producers, not only in consumer electronics. The only big European R&D programme for the sector, HDTV (analogue HD-Mac), failed, as did its

Japanese counterpart (analogue MUSE), owing to an American decision on (digital) standards for transmission.

21.2.6. Evaluation

Immediately after the war, German consumer electronics profited from strong domestic demand, technological innovation and early export activities. The initially favourable competitive position was not maintained. This analysis of the industry's development from the late 1960s onwards produces five major factors which, together, led to significant losses of competitive position:

- In important, fast-growing segments (like VCRs and CDs, but especially in components), the industry became a technological follower.
- Cost pressures were strong due to lower wages and rationalisation advantages in Japan.
- The exchange rate fluctuated strongly.
- The industry was relatively fragmented with comparatively small-sized enterprises, mostly without vertical integration of components.
- Marketing strategy, aimed at segmented diffusion and pricing, certainly eased the entry of new, low-price competitors.

It must be noted, on the other hand, that manufacturing of consumer electronics remained essentially a low-skill industry. With the increasing use of micro-electronics components, R&D was shifted to this and related segments. The reduction in the role of consumer electronics thus also reflects the transition of Germany from a low-cost producer to a knowledge-based producer.

21.3. Comparative Summary of the Consumer Electronics Industry

21.3.1. Differences in industrial structure

The domestic Japanese market has long been a scene of fierce competition led by several globally strong companies, all vying to supply similar products. All have comparable market shares, and no single company dominates the market for any particular consumer electronics product. A similar pattern of competition is evident amongst Japanese manufacturers in the global market, and in many cases, their chief rivals are the same companies with which they vie domestically. This tradition of rivalry is one of the reasons many Japanese companies are so strongly competitive in the international market today.

The German market, on the other hand, is partitioned into several product segments, and, with a few exceptions, most of the manufacturers are relatively middle-ranked, medium-scale companies. The only competitors in this environment are foreign companies.

This contrast in the scale of companies that make up the Japanese and German consumer electronics industries is closely linked to differences in competitiveness that emerged in the late 1970s. It was around that time that IC technologies began to assume critical importance as a factor in competition at the corporate level. In Japan, most major manufacturers of electric equipment are all-round manufacturers who produce not only consumer electronics but also home appliances and heavy electrical machinery. In many cases they also produce semiconductors in-house. This state of affairs has been viewed as a positive factor not only to specialised chip-fabrication ventures but also to their home-appliance and heavy electrical machinery divisions. When disparate business divisions producing consumer goods, industrial goods and materials are able to communicate closely from the early development stages, there are obviously efficiency benefits compared with companies that rely on outsourcing of materials. In Germany, Siemens is the only electronics company big enough to run its own semiconductor fabrication operation. It is this characteristic of Japanese home appliance manufacturers that has given them an advantage over their US competitors.

21.3.2. Differences in distribution strategies

Another distinguishing feature in Japan is the fact that, during the development stage of the consumer electronics industry, networks of distribution and retailing affiliations formed around each manufacturer. Consequently, even lower-ranked Japanese appliance firms were compelled to supply a full line of merchandise to their affiliated retailers in order to maintain their market share. Conversely, since such retailers handled only the products of the manufacturers with whom they were affiliated, they naturally needed to be supplied with a full line of merchandise in order to stay in business.

On the other hand, German companies have devoted their energies to maintaining their market share for relatively high-priced niche products. This has enabled foreign manufacturers to penetrate German markets for low-priced goods.

Most Japanese manufacturers have been forced to engage in similar levels of competition at all price levels and in practically every segment of the domestic market. Foreign manufacturers found that the Japanese market was relatively difficult to penetrate, however, because each segment was shaped by parallel trends towards products with many functions and features on the one hand and affordable pricing on the other. Conversely, Japanese makers found it relatively easy to obtain market share overseas by supplying well-adapted and competitive merchandise to market segments that were essentially open to penetration.

21.3.3. Differences in global strategies

It was extremely difficult for most Japanese manufacturers to expand their share of Japan's fiercely competitive domestic marketplace, and since companies were hard-pressed even to maintain their existing shares, it was imperative for them to move into overseas markets in order to sustain their own corporate growth. Once the domestic penetration rate for a product reached a certain level and domestic demand began to level off, companies tended to expand their exports rapidly. Further, companies maintained and expanded their export flows to overseas markets by flexibly shifting to offshore production as soon as they were confronted by mounting pressure from trade disputes, or by the threat of waning competitiveness due to the rising exchange value of the yen.

Most German electronics companies, however, showed comparatively little enthusiasm for moving their manufacturing facilities abroad to counter pressure from a rising D-Mark. In a significant number of cases, this caused them to lose overseas markets that they had previously gained. All in all, this contrast also seems to be linked to differences in corporate scale in the Japanese and German consumer electronics industries.

21.3.4. An assessment of the Japanese and German consumer electronics industry

One feature that the Japanese and German consumer electronics industries appear to have in common is the fact that industrial policy played no major role in their development.

In Japan, fierce competition amongst large numbers of manufacturers in the domestic market enabled companies to adopt mass-production and mass-marketing strategies to add new features and functions to their products whilst reducing prices. Partly because of their heavy emphasis on maintaining and expanding market share, most companies have relied on Europe and North America for basic research and development. Their success stems from the prioritised allocation of business resources to applied technology for use in the commercialisation of basic technology and the improvement of product functions.

German consumer electronics companies lost market share in the low-price segment and had to specialise in high-price products. This approach caused a gradual decline in their competitiveness with the trend towards more features and functions, and higher value added. Although this strategy initially fuelled new breakthroughs, such as the development of the PAL colour television format, the small scale of German companies left them unable to shoulder the massive R&D cost burden that resulted from the shift to micro-electronics. As a result, their markets in many product categories were gobbled up by Japanese rivals. In recent years, the German electronics industry has lost its international competitiveness and fallen behind on the technological front. The declining number of international patent applications by German companies is an obvious manifestation of that trend.

To meet the demands of the emerging multimedia age, the consumer electronics industry is likely to transform itself from a hardware manufacturing industry into an information industry driven by software products and other intellectual assets. Now that the US and Japanese electronics manufacturers are pursuing new alliances at home and abroad with telecommunications carriers, computer manufacturers and software houses in order to make a fresh start with a new dimension towards the twenty-first century, their German counterparts have come under growing pressure to develop a new response.

Epilogue

1 Common features of the German and Japanese postwar experiences

Germany and Japan both surrendered unconditionally in World War II, experienced Allied occupation and made heavy reparation payments. Having risen from the ashes of the war, they both achieved "miraculous" recovery, and their economic development overtook that of the victors of the war.

A number of conclusions have emerged from this study. First, the new Japan and the new Germany of the postwar period set up economic systems which are similar in that, although governments play an important role, market principles and private-sector activities maintain the predominant influence. There are, however, important differences in the economic systems, because they were formed under different political and social philosophies that evolved from different historical, and cultural backgrounds. Second, Japan and Germany have many production factors in common, including high capital efficiency, excellent technology and an industrious work force. However, they differ widely in terms of their mode of social and economic interaction. Third, while no single factor has predominantly contributed to success in either country, the synergetic functioning of various factors has enabled them to enhance their overall efficiency. Policy-makers and private sector business leaders adjusted and managed the overall system in each country in accordance with the economic environment and prevailing conditions at any given period of time. The lesson that can be learned from this is that it is extremely important for the government, industry and people of a country to create, adjust and manage their system properly in accordance with the economic environment and prevailing conditions.

2 The inevitable price of success

A significant number of policies and responses implemented during the development process can be regarded as successful. As discussed in "Challenges and Responses towards Important External Shocks (Part IV)", Japan and Germany both have had the ability to deal with a variety of obstacles through the application of resources that include knowledge, know-how, systems and mechanisms, and the efforts and zeal of their people, and, by applying these resources, they have been able to overcome a number of economic crises. As a result their economies have been held up as models of success, and their economic status in the world has risen. However, as the importance of Japan and Germany in the world economy has increased, the unique systems that each has developed have become the causes of friction and conflict with other countries. This may be the inevitable price of success.

This study was first conceived as a result of a conversation between Dr. Karl H. Oppenländer, President of Ifo Economic Research Institute, and the late Mr. Kennosuke Katayaina, the Chairman of the Sakura Institute of Research, during a luncheon meeting held in the summer of 1992. At that time, there was little doubt that the purpose of the joint research project should be nothing else than a comparative study on the factors that contributed to the post-war economic success of Japan and Germany.

However, from around that time, internal cracks and distortions in the Japanese and German systems began to come to the fore, and the Japanese and German economies, which had remained consistently strong, were both confronted with crises and challenges. In the case of Japan, it was the deepest recession of the postwar era, induced by the bursting of the economic bubble. In the case of Germany, it was the challenge derived from German reunification .

3 The laws of history

One aspect that assumed importance during the process of this study was the fact that systems and practices which had been created and maintained with the aim of ensuring the efficient functioning of economic systems in the respective countries gradually became self-serving as the economy grew. While the economic systems themselves were forced to adapt to environmental changes, efforts to maintain specific systems and practices for their own sake led both Japan and Germany into a situation in which the emergence and expansion of distortions and cracks became inevitable. Examples include employment practices, such as lifetime employment and seniority-based wages in Japan, on one hand, and labour policies and social welfare systems, including short working hours, long paid vacations, and generous pension systems in Germany, on the other. Those very systems that both countries created with considerable time and effort as the foundations for economic development in the postwar era have now become shackles that are hindering progress. It is extremely interesting that such cracks and distortions in the systems of Japan and Germany have been most clearly manifested in the areas of employment and labour relations, thus spurring the reform of economic and social structures. Neither Japan nor Germany are exempt from the laws of history that past successes eventually become hindrances.

4 Prospects for the future

The change in situation has necessitated a change of course in this joint study. It became necessary not only to conduct a comparative study of success factors, but also to focus on distortions and undesirable aspects that lurked behind those successes, and to analyze and clarify precisely the environments and conditions that existed at the time of such successes and failures.

The researchers who have participated in this joint study have done their utmost to cope with these new requirements. The extent to which they have succeeded must be judged by the readers. The situations in which Japan and Germany currently find themselves can best be characterized as a transition to the next stage, which means that further studies to make empirical verification will need to be carried out from a long-term perspective. In this sense, the joint study is still undergoing completion and will need to be modified as the reform of systems in Japan and Germany is made in response to new situations.

However, both of our institutes have agreed to publish this joint study in its present form, believing that it is capable of meeting a wide range of expectations. This is because we consider it appropriate, 50 years after the end of World War II, to publish this comprehensive analysis and clarification of the processes and results of the bold experiments undertaken in post-war Japan and Germany, and of the environment and conditions under which those results were achieved. By so doing, we believe we can offer corroborative lessons, guidelines and references that will be useful in the future, not only to the two countries directly concerned, but also to policy-makers and business managers throughout the world.

Finally, the participating researchers in both research institutes would be extremely pleased to hear the frank opinions and criticism of readers regarding the findings of this study.

Bibliography

Part I

Chapter 1

Literature to 1.1

Agency for Cultural Affairs (ed) (1993) Yearbook of religion (Shukyo Nenkan). Gyosei Corporation, Tokyo

Horie Y (1968) Readings in the history of the Japanese economy (Nihonkeizaishi Dokuhon). Toyo Keizai Shinpo-Sha, Tokyo

Kanamori H, Kosai Y (1994) Readings in the Japanese economy, 13th edn (Nihonkeizai Dokuhon, 13han). Toyo Keizai Shinpo-Sha, Tokyo

Publicity Planning Office, Nippon Steel Corporation (ed) (1987) The Japanese mind (Nihonno Kokoro). Maruzen, Tokyo

Research Office for Japanese History, College of Arts and Sciences, University of Tokyo (ed) (1961) Outline history of Japan (Nihonshi Gaisetsu). University of Tokyo Press, Tokyo

Literature to 1.2

Abramovitz M (1986) Catching up, forging ahead and falling behind. J Econ Hist 46: 385–406

Borchardt K (1982) Zwangslagen und Handlungsspielräume in der großen Weltwirtschaftskrise der frühen dreißiger Jahre: Zur Revision des überlieferten Geschichtsbildes. In: Borchardt K (ed) Wachstum, Krisen, Handlungsspielräume der Wirtschaftspolitik: Studien zur Wirtschaftsgeschichte des 19. und 20. Jahrhunderts. Göttingen

Carlin W (1994) West German growth and institutions, 1945–90. Discussion series, paper. Centre for Economic Policy Research, no 896, London

Chenery H, Syrquin M (1975) Patterns of development. Oxford University Press, Oxford

Crafts N (1985) Patterns of development: Britain in a European context. 1950–1970. British economic growth during the Industrial Revolution. Oxford University Press, Oxford, chap 3

Crafts N (1989) Revealed comparative advantage in manufacturing, 1899–1950. J Eur Econ Hist 18: 127–137

Crafts N, Thomas M (1986) Comparative advantage in UK manufacturing trade, 1910–1935. Econ J 96: 629–649

DeLong B, Eichengreen B (1993) The Marshall Plan: History's most successful structural adjustment program. In: Dornbusch R, Nölling W, Layard R (eds) Postwar economic reconstruction and lessons for the East today. MIT Press, Cambridge, MA

Eichengreen B, Uzan M (1992) The Marshall Plan: Economic implications for Eastern Europe and the former USSR. Econ Policy (1993) 7: 13–75

Gerschenkron A (1962) Economic backwardness in historical perspective. Cambridge, MA

Holtfrerich C-L (1980) Die deutsche Inflation 1914–1924, Ursachen und Folgen in internationaler Perspektive. Springer, Berlin

Maier C (1987) In search of stability. Explorations in historical political economy. Cambridge University Press, Cambridge

Olson M (1982) The rise and decline of nations. Economic growth, stagflation and social rigidities. Yale Univ. Press, New Haven

O'Mahoney M (1994) Productivity and human capital formation in UK and German manufacturing. National Institute of Economic and Social Research discussion paper no 28. National Institute of Economic and Social Research, London

Paqué K-H (1994) The causes of postwar slumps and miracles. An evaluation of Olsonian views on German economic performance in the 1920s and the 1950s. Centre for Economic Policy Research discussion paper no 981, London

Sinn H-W (1995) Schlingerkurs: Lohnpolitik und Investitionsförderung in den neuen Bundesländern.

In: Gutmann G (ed) Die Wettbewerbsfähigkeit der ostdeutschen Wirtschaft. Duncker and Humblot, Berlin, pp 23–60

Chapter 2

Literature to 2.1

Arisawa H (ed) (1994) The Showa-era history of the Japanese economy, vol 1 (Showa Keizaishi Jou). Nihon Keizai Shinbun, Tokyo

Economic Planning Agency (ed) (1992) The postwar history of the Japanese economy, vol 1 (overview). (Sengo Keizaishi 1. Soukanhen), Toyo Shorin, Tokyo

Ishikawa H (1981) The postwar history of desire (Yokubouno Sengoshi). Taihei Shuppan-Sha, Tokyo

Ministry of International Trade and Industry (ed) (1991) History of trade and industrial policy, vol 2 (Tsuushou Sangyo Seisakushi Dai 2 Kan) Tuushou Sangyo Chousakai, Tokyo

Nakamura T (1978) The Japanese economy, 1st edn (Nihonkeizai Daisanhan). University of Tokyo Press, Tokyo

Japan Federation of Certified Public Tax Accountant's Association (JFCPTA) (1987) Modern tax system series vol. 31 withholding tax (Gendai Zeimu Zensyu 31 Gensen no Zeimu). Gyousei, Tokyo

Noguchi Y (1995) The 1940 establishment (1940nen Taisei). Toyo Keizai Shinpo-Sha, Tokyo

Literature to 2.2

Abelshauser W (1975) Wirtschaft in Westdeutschland 1945–1948. Rekonstruktion und Wachstumsbedingungen in der amerikanischen und britischen Zone. DVA, Stuttgart

Buchheim C (1991) Die Währungsreform 1948 in Westdeutschland. München

DeLong B, Eichengreen B (1993) The Marshall Plan: History's most successful structural adjustment Program. In: Dornbusch R, Nölling W, Layard R (eds) Postwar economic reconstruction and lessons for the East today. MIT Press, Cambridge, MA

Dumke RH. (1990) Reassessing the Wirtschaftswunder: Reconstruction and post-war growth in West Germany in an international context. Oxf Bull Econ Stat 52 (4): 451–491

Giersch H, Paqué K-H, Schmieding H (1992). The fading miracle. Four decades of market economy in Germany. Cambridge University Press, Cambridge, MA.

Ifo Institute for Economic Research (1953) Fünf Jahre Deutsche Mark. Der Wiederaufbau der westdeutschen Wirtschaft seit der Währungsreform. Ifo-Institut, Berlin/München

Krengel J (1963) Some reasons for the rapid growth of the German Federal Republic. Banca Nazl Lav Quart Rev 64

Maddison A (1984) Phases of capitalist development. Oxford University Press, Oxford

Maddison A (1991) Dynamic forces in capitalist development, Oxford University Press, Oxford

Mendershausen H (1955). The two postwar recoveries of the German economy. Amsterdam

Paqué K-H (1994) The causes of post-war slumps and miracles. An evaluation of Olsonian views on German economic performance in the 1920s and the 1950s. Centre for Economic Policy Research discussion paper no 981, London

Ritschl A (1994) An exercise in futility: East German economic growth and decline, 1945–89. Centre for Economic Policy Research discussion paper no 984, London

Sommariva A, Tullio G (1987) German macroeconomic history, 1880–1979: A study of the effects of economic policy on inflation, currency depreciation and growth. Macmillan, Basingstoke, Hampshire

Wolf H (1993) The lucky miracle: Germany 1945–1951. In: Dornbusch R, Nölling W, Layard R (eds), Postwar economic reconstruction and lessons for the East today. MIT Press, Cambridge, MA

Part II

Chapter 3

Literature to 3.1

Japan Productivity Center (ed) (1992) Diary of the postwar Japanese economy (Sengo Nihonkeizai Nisshi). Labor Productivity Information Center, Tokyo

Research Bureau, Economic Planning Agency (ed) Survey of economic statistical figures, annual edn (Keizaiyourann). Printing Bureau, Ministry of Finance, Tokyo

Literature to 3.2

Abelshauser W (1987) Die langen fünfziger Jahre: Wirtschaft und Gesellschaft der. Bundesrepublik Deutschland 1949–1966. Schwann, Düsseldorf

Dumke RH (1990) Reassessing the Wirtschaftswunder: Reconstruction and postwar growth in West Germany in an international context. Oxf Bull Econ Stat 52 (4): 451–491

Gerstenberger W (1984) Strukturwandel unter verschlechterten Rahmenbedingungen. Strukturberichterstattung, Schriftenreihe des Ifo-Instituts, no 114, Berlin/München

Gerstenberger W (1990) Grenzen fallen, Märkte öffnen sich. Die Chancen der deutschen Wirtschaft am Beginn einer neuen Ära. Strukturberichterstattung, Schriftenreihe des Ifo-Instituts no 127, Berlin/München

Giersch H, Paqué K-H, Schmieding H (1993) Openness, wage restraint, and macroeconomic stability: West Germany's road to prosperity 1948–1959. In: Dornbusch R, Nölling W, Layard R (eds) Postwar economic reconstruction and lessons for the East today. MIT Press, Cambridge, MA, pp 1–27

Ifo-Institut (1953) Fünf Jahre Deutsche Mark. Der Wiederaufbau der west-deutschen Wirtschaft seit der Währungsreform. Ifo-Institut, Berlin/München

Chapter 4

Literature to 4.1

Ito H (1992) Introduction to local government finance (Nyumon Chihouzaisei). Gyosei Corporation, Tokyo

Nikkei Industrial Daily (ed) (1992) Secrets in the strength of Japanese manufacturing technology (Nihonno Seizougijitsu Tsuyosano Himitsu). Nihon Keizai Shinbun, Publication Department (subject: science), Tokyo

Noguchi Y (1995) The 1940 establishment (1940nen Taisei). Toyo Keizai Shinpo-Sha, Tokyo

Sato S (1994) The change in Japanese politics and its implication in external policy, in the May 1994 issue of the Sumisei Souken Report (Nihonseijino Henkato Sono Taigaiseisakueno Gani, Sumisei Souken Repouto 94.5gatsugou). Tokyo

Watanabe S (1991) Super-technology and the Japanese economy (Chougijitsuto Nihonkeizai). Shinkou-Sha, Tokyo

Literature to 4.2

Abramovitz M (1986) Catching up, forging ahead, and falling behind. J Econ Hist 46: 385–406

Barro RJ (1994) Democracy and growth. National Bureau of Economic Research, working paper series, no 4909

Dumke RH (1990) Reassessing the Wirtschaftswunder: Reconstruction and postwar growth in West Germany in an international context. Oxf Bull Econ Stat 52 (4): 451–491

Eichengreen B (1994) Institutional prerequisites for economic growth: Europe after World War II. Eur Econ Rev 38 (3/4): 883–890

Helmschrott H, Osterkamp R, Schönherr S (1992): Stagnation in der Dritten Welt—Hat die Wirtschaftspolitik versagt?—Empirische Untersuchungen über den Zusammenhang von Staat, Markt und Entwicklung. München/Köln/London

Jungfer J (1991) Grundbedürfnissstrategie oder Ordnungspolitik als Wege zur überwindung wirtschaftlicher Unterentwicklung. Bern/Stuttgart

Klump R (1995) Produktivitätslücken, Konvergenzprozesse und die Rolle der Wirtschaftsordnung: Anmerkungen zur 'Catching up'-Hypothese. Z Wirtschpol 44 (1): 29–44

Chapter 5

Literature to 5.1

Nakamura T (1993) The Japanese economy, 3rd edn (Nihonkeizai, Daisanhan). University of Tokyo Press, Tokyo

Institute for Monetary and Economic Studies (IMES) (1986) The Japanese financial system (Wagakuni no Kin-yu seido). Institute for Monetary and Economic Studies, Tokyo

Uzawa H (ed) (1989) The Japanese economy (Nihon Keizai). University of Tokyo Press, Tokyo

Literature to .5.2 (no literature quoted)

Chapter 6

Literature to 6.1

Agency of Science and Technology (ed) (1991) Indicators of science and technology (Kagakugijyutsu Shihyou). Tokyo

Economic Planning Agency (ed) Survey of economic statistics (Keizaiyouran). Printing Bureau, Ministry of Finance, Tokyo

Institute of Population Problems, Ministry of Health and Welfare (ed) (1994) Data-book of demographic statistics for 1994 (Jinkoutoukei Shiryosyu,1994). Institute of Population Problems, Ministry of Health and Welfare, Tokyo

Management and Coordination Agency (ed) Annual report on survey of the labor force (Roudouryoku Chousanenpou). Statistics Bureau Management and Coordination Agency, Tokyo

Ministry of Education, Science, Sports and Culture (ed) Report on basic survey of schools (Gakkou Kihonchousa Houkokusho). Printing Bureau, Ministry of Finance, Tokyo

Ministry of Labor (ed) Annual report on survey of monthly labor statistics (Maitsukikinro Toukei Chousa Nenpou). Institute of Labor Administration, Tokyo

Ministry of Labor (ed) Survey of labor statistics (Roudou Toukeiyouran). Printing Bureau, Ministry of Finance, Tokyo

Women's Bureau, Ministry of Labor (ed) (1994) The actual status of working women (Hataraku Joseino Jitsujou). 21seiki shokugyo zaidan, Tokyo

Ministry of Labor (ed) (1994) Compendium of wage statistics for 1995 (Chingin Toukei Souran 95). Consolidated Labor Institute, Tokyo

Literature to 6.2 (no literature quoted)

Chapter 7

Literature to 7.1

Agency of Science and Technology (ed) Indicators of science and technology, annual edn (Kagakugijutsu Shihyou). Printing Bureau, Ministry of Finance, Tokyo

Agency of Science and Technology (ed) Survey of science and technology, annual edn (Kagakugijutsuyouran). Printing Bureau, Ministry of Finance, Tokyo

Hayashi T (1990) The Japanese experience in technology. United Nations University Press, Tokyo

Hayashi T, Komota F (1993) Technological renovation and modern world economy (Gijitsukakushinto Gendaisekaikeizai). Minerva Shobo, Tokyo

Minami R, Kiyokawa Y (eds) (1987) Japanese industrialization and technological development (Nihonno Kougyoukato Gijitsuhatten). Toyo Keizai Shinpo-Sha, Tokyo

Literature to 7.2

Buckingham W (1961) Automation, its impact on business and people. New York

Bundesministerium für Forschung und Technologie (1980) Sixth report of the federal government on research. Bonn

Hallett G (1973) The social economy of West Germany. London

Ifo-Institut für Wirtschaftsforschung (1962) Soziale Auswirkungen des technischen Fortschritts. München

Ifo-Institut für Wirtschaftsforschung (ed) (1980) Technischer Fortschritt: Auswirkungen auf Wirtschaft und Arbeitsmarkt. München

Japanese Science and Technology Agency (1981) Indicators of science and technology. Tokyo, p 5

Johnson H (1974) Mercantilism, past, present, and future. Manchester School of Economic and Social Studies, vol 42, pp 1–17

Kelly RK (1977) The impact of technological innovation on international trade patterns. Staff Economic Report ER-24. Washington DC

Kendrick JW (1981) International comparisons of recent productivity trends. In: Fellner W (ed) Essays in contemporary economic problems: Demand, productivity, and pollution. Washington, DC

Kuznets S (1968) Toward a theory of economic growth. New York

Macrae N (1966) The German lesson: A survey. Economist 221 [Suppl Oct 15]: i–xxii

Matzner E, Wagner M (eds) (1990) The employment impact of new technology. Aldershot, Brookfield

OECD (1970) Gaps in technology: Analytical report. OECD, Paris

OECD (1992) Technology and the economy. Key relationships. OECD, Paris

Pollock F (1957) L'automation, ses conséquences économiques et sociales. Paris

Prognos/Mackintosh (eds) (1979) Technischer Fortschritt. Auswirkungen auf Wirtschaft und Arbeitsmarkt. Basel

Sachverständigenrat zur Begutachtung der gesamtwirtschaftlichen Entwicklung (1984) Chancen für einen langen Aufschwung. Stuttgart

Schelsky H (1957) Die sozialen Folgen der Automatisierung. Düsseldorf/Köln

Schmitt HO (1979) Mercantilism: A modern argument. Manchester School of Economic and Social Studies, vol 47

Scholz L (1977) Innovationspolitik zur Modernisierung der Produktions- und Fertigungstechnik. Berlin/München

Scholz L, Wolff H (1981) Economic growth, technical progress, and employment level. Limits of conventional theories and new approaches for theoretical and empirical investigations. In: Diettrich O, Morley J (eds) Relations between technology, capital, and labour. Proceedings of the First Community Symposium in Social Sciences, Brussels, pp 3–29

Scholz L, von Pilgrim E, Braun HG (1982) Developing countries and the international division of industrial labour: Identification of sensitive industries, technological trends and implications for technology policies of OECD countries. In: OECD (ed) North/South technology transfer. The adjustments ahead. OECD, Paris, pp 168–222

Scholz L (1995) Innovationsökonomie und -politik für die neuen Bundesländer. Beispiel: Mikroelektronik und Innovation. München

Schumpeter JA (1947) Capitalism, socialism, and democracy. New York

Vernon R (1966) International investment and international trade in the product cycle. Quart J Econ 80: 190–207

Vines D (1980) Competitiveness, technical progress and balance of trade surpluses. Manchester School of Economic and Social Studies, vol 58

Vogl F (1973) German business after the economic miracle. London

Wallich HC (1955) Mainsprings of the German revival. New Haven, CT

Part III

Chapter 8

Literature to .8.1

Hayashi T, Imai K (eds) (1994) Survey of Japanese public finances, 4th edn (Nihon Zaisei Youran, Daiyonhan). University of Tokyo Press, Tokyo

Kawaguchi S, Furukawa A (eds) (1992) The monetary policy of modern Japan (Gendai Nihonno Kinyuuseisaku). Toyo Keizai Shinpo-Sha, Tokyo

Koizumi S, Honma M (eds) (1993) Analysis of the Japanese-style market system (Nihongata Shijoushisutemuno Kaimei). Yuhikaku, Tokyo

Kuroda I (ed) (1995) The monetary system of our country, rev edn (Shinpan Wagakunino Kinyuuseido). Institute for Monetary and Economic Studies, Bank of Japan, Tokyo

Ministry of Finance, Director, Research and Planning Division, Minister's Secretariat (ed) Illustrated public finances of Japan, annual edn (Zusetsu Nihonno Zaisei). Toyo Keizai Shinpo-Sha, Tokyo

Miyazaki I (1990) The Japanese economy (Nihonkeizai). Simul, Tokyo

Moriguchi S (1988) Treatise on the Japanese economy (Nihonkeizairon). Soubun-Sha, Tokyo

Nihon Keizai Shinbun (ed) (1988) Strides in the Showa era, vol 1. The Japanese economy (Showano Ayumi 1 "Nihonno Keizai"). Nihon Keizai Shinbun, Tokyo

Nishimura Y (ed) (1994) Fiscal and monetary policy for economic rehabilitation and growth (Fukkouto Seichouno Zaiseikinyuuseisaku). Printing Bureau, Ministry of Finance, Tokyo

Suzuki Y (1993) Japanese monetary policy (Nihonno Kinyuuseisaku). Iwanami Shoten, Tokyo

Yoshida Y (1989) A macroscopic view of the Japanese economy (Makurokaramita Nihonkeizai). Nippon Hyoron-Sha, Tokyo

Literature to .8.2 (no literature quoted)

Chapter 9

Literature to 9.1

Atsutani G (1996) Introduction to the antimonopoly law of Japan (Dukusenkinshihou Nyuumon). Nihon Keizai Shinbun, Tokyo

Fair Trade Commission (ed) (1994) Annual report of the Fair Trade Commission, 1994 edn (Heisei 6nenban Kouseitorihikiiinkai Nenji Houkoku). Fair Trade Institute, Tokyo

Honjou H, Director, General Affairs Division, Commission's Secretariat, General Secretariat, Fair Trade Commission (1994) Keywords for the latest antimonopoly law (Saishin Dokusenkinshihou Kiiwaado). Economic Research Association, Tokyo

Literature to 9.2

Audretsch D (1988) Divergent views in antitrust economics. Antitrust Bull 33: 135–160

Bundeskartellamt (1944) Das Kartellverbot und seine Ausnahmen Unternehmenskooperation im Spannungsfeld zwischen nationalem und europäischem Wettbewerbsrecht. Arbeitspapier für die Sitzung des Arbeitskreises Kartellrecht. Oct 4–5, 1994, Berlin

Görgens E (1969) Wettbewerb und Wirtschaftswachstum. Freiburg

von Hayek FA (1969) Freiburger Studien. Gesammelte Aufsätze von FA v Hayek. Der Wettbewerb als Entdeckungsverfahren. Tübingen

Heuß E (1980) Wettbewerb. In: Albers W et al (eds) Handwörterbuch der Wirtschaftswissenschaften, Vol. 8. Stuttgart

Immenga U, Mestmäcker E-J (eds) (1992) GWB—Gesetz gegen Wettbewerbsbeschränkungen—Kommentar, 2nd edn, Beck, München

Kantzenbach E (1944) Wirtschaft und Wettbewerb, no 4. Unternehmenskonzentration und Wettbewerb. pp 294 ff

Kantzenbach E, Kallfass HH (1981) Das Konzept des funktionsfähigen Wettbewerbs—workable competition. In: Cox H et al (eds) Handbuch des Wettbewerbs. München

Kartte W, Holtschneider R (1981) Konzeptionelle Ansätze und Anwendungsprinzipien im Gesetz gegen Wettbewerbsbeschränkungen—Zur Geschichte des GWB. In: Cox H et al (eds) Handbuch des Wettbewerbs. München

Mestmäcker E-J, Möller H, Schwarz H-P (eds) (1987) Eine Ordnungspolitik für Europa. Baden-Baden

Monopolkommission (eds) (1994) Wettbewerbspolitik im Wandel. Baden-Baden

Schmidt I (1993) Wettbewerbspolitik und Kartellrecht. Stuttgart

Tuchtfeldt E (1978) Kartelle. In: Albers W et al (eds) Handwörterbuch der Wirtschaftswissenschaften, Vol. 4. Stuttgart

Chapter 10

Literature to 10.1

Komiya R (1988) The modern Japanese economy (Gendai Nihonkeizai). University of Tokyo Press, Tokyo

Kosai Y, Teranishi J (eds) (1993) The postwar economic reforms of Japan (Sengo Nihonno Keizaikaikaku). University of Tokyo Press, Tokyo

Shiraishi K (1983) The postwar history of Japan's international trade policy (Sengo Nihon Tsuushouseisakushi). Zeimukeiri-Kyokai, Tokyo

Literature to 10.2

Dicke H, Wieczorek N (1987) EG-Politik auf dem Prüfstand. Rationalisierungs-Kuratorium der deutschen Wirtschaft, Eschborn

Bank Deutscher Länder (1957) Geschäftsbericht für das Jahr 1956. Bank Deutscher Länder, Frankfurt

Beyfuß J (1983) Exportversicherung und Exportfinanzierung. Ein internationaler Vergleich. Beiträge zur Wirtschafts- und Sozialpolitik, no 115. Bonn

Bundesministerium für Wirtschaft (1993) Exportfibel. Bundesministerium für Wirtschaft, Bonn

Deutsche Bundesbank (1958) Monatsbericht Juni. Deutsche Bundesbank, Frankfurt

Deutsche Bundesbank (1962) Geschäftsbericht für das Jahr 1961. Deutsche Bundesbank, Frankfurt

Giersch H, Paqué K-H, Schmieding H (1992) The fading miracle: four decades of market economy in Germany. Cambridge University Press, Cambridge, MA.

Handelsblatt, (8 August 1994) 'Entwicklungspolitik. Erste Projekte mit neuer Finanzierung Bei Bonns Hilfe reiben sich die Exporteure die Haende'.

Herrmann A (1978) Anhaltend hohe Auslandsinvestitionen der deutschen Wirtschaft. Ifo

Schnelldienst, no 20, Ifo-Institut, Berlin/München
Herrmann A (1988) Wechselkursrisiko und Unternehmensverhalten—Ergebnisse einer Befragung. Diskussionsbeiträge des Sonderforschungsbereichs 178 Internationalisierung der Wirtschaft, Serie II, Nr 64, Universität Konstanz. Also in: Ifo Schnelldienst (1988) 41 (12): 7–19
Juhl P (1978) Struktur und Umfang der deutschen Exportför derungspolitik, Kieler Arbeitspapiere, no 77, Kiel
Kloten N (1976) Erfolg und Mißerfolg der Stabilisierungpolitik (1969–1974). In: Deutsche Bundesbank (ed) Währung und Wirtschaft in Deutschland 1876–1975. Frankfurt
United Nations Conference on Trade and Development (UNCTAD) (1988) Protectionism and structural adjustment. Trade and Development Board, Geneva
Weiss FD (1988) Trade policy in West Germany. Kiel

Chapter 11

Literature to 11.1

Committee for Compiling the History of International Trade and Industry, Ministry of International Trade and Industry (ed) (1992-1994) The history of international trade and industry policy, 16 vols (Tsuushousangyou Seisakushi Zen 16 Kan). International Trade and Industry Research Institute, Tokyo
Institute of International Trade and Industry, Ministry of International Trade and Industry (ed) (1994) The MITI research review, 4th edn (Tsuusan Kenkyuurebyu Daiyongou). Printing Bureau, Ministry of Finance, Tokyo
Komiya R, Okuno M, Suzumura K (eds) (1984) Industrial policy of Japan (Nihonno Sangyouseisaku). University of Tokyo Press, Tokyo
Ministry of International Trade and Industry (ed) (1990) Visions for the policy of international trade and industry for the 1990s (90nendaino Tsuusan Seisaku Bijyon). International Trade and Industry Research Institute, Tokyo
Yabushita S, Kokufuda K, Akiyama T (eds) (1992) The Japanese economy: Competition, regulation, and deregulation (Nihonkeizai—Kyousou, Kisei, Jiyuuka). Yuhikaku, Tokyo

Literature to 11.2 (no literature quoted)

Chapter 12

Literature to 12.1

Ichibangase Y (1994) Research on the history of social welfare (Shakaifukushino Rekishi Kenkyuu). Roudojunpo-Sha, Tokyo
Kaigo T (1978) A brief history of education in Japan (Nihonkyouiku Shoushi). Kodansha, Tokyo
Koga A (ed) (1994) Treatise on social securities (Shakaihoshouron). Minerva Shobo, Kyoto
Yorita M et al. (1993) The history of Japanese education (Nihonkyouikushi). Minerva Shobo, Kyoto

Literature to 12.2 (no literature quoted)

Chapter 13

Literature to 13.1

Economic Planning Agency (ed) (1992) Economic survey of Japan (Keizaihakusho). Printing Bureau, Ministry of Finance, Tokyo
Ministry of Finance (ed) (1994) Annual report on statistics of corporations (Houjin Kigyou Toukei Nenpou). Ministry of Finance, Tokyo
Noguchi Y (1995) The 1940 establishment (1940nen Taisei). Toyo Keizai Shinpo-Sha, Tokyo
Okazaki T, Okuno M (eds) (1993) Origins of the modern Japanese economic system (Gendai Nihon Keizaishisutemuno Genryuu). Nihon Keizai Shinbun, Tokyo
Tokyo Stock Exchange (ed) Research on distribution of stocks (Kabushiki Bunpujyoukyou Chousa). Tokyo Stock Exchange, Tokyo
Tsuru K (1994) The Japanese-style market economy system (Nihonteki Shijoukeizai Shisutemu). Kodansha, Tokyo
Yoshida K (1993) Advantages and disadvantages of the Japanese-style corporate management system (Nihongata Keiei Shisutemuno Kouzai). Toyo Keizai Shinpo-Sha, Tokyo

Literature to 13.2

Edwards J, Fischer K (1994) Banks, finance and investment in Germany. Cambridge University Press,

Cambridge. Study from Centre for Economic Policy Research, London
Herrhausen A (1989) Macht der Banken. Ausführungen auf dem 6. Bonner Wirtschaftsabend der Deutschen Messe AG
Hummel M, Faust K, Küddermann R, Saul C, Schedl H, Vogler-Ludwig K, Waldkircher-Heyne C, Wilhelm M, with Trojanus K (1993) Stärken und Schwächen Deutschlands im internationalen Wettbewerb um Einkommen und Arbeitsplätze. Strukturberichterstattung 1995, München
Kaen FR, Sherman HC (1994) German banking and German corporate governance. Ifo Institute for Economic Research, Munich
Monopolkommission (1990/91) Neuntes Gutachten, Bundesdrucksache 490/92, pp 204–18

Part IV

Chapter 14

Literature to 14.1

Development Bank of Japan (ed) (1991) Research (Chousa). Development Bank of Japan, Tokyo
Economic Planning Agency (ed) Economic survey of Japan, annual edn (Keizai Hakusho). Printing Bureau, Ministry of Finance, Tokyo
Institute of Energy Economics, Japan (ed) (1982) Readings in energy for Japan, 2nd edn (Nihon Energi Dokuhon, Dainihan). Toyo Keizai, Tokyo
Institute of Energy Economics, Japan (ed) (1993) Survey of energy and economic statistics (Energi Keizaitoukei Youran). Energy Conservation Center, Tokyo
Ministry of International Trade and Industry (ed) (1994) Energy—1994 (Energi'94). Denryoku Shinposha, Tokyo
Mitsuhashi N, Uchida S (1994) The Showa era: History of the Japanese economy, vol 2 (Showa Keizaishi Ge). Nihon Keizai Shinbun, Tokyo
Nakamura T (1980) The postwar Japanese economy: Its development and structure (Nihonkeizai—Sono Seichouto Kouzou Dai-Nihon). University of Tokyo Press, Tokyo
Namiki N (1986) Truth and misconceptions in popular views on the industrial economy (Sangyou Keizai Tsuusetsuno Usoto Makoto). Nihon Keizai Shinbun, Tokyo
Suetsugu K (1994) Energy renovation (Energi Kaikaku). Denryoku Shinposha, Tokyo
Tomidate T, Kifune H (1994) Introduction to the energy economy (SaishinEnergi Keizai Nyuumon). Toyo Keizai Shinpo-Sha, Tokyo
Yoshitomi M (1981) The Japanese economy (Nihon Keizai). Toyo Keizai Shinpo-Sha, Tokyo

Literature to 14.2

Bundesregierung (1986) Energiebericht der Bundesregierung, Bundesratsdrucksache 423/86, Bonn
Behring K, Adler U, Gluch E, Karl H-D, Niclas J, Rammner P, Seufert W, Söffner F (1989) Baubedarf—Perspektiven bis 2000, Ifo Studien zur Bauwirtschaft, Nr 14, München
Gerstenberger W, Hölterhoff V (1984) Wechselwirkung von Geldpolitik, Inflation und Strukturwandel. Ifo-Studien zur Strukturforschung, Nr 2, München
Gerstenberger W, Heinze J, Hummel M, Sprenger R-U (1984) Staatliche Interventionen. Ifo-Studien zur Strukturforschung, Nr. 4, München
Gerstenberger W (1988) Wettbewerbsfähige Strukturen gestatten Expansionspolitik. Strukturberichterstattung 1987, Kernbericht, Schriftenreihe des Ifo-Instituts für Wirtschaftsforschung, Nr 120, Berlin/München
Gerstenberger W (1990) Grenzen fallen, Märkte öffnen sich. Die Chancen der deutschen Wirtschaft am Beginn einer neuen Ära. Ifo-Strukturbericht 1990, Schriftenreihe des Ifo-Instituts, no 127, Berlin/München
Gerstenberger W (1992) Relative energy prices, innovation activity and economic performance in markets for energy-sensitive products. In: Commission of the European Communities (ed) The economics of limiting CO_2 emissions: European economy, special edition no 1, Brussels/Luxembourg
Hahn W, Ratzenberger R (1991) Verkehrsprognose Bayern 2005, Ifo Studien zur Verkehrswirtschaft no 24, München
Hinz S, Fischer J, Beck B (1992) Förderfibel Energie, öffentliche Finanzhilfen für den Einsatz erneuerbarer Energiequellen und die rationelle Energieverwendung, 2nd rev edn, Köln

Ifo-Institut (1980) Analyse der strukturellen Entwicklung der deutschen Wirtschaft. Schriftenreihe des Ifo-Instituts, vol 107/II, Berlin/München

IHK Kiel (1988) Finanzierungshilfen Energie, Stand: November 1988. Tips für die Praxis. IHK, Kiel

Karl HD (1986) Einfluß der Wirtschaftsentwicklung auf den Energieverbrauch. Ifo Studien zur Energiewirtschaft no 7, München

Mayer H (1990) Aufkommen und Verwendung von Energie 1978 bis 1988. Wirtsch Stat 9: 614–622

Neumann F (1990) Investment behaviour in Germany. In: Oppenländer KH, Poser G (eds) Business cycle surveys with special reference to Pacific basin economies. Papers presented to the 19th Centre for International Research on Economic Tendency Surveys (CIRET) conference proceedings, Osaka 1989

Sachverständigenrat (1994) Vollbeschäftigung für Morgen. Jahresgutachten 1974/75, Bonn

Wagner A (1994) Demographisch bedingte Arbeitslosigkeit in Deutschland. Ifo Schnelldienst, vol 47, no 25–6, München

Chapter 15

Literature to 15.1

Economic Planning Agency (ed) Questionnaire on corporate behavior, annual edn (Kigyou Koudou Ankeeto). Research Bureau, Economic Planning Agency, Tokyo

Japan External Trade Organization (ed) International trade between the world and Japan, annual edn (Sekaito Nihonno Boueki). Japan External Trade Organization, Tokyo

Japan External Trade Organization (ed) Overseas direct investment between the world and Japan, annual edn (Sekaito Nihonno Kaigai Chokusetsu Toushi). Japan External Trade Organization, Tokyo

Ministry of International Trade and Industry (ed) The white book on international trade and industry, annual edn (Tsuushouhakusho). Ministry of International Trade and Industry, Tokyo

Literature to 15.2

Emminger O (1976) Deutsche Geld- und Währungspolitik im Spannungsfeld zwischen innerem und äußerem Gleichgewicht (1948–1975). In: Deutsche Bundesbank (ed) Währung und Wirtschaft in Deutschland 1876–1975. Deutsche Bundesbank, Frankfurt

Gerstenberger W (1987) Wettbewerbsfähige Strukturen gestatten Expansionspolitik. Strukturberichterstattung 1987, Kernbericht, Berlin/München

Gerstenberger W (1992) Zur Wettbewerbssituation der deutschen Industrie im High-Tech-Bereich. Ifo Schnelldienst, no 13, Ifo-Institut, Berlin/München

Giersch H, Paqué K-H, Schmieding H (1992) The fading miracle: four decades of market economy in Germany. Cambridge University Press, Cambridge, MA.

Hardy DC, Herrmann A (1988) Effects of exchange rate fluctuations on international trade. Diskussionsbeiträge des Sonderforschungsbereichs 178 Internationalisierung der Wirtschaft, Serie II, Nr 58, Ifo-Institut, Berlin/München

Hummel M, Faust K, Köddermann R, Saul C, Schedl H, Vogler-Ludwig K, Waldkircher-Heyne C, Wilhelm M, with Trojanus K (1996) Stärken und Schwächen Deutschlands im internationalen Wettbewerb um Einkommen und Arbeitsplätze. Strukturberichterstattung 1995, München

Chapter 16

Literature to 16.1

Chikyuu Ningen Kankyou Forum (ed) (1991) GEF data-book on the environment (GEF Kankyou Deitabukku). Chikyuu Ningen Kankyou Forum, Tokyo

Earth Environment Keizai Kenkyusho (ed) (1991) The Japanese experience in environmental hazards (Nihonno Kougaikeiken). Godo Shuppan, Tokyo

Earth Environment Keizai Kenkyusho (ed) (1994) Proem to the discourse on the industries of an environment-conservation type (Kankyouhozengata Kigyouron Josetsu). Godo Shuppan, Tokyo

Environment Agency (ed) (1991) The twenty-year history of the Environment Agency (Kankyouchou 20 nenshi). Environment Agency, Tokyo

Environment Agency (ed) (1994) Illustrated basic law concerning the environment (Zudemiru Kankyoukihonhou). Chuo Hoki, Tokyo

Environment Agency (ed) Quality of the environment in Japan, annual edn (Kankyou Hakusho). Environment Agency, Tokyo

Institute of Social Science, University of Tokyo (ed) (1992) Modern Japanese society, vol 6 (Gendai Nihonshakai 6). University of Tokyo Press, Tokyo

Japan Federation of Bar Associations (ed) (1991) Japanese export of environmental hazards and environmental disruption (Nihonno Kougaiyushutsuto Kankyou Hakai). Nippon Hyoron-Sha, Tokyo

Japan Society of Industrial Machinery Manufacturers (ed) (1993) Handbook of equipment for the environment (Kankyousouchi Handobukku). Japan Society of Industrial Machinery Manufacturers, Tokyo

Ministry of International Trade and Industry (1994) Visions for the industrial environment (Sangyo Kankyou Bijyon). International Trade and Industry Research Institute, Tokyo

Ministry of International Trade and Industry (ed) (1993) Compendium of the environment—1994 (Kankyou Souran, 1994). International Trade and Industry Research Institute, Tokyo

Ministry of International Trade and Industry (ed) Capital investment projects by major industries, annual edn (Shuyousangyouno Setsubi Toushi Keikaku). Ministry of International Trade and Industry, Tokyo

Nihon Keizai Shinbun (ed) (1992) Introduction to global environmental problems (Chikyuu Kankyoumondai Nyuumon). Nihon Keizai Shinbun, Tokyo

Ueda K (1994) Keywords for the global environment (Chikyuukankyou Kiiwaado). Yuhikaku, Tokyo

Literature to 16.2

Umweltbundesamt (1993) Umweltschutz und Industriestandort. Berichte des Umweltbundesamtes, Berichte 1/93, Berlin

OECD (1993) OECD environmental performance reviews: Germany. OECD, Paris

Umweltbundesamt (1994) Environmental protection—an Economic Asset. Umweltbundesamt, Berlin

Sprenger R-U (1992) Umweltschutz als Standortfaktor. Wirschaftspolitische Diskurse no 36, Friedrich-Ebert-Stiftung, Bonn

Literature to 16.3

Keidanren (1991) Keidanren global environment charter. Tokyo

Shigeto T, Weidner H (1985) Ein Modell für uns: Die Erfolge der japanischen Umweltpolitik. Köln

International Energy Agency (1992) Climate change policy initiatives. IEA, Paris

Part V

Chapter 17

Literature to 17.1

Hamasato H (1994) Collected treatises: The Japanese chemical industry (Ronshuu Nihonno Kagakukougyou). Nippon Hyoron-Sha, Tokyo

Industrial Research Department, Industrial Bank of Japan (ed) (1993) Readings in Japanese industry, 6th edn (Nihonsangyou Dokuhon Dairokuhan). Toyo Keizai Shinpo-Sha, Tokyo

Itami N, Itami's Research Office (ed) (1991) The Japanese chemical industry: Why it has fallen behind the world in development (Nihonno Kagakusangyou, Naze Sekaini Tachiokuretaka), NTT, Tokyo

Japan Chemical Industry Association (ed) (1992/1993) Annual report on the Japanese chemical industry, 1992-1993 (Nihonno Kagakukougyou 1992/93 Nenjihoukoku). Japan Chemical Industry Association, Tokyo

Japan Chemical Industry Association (ed) (1994) A graphic depiction of the Japanese chemical industry (Gurafudemiru Nihonno Kagakukougyou). Japan Chemical Industry Association, Tokyo

Japan Petrochemical Industry Association (ed) (1971) The ten-year history of the Japanese petrochemical industry (Sekiyukagakukougyou Juunenshi). Japan Petrochemical Industry Association, Tokyo

Japan Petrochemical Industry Association (ed) (1989) Thirty-year strides in the Japanese petrochemical industry (Sekiyukagakukougyou Sanjuuneno Ayumi). Japan Petrochemical Industry Association, Tokyo

Japan Petrochemical Industry Association (ed) (1994) The petrochemical industry: Its current situation (Sekiyukagakukougyouno Genjou). Japan Petrochemical Industry Association, Tokyo

Management and Coordination Agency (ed) (1993) Standard Japanese classification of Industries

(Nihon Hyoujun Sangyou Bunrui). National Federation of Statistical Associations, Tokyo
Ministry of International Trade and Industry (ed) (1988) New chemistry developing in the 21st Century (21seikiwo hiraku Shinkagaku). International Trade and Industry Research Institute, Tokyo
Ministry of International Trade and Industry (ed) (1993) Industrial correlation tables, (prolongation tables) for 1991(1991nen Sangyoukanrenhyo (Enchouhyou)). International Trade Industry Statistics Association, Tokyo
Ministry of International Trade and Industry (ed) Tables of industrial statistics, annual edn (Kougyoutoukeihyo). Printing Bureau, Ministry of Finance, Tokyo
Tokuhisa Y (1986) Chemistry (Kagaku). Nihon Keizai Shinbun, Tokyo
Yamamoto K (1982-1989) Business circles of the Japanese chemical industry (Kagaku Gyoukai). Kyoikusha, Tokyo
Literature to 17.2 (no literature quoted)

Chapter 18

Literature to 18.1
Imai T (1994) Global strategies of the Japanese iron and steel industry (Tekkougyouno Guroubaru Senryaku). Chuo Keizai-Sha, Tokyo
Japan Iron and Steel Federation (ed) Survey of iron and steel statistics, annual edn (Tekkoutoukei Youan). Japan Iron and Steel Federation, Tokyo
Kodama M (1994) Rise and fall of the U.S. iron and steel industry (Amerikano Tekkougyouno Seisui). Japan Technical Information Service
Komiya R, Okuno M, Suzuki K (eds) (1984) Industrial policy of Japan (Nihonno Sangyouseisaku). University of Tokyo Press, Tokyo
Nihon Keizai Shinbun (ed) (1988) Strides in the Showa era, vol 2, Japanese Industry (Showano Ayumi 2 "Nihonno Sangyou"). Nihon Keizai Shinbun, Tokyo
Okazaki T (1993) Japanese industrialization and the iron and steel industry (Nihonno Kogyoukato Tekkousangyou). University of Tokyo Press, Tokyo
Research and Statistics Department, Minister's Secretariat, Ministry of International Trade and Industry (ed) Annual report on iron and steel statistics, annual edn (Tekkoutoukei Nenpoo). International Trade and Industry Research Institute, Tokyo
Shimomura T (1995) Topics in the 20th century technological history of the iron and steel industry (Nijisseiki Tekkou Gijitsushino Topikkusu). Japan Iron and Steel Federation, Tokyo
Tekko Shinbun (ed) (1992) Knowledge of new steel materials (Shinkouzaino Chishiki). Tekko Shinbun, Tokyo
Tekko Shinbun (ed) Yearbook of iron and steel (Tekkounenkan). Tekko Shinbun, Tokyo
Yonekawa S, Shimokawa K, Yamazaki H (eds) (1991) The postwar Japanese history of corporate management, vol 1 (Sengo Nihonkeieishi Daiikkan). Toyo Keizai Shinpo-Sha, Tokyo
Literature to 18.2
Commission of the European Communities (ed) (1991) Panorama of EC industry 1991—1992. EC Commission, Luxembourg
Deily M (1988) Exit barriers in the steel industry. In: Federal Reserve Board of Cleveland (ed) Economic Review, vol 24, quarter 1, pp 10–18
Eckart K (1988) Die Eisen- und Stahlindustrie in den beiden deutschen Staaten. Stuttgart
Oberender P, Rüter G (1989) Stahlindustrie. In: Oberender P (ed) Marktökonomie. Marktstruktur und Wettbewerb in ausgewählten Branchen der Bundesrepublik Deutschland. München, pp 29–77
Rahmeyer F (1992) Strukturanpassung in der eisenschaffenden Industrie. Markttheoretische Analyse und wirtschaftspolitische Strategien. Jahrbuch Sozialwiss 43: 243–266
Schafmeister H (1993) Unternehmenspolitik in der Stahlindustrie. Ein Vergleich zwischen den Vereinigten Staaten von Amerika, Japan und der Bundesrepublik Deutschland. Frankfurt am Main
United Nations (1989) The importance of the iron and steel industry for the economic activity of ECE member countries. UN, New York
Vondran R (1995a) Stahl im Umbruch. In: Oberender P (ed) Branchen im Umbruch. Schriften des Vereins für Sozialpolitik—Gesellschaft für Wirtschafts- und Sozialwissenschaften, Neue Folge, vol 238, Berlin
Vondran R (1995b) Haben private europäische Unternehmen eine Chance auf den Stahlmärkten der

Zukunft? Lecture, 6 March 1995 in London. Stahlmarkt 45 (4): 14–18
Wienert H (1983) Nachfrageschwäche und Staatsintervention—Zur Entwicklung der Stahlkrise seit 1975. Mitteilungen des Rheinisch-Westfälischen Instituts für Wirtschaftsforschung 34, Köln, pp 257–269
Wienert H (1986/87) Stahlbericht 1987. Konjunkturelle Talfahrt läuft aus, Strukturprobleme bleiben. RWI-Mitteilungen 37/38, Köln, pp 317–347
Wienert H (1993) Deutsche Stahlpolitik am Scheideweg. RWI- Konjunkturbrief 2, Köln

Literature to 18.3

Franz H-W (1988) Stahlkrise international: Schrumpfung mit und durch Modernisierung. In: Kooperationsstelle Wissenschaft-Arbeitswelt (ed) Entwicklungen in der Stahlindustrie—Lösungskonzepte zur Stahlkrise. Dortmund, pp 3–28
Schaftmeister H (1993) Unternehmenspolitik in der Stahlindustrie. Ein Vergleich zwischen den Vereinigten Staaten von Amerika, Japan und der Bundesrepublik Deutschland. Frankfurt am Main

Chapter 19

Literature to 19.1

Committee for Research on Industrial Productivity, MIT(ed) (1990) Made in America. Soshi-Sha, Tokyo
Development Bank of Japan (ed) (1988) Research, 19th issue (Chousa Daij19gou). Development Bank of Japan, Tokyo
Economic Research Institute, Japan Society for the Promotion of the Machine Tool Industry (1990) Decrease in manufacturing capacity in the machine tool industry, and its subcontracting structure (Kousakukikai Sangyouno Seisannourykuno Teikato Shitauke Kouzou). Economic Research Institute, Japan Society for the Promotion of the Machine Tool Industry, Tokyo
Friedman D (1992) The misunderstood miracle of Japan (Gokaisareta Nihonno Kiseki). Minerva Shobo, Tokyo
Kuba Y (1989) The craftsman-like high-tech group (Takumisodachino Haiteku shudan). ND Shuppan, Tokyo
Holland M (1992) Disrupted ambition (Tsuieta Yabou). Diamond, Tokyo
Japan Machine Tool Builders Association (ed) (1994) Japanese machine tool industry (Nihonno Kousakukikaisangyo). Japan Machine Tool Builders Association, Tokyo
Japan Machine Tool Builders Association (ed) Survey of machine tool statistics, annual edn (Kousakukikai Toukeiyouran). Japan Machine Tool Builders Association, Tokyo
Komiya R, Okuno M, Suzuki K (ed) (1984) Industrial policy of Japan (Niihonno Sangyouseisaku). University of Tokyo Press, Tokyo
Ministry of International Trade and Industry (ed) Annual report on machine statistics, annual edn (Kikaitoukei Nenpou). International Trade and Industry Research Institute, Tokyo
Ministry of International Trade and Industry (ed) Tables of industrial statistics (Kougyoutoukeihyou). Printing Bureau, Ministry of Finance, Tokyo
Japan Machine Tool Builders Association (ed) (1982) The thirty-year history of motherly machinery (Hahanaru Kikai Sanjuunenno Ayumi). Japan Machine Tool Builders Association, Tokyo
Takeoka Y, Takahashi H, Nakaoka T (eds) (1993) Introduction of new technology (Shingijitsuno Dounyuu). Dobunkan Shuppan, Tokyo
Yonekawa S, Shimokawa K, Yamamzaki H (eds) (1994) The postwar Japanese history of corporate management, vol 2 (Sengonihon Keieishi Dainikan). Toyo Keizai Shinpo-Sha, Tokyo
Yoshida M (1986) Structural analysis of the postwar machine tool industry (Sengo Nihon Kousakukikaikougyouno Kouzoubunseki). Mirai-Sha, Tokyo

Literature to 19.2 (no literature quoted)

Chapter 20

Literature to 20.1

Japan Automobile Manufacturers Association (ed) (1994/1995) The Japanese automobile industry (Nihonno Jidoushakougyou). Japan Automobile Manufacturers Association, Tokyo
Japan Productivity Center for Socio-Economic Development (ed) (1994) International comparison of labor productivity (Roudouseisanseino Kokusaihikaku). Japan Productivity Center for Socio-

Economic Development, Tokyo
Komiya R, Okuno M, Suzuki K (eds) (1984) Industrial policy of Japan (Nihonno Sangyou Seisaku). University of Tokyo Press, Tokyo
Nikkan Jidousha Shinbunsha (ed) (1995) Handbook of the automobile industry (Jidoushasangyou Handobukku). Nikkan Jidousha Shinbunsha, Tokyo
Ogawa E (1994) Research on Toyota Motors' production system (Toyota Seisanhoushikino Kenkyu). Nihon Keizai Shinbun, Tokyo
Ohno T, Kadota Y (1983) New development of Toyota Motors' production system (Toyota Seisanhoushikino Shintenkai). Japan Management Association, Tokyo
Shimokawa K (1993) Nikkei industry series: Automobiles (Nikkeisangyou Shiriizu "Jidousha"). Nihon Keizai Shinbun, Tokyo
Shimokawa K (1992) Rise and fall of the world automotive industries (Sekai Jidoushasangyouno Koubou). Kodansha, Tokyo
Tokudaiji A (1993) My personal history of Japanese automobiles (Bokuno Nihon Jidoouhashi). Soushi-Sha, Tokyo
Yonekawa S, Shimokawa K, Yamazaki H (eds) (1994) The postwar Japanese history of corporate management, vol 2 (Sengonihon Keieishi Dainikan). Toyo Keizai Shinpo-Sha, Tokyo
Literature to 20.2 (no literature quoted)

Chapter 21
Literature to 21.1
Aoyama Y (1991) The social history of industries in the Showa era, vol 4, electrical appliances (Sangyouno Showa Shakaishi 4 Kaden). Nihonkeizai Hyronsha, Tokyo
Japan Commission on Industrial Performance (ed) (1994) Made in Japan. Diamond, Tokyo
Wakabayashi N (1992) Locus of development of the electrical appliance industry (Kadensangyou Seichouno Kiseki). Denpa, Tokyo
Literature to 21.2 (no literature quoted)

MIX
Papier aus verantwortungsvollen Quellen
Paper from responsible sources
FSC® C105338

If you have any concerns about our products,
you can contact us on
ProductSafety@springernature.com

In case Publisher is established outside the EU,
the EU authorized representative is:
Springer Nature Customer Service Center GmbH
Europaplatz 3, 69115 Heidelberg, Germany

Printed by Libri Plureos GmbH
in Hamburg, Germany